PLAYER'S HANDBOOK®

CREDITS

D&D Lead Designers: Mike Mearls, Jeremy Crawford

Player's Handbook Lead: Jeremy Crawford
Rules Development: Rodney Thompson, Peter Lee
Writing: James Wyatt, Robert J. Schwalb, Bruce R. Cordell
Editing: Michele Carter, Chris Sims, Scott Fitzgerald Gray, Christopher Perkins
Producer: Greg Bilsland

Art Directors: Kate Irwin, Dan Gelon, Jon Schindehette, Mari Kolkowsky, Melissa Rapier, Shauna Narciso
Graphic Designers: Bree Heiss, Emi Tanji, Barry Craig
Cover Illustrator: Tyler Jacobson
Interior Illustrators: Steve Argyle, Tom Babbey, Daren Bader, Drew Baker, Mark Behm, Eric Belisle, Christopher Bradley, Noah Bradley, Sam Burley, Clint Cearley, Milivoj Ćeran, Sidharth Chaturvedi, Jedd Chevrier, jD, Allen Douglas, Jesper Ejsing, Craig Elliott, Wayne England, Scott M. Fischer, Randy Gallegos, Justin Gerard, Florian De Gesincourt, Lars Grant-West, Jon Hodgson, Ralph Horsley, Lake Hurwitz, Tyler Jacobson, Kekai Kotaki, Olly Lawson, Raphael Lübke, Titus Lunter, Slawomir Maniak, Brynn Metheney, Aaron Miller, Christopher Moeller, Mark Molnar, Scott Murphy, William O'Connor, Hector Ortiz, David Palumbo, Alessandra Pisano, Claudio Pozas, Rob Rey, Wayne Reynolds, Aaron J. Riley, Chris Seaman, Cynthia Sheppard, Craig J Spearing, John Stanko, Matt Stawicki, Alex Stone, Thom Tenery, Cory Trego-Erdner, Beth Trott, Autumn Rain Turkel, Jose Vega, Tyler Walpole, Julian Kok Joon Wen, Richard Whitters, Eva Widermann, Ben Wootten, Kieran Yanner

Additional Contributors: Kim Mohan, Matt Sernett, Chris Dupuis, Tom LaPille, Richard Baker, Miranda Horner, Jennifer Clarke Wilkes, Steve Winter, Nina Hess, Steve Townshend, Chris Youngs, Ben Petrisor, Tom Olsen

Project Management: Neil Shinkle, Kim Graham, John Hay
Production Services: Cynda Callaway, Brian Dumas, Jefferson Dunlap, David Gershman, Anita Williams

Brand and Marketing: Nathan Stewart, Liz Schuh, Chris Lindsay, Shelly Mazzanoble, Hilary Ross, Laura Tommervik, Kim Lundstrom, Trevor Kidd

Based on the original game created by
E. Gary Gygax and Dave Arneson, with Brian Blume, Rob Kuntz, James Ward, and Don Kaye
Drawing from further development by
J. Eric Holmes, Tom Moldvay, Frank Mentzer, Aaron Allston, Harold Johnson, Roger E. Moore, David "Zeb" Cook, Ed Greenwood, Tracy Hickman, Margaret Weis, Douglas Niles, Jeff Grubb, Jonathan Tweet, Monte Cook, Skip Williams, Richard Baker, Peter Adkison, Keith Baker, Bill Slavicsek, Andy Collins, and Rob Heinsoo

Playtesting provided by
over 175,000 fans of D&D. Thank you!
Additional consultation provided by
Jeff Grubb, Kenneth Hite, Kevin Kulp, Robin Laws, S. John Ross, the RPGPundit, Vincent Venturella, and Zak S.

ON THE COVER

In this fiery scene illustrated by Tyler Jacobson, the fire giant King Snurre, suffering no fools to live, calls his hell hounds to join him in confronting unwelcome guests in his home.

Disclaimer: Wizards of the Coast is not responsible for the consequences of splitting up the party, sticking appendages in the mouth of a leering green devil face, accepting a dinner invitation from bugbears, storming the feast hall of a hill giant steading, angering a dragon of any variety, or saying yes when the DM asks, "Are you really sure?"

620A9217000001 EN
ISBN: 978-0-7869-6560-1
First Printing: August 2014 (This printing includes corrections to the first printing.)

9 8 7 6 5 4

Printed in the USA. ©2014 Wizards of the Coast LLC, PO Box 707, Renton, WA 98057-0707, USA. Manufactured by Hasbro SA, Rue Emile-Boéchat 31, 2800 Delémont, CH. Represented by Hasbro Europe, 4 The Square, Stockley Park, Uxbridge, Middlesex, UB11 1ET, UK.

CONTENTS

Preface

NCE UPON A TIME, LONG, LONG AGO, IN A realm called the Midwestern United States—specifically the states of Minnesota and Wisconsin—a group of friends gathered together to forever alter the history of gaming.

It wasn't their intent to do so. They were tired of merely reading tales about worlds of magic, monsters, and adventure. They wanted to play in those worlds, rather than observe them. That they went on to invent DUNGEONS & DRAGONS, and thereby ignite a revolution in gaming that continues to this day, speaks to two things.

First, it speaks to their ingenuity and genius in figuring out that games were the perfect way to explore worlds that could not otherwise exist. Almost every modern game, whether played on a digital device or a tabletop, owes some debt to D&D.

Second, it is a testament to the inherent appeal of the game they created. DUNGEONS & DRAGONS sparked a thriving global phenomenon. It is the first roleplaying game, and it remains one of the best of its breed.

To play D&D, and to play it well, you don't need to read all the rules, memorize every detail of the game, or master the fine art of rolling funny looking dice. None of those things have any bearing on what's best about the game.

What you need are two things, the first being friends with whom you can share the game. Playing games with your friends is a lot of fun, but D&D does something more than entertain.

Playing D&D is an exercise in collaborative creation. You and your friends create epic stories filled with tension and memorable drama. You create silly in-jokes that make you laugh years later. The dice will be cruel to you, but you will soldier on. Your collective creativity will build stories that you will tell again and again, ranging from the utterly absurd to the stuff of legend.

If you don't have friends interested in playing, don't worry. There's a special alchemy that takes place around a D&D table that nothing else can match. Play the game with someone enough, and the two of you are likely to end up friends. It's a cool side effect of the game. Your next gaming group is as close as the nearest game store, online forum, or gaming convention.

The second thing you need is a lively imagination or, more importantly, the willingness to use whatever imagination you have. You don't need to be a master storyteller or a brilliant artist. You just need to aspire to create, to have the courage of someone who is willing to build something and share it with others.

Luckily, just as D&D can strengthen your friendships, it can help build in you the confidence to create and share. D&D is a game that teaches you to look for the clever solution, share the sudden idea that can overcome a problem, and push yourself to imagine what could be, rather than simply accept what is.

The first characters and adventures you create will probably be a collection of clichés. That's true of everyone, from the greatest Dungeon Masters in history on down. Accept this reality and move on to create the second character or adventure, which will be better, and then the third, which will be better still. Repeat that over the course of time, and soon you'll be able to create anything, from a character's background story to an epic world of fantasy adventure.

Once you have that skill, it's yours forever. Countless writers, artists, and other creators can trace their beginnings to a few pages of D&D notes, a handful of dice, and a kitchen table.

Above all else, D&D is yours. The friendships you make around the table will be unique to you. The adventures you embark on, the characters you create, the memories you make—these will be yours. D&D is your personal corner of the universe, a place where you have free reign to do as you wish.

Go forth now. Read the rules of the game and the story of its worlds, but always remember that you are the one who brings them to life. They are nothing without the spark of life that you give them.

Mike Mearls
May 2014

INTRODUCTION

THE DUNGEONS & DRAGONS ROLEPLAYING game is about storytelling in worlds of swords and sorcery. It shares elements with childhood games of make-believe. Like those games, D&D is driven by imagination. It's about picturing the towering castle beneath the stormy night sky and imagining how a fantasy adventurer might react to the challenges that scene presents.

Dungeon Master (DM): After passing through the craggy peaks, the road takes a sudden turn to the east and Castle Ravenloft towers before you. Crumbling towers of stone keep a silent watch over the approach. They look like abandoned guardhouses. Beyond these, a wide chasm gapes, disappearing into the deep fog below. A lowered drawbridge spans the chasm, leading to an arched entrance to the castle courtyard. The chains of the drawbridge creak in the wind, their rust-eaten iron straining with the weight. From atop the high strong walls, stone gargoyles stare at you from hollow sockets and grin hideously. A rotting wooden portcullis, green with growth, hangs in the entry tunnel. Beyond this, the main doors of Castle Ravenloft stand open, a rich warm light spilling into the courtyard.

Phillip (playing Gareth): I want to look at the gargoyles. I have a feeling they're not just statues.

Amy (playing Riva): The drawbridge looks precarious? I want to see how sturdy it is. Do I think we can cross it, or is it going to collapse under our weight?

Unlike a game of make-believe, D&D gives structure to the stories, a way of determining the consequences of the adventurers' action. Players roll dice to resolve whether their attacks hit or miss or whether their adventurers can scale a cliff, roll away from the strike of a magical lightning bolt, or pull off some other dangerous task. Anything is possible, but the dice make some outcomes more probable than others.

Dungeon Master (DM): OK, one at a time. Phillip, you're looking at the gargoyles?

Phillip: Yeah. Is there any hint they might be creatures and not decorations?

DM: Make an Intelligence check.

Phillip: Does my Investigation skill apply?

DM: Sure!

Phillip (rolling a d20): Ugh. Seven.

DM: They look like decorations to you. And Amy, Riva is checking out the drawbridge?

In the DUNGEONS & DRAGONS game, each player creates an adventurer (also called a character) and teams up with other adventurers (played by friends). Working together, the group might explore a dark dungeon, a ruined city, a haunted castle, a lost temple deep in a jungle, or a lava-filled cavern beneath a mysterious mountain. The adventurers can solve puzzles, talk with other characters, battle fantastic monsters, and discover fabulous magic items and other treasure.

One player, however, takes on the role of the Dungeon Master (DM), the game's lead storyteller and referee. The DM creates adventures for the characters, who navigate its hazards and decide which paths to explore. The DM might describe the entrance to Castle Ravenloft, and the players decide what they want their adventurers to do. Will they walk across the dangerously weathered drawbridge? Tie themselves together with rope to minimize the chance that someone will fall if the drawbridge gives way? Or cast a spell to carry them over the chasm?

Then the DM determines the results of the adventurers' actions and narrates what they experience. Because the DM can improvise to react to anything the players attempt, D&D is infinitely flexible, and each adventure can be exciting and unexpected.

The game has no real end; when one story or quest wraps up, another one can begin, creating an ongoing story called a **campaign**. Many people who play the game keep their campaigns going for months or years, meeting with their friends every week or so to pick up the story where they left off. The adventurers grow in might as the campaign continues. Each monster defeated, each adventure completed, and each treasure recovered not only adds to the continuing story, but also earns the adventurers new capabilities. This increase in power is reflected by an adventurer's level.

There's no winning and losing in the DUNGEONS & DRAGONS game—at least, not the way those terms are usually understood. Together, the DM and the players create an exciting story of bold adventurers who confront deadly perils. Sometimes an adventurer might come to a grisly end, torn apart by ferocious monsters or done in by a nefarious villain. Even so, the other adventurers can search for powerful magic to revive their fallen comrade, or the player might choose to create a new character to carry on. The group might fail to complete an adventure successfully, but if everyone had a good time and created a memorable story, they all win.

WORLDS OF ADVENTURE

The many worlds of the DUNGEONS & DRAGONS game are places of magic and monsters, of brave warriors and spectacular adventures. They begin with a foundation of medieval fantasy and then add the creatures, places, and magic that make these worlds unique.

The worlds of the DUNGEONS & DRAGONS game exist within a vast cosmos called the **multiverse**, connected in strange and mysterious ways to one another and to other planes of existence, such as the Elemental Plane of Fire and the Infinite Depths of the Abyss. Within this multiverse are an endless variety of worlds. Many of them have been published as official settings for the D&D game. The legends of the Forgotten Realms, Dragonlance, Greyhawk, Dark Sun, Mystara, and Eberron settings are woven together in the fabric of the multiverse. Alongside these worlds are hundreds of thousands more, created by generations of D&D players for their own games. And amid all the richness of the multiverse, you might create a world of your own.

All these worlds share characteristics, but each world is set apart by its own history and cultures, distinctive monsters and races, fantastic geography, ancient dungeons, and scheming villains. Some races have unusual traits in different worlds. The halflings of the Dark Sun setting, for example, are jungle-dwelling cannibals, and the elves are desert nomads. Some worlds feature races unknown in other settings, such as Eberron's warforged, soldiers created and imbued with life to fight in the Last War. Some worlds are dominated by one great story, like the War of the Lance that plays a central role in the Dragonlance setting. But they're all D&D worlds, and you can use the rules in this book to create a character and play in any one of them.

Your DM might set the campaign on one of these worlds or on one that he or she created. Because there is so much diversity among the worlds of D&D, you should check with your DM about any house rules that will affect your play of the game. Ultimately, the Dungeon Master is the authority on the campaign and its setting, even if the setting is a published world.

USING THIS BOOK

The *Player's Handbook* is divided into three parts.

Part 1 (chapters 1–6) is about creating a character, providing the rules and guidance you need to make the character you'll play in the game. It includes information on the various races, classes, backgrounds, equipment, and other customization options that you can choose from. Many of the rules in part 1 rely on material in parts 2 and 3. If you come across a game concept in part 1 that you don't understand, consult the book's index.

Part 2 (chapters 7–9) details the rules of how to play the game, beyond the basics described in this introduction. That part covers the kinds of die rolls you make to determine success or failure at the tasks your character attempts, and describes the three broad categories of activity in the game: exploration, interaction, and combat.

Part 3 (chapters 10–11) is all about magic. It covers the nature of magic in the worlds of D&D, the rules for spellcasting, and the huge variety of spells available to magic-using characters (and monsters) in the game.

HOW TO PLAY

The play of the DUNGEONS & DRAGONS game unfolds according to this basic pattern.

1. The DM describes the environment. The DM tells the players where their adventurers are and what's around them, presenting the basic scope of options that present themselves (how many doors lead out of a room, what's on a table, who's in the tavern, and so on).

2. The players describe what they want to do. Sometimes one player speaks for the whole party, saying, "We'll take the east door," for example. Other times, different adventurers do different things: one adventurer might search a treasure chest while a second examines an esoteric symbol engraved on a wall and a third keeps watch for monsters. The players don't need to take turns, but the DM listens to every player and decides how to resolve those actions.

Sometimes, resolving a task is easy. If an adventurer wants to walk across a room and open a door, the DM might just say that the door opens and describe what lies beyond. But the door might be locked, the floor might hide a deadly trap, or some other circumstance might make it challenging for an adventurer to complete a task. In those cases, the DM decides what happens, often relying on the roll of a die to determine the results of an action.

3. The DM narrates the results of the adventurers' actions. Describing the results often leads to another decision point, which brings the flow of the game right back to step 1.

This pattern holds whether the adventurers are cautiously exploring a ruin, talking to a devious prince, or locked in mortal combat against a mighty dragon. In certain situations, particularly combat, the action is more structured and the players (and DM) do take turns choosing and resolving actions. But most of the time, play is fluid and flexible, adapting to the circumstances of the adventure.

Often the action of an adventure takes place in the imagination of the players and DM, relying on the DM's verbal descriptions to set the scene. Some DMs like to use music, art, or recorded sound effects to help set the mood, and many players and DMs alike adopt different voices for the various adventurers, monsters, and other characters they play in the game. Sometimes, a DM might lay out a map and use tokens or miniature figures to represent each creature involved in a scene to help the players keep track of where everyone is.

GAME DICE

The game uses polyhedral dice with different numbers of sides. You can find dice like these in game stores and in many bookstores.

In these rules, the different dice are referred to by the letter d followed by the number of sides: d4, d6, d8, d10, d12, and d20. For instance, a d6 is a six-sided die (the typical cube that many games use).

Percentile dice, or d100, work a little differently. You generate a number between 1 and 100 by rolling two different ten-sided dice numbered from 0 to 9. One die (designated before you roll) gives the tens digit, and the other gives the ones digit. If you roll a 7 and a 1, for example, the number rolled is 71. Two 0s represent 100. Some ten-sided dice are numbered in tens (00, 10, 20, and so on), making it easier to distinguish the tens digit from the ones digit. In this case, a roll of 70 and 1 is 71, and 00 and 0 is 100.

When you need to roll dice, the rules tell you how many dice to roll of a certain type, as well as what modifiers to add. For example, "3d8 + 5" means you roll three eight-sided dice, add them together, and add 5 to the total.

The same d notation appears in the expressions "1d3" and "1d2." To simulate the roll of 1d3, roll a d6 and divide the number rolled by 2 (round up). To simulate the roll of 1d2, roll any die and assign a 1 or 2 to the roll depending on whether it was odd or even. (Alternatively, if the number rolled is more than half the number of sides on the die, it's a 2.)

THE D20

Does an adventurer's sword swing hurt a dragon or just bounce off its iron-hard scales? Will the ogre believe an outrageous bluff? Can a character swim across a raging river? Can a character avoid the main blast of a fireball, or does he or she take full damage from the blaze? In cases where the outcome of an action is uncertain, the DUNGEONS & DRAGONS game relies on rolls of a 20-sided die, a d20, to determine success or failure.

Every character and monster in the game has capabilities defined by six **ability scores**. The abilities are Strength, Dexterity, Constitution, Intelligence, Wisdom, and Charisma, and they typically range from 3 to 18 for most adventurers. (Monsters might have scores as low as 1 or as high as 30.) These ability scores, and the **ability modifiers** derived from them, are the basis for almost every d20 roll that a player makes on a character's or monster's behalf.

Ability checks, attack rolls, and saving throws are the three main kinds of d20 rolls, forming the core of the rules of the game. All three follow these simple steps.

1. Roll the die and add a modifier. Roll a d20 and add the relevant modifier. This is typically the modifier derived from one of the six ability scores, and it sometimes includes a proficiency bonus to reflect a character's particular skill. (See chapter 1 for details on each ability and how to determine an ability's modifier.)

2. Apply circumstantial bonuses and penalties. A class feature, a spell, a particular circumstance, or some other effect might give a bonus or penalty to the check.

3. Compare the total to a target number. If the total equals or exceeds the target number, the ability check, attack roll, or saving throw is a success. Otherwise, it's a failure. The DM is usually the one who determines target numbers and tells players whether their ability checks, attack rolls, and saving throws succeed or fail.

The target number for an ability check or a saving throw is called a **Difficulty Class** (DC). The target number for an attack roll is called an **Armor Class** (AC).

This simple rule governs the resolution of most tasks in D&D play. Chapter 7, "Using Ability Scores," provides more detailed rules for using the d20 in the game.

ADVANTAGE AND DISADVANTAGE

Sometimes an ability check, attack roll, or saving throw is modified by special situations called advantage and disadvantage. Advantage reflects the positive circumstances surrounding a d20 roll, while disadvantage reflects the opposite. When you have either advantage or disadvantage, you roll a second d20 when you make the roll. Use the higher of the two rolls if you have advantage, and use the lower roll if you have disadvantage. For example, if you have disadvantage and roll a 17 and a 5, you use the 5. If you instead have advantage and roll those numbers, you use the 17.

More detailed rules for advantage and disadvantage are presented in chapter 7.

SPECIFIC BEATS GENERAL

This book contains rules, especially in parts 2 and 3, that govern how the game plays. That said, many racial traits, class features, spells, magic items, monster abilities, and other game elements break the general rules in some way, creating an exception to how the rest of the game works. Remember this: If a specific rule contradicts a general rule, the specific rule wins.

Exceptions to the rules are often minor. For instance, many adventurers don't have proficiency with longbows, but every wood elf does because of a racial trait. That trait creates a minor exception in the game. Other examples of rule-breaking are more conspicuous. For instance, an adventurer can't normally pass through walls, but some spells make that possible. Magic accounts for most of the major exceptions to the rules.

ROUND DOWN

There's one more general rule you need to know at the outset. Whenever you divide a number in the game, round down if you end up with a fraction, even if the fraction is one-half or greater.

ADVENTURES

The DUNGEONS & DRAGONS game consists of a group of characters embarking on an adventure that the Dungeon Master presents to them. Each character brings particular capabilities to the adventure in the form of ability scores and skills, class features, racial traits, equipment, and magic items. Every character is different, with various strengths and weaknesses, so the best party of adventurers is one in which the characters complement each other and cover the weaknesses of their companions. The adventurers must cooperate to successfully complete the adventure.

The adventure is the heart of the game, a story with a beginning, a middle, and an end. An adventure might be created by the Dungeon Master or purchased off the shelf, tweaked and modified to suit the DM's needs and desires. In either case, an adventure features a fantastic setting, whether it's an underground dungeon, a crumbling castle, a stretch of wilderness, or a bustling city. It features a rich cast of characters: the adventurers created and played by the other players at the table, as well as nonplayer characters (NPCs). Those characters might be patrons, allies, enemies, hirelings, or just background extras in an adventure. Often, one of the NPCs is a villain whose agenda drives much of an adventure's action.

Over the course of their adventures, the characters are confronted by a variety of creatures, objects, and situations that they must deal with in some way. Sometimes the adventurers and other creatures do their best to kill or capture each other in combat. At other times, the adventurers talk to another creature (or even a magical object) with a goal in mind. And often, the adventurers spend time trying to solve a puzzle, bypass an obstacle, find something hidden, or unravel the current situation. Meanwhile, the adventurers explore the world, making decisions about which way to travel and what they'll try to do next.

Adventures vary in length and complexity. A short adventure might present only a few challenges, and it might take no more than a single game session to complete. A long adventure can involve hundreds of combats, interactions, and other challenges, and take dozens of sessions to play through, stretching over weeks or months of real time. Usually, the end of an adventure is marked by the adventurers heading back to civilization to rest and enjoy the spoils of their labors.

But that's not the end of the story. You can think of an adventure as a single episode of a TV series, made up of multiple exciting scenes. A campaign is the whole series—a string of adventures joined together, with a consistent group of adventurers following the narrative from start to finish.

THE THREE PILLARS OF ADVENTURE

Adventurers can try to do anything their players can imagine, but it can be helpful to talk about their activities in three broad categories: exploration, social interaction, and combat.

Exploration includes both the adventurers' movement through the world and their interaction with objects and situations that require their attention. Exploration is the give-and-take of the players describing what they want their characters to do, and the Dungeon Master telling the players what happens as a result. On a large scale, that might involve the characters spending a day crossing a rolling plain or an hour making their way through caverns underground. On the smallest scale, it could mean one character pulling a lever in a dungeon room to see what happens.

Social interaction features the adventurers talking to someone (or something) else. It might mean demanding

that a captured scout reveal the secret entrance to the goblin lair, getting information from a rescued prisoner, pleading for mercy from an orc chieftain, or persuading a talkative magic mirror to show a distant location to the adventurers.

The rules in part 2 (especially chapters 7 and 8) support exploration and social interaction, as do many class features and personality traits in part 1.

Combat, the focus of chapter 9, involves characters and other creatures swinging weapons, casting spells, maneuvering for position, and so on—all in an effort to defeat their opponents, whether that means killing every enemy, taking captives, or forcing a rout. Combat is the most structured element of a D&D session, with creatures taking turns to make sure that everyone gets a chance to act. Even in the context of a pitched battle, there's still plenty of opportunity for adventurers to attempt wacky stunts like surfing down a flight of stairs on a shield, to examine the environment (perhaps by pulling a mysterious lever), and to interact with other creatures, including allies, enemies, and neutral parties.

THE WONDERS OF MAGIC

Few D&D adventures end without something magical happening. Whether helpful or harmful, magic appears frequently in the life of an adventurer, and it is the focus of part 3.

In the worlds of DUNGEONS & DRAGONS, practitioners of magic are rare, set apart from the masses of people by their extraordinary talent. Common folk might see evidence of magic on a regular basis, but it's usually minor—a fantastic monster, a visibly answered prayer, a wizard walking through the streets with an animated shield guardian as a bodyguard.

For adventurers, though, magic is key to their survival. Without the healing magic of clerics and paladins, adventurers would quickly succumb to their wounds. Without the uplifting magical support of bards and clerics, warriors might be overwhelmed by powerful foes. Without the sheer magical power and versatility of wizards and druids, every threat would be magnified tenfold.

Magic is also a favored tool of villains. Many adventures are driven by the machinations of spellcasters who are hellbent on using magic for some ill end. A cult leader seeks to awaken a god who slumbers beneath the sea, a hag kidnaps youths to magically drain them of their vigor, a mad wizard labors to invest an army of automatons with a facsimile of life, a dragon begins a mystical ritual to rise up as a god of destruction—these are just a few of the magical threats that adventurers might face. With magic of their own, in the form of spells and magic items, the adventurers might prevail!

PART 1
Creating a Character

Chapter 1: Step-by-Step Characters

YOUR FIRST STEP IN PLAYING AN ADVENTURER IN THE DUNGEONS & DRAGONS game is to imagine and create a character of your own. Your character is a combination of game statistics, roleplaying hooks, and your imagination. You choose a race (such as human or halfling) and a class (such as fighter or wizard). You also invent the personality, appearance, and backstory of your character. Once completed, your character serves as your representative in the game, your avatar in the DUNGEONS & DRAGONS world.

Before you dive into step 1 below, think about the kind of adventurer you want to play. You might be a courageous fighter, a skulking rogue, a fervent cleric, or a flamboyant wizard. Or you might be more interested in an unconventional character, such as a brawny rogue who likes hand-to-hand combat, or a sharpshooter who picks off enemies from afar. Do you like fantasy fiction featuring dwarves or elves? Try building a character of one of those races. Do you want your character to be the toughest adventurer at the table? Consider a class like barbarian or paladin. If you don't know where else to begin, take a look at the illustrations in this book to see what catches your interest.

Once you have a character in mind, follow these steps in order, making decisions that reflect the character you want. Your conception of your character might evolve with each choice you make. What's important is that you come to the table with a character you're excited to play.

Throughout this chapter, we use the term **character sheet** to mean whatever you use to track your character, whether it's a formal character sheet (like the one at the end of this book), some form of digital record, or a piece of notebook paper. An official D&D character sheet is a fine place to start until you know what information you need and how you use it during the game.

Building Bruenor

Each step of character creation includes an example of that step, with a player named Bob building his dwarf character, Bruenor.

1. Choose a Race

Every character belongs to a race, one of the many intelligent humanoid species in the D&D world. The most common player character races are dwarves, elves, halflings, and humans. Some races also have **subraces**, such as mountain dwarf or wood elf. Chapter 2 provides more information about these races, as well as the less widespread races of dragonborn, gnomes, half-elves, half-orcs, and tieflings.

The race you choose contributes to your character's identity in an important way, by establishing a general appearance and the natural talents gained from culture and ancestry. Your character's race grants particular racial traits, such as special senses, proficiency with certain weapons or tools, proficiency in one or more skills, or the ability to use minor spells. These traits sometimes dovetail with the capabilities of certain classes (see step 2). For example, the racial traits of lightfoot halflings make them exceptional rogues, and high elves tend to be powerful wizards. Sometimes playing against type can be fun, too. Half-orc paladins and mountain dwarf wizards, for example, can be unusual but memorable characters.

Your race also increases one or more of your ability scores, which you determine in step 3. Note these increases and remember to apply them later.

Record the traits granted by your race on your character sheet. Be sure to note your starting languages and your base speed as well.

Building Bruenor, Step 1

Bob is sitting down to create his character. He decides that a gruff mountain dwarf fits the character he wants to play. He notes all the racial traits of dwarves on his character sheet, including his speed of 25 feet and the languages he knows: Common and Dwarvish.

2. Choose a Class

Every adventurer is a member of a class. Class broadly describes a character's vocation, what special talents he or she possesses, and the tactics he or she is most likely to employ when exploring a dungeon, fighting monsters, or engaging in a tense negotiation. The character classes are described in chapter 3, "Classes."

Your character receives a number of benefits from your choice of class. Many of these benefits are **class features**—capabilities (including spellcasting) that set your character apart from members of other classes. You also gain a number of **proficiencies**: armor, weapons, skills, saving throws, and sometimes tools. Your proficiencies define many of the things your character can do particularly well, from using certain weapons to telling a convincing lie.

On your character sheet, record all the features that your class gives you at 1st level.

Level

Typically, a character starts at 1st level and advances in level by adventuring and gaining **experience points** (XP). A 1st-level character is inexperienced in the adventuring world, although he or she might have been a soldier or a pirate and done dangerous things before.

Starting off at 1st level marks your character's entry into the adventuring life. If you're already familiar with the game, or if you are joining an existing D&D campaign, your DM might decide to have you begin at a higher level, on the assumption that your character has already survived a few harrowing adventures.

> ### Quick Build
> Each class description in chapter 3 includes a section offering suggestions to quickly build a character of that class, including how to assign your highest ability scores, a background suitable to the class, and starting spells.

Record your level on your character sheet. If you're starting at a higher level, record the additional elements your class gives you for your levels past 1st. Also record your experience points. A 1st-level character has 0 XP. A higher-level character typically begins with the minimum amount of XP required to reach that level (see "Beyond 1st Level" later in this chapter).

HIT POINTS AND HIT DICE

Your character's hit points define how tough your character is in combat and other dangerous situations. Your hit points are determined by your Hit Dice (short for Hit Point Dice).

ABILITY SCORE SUMMARY

Strength
Measures: Natural athleticism, bodily power
Important for: Barbarian, fighter, paladin
Racial Increases:

Mountain dwarf (+2)	Half-orc (+2)
Dragonborn (+2)	Human (+1)

Dexterity
Measures: Physical agility, reflexes, balance, poise
Important for: Monk, ranger, rogue
Racial Increases:

Elf (+2)	Forest gnome (+1)
Halfling (+2)	Human (+1)

Constitution
Measures: Health, stamina, vital force
Important for: Everyone
Racial Increases:

Dwarf (+2)	Half-orc (+1)
Stout halfling (+1)	Human (+1)
Rock gnome (+1)	

Intelligence
Measures: Mental acuity, information recall, analytical skill
Important for: Wizard
Racial Increases:

High elf (+1)	Tiefling (+1)
Gnome (+2)	Human (+1)

Wisdom
Measures: Awareness, intuition, insight
Important for: Cleric, druid
Racial Increases:

Hill dwarf (+1)	Human (+1)
Wood elf (+1)	

Charisma
Measures: Confidence, eloquence, leadership
Important for: Bard, sorcerer, warlock
Racial Increases:

Half-elf (+2)	Dragonborn (+1)
Drow (+1)	Human (+1)
Lightfoot halfling (+1)	Tiefling (+2)

At 1st level, your character has 1 Hit Die, and the die type is determined by your class. You start with hit points equal to the highest roll of that die, as indicated in your class description. (You also add your Constitution modifier, which you'll determine in step 3.) This is also your **hit point maximum**.

Record your character's hit points on your character sheet. Also record the type of Hit Die your character uses and the number of Hit Dice you have. After you rest, you can spend Hit Dice to regain hit points (see "Resting" in chapter 8, "Adventuring").

PROFICIENCY BONUS

The table that appears in your class description shows your proficiency bonus, which is +2 for a 1st-level character. Your proficiency bonus applies to many of the numbers you'll be recording on your character sheet:

- Attack rolls using weapons you're proficient with
- Attack rolls with spells you cast
- Ability checks using skills you're proficient in
- Ability checks using tools you're proficient with
- Saving throws you're proficient in
- Saving throw DCs for spells you cast (explained in each spellcasting class)

Your class determines your weapon proficiencies, your saving throw proficiencies, and some of your skill and tool proficiencies. (Skills are described in chapter 7, "Using Ability Scores," and tools in chapter 5, "Equipment.") Your background gives you additional skill and tool proficiencies, and some races give you more proficiencies. Be sure to note all of these proficiencies, as well as your proficiency bonus, on your character sheet.

Your proficiency bonus can't be added to a single die roll or other number more than once. Occasionally, your proficiency bonus might be modified (doubled or halved, for example) before you apply it. If a circumstance suggests that your proficiency bonus applies more than once to the same roll or that it should be multiplied more than once, you nevertheless add it only once, multiply it only once, and halve it only once.

BUILDING BRUENOR, STEP 2

Bob imagines Bruenor charging into battle with an axe, one horn on his helmet broken off. He makes Bruenor a fighter and notes the fighter's proficiencies and 1st-level class features on his character sheet.

As a 1st-level fighter, Bruenor has 1 Hit Die—a d10—and starts with hit points equal to 10 + his Constitution modifier. Bob notes this, and will record the final number after he determines Bruenor's Constitution score (see step 3). Bob also notes the proficiency bonus for a 1st-level character, which is +2.

3. DETERMINE ABILITY SCORES

Much of what your character does in the game depends on his or her six abilities: **Strength**, **Dexterity**, **Constitution**, **Intelligence**, **Wisdom**, and **Charisma**. Each ability has a score, which is a number you record on your character sheet.

The six abilities and their use in the game are described in chapter 7. The Ability Score Summary table provides a quick reference for what qualities are measured by each ability, what races increases which abilities, and what classes consider each ability particularly important.

You generate your character's six **ability scores** randomly. Roll four 6-sided dice and record the total of the highest three dice on a piece of scratch paper. Do this five more times, so that you have six numbers. If you want to save time or don't like the idea of randomly determining ability scores, you can use the following scores instead: 15, 14, 13, 12, 10, 8.

Now take your six numbers and write each number beside one of your character's six abilities to assign scores to Strength, Dexterity, Constitution, Intelligence, Wisdom, and Charisma. Afterward, make any changes to your ability scores as a result of your race choice.

After assigning your ability scores, determine your **ability modifiers** using the Ability Scores and Modifiers table. To determine an ability modifier without consulting the table, subtract 10 from the ability score and then divide the result by 2 (round down). Write the modifier next to each of your scores.

BUILDING BRUENOR, STEP 3

Bob decides to use the standard set of scores (15, 14, 13, 12, 10, 8) for Bruenor's abilities. Since he's a fighter, he puts his highest score, 15, in Strength. His next-highest, 14, goes in Constitution. Bruenor might be a brash fighter, but Bob decides he wants the dwarf to be older, wiser, and a good leader, so he puts decent scores in Wisdom and Charisma. After applying his racial benefits (increasing Bruenor's Constitution by 2 and his Strength by 2), Bruenor's ability scores and modifiers look like this: Strength 17 (+3), Dexterity 10 (+0), Constitution 16 (+3), Intelligence 8 (–1), Wisdom 13 (+1), Charisma 12 (+1).

Bob fills in Bruenor's final hit points: 10 + his Constitution modifier of +3, for a total of 13 hit points.

VARIANT: CUSTOMIZING ABILITY SCORES

At your Dungeon Master's option, you can use this variant for determining your ability scores. The method described here allows you to build a character with a set of ability scores you choose individually.

You have 27 points to spend on your ability scores. The cost of each score is shown on the Ability Score Point Cost table. For example, a score of 14 costs 7 points. Using this method, 15 is the highest ability score you can end up with, before applying racial increases. You can't have a score lower than 8.

This method of determining ability scores enables you to create a set of three high numbers and three low ones (15, 15, 15, 8, 8, 8), a set of numbers that are above

ABILITY SCORES AND MODIFIERS

Score	Modifier	Score	Modifier
1	–5	16–17	+3
2–3	–4	18–19	+4
4–5	–3	20–21	+5
6–7	–2	22–23	+6
8–9	–1	24–25	+7
10–11	+0	26–27	+8
12–13	+1	28–29	+9
14–15	+2	30	+10

average and nearly equal (13, 13, 13, 12, 12, 12), or any set of numbers between those extremes.

4. DESCRIBE YOUR CHARACTER

Once you know the basic game aspects of your character, it's time to flesh him or her out as a person. Your character needs a name. Spend a few minutes thinking about what he or she looks like and how he or she behaves in general terms.

Using the information in chapter 4, "Personality and Background," you can flesh out your character's appearance and personality. Choose your character's **alignment** (the moral compass that guides his or her decisions) and **ideals**. Chapter 4 also helps you identify the things your character holds most dear, called **bonds**, and the **flaws** that could one day undermine him or her.

Your character's **background** describes where he or she came from, his or her original occupation, and the character's place in the D&D world. Your DM might offer additional backgrounds beyond the ones included

BRUENOR

ABILITY SCORE POINT COST

Score	Cost	Score	Cost
8	0	12	4
9	1	13	5
10	2	14	7
11	3	15	9

in chapter 4, and might be willing to work with you to craft a background that's a more precise fit for your character concept.

A background gives your character a background feature (a general benefit) and proficiency in two skills, and it might also give you additional languages or proficiency with certain kinds of tools. Record this information, along with the personality information you develop, on your character sheet.

YOUR CHARACTER'S ABILITIES

Take your character's ability scores and race into account as you flesh out his or her appearance and personality. A very strong character with low Intelligence might think and behave very differently from a very smart character with low Strength.

For example, high Strength usually corresponds with a burly or athletic body, while a character with low Strength might be scrawny or plump.

A character with high Dexterity is probably lithe and slim, while a character with low Dexterity might be either gangly and awkward or heavy and thick-fingered.

A character with high Constitution usually looks healthy, with bright eyes and abundant energy. A character with low Constitution might be sickly or frail.

A character with high Intelligence might be highly inquisitive and studious, while a character with low Intelligence might speak simply or easily forget details.

A character with high Wisdom has good judgment, empathy, and a general awareness of what's going on. A character with low Wisdom might be absent-minded, foolhardy, or oblivious.

A character with high Charisma exudes confidence, which is usually mixed with a graceful or intimidating presence. A character with a low Charisma might come across as abrasive, inarticulate, or timid.

BUILDING BRUENOR, STEP 4

Bob fills in some of Bruenor's basic details: his name, his sex (male), his height and weight, and his alignment (lawful good). His high Strength and Constitution suggest a healthy, athletic body, and his low Intelligence suggests a degree of forgetfulness.

Bob decides that Bruenor comes from a noble line, but his clan was expelled from its homeland when Bruenor was very young. He grew up working as a smith in the remote villages of Icewind Dale. But Bruenor has a heroic destiny—to reclaim his homeland—so Bob chooses the folk hero background for his dwarf. He notes the proficiencies and special feature this background gives him.

Bob has a pretty clear picture of Bruenor's personality in mind, so he skips the personality traits suggested in the folk hero background, noting instead that Bruenor is a caring, sensitive dwarf who genuinely loves his friends and allies, but he hides this soft heart behind a gruff, snarling demeanor. He chooses the ideal of fairness from the list in his background, noting that Bruenor believes that no one is above the law.

Given his history, Bruenor's bond is obvious: he aspires to someday reclaim Mithral Hall, his homeland, from the shadow dragon that drove the dwarves out.

His flaw is tied to his caring, sensitive nature—he has a soft spot for orphans and wayward souls, leading him to show mercy even when it might not be warranted.

5. CHOOSE EQUIPMENT

Your class and background determine your character's **starting equipment**, including weapons, armor, and other adventuring gear. Record this equipment on your character sheet. All such items are detailed in chapter 5, "Equipment."

Instead of taking the gear given to you by your class and background, you can purchase your starting equipment. You have a number of **gold pieces** (gp) to spend based on your class, as shown in chapter 5. Extensive lists of equipment, with prices, also appear in that chapter. If you wish, you can also have one trinket at no cost (see the Trinkets table at the end of chapter 5).

Your Strength score limits the amount of gear you can carry. Try not to purchase equipment with a total weight (in pounds) exceeding your Strength score times 15. Chapter 7 has more information on carrying capacity.

ARMOR CLASS

Your **Armor Class** (AC) represents how well your character avoids being wounded in battle. Things that contribute to your AC include the armor you wear, the shield you carry, and your Dexterity modifier. Not all characters wear armor or carry shields, however.

Without armor or a shield, your character's AC equals 10 + his or her Dexterity modifier. If your character wears armor, carries a shield, or both, calculate your AC using the rules in chapter 5. Record your AC on your character sheet.

Your character needs to be proficient with armor and shields to wear and use them effectively, and your armor and shield proficiencies are determined by your class. There are drawbacks to wearing armor or carrying a shield if you lack the required proficiency, as explained in chapter 5.

Some spells and class features give you a different way to calculate your AC. If you have multiple features that give you different ways to calculate your AC, you choose which one to use.

WEAPONS

For each weapon your character wields, calculate the modifier you use when you attack with the weapon and the damage you deal when you hit.

When you make an attack with a weapon, you roll a d20 and add your proficiency bonus (but only if you are proficient with the weapon) and the appropriate ability modifier.

- For attacks with **melee weapons**, use your Strength modifier for attack and damage rolls. A weapon that has the finesse property, such as a rapier, can use your Dexterity modifier instead.
- For attacks with **ranged weapons**, use your Dexterity modifier for attack and damage rolls. A weapon that has the thrown property, such as a handaxe, can use your Strength modifier instead.

BUILDING BRUENOR, STEP 5

Bob writes down the starting equipment from the fighter class and the folk hero background. His starting equipment includes chain mail and a shield, which combine to give Bruenor an Armor Class of 18.

For Bruenor's weapons, Bob chooses a battleaxe and two handaxes. His battleaxe is a melee weapon, so Bruenor uses his Strength modifier for his attacks and damage. His attack bonus is his Strength modifier (+3) plus his proficiency bonus (+2), for a total of +5. The battleaxe deals 1d8 slashing damage, and Bruenor adds his Strength modifier to the damage when he hits, for a total of 1d8 + 3 slashing damage. When throwing a handaxe, Bruenor has the same attack bonus (handaxes, as thrown weapons, use Strength for attacks and damage), and the weapon deals 1d6 + 3 slashing damage when it hits.

6. Come Together

Most D&D characters don't work alone. Each character plays a role within a **party**, a group of adventurers working together for a common purpose. Teamwork and cooperation greatly improve your party's chances to survive the many perils in the worlds of Dungeons & Dragons. Talk to your fellow players and your DM to decide whether your characters know one another, how they met, and what sorts of quests the group might undertake.

Beyond 1st Level

As your character goes on adventures and overcomes challenges, he or she gains experience, represented by experience points. A character who reaches a specified experience point total advances in capability. This advancement is called **gaining a level**.

When your character gains a level, his or her class often grants additional features, as detailed in the class description. Some of these features allow you to increase your ability scores, either increasing two scores by 1 each or increasing one score by 2. You can't increase an ability score above 20. In addition, every character's proficiency bonus increases at certain levels.

Each time you gain a level, you gain 1 additional Hit Die. Roll that Hit Die, add your Constitution modifier to the roll, and add the total to your hit point maximum. Alternatively, you can use the fixed value shown in your class entry, which is the average result of the die roll (rounded up).

When your Constitution modifier increases by 1, your hit point maximum increases by 1 for each level you have attained. For example, when Bruenor reaches 8th level as a fighter, he increases his Constitution score from 17 to 18, thus increasing his Constitution modifier from +3 to +4. His hit point maximum then increases by 8.

The Character Advancement table summarizes the XP you need to advance in levels from level 1 through level 20, and the proficiency bonus for a character of that level. Consult the information in your character's class description to see what other improvements you gain at each level.

Tiers of Play

The shading in the Character Advancement table shows the four tiers of play. The tiers don't have any rules associated with them; they are a general description of how the play experience changes as characters gain levels.

In the first tier (levels 1–4), characters are effectively apprentice adventurers. They are learning the features that define them as members of particular classes, including the major choices that flavor their class features as they advance (such as a wizard's Arcane Tradition or a fighter's Martial Archetype). The threats they face are relatively minor, usually posing a danger to local farmsteads or villages.

In the second tier (levels 5–10), characters come into their own. Many spellcasters gain access to 3rd-level spells at the start of this tier, crossing a new threshold of magical power with spells such as *fireball* and *lightning bolt*. At this tier, many weapon-using classes gain the ability to make multiple attacks in one round. These characters have become important, facing dangers that threaten cities and kingdoms.

In the third tier (levels 11–16), characters have reached a level of power that sets them high above the ordinary populace and makes them special even among adventurers. At 11th level, many spellcasters gain access to 6th-level spells, some of which create effects previously impossible for player characters to achieve. Other characters gain features that allow them to make more attacks or do more impressive things with those attacks. These mighty adventurers often confront threats to whole regions and continents.

At the fourth tier (levels 17–20), characters achieve the pinnacle of their class features, becoming heroic (or villainous) archetypes in their own right. The fate of the world or even the fundamental order of the multiverse might hang in the balance during their adventures.

Character Advancement

Experience Points	Level	Proficiency Bonus
0	1	+2
300	2	+2
900	3	+2
2,700	4	+2
6,500	5	+3
14,000	6	+3
23,000	7	+3
34,000	8	+3
48,000	9	+4
64,000	10	+4
85,000	11	+4
100,000	12	+4
120,000	13	+5
140,000	14	+5
165,000	15	+5
195,000	16	+5
225,000	17	+6
265,000	18	+6
305,000	19	+6
355,000	20	+6

Chapter 2: Races

A VISIT TO ONE OF THE GREAT CITIES IN THE worlds of DUNGEONS & DRAGONS— Waterdeep, the Free City of Greyhawk, or even uncanny Sigil, the City of Doors— overwhelms the senses. Voices chatter in countless different languages. The smells of cooking in dozens of different cuisines mingle with the odors of crowded streets and poor sanitation. Buildings in myriad architectural styles display the diverse origins of their inhabitants.

And the people themselves—people of varying size, shape, and color, dressed in a dazzling spectrum of styles and hues—represent many different races, from diminutive halflings and stout dwarves to majestically beautiful elves, mingling among a variety of human ethnicities.

Scattered among the members of these more common races are the true exotics: a hulking dragonborn here, pushing his way through the crowd, and a sly tiefling there, lurking in the shadows with mischief in her eyes. A group of gnomes laughs as one of them activates a clever wooden toy that moves of its own accord. Half-elves and half-orcs live and work alongside humans, without fully belonging to the races of either of their parents. And there, well out of the sunlight, is a lone drow—a fugitive from the subterranean expanse of the Underdark, trying to make his way in a world that fears his kind.

Choosing a Race

Humans are the most common people in the worlds of D&D, but they live and work alongside dwarves, elves, halflings, and countless other fantastic species. Your character belongs to one of these peoples.

Not every intelligent race of the multiverse is appropriate for a player-controlled adventurer. Dwarves, elves, halflings, and humans are the most common races to produce the sort of adventurers who make up typical parties. Dragonborn, gnomes, half-elves, half-orcs, and tieflings are less common as adventurers. Drow, a subrace of elves, are also uncommon.

Your choice of race affects many different aspects of your character. It establishes fundamental qualities that exist throughout your character's adventuring career. When making this decision, keep in mind the kind of character you want to play. For example, a halfling could be a good choice for a sneaky rogue, a dwarf makes a tough warrior, and an elf can be a master of arcane magic.

Your character race not only affects your ability scores and traits but also provides the cues for building your character's story. Each race's description in this chapter includes information to help you roleplay a character of that race, including personality, physical appearance, features of society, and racial alignment tendencies. These details are suggestions to help you think about your character; adventurers can deviate widely from the norm for their race. It's worthwhile to consider why your character is different, as a helpful way to think about your character's background and personality.

Racial Traits

The description of each race includes racial traits that are common to members of that race. The following entries appear among the traits of most races.

Ability Score Increase
Every race increases one or more of a character's ability scores.

Age
The age entry notes the age when a member of the race is considered an adult, as well as the race's expected lifespan. This information can help you decide how old your character is at the start of the game. You can choose any age for your character, which could provide an explanation for some of your ability scores. For example, if you play a young or very old character, your age could explain a particularly low Strength or Constitution score, while advanced age could account for a high Intelligence or Wisdom.

Alignment
Most races have tendencies toward certain alignments, described in this entry. These are not binding for player characters, but considering why your dwarf is chaotic, for example, in defiance of lawful dwarf society can help you better define your character.

Size
Characters of most races are Medium, a size category including creatures that are roughly 4 to 8 feet tall. Members of a few races are Small (between 2 and 4 feet tall), which means that certain rules of the game affect them differently. The most important of these rules is that Small characters have trouble wielding heavy weapons, as explained in chapter 5, "Equipment."

Speed
Your speed determines how far you can move when traveling (chapter 8, "Adventuring") and fighting (chapter 9, "Combat").

Languages
By virtue of your race, your character can speak, read, and write certain languages. Chapter 4, "Personality and Background," lists the most common languages of the D&D multiverse.

Subraces
Some races have subraces. Members of a subrace have the traits of the parent race in addition to the traits specified for their subrace. Relationships among subraces vary significantly from race to race and world to world. In the Dragonlance campaign setting, for example, mountain dwarves and hill dwarves live together as different clans of the same people, but in the Forgotten Realms, they live far apart in separate kingdoms and call themselves shield dwarves and gold dwarves, respectively.

DWARF

"YER LATE, ELF!" CAME THE ROUGH EDGE OF A FAMILIAR voice. Bruenor Battlehammer walked up the back of his dead foe, disregarding the fact that the heavy monster lay on top of his elven friend. In spite of the added discomfort, the dwarf's long, pointed, often-broken nose and gray-streaked though still-fiery red beard came as a welcome sight to Drizzt. "Knew I'd find ye in trouble if I came out an' looked for ye!"

—R. A. Salvatore, *The Crystal Shard*

Kingdoms rich in ancient grandeur, halls carved into the roots of mountains, the echoing of picks and hammers in deep mines and blazing forges, a commitment to clan and tradition, and a burning hatred of goblins and orcs—these common threads unite all dwarves.

SHORT AND STOUT

Bold and hardy, dwarves are known as skilled warriors, miners, and workers of stone and metal. Though they stand well under 5 feet tall, dwarves are so broad and compact that they can weigh as much as a human standing nearly two feet taller. Their courage and endurance are also easily a match for any of the larger folk.

Dwarven skin ranges from deep brown to a paler hue tinged with red, but the most common shades are light brown or deep tan, like certain tones of earth. Their hair, worn long but in simple styles, is usually black, gray, or brown, though paler dwarves often have red hair. Male dwarves value their beards highly and groom them carefully.

LONG MEMORY, LONG GRUDGES

Dwarves can live to be more than 400 years old, so the oldest living dwarves often remember a very different world. For example, some of the oldest dwarves living in Citadel Felbarr (in the world of the Forgotten Realms) can recall the day, more than three centuries ago, when orcs conquered the fortress and drove them into an exile that lasted over 250 years. This longevity grants them a perspective on the world that shorter-lived races such as humans and halflings lack.

Dwarves are solid and enduring like the mountains they love, weathering the passage of centuries with stoic endurance and little change. They respect the traditions of their clans, tracing their ancestry back to the founding of their most ancient strongholds in the youth of the world, and don't abandon those traditions lightly. Part of those traditions is devotion to the gods of the dwarves, who uphold the dwarven ideals of industrious labor, skill in battle, and devotion to the forge.

Individual dwarves are determined and loyal, true to their word and decisive in action, sometimes to the point of stubbornness. Many dwarves have a strong sense of justice, and they are slow to forget wrongs they have suffered. A wrong done to one dwarf is a wrong done to the dwarf's entire clan, so what begins as one dwarf's hunt for vengeance can become a full-blown clan feud.

CLANS AND KINGDOMS

Dwarven kingdoms stretch deep beneath the mountains where the dwarves mine gems and precious metals and forge items of wonder. They love the beauty and artistry of precious metals and fine jewelry, and in some dwarves this love festers into avarice. Whatever wealth they can't find in their mountains, they gain through trade. They dislike boats, so enterprising humans and halflings frequently handle trade in dwarven goods along water routes. Trustworthy members of other races are welcome in dwarf settlements, though some areas are off limits even to them.

The chief unit of dwarven society is the clan, and dwarves highly value social standing. Even dwarves who live far from their own kingdoms cherish their clan identities and affiliations, recognize related dwarves, and invoke their ancestors' names in oaths and curses. To be clanless is the worst fate that can befall a dwarf.

Dwarves in other lands are typically artisans, especially weaponsmiths, armorers, and jewelers. Some become mercenaries or bodyguards, highly sought after for their courage and loyalty.

GODS, GOLD, AND CLAN

Dwarves who take up the adventuring life might be motivated by a desire for treasure—for its own sake, for a specific purpose, or even out of an altruistic desire to help others. Other dwarves are driven by the command or inspiration of a deity, a direct calling or simply a desire to bring glory to one of the dwarf gods. Clan and ancestry are also important motivators. A dwarf might seek to restore a clan's lost honor, avenge an ancient wrong the clan suffered, or earn a new place within the clan after having been exiled. Or a dwarf might search for the axe wielded by a mighty ancestor, lost on the field of battle centuries ago.

SLOW TO TRUST

Dwarves get along passably well with most other races. "The difference between an acquaintance and a friend is about a hundred years," is a dwarf saying that might be hyperbole, but certainly points to how difficult it can be for a member of a short-lived race like humans to earn a dwarf's trust.

Elves. "It's not wise to depend on the elves. No telling what an elf will do next; when the hammer meets the orc's head, they're as apt to start singing as to pull out a sword. They're flighty and frivolous. Two things to be said for them, though: They don't have many smiths, but the ones they have do very fine work. And when orcs or goblins come streaming down out of the mountains, an elf's good to have at your back. Not as good as a dwarf, maybe, but no doubt they hate the orcs as much as we do."

Halflings. "Sure, they're pleasant folk. But show me a halfling hero. An empire, a triumphant army. Even a treasure for the ages made by halfling hands. Nothing. How can you take them seriously?"

Humans. "You take the time to get to know a human, and by then the human's on her deathbed. If you're lucky, she's got kin—a daughter or granddaughter, maybe—who's got hands and heart as good as hers. That's when you can make a human friend. And watch them go! They set their hearts on something, they'll get it, whether it's a dragon's hoard or an empire's throne. You have to admire that kind of dedication, even if it gets them in trouble more often than not."

DWARF NAMES

A dwarf's name is granted by a clan elder, in accordance with tradition. Every proper dwarven name has been used and reused down through the generations. A dwarf's name belongs to the clan, not to the individual. A dwarf who misuses or brings shame to a clan name is stripped of the name and forbidden by law to use any dwarven name in its place.

Male Names: Adrik, Alberich, Baern, Barendd, Brottor, Bruenor, Dain, Darrak, Delg, Eberk, Einkil, Fargrim, Flint, Gardain, Harbek, Kildrak, Morgran, Orsik, Oskar, Rangrim, Rurik, Taklinn, Thoradin, Thorin, Tordek, Traubon, Travok, Ulfgar, Veit, Vondal

Female Names: Amber, Artin, Audhild, Bardryn, Dagnal, Diesa, Eldeth, Falkrunn, Finellen, Gunnloda, Gurdis, Helja, Hlin, Kathra, Kristryd, Ilde, Liftrasa, Mardred, Riswynn, Sannl, Torbera, Torgga, Vistra

Clan Names: Balderk, Battlehammer, Brawnanvil, Dankil, Fireforge, Frostbeard, Gorunn, Holderhek, Ironfist, Loderr, Lutgehr, Rumnaheim, Strakeln, Torunn, Ungart

DWARF TRAITS

Your dwarf character has an assortment of inborn abilities, part and parcel of dwarven nature.

Ability Score Increase. Your Constitution score increases by 2.

Age. Dwarves mature at the same rate as humans, but they're considered young until they reach the age of 50. On average, they live about 350 years.

Alignment. Most dwarves are lawful, believing firmly in the benefits of a well-ordered society. They tend toward good as well, with a strong sense of fair play and a belief that everyone deserves to share in the benefits of a just order.

Size. Dwarves stand between 4 and 5 feet tall and average about 150 pounds. Your size is Medium.

Speed. Your base walking speed is 25 feet. Your speed is not reduced by wearing heavy armor.

Darkvision. Accustomed to life underground, you have superior vision in dark and dim conditions. You can see in dim light within 60 feet of you as if it were bright light, and in darkness as if it were dim light. You can't discern color in darkness, only shades of gray.

Dwarven Resilience. You have advantage on saving throws against poison, and you have resistance against poison damage (explained in chapter 9, "Combat").

Dwarven Combat Training. You have proficiency with the battleaxe, handaxe, light hammer, and warhammer.

Tool Proficiency. You gain proficiency with the artisan's tools of your choice: smith's tools, brewer's supplies, or mason's tools.

Stonecunning. Whenever you make an Intelligence (History) check related to the origin of stonework, you are considered proficient in the History skill and add double your proficiency bonus to the check, instead of your normal proficiency bonus.

Languages. You can speak, read, and write Common and Dwarvish. Dwarvish is full of hard consonants and guttural sounds, and those characteristics spill over into whatever other language a dwarf might speak.

Subrace. Two main subraces of dwarves populate the worlds of D&D: hill dwarves and mountain dwarves. Choose one of these subraces.

HILL DWARF

As a hill dwarf, you have keen senses, deep intuition, and remarkable resilience. The gold dwarves of Faerûn in their mighty southern kingdom are hill dwarves, as are the exiled Neidar and the debased Klar of Krynn in the Dragonlance setting.

Ability Score Increase. Your Wisdom score increases by 1.

Dwarven Toughness. Your hit point maximum increases by 1, and it increases by 1 every time you gain a level.

MOUNTAIN DWARF

As a mountain dwarf, you're strong and hardy, accustomed to a difficult life in rugged terrain. You're probably on the tall side (for a dwarf), and tend toward lighter coloration. The shield dwarves of northern Faerûn, as well as the ruling Hylar clan and the noble Daewar clan of Dragonlance, are mountain dwarves.

Ability Score Increase. Your Strength score increases by 2.

Dwarven Armor Training. You have proficiency with light and medium armor.

> ### DUERGAR
> In cities deep in the Underdark live the duergar, or gray dwarves. These vicious, stealthy slave traders raid the surface world for captives, then sell their prey to the other races of the Underdark. They have innate magical abilities to become invisible and to temporarily grow to giant size.

Elf

"I have never imagined such beauty existed,"
Goldmoon said softly. The day's march had been difficult,
but the reward at the end was beyond their dreams.
The companions stood on a high cliff over the fabled
city of Qualinost.

Four slender spires rose from the city's corners like glisten-
ing spindles, their brilliant white stone marbled with shining
silver. Graceful arches, swooping from spire to spire, soared
through the air. Crafted by ancient dwarven metalsmiths,
they were strong enough to hold the weight of an army, yet
they appeared so delicate that a bird lighting on them might
overthrow the balance. These glistening arches were the
city's only boundaries; there was no wall around Qualinost.
The elven city opened its arms lovingly to the wilderness.

—Margaret Weis & Tracy Hickman,
Dragons of Autumn Twilight

DRIZZT DO'URDEN

Elves are a magical people of otherworldly grace, living
in the world but not entirely part of it. They live in
places of ethereal beauty, in the midst of ancient forests
or in silvery spires glittering with faerie light, where
soft music drifts through the air and gentle fragrances
waft on the breeze. Elves love nature and magic, art
and artistry, music and poetry, and the good things
of the world.

Slender and Graceful

With their unearthly grace and fine features, elves
appear hauntingly beautiful to humans and members
of many other races. They are slightly shorter than
humans on average, ranging from well under 5 feet
tall to just over 6 feet. They are more slender than
humans, weighing only 100 to 145 pounds. Males and
females are about the same height, and males are only
marginally heavier than females.

Elves' coloration encompasses the normal human
range and also includes skin in shades of copper,
bronze, and almost bluish-white, hair of green or blue,
and eyes like pools of liquid gold or silver. Elves have no
facial and little body hair. They favor elegant clothing in
bright colors, and they enjoy simple yet lovely jewelry.

A Timeless Perspective

Elves can live well over 700 years, giving them a broad
perspective on events that might trouble the shorter-
lived races more deeply. They are more often amused
than excited, and more likely to be curious than
greedy. They tend to remain aloof and unfazed by petty
happenstance. When pursuing a goal, however, whether

adventuring on a mission or learning a new skill or art, elves can be focused and relentless. They are slow to make friends and enemies, and even slower to forget them. They reply to petty insults with disdain and to serious insults with vengeance.

Like the branches of a young tree, elves are flexible in the face of danger. They trust in diplomacy and compromise to resolve differences before they escalate to violence. They have been known to retreat from intrusions into their woodland homes, confident that they can simply wait the invaders out. But when the need arises, elves reveal a stern martial side, demonstrating skill with sword, bow, and strategy.

HIDDEN WOODLAND REALMS

Most elves dwell in small forest villages hidden among the trees. Elves hunt game, gather food, and grow vegetables, and their skill and magic allow them to support themselves without the need for clearing and plowing land. They are talented artisans, crafting finely worked clothes and art objects. Their contact with outsiders is usually limited, though a few elves make a good living by trading crafted items for metals (which they have no interest in mining).

Elves encountered outside their own lands are commonly traveling minstrels, artists, or sages. Human nobles compete for the services of elf instructors to teach swordplay or magic to their children.

EXPLORATION AND ADVENTURE

Elves take up adventuring out of wanderlust. Since they are so long-lived, they can enjoy centuries of exploration and discovery. They dislike the pace of human society, which is regimented from day to day but constantly changing over decades, so they find careers that let them travel freely and set their own pace. Elves also enjoy exercising their martial prowess or gaining greater magical power, and adventuring allows them

to do so. Some might join with rebels fighting against oppression, and others might become champions of moral causes.

ELF NAMES

Elves are considered children until they declare themselves adults, some time after the hundredth birthday, and before this period they are called by child names.

On declaring adulthood, an elf selects an adult name, although those who knew him or her as a youngster might continue to use the child name. Each elf's adult name is a unique creation, though it might reflect the names of respected individuals or other family members. Little distinction exists between male names and female names; the groupings here reflect only general tendencies. In addition, every elf bears a family name, typically a combination of other Elvish words. Some elves traveling among humans translate their family names into Common, but others retain the Elvish version.

Child Names: Ara, Bryn, Del, Eryn, Faen, Innil, Lael, Mella, Naill, Naeris, Phann, Rael, Rinn, Sai, Syllin, Thia, Vall

Male Adult Names: Adran, Aelar, Aramil, Arannis, Aust, Beiro, Berrian, Carric, Enialis, Erdan, Erevan, Galinndan, Hadarai, Heian, Himo, Immeral, Ivellios, Laucian, Mindartis, Paelias, Peren, Quarion, Riardon, Rolen, Soveliss, Thamior, Tharivol, Theren, Varis

Female Adult Names: Adrie, Althaea, Anastrianna, Andraste, Antinua, Bethrynna, Birel, Caelynn, Drusilia, Enna, Felosial, Ielenia, Jelenneth, Keyleth, Leshanna, Lia, Meriele, Mialee, Naivara, Quelenna, Quillathe, Sariel, Shanairra, Shava, Silaqui, Theirastra, Thia, Vadania, Valanthe, Xanaphia

Family Names (Common Translations): Amakiir (Gemflower), Amastacia (Starflower), Galanodel (Moonwhisper), Holimion (Diamonddew), Ilphelkiir (Gemblossom), Liadon (Silverfrond), Meliamne (Oakenheel), Naïlo (Nightbreeze), Siannodel (Moonbrook), Xiloscient (Goldpetal)

ELF TRAITS

Your elf character has a variety of natural abilities, the result of thousands of years of elven refinement.

Ability Score Increase. Your Dexterity score increases by 2.

Age. Although elves reach physical maturity at about the same age as humans, the elven understanding of adulthood goes beyond physical growth to encompass worldly experience. An elf typically claims adulthood and an adult name around the age of 100 and can live to be 750 years old.

Alignment. Elves love freedom, variety, and self-expression, so they lean strongly toward the gentler aspects of chaos. They value and protect others' freedom as well as their own, and they are more often good than not. The drow are an exception; their exile into the Underdark has made them vicious and dangerous. Drow are more often evil than not.

Size. Elves range from under 5 to over 6 feet tall and have slender builds. Your size is Medium.

Speed. Your base walking speed is 30 feet.

Darkvision. Accustomed to twilit forests and the night sky, you have superior vision in dark and dim conditions. You can see in dim light within 60 feet of you as if it were bright light, and in darkness as if it were dim light. You can't discern color in darkness, only shades of gray.

Keen Senses. You have proficiency in the Perception skill.

Fey Ancestry. You have advantage on saving throws against being charmed, and magic can't put you to sleep.

Trance. Elves don't need to sleep. Instead, they meditate deeply, remaining semiconscious, for 4 hours a day. (The Common word for such meditation is "trance.") While meditating, you can dream after a fashion; such dreams are actually mental exercises that have become reflexive through years of practice. After resting in this way, you gain the same benefit that a human does from 8 hours of sleep.

Languages. You can speak, read, and write Common and Elvish. Elvish is fluid, with subtle intonations and intricate grammar. Elven literature is rich and varied, and their songs and poems are famous among other races. Many bards learn their language so they can add Elvish ballads to their repertoires.

Subrace. Ancient divides among the elven people resulted in three main subraces: high elves, wood elves, and dark elves, who are commonly called drow. Choose one of these subraces. In some worlds, these subraces are divided still further (such as the sun elves and moon elves of the Forgotten Realms), so if you wish, you can choose a narrower subrace.

HIGH ELF

As a high elf, you have a keen mind and a mastery of at least the basics of magic. In many of the worlds of D&D, there are two kinds of high elves. One type (which includes the gray elves and valley elves of Greyhawk, the Silvanesti of Dragonlance, and the sun elves of the Forgotten Realms) is haughty and reclusive, believing themselves to be superior to non-elves and even other elves. The other type (including the high elves of Greyhawk, the Qualinesti of Dragonlance, and the moon elves of the Forgotten Realms) are more common and more friendly, and often encountered among humans and other races.

The sun elves of Faerûn (also called gold elves or sunrise elves) have bronze skin and hair of copper, black, or golden blond. Their eyes are golden, silver, or black. Moon elves (also called silver elves or gray elves) are much paler, with alabaster skin sometimes tinged with blue. They often have hair of silver-white, black, or blue, but various shades of blond, brown, and red are not uncommon. Their eyes are blue or green and flecked with gold.

Ability Score Increase. Your Intelligence score increases by 1.

Elf Weapon Training. You have proficiency with the longsword, shortsword, shortbow, and longbow.

Cantrip. You know one cantrip of your choice from the wizard spell list. Intelligence is your spellcasting ability for it.

Extra Language. You can speak, read, and write one extra language of your choice.

Wood Elf

As a wood elf, you have keen senses and intuition, and your fleet feet carry you quickly and stealthily through your native forests. This category includes the wild elves (grugach) of Greyhawk and the Kagonesti of Dragonlance, as well as the races called wood elves in Greyhawk and the Forgotten Realms. In Faerûn, wood elves (also called wild elves, green elves, or forest elves) are reclusive and distrusting of non-elves.

Wood elves' skin tends to be copperish in hue, sometimes with traces of green. Their hair tends toward browns and blacks, but it is occasionally blond or copper-colored. Their eyes are green, brown, or hazel.

Ability Score Increase. Your Wisdom score increases by 1.

Elf Weapon Training. You have proficiency with the longsword, shortsword, shortbow, and longbow.

Fleet of Foot. Your base walking speed increases to 35 feet.

Mask of the Wild. You can attempt to hide even when you are only lightly obscured by foliage, heavy rain, falling snow, mist, and other natural phenomena.

Dark Elf (Drow)

Descended from an earlier subrace of elves, the drow were banished from the surface world for following the goddess Lolth down the path of evil. Now they have built their own civilization in the depths of the Underdark, patterned after the Way of Lolth. Also called dark elves, the drow have skin that resembles charcoal or obsidian, as well as stark white or pale yellow hair. They commonly have very pale eyes (so pale as to be mistaken for white) in shades of lilac, silver, pink, red, and blue. They tend to be smaller and thinner than most elves.

Drow adventurers are rare. Check with your Dungeon Master to see if you can play one.

Ability Score Increase. Your Charisma score increases by 1.

Superior Darkvision. Your darkvision has a radius of 120 feet.

Sunlight Sensitivity. You have disadvantage on attack rolls and on Wisdom (Perception) checks that rely on sight when you, the target of your attack, or whatever you are trying to perceive is in direct sunlight.

Drow Magic. You know the *dancing lights* cantrip. When you reach 3rd level, you can cast the *faerie fire* spell once with this trait and regain the ability to do so when you finish a long rest. When you reach 5th level, you can cast the *darkness* spell once with this trait and regain the ability to do so when you finish a long rest. Charisma is your spellcasting ability for these spells.

Drow Weapon Training. You have proficiency with rapiers, shortswords, and hand crossbows.

THE DARKNESS OF THE DROW

Were it not for one renowned exception, the race of drow would be universally reviled. To most, they are a race of demon-worshiping marauders dwelling in the subterranean depths of the Underdark, emerging only on the blackest nights to pillage and slaughter the surface dwellers they despise. Their society is depraved and preoccupied with the favor of Lolth, their spider-goddess, who sanctions murder and the extermination of entire families as noble houses vie for position.

Yet one drow, at least, broke the mold. In the world of the Forgotten Realms, Drizzt Do'Urden, ranger of the North, has proven his quality as a good-hearted defender of the weak and innocent. Rejecting his heritage and adrift in a world that looks upon him with terror and loathing, Drizzt is a model for those few drow who follow in his footsteps, trying to find a life apart from the evil society of their Underdark homes.

Drow grow up believing that surface-dwelling races are inferior, worthless except as slaves. Drow who develop a conscience or find it necessary to cooperate with members of other races find it hard to overcome that prejudice, especially when they are so often on the receiving end of hatred.

HALFLING

REGIS THE HALFLING, THE ONLY ONE OF HIS KIND FOR *hundreds of miles in any direction, locked his fingers behind his head and leaned back against the mossy blanket of the tree trunk. Regis was short, even by the standards of his diminutive race, with the fluff of his curly brown locks barely cresting the three-foot mark, but his belly was amply thickened by his love of a good meal, or several, as the opportunities presented themselves. The crooked stick that served as his fishing pole rose up above him, clenched between two of his toes, and hung out over the quiet lake, mirrored perfectly in the glassy surface of Maer Dualdon.*

—R.A. Salvatore, *The Crystal Shard*

The comforts of home are the goals of most halflings' lives: a place to settle in peace and quiet, far from marauding monsters and clashing armies; a blazing fire and a generous meal; fine drink and fine conversation. Though some halflings live out their days in remote agricultural communities, others form nomadic bands that travel constantly, lured by the open road and the wide horizon to discover the wonders of new lands and peoples. But even these wanderers love peace, food, hearth, and home, though home might be a wagon jostling along an dirt road or a raft floating downriver.

SMALL AND PRACTICAL

The diminutive halflings survive in a world full of larger creatures by avoiding notice or, barring that, avoiding offense. Standing about 3 feet tall, they appear relatively harmless and so have managed to survive for centuries in the shadow of empires and on the edges of wars and political strife. They are inclined to be stout, weighing between 40 and 45 pounds.

Halflings' skin ranges from tan to pale with a ruddy cast, and their hair is usually brown or sandy brown and wavy. They have brown or hazel eyes. Halfling men often sport long sideburns, but beards are rare among them and mustaches even more so. They like to wear simple, comfortable, and practical clothes, favoring bright colors.

Halfling practicality extends beyond their clothing. They're concerned with basic needs and simple pleasures and have little use for ostentation. Even the wealthiest of halflings keep their treasures locked in a cellar rather than on display for all to see. They have a knack for finding the most straightforward solution to a problem, and have little patience for dithering.

KIND AND CURIOUS

Halflings are an affable and cheerful people. They cherish the bonds of family and friendship as well as the comforts of hearth and home, harboring few dreams of gold or glory. Even adventurers among them usually venture into the world for reasons of community, friendship, wanderlust, or curiosity. They love discovering new things, even simple things, such as an exotic food or an unfamiliar style of clothing.

Halflings are easily moved to pity and hate to see any living thing suffer. They are generous, happily sharing what they have even in lean times.

Blend into the Crowd

Halflings are adept at fitting into a community of humans, dwarves, or elves, making themselves valuable and welcome. The combination of their inherent stealth and their unassuming nature helps halflings to avoid unwanted attention.

Halflings work readily with others, and they are loyal to their friends, whether halfling or otherwise. They can display remarkable ferocity when their friends, families, or communities are threatened.

Pastoral Pleasantries

Most halflings live in small, peaceful communities with large farms and well-kept groves. They rarely build kingdoms of their own or even hold much land beyond their quiet shires. They typically don't recognize any sort of halfling nobility or royalty, instead looking to family elders to guide them. Families preserve their traditional ways despite the rise and fall of empires.

Many halflings live among other races, where the halflings' hard work and loyal outlook offer them abundant rewards and creature comforts. Some halfling communities travel as a way of life, driving wagons or guiding boats from place to place and maintaining no permanent home.

Affable and Positive

Halflings try to get along with everyone else and are loath to make sweeping generalizations—especially negative ones.

Dwarves. "Dwarves make loyal friends, and you can count on them to keep their word. But would it hurt them to smile once in a while?"

Elves. "They're so beautiful! Their faces, their music, their grace and all. It's like they stepped out of a wonderful dream. But there's no telling what's going on behind their smiling faces—surely more than they ever let on."

Humans. "Humans are a lot like us, really. At least some of them are. Step out of the castles and keeps, go talk to the farmers and herders and you'll find good, solid folk. Not that there's anything wrong with the barons and soldiers—you have to admire their conviction. And by protecting their own lands, they protect us as well."

Exploring Opportunities

Halflings usually set out on the adventurer's path to defend their communities, support their friends, or explore a wide and wonder-filled world. For them, adventuring is less a career than an opportunity or sometimes a necessity.

Halfling Names

A halfling has a given name, a family name, and possibly a nickname. Family names are often nicknames that stuck so tenaciously they have been passed down through the generations.

Male Names: Alton, Ander, Cade, Corrin, Eldon, Errich, Finnan, Garret, Lindal, Lyle, Merric, Milo, Osborn, Perrin, Reed, Roscoe, Wellby

Female Names: Andry, Bree, Callie, Cora, Euphemia, Jillian, Kithri, Lavinia, Lidda, Merla, Nedda, Paela, Portia, Seraphina, Shaena, Trym, Vani, Verna

Family Names: Brushgather, Goodbarrel, Greenbottle, High-hill, Hilltopple, Leagallow, Tealeaf, Thorngage, Tosscobble, Underbough

HALFLING TRAITS

Your halfling character has a number of traits in common with all other halflings.

Ability Score Increase. Your Dexterity score increases by 2.

Age. A halfling reaches adulthood at the age of 20 and generally lives into the middle of his or her second century.

Alignment. Most halflings are lawful good. As a rule, they are good-hearted and kind, hate to see others in pain, and have no tolerance for oppression. They are also very orderly and traditional, leaning heavily on the support of their community and the comfort of their old ways.

Size. Halflings average about 3 feet tall and weigh about 40 pounds. Your size is Small.

Speed. Your base walking speed is 25 feet.

Lucky. When you roll a 1 on the d20 for an attack roll, ability check, or saving throw, you can reroll the die and must use the new roll.

Brave. You have advantage on saving throws against being frightened.

Halfling Nimbleness. You can move through the space of any creature that is of a size larger than yours.

Languages. You can speak, read, and write Common and Halfling. The Halfling language isn't secret, but halflings are loath to share it with others. They write very little, so they don't have a rich body of literature. Their oral tradition, however, is very strong. Almost all halflings speak Common to converse with the people in whose lands they dwell or through which they are traveling.

Subrace. The two main kinds of halfling, lightfoot and stout, are more like closely related families than true subraces. Choose one of these subraces.

LIGHTFOOT

As a lightfoot halfling, you can easily hide from notice, even using other people as cover. You're inclined to be affable and get along well with others. In the Forgotten Realms, lightfoot halflings have spread the farthest and thus are the most common variety.

Lightfoots are more prone to wanderlust than other halflings, and often dwell alongside other races or take up a nomadic life. In the world of Greyhawk, these halflings are called hairfeet or tallfellows.

Ability Score Increase. Your Charisma score increases by 1.

Naturally Stealthy. You can attempt to hide even when you are obscured only by a creature that is at least one size larger than you.

STOUT

As a stout halfling, you're hardier than average and have some resistance to poison. Some say that stouts have dwarven blood. In the Forgotten Realms, these halflings are called stronghearts, and they're most common in the south.

Ability Score Increase. Your Constitution score increases by 1.

Stout Resilience. You have advantage on saving throws against poison, and you have resistance against poison damage.

Human

THESE WERE THE STORIES OF A RESTLESS PEOPLE WHO *long ago took to the seas and rivers in longboats, first to pillage and terrorize, then to settle. Yet there was an energy, a love of adventure, that sang from every page. Long into the night Liriel read, lighting candle after precious candle.*

She'd never given much thought to humans, but these stories fascinated her. In these yellowed pages were tales of bold heroes, strange and fierce animals, mighty primitive gods, and a magic that was part and fabric of that distant land.

—Elaine Cunningham, *Daughter of the Drow*

In the reckonings of most worlds, humans are the youngest of the common races, late to arrive on the world scene and short-lived in comparison to dwarves, elves, and dragons. Perhaps it is because of their shorter lives that they strive to achieve as much as they can in the years they are given. Or maybe they feel they have something to prove to the elder races, and that's why they build their mighty empires on the foundation of conquest and trade. Whatever drives them, humans are the innovators, the achievers, and the pioneers of the worlds.

A Broad Spectrum

With their penchant for migration and conquest, humans are more physically diverse than other common races. There is no typical human. An individual can stand from 5 feet to a little over 6 feet tall and weigh from 125 to 250 pounds. Human skin shades range from nearly black to very pale, and hair colors from black to blond (curly, kinky, or straight); males might sport facial hair that is sparse or thick. A lot of humans have a dash of nonhuman blood, revealing hints of elf, orc, or other lineages. Humans reach adulthood in their late teens and rarely live even a single century.

Variety in All Things

Humans are the most adaptable and ambitious people among the common races. They have widely varying tastes, morals, and customs in the many different lands where they have settled. When they settle, though, they stay: they build cities to last for the ages, and great kingdoms that can persist for long centuries. An individual human might have a relatively short life span, but a human nation or culture preserves traditions with origins far beyond the reach of any single human's memory. They live fully in the present—making them well suited to the adventuring life—but also plan for the future, striving to leave a lasting legacy. Individually and as a group, humans are adaptable opportunists, and they stay alert to changing political and social dynamics.

LASTING INSTITUTIONS

Where a single elf or dwarf might take on the responsibility of guarding a special location or a powerful secret, humans found sacred orders and institutions for such purposes. While dwarf clans and halfling elders pass on the ancient traditions to each new generation, human temples, governments, libraries, and codes of law fix their traditions in the bedrock of history. Humans dream of immortality, but (except for those few who seek undeath or divine ascension to escape death's clutches) they achieve it by ensuring that they will be remembered when they are gone.

Although some humans can be xenophobic, in general their societies are inclusive. Human lands welcome large numbers of nonhumans compared to the proportion of humans who live in nonhuman lands.

EXEMPLARS OF AMBITION

Humans who seek adventure are the most daring and ambitious members of a daring and ambitious race. They seek to earn glory in the eyes of their fellows by amassing power, wealth, and fame. More than other people, humans champion causes rather than territories or groups.

HUMAN NAMES AND ETHNICITIES

Having so much more variety than other cultures, humans as a whole have no typical names. Some human parents give their children names from other languages, such as Dwarvish or Elvish (pronounced more or less correctly), but most parents give names that are linked to their region's culture or to the naming traditions of their ancestors.

The material culture and physical characteristics of humans can change wildly from region to region. In the Forgotten Realms, for example, the clothing, architecture, cuisine, music, and literature are different in the northwestern lands of the Silver Marches than in distant Turmish or Impiltur to the east—and even more distinctive in far-off Kara-Tur. Human physical characteristics, though, vary according to the ancient migrations of the earliest humans, so that the humans of the Silver Marches have every possible variation of coloration and features.

In the Forgotten Realms, nine human ethnic groups are widely recognized, though over a dozen others are found in more localized areas of Faerûn. These groups, and the typical names of their members, can be used as inspiration no matter which world your human is in.

CALISHITE

Shorter and slighter in build than most other humans, Calishites have dusky brown skin, hair, and eyes. They're found primarily in southwest Faerûn.

Calishite Names: (Male) Aseir, Bardeid, Haseid, Khemed, Mehmen, Sudeiman, Zasheir; (female) Atala, Ceidil, Hama, Jasmal, Meilil, Seipora, Yasheira, Zasheida; (surnames) Basha, Dumein, Jassan, Khalid, Mostana, Pashar, Rein

CHONDATHAN

Chondathans are slender, tawny-skinned folk with brown hair that ranges from almost blond to almost black. Most are tall and have green or brown eyes, but these traits are hardly universal. Humans of Chondathan descent dominate the central lands of Faerûn, around the Inner Sea.

Chondathan Names: (Male) Darvin, Dorn, Evendur, Gorstag, Grim, Helm, Malark, Morn, Randal, Stedd; (female) Arveene, Esvele, Jhessail, Kerri, Lureene, Miri, Rowan, Shandri, Tessele; (surnames) Amblecrown, Buckman, Dundragon, Evenwood, Greycastle, Tallstag

DAMARAN

Found primarily in the northwest of Faerûn, Damarans are of moderate height and build, with skin hues ranging from tawny to fair. Their hair is usually brown or black, and their eye color varies widely, though brown is most common.

Damaran Names: (Male) Bor, Fodel, Glar, Grigor, Igan, Ivor, Kosef, Mival, Orel, Pavel, Sergor; (female) Alethra, Kara, Katernin, Mara, Natali, Olma, Tana, Zora; (surnames) Bersk, Chernin, Dotsk, Kulenov, Marsk, Nemetsk, Shemov, Starag

ILLUSKAN

Illuskans are tall, fair-skinned folk with blue or steely gray eyes. Most have raven-black hair, but those who inhabit the extreme northwest have blond, red, or light brown hair.

Illuskan Names: (Male) Ander, Blath, Bran, Frath, Geth, Lander, Luth, Malcer, Stor, Taman, Urth; (female) Amafrey, Betha, Cefrey, Kethra, Mara, Olga, Silifrey, Westra; (surnames) Brightwood, Helder, Hornraven, Lackman, Stormwind, Windrivver

MULAN

Dominant in the eastern and southeastern shores of the Inner Sea, the Mulan are generally tall, slim, and amber-skinned, with eyes of hazel or brown. Their hair ranges from black to dark brown, but in the lands where the Mulan are most prominent, nobles and many other Mulan shave off all their hair.

Mulan Names: (Male) Aoth, Bareris, Ehput-Ki, Kethoth, Mumed, Ramas, So-Kehur, Thazar-De, Urhur; (female) Arizima, Chathi, Nephis, Nulara, Murithi, Sefris, Thola, Umara, Zolis; (surnames) Ankhalab, Anskuld, Fezim, Hahpet, Nathandem, Sepret, Uuthrakt

RASHEMI

Most often found east of the Inner Sea and often intermingled with the Mulan, Rashemis tend to be short, stout, and muscular. They usually have dusky skin, dark eyes, and thick black hair.

Rashemi Names: (Male) Borivik, Faurgar, Jandar, Kanithar, Madislak, Ralmevik, Shaumar, Vladislak; (female) Fyevarra, Hulmarra, Immith, Imzel, Navarra, Shevarra, Tammith, Yuldra; (surnames) Chergoba, Dyernina, Iltazyara, Murnyethara, Stayanoga, Ulmokina

SHOU

The Shou are the most numerous and powerful ethnic group in Kara-Tur, far to the east of Faerûn. They are yellowish-bronze in hue, with black hair and dark eyes. Shou surnames are usually presented before the given name.

Shou Names: (Male) An, Chen, Chi, Fai, Jiang, Jun, Lian, Long, Meng, On, Shan, Shui, Wen; (female) Bai, Chao, Jia, Lei, Mei, Qiao, Shui, Tai; (surnames) Chien, Huang, Kao, Kung, Lao, Ling, Mei, Pin, Shin, Sum, Tan, Wan

TETHYRIAN

Widespread along the entire Sword Coast at the western edge of Faerûn, Tethyrians are of medium build and height, with dusky skin that tends to grow fairer the farther north they dwell. Their hair and eye color varies widely, but brown hair and blue eyes are the most common. Tethyrians primarily use Chondathan names.

TURAMI

Native to the southern shore of the Inner Sea, the Turami people are generally tall and muscular, with dark mahogany skin, curly black hair, and dark eyes.

Turami Names: (Male) Anton, Diero, Marcon, Pieron, Rimardo, Romero, Salazar, Umbero; (female) Balama, Dona, Faila, Jalana, Luisa, Marta, Quara, Selise, Vonda; (surnames) Agosto, Astorio, Calabra, Domine, Falone, Marivaldi, Pisacar, Ramondo

HUMAN TRAITS

It's hard to make generalizations about humans, but your human character has these traits.

Ability Score Increase. Your ability scores each increase by 1.

Age. Humans reach adulthood in their late teens and live less than a century.

Alignment. Humans tend toward no particular alignment. The best and the worst are found among them.

Size. Humans vary widely in height and build, from barely 5 feet to well over 6 feet tall. Regardless of your position in that range, your size is Medium.

Speed. Your base walking speed is 30 feet.

Languages. You can speak, read, and write Common and one extra language of your choice. Humans typically learn the languages of other peoples they deal with, including obscure dialects. They are fond of sprinkling their speech with words borrowed from other tongues: Orc curses, Elvish musical expressions, Dwarvish military phrases, and so on.

VARIANT HUMAN TRAITS

If your campaign uses the optional feat rules from chapter 6, your Dungeon Master might allow these variant traits, all of which replace the human's Ability Score Increase trait.

Ability Score Increase. Two different ability scores of your choice increase by 1.

Skills. You gain proficiency in one skill of your choice.

Feat. You gain one feat of your choice.

For all her life, Farideh had known that reading her father's face was a skill she'd been fortunate to learn. A human who couldn't spot the shift of her eyes or Havilar's would certainly see only the indifference of a dragon in Clanless Mehen's face. But the shift of scales, the arch of a ridge, the set of his eyes, the gape of his teeth—her father's face spoke volumes.

But every scale of it, this time, seemed completely still— the indifference of a dragon, even to Farideh.

—Erin M. Evans, *The Adversary*

Born of dragons, as their name proclaims, the dragonborn walk proudly through a world that greets them with fearful incomprehension. Shaped by draconic gods or the dragons themselves, dragonborn originally hatched from dragon eggs as a unique race, combining the best attributes of dragons and humanoids. Some dragonborn are faithful servants to true dragons, others form the ranks of soldiers in great wars, and still others find themselves adrift, with no clear calling in life.

PROUD DRAGON KIN

Dragonborn look very much like dragons standing erect in humanoid form, though they lack wings or a tail. The first dragonborn had scales of vibrant hues matching the colors of their dragon kin, but generations of interbreeding have created a more uniform appearance. Their small, fine scales are usually brass or bronze in color, sometimes ranging to scarlet, rust, gold, or copper-green. They are tall and strongly built, often standing close to 6½ feet tall and weighing 300 pounds or more. Their hands and feet are strong, talonlike claws with three fingers and a thumb on each hand.

The blood of a particular type of dragon runs very strong through some dragonborn clans. These dragonborn often boast scales that more closely match those of their dragon ancestor—bright red, green, blue, or white, lustrous black, or gleaming metallic gold, silver, brass, copper, or bronze.

DRAGONBORN

HER FATHER STOOD ON THE FIRST OF THE THREE STAIRS *that led down from the portal, unmoving. The scales of his face had grown paler around the edges, but Clanless Mehen still looked as if he could wrestle down a dire bear himself. His familiar well-worn armor was gone, replaced by violet-tinted scale armor with bright silvery tracings. There was a blazon on his arm as well, the mark of some foreign house. The sword at his back was the same, though, the one he had carried since even before he had found the twins left in swaddling at the gates of Arush Vayem.*

SELF-SUFFICIENT CLANS

To any dragonborn, the clan is more important than life itself. Dragonborn owe their devotion and respect to their clan above all else, even the gods. Each dragonborn's conduct reflects on the honor of his or her clan, and bringing dishonor to the clan can result in expulsion and exile. Each dragonborn knows his or her station and duties within the clan, and honor demands maintaining the bounds of that position.

A continual drive for self-improvement reflects the self-sufficiency of the race as a whole. Dragonborn value skill and excellence in all endeavors. They hate to fail, and they push themselves to extreme efforts before they give up on something. A dragonborn holds mastery of a particular skill as a lifetime goal. Members of other races who share the same commitment find it easy to earn the respect of a dragonborn.

Though all dragonborn strive to be self-sufficient, they recognize that help is sometimes needed in difficult situations. But the best source for such help is the clan, and when a clan needs help, it turns to another dragonborn clan before seeking aid from other races—or even from the gods.

DRAGONBORN NAMES

Dragonborn have personal names given at birth, but they put their clan names first as a mark of honor. A childhood name or nickname is often used among clutchmates as a descriptive term or a term of endearment. The name might recall an event or center on a habit.

Male Names: Arjhan, Balasar, Bharash, Donaar, Ghesh, Heskan, Kriv, Medrash, Mehen, Nadarr, Pandjed, Patrin, Rhogar, Shamash, Shedinn, Tarhun, Torinn
Female Names: Akra, Biri, Daar, Farideh, Harann, Havilar, Jheri, Kava, Korinn, Mishann, Nala, Perra, Raiann, Sora, Surina, Thava, Uadjit

UNCOMMON RACES

The dragonborn and the rest of the races in this chapter are uncommon. They don't exist in every world of D&D, and even where they are found, they are less widespread than dwarves, elves, halflings, and humans.

In the cosmopolitan cities of the D&D multiverse, most people hardly look twice at members of even the most exotic races. But the small towns and villages that dot the countryside are different. The common folk aren't accustomed to seeing members of these races, and they react accordingly.

Dragonborn. It's easy to assume that a dragonborn is a monster, especially if his or her scales betray a chromatic heritage. Unless the dragonborn starts breathing fire and causing destruction, though, people are likely to respond with caution rather than outright fear.

Gnome. Gnomes don't look like a threat and can quickly disarm suspicion with good humor. The common folk are often curious about gnomes, likely never having seen one before, but they are rarely hostile or fearful.

Half-Elf. Although many people have never seen a half-elf, virtually everyone knows they exist. A half-elf stranger's arrival is followed by gossip behind the half-elf's back and stolen glances across the common room, rather than any confrontation or open curiosity.

Half-Orc. It's usually safe to assume that a half-orc is belligerent and quick to anger, so people watch themselves around an unfamiliar half-orc. Shopkeepers might surreptitiously hide valuable or fragile goods when a half-orc comes in, and people slowly clear out of a tavern, assuming a fight will break out soon.

Tiefling. Half-orcs are greeted with a practical caution, but tieflings are the subject of supernatural fear. The evil of their heritage is plainly visible in their features, and as far as most people are concerned, a tiefling could very well be a devil straight from the Nine Hells. People might make warding signs as a tiefling approaches, cross the street to avoid passing near, or bar shop doors before a tiefling can enter.

Childhood Names: Climber, Earbender, Leaper, Pious, Shieldbiter, Zealous

Clan Names: Clethtinthiallor, Daardendrian, Delmirev, Drachedandion, Fenkenkabradon, Kepeshkmolik, Kerrhylon, Kimbatuul, Linxakasendalor, Myastan, Nemmonis, Norixius, Ophinshtalajiir, Prexijandilin, Shestendeliath, Turnuroth, Verthisathurgiesh, Yarjerit

Dragonborn Traits

Your draconic heritage manifests in a variety of traits you share with other dragonborn.

Ability Score Increase. Your Strength score increases by 2, and your Charisma score increases by 1.

Age. Young dragonborn grow quickly. They walk hours after hatching, attain the size and development of a 10-year-old human child by the age of 3, and reach adulthood by 15. They live to be around 80.

Alignment. Dragonborn tend to extremes, making a conscious choice for one side or the other in the cosmic war between good and evil (represented by Bahamut and Tiamat, respectively). Most dragonborn are good, but those who side with Tiamat can be terrible villains.

Size. Dragonborn are taller and heavier than humans, standing well over 6 feet tall and averaging almost 250 pounds. Your size is Medium.

Speed. Your base walking speed is 30 feet.

Draconic Ancestry

Dragon	Damage Type	Breath Weapon
Black	Acid	5 by 30 ft. line (Dex. save)
Blue	Lightning	5 by 30 ft. line (Dex. save)
Brass	Fire	5 by 30 ft. line (Dex. save)
Bronze	Lightning	5 by 30 ft. line (Dex. save)
Copper	Acid	5 by 30 ft. line (Dex. save)
Gold	Fire	15 ft. cone (Dex. save)
Green	Poison	15 ft. cone (Con. save)
Red	Fire	15 ft. cone (Dex. save)
Silver	Cold	15 ft. cone (Con. save)
White	Cold	15 ft. cone (Con. save)

Draconians

In the Dragonlance setting, the followers of the evil goddess Takhisis learned a dark ritual that let them corrupt the eggs of metallic dragons, producing evil dragonborn called draconians. Five types of draconians, corresponding to the five types of metallic dragons, fought for Takhisis in the War of the Lance: auraks (gold), baaz (brass), bozak (bronze), kapak (copper), and sivak (silver). In place of their draconic breath weapons, they have unique magical abilities.

Draconic Ancestry. You have draconic ancestry. Choose one type of dragon from the Draconic Ancestry table. Your breath weapon and damage resistance are determined by the dragon type, as shown in the table.

Breath Weapon. You can use your action to exhale destructive energy. Your draconic ancestry determines the size, shape, and damage type of the exhalation.

When you use your breath weapon, each creature in the area of the exhalation must make a saving throw, the type of which is determined by your draconic ancestry. The DC for this saving throw equals 8 + your Constitution modifier + your proficiency bonus. A creature takes 2d6 damage on a failed save, and half as much damage on a successful one. The damage increases to 3d6 at 6th level, 4d6 at 11th level, and 5d6 at 16th level.

After you use your breath weapon, you can't use it again until you complete a short or long rest.

Damage Resistance. You have resistance to the damage type associated with your draconic ancestry.

Languages. You can speak, read, and write Common and Draconic. Draconic is thought to be one of the oldest languages and is often used in the study of magic. The language sounds harsh to most other creatures and includes numerous hard consonants and sibilants.

Gnome

Skinny and flaxen-haired, his skin
*walnut brown and his eyes a startling
turquoise, Burgell stood half as tall as Aeron and had to
climb up on a stool to look out the peephole. Like most hab-
itations in Oeble, that particular tenement had been built
for humans, and smaller residents coped with the resulting
awkwardness as best they could.*

*But at least the relative largeness of the apartment gave
Burgell room to pack in all his gnome-sized gear. The front
room was his workshop, and it contained a bewildering
miscellany of tools: hammers, chisels, saws, lockpicks,
tinted lenses, jeweler's loupes, and jars of powdered and
shredded ingredients for casting spells. A fat gray cat, the
mage's familiar, lay curled atop a grimoire. It opened its
eyes, gave Aeron a disdainful yellow stare, then appeared
to go back to sleep.*

—Richard Lee Byers, *The Black Bouquet*

A constant hum of busy activity pervades the warrens
and neighborhoods where gnomes form their close-
knit communities. Louder sounds punctuate the hum:
a crunch of grinding gears here, a minor explosion
there, a yelp of surprise or triumph, and especially
bursts of laughter. Gnomes take delight in life, enjoying
every moment of invention, exploration, investigation,
creation, and play.

Vibrant Expression

A gnome's energy and enthusiasm for living shines
through every inch of his or her tiny body. Gnomes
average slightly over 3 feet tall and weigh 40 to 45
pounds. Their tan or brown faces are usually adorned
with broad smiles (beneath their prodigious noses),
and their bright eyes shine with excitement. Their
fair hair has a tendency to stick out in every direction,
as if expressing the gnome's insatiable interest in
everything around.

A gnome's personality is writ large in his or her
appearance. A male gnome's beard, in contrast to
his wild hair, is kept carefully trimmed but often
styled into curious forks or neat points. A gnome's
clothing, though usually made in modest earth tones,
is elaborately decorated with embroidery, embossing,
or gleaming jewels.

Delighted Dedication

As far as gnomes are concerned, being alive is a
wonderful thing, and they squeeze every ounce of
enjoyment out of their three to five centuries of life.
Humans might wonder about getting bored over the
course of such a long life, and elves take plenty of time
to savor the beauties of the world in their long years, but
gnomes seem to worry that even with all that time, they
can't get in enough of the things they want to do and see.

Gnomes speak as if they can't get the thoughts
out of their heads fast enough. Even as they offer
ideas and opinions on a range of subjects, they still
manage to listen carefully to others, adding the
appropriate exclamations of surprise and appreciation
along the way.

Though gnomes love jokes of all kinds, particularly puns and pranks, they're just as dedicated to the more serious tasks they undertake. Many gnomes are skilled engineers, alchemists, tinkers, and inventors. They're willing to make mistakes and laugh at themselves in the process of perfecting what they do, taking bold (sometimes foolhardy) risks and dreaming large.

BRIGHT BURROWS

Gnomes make their homes in hilly, wooded lands. They live underground but get more fresh air than dwarves do, enjoying the natural, living world on the surface whenever they can. Their homes are well hidden by both clever construction and simple illusions. Welcome visitors are quickly ushered into the bright, warm burrows. Those who are not welcome are unlikely to find the burrows in the first place.

Gnomes who settle in human lands are commonly gemcutters, engineers, sages, or tinkers. Some human families retain gnome tutors, ensuring that their pupils enjoy a mix of serious learning and delighted enjoyment. A gnome might tutor several generations of a single human family over the course of his or her long life.

GNOME NAMES

Gnomes love names, and most have half a dozen or so. A gnome's mother, father, clan elder, aunts, and uncles each give the gnome a name, and various nicknames from just about everyone else might or might not stick over time. Gnome names are typically variants on the names of ancestors or distant relatives, though some are purely new inventions. When dealing with humans and others who are "stuffy" about names, a gnome learns to use no more than three names: a personal name, a clan name, and a nickname, choosing the one in each category that's the most fun to say.

> ### DEEP GNOMES
> A third subrace of gnomes, the deep gnomes (or svirfneblin), live in small communities scattered in the Underdark. Unlike the duergar and the drow, svirfneblin are as good as their surface cousins. However, their humor and enthusiasm are dampened by their oppressive environment, and their inventive expertise is directed mostly toward stonework.

Male Names: Alston, Alvyn, Boddynock, Brocc, Burgell, Dimble, Eldon, Erky, Fonkin, Frug, Gerbo, Gimble, Glim, Jebeddo, Kellen, Namfoodle, Orryn, Roondar, Seebo, Sindri, Warryn, Wrenn, Zook

Female Names: Bimpnottin, Breena, Caramip, Carlin, Donella, Duvamil, Ella, Ellyjobell, Ellywick, Lilli, Loopmottin, Lorilla, Mardnab, Nissa, Nyx, Oda, Orla, Roywyn, Shamil, Tana, Waywocket, Zanna

Clan Names: Beren, Daergel, Folkor, Garrick, Nackle, Murnig, Ningel, Raulnor, Scheppen, Timbers, Turen

Nicknames: Aleslosh, Ashhearth, Badger, Cloak, Doublelock, Filchbatter, Fnipper, Ku, Nim, Oneshoe, Pock, Sparklegem, Stumbleduck

SEEING THE WORLD

Curious and impulsive, gnomes might take up adventuring as a way to see the world or for the love of exploring. As lovers of gems and other fine items, some gnomes take to adventuring as a quick, if dangerous, path to wealth. Regardless of what spurs them to adventure, gnomes who adopt this way of life eke as much enjoyment out of it as they do out of any other activity they undertake, sometimes to the great annoyance of their adventuring companions.

GNOME TRAITS

Your gnome character has certain characteristics in common with all other gnomes.

Ability Score Increase. Your Intelligence score increases by 2.

Age. Gnomes mature at the same rate humans do, and most are expected to settle down into an adult life by around age 40. They can live 350 to almost 500 years.

Alignment. Gnomes are most often good. Those who tend toward law are sages, engineers, researchers, scholars, investigators, or inventors. Those who tend toward chaos are minstrels, tricksters, wanderers, or fanciful jewelers. Gnomes are good-hearted, and even the tricksters among them are more playful than vicious.

Size. Gnomes are between 3 and 4 feet tall and average about 40 pounds. Your size is Small.

Speed. Your base walking speed is 25 feet.

Darkvision. Accustomed to life underground, you have superior vision in dark and dim conditions. You can see in dim light within 60 feet of you as if it were bright light, and in darkness as if it were dim light. You can't discern color in darkness, only shades of gray.

Gnome Cunning. You have advantage on all Intelligence, Wisdom, and Charisma saving throws against magic.

Languages. You can speak, read, and write Common and Gnomish. The Gnomish language, which uses the Dwarvish script, is renowned for its technical treatises and its catalogs of knowledge about the natural world.

Subrace. Two subraces of gnomes are found among the worlds of D&D: forest gnomes and rock gnomes. Choose one of these subraces.

FOREST GNOME

As a forest gnome, you have a natural knack for illusion and inherent quickness and stealth. In the worlds of D&D, forest gnomes are rare and secretive. They gather in hidden communities in sylvan forests, using illusions and trickery to conceal themselves from threats or to mask their escape should they be detected. Forest gnomes tend to be friendly with other good-spirited woodland folk, and they regard elves and good fey as their most important allies. These gnomes also befriend small forest animals and rely on them for information about threats that might prowl their lands.

Ability Score Increase. Your Dexterity score increases by 1.

Natural Illusionist. You know the *minor illusion* cantrip. Intelligence is your spellcasting ability for it.

Speak with Small Beasts. Through sounds and gestures, you can communicate simple ideas with Small or smaller beasts. Forest gnomes love animals and often keep squirrels, badgers, rabbits, moles, woodpeckers, and other creatures as beloved pets.

ROCK GNOME

As a rock gnome, you have a natural inventiveness and hardiness beyond that of other gnomes. Most gnomes in the worlds of D&D are rock gnomes, including the tinker gnomes of the Dragonlance setting.

Ability Score Increase. Your Constitution score increases by 1.

Artificer's Lore. Whenever you make an Intelligence (History) check related to magic items, alchemical objects, or technological devices, you can add twice your proficiency bonus, instead of any proficiency bonus you normally apply.

Tinker. You have proficiency with artisan's tools (tinker's tools). Using those tools, you can spend 1 hour and 10 gp worth of materials to construct a Tiny clockwork device (AC 5, 1 hp). The device ceases to function after 24 hours (unless you spend 1 hour repairing it to keep the device functioning), or when you use your action to dismantle it; at that time, you can reclaim the materials used to create it. You can have up to three such devices active at a time.

When you create a device, choose one of the following options:

Clockwork Toy. This toy is a clockwork animal, monster, or person, such as a frog, mouse, bird, dragon, or soldier. When placed on the ground, the toy moves 5 feet across the ground on each of your turns in a random direction. It makes noises as appropriate to the creature it represents.

Fire Starter. The device produces a miniature flame, which you can use to light a candle, torch, or campfire. Using the device requires your action.

Music Box. When opened, this music box plays a single song at a moderate volume. The box stops playing when it reaches the song's end or when it is closed.

HALF-ELF

FLINT SQUINTED INTO THE SETTING SUN. HE THOUGHT
he saw the figure of a man striding up the path. Standing,
Flint drew back into the shadow of a tall pine to see better.
The man's walk was marked by an easy grace—an elvish
grace, Flint would have said; yet the man's body had the
thickness and tight muscles of a human, while the facial
hair was definitely humankind's. All the dwarf could see
of the man's face beneath a green hood was tan skin and a
brownish-red beard. A longbow was slung over one shoulder
and a sword hung at his left side. He was dressed in soft
leather, carefully tooled in the intricate designs the elves
loved. But no elf in the world of Krynn could grow a beard
. . . no elf, but . . .

"Tanis?" said Flint hesitantly as the man neared.

"The same." The newcomer's bearded face split in a wide
grin. He held open his arms and, before the dwarf could
stop him, engulfed Flint in a hug that lifted him off the
ground. The dwarf clasped his old friend close for a brief
instant, then, remembering his dignity, squirmed and freed
himself from the half-elf's embrace.

—Margaret Weis and Tracy Hickman,
Dragons of Autumn Twilight

Walking in two worlds but truly belonging to neither,
half-elves combine what some say are the best qualities
of their elf and human parents: human curiosity,
inventiveness, and ambition tempered by the refined
senses, love of nature, and artistic tastes of the elves.
Some half-elves live among humans, set apart by their
emotional and physical differences, watching friends
and loved ones age while time barely touches them.
Others live with the elves, growing restless as they
reach adulthood in the timeless elven realms, while
their peers continue to live as children. Many half-elves,
unable to fit into either society, choose lives of solitary
wandering or join with other misfits and outcasts in
the adventuring life.

OF TWO WORLDS

To humans, half-elves look like elves, and to elves, they
look human. In height, they're on par with both parents,
though they're neither as slender as elves nor as broad
as humans. They range from under 5 feet to about 6 feet
tall, and from 100 to 180 pounds, with men only slightly
taller and heavier than women. Half-elf men do have
facial hair, and sometimes grow beards to mask their
elven ancestry. Half-elven coloration and features lie
somewhere between their human and elf parents, and
thus show a variety even more pronounced than that
found among either race. They tend to have the eyes
of their elven parents.

Diplomats or Wanderers

Half-elves have no lands of their own, though they are welcome in human cities and somewhat less welcome in elven forests. In large cities in regions where elves and humans interact often, half-elves are sometimes numerous enough to form small communities of their own. They enjoy the company of other half-elves, the only people who truly understand what it is to live between these two worlds.

In most parts of the world, though, half-elves are uncommon enough that one might live for years without meeting another. Some half-elves prefer to avoid company altogether, wandering the wilds as trappers, foresters, hunters, or adventurers and visiting civilization only rarely. Like elves, they are driven by the wanderlust that comes of their longevity. Others, in contrast, throw themselves into the thick of society, putting their charisma and social skills to great use in diplomatic roles or as swindlers.

Half-Elf Names

Half-elves use either human or elven naming conventions. As if to emphasize that they don't really fit in to either society, half-elves raised among humans are often given elven names, and those raised among elves often take human names.

Half-Elf Traits

Your half-elf character has some qualities in common with elves and some that are unique to half-elves.

Ability Score Increase. Your Charisma score increases by 2, and two other ability scores of your choice increase by 1.

Age. Half-elves mature at the same rate humans do and reach adulthood around the age of 20. They live much longer than humans, however, often exceeding 180 years.

Alignment. Half-elves share the chaotic bent of their elven heritage. They value both personal freedom and creative expression, demonstrating neither love of leaders nor desire for followers. They chafe at rules, resent others' demands, and sometimes prove unreliable, or at least unpredictable.

Size. Half-elves are about the same size as humans, ranging from 5 to 6 feet tall. Your size is Medium.

Speed. Your base walking speed is 30 feet.

Darkvision. Thanks to your elf blood, you have superior vision in dark and dim conditions. You can see in dim light within 60 feet of you as if it were bright light, and in darkness as if it were dim light. You can't discern color in darkness, only shades of gray.

Fey Ancestry. You have advantage on saving throws against being charmed, and magic can't put you to sleep.

Skill Versatility. You gain proficiency in two skills of your choice.

Languages. You can speak, read, and write Common, Elvish, and one extra language of your choice.

Excellent Ambassadors

Many half-elves learn at an early age to get along with everyone, defusing hostility and finding common ground. As a race, they have elven grace without elven aloofness and human energy without human boorishness. They often make excellent ambassadors and go-betweens (except between elves and humans, since each side suspects the half-elf of favoring the other).

Half-Orc

THE WARCHIEF MHURREN ROUSED HIMSELF FROM HIS *sleeping-furs and his women and pulled a short hauberk of heavy steel rings over his thick, well-muscled torso. He usually rose before most of his warriors, since he had a strong streak of human blood in him, and he found the daylight less bothersome than most of his tribe did. Among the Bloody Skulls, a warrior was judged by his strength, his fierceness, and his wits. Human ancestry was no blemish against a warrior—provided he was every bit as strong, enduring, and bloodthirsty as his full-blooded kin. Half-orcs who were weaker than their orc comrades didn't last long among the Bloody Skulls or any other orc tribe for that matter. But it was often true that a bit of human blood gave a warrior just the right mix of cunning, ambition, and self-discipline to go far indeed, as Mhurren had. He was master of a tribe that could muster two thousand spears, and the strongest chief in Thar.*

—Richard Baker, *Swordmage*

Whether united under the leadership of a mighty warlock or having fought to a standstill after years of conflict, orc and human tribes sometimes form alliances, joining forces into a larger horde to the terror of civilized lands nearby. When these alliances are sealed by marriages, half-orcs are born. Some half-orcs rise to become proud chiefs of orc tribes, their human blood giving them an edge over their full-blooded orc rivals. Some venture into the world to prove their worth among humans and other more civilized races. Many of these become adventurers, achieving greatness for their mighty deeds and notoriety for their barbaric customs and savage fury.

SCARRED AND STRONG

Half-orcs' grayish pigmentation, sloping foreheads, jutting jaws, prominent teeth, and towering builds make their orcish heritage plain for all to see. Half-orcs stand between 6 and 7 feet tall and usually weigh between 180 and 250 pounds.

Orcs regard battle scars as tokens of pride and ornamental scars as things of beauty. Other scars, though, mark an orc or half-orc as a former slave or a disgraced exile. Any half-orc who has lived among or near orcs has scars, whether they are marks of humiliation or of pride, recounting their past exploits and injuries. Such a half-orc living among humans might display these scars proudly or hide them in shame.

THE MARK OF GRUUMSH

The one-eyed god Gruumsh created the orcs, and even those orcs who turn away from his worship can't fully escape his influence. The same is true of half-orcs, though their human blood moderates the impact of their orcish heritage. Some half-orcs hear the whispers of Gruumsh in their dreams, calling them to unleash the rage that simmers within them. Others feel Gruumsh's exultation when they join in melee combat—and either exult along with him or shiver with fear and loathing. Half-orcs are not evil by nature, but evil does lurk within them, whether they embrace it or rebel against it.

Beyond the rage of Gruumsh, half-orcs feel emotion powerfully. Rage doesn't just quicken their pulse, it makes their bodies burn. An insult stings like acid, and sadness saps their strength. But they laugh loudly and heartily, and simple bodily pleasures—feasting, drinking, wrestling, drumming, and wild dancing—fill their hearts with joy. They tend to be short-tempered and sometimes sullen, more inclined to action than contemplation and to fighting than arguing. The most accomplished half-orcs are those with enough self-control to get by in a civilized land.

TRIBES AND SLUMS

Half-orcs most often live among orcs. Of the other races, humans are most likely to accept half-orcs, and half-orcs almost always live in human lands when not living among orc tribes. Whether proving themselves among rough barbarian tribes or scrabbling to survive in the slums of larger cities, half-orcs get by on their physical might, their endurance, and the sheer determination they inherit from their human ancestry.

HALF-ORC NAMES

Half-orcs usually have names appropriate to the culture in which they were raised. A half-orc who wants to fit in among humans might trade an orc name for a human name. Some half-orcs with human names decide to adopt a guttural orc name because they think it makes them more intimidating.

Male Orc Names: Dench, Feng, Gell, Henk, Holg, Imsh, Keth, Krusk, Mhurren, Ront, Shump, Thokk
Female Orc Names: Baggi, Emen, Engong, Kansif, Myev, Neega, Ovak, Ownka, Shautha, Sutha, Vola, Volen, Yevelda

HALF-ORC TRAITS

Your half-orc character has certain traits deriving from your orc ancestry.

GRUDGING ACCEPTANCE

Each half-orc finds a way to gain acceptance from those who hate orcs. Some are reserved, trying not to draw attention to themselves. A few demonstrate piety and good-heartedness as publicly as they can (whether or not such demonstrations are genuine). And some simply try to be so tough that others just avoid them.

Ability Score Increase. Your Strength score increases by 2, and your Constitution score increases by 1.

Age. Half-orcs mature a little faster than humans, reaching adulthood around age 14. They age noticeably faster and rarely live longer than 75 years.

Alignment. Half-orcs inherit a tendency toward chaos from their orc parents and are not strongly inclined toward good. Half-orcs raised among orcs and willing to live out their lives among them are usually evil.

Size. Half-orcs are somewhat larger and bulkier than humans, and they range from 5 to well over 6 feet tall. Your size is Medium.

Speed. Your base walking speed is 30 feet.

Darkvision. Thanks to your orc blood, you have superior vision in dark and dim conditions. You can see in dim light within 60 feet of you as if it were bright light, and in darkness as if it were dim light. You can't discern color in darkness, only shades of gray.

Menacing. You gain proficiency in the Intimidation skill.

Relentless Endurance. When you are reduced to 0 hit points but not killed outright, you can drop to 1 hit point instead. You can't use this feature again until you finish a long rest.

Savage Attacks. When you score a critical hit with a melee weapon attack, you can roll one of the weapon's damage dice one additional time and add it to the extra damage of the critical hit.

Languages. You can speak, read, and write Common and Orc. Orc is a harsh, grating language with hard consonants. It has no script of its own but is written in the Dwarvish script.

TIEFLING

"BUT YOU DO SEE THE WAY PEOPLE LOOK AT YOU, *devil's child.*"

Those black eyes, cold as a winter storm, were staring right into her heart and the sudden seriousness in his voice jolted her.

"What is it they say?" he asked. "One's a curiosity, two's a conspiracy—"

"Three's a curse," she finished. "You think I haven't heard that rubbish before?"

"I know you have." When she glared at him, he added, "It's not as if I'm plumbing the depths of your mind, dear girl. That is the burden of every tiefling. Some break under it, some make it the millstone around their neck, some revel in it." He tilted his head again, scrutinizing her, with that wicked glint in his eyes. *"You fight it, don't you? Like a little wildcat, I wager. Every little jab and comment just sharpens your claws."*

—Erin M. Evans, *Brimstone Angels*

To be greeted with stares and whispers, to suffer violence and insult on the street, to see mistrust and fear in every eye: this is the lot of the tiefling. And to twist the knife, tieflings know that this is because a pact struck generations ago infused the essence of Asmodeus—overlord of the Nine Hells—into their bloodline. Their appearance and their nature are not their fault but the result of an ancient sin, for which they and their children and their children's children will always be held accountable.

INFERNAL BLOODLINE

Tieflings are derived from human bloodlines, and in the broadest possible sense, they still look human. However, their infernal heritage has left a clear imprint on their appearance. Tieflings have large horns that take any of a variety of shapes: some have curling horns like a ram, others have straight and tall horns like a gazelle's, and some spiral upward like an antelopes' horns. They have thick tails, four to five feet long, which lash or coil around their legs when they get upset or nervous. Their canine teeth are sharply pointed, and their eyes are solid colors—black, red, white, silver, or gold—with no visible sclera or pupil. Their skin tones cover the full range of human coloration, but also include various shades of red. Their hair, cascading down from behind their horns, is usually dark, from black or brown to dark red, blue, or purple.

SELF-RELIANT AND SUSPICIOUS

Tieflings subsist in small minorities found mostly in human cities or towns, often in the roughest quarters of those places, where they grow up to be swindlers, thieves, or crime lords. Sometimes they live among other minority populations in enclaves where they are treated with more respect.

Lacking a homeland, tieflings know that they have to make their own way in the world and that they have to be strong to survive. They are not quick to trust anyone who claims to be a friend, but when a tiefling's companions demonstrate that they trust him or her, the tiefling learns to extend the same trust to them. And once a tiefling gives someone loyalty, the tiefling is a firm friend or ally for life.

TIEFLING NAMES

Tiefling names fall into three broad categories. Tieflings born into another culture typically have names reflective of that culture. Some have names derived from the Infernal language, passed down through generations, that reflect their fiendish heritage. And some younger tieflings, striving to find a place in the world, adopt a name that signifies a virtue or other concept and then try to embody that concept. For some, the chosen name is a noble quest. For others, it's a grim destiny.

Male Infernal Names: Akmenos, Amnon, Barakas, Damakos, Ekemon, Iados, Kairon, Leucis, Melech, Mordai, Morthos, Pelaios, Skamos, Therai

Female Infernal Names: Akta, Anakis, Bryseis, Criella, Damaia, Ea, Kallista, Lerissa, Makaria, Nemeia, Orianna, Phelaia, Rieta

"Virtue" Names: Art, Carrion, Chant, Creed, Despair, Excellence, Fear, Glory, Hope, Ideal, Music, Nowhere, Open, Poetry, Quest, Random, Reverence, Sorrow, Temerity, Torment, Weary

MUTUAL MISTRUST

People tend to be suspicious of tieflings, assuming that their infernal heritage has left its mark on their personality and morality, not just their appearance. Shopkeepers keep a close eye on their goods when tieflings enter their stores, the town watch might follow a tiefling around for a while, and demagogues blame tieflings for strange happenings. The reality, though, is that a tiefling's bloodline doesn't affect his or her personality to any great degree. Years of dealing with mistrust does leave its mark on most tieflings, and they respond to it in different ways. Some choose to live up to the wicked stereotype, but others are virtuous. Most are simply very aware of how people respond to them. After dealing with this mistrust throughout youth, a tiefling often develops the ability to overcome prejudice through charm or intimidation.

TIEFLING TRAITS

Tieflings share certain racial traits as a result of their infernal descent.

Ability Score Increase. Your Intelligence score increases by 1, and your Charisma score increases by 2.

Age. Tieflings mature at the same rate as humans but live a few years longer.

Alignment. Tieflings might not have an innate tendency toward evil, but many of them end up there. Evil or not, an independent nature inclines many tieflings toward a chaotic alignment.

Size. Tieflings are about the same size and build as humans. Your size is Medium.

Speed. Your base walking speed is 30 feet.

Darkvision. Thanks to your infernal heritage, you have superior vision in dark and dim conditions. You can see in dim light within 60 feet of you as if it were bright light, and in darkness as if it were dim light. You can't discern color in darkness, only shades of gray.

Hellish Resistance. You have resistance to fire damage.

Infernal Legacy. You know the *thaumaturgy* cantrip. When you reach 3rd level, you can cast the *hellish rebuke* spell as a 2nd-level spell once with this trait and regain the ability to do so when you finish a long rest. When you reach 5th level, you can cast the *darkness* spell once with this trait and regain the ability to do so when you finish a long rest. Charisma is your spellcasting ability for these spells.

Languages. You can speak, read, and write Common and Infernal.

PART 1 | RACES

43

CHAPTER 3: CLASSES

ADVENTURERS ARE EXTRAORDINARY PEOPLE, driven by a thirst for excitement into a life that others would never dare lead. They are heroes, compelled to explore the dark places of the world and take on the challenges that lesser women and men can't stand against.

Class is the primary definition of what your character can do. It's more than a profession; it's your character's calling. Class shapes the way you think about the world and interact with it and your relationship with other people and powers in the multiverse. A fighter, for example, might view the world in pragmatic terms of strategy and maneuvering, and see herself as just a pawn in a much larger game. A cleric, by contrast, might see himself as a willing servant in a god's unfolding plan or a conflict brewing among various deities. While the fighter has contacts in a mercenary company or army, the cleric might know a number of priests, paladins, and devotees who share his faith.

Your class gives you a variety of special features, such as a fighter's mastery of weapons and armor, and a wizard's spells. At low levels, your class gives you only two or three features, but as you advance in level you gain more and your existing features often improve. Each class entry in this chapter includes a table summarizing the benefits you gain at every level, and a detailed explanation of each one.

Adventurers sometimes advance in more than one class. A rogue might switch direction in life and swear the oath of a paladin. A barbarian might discover latent magical ability and dabble in the sorcerer class while continuing to advance as a barbarian. Elves are known to combine martial mastery with magical training and advance as fighters and wizards simultaneously. Optional rules for combining classes in this way, called multiclassing, appear in chapter 6.

Twelve classes—listed in the Classes table—are found in almost every D&D world and define the spectrum of typical adventurers.

CLASSES

Class	Description	Hit Die	Primary Ability	Saving Throw Proficiencies	Armor and Weapon Proficiencies
Barbarian	A fierce warrior of primitive background who can enter a battle rage	d12	Strength	Strength & Constitution	Light and medium armor, shields, simple and martial weapons
Bard	An inspiring magician whose power echoes the music of creation	d8	Charisma	Dexterity & Charisma	Light armor, simple weapons, hand crossbows, longswords, rapiers, shortswords
Cleric	A priestly champion who wields divine magic in service of a higher power	d8	Wisdom	Wisdom & Charisma	Light and medium armor, shields, simple weapons
Druid	A priest of the Old Faith, wielding the powers of nature—moonlight and plant growth, fire and lightning—and adopting animal forms	d8	Wisdom	Intelligence & Wisdom	Light and medium armor (nonmetal), shields (nonmetal), clubs, daggers, darts, javelins, maces, quarterstaffs, scimitars, sickles, slings, spears
Fighter	A master of martial combat, skilled with a variety of weapons and armor	d10	Strength or Dexterity	Strength & Constitution	All armor, shields, simple and martial weapons
Monk	A master of martial arts, harnessing the power of the body in pursuit of physical and spiritual perfection	d8	Dexterity & Wisdom	Strength & Dexterity	Simple weapons, shortswords
Paladin	A holy warrior bound to a sacred oath	d10	Strength & Charisma	Wisdom & Charisma	All armor, shields, simple and martial weapons
Ranger	A warrior who uses martial prowess and nature magic to combat threats on the edges of civilization	d10	Dexterity & Wisdom	Strength & Dexterity	Light and medium armor, shields, simple and martial weapons
Rogue	A scoundrel who uses stealth and trickery to overcome obstacles and enemies	d8	Dexterity	Dexterity & Intelligence	Light armor, simple weapons, hand crossbows, longswords, rapiers, shortswords
Sorcerer	A spellcaster who draws on inherent magic from a gift or bloodline	d6	Charisma	Constitution & Charisma	Daggers, darts, slings, quarterstaffs, light crossbows
Warlock	A wielder of magic that is derived from a bargain with an extraplanar entity	d8	Charisma	Wisdom & Charisma	Light armor, simple weapons
Wizard	A scholarly magic-user capable of manipulating the structures of reality	d6	Intelligence	Intelligence & Wisdom	Daggers, darts, slings, quarterstaffs, light crossbows

BARBARIAN

A tall human tribesman strides through a blizzard, draped in fur and hefting his axe. He laughs as he charges toward the frost giant who dared poach his people's elk herd.

A half-orc snarls at the latest challenger to her authority over their savage tribe, ready to break his neck with her bare hands as she did to the last six rivals.

Frothing at the mouth, a dwarf slams his helmet into the face of his drow foe, then turns to drive his armored elbow into the gut of another.

These barbarians, different as they might be, are defined by their rage: unbridled, unquenchable, and unthinking fury. More than a mere emotion, their anger is the ferocity of a cornered predator, the unrelenting assault of a storm, the churning turmoil of the sea.

For some, their rage springs from a communion with fierce animal spirits. Others draw from a roiling reservoir of anger at a world full of pain. For every barbarian, rage is a power that fuels not just a battle frenzy but also uncanny reflexes, resilience, and feats of strength.

PRIMAL INSTINCT

People of towns and cities take pride in how their civilized ways set them apart from animals, as if denying one's own nature was a mark of superiority. To a barbarian, though, civilization is no virtue, but a sign of weakness. The strong embrace their animal nature—keen instincts, primal physicality, and ferocious rage. Barbarians are uncomfortable when hedged in by walls and crowds. They thrive in the wilds of their homelands: the tundra, jungle, or grasslands where their tribes live and hunt.

Barbarians come alive in the chaos of combat. They can enter a berserk state where rage takes over, giving them superhuman strength and resilience. A barbarian can draw on this reservoir of fury only a few times without resting, but those few rages are usually sufficient to defeat whatever threats arise.

A LIFE OF DANGER

Not every member of the tribes deemed "barbarians" by scions of civilized society has the barbarian class. A true barbarian among these people is as uncommon as a skilled fighter in a town, and he or she plays a similar role as a protector of the people and a leader in times of war. Life in the wild places of the world is fraught with peril: rival tribes, deadly weather, and terrifying

THE BARBARIAN

Level	Proficiency Bonus	Features	Rages	Rage Damage
1st	+2	Rage, Unarmored Defense	2	+2
2nd	+2	Reckless Attack, Danger Sense	2	+2
3rd	+2	Primal Path	3	+2
4th	+2	Ability Score Improvement	3	+2
5th	+3	Extra Attack, Fast Movement	3	+2
6th	+3	Path feature	4	+2
7th	+3	Feral Instinct	4	+2
8th	+3	Ability Score Improvement	4	+2
9th	+4	Brutal Critical (1 die)	4	+3
10th	+4	Path feature	4	+3
11th	+4	Relentless Rage	4	+3
12th	+4	Ability Score Improvement	5	+3
13th	+5	Brutal Critical (2 dice)	5	+3
14th	+5	Path feature	5	+3
15th	+5	Persistent Rage	5	+3
16th	+5	Ability Score Improvement	5	+4
17th	+6	Brutal Critical (3 dice)	6	+4
18th	+6	Indomitable Might	6	+4
19th	+6	Ability Score Improvement	6	+4
20th	+6	Primal Champion	Unlimited	+4

monsters. Barbarians charge headlong into that danger so that their people don't have to.

Their courage in the face of danger makes barbarians perfectly suited for adventuring. Wandering is often a way of life for their native tribes, and the rootless life of the adventurer is little hardship for a barbarian. Some barbarians miss the close-knit family structures of the tribe, but eventually find them replaced by the bonds formed among the members of their adventuring parties.

CREATING A BARBARIAN

When creating a barbarian character, think about where your character comes from and his or her place in the world. Talk with your DM about an appropriate origin for your barbarian. Did you come from a distant land, making you a stranger in the area of the campaign? Or is the campaign set in a rough-and-tumble frontier where barbarians are common?

What led you to take up the adventuring life? Were you lured to settled lands by the promise of riches? Did you join forces with soldiers of those lands to face a shared threat? Did monsters or an invading horde drive you out of your homeland, making you a rootless refugee? Perhaps you were a prisoner of war, brought in chains to "civilized" lands and only now able to win your freedom. Or you might have been cast out from your people because of a crime you committed, a taboo you violated, or a coup that removed you from a position of authority.

QUICK BUILD

You can make a barbarian quickly by following these suggestions. First, put your highest ability score in Strength, followed by Constitution. Second, choose the outlander background.

CLASS FEATURES

As a barbarian, you gain the following class features.

HIT POINTS
Hit Dice: 1d12 per barbarian level
Hit Points at 1st Level: 12 + your Constitution modifier
Hit Points at Higher Levels: 1d12 (or 7) + your Constitution modifier per barbarian level after 1st

PROFICIENCIES
Armor: Light armor, medium armor, shields
Weapons: Simple weapons, martial weapons
Tools: None

Saving Throws: Strength, Constitution
Skills: Choose two from Animal Handling, Athletics, Intimidation, Nature, Perception, and Survival

Equipment

You start with the following equipment, in addition to the equipment granted by your background:

- (a) a greataxe or (b) any martial melee weapon
- (a) two handaxes or (b) any simple weapon
- An explorer's pack and four javelins

Rage

In battle, you fight with primal ferocity. On your turn, you can enter a rage as a bonus action.

While raging, you gain the following benefits if you aren't wearing heavy armor:

- You have advantage on Strength checks and Strength saving throws.
- When you make a melee weapon attack using Strength, you gain a bonus to the damage roll that increases as you gain levels as a barbarian, as shown in the Rage Damage column of the Barbarian table.
- You have resistance to bludgeoning, piercing, and slashing damage.

If you are able to cast spells, you can't cast them or concentrate on them while raging.

Your rage lasts for 1 minute. It ends early if you are knocked unconscious or if your turn ends and you haven't attacked a hostile creature since your last turn or taken damage since then. You can also end your rage on your turn as a bonus action.

Once you have raged the number of times shown for your barbarian level in the Rages column of the Barbarian table, you must finish a long rest before you can rage again.

Unarmored Defense

While you are not wearing any armor, your Armor Class equals 10 + your Dexterity modifier + your Constitution modifier. You can use a shield and still gain this benefit.

Reckless Attack

Starting at 2nd level, you can throw aside all concern for defense to attack with fierce desperation. When you make your first attack on your turn, you can decide to attack recklessly. Doing so gives you advantage on melee weapon attack rolls using Strength during this turn, but attack rolls against you have advantage until your next turn.

Danger Sense

At 2nd level, you gain an uncanny sense of when things nearby aren't as they should be, giving you an edge when you dodge away from danger.

You have advantage on Dexterity saving throws against effects that you can see, such as traps and spells. To gain this benefit, you can't be blinded, deafened, or incapacitated.

Primal Path

At 3rd level, you choose a path that shapes the nature of your rage. Choose the Path of the Berserker or the Path of the Totem Warrior, both detailed at the end of the class description. Your choice grants you features at 3rd level and again at 6th, 10th, and 14th levels.

Ability Score Improvement

When you reach 4th level, and again at 8th, 12th, 16th, and 19th level, you can increase one ability score of your choice by 2, or you can increase two ability scores of your choice by 1. As normal, you can't increase an ability score above 20 using this feature.

Extra Attack

Beginning at 5th level, you can attack twice, instead of once, whenever you take the Attack action on your turn.

Fast Movement

Starting at 5th level, your speed increases by 10 feet while you aren't wearing heavy armor.

Feral Instinct

By 7th level, your instincts are so honed that you have advantage on initiative rolls.

Additionally, if you are surprised at the beginning of combat and aren't incapacitated, you can act normally on your first turn, but only if you enter your rage before doing anything else on that turn.

Brutal Critical

Beginning at 9th level, you can roll one additional weapon damage die when determining the extra damage for a critical hit with a melee attack.

This increases to two additional dice at 13th level and three additional dice at 17th level.

Relentless Rage

Starting at 11th level, your rage can keep you fighting despite grievous wounds. If you drop to 0 hit points while you're raging and don't die outright, you can make a DC 10 Constitution saving throw. If you succeed, you drop to 1 hit point instead.

Each time you use this feature after the first, the DC increases by 5. When you finish a short or long rest, the DC resets to 10.

Persistent Rage

Beginning at 15th level, your rage is so fierce that it ends early only if you fall unconscious or if you choose to end it.

Indomitable Might

Beginning at 18th level, if your total for a Strength check is less than your Strength score, you can use that score in place of the total.

Primal Champion

At 20th level, you embody the power of the wilds. Your Strength and Constitution scores increase by 4. Your maximum for those scores is now 24.

Primal Paths

Rage burns in every barbarian's heart, a furnace that drives him or her toward greatness. Different barbarians attribute their rage to different sources, however. For some, it is an internal reservoir where pain, grief, and anger are forged into a fury hard as steel. Others see it as a spiritual blessing, a gift of a totem animal.

Path of the Berserker

For some barbarians, rage is a means to an end—that end being violence. The Path of the Berserker is a path of untrammeled fury, slick with blood. As you enter the berserker's rage, you thrill in the chaos of battle, heedless of your own health or well-being.

Frenzy

Starting when you choose this path at 3rd level, you can go into a frenzy when you rage. If you do so, for the duration of your rage you can make a single melee weapon attack as a bonus action on each of your turns after this one. When your rage ends, you suffer one level of exhaustion (as described in appendix A).

Mindless Rage

Beginning at 6th level, you can't be charmed or frightened while raging. If you are charmed or frightened when you enter your rage, the effect is suspended for the duration of the rage.

Intimidating Presence

Beginning at 10th level, you can use your action to frighten someone with your menacing presence. When you do so, choose one creature that you can see within 30 feet of you. If the creature can see or hear you, it must succeed on a Wisdom saving throw (DC equal to 8 + your proficiency bonus + your Charisma modifier) or be frightened of you until the end of your next turn. On subsequent turns, you can use your action to extend the duration of this effect on the frightened

creature until the end of your next turn. This effect ends if the creature ends its turn out of line of sight or more than 60 feet away from you.

If the creature succeeds on its saving throw, you can't use this feature on that creature again for 24 hours.

RETALIATION

Starting at 14th level, when you take damage from a creature that is within 5 feet of you, you can use your reaction to make a melee weapon attack against that creature.

PATH OF THE TOTEM WARRIOR

The Path of the Totem Warrior is a spiritual journey, as the barbarian accepts a spirit animal as guide, protector, and inspiration. In battle, your totem spirit fills you with supernatural might, adding magical fuel to your barbarian rage.

Most barbarian tribes consider a totem animal to be kin to a particular clan. In such cases, it is unusual for an individual to have more than one totem animal spirit, though exceptions exist.

SPIRIT SEEKER

Yours is a path that seeks attunement with the natural world, giving you a kinship with beasts. At 3rd level when you adopt this path, you gain the ability to cast the *beast sense* and *speak with animals* spells, but only as rituals, as described in chapter 10, "Spellcasting."

TOTEM SPIRIT

At 3rd level, when you adopt this path, you choose a totem spirit and gain its feature. You must make or acquire a physical totem object—an amulet or similar adornment—that incorporates fur or feathers, claws, teeth, or bones of the totem animal. At your option, you also gain minor physical attributes that are reminiscent of your totem spirit. For example, if you have a bear totem spirit, you might be unusually hairy and thick-skinned, or if your totem is the eagle, your eyes turn bright yellow.

Your totem animal might be an animal related to those listed here but more appropriate to your homeland. For example, you could choose a hawk or vulture in place of an eagle.

Bear. While raging, you have resistance to all damage except psychic damage. The spirit of the bear makes you tough enough to stand up to any punishment.

Eagle. While you're raging and aren't wearing heavy armor, other creatures have disadvantage on opportunity attack rolls against you, and you can use the Dash action as a bonus action on your turn. The spirit of the eagle makes you into a predator who can weave through the fray with ease.

Wolf. While you're raging, your friends have advantage on melee attack rolls against any creature within 5 feet of you that is hostile to you. The spirit of the wolf makes you a leader of hunters.

ASPECT OF THE BEAST

At 6th level, you gain a magical benefit based on the totem animal of your choice. You can choose the same animal you selected at 3rd level or a different one.

Bear. You gain the might of a bear. Your carrying capacity (including maximum load and maximum lift) is doubled, and you have advantage on Strength checks made to push, pull, lift, or break objects.

Eagle. You gain the eyesight of an eagle. You can see up to 1 mile away with no difficulty, able to discern even fine details as though looking at something no more than 100 feet away from you. Additionally, dim light doesn't impose disadvantage on your Wisdom (Perception) checks.

Wolf. You gain the hunting sensibilities of a wolf. You can track other creatures while traveling at a fast pace, and you can move stealthily while traveling at a normal pace (see chapter 8, "Adventuring," for rules on travel pace).

SPIRIT WALKER

At 10th level, you can cast the *commune with nature* spell, but only as a ritual. When you do so, a spiritual version of one of the animals you chose for Totem Spirit or Aspect of the Beast appears to you to convey the information you seek.

TOTEMIC ATTUNEMENT

At 14th level, you gain a magical benefit based on a totem animal of your choice. You can choose the same animal you selected previously or a different one.

Bear. While you're raging, any creature within 5 feet of you that's hostile to you has disadvantage on attack rolls against targets other than you or another character with this feature. An enemy is immune to this effect if it can't see or hear you or if it can't be frightened.

Eagle. While raging, you have a flying speed equal to your current walking speed. This benefit works only in short bursts; you fall if you end your turn in the air and nothing else is holding you aloft.

Wolf. While you're raging, you can use a bonus action on your turn to knock a Large or smaller creature prone when you hit it with melee weapon attack.

BARD

Humming as she traces her fingers over an ancient monument in a long-forgotten ruin, a half-elf in rugged leathers finds knowledge springing into her mind, conjured forth by the magic of her song—knowledge of the people who constructed the monument and the mythic saga it depicts.

A stern human warrior bangs his sword rhythmically against his scale mail, setting the tempo for his war chant and exhorting his companions to bravery and heroism. The magic of his song fortifies and emboldens them.

Laughing as she tunes her cittern, a gnome weaves her subtle magic over the assembled nobles, ensuring that her companions' words will be well received.

Whether scholar, skald, or scoundrel, a bard weaves magic through words and music to inspire allies, demoralize foes, manipulate minds, create illusions, and even heal wounds.

MUSIC AND MAGIC

In the worlds of D&D, words and music are not just vibrations of air, but vocalizations with power all their own. The bard is a master of song, speech, and the magic they contain. Bards say that the multiverse was spoken into existence, that the words of the gods gave it shape, and that echoes of these primordial Words of Creation still resound throughout the cosmos. The music of bards is an attempt to snatch and harness those echoes, subtly woven into their spells and powers.

The greatest strength of bards is their sheer versatility. Many bards prefer to stick to the sidelines in combat, using their magic to inspire their allies and hinder their foes from a distance. But bards are capable of defending themselves in melee if necessary, using their magic to bolster their swords and armor. Their spells lean toward charms and illusions rather than blatantly destructive spells. They have a wide-ranging knowledge of many subjects and a natural aptitude that lets them do almost anything well. Bards become masters of the talents they set their minds to perfecting, from musical performance to esoteric knowledge.

LEARNING FROM EXPERIENCE

True bards are not common in the world. Not every minstrel singing in a tavern or jester cavorting in a royal court is a bard. Discovering the magic hidden in music requires hard study and some measure of natural talent that most troubadours and jongleurs lack. It can be hard to spot the difference between these performers and true bards, though. A bard's life is spent wandering across the land gathering lore, telling stories, and living on the gratitude of audiences, much like any other entertainer. But a depth of knowledge, a level of musical skill, and a touch of magic set bards apart from their fellows.

Only rarely do bards settle in one place for long, and their natural desire to travel—to find new tales to tell, new skills to learn, and new discoveries beyond the horizon—makes an adventuring career a natural calling. Every adventure is an opportunity to learn, practice a variety of skills, enter long-forgotten tombs, discover lost works of magic, decipher old tomes, travel to strange places, or encounter exotic creatures. Bards love to accompany heroes to witness their deeds firsthand. A bard who can tell an awe-inspiring story from personal experience earns renown among other bards. Indeed, after telling so many stories about heroes accomplishing mighty deeds, many bards take these themes to heart and assume heroic roles themselves.

CREATING A BARD

Bards thrive on stories, whether those stories are true or not. Your character's background and motivations are not as important as the stories that he or she tells about them. Perhaps you had a secure and mundane childhood. There's no good story to be told about that, so you might paint yourself as an orphan raised by a hag in a dismal swamp. Or your childhood might be worthy of a story. Some bards acquire their magical music through extraordinary means, including the inspiration of fey or other supernatural creatures.

Did you serve an apprenticeship, studying under a master, following the more experienced bard until you were ready to strike out on your own? Or did you attend a college where you studied bardic lore and practiced your musical magic? Perhaps you were a young runaway or orphan, befriended by a wandering bard who became your mentor. Or you might have been a spoiled noble child tutored by a master. Perhaps you stumbled into the clutches of a hag, making a bargain for a musical gift in addition to your life and freedom, but at what cost?

QUICK BUILD

You can make a bard quickly by following these suggestions. First, Charisma should be your highest ability score, followed by Dexterity. Second, choose the entertainer background. Third, choose the *dancing lights* and *vicious mockery* cantrips, along with the following 1st-level spells: *charm person*, *detect magic*, *healing word*, and *thunderwave*.

CLASS FEATURES

As a bard, you gain the following class features.

HIT POINTS

Hit Dice: 1d8 per bard level
Hit Points at 1st Level: 8 + your Constitution modifier
Hit Points at Higher Levels: 1d8 (or 5) + your Constitution modifier per bard level after 1st

PROFICIENCIES

Armor: Light armor
Weapons: Simple weapons, hand crossbows, longswords, rapiers, shortswords
Tools: Three musical instruments of your choice

Saving Throws: Dexterity, Charisma
Skills: Choose any three

EQUIPMENT

You start with the following equipment, in addition to the equipment granted by your background:

- (*a*) a rapier, (*b*) a longsword, or (*c*) any simple weapon
- (*a*) a diplomat's pack or (*b*) an entertainer's pack
- (*a*) a lute or (*b*) any other musical instrument
- Leather armor and a dagger

SPELLCASTING

You have learned to untangle and reshape the fabric of reality in harmony with your wishes and music. Your spells are part of your vast repertoire, magic that you can tune to different situations. See chapter 10 for the general rules of spellcasting and chapter 11 for the bard spell list.

CANTRIPS

You know two cantrips of your choice from the bard spell list. You learn additional bard cantrips of your choice at higher levels, as shown in the Cantrips Known column of the Bard table.

THE BARD

Level	Proficiency Bonus	Features	Cantrips Known	Spells Known	Spell Slots per Spell Level								
					1st	2nd	3rd	4th	5th	6th	7th	8th	9th
1st	+2	Spellcasting, Bardic Inspiration (d6)	2	4	2	—	—	—	—	—	—	—	—
2nd	+2	Jack of All Trades, Song of Rest (d6)	2	5	3	—	—	—	—	—	—	—	—
3rd	+2	Bard College, Expertise	2	6	4	2	—	—	—	—	—	—	—
4th	+2	Ability Score Improvement	3	7	4	3	—	—	—	—	—	—	—
5th	+3	Bardic Inspiration (d8), Font of Inspiration	3	8	4	3	2	—	—	—	—	—	—
6th	+3	Countercharm, Bard College feature	3	9	4	3	3	—	—	—	—	—	—
7th	+3	—	3	10	4	3	3	1	—	—	—	—	—
8th	+3	Ability Score Improvement	3	11	4	3	3	2	—	—	—	—	—
9th	+4	Song of Rest (d8)	3	12	4	3	3	3	1	—	—	—	—
10th	+4	Bardic Inspiration (d10), Expertise, Magical Secrets	4	14	4	3	3	3	2	—	—	—	—
11th	+4	—	4	15	4	3	3	3	2	1	—	—	—
12th	+4	Ability Score Improvement	4	15	4	3	3	3	2	1	—	—	—
13th	+5	Song of Rest (d10)	4	16	4	3	3	3	2	1	1	—	—
14th	+5	Magical Secrets, Bard College feature	4	18	4	3	3	3	2	1	1	—	—
15th	+5	Bardic Inspiration (d12)	4	19	4	3	3	3	2	1	1	1	—
16th	+5	Ability Score Improvement	4	19	4	3	3	3	2	1	1	1	—
17th	+6	Song of Rest (d12)	4	20	4	3	3	3	2	1	1	1	1
18th	+6	Magical Secrets	4	22	4	3	3	3	3	1	1	1	1
19th	+6	Ability Score Improvement	4	22	4	3	3	3	3	2	1	1	1
20th	+6	Superior Inspiration	4	22	4	3	3	3	3	2	2	1	1

SPELL SLOTS

The Bard table shows how many spell slots you have to cast your spells of 1st level and higher. To cast one of these spells, you must expend a slot of the spell's level or higher. You regain all expended spell slots when you finish a long rest.

For example, if you know the 1st-level spell *cure wounds* and have a 1st-level and a 2nd-level spell slot available, you can cast *cure wounds* using either slot.

SPELLS KNOWN OF 1ST LEVEL AND HIGHER

You know four 1st-level spells of your choice from the bard spell list.

The Spells Known column of the Bard table shows when you learn more bard spells of your choice. Each of these spells must be of a level for which you have spell slots, as shown on the table. For instance, when you reach 3rd level in this class, you can learn one new spell of 1st or 2nd level.

Additionally, when you gain a level in this class, you can choose one of the bard spells you know and replace it with another spell from the bard spell list, which also must be of a level for which you have spell slots.

SPELLCASTING ABILITY

Charisma is your spellcasting ability for your bard spells. Your magic comes from the heart and soul you pour into the performance of your music or oration. You use your Charisma whenever a spell refers to your spellcasting ability. In addition, you use your Charisma modifier when setting the saving throw DC for a bard spell you cast and when making an attack roll with one.

Spell save DC = 8 + your proficiency bonus + your Charisma modifier

Spell attack modifier = your proficiency bonus + your Charisma modifier

RITUAL CASTING

You can cast any bard spell you know as a ritual if that spell has the ritual tag.

SPELLCASTING FOCUS

You can use a musical instrument (see chapter 5, "Equipment") as a spellcasting focus for your bard spells.

BARDIC INSPIRATION

You can inspire others through stirring words or music. To do so, you use a bonus action on your turn to choose one creature other than yourself within 60 feet of you who can hear you. That creature gains one Bardic Inspiration die, a d6.

Once within the next 10 minutes, the creature can roll the die and add the number rolled to one ability check, attack roll, or saving throw it makes. The creature can wait until after it rolls the d20 before deciding to use the Bardic Inspiration die, but must decide before the DM says whether the roll succeeds or fails. Once the Bardic Inspiration die is rolled, it is lost. A creature can have only one Bardic Inspiration die at a time.

You can use this feature a number of times equal to your Charisma modifier (a minimum of once). You regain any expended uses when you finish a long rest.

Your Bardic Inspiration die changes when you reach certain levels in this class. The die becomes a d8 at 5th level, a d10 at 10th level, and a d12 at 15th level.

JACK OF ALL TRADES

Starting at 2nd level, you can add half your proficiency bonus, rounded down, to any ability check you make that doesn't already include your proficiency bonus.

SONG OF REST

Beginning at 2nd level, you can use soothing music or oration to help revitalize your wounded allies during a short rest. If you or any friendly creatures who can hear your performance regain hit points at the end of the short rest by spending one or more Hit Dice, each of those creatures regains an extra 1d6 hit points.

The extra hit points increase when you reach certain levels in this class: to 1d8 at 9th level, to 1d10 at 13th level, and to 1d12 at 17th level.

BARD COLLEGE

At 3rd level, you delve into the advanced techniques of a bard college of your choice: the College of Lore or the College of Valor, both detailed at the end of the class description. Your choice grants you features at 3rd level and again at 6th and 14th level.

EXPERTISE

At 3rd level, choose two of your skill proficiencies. Your proficiency bonus is doubled for any ability check you make that uses either of the chosen proficiencies.

At 10th level, you can choose another two skill proficiencies to gain this benefit.

ABILITY SCORE IMPROVEMENT

When you reach 4th level, and again at 8th, 12th, 16th, and 19th level, you can increase one ability score of your choice by 2, or you can increase two ability scores of your choice by 1. As normal, you can't increase an ability score above 20 using this feature.

FONT OF INSPIRATION

Beginning when you reach 5th level, you regain all of your expended uses of Bardic Inspiration when you finish a short or long rest.

COUNTERCHARM

At 6th level, you gain the ability to use musical notes or words of power to disrupt mind-influencing effects. As an action, you can start a performance that lasts until the end of your next turn. During that time, you and any friendly creatures within 30 feet of you have advantage on saving throws against being frightened or charmed. A creature must be able to hear you to gain this benefit. The performance ends early if you are incapacitated or silenced or if you voluntarily end it (no action required).

MAGICAL SECRETS

By 10th level, you have plundered magical knowledge from a wide spectrum of disciplines. Choose two spells from any class, including this one. A spell you choose must be of a level you can cast, as shown on the Bard table, or a cantrip.

The chosen spells count as bard spells for you and are included in the number in the Spells Known column of the Bard table.

You learn two additional spells from any class at 14th level and again at 18th level.

SUPERIOR INSPIRATION

At 20th level, when you roll initiative and have no uses of Bardic Inspiration left, you regain one use.

BARD COLLEGES

The way of a bard is gregarious. Bards seek each other out to swap songs and stories, boast of their accomplishments, and share their knowledge. Bards form loose associations, which they call colleges, to facilitate their gatherings and preserve their traditions.

COLLEGE OF LORE

Bards of the College of Lore know something about most things, collecting bits of knowledge from sources as diverse as scholarly tomes and peasant tales. Whether singing folk ballads in taverns or elaborate compositions in royal courts, these bards use their gifts to hold audiences spellbound. When the applause dies down, the audience members might find themselves questioning everything they held to be true, from their faith in the priesthood of the local temple to their loyalty to the king.

The loyalty of these bards lies in the pursuit of beauty and truth, not in fealty to a monarch or following the tenets of a deity. A noble who keeps such a bard as a herald or advisor knows that the bard would rather be honest than politic.

The college's members gather in libraries and sometimes in actual colleges, complete with classrooms and dormitories, to share their lore with one another. They also meet at festivals or affairs of state, where they can expose corruption, unravel lies, and poke fun at self-important figures of authority.

BONUS PROFICIENCIES

When you join the College of Lore at 3rd level, you gain proficiency with three skills of your choice.

CUTTING WORDS

Also at 3rd level, you learn how to use your wit to distract, confuse, and otherwise sap the confidence and competence of others. When a creature that you can see within 60 feet of you makes an attack roll, an ability check, or a damage roll, you can use your reaction to expend one of your uses of Bardic Inspiration, rolling a Bardic Inspiration die and subtracting the number rolled from the creature's roll. You can choose to use this feature after the creature makes its roll, but before the DM determines whether the attack roll or ability

check succeeds or fails, or before the creature deals its damage. The creature is immune if it can't hear you or if it's immune to being charmed.

ADDITIONAL MAGICAL SECRETS

At 6th level, you learn two spells of your choice from any class. A spell you choose must be of a level you can cast, as shown on the Bard table, or a cantrip. The chosen spells count as bard spells for you but don't count against the number of bard spells you know.

PEERLESS SKILL

Starting at 14th level, when you make an ability check, you can expend one use of Bardic Inspiration. Roll a Bardic Inspiration die and add the number rolled to your ability check. You can choose to do so after you roll the die for the ability check, but before the DM tells you whether you succeed or fail.

COLLEGE OF VALOR

Bards of the College of Valor are daring skalds whose tales keep alive the memory of the great heroes of the past, and thereby inspire a new generation of heroes. These bards gather in mead halls or around great bonfires to sing the deeds of the mighty, both past and present. They travel the land to witness great events firsthand and to ensure that the memory of those events doesn't pass from the world. With their songs, they inspire others to reach the same heights of accomplishment as the heroes of old.

BONUS PROFICIENCIES

When you join the College of Valor at 3rd level, you gain proficiency with medium armor, shields, and martial weapons.

COMBAT INSPIRATION

Also at 3rd level, you learn to inspire others in battle. A creature that has a Bardic Inspiration die from you can roll that die and add the number rolled to a weapon damage roll it just made. Alternatively, when an attack roll is made against the creature, it can use its reaction to roll the Bardic Inspiration die and add the number rolled to its AC against that attack, after seeing the roll but before knowing whether it hits or misses.

EXTRA ATTACK

Starting at 6th level, you can attack twice, instead of once, whenever you take the Attack action on your turn.

BATTLE MAGIC

At 14th level, you have mastered the art of weaving spellcasting and weapon use into a single harmonious act. When you use your action to cast a bard spell, you can make one weapon attack as a bonus action.

CLERIC

Arms and eyes upraised toward the sun and a prayer on his lips, an elf begins to glow with an inner light that spills out to heal his battle-worn companions.

Chanting a song of glory, a dwarf swings his axe in wide swaths to cut through the ranks of orcs arrayed against him, shouting praise to the gods with every foe's fall.

Calling down a curse upon the forces of undeath, a human lifts her holy symbol as light pours from it to drive back the zombies crowding in on her companions.

Clerics are intermediaries between the mortal world and the distant planes of the gods. As varied as the gods they serve, clerics strive to embody the handiwork of their deities. No ordinary priest, a cleric is imbued with divine magic.

HEALERS AND WARRIORS

Divine magic, as the name suggests, is the power of the gods, flowing from them into the world. Clerics are conduits for that power, manifesting it as miraculous effects. The gods don't grant this power to everyone who seeks it, but only to those chosen to fulfill a high calling.

Harnessing divine magic doesn't rely on study or training. A cleric might learn formulaic prayers and ancient rites, but the ability to cast cleric spells relies on devotion and an intuitive sense of a deity's wishes.

Clerics combine the helpful magic of healing and inspiring their allies with spells that harm and hinder foes. They can provoke awe and dread, lay curses of plague or poison, and even call down flames from heaven to consume their enemies. For those evildoers who will benefit most from a mace to the head, clerics depend on their combat training to let them wade into melee with the power of the gods on their side.

DIVINE AGENTS

Not every acolyte or officiant at a temple or shrine is a cleric. Some priests are called to a simple life of temple service, carrying out their gods' will through prayer and sacrifice, not by magic and strength of arms. In some cities, priesthood amounts to a political office, viewed as a stepping stone to higher positions of authority and involving no communion with a god at all. True clerics are rare in most hierarchies.

When a cleric takes up an adventuring life, it is usually because his or her god demands it. Pursuing the goals of the gods often involves braving dangers beyond the walls of civilization, smiting evil or seeking holy relics in ancient tombs. Many clerics are also expected to protect

The Cleric

Level	Proficiency Bonus	Features	Cantrips Known	1st	2nd	3rd	4th	5th	6th	7th	8th	9th
1st	+2	Spellcasting, Divine Domain	3	2	—	—	—	—	—	—	—	—
2nd	+2	Channel Divinity (1/rest), Divine Domain feature	3	3	—	—	—	—	—	—	—	—
3rd	+2	—	3	4	2	—	—	—	—	—	—	—
4th	+2	Ability Score Improvement	4	4	3	—	—	—	—	—	—	—
5th	+3	Destroy Undead (CR 1/2)	4	4	3	2	—	—	—	—	—	—
6th	+3	Channel Divinity (2/rest), Divine Domain feature	4	4	3	3	—	—	—	—	—	—
7th	+3	—	4	4	3	3	1	—	—	—	—	—
8th	+3	Ability Score Improvement, Destroy Undead (CR 1), Divine Domain feature	4	4	3	3	2	—	—	—	—	—
9th	+4	—	4	4	3	3	3	1	—	—	—	—
10th	+4	Divine Intervention	5	4	3	3	3	2	—	—	—	—
11th	+4	Destroy Undead (CR 2)	5	4	3	3	3	2	1	—	—	—
12th	+4	Ability Score Improvement	5	4	3	3	3	2	1	—	—	—
13th	+5	—	5	4	3	3	3	2	1	1	—	—
14th	+5	Destroy Undead (CR 3)	5	4	3	3	3	2	1	1	—	—
15th	+5	—	5	4	3	3	3	2	1	1	1	—
16th	+5	Ability Score Improvement	5	4	3	3	3	2	1	1	1	—
17th	+6	Destroy Undead (CR 4), Divine Domain feature	5	4	3	3	3	2	1	1	1	1
18th	+6	Channel Divinity (3/rest)	5	4	3	3	3	3	1	1	1	1
19th	+6	Ability Score Improvement	5	4	3	3	3	3	2	1	1	1
20th	+6	Divine Intervention improvement	5	4	3	3	3	3	2	2	1	1

their deities' worshipers, which can mean fighting rampaging orcs, negotiating peace between warring nations, or sealing a portal that would allow a demon prince to enter the world.

Most adventuring clerics maintain some connection to established temples and orders of their faiths. A temple might ask for a cleric's aid, or a high priest might be in a position to demand it.

Creating a Cleric

As you create a cleric, the most important question to consider is which deity to serve and what principles you want your character to embody. Appendix B includes lists of many of the gods of the multiverse. Check with your DM to learn which deities are in your campaign.

Once you've chosen a deity, consider your cleric's relationship to that god. Did you enter this service willingly? Or did the god choose you, impelling you into service with no regard for your wishes? How do the temple priests of your faith regard you: as a champion or a troublemaker? What are your ultimate goals? Does your deity have a special task in mind for you? Or are you striving to prove yourself worthy of a great quest?

Quick Build

You can make a cleric quickly by following these suggestions. First, Wisdom should be your highest ability score, followed by Strength or Constitution. Second, choose the acolyte background.

Class Features

As a cleric, you gain the following class features.

Hit Points

Hit Dice: 1d8 per cleric level
Hit Points at 1st Level: 8 + your Constitution modifier
Hit Points at Higher Levels: 1d8 (or 5) + your Constitution modifier per cleric level after 1st

Proficiencies

Armor: Light armor, medium armor, shields
Weapons: Simple weapons
Tools: None

Saving Throws: Wisdom, Charisma
Skills: Choose two from History, Insight, Medicine, Persuasion, and Religion

Equipment

You start with the following equipment, in addition to the equipment granted by your background:

- (a) a mace or (b) a warhammer (if proficient)
- (a) scale mail, (b) leather armor, or (c) chain mail (if proficient)
- (a) a light crossbow and 20 bolts or (b) any simple weapon
- (a) a priest's pack or (b) an explorer's pack
- A shield and a holy symbol

SPELLCASTING

As a conduit for divine power, you can cast cleric spells. See chapter 10 for the general rules of spellcasting and chapter 11 for the cleric spell list.

CANTRIPS

At 1st level, you know three cantrips of your choice from the cleric spell list. You learn additional cleric cantrips of your choice at higher levels, as shown in the Cantrips Known column of the Cleric table.

PREPARING AND CASTING SPELLS

The Cleric table shows how many spell slots you have to cast your spells of 1st level and higher. To cast one of these spells, you must expend a slot of the spell's level or higher. You regain all expended spell slots when you finish a long rest.

You prepare the list of cleric spells that are available for you to cast, choosing from the cleric spell list. When you do so, choose a number of cleric spells equal to your Wisdom modifier + your cleric level (minimum of one spell). The spells must be of a level for which you have spell slots.

For example, if you are a 3rd-level cleric, you have four 1st-level and two 2nd-level spell slots. With a Wisdom of 16, your list of prepared spells can include six spells of 1st or 2nd level, in any combination. If you prepare the 1st-level spell *cure wounds*, you can cast it using a 1st-level or 2nd-level slot. Casting the spell doesn't remove it from your list of prepared spells.

You can change your list of prepared spells when you finish a long rest. Preparing a new list of cleric spells requires time spent in prayer and meditation: at least 1 minute per spell level for each spell on your list.

SPELLCASTING ABILITY

Wisdom is your spellcasting ability for your cleric spells. The power of your spells comes from your devotion to your deity. You use your Wisdom whenever a cleric spell refers to your spellcasting ability. In addition, you use your Wisdom modifier when setting the saving throw DC for a cleric spell you cast and when making an attack roll with one.

Spell save DC = 8 + your proficiency bonus + your Wisdom modifier

Spell attack modifier = your proficiency bonus + your Wisdom modifier

RITUAL CASTING

You can cast a cleric spell as a ritual if that spell has the ritual tag and you have the spell prepared.

SPELLCASTING FOCUS

You can use a holy symbol (found in chapter 5) as a spellcasting focus for your cleric spells.

DIVINE DOMAIN

Choose one domain related to your deity: Knowledge, Life, Light, Nature, Tempest, Trickery, or War. Each domain is detailed at the end of the class description, and each one provides examples of gods associated with it. Your choice grants you domain spells and other features when you choose it at 1st level. It also grants you additional ways to use Channel Divinity when you gain that feature at 2nd level, and additional benefits at 6th, 8th, and 17th levels.

DOMAIN SPELLS

Each domain has a list of spells—its domain spells—that you gain at the cleric levels noted in the domain description. Once you gain a domain spell, you always have it prepared, and it doesn't count against the number of spells you can prepare each day.

If you have a domain spell that doesn't appear on the cleric spell list, the spell is nonetheless a cleric spell for you.

CHANNEL DIVINITY

At 2nd level, you gain the ability to channel divine energy directly from your deity, using that energy to fuel magical effects. You start with two such effects: Turn Undead and an effect determined by your domain. Some domains grant you additional effects as you advance in levels, as noted in the domain description.

When you use your Channel Divinity, you choose which effect to create. You must then finish a short or long rest to use your Channel Divinity again.

Some Channel Divinity effects require saving throws. When you use such an effect from this class, the DC equals your cleric spell save DC.

Beginning at 6th level, you can use your Channel Divinity twice between rests, and beginning at 18th level, you can use it three times between rests. When you finish a short or long rest, you regain your expended uses.

CHANNEL DIVINITY: TURN UNDEAD

As an action, you present your holy symbol and speak a prayer censuring the undead. Each undead that can see or hear you within 30 feet of you must make a Wisdom saving throw. If the creature fails its saving throw, it is turned for 1 minute or until it takes any damage.

A turned creature must spend its turns trying to move as far away from you as it can, and it can't willingly move to a space within 30 feet of you. It also can't take reactions. For its action, it can use only the Dash action or try to escape from an effect that prevents it from moving. If there's nowhere to move, the creature can use the Dodge action.

ABILITY SCORE IMPROVEMENT

When you reach 4th level, and again at 8th, 12th, 16th, and 19th level, you can increase one ability score of your choice by 2, or you can increase two ability scores of your choice by 1. As normal, you can't increase an ability score above 20 using this feature.

DESTROY UNDEAD

Starting at 5th level, when an undead fails its saving throw against your Turn Undead feature, the creature is instantly destroyed if its challenge rating is at or below a certain threshold, as shown in the Destroy Undead table.

DESTROY UNDEAD

Cleric Level	Destroys Undead of CR . . .
5th	1/2 or lower
8th	1 or lower
11th	2 or lower
14th	3 or lower
17th	4 or lower

DIVINE INTERVENTION

Beginning at 10th level, you can call on your deity to intervene on your behalf when your need is great.

Imploring your deity's aid requires you to use your action. Describe the assistance you seek, and roll percentile dice. If you roll a number equal to or lower than your cleric level, your deity intervenes. The DM chooses the nature of the intervention; the effect of any cleric spell or cleric domain spell would be appropriate.

If your deity intervenes, you can't use this feature again for 7 days. Otherwise, you can use it again after you finish a long rest.

At 20th level, your call for intervention succeeds automatically, no roll required.

DIVINE DOMAINS

In a pantheon, every deity has influence over different aspects of mortal life and civilization, called a deity's domain. All the domains over which a deity has influence are called the deity's portfolio. For example, the portfolio of the Greek god Apollo includes the domains of Knowledge, Life, and Light. As a cleric, you choose one aspect of your deity's portfolio to emphasize, and you are granted powers related to that domain.

Your choice might correspond to a particular sect dedicated to your deity. Apollo, for example, could be worshiped in one region as Phoebus ("radiant") Apollo, emphasizing his influence over the Light domain, and in a different place as Apollo Acesius ("healing"), emphasizing his association with the Life domain. Alternatively, your choice of domain could simply be a matter of personal preference, the aspect of the deity that appeals to you most.

Each domain's description gives examples of deities who have influence over that domain. Gods are included from the worlds of the Forgotten Realms, Greyhawk, Dragonlance, and Eberron campaign settings, as well as from the Celtic, Greek, Norse, and Egyptian pantheons of antiquity.

KNOWLEDGE DOMAIN

The gods of knowledge—including Oghma, Boccob, Gilean, Aureon, and Thoth—value learning and understanding above all. Some teach that knowledge is to be gathered and shared in libraries and universities, or promote the practical knowledge of craft and invention. Some deities hoard knowledge and keep its secrets to themselves. And some promise their followers that they will gain tremendous power if they unlock the secrets of the multiverse. Followers of these gods study esoteric lore, collect old tomes, delve into the secret places of the earth, and learn all they can. Some gods of knowledge promote the practical knowledge of craft and invention, including smith deities like Gond, Reorx, Onatar, Moradin, Hephaestus, and Goibhniu.

KNOWLEDGE DOMAIN SPELLS

Cleric Level	Spells
1st	*command, identify*
3rd	*augury, suggestion*
5th	*nondetection, speak with dead*
7th	*arcane eye, confusion*
9th	*legend lore, scrying*

BLESSINGS OF KNOWLEDGE

At 1st level, you learn two languages of your choice. You also become proficient in your choice of two of the following skills: Arcana, History, Nature, or Religion.

Your proficiency bonus is doubled for any ability check you make that uses either of those skills.

CHANNEL DIVINITY: KNOWLEDGE OF THE AGES

Starting at 2nd level, you can use your Channel Divinity to tap into a divine well of knowledge. As an action, you choose one skill or tool. For 10 minutes, you have proficiency with the chosen skill or tool.

CHANNEL DIVINITY: READ THOUGHTS

At 6th level, you can use your Channel Divinity to read a creature's thoughts. You can then use your access to the creature's mind to command it.

As an action, choose one creature that you can see within 60 feet of you. That creature must make a Wisdom saving throw. If the creature succeeds on the saving throw, you can't use this feature on it again until you finish a long rest.

If the creature fails its save, you can read its surface thoughts (those foremost in its mind, reflecting its current emotions and what it is actively thinking about) when it is within 60 feet of you. This effect lasts for 1 minute.

During that time, you can use your action to end this effect and cast the *suggestion* spell on the creature without expending a spell slot. The target automatically fails its saving throw against the spell.

POTENT SPELLCASTING

Starting at 8th level, you add your Wisdom modifier to the damage you deal with any cleric cantrip.

VISIONS OF THE PAST

Starting at 17th level, you can call up visions of the past that relate to an object you hold or your immediate surroundings. You spend at least 1 minute in meditation and prayer, then receive dreamlike, shadowy glimpses of recent events. You can meditate in this way for a number of minutes equal to your Wisdom score and must maintain concentration during that time, as if you were casting a spell.

Once you use this feature, you can't use it again until you finish a short or long rest.

Object Reading. Holding an object as you meditate, you can see visions of the object's previous owner. After meditating for 1 minute, you learn how the owner acquired and lost the object, as well as the most recent significant event involving the object and that owner. If the object was owned by another creature in the recent past (within a number of days equal to your Wisdom score), you can spend 1 additional minute for each owner to learn the same information about that creature.

Area Reading. As you meditate, you see visions of recent events in your immediate vicinity (a room, street, tunnel, clearing, or the like, up to a 50-foot cube), going back a number of days equal to your Wisdom score. For each minute you meditate, you learn about one significant event, beginning with the most recent. Significant events typically involve powerful emotions, such as battles and betrayals, marriages and murders, births and funerals. However, they might also include more mundane events that are nevertheless important in your current situation.

LIFE DOMAIN

The Life domain focuses on the vibrant positive energy—one of the fundamental forces of the universe—that sustains all life. The gods of life promote vitality and health through healing the sick and wounded, caring for those in need, and driving away the forces of death and undeath. Almost any non-evil deity can claim influence over this domain, particularly agricultural deities (such as Chauntea, Arawai, and Demeter), sun gods (such as Lathander, Pelor, and Re-Horakhty), gods

of healing or endurance (such as Ilmater, Mishakal, Apollo, and Diancecht), and gods of home and community (such as Hestia, Hathor, and Boldrei).

LIFE DOMAIN SPELLS

Cleric Level	Spells
1st	*bless, cure wounds*
3rd	*lesser restoration, spiritual weapon*
5th	*beacon of hope, revivify*
7th	*death ward, guardian of faith*
9th	*mass cure wounds, raise dead*

BONUS PROFICIENCY

When you choose this domain at 1st level, you gain proficiency with heavy armor.

DISCIPLE OF LIFE

Also starting at 1st level, your healing spells are more effective. Whenever you use a spell of 1st level or higher to restore hit points to a creature, the creature regains additional hit points equal to 2 + the spell's level.

CHANNEL DIVINITY: PRESERVE LIFE

Starting at 2nd level, you can use your Channel Divinity to heal the badly injured.

As an action, you present your holy symbol and evoke healing energy that can restore a number of hit points equal to five times your cleric level. Choose any creatures within 30 feet of you, and divide those hit points among them. This feature can restore a creature to no more than half of its hit point maximum. You can't use this feature on an undead or a construct.

BLESSED HEALER

Beginning at 6th level, the healing spells you cast on others heal you as well. When you cast a spell of 1st level or higher that restores hit points to a creature other than you, you regain hit points equal to 2 + the spell's level.

DIVINE STRIKE

At 8th level, you gain the ability to infuse your weapon strikes with divine energy. Once on each of your turns when you hit a creature with a weapon attack, you can cause the attack to deal an extra 1d8 radiant damage to the target. When you reach 14th level, the extra damage increases to 2d8.

SUPREME HEALING

Starting at 17th level, when you would normally roll one or more dice to restore hit points with a spell, you instead use the highest number possible for each die. For example, instead of restoring 2d6 hit points to a creature, you restore 12.

LIGHT DOMAIN

Gods of light—including Helm, Lathander, Pholtus, Branchala, the Silver Flame, Belenus, Apollo, and Re-Horakhty—promote the ideals of rebirth and renewal, truth, vigilance, and beauty, often using the symbol of the sun. Some of these gods are portrayed as the sun itself or as a charioteer who guides the sun across the sky. Others are tireless sentinels whose eyes pierce every shadow and see through every deception. Some are deities of beauty and artistry, who teach that art is a vehicle for the soul's improvement. Clerics of a god of light are enlightened souls infused with radiance and the power of their gods' discerning vision, charged with chasing away lies and burning away darkness.

LIGHT DOMAIN SPELLS

Cleric Level	Spells
1st	burning hands, faerie fire
3rd	flaming sphere, scorching ray
5th	daylight, fireball
7th	guardian of faith, wall of fire
9th	flame strike, scrying

BONUS CANTRIP
When you choose this domain at 1st level, you gain the *light* cantrip if you don't already know it.

WARDING FLARE
Also at 1st level, you can interpose divine light between yourself and an attacking enemy. When you are attacked by a creature within 30 feet of you that you can see, you can use your reaction to impose disadvantage on the attack roll, causing light to flare before the attacker before it hits or misses. An attacker that can't be blinded is immune to this feature.

You can use this feature a number of times equal to your Wisdom modifier (a minimum of once). You regain all expended uses when you finish a long rest.

CHANNEL DIVINITY: RADIANCE OF THE DAWN
Starting at 2nd level, you can use your Channel Divinity to harness sunlight, banishing darkness and dealing radiant damage to your foes.

As an action, you present your holy symbol, and any magical darkness within 30 feet of you is dispelled. Additionally, each hostile creature within 30 feet of you must make a Constitution saving throw. A creature takes radiant damage equal to 2d10 + your cleric level on a failed saving throw, and half as much damage on a successful one. A creature that has total cover from you is not affected.

IMPROVED FLARE
Starting at 6th level, you can also use your Warding Flare feature when a creature that you can see within 30 feet of you attacks a creature other than you.

POTENT SPELLCASTING
Starting at 8th level, you add your Wisdom modifier to the damage you deal with any cleric cantrip.

CORONA OF LIGHT
Starting at 17th level, you can use your action to activate an aura of sunlight that lasts for 1 minute or until you dismiss it using another action. You emit bright light in a 60-foot radius and dim light 30 feet beyond that. Your enemies in the bright light have disadvantage on saving throws against any spell that deals fire or radiant damage.

NATURE DOMAIN

Gods of nature are as varied as the natural world itself, from inscrutable gods of the deep forests (such as Silvanus, Obad-Hai, Chislev, Balinor, and Pan) to friendly deities associated with particular springs and groves (such as Eldath). Druids revere nature as a whole and might serve one of these deities, practicing mysterious rites and reciting all-but-forgotten prayers in their own secret tongue. But many of these gods have clerics as well, champions who take a more active role in advancing the interests of a particular nature god. These clerics might hunt the evil monstrosities that despoil the woodlands, bless the harvest of the faithful, or wither the crops of those who anger their gods.

NATURE DOMAIN SPELLS

Cleric Level	Spells
1st	animal friendship, speak with animals
3rd	barkskin, spike growth
5th	plant growth, wind wall
7th	dominate beast, grasping vine
9th	insect plague, tree stride

ACOLYTE OF NATURE

At 1st level, you learn one druid cantrip of your choice. You also gain proficiency in one of the following skills of your choice: Animal Handling, Nature, or Survival.

BONUS PROFICIENCY

Also at 1st level, you gain proficiency with heavy armor.

CHANNEL DIVINITY: CHARM ANIMALS AND PLANTS

Starting at 2nd level, you can use your Channel Divinity to charm animals and plants.

As an action, you present your holy symbol and invoke the name of your deity. Each beast or plant creature that can see you within 30 feet of you must make a Wisdom saving throw. If the creature fails its saving throw, it is charmed by you for 1 minute or until it takes damage. While it is charmed by you, it is friendly to you and other creatures you designate.

DAMPEN ELEMENTS

Starting at 6th level, when you or a creature within 30 feet of you takes acid, cold, fire, lightning, or thunder damage, you can use your reaction to grant resistance to the creature against that instance of the damage.

DIVINE STRIKE

At 8th level, you gain the ability to infuse your weapon strikes with divine energy. Once on each of your turns when you hit a creature with a weapon attack, you can cause the attack to deal an extra 1d8 cold, fire, or lightning damage (your choice) to the target. When you reach 14th level, the extra damage increases to 2d8.

MASTER OF NATURE

At 17th level, you gain the ability to command animals and plant creatures. While creatures are charmed by your Charm Animals and Plants feature, you can take a bonus action on your turn to verbally command what each of those creatures will do on its next turn.

TEMPEST DOMAIN

Gods whose portfolios include the Tempest domain—including Talos, Umberlee, Kord, Zeboim, the Devourer, Zeus, and Thor—govern storms, sea, and sky. They include gods of lightning and thunder, gods of earthquakes, some fire gods, and certain gods of violence, physical strength, and courage. In some pantheons, a god of this domain rules over other deities and is known for swift justice delivered by thunderbolts. In the pantheons of seafaring people, gods of this domain are ocean deities and the patrons of sailors. Tempest gods send their clerics to inspire fear in the common folk, either to keep those folk on the path of righteousness or to encourage them to offer sacrifices of propitiation to ward off divine wrath.

TEMPEST DOMAIN SPELLS

Cleric Level	Spells
1st	fog cloud, thunderwave
3rd	gust of wind, shatter
5th	call lightning, sleet storm
7th	control water, ice storm
9th	destructive wave, insect plague

BONUS PROFICIENCIES

At 1st level, you gain proficiency with martial weapons and heavy armor.

WRATH OF THE STORM

Also at 1st level, you can thunderously rebuke attackers. When a creature within 5 feet of you that you can see hits you with an attack, you can use your reaction to cause the creature to make a Dexterity saving throw. The creature takes 2d8 lightning or thunder damage (your choice) on a failed saving throw, and half as much damage on a successful one.

You can use this feature a number of times equal to your Wisdom modifier (a minimum of once). You regain all expended uses when you finish a long rest.

CHANNEL DIVINITY: DESTRUCTIVE WRATH

Starting at 2nd level, you can use your Channel Divinity to wield the power of the storm with unchecked ferocity.

When you roll lightning or thunder damage, you can use your Channel Divinity to deal maximum damage, instead of rolling.

THUNDERBOLT STRIKE

At 6th level, when you deal lightning damage to a Large or smaller creature, you can also push it up to 10 feet away from you.

DIVINE STRIKE

At 8th level, you gain the ability to infuse your weapon strikes with divine energy. Once on each of your turns when you hit a creature with a weapon attack, you can cause the attack to deal an extra 1d8 thunder damage to the target. When you reach 14th level, the extra damage increases to 2d8.

STORMBORN

At 17th level, you have a flying speed equal to your current walking speed whenever you are not underground or indoors.

TRICKERY DOMAIN

Gods of trickery—such as Tymora, Beshaba, Olidammara, the Traveler, Garl Glittergold, and Loki—are mischief-makers and instigators who stand as a constant challenge to the accepted order among both gods and mortals. They're patrons of thieves, scoundrels, gamblers, rebels, and liberators. Their clerics are a disruptive force in the world, puncturing pride, mocking tyrants, stealing from the rich, freeing captives, and flouting hollow traditions. They prefer subterfuge, pranks, deception, and theft rather than direct confrontation.

TRICKERY DOMAIN SPELLS

Cleric Level	Spells
1st	charm person, disguise self
3rd	mirror image, pass without trace
5th	blink, dispel magic
7th	dimension door, polymorph
9th	dominate person, modify memory

BLESSING OF THE TRICKSTER

Starting when you choose this domain at 1st level, you can use your action to touch a willing creature other than yourself to give it advantage on Dexterity (Stealth) checks. This blessing lasts for 1 hour or until you use this feature again.

CHANNEL DIVINITY: INVOKE DUPLICITY

Starting at 2nd level, you can use your Channel Divinity to create an illusory duplicate of yourself.

As an action, you create a perfect illusion of yourself that lasts for 1 minute, or until you lose your concentration (as if you were concentrating on a spell). The illusion appears in an unoccupied space that you can see within 30 feet of you. As a bonus action on your turn, you can move the illusion up to 30 feet to a space you can see, but it must remain within 120 feet of you.

For the duration, you can cast spells as though you were in the illusion's space, but you must use your own senses. Additionally, when both you and your illusion are within 5 feet of a creature that can see the illusion, you have advantage on attack rolls against that creature, given how distracting the illusion is to the target.

CHANNEL DIVINITY: CLOAK OF SHADOWS

Starting at 6th level, you can use your Channel Divinity to vanish.

As an action, you become invisible until the end of your next turn. You become visible if you attack or cast a spell.

DIVINE STRIKE

At 8th level, you gain the ability to infuse your weapon strikes with poison—a gift from your deity. Once on each of your turns when you hit a creature with a weapon attack, you can cause the attack to deal an extra 1d8 poison damage to the target. When you reach 14th level, the extra damage increases to 2d8.

IMPROVED DUPLICITY

At 17th level, you can create up to four duplicates of yourself, instead of one, when you use Invoke Duplicity. As a bonus action on your turn, you can move any number of them up to 30 feet, to a maximum range of 120 feet.

WAR DOMAIN

War has many manifestations. It can make heroes of ordinary people. It can be desperate and horrific, with acts of cruelty and cowardice eclipsing instances of excellence and courage. In either case, the gods of war watch over warriors and reward them for their great deeds. The clerics of such gods excel in battle, inspiring others to fight the good fight or offering acts of violence as prayers. Gods of war include champions of honor and chivalry (such as Torm, Heironeous, and Kiri-Jolith) as well as gods of destruction and pillage (such as Erythnul, the Fury, Gruumsh, and Ares) and gods of conquest and domination (such as Bane, Hextor, and Maglubiyet). Other war gods (such as Tempus, Nike, and Nuada) take a more neutral stance, promoting war in all its manifestations and supporting warriors in any circumstance.

WAR DOMAIN SPELLS

Cleric Level	Spells
1st	divine favor, shield of faith
3rd	magic weapon, spiritual weapon
5th	crusader's mantle, spirit guardians
7th	freedom of movement, stoneskin
9th	flame strike, hold monster

BONUS PROFICIENCIES

At 1st level, you gain proficiency with martial weapons and heavy armor.

WAR PRIEST

From 1st level, your god delivers bolts of inspiration to you while you are engaged in battle. When you use the Attack action, you can make one weapon attack as a bonus action.

You can use this feature a number of times equal to your Wisdom modifier (a minimum of once). You regain all expended uses when you finish a long rest.

CHANNEL DIVINITY: GUIDED STRIKE

Starting at 2nd level, you can use your Channel Divinity to strike with supernatural accuracy. When you make an attack roll, you can use your Channel Divinity to gain a +10 bonus to the roll. You make this choice after you see the roll, but before the DM says whether the attack hits or misses.

CHANNEL DIVINITY: WAR GOD'S BLESSING

At 6th level, when a creature within 30 feet of you makes an attack roll, you can use your reaction to grant that creature a +10 bonus to the roll, using your Channel Divinity. You make this choice after you see the roll, but before the DM says whether the attack hits or misses.

DIVINE STRIKE

At 8th level, you gain the ability to infuse your weapon strikes with divine energy. Once on each of your turns when you hit a creature with a weapon attack, you can cause the attack to deal an extra 1d8 damage of the same type dealt by the weapon to the target. When you reach 14th level, the extra damage increases to 2d8.

AVATAR OF BATTLE

At 17th level, you gain resistance to bludgeoning, piercing, and slashing damage from nonmagical weapons.

Druid

Holding high a gnarled staff wreathed with holly, an elf summons the fury of the storm and calls down explosive bolts of lightning to smite the torch-carrying orcs who threaten her forest.

Crouching out of sight on a high tree branch in the form of a leopard, a human peers out of the jungle at the strange construction of a temple of Evil Elemental Air, keeping a close eye on the cultists' activities.

Swinging a blade formed of pure fire, a half-elf charges into a mass of skeletal soldiers, sundering the unnatural magic that gives the foul creatures the mocking semblance of life.

Whether calling on the elemental forces of nature or emulating the creatures of the animal world, druids are an embodiment of nature's resilience, cunning, and fury. They claim no mastery over nature. Instead, they see themselves as extensions of nature's indomitable will.

Power of Nature

Druids revere nature above all, gaining their spells and other magical powers either from the force of nature itself or from a nature deity. Many druids pursue a mystic spirituality of transcendent union with nature rather than devotion to a divine entity, while others serve gods of wild nature, animals, or elemental forces. The ancient druidic traditions are sometimes called the Old Faith, in contrast to the worship of gods in temples and shrines.

Druid spells are oriented toward nature and animals—the power of tooth and claw, of sun and moon, of fire and storm. Druids also gain the ability to take on animal forms, and some druids make a particular study of this practice, even to the point where they prefer animal form to their natural form.

Preserve the Balance

For druids, nature exists in a precarious balance. The four elements that make up a world—air, earth, fire,

THE DRUID

Level	Proficiency Bonus	Features	Cantrips Known	Spell Slots per Spell Level								
				1st	2nd	3rd	4th	5th	6th	7th	8th	9th
1st	+2	Druidic, Spellcasting	2	2	—	—	—	—	—	—	—	—
2nd	+2	Wild Shape, Druid Circle	2	3	—	—	—	—	—	—	—	—
3rd	+2	—	2	4	2	—	—	—	—	—	—	—
4th	+2	Wild Shape improvement, Ability Score Improvement	3	4	3	—	—	—	—	—	—	—
5th	+3	—	3	4	3	2	—	—	—	—	—	—
6th	+3	Druid Circle feature	3	4	3	3	—	—	—	—	—	—
7th	+3	—	3	4	3	3	1	—	—	—	—	—
8th	+3	Wild Shape improvement, Ability Score Improvement	3	4	3	3	2	—	—	—	—	—
9th	+4	—	3	4	3	3	3	1	—	—	—	—
10th	+4	Druid Circle feature	4	4	3	3	3	2	—	—	—	—
11th	+4	—	4	4	3	3	3	2	1	—	—	—
12th	+4	Ability Score Improvement	4	4	3	3	3	2	1	—	—	—
13th	+5	—	4	4	3	3	3	2	1	1	—	—
14th	+5	Druid Circle feature	4	4	3	3	3	2	1	1	—	—
15th	+5	—	4	4	3	3	3	2	1	1	1	—
16th	+5	Ability Score Improvement	4	4	3	3	3	2	1	1	1	—
17th	+6	—	4	4	3	3	3	2	1	1	1	1
18th	+6	Timeless Body, Beast Spells	4	4	3	3	3	3	1	1	1	1
19th	+6	Ability Score Improvement	4	4	3	3	3	3	2	1	1	1
20th	+6	Archdruid	4	4	3	3	3	3	2	2	1	1

and water—must remain in equilibrium. If one element were to gain power over the others, the world could be destroyed, drawn into one of the elemental planes and broken apart into its component elements. Thus, druids oppose cults of Elemental Evil and others who promote one element to the exclusion of others.

Druids are also concerned with the delicate ecological balance that sustains plant and animal life, and the need for civilized folk to live in harmony with nature, not in opposition to it. Druids accept that which is cruel in nature, and they hate that which is unnatural, including aberrations (such as beholders and mind flayers) and undead (such as zombies and vampires). Druids sometimes lead raids against such creatures, especially when the monsters encroach on the druids' territory.

Druids are often found guarding sacred sites or watching over regions of unspoiled nature. But when a significant danger arises, threatening nature's balance or the lands they protect, druids take on a more active role in combating the threat, as adventurers.

CREATING A DRUID

When making a druid, consider why your character has such a close bond with nature. Perhaps your character lives in a society where the Old Faith still thrives, or was raised by a druid after being abandoned in the depths of a forest. Perhaps your character had a dramatic encounter with the spirits of nature, coming face to face with a giant eagle or dire wolf and surviving the experience. Maybe your character was born during an epic storm or a volcanic eruption, which was interpreted as a sign that becoming a druid was part of your character's destiny.

Have you always been an adventurer as part of your druidic calling, or did you first spend time as a caretaker of a sacred grove or spring? Perhaps your homeland was befouled by evil, and you took up an adventuring life in hopes of finding a new home or purpose.

QUICK BUILD

You can make a druid quickly by following these suggestions. First, Wisdom should be your highest ability score, followed by Constitution. Second, choose the hermit background.

CLASS FEATURES

As a druid, you gain the following class features.

HIT POINTS

Hit Dice: 1d8 per druid level
Hit Points at 1st Level: 8 + your Constitution modifier
Hit Points at Higher Levels: 1d8 (or 5) + your Constitution modifier per druid level after 1st

PROFICIENCIES

Armor: Light armor, medium armor, shields (druids will not wear armor or use shields made of metal)
Weapons: Clubs, daggers, darts, javelins, maces, quarterstaffs, scimitars, sickles, slings, spears
Tools: Herbalism kit

Saving Throws: Intelligence, Wisdom

Skills: Choose two from Arcana, Animal Handling, Insight, Medicine, Nature, Perception, Religion, and Survival

EQUIPMENT

You start with the following equipment, in addition to the equipment granted by your background:

- (a) a wooden shield or (b) any simple weapon
- (a) a scimitar or (b) any simple melee weapon
- Leather armor, an explorer's pack, and a druidic focus

DRUIDIC

You know Druidic, the secret language of druids. You can speak the language and use it to leave hidden messages. You and others who know this language automatically spot such a message. Others spot the message's presence with a successful DC 15 Wisdom (Perception) check but can't decipher it without magic.

SPELLCASTING

Drawing on the divine essence of nature itself, you can cast spells to shape that essence to your will. See chapter 10 for the general rules of spellcasting and chapter 11 for the druid spell list.

CANTRIPS

At 1st level, you know two cantrips of your choice from the druid spell list. You learn additional druid cantrips of your choice at higher levels, as shown in the Cantrips Known column of the Druid table.

PREPARING AND CASTING SPELLS

The Druid table shows how many spell slots you have to cast your spells of 1st level and higher. To cast one of these druid spells, you must expend a slot of the spell's level or higher. You regain all expended spell slots when you finish a long rest.

You prepare the list of druid spells that are available for you to cast, choosing from the druid spell list. When you do so, choose a number of druid spells equal to your Wisdom modifier + your druid level (minimum of

---

SACRED PLANTS AND WOOD

A druid holds certain plants to be sacred, particularly alder, ash, birch, elder, hazel, holly, juniper, mistletoe, oak, rowan, willow, and yew. Druids often use such plants as part of a spellcasting focus, incorporating lengths of oak or yew or sprigs of mistletoe.

Similarly, a druid uses such woods to make other objects, such as weapons and shields. Yew is associated with death and rebirth, so weapon handles for scimitars or sickles might be fashioned from it. Ash is associated with life and oak with strength. These woods make excellent hafts or whole weapons, such as clubs or quarterstaffs, as well as shields. Alder is associated with air, and it might be used for thrown weapons, such as darts or javelins.

Druids from regions that lack the plants described here have chosen other plants to take on similar uses. For instance, a druid of a desert region might value the yucca tree and cactus plants.

---

one spell). The spells must be of a level for which you have spell slots.

For example, if you are a 3rd-level druid, you have four 1st-level and two 2nd-level spell slots. With a Wisdom of 16, your list of prepared spells can include six spells of 1st or 2nd level, in any combination. If you prepare the 1st-level spell *cure wounds,* you can cast it using a 1st-level or 2nd-level slot. Casting the spell doesn't remove it from your list of prepared spells.

You can also change your list of prepared spells when you finish a long rest. Preparing a new list of druid spells requires time spent in prayer and meditation: at least 1 minute per spell level for each spell on your list.

SPELLCASTING ABILITY

Wisdom is your spellcasting ability for your druid spells, since your magic draws upon your devotion and attunement to nature. You use your Wisdom whenever a spell refers to your spellcasting ability. In addition, you use your Wisdom modifier when setting the saving throw DC for a druid spell you cast and when making an attack roll with one.

Spell save DC = 8 + your proficiency bonus + your Wisdom modifier

Spell attack modifier = your proficiency bonus + your Wisdom modifier

RITUAL CASTING

You can cast a druid spell as a ritual if that spell has the ritual tag and you have the spell prepared.

SPELLCASTING FOCUS

You can use a druidic focus (see chapter 5, "Equipment") as a spellcasting focus for your druid spells.

WILD SHAPE

Starting at 2nd level, you can use your action to magically assume the shape of a beast that you have seen before. You can use this feature twice. You regain expended uses when you finish a short or long rest.

Your druid level determines the beasts you can transform into, as shown in the Beast Shapes table. At 2nd level, for example, you can transform into any beast that has a challenge rating of 1/4 or lower that doesn't have a flying or swimming speed.

BEAST SHAPES

Level	Max. CR	Limitations	Example
2nd	1/4	No flying or swimming speed	Wolf
4th	1/2	No flying speed	Crocodile
8th	1	—	Giant eagle

You can stay in a beast shape for a number of hours equal to half your druid level (rounded down). You then revert to your normal form unless you expend another use of this feature. You can revert to your normal form earlier by using a bonus action on your turn. You automatically revert if you fall unconscious, drop to 0 hit points, or die.

While you are transformed, the following rules apply:

- Your game statistics are replaced by the statistics of the beast, but you retain your alignment, personality, and Intelligence, Wisdom, and Charisma scores. You also retain all of your skill and saving throw proficiencies, in addition to gaining those of the creature. If the creature has the same proficiency as you and the bonus in its stat block is higher than yours, use the creature's bonus instead of yours. If the creature has any legendary or lair actions, you can't use them.
- When you transform, you assume the beast's hit points and Hit Dice. When you revert to your normal form, you return to the number of hit points you had before you transformed. However, if you revert as a result of dropping to 0 hit points, any excess damage carries over to your normal form. For example, if you take 10 damage in animal form and have only 1 hit point left, you revert and take 9 damage. As long as the excess damage doesn't reduce your normal form to 0 hit points, you aren't knocked unconscious.
- You can't cast spells, and your ability to speak or take any action that requires hands is limited to the capabilities of your beast form. Transforming doesn't break your concentration on a spell you've already cast, however, or prevent you from taking actions that are part of a spell, such as *call lightning*, that you've already cast.
- You retain the benefit of any features from your class, race, or other source and can use them if the new form is physically capable of doing so. However, you can't use any of your special senses, such as darkvision, unless your new form also has that sense.
- You choose whether your equipment falls to the ground in your space, merges into your new form, or is worn by it. Worn equipment functions as normal, but the DM decides whether it is practical for the new form to wear a piece of equipment, based on the creature's shape and size. Your equipment doesn't change size or shape to match the new form, and any equipment that the new form can't wear must either fall to the ground or merge with it. Equipment that merges with the form has no effect until you leave the form.

DRUID CIRCLE

At 2nd level, you choose to identify with a circle of druids: the Circle of the Land or the Circle of the Moon, both detailed at the end of the class description. Your choice grants you features at 2nd level and again at 6th, 10th, and 14th level.

ABILITY SCORE IMPROVEMENT

When you reach 4th level, and again at 8th, 12th, 16th, and 19th level, you can increase one ability score of your choice by 2, or you can increase two ability scores of your choice by 1. As normal, you can't increase an ability score above 20 using this feature.

TIMELESS BODY

Starting at 18th level, the primal magic that you wield causes you to age more slowly. For every 10 years that pass, your body ages only 1 year.

BEAST SPELLS

Beginning at 18th level, you can cast many of your druid spells in any shape you assume using Wild Shape. You can perform the somatic and verbal components of a druid spell while in a beast shape, but you aren't able to provide material components.

ARCHDRUID

At 20th level, you can use your Wild Shape an unlimited number of times.

Additionally, you can ignore the verbal and somatic components of your druid spells, as well as any material components that lack a cost and aren't consumed by a spell. You gain this benefit in both your normal shape and your beast shape from Wild Shape.

DRUID CIRCLES

Though their organization is invisible to most outsiders, druids are part of a society that spans the land, ignoring political borders. All druids are nominally members of this druidic society, though some individuals are so isolated that they have never seen any high-ranking members of the society or participated in druidic gatherings. Druids recognize each other as brothers and sisters. Like creatures of the wilderness, however, druids sometimes compete with or even prey on each other.

At a local scale, druids are organized into circles that share certain perspectives on nature, balance, and the way of the druid.

CIRCLE OF THE LAND

The Circle of the Land is made up of mystics and sages who safeguard ancient knowledge and rites through a vast oral tradition. These druids meet within sacred circles of trees or standing stones to whisper primal secrets in Druidic. The circle's wisest members preside as the chief priests of communities that hold to the Old Faith and serve as advisors to the rulers of those folk. As a member of this circle, your magic is influenced by the land where you were initiated into the circle's mysterious rites.

BONUS CANTRIP

When you choose this circle at 2nd level, you learn one additional druid cantrip of your choice.

NATURAL RECOVERY

Starting at 2nd level, you can regain some of your magical energy by sitting in meditation and communing with nature. During a short rest, you choose expended spell slots to recover. The spell slots can have a combined level that is equal to or less than half your druid level (rounded up), and none of the slots can be 6th level or higher. You can't use this feature again until you finish a long rest

For example, when you are a 4th-level druid, you can recover up to two levels worth of spell slots. You can recover either a 2nd-level slot or two 1st-level slots.

CIRCLE SPELLS

Your mystical connection to the land infuses you with the ability to cast certain spells. At 3rd, 5th, 7th, and 9th level you gain access to circle spells connected to the land where you became a druid. Choose that land—arctic, coast, desert, forest, grassland, mountain, swamp, or Underdark—and consult the associated list of spells.

Once you gain access to a circle spell, you always have it prepared, and it doesn't count against the number of spells you can prepare each day. If you gain access to a spell that doesn't appear on the druid spell list, the spell is nonetheless a druid spell for you.

ARCTIC

Druid Level	Circle Spells
3rd	hold person, spike growth
5th	sleet storm, slow
7th	freedom of movement, ice storm
9th	commune with nature, cone of cold

COAST

Druid Level	Circle Spells
3rd	mirror image, misty step
5th	water breathing, water walk
7th	control water, freedom of movement
9th	conjure elemental, scrying

DESERT

Druid Level	Circle Spells
3rd	blur, silence
5th	create food and water, protection from energy
7th	blight, hallucinatory terrain
9th	insect plague, wall of stone

FOREST

Druid Level	Circle Spells
3rd	barkskin, spider climb
5th	call lightning, plant growth
7th	divination, freedom of movement
9th	commune with nature, tree stride

GRASSLAND

Druid Level	Circle Spells
3rd	invisibility, pass without trace
5th	daylight, haste
7th	divination, freedom of movement
9th	dream, insect plague

MOUNTAIN

Druid Level	Circle Spells
3rd	spider climb, spike growth
5th	lightning bolt, meld into stone
7th	stone shape, stoneskin
9th	passwall, wall of stone

SWAMP

Druid Level	Circle Spells
3rd	darkness, Melf's acid arrow
5th	water walk, stinking cloud
7th	freedom of movement, locate creature
9th	insect plague, scrying

UNDERDARK

Druid Level	Circle Spells
3rd	spider climb, web
5th	gaseous form, stinking cloud
7th	greater invisibility, stone shape
9th	cloudkill, insect plague

Land's Stride

Starting at 6th level, moving through nonmagical difficult terrain costs you no extra movement. You can also pass through nonmagical plants without being slowed by them and without taking damage from them if they have thorns, spines, or a similar hazard.

In addition, you have advantage on saving throws against plants that are magically created or manipulated to impede movement, such those created by the *entangle* spell.

Nature's Ward

When you reach 10th level, you can't be charmed or frightened by elementals or fey, and you are immune to poison and disease.

Nature's Sanctuary

When you reach 14th level, creatures of the natural world sense your connection to nature and become hesitant to attack you. When a beast or plant creature attacks you, that creature must make a Wisdom saving throw against your druid spell save DC. On a failed save, the creature must choose a different target, or the attack automatically misses. On a successful save, the creature is immune to this effect for 24 hours.

The creature is aware of this effect before it makes its attack against you.

Circle of the Moon

Druids of the Circle of the Moon are fierce guardians of the wilds. Their order gathers under the full moon to share news and trade warnings. They haunt the deepest parts of the wilderness, where they might go for weeks on end before crossing paths with another humanoid creature, let alone another druid.

Changeable as the moon, a druid of this circle might prowl as a great cat one night, soar over the treetops as an eagle the next day, and crash through the undergrowth in bear form to drive off a trespassing monster. The wild is in the druid's blood.

Combat Wild Shape

When you choose this circle at 2nd level, you gain the ability to use Wild Shape on your turn as a bonus action, rather than as an action.

Additionally, while you are transformed by Wild Shape, you can use a bonus action to expend one spell slot to regain 1d8 hit points per level of the spell slot expended.

Circle Forms

The rites of your circle grant you the ability to transform into more dangerous animal forms. Starting at 2nd level, you can use your Wild Shape to transform into a beast with a challenge rating as high as 1 (you ignore the Max. CR column of the Beast Shapes table, but must abide by the other limitations there).

Starting at 6th level, you can transform into a beast with a challenge rating as high as your druid level divided by 3, rounded down.

Primal Strike

Starting at 6th level, your attacks in beast form count as magical for the purpose of overcoming resistance and immunity to nonmagical attacks and damage.

Elemental Wild Shape

At 10th level, you can expend two uses of Wild Shape at the same time to transform into an air elemental, an earth elemental, a fire elemental, or a water elemental.

Thousand Forms

By 14th level, you have learned to use magic to alter your physical form in more subtle ways. You can cast the *alter self* spell at will.

DRUIDS AND THE GODS

Some druids venerate the forces of nature themselves, but most druids are devoted to one of the many nature deities worshiped in the multiverse (the lists of gods in appendix B include many such deities). The worship of these deities is often considered a more ancient tradition than the faiths of clerics and urbanized peoples. In fact, in the world of Greyhawk, the druidic faith is called the Old Faith, and it claims many adherents among farmers, foresters, fishers, and others who live closely with nature. This tradition includes the worship of Nature as a primal force beyond personification, but also encompasses the worship of Beory, the Oerth Mother, as well as devotees of Obad-Hai, Ehlonna, and Ulaa.

In the worlds of Greyhawk and the Forgotten Realms, druidic circles are not usually connected to the faith of a single nature deity. Any given circle in the Forgotten Realms, for example, might include druids who revere Silvanus, Mielikki, Eldath, Chauntea, or even the harsh Gods of Fury: Talos, Malar, Auril, and Umberlee. These nature gods are often called the First Circle, the first among the druids, and most druids count them all (even the violent ones) as worthy of veneration.

The druids of Eberron hold animistic beliefs completely unconnected to the Sovereign Host, the Dark Six, or any of the other religions of the world. They believe that every living thing and every natural phenomenon—sun, moon, wind, fire, and the world itself—has a spirit. Their spells, then, are a means to communicate with and command these spirits. Different druidic sects, though, hold different philosophies about the proper relationship of these spirits to each other and to the forces of civilization. The Ashbound, for example, believe that arcane magic is an abomination against nature, the Children of Winter venerate the forces of death, and the Gatekeepers preserve ancient traditions meant to protect the world from the incursion of aberrations.

FIGHTER

A human in clanging plate armor holds her shield before her as she runs toward the massed goblins. An elf behind her, clad in studded leather armor, peppers the goblins with arrows loosed from his exquisite bow. The half-orc nearby shouts orders, helping the two combatants coordinate their assault to the best advantage.

A dwarf in chain mail interposes his shield between the ogre's club and his companion, knocking the deadly blow aside. His companion, a half-elf in scale armor, swings two scimitars in a blinding whirl as she circles the ogre, looking for a blind spot in its defenses.

A gladiator fights for sport in an arena, a master with his trident and net, skilled at toppling foes and moving them around for the crowd's delight—and his own tactical advantage. His opponent's sword flares with blue light an instant before she sends lightning flashing forth to smite him.

All of these heroes are fighters, perhaps the most diverse class of characters in the worlds of Dungeons & Dragons. Questing knights, conquering overlords, royal champions, elite foot soldiers, hardened mercenaries, and bandit kings—as fighters, they all share an unparalleled mastery with weapons and armor, and a thorough knowledge of the skills of combat. And they are well acquainted with death, both meting it out and staring it defiantly in the face.

WELL-ROUNDED SPECIALISTS

Fighters learn the basics of all combat styles. Every fighter can swing an axe, fence with a rapier, wield a longsword or a greatsword, use a bow, and even trap foes in a net with some degree of skill. Likewise, a fighter is adept with shields and every form of armor. Beyond that basic degree of familiarity, each fighter specializes in a certain style of combat. Some concentrate on archery, some on fighting with two weapons at once, and some on augmenting their martial skills with magic. This combination of broad general ability and extensive specialization makes fighters superior combatants on battlefields and in dungeons alike.

TRAINED FOR DANGER

Not every member of the city watch, the village militia, or the queen's army is a fighter. Most of these troops are relatively untrained soldiers with only the most basic combat knowledge. Veteran soldiers, military officers, trained bodyguards, dedicated knights, and similar figures are fighters.

THE FIGHTER

Level	Proficiency Bonus	Features
1st	+2	Fighting Style, Second Wind
2nd	+2	Action Surge (one use)
3rd	+2	Martial Archetype
4th	+2	Ability Score Improvement
5th	+3	Extra Attack
6th	+3	Ability Score Improvement
7th	+3	Martial Archetype feature
8th	+3	Ability Score Improvement
9th	+4	Indomitable (one use)
10th	+4	Martial Archetype feature
11th	+4	Extra Attack (2)
12th	+4	Ability Score Improvement
13th	+5	Indomitable (two uses)
14th	+5	Ability Score Improvement
15th	+5	Martial Archetype feature
16th	+5	Ability Score Improvement
17th	+6	Action Surge (two uses), Indomitable (three uses)
18th	+6	Martial Archetype feature
19th	+6	Ability Score Improvement
20th	+6	Extra Attack (3)

Some fighters feel drawn to use their training as adventurers. The dungeon delving, monster slaying, and other dangerous work common among adventurers is second nature for a fighter, not all that different from the life he or she left behind. There are greater risks, perhaps, but also much greater rewards—few fighters in the city watch have the opportunity to discover a magic *flame tongue* sword, for example.

CREATING A FIGHTER

As you build your fighter, think about two related elements of your character's background: Where did you get your combat training, and what set you apart from the mundane warriors around you? Were you particularly ruthless? Did you get extra help from a mentor, perhaps because of your exceptional dedication? What drove you to this training in the first place? A threat to your homeland, a thirst for.revenge, or a need to prove yourself might all have been factors.

You might have enjoyed formal training in a noble's army or in a local militia. Perhaps you trained in a war academy, learning strategy, tactics, and military history. Or you might be self-taught—unpolished but well tested. Did you take up the sword as a way to escape the limits of life on a farm, or are you following a proud family tradition? Where did you acquire your weapons and armor? They might have been military issue or family heirlooms, or perhaps you scrimped and saved for years

to buy them. Your armaments are now among your most important possessions—the only things that stand between you and death's embrace.

QUICK BUILD

You can make a fighter quickly by following these suggestions. First, make Strength or Dexterity your highest ability score, depending on whether you want to focus on melee weapons or on archery (or finesse weapons). Your next-highest score should be Constitution, or Intelligence if you plan to adopt the Eldritch Knight martial archetype. Second, choose the soldier background.

CLASS FEATURES

As a fighter, you gain the following class features.

HIT POINTS

Hit Dice: 1d10 per fighter level
Hit Points at 1st Level: 10 + your Constitution modifier
Hit Points at Higher Levels: 1d10 (or 6) + your Constitution modifier per fighter level after 1st

PROFICIENCIES

Armor: All armor, shields
Weapons: Simple weapons, martial weapons
Tools: None

Saving Throws: Strength, Constitution

Skills: Choose two skills from Acrobatics, Animal Handling, Athletics, History, Insight, Intimidation, Perception, and Survival

EQUIPMENT

You start with the following equipment, in addition to the equipment granted by your background:

- (*a*) chain mail or (*b*) leather armor, longbow, and 20 arrows
- (*a*) a martial weapon and a shield or (*b*) two martial weapons
- (*a*) a light crossbow and 20 bolts or (*b*) two handaxes
- (*a*) a dungeoneer's pack or (*b*) an explorer's pack

FIGHTING STYLE

You adopt a particular style of fighting as your specialty. Choose one of the following options. You can't take a Fighting Style option more than once, even if you later get to choose again.

ARCHERY

You gain a +2 bonus to attack rolls you make with ranged weapons.

DEFENSE

While you are wearing armor, you gain a +1 bonus to AC.

DUELING

When you are wielding a melee weapon in one hand and no other weapons, you gain a +2 bonus to damage rolls with that weapon.

GREAT WEAPON FIGHTING

When you roll a 1 or 2 on a damage die for an attack you make with a melee weapon that you are wielding with two hands, you can reroll the die and must use the new roll, even if the new roll is a 1 or a 2. The weapon must have the two-handed or versatile property for you to gain this benefit.

PROTECTION

When a creature you can see attacks a target other than you that is within 5 feet of you, you can use your reaction to impose disadvantage on the attack roll. You must be wielding a shield.

TWO-WEAPON FIGHTING

When you engage in two-weapon fighting, you can add your ability modifier to the damage of the second attack.

SECOND WIND

You have a limited well of stamina that you can draw on to protect yourself from harm. On your turn, you can use a bonus action to regain hit points equal to 1d10 + your fighter level. Once you use this feature, you must finish a short or long rest before you can use it again.

ACTION SURGE

Starting at 2nd level, you can push yourself beyond your normal limits for a moment. On your turn, you can take one additional action on top of your regular action and a possible bonus action.

Once you use this feature, you must finish a short or long rest before you can use it again. Starting at 17th level, you can use it twice before a rest, but only once on the same turn.

MARTIAL ARCHETYPE

At 3rd level, you choose an archetype that you strive to emulate in your combat styles and techniques. Choose Champion, Battle Master, or Eldritch Knight, all detailed at the end of the class description. The archetype you choose grants you features at 3rd level and again at 7th, 10th, 15th, and 18th level.

ABILITY SCORE IMPROVEMENT

When you reach 4th level, and again at 6th, 8th, 12th, 14th, 16th, and 19th level, you can increase one ability score of your choice by 2, or you can increase two ability scores of your choice by 1. As normal, you can't increase an ability score above 20 using this feature.

EXTRA ATTACK

Beginning at 5th level, you can attack twice, instead of once, whenever you take the Attack action on your turn.

The number of attacks increases to three when you reach 11th level in this class and to four when you reach 20th level in this class.

INDOMITABLE

Beginning at 9th level, you can reroll a saving throw that you fail. If you do so, you must use the new roll, and you can't use this feature again until you finish a long rest.

You can use this feature twice between long rests starting at 13th level and three times between long rests starting at 17th level.

MARTIAL ARCHETYPES

Different fighters choose different approaches to perfecting their fighting prowess. The martial archetype you choose to emulate reflects your approach.

CHAMPION

The archetypal Champion focuses on the development of raw physical power honed to deadly perfection. Those who model themselves on this archetype combine rigorous training with physical excellence to deal devastating blows.

IMPROVED CRITICAL

Beginning when you choose this archetype at 3rd level, your weapon attacks score a critical hit on a roll of 19 or 20.

REMARKABLE ATHLETE

Starting at 7th level, you can add half your proficiency bonus (round up) to any Strength, Dexterity, or Constitution check you make that doesn't already use your proficiency bonus.

In addition, when you make a running long jump, the distance you can cover increases by a number of feet equal to your Strength modifier.

ADDITIONAL FIGHTING STYLE

At 10th level, you can choose a second option from the Fighting Style class feature.

SUPERIOR CRITICAL

Starting at 15th level, your weapon attacks score a critical hit on a roll of 18–20.

SURVIVOR

At 18th level, you attain the pinnacle of resilience in battle. At the start of each of your turns, you regain hit points equal to 5 + your Constitution modifier if you have no more than half of your hit points left. You don't gain this benefit if you have 0 hit points.

BATTLE MASTER

Those who emulate the archetypal Battle Master employ martial techniques passed down through generations. To a Battle Master, combat is an academic field, sometimes including subjects beyond battle such as weaponsmithing and calligraphy. Not every fighter absorbs the lessons of history, theory, and artistry that are reflected in the Battle Master archetype, but those who do are well-rounded fighters of great skill and knowledge.

COMBAT SUPERIORITY

When you choose this archetype at 3rd level, you learn maneuvers that are fueled by special dice called superiority dice.

Maneuvers. You learn three maneuvers of your choice, which are detailed under "Maneuvers" below. Many maneuvers enhance an attack in some way. You can use only one maneuver per attack.

You learn two additional maneuvers of your choice at 7th, 10th, and 15th level. Each time you learn new maneuvers, you can also replace one maneuver you know with a different one.

Superiority Dice. You have four superiority dice, which are d8s. A superiority die is expended when you use it. You regain all of your expended superiority dice when you finish a short or long rest.

You gain another superiority die at 7th level and one more at 15th level.

Saving Throws. Some of your maneuvers require your target to make a saving throw to resist the maneuver's effects. The saving throw DC is calculated as follows:

> **Maneuver save DC** = 8 + your proficiency bonus + your Strength or Dexterity modifier (your choice)

STUDENT OF WAR

At 3rd level, you gain proficiency with one type of artisan's tools of your choice.

KNOW YOUR ENEMY

Starting at 7th level, if you spend at least 1 minute observing or interacting with another creature outside combat, you can learn certain information about its capabilities compared to your own. The DM tells you if the creature is your equal, superior, or inferior in regard to two of the following characteristics of your choice:

- Strength score
- Dexterity score
- Constitution score
- Armor Class
- Current hit points
- Total class levels (if any)
- Fighter class levels (if any)

Improved Combat Superiority

At 10th level, your superiority dice turn into d10s. At 18th level, they turn into d12s.

Relentless

Starting at 15th level, when you roll initiative and have no superiority dice remaining, you regain 1 superiority die.

Maneuvers

The maneuvers are presented in alphabetical order.

Commander's Strike. When you take the Attack action on your turn, you can forgo one of your attacks and use a bonus action to direct one of your companions to strike. When you do so, choose a friendly creature who can see or hear you and expend one superiority die. That creature can immediately use its reaction to make one weapon attack, adding the superiority die to the attack's damage roll.

Disarming Attack. When you hit a creature with a weapon attack, you can expend one superiority die to attempt to disarm the target, forcing it to drop one item of your choice that it's holding. You add the superiority die to the attack's damage roll, and the target must make a Strength saving throw. On a failed save, it drops the object you choose. The object lands at its feet.

Distracting Strike. When you hit a creature with a weapon attack, you can expend one superiority die to distract the creature, giving your allies an opening. You add the superiority die to the attack's damage roll. The next attack roll against the target by an attacker other than you has advantage if the attack is made before the start of your next turn.

Evasive Footwork. When you move, you can expend one superiority die, rolling the die and adding the number rolled to your AC until you stop moving.

Feinting Attack. You can expend one superiority die and use a bonus action on your turn to feint, choosing one creature within 5 feet of you as your target. You have advantage on your next attack roll against that creature this turn. If that attack hits, add the superiority die to the attack's damage roll.

Goading Attack. When you hit a creature with a weapon attack, you can expend one superiority die to attempt to goad the target into attacking you. You add the superiority die to the attack's damage roll, and the target must make a Wisdom saving throw. On a failed save, the target has disadvantage on all attack rolls against targets other than you until the end of your next turn.

Lunging Attack. When you make a melee weapon attack on your turn, you can expend one superiority die to increase your reach for that attack by 5 feet. If you hit, you add the superiority die to the attack's damage roll.

Maneuvering Attack. When you hit a creature with a weapon attack, you can expend one superiority die to maneuver one of your comrades into a more advantageous position. You add the superiority die to the attack's damage roll, and you choose a friendly creature who can see or hear you. That creature can use its reaction to move up to half its speed without provoking opportunity attacks from the target of your attack.

Menacing Attack. When you hit a creature with a weapon attack, you can expend one superiority die to attempt to frighten the target. You add the superiority die to the attack's damage roll, and the target must make a Wisdom saving throw. On a failed save, it is frightened of you until the end of your next turn.

Parry. When another creature damages you with a melee attack, you can use your reaction and expend one superiority die to reduce the damage by the number you roll on your superiority die + your Dexterity modifier.

Precision Attack. When you make a weapon attack roll against a creature, you can expend one superiority die to add it to the roll. You can use this maneuver before or after making the attack roll, but before any effects of the attack are applied.

Pushing Attack. When you hit a creature with a weapon attack, you can expend one superiority die to attempt to drive the target back. You add the superiority die to the attack's damage roll, and if the target is Large or smaller, it must make a Strength saving throw. On a failed save, you push the target up to 15 feet away from you.

Rally. On your turn, you can use a bonus action and expend one superiority die to bolster the resolve of one of your companions. When you do so, choose a friendly creature who can see or hear you. That creature gains temporary hit points equal to the superiority die roll + your Charisma modifier.

Riposte. When a creature misses you with a melee attack, you can use your reaction and expend one superiority die to make a melee weapon attack against the creature. If you hit, you add the superiority die to the attack's damage roll.

Sweeping Attack. When you hit a creature with a melee weapon attack, you can expend one superiority die to attempt to damage another creature with the same attack. Choose another creature within 5 feet of the original target and within your reach. If the original attack roll would hit the second creature, it takes damage equal to the number you roll on your superiority die. The damage is of the same type dealt by the original attack.

Trip Attack. When you hit a creature with a weapon attack, you can expend one superiority die to attempt to knock the target down. You add the superiority die to the attack's damage roll, and if the target is Large or smaller, it must make a Strength saving throw. On a failed save, you knock the target prone.

Eldritch Knight

The archetypal Eldritch Knight combines the martial mastery common to all fighters with a careful study of magic. Eldritch Knights use magical techniques similar to those practiced by wizards. They focus their study on two of the eight schools of magic: abjuration and evocation. Abjuration spells grant an Eldritch Knight additional protection in battle, and evocation spells deal damage to many foes at once, extending the fighter's reach in combat. These knights learn a comparatively small number of spells, committing them to memory instead of keeping them in a spellbook.

SPELLCASTING

When you reach 3rd level, you augment your martial prowess with the ability to cast spells. See chapter 10 for the general rules of spellcasting and chapter 11 for the wizard spell list.

Cantrips. You learn two cantrips of your choice from the wizard spell list. You learn an additional wizard cantrip of your choice at 10th level.

Spell Slots. The Eldritch Knight Spellcasting table shows how many spell slots you have to cast your spells of 1st level and higher. To cast one of these spells, you must expend a slot of the spell's level or higher. You regain all expended spell slots when you finish a long rest.

For example, if you know the 1st-level spell *shield* and have a 1st-level and a 2nd-level spell slot available, you can cast *shield* using either slot.

Spells Known of 1st-Level and Higher. You know three 1st-level wizard spells of your choice, two of which you must choose from the abjuration and evocation spells on the wizard spell list.

The Spells Known column of the Eldritch Knight Spellcasting table shows when you learn more wizard spells of 1st level or higher. Each of these spells must be an abjuration or evocation spell of your choice, and must be of a level for which you have spell slots. For instance, when you reach 7th level in this class, you can learn one new spell of 1st or 2nd level.

The spells you learn at 8th, 14th, and 20th level can come from any school of magic.

Whenever you gain a level in this class, you can replace one of the wizard spells you know with another spell of your choice from the wizard spell list. The new spell must be of a level for which you have spell slots, and it must be an abjuration or evocation spell, unless you're replacing the spell you gained at 8th, 14th, or 20th level.

Spellcasting Ability. Intelligence is your spellcasting ability for your wizard spells, since you learn your spells through study and memorization. You use your Intelligence whenever a spell refers to your spellcasting ability. In addition, you use your Intelligence modifier when setting the saving throw DC for a wizard spell you cast and when making an attack roll with one.

> **Spell save DC** = 8 + your proficiency bonus + your Intelligence modifier
>
> **Spell attack modifier** = your proficiency bonus + your Intelligence modifier

WEAPON BOND

At 3rd level, you learn a ritual that creates a magical bond between yourself and one weapon. You perform the ritual over the course of 1 hour, which can be done

ELDRITCH KNIGHT SPELLCASTING

Fighter Level	Cantrips Known	Spells Known	—Spell Slots per Spell Level—			
			1st	2nd	3rd	4th
3rd	2	3	2	—	—	—
4th	2	4	3	—	—	—
5th	2	4	3	—	—	—
6th	2	4	3	—	—	—
7th	2	5	4	2	—	—
8th	2	6	4	2	—	—
9th	2	6	4	2	—	—
10th	3	7	4	3	—	—
11th	3	8	4	3	—	—
12th	3	8	4	3	—	—
13th	3	9	4	3	2	—
14th	3	10	4	3	2	—
15th	3	10	4	3	2	—
16th	3	11	4	3	3	—
17th	3	11	4	3	3	—
18th	3	11	4	3	3	—
19th	3	12	4	3	3	1
20th	3	13	4	3	3	1

during a short rest. The weapon must be within your reach throughout the ritual, at the conclusion of which you touch the weapon and forge the bond.

Once you have bonded a weapon to yourself, you can't be disarmed of that weapon unless you are incapacitated. If it is on the same plane of existence, you can summon that weapon as a bonus action on your turn, causing it to teleport instantly to your hand.

You can have up to two bonded weapons, but can summon only one at a time with your bonus action. If you attempt to bond with a third weapon, you must break the bond with one of the other two.

WAR MAGIC

Beginning at 7th level, when you use your action to cast a cantrip, you can make one weapon attack as a bonus action.

ELDRITCH STRIKE

At 10th level, you learn how to make your weapon strikes undercut a creature's resistance to your spells. When you hit a creature with a weapon attack, that creature has disadvantage on the next saving throw it makes against a spell you cast before the end of your next turn.

ARCANE CHARGE

At 15th level, you gain the ability to teleport up to 30 feet to an unoccupied space you can see when you use your Action Surge. You can teleport before or after the additional action.

IMPROVED WAR MAGIC

Starting at 18th level, when you use your action to cast a spell, you can make one weapon attack as a bonus action.

Monk

Her fists a blur as they deflect an incoming hail of arrows, a half-elf springs over a barricade and throws herself into the massed ranks of hobgoblins on the other side. She whirls among them, knocking their blows aside and sending them reeling, until at last she stands alone.

Taking a deep breath, a human covered in tattoos settles into a battle stance. As the first charging orcs reach him, he exhales and a blast of fire roars from his mouth, engulfing his foes.

Moving with the silence of the night, a black-clad halfling steps into a shadow beneath an arch and emerges from another inky shadow on a balcony a stone's throw away. She slides her blade free of its cloth-wrapped scabbard and peers through the open window at the tyrant prince, so vulnerable in the grip of sleep.

Whatever their discipline, monks are united in their ability to magically harness the energy that flows in their bodies. Whether channeled as a striking display of combat prowess or a subtler focus of defensive ability and speed, this energy infuses all that a monk does.

The Magic of Ki

Monks make careful study of a magical energy that most monastic traditions call ki. This energy is an element of the magic that suffuses the multiverse—specifically, the element that flows through living bodies. Monks harness this power within themselves to create magical effects and exceed their bodies' physical capabilities, and some of their special attacks can hinder the flow of ki in their opponents. Using this energy, monks channel uncanny speed and strength into their unarmed strikes. As they gain experience, their martial training and their mastery of ki gives them more power over their bodies and the bodies of their foes.

Training and Asceticism

Small walled cloisters dot the landscapes of the worlds of D&D, tiny refuges from the flow of ordinary life, where time seems to stand still. The monks who live there seek personal perfection through contemplation and rigorous training. Many entered the monastery as children, sent to live there when their parents died, when food couldn't be found to support them, or in return for some kindness that the monks had performed for their families.

Some monks live entirely apart from the surrounding population, secluded from anything that might impede their spiritual progress. Others are sworn to isolation,

The Monk

Level	Proficiency Bonus	Martial Arts	Ki Points	Unarmored Movement	Features
1st	+2	1d4	—	—	Unarmored Defense, Martial Arts
2nd	+2	1d4	2	+10 ft.	Ki, Unarmored Movement
3rd	+2	1d4	3	+10 ft.	Monastic Tradition, Deflect Missiles
4th	+2	1d4	4	+10 ft.	Ability Score Improvement, Slow Fall
5th	+3	1d6	5	+10 ft.	Extra Attack, Stunning Strike
6th	+3	1d6	6	+15 ft.	Ki-Empowered Strikes, Monastic Tradition feature
7th	+3	1d6	7	+15 ft.	Evasion, Stillness of Mind
8th	+3	1d6	8	+15 ft.	Ability Score Improvement
9th	+4	1d6	9	+15 ft.	Unarmored Movement improvement
10th	+4	1d6	10	+20 ft.	Purity of Body
11th	+4	1d8	11	+20 ft.	Monastic Tradition feature
12th	+4	1d8	12	+20 ft.	Ability Score Improvement
13th	+5	1d8	13	+20 ft.	Tongue of the Sun and Moon
14th	+5	1d8	14	+25 ft.	Diamond Soul
15th	+5	1d8	15	+25 ft.	Timeless Body
16th	+5	1d8	16	+25 ft.	Ability Score Improvement
17th	+6	1d10	17	+25 ft.	Monastic Tradition feature
18th	+6	1d10	18	+30 ft.	Empty Body
19th	+6	1d10	19	+30 ft.	Ability Score Improvement
20th	+6	1d10	20	+30 ft.	Perfect Self

emerging only to serve as spies or assassins at the command of their leader, a noble patron, or some other mortal or divine power.

The majority of monks don't shun their neighbors, making frequent visits to nearby towns or villages and exchanging their service for food and other goods. As versatile warriors, monks often end up protecting their neighbors from monsters or tyrants.

For a monk, becoming an adventurer means leaving a structured, communal lifestyle to become a wanderer. This can be a harsh transition, and monks don't undertake it lightly. Those who leave their cloisters take their work seriously, approaching their adventures as personal tests of their physical and spiritual growth. As a rule, monks care little for material wealth and are driven by a desire to accomplish a greater mission than merely slaying monsters and plundering their treasure.

CREATING A MONK

As you make your monk character, think about your connection to the monastery where you learned your skills and spent your formative years. Were you an orphan or a child left on the monastery's threshold? Did your parents promise you to the monastery in gratitude for a service performed by the monks? Did you enter this secluded life to hide from a crime you committed? Or did you choose the monastic life for yourself?

Consider why you left. Did the head of your monastery choose you for a particularly important mission beyond the cloister? Perhaps you were cast out because of some violation of the community's rules. Did you dread leaving, or were you happy to go? Is there something you hope to accomplish outside the monastery? Are you eager to return to your home?

As a result of the structured life of a monastic community and the discipline required to harness ki, monks are almost always lawful in alignment.

QUICK BUILD

You can make a monk quickly by following these suggestions. First, make Dexterity your highest ability score, followed by Wisdom. Second, choose the hermit background.

CLASS FEATURES

As a monk, you gain the following class features.

HIT POINTS

Hit Dice: 1d8 per monk level
Hit Points at 1st Level: 8 + your Constitution modifier
Hit Points at Higher Levels: 1d8 (or 5) + your Constitution modifier per monk level after 1st

PROFICIENCIES

Armor: None
Weapons: Simple weapons, shortswords
Tools: Choose one type of artisan's tools or one musical instrument

Saving Throws: Strength, Dexterity
Skills: Choose two from Acrobatics, Athletics, History, Insight, Religion, and Stealth

EQUIPMENT

You start with the following equipment, in addition to the equipment granted by your background:

- (a) a shortsword or (b) any simple weapon
- (a) a dungeoneer's pack or (b) an explorer's pack
- 10 darts

UNARMORED DEFENSE

Beginning at 1st level, while you are wearing no armor and not wielding a shield, your AC equals 10 + your Dexterity modifier + your Wisdom modifier.

MARTIAL ARTS

At 1st level, your practice of martial arts gives you mastery of combat styles that use unarmed strikes and monk weapons, which are shortswords and any simple melee weapons that don't have the two-handed or heavy property.

You gain the following benefits while you are unarmed or wielding only monk weapons and you aren't wearing armor or wielding a shield:

- You can use Dexterity instead of Strength for the attack and damage rolls of your unarmed strikes and monk weapons.
- You can roll a d4 in place of the normal damage of your unarmed strike or monk weapon. This die changes as you gain monk levels, as shown in the Martial Arts column of the Monk table.
- When you use the Attack action with an unarmed strike or a monk weapon on your turn, you can make one unarmed strike as a bonus action. For example, if you take the Attack action and attack with a quarter-staff, you can also make an unarmed strike as a bonus action, assuming you haven't already taken a bonus action this turn.

Certain monasteries use specialized forms of the monk weapons. For example, you might use a club that is two lengths of wood connected by a short chain (called a nunchaku) or a sickle with a shorter, straighter blade (called a kama). Whatever name you use for a monk weapon, you can use the game statistics provided for the weapon in chapter 5, "Equipment."

KI

Starting at 2nd level, your training allows you to harness the mystic energy of ki. Your access to this energy is represented by a number of ki points. Your monk level determines the number of points you have, as shown in the Ki Points column of the Monk table.

You can spend these points to fuel various ki features. You start knowing three such features: Flurry of Blows, Patient Defense, and Step of the Wind. You learn more ki features as you gain levels in this class.

When you spend a ki point, it is unavailable until you finish a short or long rest, at the end of which you draw all of your expended ki back into yourself. You must spend at least 30 minutes of the rest meditating to regain your ki points.

Some of your ki features require your target to make a saving throw to resist the feature's effects. The saving throw DC is calculated as follows:

Ki save DC = 8 + your proficiency bonus + your Wisdom modifier

FLURRY OF BLOWS

Immediately after you take the Attack action on your turn, you can spend 1 ki point to make two unarmed strikes as a bonus action.

PATIENT DEFENSE

You can spend 1 ki point to take the Dodge action as a bonus action on your turn.

STEP OF THE WIND

You can spend 1 ki point to take the Disengage or Dash action as a bonus action on your turn, and your jump distance is doubled for the turn.

UNARMORED MOVEMENT

Starting at 2nd level, your speed increases by 10 feet while you are not wearing armor or wielding a shield. This bonus increases when you reach certain monk levels, as shown in the Monk table.

At 9th level, you gain the ability to move along vertical surfaces and across liquids on your turn without falling during the move.

MONASTIC TRADITION

When you reach 3rd level, you commit yourself to a monastic tradition: the Way of the Open Hand, the Way of Shadow, or the Way of the Four Elements, all detailed at the end of the class description. Your tradition grants you features at 3rd level and again at 6th, 11th, and 17th level.

DEFLECT MISSILES

Starting at 3rd level, you can use your reaction to deflect or catch the missile when you are hit by a ranged weapon attack. When you do so, the damage you take from the attack is reduced by 1d10 + your Dexterity modifier + your monk level.

If you reduce the damage to 0, you can catch the missile if it is small enough for you to hold in one hand and you have at least one hand free. If you catch a missile in this way, you can spend 1 ki point to make a ranged attack with the weapon or piece of ammunition you just caught, as part of the same reaction. You make this attack with proficiency, regardless of your weapon proficiencies, and the missile counts as a monk weapon for the attack, which has a normal range of 20 feet and a long range of 60 feet.

ABILITY SCORE IMPROVEMENT

When you reach 4th level, and again at 8th, 12th, 16th, and 19th level, you can increase one ability score of your choice by 2, or you can increase two ability scores of your choice by 1. As normal, you can't increase an ability score above 20 using this feature.

SLOW FALL

Beginning at 4th level, you can use your reaction when you fall to reduce any falling damage you take by an amount equal to five times your monk level.

Extra Attack

Beginning at 5th level, you can attack twice, instead of once, whenever you take the Attack action on your turn.

Stunning Strike

Starting at 5th level, you can interfere with the flow of ki in an opponent's body. When you hit another creature with a melee weapon attack, you can spend 1 ki point to attempt a stunning strike. The target must succeed on a Constitution saving throw or be stunned until the end of your next turn.

Ki-Empowered Strikes

Starting at 6th level, your unarmed strikes count as magical for the purpose of overcoming resistance and immunity to nonmagical attacks and damage.

Evasion

At 7th level, your instinctive agility lets you dodge out of the way of certain area effects, such as a blue dragon's lightning breath or a *fireball* spell. When you are subjected to an effect that allows you to make a Dexterity saving throw to take only half damage, you instead take no damage if you succeed on the saving throw, and only half damage if you fail.

Stillness of Mind

Starting at 7th level, you can use your action to end one effect on yourself that is causing you to be charmed or frightened.

Purity of Body

At 10th level, your mastery of the ki flowing through you makes you immune to disease and poison.

Tongue of the Sun and Moon

Starting at 13th level, you learn to touch the ki of other minds so that you understand all spoken languages. Moreover, any creature that can understand a language can understand what you say.

Diamond Soul

Beginning at 14th level, your mastery of ki grants you proficiency in all saving throws.

Additionally, whenever you make a saving throw and fail, you can spend 1 ki point to reroll it and take the second result.

Timeless Body

At 15th level, your ki sustains you so that you suffer none of the frailty of old age, and you can't be aged magically. You can still die of old age, however. In addition, you no longer need food or water.

Empty Body

Beginning at 18th level, you can use your action to spend 4 ki points to become invisible for 1 minute.

During that time, you also have resistance to all damage but force damage.

Additionally, you can spend 8 ki points to cast the *astral projection* spell, without needing material components. When you do so, you can't take any other creatures with you.

Perfect Self

At 20th level, when you roll for initiative and have no ki points remaining, you regain 4 ki points.

Monastic Traditions

Three traditions of monastic pursuit are common in the monasteries scattered across the multiverse. Most monasteries practice one tradition exclusively, but a few honor the three traditions and instruct each monk according to his or her aptitude and interest. All three traditions rely on the same basic techniques, diverging as the student grows more adept. Thus, a monk need choose a tradition only upon reaching 3rd level.

Way of the Open Hand

Monks of the Way of the Open Hand are the ultimate masters of martial arts combat, whether armed or unarmed. They learn techniques to push and trip their opponents, manipulate ki to heal damage to their bodies, and practice advanced meditation that can protect them from harm.

Open Hand Technique

Starting when you choose this tradition at 3rd level, you can manipulate your enemy's ki when you harness your own. Whenever you hit a creature with one of the attacks granted by your Flurry of Blows, you can impose one of the following effects on that target:

- It must succeed on a Dexterity saving throw or be knocked prone.
- It must make a Strength saving throw. If it fails, you can push it up to 15 feet away from you.
- It can't take reactions until the end of your next turn.

Wholeness of Body

At 6th level, you gain the ability to heal yourself. As an action, you can regain hit points equal to three times

your monk level. You must finish a long rest before you can use this feature again.

TRANQUILITY

Beginning at 11th level, you can enter a special meditation that surrounds you with an aura of peace. At the end of a long rest, you gain the effect of a *sanctuary* spell that lasts until the start of your next long rest (the spell can end early as normal). The saving throw DC for the spell equals 8 + your Wisdom modifier + your proficiency bonus.

QUIVERING PALM

At 17th level, you gain the ability to set up lethal vibrations in someone's body. When you hit a creature with an unarmed strike, you can spend 3 ki points to start these imperceptible vibrations, which last for a number of days equal to your monk level. The vibrations are harmless unless you use your action to end them. To do so, you and the target must be on the same plane of existence. When you use this action, the creature must make a Constitution saving throw. If it fails, it is reduced to 0 hit points. If it succeeds, it takes 10d10 necrotic damage.

You can have only one creature under the effect of this feature at a time. You can choose to end the vibrations harmlessly without using an action.

WAY OF SHADOW

Monks of the Way of Shadow follow a tradition that values stealth and subterfuge. These monks might be called ninjas or shadowdancers, and they serve as spies and assassins. Sometimes the members of a ninja monastery are family members, forming a clan sworn to secrecy about their arts and missions. Other monasteries are more like thieves' guilds, hiring out their services to nobles, rich merchants, or anyone else who can pay their fees. Regardless of their methods, the heads of these monasteries expect the unquestioning obedience of their students.

SHADOW ARTS

Starting when you choose this tradition at 3rd level, you can use your ki to duplicate the effects of certain spells. As an action, you can spend 2 ki points to cast *darkness*, *darkvision*, *pass without trace*, or *silence*, without providing material components. Additionally, you gain the *minor illusion* cantrip if you don't already know it.

SHADOW STEP

At 6th level, you gain the ability to step from one shadow into another. When you are in dim light or darkness, as a bonus action you can teleport up to 60 feet to an unoccupied space you can see that is also in dim light or darkness. You then have advantage on the first melee attack you make before the end of the turn.

CLOAK OF SHADOWS

By 11th level, you have learned to become one with the shadows. When you are in an area of dim light or darkness, you can use your action to become invisible. You remain invisible until you make an attack, cast a spell, or are in an area of bright light.

OPPORTUNIST

At 17th level, you can exploit a creature's momentary distraction when it is hit by an attack. Whenever a creature within 5 feet of you is hit by an attack made by a creature other than you, you can use your reaction to make a melee attack against that creature.

WAY OF THE FOUR ELEMENTS

You follow a monastic tradition that teaches you to harness the elements. When you focus your ki, you can align yourself with the forces of creation and bend the four elements to your will, using them as an extension of your body. Some members of this tradition dedicate themselves to a single element, but others weave the elements together.

Many monks of this tradition tattoo their bodies with representations of their ki powers, commonly imagined as coiling dragons, but also as phoenixes, fish, plants, mountains, and cresting waves.

DISCIPLE OF THE ELEMENTS

When you choose this tradition at 3rd level, you learn magical disciplines that harness the power of the four elements. A discipline requires you to spend ki points each time you use it.

You know the Elemental Attunement discipline and one other elemental discipline of your choice, which are detailed in the "Elemental Disciplines" section below. You learn one additional elemental discipline of your choice at 6th, 11th, and 17th level.

Whenever you learn a new elemental discipline, you can also replace one elemental discipline that you already know with a different discipline.

Casting Elemental Spells. Some elemental disciplines allow you to cast spells. See chapter 10 for the general rules of spellcasting. To cast one of these spells, you use its casting time and other rules, but you don't need to provide material components for it.

Once you reach 5th level in this class, you can spend additional ki points to increase the level of an elemental discipline spell that you cast, provided that the spell has an enhanced effect at a higher level, as *burning hands* does. The spell's level increases by 1 for each additional ki point you spend. For example, if you are a 5th-level monk and use Sweeping Cinder Strike to cast *burning hands*, you can spend 3 ki points to cast it as a 2nd-level spell (the discipline's base cost of 2 ki points plus 1).

The maximum number of ki points you can spend to cast a spell in this way (including its base ki point cost and any additional ki points you spend to increase its level) is determined by your monk level, as shown in the Spells and Ki Points table.

SPELLS AND KI POINTS

Monk Levels	Maximum Ki Points for a Spell
5th–8th	3
9th–12th	4
13th–16th	5
17th–20th	6

ELEMENTAL DISCIPLINES

The elemental disciplines are presented in alphabetical order. If a discipline requires a level, you must be that level in this class to learn the discipline.

Breath of Winter (17th Level Required). You can spend 6 ki points to cast *cone of cold*.

Clench of the North Wind (6th Level Required). You can spend 3 ki points to cast *hold person*.

Elemental Attunement. You can use your action to briefly control elemental forces nearby, causing one of the following effects of your choice:

- Create a harmless, instantaneous sensory effect related to air, earth, fire, or water, such as a shower of sparks, a puff of wind, a spray of light mist, or a gentle rumbling of stone.
- Instantaneously light or snuff out a candle, a torch, or a small campfire.
- Chill or warm up to 1 pound of nonliving material for up to 1 hour.
- Cause earth, fire, water, or mist that can fit within a 1-foot cube to shape itself into a crude form you designate for 1 minute.

Eternal Mountain Defense (17th Level Required). You can spend 5 ki points to cast *stoneskin*, targeting yourself.

Fangs of the Fire Snake. When you use the Attack action on your turn, you can spend 1 ki point to cause tendrils of flame to stretch out from your fists and feet. Your reach with your unarmed strikes increases by 10 feet for that action, as well as the rest of the turn. A hit with such an attack deals fire damage instead of bludgeoning damage, and if you spend 1 ki point when the attack hits, it also deals an extra 1d10 fire damage.

Fist of Four Thunders. You can spend 2 ki points to cast *thunderwave*.

Fist of Unbroken Air. You can create a blast of compressed air that strikes like a mighty fist. As an action, you can spend 2 ki points and choose a creature within 30 feet of you. That creature must make a Strength saving throw. On a failed save, the creature takes 3d10 bludgeoning damage, plus an extra 1d10 bludgeoning damage for each additional ki point you spend, and you can push the creature up to 20 feet away from you and knock it prone. On a successful save, the creature takes half as much damage, and you don't push it or knock it prone.

Flames of the Phoenix (11th Level Required). You can spend 4 ki points to cast *fireball*.

Gong of the Summit (6th Level Required). You can spend 3 ki points to cast *shatter*.

Mist Stance (11th Level Required). You can spend 4 ki points to cast *gaseous form*, targeting yourself.

Ride the Wind (11th Level Required). You can spend 4 ki points to cast *fly*, targeting yourself.

River of Hungry Flame (17th Level Required). You can spend 5 ki points to cast *wall of fire*.

Rush of the Gale Spirits. You can spend 2 ki points to cast *gust of wind*.

Shape the Flowing River. As an action, you can spend 1 ki point to choose an area of ice or water no larger than 30 feet on a side within 120 feet of you. You can change water to ice within the area and vice versa, and you can reshape ice in the area in any manner you choose. You can raise or lower the ice's elevation, create or fill in a trench, erect or flatten a wall, or form a pillar. The extent of any such changes can't exceed half the area's largest dimension. For example, if you affect a 30-foot square, you can create a pillar up to 15 feet high, raise or lower the square's elevation by up to 15 feet, dig a trench up to 15 feet deep, and so on. You can't shape the ice to trap or damage a creature in the area.

Sweeping Cinder Strike. You can spend 2 ki points to cast *burning hands*.

Water Whip. You can spend 2 ki points as an action to create a whip of water that shoves and pulls a creature to unbalance it. A creature that you can see that is within 30 feet of you must make a Dexterity saving throw. On a failed save, the creature takes 3d10 bludgeoning damage, plus an extra 1d10 bludgeoning damage for each additional ki point you spend, and you can either knock it prone or pull it up to 25 feet closer to you. On a successful save, the creature takes half as much damage, and you don't pull it or knock it prone.

Wave of Rolling Earth (17th Level Required). You can spend 6 ki points to cast *wall of stone*.

MONASTIC ORDERS

The worlds of D&D contain a multitude of monasteries and monastic traditions. In lands with an Asian cultural flavor, such as Shou Lung far to the east of the Forgotten Realms, these monasteries are associated with philosophical traditions and martial arts practice. The Iron Hand School, the Five Stars School, the Northern Fist School, and the Southern Star School of Shou Lung teach different approaches to the physical, mental, and spiritual disciplines of the monk. Some of these monasteries have spread to the western lands of Faerûn, particularly in places with large Shou immigrant communities, such as Thesk and Westgate.

Other monastic traditions are associated with deities who teach the value of physical excellence and mental discipline. In the Forgotten Realms, the order of the Dark Moon is made up of monks dedicated to Shar (goddess of loss), who maintain secret communities in remote hills, back allies, and subterranean hideaways. Monasteries of Ilmater (god of endurance) are named after flowers, and their orders carry the names of great heroes of the faith; the Disciples of Saint Sollars the Twice-Martyred reside in the Monastery of the Yellow Rose near Damara. The monasteries of Eberron combine the study of martial arts with a life of scholarship. Most are devoted to the deities of the Sovereign Host. In the world of Dragonlance, most monks are devoted to Majere, god of meditation and thought. In Greyhawk, many monasteries are dedicated to Xan Yae, the goddess of twilight and the superiority of mind over matter, or to Zuoken, god of mental and physical mastery.

The evil monks of the Scarlet Brotherhood in the world of Greyhawk derive their fanatic zeal not from devotion to a god but from dedication to the principles of their nation and their race—the belief that the Suel strand of humanity are meant to rule the world.

PALADIN

Clad in plate armor that gleams in the sunlight despite the dust and grime of long travel, a human lays down her sword and shield and places her hands on a mortally wounded man. Divine radiance shines from her hands, the man's wounds knit closed, and his eyes open wide with amazement.

A dwarf crouches behind an outcrop, his black cloak making him nearly invisible in the night, and watches an orc war band celebrating its recent victory. Silently, he stalks into their midst and whispers an oath, and two orcs are dead before they even realize he is there.

Silver hair shining in a shaft of light that seems to illuminate only him, an elf laughs with exultation. His spear flashes like his eyes as he jabs again and again at a twisted giant, until at last his light overcomes its hideous darkness.

Whatever their origin and their mission, paladins are united by their oaths to stand against the forces of evil. Whether sworn before a god's altar and the witness of a priest, in a sacred glade before nature spirits and fey beings, or in a moment of desperation and grief with the dead as the only witness, a paladin's oath is a powerful bond. It is a source of power that turns a devout warrior into a blessed champion.

THE CAUSE OF RIGHTEOUSNESS

A paladin swears to uphold justice and righteousness, to stand with the good things of the world against the encroaching darkness, and to hunt the forces of evil wherever they lurk. Different paladins focus on various aspects of the cause of righteousness, but all are bound by the oaths that grant them power to do their sacred work. Although many paladins are devoted to gods of good, a paladin's power comes as much from a commitment to justice itself as it does from a god.

Paladins train for years to learn the skills of combat, mastering a variety of weapons and armor. Even so, their martial skills are secondary to the magical power they wield: power to heal the sick and injured, to smite the wicked and the undead, and to protect the innocent and those who join them in the fight for justice.

BEYOND THE MUNDANE LIFE

Almost by definition, the life of a paladin is an adventuring life. Unless a lasting injury has taken him or her away from adventuring for a time, every paladin lives on the front lines of the cosmic struggle against

THE PALADIN

Level	Proficiency Bonus	Features	Spell Slots per Spell Level				
			1st	2nd	3rd	4th	5th
1st	+2	Divine Sense, Lay on Hands	—	—	—	—	—
2nd	+2	Fighting Style, Spellcasting, Divine Smite	2	—	—	—	—
3rd	+2	Divine Health, Sacred Oath	3	—	—	—	—
4th	+2	Ability Score Improvement	3	—	—	—	—
5th	+3	Extra Attack	4	2	—	—	—
6th	+3	Aura of Protection	4	2	—	—	—
7th	+3	Sacred Oath feature	4	3	—	—	—
8th	+3	Ability Score Improvement	4	3	—	—	—
9th	+4	—	4	3	2	—	—
10th	+4	Aura of Courage	4	3	2	—	—
11th	+4	Improved Divine Smite	4	3	3	—	—
12th	+4	Ability Score Improvement	4	3	3	—	—
13th	+5	—	4	3	3	1	—
14th	+5	Cleansing Touch	4	3	3	1	—
15th	+5	Sacred Oath feature	4	3	3	2	—
16th	+5	Ability Score Improvement	4	3	3	2	—
17th	+6	—	4	3	3	3	1
18th	+6	Aura improvements	4	3	3	3	1
19th	+6	Ability Score Improvement	4	3	3	3	2
20th	+6	Sacred Oath feature	4	3	3	3	2

evil. Fighters are rare enough among the ranks of the militias and armies of the world, but even fewer people can claim the true calling of a paladin. When they do receive the call, these warriors turn from their former occupations and take up arms to fight evil. Sometimes their oaths lead them into the service of the crown as leaders of elite groups of knights, but even then their loyalty is first to the cause of righteousness, not to crown and country.

Adventuring paladins take their work seriously. A delve into an ancient ruin or dusty crypt can be a quest driven by a higher purpose than the acquisition of treasure. Evil lurks in dungeons and primeval forests, and even the smallest victory against it can tilt the cosmic balance away from oblivion.

CREATING A PALADIN

The most important aspect of a paladin character is the nature of his or her holy quest. Although the class features related to your oath don't appear until you reach 3rd level, plan ahead for that choice by reading the oath descriptions at the end of the class. Are you a devoted servant of good, loyal to the gods of justice and honor, a holy knight in shining armor venturing forth to smite evil? Are you a glorious champion of the light, cherishing everything beautiful that stands against the shadow, a knight whose oath descends from traditions older than many of the gods? Or are you an embittered loner sworn to take vengeance on those who have done great evil, sent as an angel of death by the gods or driven by your need for revenge? Appendix B lists many deities worshiped by paladins throughout the multiverse, such

as Torm, Tyr, Heironeous, Paladine, Kiri-Jolith, Dol Arrah, the Silver Flame, Bahamut, Athena, Re-Horakhty, and Heimdall.

How did you experience your call to serve as a paladin? Did you hear a whisper from an unseen god or angel while you were at prayer? Did another paladin sense the potential within you and decide to train you as a squire? Or did some terrible event—the destruction of your home, perhaps—drive you to your quests? Perhaps you stumbled into a sacred grove or a hidden elven enclave and found yourself called to protect all such refuges of goodness and beauty. Or you might have known from your earliest memories that the paladin's life was your calling, almost as if you had been sent into the world with that purpose stamped on your soul.

As guardians against the forces of wickedness, paladins are rarely of any evil alignment. Most of them walk the paths of charity and justice. Consider how your alignment colors the way you pursue your holy quest and the manner in which you conduct yourself before gods and mortals. Your oath and alignment might be in harmony, or your oath might represent standards of behavior that you have not yet attained.

QUICK BUILD

You can make a paladin quickly by following these suggestions. First, Strength should be your highest ability score, followed by Charisma. Second, choose the noble background.

Class Features

As a paladin, you gain the following class features.

Hit Points

Hit Dice: 1d10 per paladin level
Hit Points at 1st Level: 10 + your Constitution modifier
Hit Points at Higher Levels: 1d10 (or 6) + your Constitution modifier per paladin level after 1st

Proficiencies

Armor: All armor, shields
Weapons: Simple weapons, martial weapons
Tools: None

Saving Throws: Wisdom, Charisma
Skills: Choose two from Athletics, Insight, Intimidation, Medicine, Persuasion, and Religion

Equipment

You start with the following equipment, in addition to the equipment granted by your background:

- (*a*) a martial weapon and a shield or (*b*) two martial weapons
- (*a*) five javelins or (*b*) any simple melee weapon
- (*a*) a priest's pack or (*b*) an explorer's pack
- Chain mail and a holy symbol

Divine Sense

The presence of strong evil registers on your senses like a noxious odor, and powerful good rings like heavenly music in your ears. As an action, you can open your awareness to detect such forces. Until the end of your next turn, you know the location of any celestial, fiend, or undead within 60 feet of you that is not behind total cover. You know the type (celestial, fiend, or undead) of any being whose presence you sense, but not its identity (the vampire Count Strahd von Zarovich, for instance). Within the same radius, you also detect the presence of any place or object that has been consecrated or desecrated, as with the *hallow* spell.

You can use this feature a number of times equal to 1 + your Charisma modifier. When you finish a long rest, you regain all expended uses.

Lay on Hands

Your blessed touch can heal wounds. You have a pool of healing power that replenishes when you take a long rest. With that pool, you can restore a total number of hit points equal to your paladin level × 5.

As an action, you can touch a creature and draw power from the pool to restore a number of hit points to that creature, up to the maximum amount remaining in your pool.

Alternatively, you can expend 5 hit points from your pool of healing to cure the target of one disease or neutralize one poison affecting it. You can cure multiple diseases and neutralize multiple poisons with a single use of Lay on Hands, expending hit points separately for each one.

This feature has no effect on undead and constructs.

Fighting Style

At 2nd level, you adopt a style of fighting as your specialty. Choose one of the following options. You can't take a Fighting Style option more than once, even if you later get to choose again.

Defense

While you are wearing armor, you gain a +1 bonus to AC.

Dueling

When you are wielding a melee weapon in one hand and no other weapons, you gain a +2 bonus to damage rolls with that weapon.

Great Weapon Fighting

When you roll a 1 or 2 on a damage die for an attack you make with a melee weapon that you are wielding with two hands, you can reroll the die and must use the new roll. The weapon must have the two-handed or versatile property for you to gain this benefit.

Protection

When a creature you can see attacks a target other than you that is within 5 feet of you, you can use your reaction to impose disadvantage on the attack roll. You must be wielding a shield.

Spellcasting

By 2nd level, you have learned to draw on divine magic through meditation and prayer to cast spells as a cleric does. See chapter 10 for the general rules of spellcasting and chapter 11 for the paladin spell list.

Preparing and Casting Spells

The Paladin table shows how many spell slots you have to cast your spells. To cast one of your paladin spells of 1st level or higher, you must expend a slot of the spell's level or higher. You regain all expended spell slots when you finish a long rest.

You prepare the list of paladin spells that are available for you to cast, choosing from the paladin spell list. When you do so, choose a number of paladin spells equal to your Charisma modifier + half your paladin level, rounded down (minimum of one spell). The spells must be of a level for which you have spell slots.

For example, if you are a 5th-level paladin, you have four 1st-level and two 2nd-level spell slots. With a Charisma of 14, your list of prepared spells can include four spells of 1st or 2nd level, in any combination. If you prepare the 1st-level spell *cure wounds*, you can cast it using a 1st-level or a 2nd-level slot. Casting the spell doesn't remove it from your list of prepared spells.

You can change your list of prepared spells when you finish a long rest. Preparing a new list of paladin spells requires time spent in prayer and meditation: at least 1 minute per spell level for each spell on your list.

Spellcasting Ability

Charisma is your spellcasting ability for your paladin spells, since their power derives from the strength of your convictions. You use your Charisma whenever a spell refers to your spellcasting ability. In addition, you use your Charisma modifier when setting the saving throw DC for a paladin spell you cast and when making an attack roll with one.

Spell save DC = 8 + your proficiency bonus + your Charisma modifier

Spell attack modifier = your proficiency bonus + your Charisma modifier

SPELLCASTING FOCUS

You can use a holy symbol (see chapter 5, "Equipment") as a spellcasting focus for your paladin spells.

DIVINE SMITE

Starting at 2nd level, when you hit a creature with a melee weapon attack, you can expend one spell slot to deal radiant damage to the target, in addition to the weapon's damage. The extra damage is 2d8 for a 1st-level spell slot, plus 1d8 for each spell level higher than 1st, to a maximum of 5d8. The damage increases by 1d8 if the target is an undead or a fiend.

DIVINE HEALTH

By 3rd level, the divine magic flowing through you makes you immune to disease.

SACRED OATH

When you reach 3rd level, you swear the oath that binds you as a paladin forever. Up to this time you have been in a preparatory stage, committed to the path but not yet sworn to it. Now you choose the Oath of Devotion, the Oath of the Ancients, or the Oath of Vengeance, all detailed at the end of the class description.

Your choice grants you features at 3rd level and again at 7th, 15th, and 20th level. Those features include oath spells and the Channel Divinity feature.

OATH SPELLS

Each oath has a list of associated spells. You gain access to these spells at the levels specified in the oath description. Once you gain access to an oath spell, you always have it prepared. Oath spells don't count against the number of spells you can prepare each day.

If you gain an oath spell that doesn't appear on the paladin spell list, the spell is nonetheless a paladin spell for you.

CHANNEL DIVINITY

Your oath allows you to channel divine energy to fuel magical effects. Each Channel Divinity option provided by your oath explains how to use it.

When you use your Channel Divinity, you choose which option to use. You must then finish a short or long rest to use your Channel Divinity again.

Some Channel Divinity effects require saving throws. When you use such an effect from this class, the DC equals your paladin spell save DC.

ABILITY SCORE IMPROVEMENT

When you reach 4th level, and again at 8th, 12th, 16th, and 19th level, you can increase one ability score of your choice by 2, or you can increase two ability scores of your choice by 1. As normal, you can't increase an ability score above 20 using this feature.

EXTRA ATTACK

Beginning at 5th level, you can attack twice, instead of once, whenever you take the Attack action on your turn.

AURA OF PROTECTION

Starting at 6th level, whenever you or a friendly creature within 10 feet of you must make a saving throw, the creature gains a bonus to the saving throw equal to your Charisma modifier (with a minimum bonus of +1). You must be conscious to grant this bonus.

At 18th level, the range of this aura increases to 30 feet.

AURA OF COURAGE

Starting at 10th level, you and friendly creatures within 10 feet of you can't be frightened while you are conscious.

At 18th level, the range of this aura increases to 30 feet.

IMPROVED DIVINE SMITE

By 11th level, you are so suffused with righteous might that all your melee weapon strikes carry divine power with them. Whenever you hit a creature with a melee weapon, the creature takes an extra 1d8 radiant damage. If you also use your Divine Smite with an attack, you add this damage to the extra damage of your Divine Smite.

CLEANSING TOUCH

Beginning at 14th level, you can use your action to end one spell on yourself or on one willing creature that you touch.

You can use this feature a number of times equal to your Charisma modifier (a minimum of once). You regain expended uses when you finish a long rest.

SACRED OATHS

Becoming a paladin involves taking vows that commit the paladin to the cause of righteousness, an active path of fighting wickedness. The final oath, taken when he or she reaches 3rd level, is the culmination of all the paladin's training. Some characters with this class don't consider themselves true paladins until they have reached 3rd level and made this oath. For others, the actual swearing of the oath is a formality, an official stamp on what has always been true in the paladin's heart.

OATH OF DEVOTION

The Oath of Devotion binds a paladin to the loftiest ideals of justice, virtue, and order. Sometimes called cavaliers, white knights, or holy warriors, these paladins meet the ideal of the knight in shining armor, acting with honor in pursuit of justice and the greater good. They hold themselves to the highest standards of conduct, and some, for better or worse, hold the rest of the world to the same standards. Many who swear this oath are devoted to gods of law and good and use their gods' tenets as the measure of their devotion. They hold angels—the perfect servants of good—as their ideals, and incorporate images of angelic wings into their helmets or coats of arms.

Tenets of Devotion

Though the exact words and strictures of the Oath of Devotion vary, paladins of this oath share these tenets.

Honesty. Don't lie or cheat. Let your word be your promise.

Courage. Never fear to act, though caution is wise.

Compassion. Aid others, protect the weak, and punish those who threaten them. Show mercy to your foes, but temper it with wisdom.

Honor. Treat others with fairness, and let your honorable deeds be an example to them. Do as much good as possible while causing the least amount of harm.

Duty. Be responsible for your actions and their consequences, protect those entrusted to your care, and obey those who have just authority over you.

Oath Spells

You gain oath spells at the paladin levels listed.

Oath of Devotion Spells

Paladin Level	Spells
3rd	protection from evil and good, sanctuary
5th	lesser restoration, zone of truth
9th	beacon of hope, dispel magic
13th	freedom of movement, guardian of faith
17th	commune, flame strike

Channel Divinity

When you take this oath at 3rd level, you gain the following two Channel Divinity options.

Sacred Weapon. As an action, you can imbue one weapon that you are holding with positive energy, using your Channel Divinity. For 1 minute, you add your Charisma modifier to attack rolls made with that weapon (with a minimum bonus of +1). The weapon also emits bright light in a 20-foot radius and dim light 20 feet beyond that. If the weapon is not already magical, it becomes magical for the duration.

You can end this effect on your turn as part of any other action. If you are no longer holding or carrying this weapon, or if you fall unconscious, this effect ends.

Turn the Unholy. As an action, you present your holy symbol and speak a prayer censuring fiends and undead, using your Channel Divinity. Each fiend or undead that can see or hear you within 30 feet of you must make a Wisdom saving throw. If the creature fails its saving throw, it is turned for 1 minute or until it takes damage.

A turned creature must spend its turns trying to move as far away from you as it can, and it can't willingly move to a space within 30 feet of you. It also can't take

reactions. For its action, it can use only the Dash action or try to escape from an effect that prevents it from moving. If there's nowhere to move, the creature can use the Dodge action.

Aura of Devotion

Starting at 7th level, you and friendly creatures within 10 feet of you can't be charmed while you are conscious.

At 18th level, the range of this aura increases to 30 feet.

Purity of Spirit

Beginning at 15th level, you are always under the effects of a *protection from evil and good* spell.

Holy Nimbus

At 20th level, as an action, you can emanate an aura of sunlight. For 1 minute, bright light shines from you in a 30-foot radius, and dim light shines 30 feet beyond that.

Whenever an enemy creature starts its turn in the bright light, the creature takes 10 radiant damage.

In addition, for the duration, you have advantage on saving throws against spells cast by fiends or undead.

Once you use this feature, you can't use it again until you finish a long rest.

Oath of the Ancients

The Oath of the Ancients is as old as the race of elves and the rituals of the druids. Sometimes called fey knights, green knights, or horned knights, paladins who swear this oath cast their lot with the side of the light in the cosmic struggle against darkness because they love the beautiful and life-giving things of the world, not necessarily because they believe in principles of honor, courage, and justice. They adorn their armor and clothing with images of growing things—leaves, antlers, or flowers—to reflect their commitment to preserving life and light in the world.

Tenets of the Ancients

The tenets of the Oath of the Ancients have been preserved for uncounted centuries. This oath emphasizes the principles of good above any concerns of law or chaos. Its four central principles are simple.

Kindle the Light. Through your acts of mercy, kindness, and forgiveness, kindle the light of hope in the world, beating back despair.

Shelter the Light. Where there is good, beauty, love, and laughter in the world, stand against the wickedness that would swallow it. Where life flourishes, stand against the forces that would render it barren.

Preserve Your Own Light. Delight in song and laughter, in beauty and art. If you allow the light to die in your own heart, you can't preserve it in the world.

Be the Light. Be a glorious beacon for all who live in despair. Let the light of your joy and courage shine forth in all your deeds.

Oath Spells

You gain oath spells at the paladin levels listed.

Oath of the Ancients Spells

Paladin Level	Spells
3rd	*ensnaring strike, speak with animals*
5th	*misty step, moonbeam*
9th	*plant growth, protection from energy*
13th	*ice storm, stoneskin*
17th	*commune with nature, tree stride*

Channel Divinity

When you take this oath at 3rd level, you gain the following two Channel Divinity options.

Nature's Wrath. You can use your Channel Divinity to invoke primeval forces to ensnare a foe. As an action, you can cause spectral vines to spring up and reach for a creature within 10 feet of you that you can see. The creature must succeed on a Strength or Dexterity saving throw (its choice) or be restrained. While restrained by the vines, the creature repeats the saving throw at the end of each of its turns. On a success, it frees itself and the vines vanish.

Turn the Faithless. You can use your Channel Divinity to utter ancient words that are painful for fey and fiends to hear. As an action, you present your holy symbol, and each fey or fiend within 30 feet of you that can hear you must make a Wisdom saving throw. On a failed save, the creature is turned for 1 minute or until it takes damage.

A turned creature must spend its turns trying to move as far away from you as it can, and it can't willingly move to a space within 30 feet of you. It also can't take reactions. For its action, it can use only the Dash action or try to escape from an effect that prevents it from moving. If there's nowhere to move, the creature can use the Dodge action.

If the creature's true form is concealed by an illusion, shapeshifting, or other effect, that form is revealed while it is turned.

Aura of Warding

Beginning at 7th level, ancient magic lies so heavily upon you that it forms an eldritch ward. You and friendly creatures within 10 feet of you have resistance to damage from spells.

At 18th level, the range of this aura increases to 30 feet.

Undying Sentinel

Starting at 15th level, when you are reduced to 0 hit points and are not killed outright, you can choose to drop to 1 hit point instead. Once you use this ability, you can't use it again until you finish a long rest.

Additionally, you suffer none of the drawbacks of old age, and you can't be aged magically.

Elder Champion

At 20th level, you can assume the form of an ancient force of nature, taking on an appearance you choose. For example, your skin might turn green or take on a bark-like texture, your hair might become leafy or moss-like, or you might sprout antlers or a lion-like mane.

Using your action, you undergo a transformation. For 1 minute, you gain the following benefits:

- At the start of each of your turns, you regain 10 hit points.
- Whenever you cast a paladin spell that has a casting time of 1 action, you can cast it using a bonus action instead.
- Enemy creatures within 10 feet of you have disadvantage on saving throws against your paladin spells and Channel Divinity options.

Once you use this feature, you can't use it again until you finish a long rest.

Oath of Vengeance

The Oath of Vengeance is a solemn commitment to punish those who have committed a grievous sin. When evil forces slaughter helpless villagers, when an entire people turns against the will of the gods, when a thieves' guild grows too violent and powerful, when a dragon rampages through the countryside—at times like these, paladins arise and swear an Oath of Vengeance to set right that which has gone wrong. To these paladins—sometimes called avengers or dark knights—their own purity is not as important as delivering justice.

Tenets of Vengeance

The tenets of the Oath of Vengeance vary by paladin, but all the tenets revolve around punishing wrongdoers by any means necessary. Paladins who uphold these tenets are willing to sacrifice even their own righteousness to mete out justice upon those who do evil, so the paladins are often neutral or lawful neutral in alignment. The core principles of the tenets are brutally simple.

Fight the Greater Evil. Faced with a choice of fighting my sworn foes or combating a lesser evil, I choose the greater evil.

No Mercy for the Wicked. Ordinary foes might win my mercy, but my sworn enemies do not.

By Any Means Necessary. My qualms can't get in the way of exterminating my foes.

Restitution. If my foes wreak ruin on the world, it is because I failed to stop them. I must help those harmed by their misdeeds.

Oath Spells

You gain oath spells at the paladin levels listed.

Oath of Vengeance Spells

Paladin Level	Spells
3rd	bane, hunter's mark
5th	hold person, misty step
9th	haste, protection from energy
13th	banishment, dimension door
17th	hold monster, scrying

Channel Divinity

When you take this oath at 3rd level, you gain the following two Channel Divinity options.

Abjure Enemy. As an action, you present your holy symbol and speak a prayer of denunciation, using your Channel Divinity. Choose one creature within 60 feet of you that you can see. That creature must make a Wisdom saving throw, unless it is immune to being frightened. Fiends and undead have disadvantage on this saving throw.

On a failed save, the creature is frightened for 1 minute or until it takes any damage. While frightened, the creature's speed is 0, and it can't benefit from any bonus to its speed.

On a successful save, the creature's speed is halved for 1 minute or until the creature takes any damage.

Vow of Enmity. As a bonus action, you can utter a vow of enmity against a creature you can see within 10 feet of you, using your Channel Divinity. You gain advantage on attack rolls against the creature for 1 minute or until it drops to 0 hit points or falls unconscious.

Relentless Avenger

By 7th level, your supernatural focus helps you close off a foe's retreat. When you hit a creature with an opportunity attack, you can move up to half your speed immediately after the attack and as part of the same reaction. This movement doesn't provoke opportunity attacks.

Soul of Vengeance

Starting at 15th level, the authority with which you speak your Vow of Enmity gives you greater power over your foe. When a creature under the effect of your Vow of Enmity makes an attack, you can use your reaction to make a melee weapon attack against that creature if it is within range.

Avenging Angel

At 20th level, you can assume the form of an angelic avenger. Using your action, you undergo a transformation. For 1 hour, you gain the following benefits:

- Wings sprout from your back and grant you a flying speed of 60 feet.
- You emanate an aura of menace in a 30-foot radius. The first time any enemy creature enters the aura or starts its turn there during a battle, the creature must succeed on a Wisdom saving throw or become frightened of you for 1 minute or until it takes any damage. Attack rolls against the frightened creature have advantage.

Once you use this feature, you can't use it again until you finish a long rest.

Ranger

Rough and wild looking, a human stalks alone through the shadows of trees, hunting the orcs he knows are planning a raid on a nearby farm. Clutching a shortsword in each hand, he becomes a whirlwind of steel, cutting down one enemy after another.

After tumbling away from a cone of freezing air, an elf finds her feet and draws back her bow to loose an arrow at the white dragon. Shrugging off the wave of fear that emanates from the dragon like the cold of its breath, she sends one arrow after another to find the gaps between the dragon's thick scales.

Holding his hand high, a half-elf whistles to the hawk that circles high above him, calling the bird back to his side. Whispering instructions in Elvish, he points to the owlbear he's been tracking and sends the hawk to distract the creature while he readies his bow.

Far from the bustle of cities and towns, past the hedges that shelter the most distant farms from the terrors of the wild, amid the dense-packed trees of trackless forests and across wide and empty plains, rangers keep their unending watch.

Deadly Hunters

Warriors of the wilderness, rangers specialize in hunting the monsters that threaten the edges of civilization—humanoid raiders, rampaging beasts and monstrosities, terrible giants, and deadly dragons. They learn to track their quarry as a predator does, moving stealthily through the wilds and hiding themselves in brush and rubble. Rangers focus their combat training on techniques that are particularly useful against their specific favored foes.

Thanks to their familiarity with the wilds, rangers acquire the ability to cast spells that harness nature's power, much as a druid does. Their spells, like their combat abilities, emphasize speed, stealth, and the hunt. A ranger's talents and abilities are honed with deadly focus on the grim task of protecting the borderlands.

Independent Adventurers

Though a ranger might make a living as a hunter, a guide, or a tracker, a ranger's true calling is to defend the outskirts of civilization from the ravages of monsters and humanoid hordes that press in from the wild. In some places, rangers gather in secretive orders or join forces with druidic circles. Many rangers, though, are independent almost to a fault, knowing that, when a dragon or a band of orcs attacks, a ranger might be the first—and possibly the last—line of defense.

This fierce independence makes rangers well suited to adventuring, since they are accustomed to life far from the comforts of a dry bed and a hot bath. Faced with city-bred adventurers who grouse and whine about the hardships of the wild, rangers respond with some

The Ranger

Level	Proficiency Bonus	Features	Spells Known	Spell Slots per Spell Level				
				1st	2nd	3rd	4th	5th
1st	+2	Favored Enemy, Natural Explorer	—	—	—	—	—	—
2nd	+2	Fighting Style, Spellcasting	2	2	—	—	—	—
3rd	+2	Ranger Archetype, Primeval Awareness	3	3	—	—	—	—
4th	+2	Ability Score Improvement	3	3	—	—	—	—
5th	+3	Extra Attack	4	4	2	—	—	—
6th	+3	Favored Enemy and Natural Explorer improvements	4	4	2	—	—	—
7th	+3	Ranger Archetype feature	5	4	3	—	—	—
8th	+3	Ability Score Improvement, Land's Stride	5	4	3	—	—	—
9th	+4	—	6	4	3	2	—	—
10th	+4	Natural Explorer improvement, Hide in Plain Sight	6	4	3	2	—	—
11th	+4	Ranger Archetype feature	7	4	3	3	—	—
12th	+4	Ability Score Improvement	7	4	3	3	—	—
13th	+5	—	8	4	3	3	1	—
14th	+5	Favored Enemy improvement, Vanish	8	4	3	3	1	—
15th	+5	Ranger Archetype feature	9	4	3	3	2	—
16th	+5	Ability Score Improvement	9	4	3	3	2	—
17th	+6	—	10	4	3	3	3	1
18th	+6	Feral Senses	10	4	3	3	3	1
19th	+6	Ability Score Improvement	11	4	3	3	3	2
20th	+6	Foe Slayer	11	4	3	3	3	2

mixture of amusement, frustration, and compassion. But they quickly learn that other adventurers who can carry their own weight in a fight against civilization's foes are worth any extra burden. Coddled city folk might not know how to feed themselves or find fresh water in the wild, but they make up for it in other ways.

CREATING A RANGER

As you create your ranger character, consider the nature of the training that gave you your particular capabilities. Did you train with a single mentor, wandering the wilds together until you mastered the ranger's ways? Did you leave your apprenticeship, or was your mentor slain—perhaps by the same kind of monster that became your favored enemy? Or perhaps you learned your skills as part of a band of rangers affiliated with a druidic circle, trained in mystic paths as well as wilderness lore. You might be self-taught, a recluse who learned combat skills, tracking, and even a magical connection to nature through the necessity of surviving in the wilds.

What's the source of your particular hatred of a certain kind of enemy? Did a monster kill someone you loved or destroy your home village? Or did you see too much of the destruction these monsters cause and commit yourself to reining in their depredations? Is your adventuring career a continuation of your work in protecting the borderlands, or a significant change?

What made you join up with a band of adventurers? Do you find it challenging to teach new allies the ways of the wild, or do you welcome the relief from solitude that they offer?

QUICK BUILD

You can make a ranger quickly by following these suggestions. First, make Dexterity your highest ability score, followed by Wisdom. (Some rangers who focus on two-weapon fighting make Strength higher than Dexterity.) Second, choose the outlander background.

CLASS FEATURES

As a ranger, you gain the following class features.

HIT POINTS

Hit Dice: 1d10 per ranger level
Hit Points at 1st Level: 10 + your Constitution modifier
Hit Points at Higher Levels: 1d10 (or 6) + your Constitution modifier per ranger level after 1st

PROFICIENCIES

Armor: Light armor, medium armor, shields
Weapons: Simple weapons, martial weapons
Tools: None

Saving Throws: Strength, Dexterity
Skills: Choose three from Animal Handling, Athletics, Insight, Investigation, Nature, Perception, Stealth, and Survival

EQUIPMENT

You start with the following equipment, in addition to the equipment granted by your background:

- (*a*) scale mail or (*b*) leather armor
- (*a*) two shortswords or (*b*) two simple melee weapons
- (*a*) a dungeoneer's pack or (*b*) an explorer's pack
- A longbow and a quiver of 20 arrows

FAVORED ENEMY

Beginning at 1st level, you have significant experience studying, tracking, hunting, and even talking to a certain type of enemy.

Choose a type of favored enemy: aberrations, beasts, celestials, constructs, dragons, elementals, fey, fiends, giants, monstrosities, oozes, plants, or undead. Alternatively, you can select two races of humanoid (such as gnolls and orcs) as favored enemies.

You have advantage on Wisdom (Survival) checks to track your favored enemies, as well as on Intelligence checks to recall information about them.

When you gain this feature, you also learn one language of your choice that is spoken by your favored enemies, if they speak one at all.

You choose one additional favored enemy, as well as an associated language, at 6th and 14th level. As you gain levels, your choices should reflect the types of monsters you have encountered on your adventures.

NATURAL EXPLORER

You are particularly familiar with one type of natural environment and are adept at traveling and surviving in such regions. Choose one type of favored terrain: arctic, coast, desert, forest, grassland, mountain, swamp, or the Underdark. When you make an Intelligence or Wisdom check related to your favored terrain, your proficiency bonus is doubled if you are using a skill that you're proficient in.

While traveling for an hour or more in your favored terrain, you gain the following benefits:

- Difficult terrain doesn't slow your group's travel.
- Your group can't become lost except by magical means.
- Even when you are engaged in another activity while traveling (such as foraging, navigating, or tracking), you remain alert to danger.
- If you are traveling alone, you can move stealthily at a normal pace.
- When you forage, you find twice as much food as you normally would.
- While tracking other creatures, you also learn their exact number, their sizes, and how long ago they passed through the area.

You choose additional favored terrain types at 6th and 10th level.

FIGHTING STYLE

At 2nd level, you adopt a particular style of fighting as your specialty. Choose one of the following options. You can't take a Fighting Style option more than once, even if you later get to choose again.

ARCHERY

You gain a +2 bonus to attack rolls you make with ranged weapons.

DEFENSE

While you are wearing armor, you gain a +1 bonus to AC.

DUELING

When you are wielding a melee weapon in one hand and no other weapons, you gain a +2 bonus to damage rolls with that weapon.

TWO-WEAPON FIGHTING

When you engage in two-weapon fighting, you can add your ability modifier to the damage of the second attack.

SPELLCASTING

By the time you reach 2nd level, you have learned to use the magical essence of nature to cast spells, much as a druid does. See chapter 10 for the general rules of spellcasting and chapter 11 for the ranger spell list.

SPELL SLOTS

The Ranger table shows how many spell slots you have to cast your spells of 1st level and higher. To cast one of these spells, you must expend a slot of the spell's level or higher. You regain all expended spell slots when you finish a long rest.

For example, if you know the 1st-level spell *animal friendship* and have a 1st-level and a 2nd-level spell slot available, you can cast *animal friendship* using either slot.

SPELLS KNOWN OF 1ST LEVEL AND HIGHER

You know two 1st-level spells of your choice from the ranger spell list.

The Spells Known column of the Ranger table shows when you learn more ranger spells of your choice. Each of these spells must be of a level for which you have spell slots. For instance, when you reach 5th level in this class, you can learn one new spell of 1st or 2nd level.

Additionally, when you gain a level in this class, you can choose one of the ranger spells you know and replace it with another spell from the ranger spell list, which also must be of a level for which you have spell slots.

Spellcasting Ability

Wisdom is your spellcasting ability for your ranger spells, since your magic draws on your attunement to nature. You use your Wisdom whenever a spell refers to your spellcasting ability. In addition, you use your Wisdom modifier when setting the saving throw DC for a ranger spell you cast and when making an attack roll with one.

Spell save DC = 8 + your proficiency bonus + your Wisdom modifier

Spell attack modifier = your proficiency bonus + your Wisdom modifier

Ranger Archetype

At 3rd level, you choose an archetype that you strive to emulate: Hunter or Beast Master, both detailed at the end of the class description. Your choice grants you features at 3rd level and again at 7th, 11th, and 15th level.

Primeval Awareness

Beginning at 3rd level, you can use your action and expend one ranger spell slot to focus your awareness on the region around you. For 1 minute per level of the spell slot you expend, you can sense whether the following types of creatures are present within 1 mile of you (or within up to 6 miles if you are in your favored terrain): aberrations, celestials, dragons, elementals, fey, fiends, and undead. This feature doesn't reveal the creatures' location or number.

Ability Score Improvement

When you reach 4th level, and again at 8th, 12th, 16th, and 19th level, you can increase one ability score of your choice by 2, or you can increase two ability scores of your choice by 1. As normal, you can't increase an ability score above 20 using this feature.

Extra Attack

Beginning at 5th level, you can attack twice, instead of once, whenever you take the Attack action on your turn.

Land's Stride

Starting at 8th level, moving through nonmagical difficult terrain costs you no extra movement. You can also pass through nonmagical plants without being slowed by them and without taking damage from them if they have thorns, spines, or a similar hazard.

In addition, you have advantage on saving throws against plants that are magically created or manipulated to impede movement, such those created by the *entangle* spell.

Hide in Plain Sight

Starting at 10th level, you can spend 1 minute creating camouflage for yourself. You must have access to fresh mud, dirt, plants, soot, and other naturally occurring materials with which to create your camouflage.

Once you are camouflaged in this way, you can try to hide by pressing yourself up against a solid surface, such as a tree or wall, that is at least as tall and wide as you are. You gain a +10 bonus to Dexterity (Stealth) checks as long as you remain there without moving or taking actions. Once you move or take an action or a reaction, you must camouflage yourself again to gain this benefit.

Vanish

Starting at 14th level, you can use the Hide action as a bonus action on your turn. Also, you can't be tracked by nonmagical means, unless you choose to leave a trail.

Feral Senses

At 18th level, you gain preternatural senses that help you fight creatures you can't see. When you attack a creature you can't see, your inability to see it doesn't impose disadvantage on your attack rolls against it.

You are also aware of the location of any invisible creature within 30 feet of you, provided that the creature isn't hidden from you and you aren't blinded or deafened.

Foe Slayer

At 20th level, you become an unparalleled hunter of your enemies. Once on each of your turns, you can add your Wisdom modifier to the attack roll or the damage roll of an attack you make against one of your favored enemies. You can choose to use this feature before or after the roll, but before any effects of the roll are applied.

Ranger Archetypes

The ideal of the ranger has two classic expressions: the Hunter and the Beast Master.

Hunter

Emulating the Hunter archetype means accepting your place as a bulwark between civilization and the terrors of the wilderness. As you walk the Hunter's path, you learn specialized techniques for fighting the threats you face, from rampaging ogres and hordes of orcs to towering giants and terrifying dragons.

Hunter's Prey

At 3rd level, you gain one of the following features of your choice.

Colossus Slayer. Your tenacity can wear down the most potent foes. When you hit a creature with a weapon attack, the creature takes an extra 1d8 damage if it's below its hit point maximum. You can deal this extra damage only once per turn.

Giant Killer. When a Large or larger creature within 5 feet of you hits or misses you with an attack, you can use your reaction to attack that creature immediately after its attack, provided that you can see the creature.

Horde Breaker. Once on each of your turns when you make a weapon attack, you can make another attack with the same weapon against a different creature that is within 5 feet of the original target and within range of your weapon.

Defensive Tactics

At 7th level, you gain one of the following features of your choice.

Escape the Horde. Opportunity attacks against you are made with disadvantage.

Multiattack Defense. When a creature hits you with an attack, you gain a +4 bonus to AC against all subsequent attacks made by that creature for the rest of the turn.

Steel Will. You have advantage on saving throws against being frightened.

Multiattack

At 11th level, you gain one of the following features of your choice.

Volley. You can use your action to make a ranged attack against any number of creatures within 10 feet of a point you can see within your weapon's range. You must have ammunition for each target, as normal, and you make a separate attack roll for each target.

Whirlwind Attack. You can use your action to make a melee attack against any number of creatures within 5 feet of you, with a separate attack roll for each target.

Superior Hunter's Defense

At 15th level, you gain one of the following features of your choice.

Evasion. When you are subjected to an effect, such as a red dragon's fiery breath or a *lightning bolt* spell, that allows you to make a Dexterity saving throw to take only half damage, you instead take no damage if you succeed on the saving throw, and only half damage if you fail.

Stand Against the Tide. When a hostile creature misses you with a melee attack, you can use your reaction to force that creature to repeat the same attack against another creature (other than itself) of your choice.

Uncanny Dodge. When an attacker that you can see hits you with an attack, you can use your reaction to halve the attack's damage against you.

Beast Master

The Beast Master archetype embodies a friendship between the civilized races and the beasts of the wild. United in focus, beast and ranger fight the monsters that threaten civilization and the wilderness alike.

Ranger's Companion

At 3rd level, you gain a beast companion that accompanies you on your adventures and is trained to fight alongside you. Choose a beast that is no larger than Medium and that has a challenge rating of 1/4 or lower (appendix D presents statistics for the hawk, mastiff, and panther as examples). Add your proficiency bonus to the beast's AC, attack rolls, and damage rolls, as well as to any saving throws and skills it is proficient in. Its hit point maximum equals the hit point number in its stat block or four times your ranger level, whichever is higher. Like any creature, it can spend Hit Dice during a short rest to regain hit points.

The beast obeys your commands as best as it can. It takes its turn on your initiative, though it doesn't take an action unless you command it to. On your turn, you can verbally command the beast where to move (no action required by you). You can use your action to verbally command it to take the Attack, Dash, Disengage, Dodge, or Help action. Once you have the Extra Attack feature, you can make one weapon attack yourself when you command the beast to take the Attack action.

If you are incapacitated or absent, the beast acts on its own, focusing on protecting you and itself. The beast never requires your command to use its reaction, such as when making an opportunity attack.

While traveling through your favored terrain with only the beast, you can move stealthily at a normal pace.

If the beast dies, you can obtain a new companion by spending 8 hours magically bonding with a beast that isn't hostile to you and that meets the requirements.

Exceptional Training

Beginning at 7th level, on any of your turns when your beast companion doesn't attack, you can use a bonus action to command the beast to take the Dash, Disengage, Dodge, or Help action on its turn.

Bestial Fury

Starting at 11th level, when you command your beast companion to take the Attack action, the beast can make two attacks, or it can take the Multiattack action if it has that action.

Share Spells

Beginning at 15th level, when you cast a spell targeting yourself, you can also affect your beast companion with the spell if the beast is within 30 feet of you.

ROGUE

Signaling for her companions to wait, a halfling creeps forward through the dungeon hall. She presses an ear to the door, then pulls out a set of tools and picks the lock in the blink of an eye. Then she disappears into the shadows as her fighter friend moves forward to kick the door open.

A human lurks in the shadows of an alley while his accomplice prepares for her part in the ambush. When their target—a notorious slaver—passes the alleyway, the accomplice cries out, the slaver comes to investigate, and the assassin's blade cuts his throat before he can make a sound.

Suppressing a giggle, a gnome waggles her fingers and magically lifts the key ring from the guard's belt. In a moment, the keys are in her hand, the cell door is open, and she and her companions are free to make their escape.

Rogues rely on skill, stealth, and their foes' vulnerabilities to get the upper hand in any situation. They have a knack for finding the solution to just about any problem, demonstrating a resourcefulness and versatility that is the cornerstone of any successful adventuring party.

SKILL AND PRECISION

Rogues devote as much effort to mastering the use of a variety of skills as they do to perfecting their combat abilities, giving them a broad expertise that few other characters can match. Many rogues focus on stealth and deception, while others refine the skills that help them in a dungeon environment, such as climbing, finding and disarming traps, and opening locks.

When it comes to combat, rogues prioritize cunning over brute strength. A rogue would rather make one precise strike, placing it exactly where the attack will hurt the target most, than wear an opponent down with a barrage of attacks. Rogues have an almost supernatural knack for avoiding danger, and a few learn magical tricks to supplement their other abilities.

A SHADY LIVING

Every town and city has its share of rogues. Most of them live up to the worst stereotypes of the class, making a living as burglars, assassins, cutpurses, and con artists. Often, these scoundrels are organized into thieves' guilds or crime families. Plenty of rogues operate independently, but even they sometimes recruit apprentices to help them in their scams and heists. A few rogues make an honest living as

The Rogue

Level	Proficiency Bonus	Sneak Attack	Features
1st	+2	1d6	Expertise, Sneak Attack, Thieves' Cant
2nd	+2	1d6	Cunning Action
3rd	+2	2d6	Roguish Archetype
4th	+2	2d6	Ability Score Improvement
5th	+3	3d6	Uncanny Dodge
6th	+3	3d6	Expertise
7th	+3	4d6	Evasion
8th	+3	4d6	Ability Score Improvement
9th	+4	5d6	Roguish Archetype feature
10th	+4	5d6	Ability Score Improvement
11th	+4	6d6	Reliable Talent
12th	+4	6d6	Ability Score Improvement
13th	+5	7d6	Roguish Archetype feature
14th	+5	7d6	Blindsense
15th	+5	8d6	Slippery Mind
16th	+5	8d6	Ability Score Improvement
17th	+6	9d6	Roguish Archetype feature
18th	+6	9d6	Elusive
19th	+6	10d6	Ability Score Improvement
20th	+6	10d6	Stroke of Luck

locksmiths, investigators, or exterminators, which can be a dangerous job in a world where dire rats—and wererats—haunt the sewers.

As adventurers, rogues fall on both sides of the law. Some are hardened criminals who decide to seek their fortune in treasure hoards, while others take up a life of adventure to escape from the law. Some have learned and perfected their skills with the explicit purpose of infiltrating ancient ruins and hidden crypts in search of treasure.

Creating a Rogue

As you create your rogue character, consider the character's relationship to the law. Do you have a criminal past—or present? Are you on the run from the law or from an angry thieves' guild master? Or did you leave your guild in search of bigger risks and bigger rewards? Is it greed that drives you in your adventures, or some other desire or ideal?

What was the trigger that led you away from your previous life? Did a great con or heist gone terribly wrong cause you to reevaluate your career? Maybe you were lucky and a successful robbery gave you the coin you needed to escape the squalor of your life. Did wanderlust finally call you away from your home? Perhaps you suddenly found yourself cut off from your family or your mentor, and you had to find a new means of support. Or maybe you made a new friend—another member of your adventuring party—who showed you new possibilities for earning a living and employing your particular talents.

Quick Build

You can make a rogue quickly by following these suggestions. First, Dexterity should be your highest ability score. Make Intelligence your next-highest if you want to excel at Investigation or plan to take up the Arcane Trickster archetype. Choose Charisma instead if you plan to emphasize deception and social interaction. Second, choose the charlatan background.

Class Features

As a rogue, you have the following class features.

Hit Points

Hit Dice: 1d8 per rogue level
Hit Points at 1st Level: 8 + your Constitution modifier
Hit Points at Higher Levels: 1d8 (or 5) + your Constitution modifier per rogue level after 1st

Proficiencies

Armor: Light armor
Weapons: Simple weapons, hand crossbows, longswords, rapiers, shortswords
Tools: Thieves' tools

Saving Throws: Dexterity, Intelligence
Skills: Choose four from Acrobatics, Athletics, Deception, Insight, Intimidation, Investigation, Perception, Performance, Persuasion, Sleight of Hand, and Stealth

EQUIPMENT

You start with the following equipment, in addition to the equipment granted by your background:

- (a) a rapier or (b) a shortsword
- (a) a shortbow and quiver of 20 arrows or (b) a shortsword
- (a) a burglar's pack, (b) a dungeoneer's pack, or (c) an explorer's pack
- Leather armor, two daggers, and thieves' tools

EXPERTISE

At 1st level, choose two of your skill proficiencies, or one of your skill proficiencies and your proficiency with thieves' tools. Your proficiency bonus is doubled for any ability check you make that uses either of the chosen proficiencies.

At 6th level, you can choose two more of your proficiencies (in skills or with thieves' tools) to gain this benefit.

SNEAK ATTACK

Beginning at 1st level, you know how to strike subtly and exploit a foe's distraction. Once per turn, you can deal an extra 1d6 damage to one creature you hit with an attack if you have advantage on the attack roll. The attack must use a finesse or a ranged weapon.

You don't need advantage on the attack roll if another enemy of the target is within 5 feet of it, that enemy isn't incapacitated, and you don't have disadvantage on the attack roll.

The amount of the extra damage increases as you gain levels in this class, as shown in the Sneak Attack column of the Rogue table.

THIEVES' CANT

During your rogue training you learned thieves' cant, a secret mix of dialect, jargon, and code that allows you to hide messages in seemingly normal conversation. Only another creature that knows thieves' cant understands such messages. It takes four times longer to convey such a message than it does to speak the same idea plainly.

In addition, you understand a set of secret signs and symbols used to convey short, simple messages, such as whether an area is dangerous or the territory of a thieves' guild, whether loot is nearby, or whether the

people in an area are easy marks or will provide a safe house for thieves on the run.

CUNNING ACTION

Starting at 2nd level, your quick thinking and agility allow you to move and act quickly. You can take a bonus action on each of your turns in combat. This action can be used only to take the Dash, Disengage, or Hide action.

ROGUISH ARCHETYPE

At 3rd level, you choose an archetype that you emulate in the exercise of your rogue abilities: Thief, Assassin, or Arcane Trickster, all detailed at the end of the class description. Your archetype choice grants you features at 3rd level and then again at 9th, 13th, and 17th level.

ABILITY SCORE IMPROVEMENT

When you reach 4th level, and again at 8th, 10th, 12th, 16th, and 19th level, you can increase one ability score of your choice by 2, or you can increase two ability scores of your choice by 1. As normal, you can't increase an ability score above 20 using this feature.

UNCANNY DODGE

Starting at 5th level, when an attacker that you can see hits you with an attack, you can use your reaction to halve the attack's damage against you.

EVASION

Beginning at 7th level, you can nimbly dodge out of the way of certain area effects, such as a red dragon's fiery breath or an *ice storm* spell. When you are subjected to an effect that allows you to make a Dexterity saving throw to take only half damage, you instead take no damage if you succeed on the saving throw, and only half damage if you fail.

RELIABLE TALENT

By 11th level, you have refined your chosen skills until they approach perfection. Whenever you make an ability check that lets you add your proficiency bonus, you can treat a d20 roll of 9 or lower as a 10.

BLINDSENSE

Starting at 14th level, if you are able to hear, you are aware of the location of any hidden or invisible creature within 10 feet of you.

SLIPPERY MIND

By 15th level, you have acquired greater mental strength. You gain proficiency in Wisdom saving throws.

ELUSIVE

Beginning at 18th level, you are so evasive that attackers rarely gain the upper hand against you. No attack roll has advantage against you while you aren't incapacitated.

Stroke of Luck

At 20th level, you have an uncanny knack for succeeding when you need to. If your attack misses a target within range, you can turn the miss into a hit. Alternatively, if you fail an ability check, you can treat the d20 roll as a 20.

Once you use this feature, you can't use it again until you finish a short or long rest.

Roguish Archetypes

Rogues have many features in common, including their emphasis on perfecting their skills, their precise and deadly approach to combat, and their increasingly quick reflexes. But different rogues steer those talents in varying directions, embodied by the rogue archetypes. Your choice of archetype is a reflection of your focus—not necessarily an indication of your chosen profession, but a description of your preferred techniques.

Thief

You hone your skills in the larcenous arts. Burglars, bandits, cutpurses, and other criminals typically follow this archetype, but so do rogues who prefer to think of themselves as professional treasure seekers, explorers, delvers, and investigators. In addition to improving your agility and stealth, you learn skills useful for delving into ancient ruins, reading unfamiliar languages, and using magic items you normally couldn't employ.

Fast Hands

Starting at 3rd level, you can use the bonus action granted by your Cunning Action to make a Dexterity (Sleight of Hand) check, use your thieves' tools to disarm a trap or open a lock, or take the Use an Object action.

Second-Story Work

When you choose this archetype at 3rd level, you gain the ability to climb faster than normal; climbing no longer costs you extra movement.

In addition, when you make a running jump, the distance you cover increases by a number of feet equal to your Dexterity modifier.

Supreme Sneak

Starting at 9th level, you have advantage on a Dexterity (Stealth) check if you move no more than half your speed on the same turn.

Use Magic Device

By 13th level, you have learned enough about the workings of magic that you can improvise the use of items even when they are not intended for you. You ignore all class, race, and level requirements on the use of magic items.

Thief's Reflexes

When you reach 17th level, you have become adept at laying ambushes and quickly escaping danger. You can take two turns during the first round of any combat. You take your first turn at your normal initiative and your second turn at your initiative minus 10. You can't use this feature when you are surprised.

Assassin

You focus your training on the grim art of death. Those who adhere to this archetype are diverse: hired killers, spies, bounty hunters, and even specially anointed priests trained to exterminate the enemies of their deity. Stealth, poison, and disguise help you eliminate your foes with deadly efficiency.

Bonus Proficiencies

When you choose this archetype at 3rd level, you gain proficiency with the disguise kit and the poisoner's kit.

Assassinate

Starting at 3rd level, you are at your deadliest when you get the drop on your enemies. You have advantage on attack rolls against any creature that hasn't taken a turn in the combat yet. In addition, any hit you score against a creature that is surprised is a critical hit.

Infiltration Expertise

Starting at 9th level, you can unfailingly create false identities for yourself. You must spend seven days and 25 gp to establish the history, profession, and affiliations for an identity. You can't establish an identity that belongs to someone else. For example, you might acquire appropriate clothing, letters of introduction, and official-looking certification to establish yourself as a member of a trading house from a remote city so you can insinuate yourself into the company of other wealthy merchants.

Thereafter, if you adopt the new identity as a disguise, other creatures believe you to be that person until given an obvious reason not to.

Impostor

At 13th level, you gain the ability to unerringly mimic another person's speech, writing, and behavior. You must spend at least three hours studying these three components of the person's behavior, listening to speech, examining handwriting, and observing mannerisms.

Your ruse is indiscernible to the casual observer. If a wary creature suspects something is amiss, you have advantage on any Charisma (Deception) check you make to avoid detection.

Death Strike

Starting at 17th level, you become a master of instant death. When you attack and hit a creature that is surprised, it must make a Constitution saving throw (DC 8 + your Dexterity modifier + your proficiency bonus). On a failed save, double the damage of your attack against the creature.

Arcane Trickster

Some rogues enhance their fine-honed skills of stealth and agility with magic, learning tricks of enchantment and illusion. These rogues include pickpockets and burglars, but also pranksters, mischief-makers, and a significant number of adventurers.

Spellcasting

When you reach 3rd level, you gain the ability to cast spells. See chapter 10 for the general rules of spellcasting and chapter 11 for the wizard spell list.

Cantrips. You learn three cantrips: *mage hand* and two other cantrips of your choice from the wizard spell list. You learn another wizard cantrip of your choice at 10th level.

Spell Slots. The Arcane Trickster Spellcasting table shows how many spell slots you have to cast your spells of 1st level and higher. To cast one of these spells, you must expend a slot of the spell's level or higher. You regain all expended spell slots when you finish a long rest.

For example, if you know the 1st-level spell *charm person* and have a 1st-level and a 2nd-level spell slot available, you can cast *charm person* using either slot.

Spells Known of 1st-Level and Higher. You know three 1st-level wizard spells of your choice, two of which you must choose from the enchantment and illusion spells on the wizard spell list.

The Spells Known column of the Arcane Trickster Spellcasting table shows when you learn more wizard spells of 1st level or higher. Each of these spells must be an enchantment or illusion spell of your choice, and must be of a level for which you have spell slots. For instance, when you reach 7th level in this class, you can learn one new spell of 1st or 2nd level.

The spells you learn at 8th, 14th, and 20th level can come from any school of magic.

Whenever you gain a level in this class, you can replace one of the wizard spells you know with another spell of your choice from the wizard spell list. The new spell must be of a level for which you have spell slots, and it must be an enchantment or illusion spell, unless you're replacing the spell you gained at 8th, 14th, or 20th level.

Spellcasting Ability. Intelligence is your spellcasting ability for your wizard spells, since you learn your spells through dedicated study and memorization. You use your Intelligence whenever a spell refers to your spellcasting ability. In addition, you use your Intelligence modifier when setting the saving throw DC for a wizard spell you cast and when making an attack roll with one.

Spell save DC = 8 + your proficiency bonus + your Intelligence modifier

Spell attack modifier = your proficiency bonus + your Intelligence modifier

MAGE HAND LEGERDEMAIN

Starting at 3rd level, when you cast *mage hand*, you can make the spectral hand invisible, and you can perform the following additional tasks with it:

- You can stow one object the hand is holding in a container worn or carried by another creature.
- You can retrieve an object in a container worn or carried by another creature.
- You can use thieves' tools to pick locks and disarm traps at range.

ARCANE TRICKSTER SPELLCASTING

Rogue Level	Cantrips Known	Spells Known	—Spell Slots per Spell Level—			
			1st	2nd	3rd	4th
3rd	3	3	2	—	—	—
4th	3	4	3	—	—	—
5th	3	4	3	—	—	—
6th	3	4	3	—	—	—
7th	3	5	4	2	—	—
8th	3	6	4	2	—	—
9th	3	6	4	2	—	—
10th	4	7	4	3	—	—
11th	4	8	4	3	—	—
12th	4	8	4	3	—	—
13th	4	9	4	3	2	—
14th	4	10	4	3	2	—
15th	4	10	4	3	2	—
16th	4	11	4	3	3	—
17th	4	11	4	3	3	—
18th	4	11	4	3	3	—
19th	4	12	4	3	3	1
20th	4	13	4	3	3	1

You can perform one of these tasks without being noticed by a creature if you succeed on a Dexterity (Sleight of Hand) check contested by the creature's Wisdom (Perception) check.

In addition, you can use the bonus action granted by your Cunning Action to control the hand.

MAGICAL AMBUSH

Starting at 9th level, if you are hidden from a creature when you cast a spell on it, the creature has disadvantage on any saving throw it makes against the spell this turn.

VERSATILE TRICKSTER

At 13th level, you gain the ability to distract targets with your *mage hand*. As a bonus action on your turn, you can designate a creature within 5 feet of the spectral hand created by the spell. Doing so gives you advantage on attack rolls against that creature until the end of the turn.

SPELL THIEF

At 17th level, you gain the ability to magically steal the knowledge of how to cast a spell from another spellcaster.

Immediately after a creature casts a spell that targets you or includes you in its area of effect, you can use your reaction to force the creature to make a saving throw with its spellcasting ability modifier. The DC equals your spell save DC. On a failed save, you negate the spell's effect against you, and you steal the knowledge of the spell if it is at least 1st level and of a level you can cast (it doesn't need to be a wizard spell). For the next 8 hours, you know the spell and can cast it using your spell slots. The creature can't cast that spell until the 8 hours have passed.

Once you use this feature, you can't use it again until you finish a long rest.

Sorcerer

Golden eyes flashing, a human stretches out her hand and unleashes the dragonfire that burns in her veins. As an inferno rages around her foes, leathery wings spread from her back and she takes to the air.

Long hair whipped by a conjured wind, a half-elf spreads his arms wide and throws his head back. Lifting him momentarily off the ground, a wave of magic surges up in him, through him, and out from him in a mighty blast of lightning.

Crouching behind a stalagmite, a halfling points a finger at a charging troglodyte. A blast of fire springs from her finger to strike the creature. She ducks back behind the rock formation with a grin, unaware that her wild magic has turned her skin bright blue.

Sorcerers carry a magical birthright conferred upon them by an exotic bloodline, some otherworldly influence, or exposure to unknown cosmic forces. One can't study sorcery as one learns a language, any more than one can learn to live a legendary life. No one chooses sorcery; the power chooses the sorcerer.

Raw Magic

Magic is a part of every sorcerer, suffusing body, mind, and spirit with a latent power that waits to be tapped. Some sorcerers wield magic that springs from an ancient bloodline infused with the magic of dragons. Others carry a raw, uncontrolled magic within them, a chaotic storm that manifests in unexpected ways.

The appearance of sorcerous powers is wildly unpredictable. Some draconic bloodlines produce exactly one sorcerer in every generation, but in other lines of descent every individual is a sorcerer. Most of the time, the talents of sorcery appear as apparent flukes. Some sorcerers can't name the origin of their power, while others trace it to strange events in their own lives. The touch of a demon, the blessing of a dryad at a baby's birth, or a taste of the water from a mysterious spring might spark the gift of sorcery. So too might the gift of a deity of magic, exposure to the elemental forces of the Inner Planes or the maddening chaos of Limbo, or a glimpse into the inner workings of reality.

Sorcerers have no use for the spellbooks and ancient tomes of magic lore that wizards rely on, nor do they rely on a patron to grant their spells as warlocks do. By learning to harness and channel their own inborn magic, they can discover new and staggering ways to unleash that power.

Unexplained Powers

Sorcerers are rare in the world, and it's unusual to find a sorcerer who is not involved in the adventuring life in some way. People with magical power seething in their veins soon discover that the power doesn't like to stay quiet. A sorcerer's magic wants to be wielded, and it has a tendency to spill out in unpredictable ways if it isn't called on.

Level	Proficiency Bonus	Sorcery Points	Features	Cantrips Known	Spells Known	Spell Slots per Spell Level								
						1st	2nd	3rd	4th	5th	6th	7th	8th	9th
1st	+2	—	Spellcasting, Sorcerous Origin	4	2	2	—	—	—	—	—	—	—	—
2nd	+2	2	Font of Magic	4	3	3	—	—	—	—	—	—	—	—
3rd	+2	3	Metamagic	4	4	4	2	—	—	—	—	—	—	—
4th	+2	4	Ability Score Improvement	5	5	4	3	—	—	—	—	—	—	—
5th	+3	5	—	5	6	4	3	2	—	—	—	—	—	—
6th	+3	6	Sorcerous Origin feature	5	7	4	3	3	—	—	—	—	—	—
7th	+3	7	—	5	8	4	3	3	1	—	—	—	—	—
8th	+3	8	Ability Score Improvement	5	9	4	3	3	2	—	—	—	—	—
9th	+4	9	—	5	10	4	3	3	3	1	—	—	—	—
10th	+4	10	Metamagic	6	11	4	3	3	3	2	—	—	—	—
11th	+4	11	—	6	12	4	3	3	3	2	1	—	—	—
12th	+4	12	Ability Score Improvement	6	12	4	3	3	3	2	1	—	—	—
13th	+5	13	—	6	13	4	3	3	3	2	1	1	—	—
14th	+5	14	Sorcerous Origin feature	6	13	4	3	3	3	2	1	1	—	—
15th	+5	15	—	6	14	4	3	3	3	2	1	1	1	—
16th	+5	16	Ability Score Improvement	6	14	4	3	3	3	2	1	1	1	—
17th	+6	17	Metamagic	6	15	4	3	3	3	2	1	1	1	1
18th	+6	18	Sorcerous Origin feature	6	15	4	3	3	3	3	1	1	1	1
19th	+6	19	Ability Score Improvement	6	15	4	3	3	3	3	2	1	1	1
20th	+6	20	Sorcerous Restoration	6	15	4	3	3	3	3	2	2	1	1

Sorcerers often have obscure or quixotic motivations driving them to adventure. Some seek a greater understanding of the magical force that infuses them, or the answer to the mystery of its origin. Others hope to find a way to get rid of it, or to unleash its full potential. Whatever their goals, sorcerers are every bit as useful to an adventuring party as wizards, making up for a comparative lack of breadth in their magical knowledge with enormous flexibility in using the spells they know.

CREATING A SORCERER

The most important question to consider when creating your sorcerer is the origin of your power. As a starting character, you'll choose an origin that ties to a draconic bloodline or the influence of wild magic, but the exact source of your power is up to you to decide. Is it a family curse, passed down to you from distant ancestors? Or did some extraordinary event leave you blessed with inherent magic but perhaps scarred as well?

How do you feel about the magical power coursing through you? Do you embrace it, try to master it, or revel in its unpredictable nature? Is it a blessing or a curse? Did you seek it out, or did it find you? Did you have the option to refuse it, and do you wish you had? What do you intend to do with it? Perhaps you feel like you've been given this power for some lofty purpose. Or you might decide that the power gives you the right to do what you want, to take what you want from those who lack such power. Perhaps your power links you to a powerful individual in the world—the fey creature that blessed you at birth, the dragon who put a drop of its blood into your veins, the lich who created you as an experiment, or the deity who chose you to carry this power.

QUICK BUILD

You can make a sorcerer quickly by following these suggestions. First, Charisma should be your highest ability score, followed by Constitution. Second, choose the hermit background. Third, choose the *light*, *prestidigitation*, *ray of frost*, and *shocking grasp* cantrips, along with the 1st-level spells *shield* and *magic missile*.

CLASS FEATURES

As a sorcerer, you gain the following class features.

HIT POINTS
Hit Dice: 1d6 per sorcerer level
Hit Points at 1st Level: 6 + your Constitution modifier
Hit Points at Higher Levels: 1d6 (or 4) + your Constitution modifier per sorcerer level after 1st

PROFICIENCIES
Armor: None
Weapons: Daggers, darts, slings, quarterstaffs, light crossbows
Tools: None

Saving Throws: Constitution, Charisma
Skills: Choose two from Arcana, Deception, Insight, Intimidation, Persuasion, and Religion

EQUIPMENT

You start with the following equipment, in addition to the equipment granted by your background:

- (*a*) a light crossbow and 20 bolts or (*b*) any simple weapon
- (*a*) a component pouch or (*b*) an arcane focus
- (*a*) a dungeoneer's pack or (*b*) an explorer's pack
- Two daggers

SPELLCASTING

An event in your past, or in the life of a parent or ancestor, left an indelible mark on you, infusing you with arcane magic. This font of magic, whatever its origin, fuels your spells. See chapter 10 for the general rules of spellcasting and chapter 11 for the sorcerer spell list.

CANTRIPS

At 1st level, you know four cantrips of your choice from the sorcerer spell list. You learn additional sorcerer cantrips of your choice at higher levels, as shown in the Cantrips Known column of the Sorcerer table.

SPELL SLOTS

The Sorcerer table shows how many spell slots you have to cast your spells of 1st level and higher. To cast one of these sorcerer spells, you must expend a slot of the spell's level or higher. You regain all expended spell slots when you finish a long rest.

For example, if you know the 1st-level spell *burning hands* and have a 1st-level and a 2nd-level spell slot available, you can cast *burning hands* using either slot.

SPELLS KNOWN OF 1ST LEVEL AND HIGHER

You know two 1st-level spells of your choice from the sorcerer spell list.

The Spells Known column of the Sorcerer table shows when you learn more sorcerer spells of your choice. Each of these spells must be of a level for which you have spell slots. For instance, when you reach 3rd level in this class, you can learn one new spell of 1st or 2nd level.

Additionally, when you gain a level in this class, you can choose one of the sorcerer spells you know and replace it with another spell from the sorcerer spell list, which also must be of a level for which you have spell slots.

SPELLCASTING ABILITY

Charisma is your spellcasting ability for your sorcerer spells, since the power of your magic relies on your ability to project your will into the world. You use your Charisma whenever a spell refers to your spellcasting ability. In addition, you use your Charisma modifier when setting the saving throw DC for a sorcerer spell you cast and when making an attack roll with one.

Spell save DC = 8 + your proficiency bonus + your Charisma modifier

Spell attack modifier = your proficiency bonus + your Charisma modifier

SPELLCASTING FOCUS

You can use an arcane focus (see chapter 5, "Equipment") as a spellcasting focus for your sorcerer spells.

SORCEROUS ORIGIN

Choose a sorcerous origin, which describes the source of your innate magical power: Draconic Bloodline or Wild Magic, both detailed at the end of the class description.

Your choice grants you features when you choose it at 1st level and again at 6th, 14th, and 18th level.

FONT OF MAGIC

At 2nd level, you tap into a deep wellspring of magic within yourself. This wellspring is represented by sorcery points, which allow you to create a variety of magical effects.

SORCERY POINTS

You have 2 sorcery points, and you gain more as you reach higher levels, as shown in the Sorcery Points column of the Sorcerer table. You can never have more sorcery points than shown on the table for your level. You regain all spent sorcery points when you finish a long rest.

FLEXIBLE CASTING

You can use your sorcery points to gain additional spell slots, or sacrifice spell slots to gain additional sorcery points. You learn other ways to use your sorcery points as you reach higher levels.

Creating Spell Slots. You can transform unexpended sorcery points into one spell slot as a bonus action on your turn. The Creating Spell Slots table shows the cost of creating a spell slot of a given level. You can create spell slots no higher in level than 5th.

Any spell slot you create with this feature vanishes when you finish a long rest.

CREATING SPELL SLOTS

Spell Slot Level	Sorcery Point Cost
1st	2
2nd	3
3rd	5
4th	6
5th	7

Converting a Spell Slot to Sorcery Points. As a bonus action on your turn, you can expend one spell slot and gain a number of sorcery points equal to the slot's level.

METAMAGIC

At 3rd level, you gain the ability to twist your spells to suit your needs. You gain two of the following Metamagic options of your choice. You gain another one at 10th and 17th level.

You can use only one Metamagic option on a spell when you cast it, unless otherwise noted.

Careful Spell

When you cast a spell that forces other creatures to make a saving throw, you can protect some of those creatures from the spell's full force. To do so, you spend 1 sorcery point and choose a number of those creatures up to your Charisma modifier (minimum of one creature). A chosen creature automatically succeeds on its saving throw against the spell.

Distant Spell

When you cast a spell that has a range of 5 feet or greater, you can spend 1 sorcery point to double the range of the spell.

When you cast a spell that has a range of touch, you can spend 1 sorcery point to make the range of the spell 30 feet.

Empowered Spell

When you roll damage for a spell, you can spend 1 sorcery point to reroll a number of the damage dice up to your Charisma modifier (minimum of one). You must use the new rolls.

You can use Empowered Spell even if you have already used a different Metamagic option during the casting of the spell.

Extended Spell

When you cast a spell that has a duration of 1 minute or longer, you can spend 1 sorcery point to double its duration, to a maximum duration of 24 hours.

Heightened Spell

When you cast a spell that forces a creature to make a saving throw to resist its effects, you can spend 3 sorcery points to give one target of the spell disadvantage on its first saving throw made against the spell.

Quickened Spell

When you cast a spell that has a casting time of 1 action, you can spend 2 sorcery points to change the casting time to 1 bonus action for this casting.

Subtle Spell

When you cast a spell, you can spend 1 sorcery point to cast it without any somatic or verbal components.

Twinned Spell

When you cast a spell that targets only one creature and doesn't have a range of self, you can spend a number of sorcery points equal to the spell's level to target a second creature in range with the same spell (1 sorcery point if the spell is a cantrip).

To be eligible, a spell must be incapable of targeting more than one creature at the spell's current level. For example, *magic missile* and *scorching ray* aren't eligible, but *ray of frost* and *chromatic orb* are.

Ability Score Improvement

When you reach 4th level, and again at 8th, 12th, 16th, and 19th level, you can increase one ability score of your choice by 2, or you can increase two ability scores of your choice by 1. As normal, you can't increase an ability score above 20 using this feature.

Sorcerous Restoration

At 20th level, you regain 4 expended sorcery points whenever you finish a short rest.

Sorcerous Origins

Different sorcerers claim different origins for their innate magic. Although many variations exist, most of these origins fall into two categories: a draconic bloodline and wild magic.

Draconic Bloodline

Your innate magic comes from draconic magic that was mingled with your blood or that of your ancestors. Most often, sorcerers with this origin trace their descent back to a mighty sorcerer of ancient times who made a bargain with a dragon or who might even have claimed a dragon parent. Some of these bloodlines are well established in the world, but most are obscure. Any given sorcerer could be the first of a new bloodline, as a result of a pact or some other exceptional circumstance.

Dragon Ancestor

At 1st level, you choose one type of dragon as your ancestor. The damage type associated with each dragon is used by features you gain later.

Draconic Ancestry

Dragon	Damage Type
Black	Acid
Blue	Lightning
Brass	Fire
Bronze	Lightning
Copper	Acid
Gold	Fire
Green	Poison
Red	Fire
Silver	Cold
White	Cold

You can speak, read, and write Draconic. Additionally, whenever you make a Charisma check when interacting with dragons, your proficiency bonus is doubled if it applies to the check.

Draconic Resilience

As magic flows through your body, it causes physical traits of your dragon ancestors to emerge. At 1st level, your hit point maximum increases by 1 and increases by 1 again whenever you gain a level in this class.

Additionally, parts of your skin are covered by a thin sheen of dragon-like scales. When you aren't wearing armor, your AC equals 13 + your Dexterity modifier.

Elemental Affinity

Starting at 6th level, when you cast a spell that deals damage of the type associated with your draconic ancestry, you can add your Charisma modifier to one damage roll of that spell. At the same time, you can spend 1 sorcery point to gain resistance to that damage type for 1 hour.

DRAGON WINGS

At 14th level, you gain the ability to sprout a pair of dragon wings from your back, gaining a flying speed equal to your current speed. You can create these wings as a bonus action on your turn. They last until you dismiss them as a bonus action on your turn.

You can't manifest your wings while wearing armor unless the armor is made to accommodate them, and clothing not made to accommodate your wings might be destroyed when you manifest them.

DRACONIC PRESENCE

Beginning at 18th level, you can channel the dread presence of your dragon ancestor, causing those around you to become awestruck or frightened. As an action, you can spend 5 sorcery points to draw on this power and exude an aura of awe or fear (your choice) to a distance of 60 feet. For 1 minute or until you lose your concentration (as if you were casting a concentration spell), each hostile creature that starts its turn in this aura must succeed on a Wisdom saving throw or be charmed (if you chose awe) or frightened (if you chose fear) until the aura ends. A creature that succeeds on this saving throw is immune to your aura for 24 hours.

WILD MAGIC

Your innate magic comes from the forces of chaos that underlie the order of creation. You might have endured exposure to raw magic, perhaps through a planar portal leading to Limbo, the Elemental Planes, or the Far Realm. Perhaps you were blessed by a fey being or marked by a demon. Or your magic could be a fluke of your birth, with no apparent cause. However it came to be, this magic churns within you, waiting for any outlet.

WILD MAGIC SURGE

Starting when you choose this origin at 1st level, your spellcasting can unleash surges of untamed magic. Once per turn, the DM can have you roll a d20 immediately after you cast a sorcerer spell of 1st level or higher. If you roll a 1, roll on the Wild Magic Surge table to create a magical effect. If that effect is a spell, it is too wild to be affected by your Metamagic, and if it normally requires concentration, it doesn't require concentration in this case; the spell lasts for its full duration.

TIDES OF CHAOS

Starting at 1st level, you can manipulate the forces of chance and chaos to gain advantage on one attack roll, ability check, or saving throw. Once you do so, you must finish a long rest before you can use this feature again.

Any time before you regain the use of this feature, the DM can have you roll on the Wild Magic Surge table immediately after you cast a sorcerer spell of 1st level or higher. You then regain the use of this feature.

BEND LUCK

Starting at 6th level, you have the ability to twist fate using your wild magic. When another creature you can see makes an attack roll, an ability check, or a saving throw, you can use your reaction and spend 2 sorcery points to roll 1d4 and apply the number rolled as a bonus or penalty (your choice) to the creature's roll. You

can do so after the creature rolls but before any effects of the roll occur.

CONTROLLED CHAOS

At 14th level, you gain a modicum of control over the surges of your wild magic. Whenever you roll on the Wild Magic Surge table, you can roll twice and use either number.

SPELL BOMBARDMENT

Beginning at 18th level, the harmful energy of your spells intensifies. When you roll damage for a spell and roll the highest number possible on any of the dice, choose one of those dice, roll it again and add that roll to the damage. You can use the feature only once per turn.

WILD MAGIC SURGE

d100	Effect
01–02	Roll on this table at the start of each of your turns for the next minute, ignoring this result on subsequent rolls.
03–04	For the next minute, you can see any invisible creature if you have line of sight to it.
05–06	A modron chosen and controlled by the DM appears in an unoccupied space within 5 feet of you, then disappears 1 minute later.
07–08	You cast *fireball* as a 3rd-level spell centered on yourself.
09–10	You cast *magic missile* as a 5th-level spell.
11–12	Roll a d10. Your height changes by a number of inches equal to the roll. If the roll is odd, you shrink. If the roll is even, you grow.
13–14	You cast *confusion* centered on yourself.
15–16	For the next minute, you regain 5 hit points at the start of each of your turns.
17–18	You grow a long beard made of feathers that remains until you sneeze, at which point the feathers explode out from your face.
19–20	You cast *grease* centered on yourself.
21–22	Creatures have disadvantage on saving throws against the next spell you cast in the next minute that involves a saving throw.
23–24	Your skin turns a vibrant shade of blue. A *remove curse* spell can end this effect.
25–26	An eye appears on your forehead for the next minute. During that time, you have advantage on Wisdom (Perception) checks that rely on sight.
27–28	For the next minute, all your spells with a casting time of 1 action have a casting time of 1 bonus action.
29–30	You teleport up to 60 feet to an unoccupied space of your choice that you can see.
31–32	You are transported to the Astral Plane until the end of your next turn, after which time you return to the space you previously occupied or the nearest unoccupied space if that space is occupied.
33–34	Maximize the damage of the next damaging spell you cast within the next minute.
35–36	Roll a d10. Your age changes by a number of years equal to the roll. If the roll is odd, you get younger (minimum 1 year old). If the roll is even, you get older.
37–38	1d6 flumphs controlled by the DM appear in unoccupied spaces within 60 feet of you and are frightened of you. They vanish after 1 minute.
39–40	You regain 2d10 hit points.
41–42	You turn into a potted plant until the start of your next turn. While a plant, you are incapacitated and have vulnerability to all damage. If you drop to 0 hit points, your pot breaks, and your form reverts.
43–44	For the next minute, you can teleport up to 20 feet as a bonus action on each of your turns.
45–46	You cast *levitate* on yourself.
47–48	A unicorn controlled by the DM appears in a space within 5 feet of you, then disappears 1 minute later.
49–50	You can't speak for the next minute. Whenever you try, pink bubbles float out of your mouth.
51–52	A spectral shield hovers near you for the next minute, granting you a +2 bonus to AC and immunity to *magic missile*.
53–54	You are immune to being intoxicated by alcohol for the next 5d6 days.
55–56	Your hair falls out but grows back within 24 hours.
57–58	For the next minute, any flammable object you touch that isn't being worn or carried by another creature bursts into flame.
59–60	You regain your lowest-level expended spell slot.
61–62	For the next minute, you must shout when you speak.
63–64	You cast *fog cloud* centered on yourself.
65–66	Up to three creatures you choose within 30 feet of you take 4d10 lightning damage.
67–68	You are frightened by the nearest creature until the end of your next turn.
69–70	Each creature within 30 feet of you becomes invisible for the next minute. The invisibility ends on a creature when it attacks or casts a spell.
71–72	You gain resistance to all damage for the next minute.
73–74	A random creature within 60 feet of you becomes poisoned for 1d4 hours.
75–76	You glow with bright light in a 30-foot radius for the next minute. Any creature that ends its turn within 5 feet of you is blinded until the end of its next turn.
77–78	You cast *polymorph* on yourself. If you fail the saving throw, you turn into a sheep for the spell's duration.
79–80	Illusory butterflies and flower petals flutter in the air within 10 feet of you for the next minute.
81–82	You can take one additional action immediately.
83–84	Each creature within 30 feet of you takes 1d10 necrotic damage. You regain hit points equal to the sum of the necrotic damage dealt.
85–86	You cast *mirror image*.
87–88	You cast *fly* on a random creature within 60 feet of you.
89–90	You become invisible for the next minute. During that time, other creatures can't hear you. The invisibility ends if you attack or cast a spell.
91–92	If you die within the next minute, you immediately come back to life as if by the *reincarnate* spell.
93–94	Your size increases by one size category for the next minute.
95–96	You and all creatures within 30 feet of you gain vulnerability to piercing damage for the next minute.
97–98	You are surrounded by faint, ethereal music for the next minute.
99–00	You regain all expended sorcery points.

WARLOCK

With a pseudodragon curled on his shoulder, a young elf in golden robes smiles warmly, weaving a magical charm into his honeyed words and bending the palace sentinel to his will.

As flames spring to life in her hands, a wizened human whispers the secret name of her demonic patron, infusing her spell with fiendish magic.

Shifting his gaze between a battered tome and the odd alignment of the stars overhead, a wild-eyed tiefling chants the mystic ritual that will open a doorway to a distant world.

Warlocks are seekers of the knowledge that lies hidden in the fabric of the multiverse. Through pacts made with mysterious beings of supernatural power, warlocks unlock magical effects both subtle and spectacular. Drawing on the ancient knowledge of beings such as fey nobles, demons, devils, hags, and alien entities of the Far Realm, warlocks piece together arcane secrets to bolster their own power.

SWORN AND BEHOLDEN

A warlock is defined by a pact with an otherworldly being. Sometimes the relationship between warlock and patron is like that of a cleric and a deity, though the beings that serve as patrons for warlocks are not gods. A warlock might lead a cult dedicated to a demon prince, an archdevil, or an utterly alien entity—beings not typically served by clerics. More often, though, the arrangement is similar to that between a master and an apprentice. The warlock learns and grows in power, at the cost of occasional services performed on the patron's behalf.

The magic bestowed on a warlock ranges from minor but lasting alterations to the warlock's being (such as the ability to see in darkness or to read any language) to access to powerful spells. Unlike bookish wizards, warlocks supplement their magic with some facility at hand-to-hand combat. They are comfortable in light armor and know how to use simple weapons.

DELVERS INTO SECRETS

Warlocks are driven by an insatiable need for knowledge and power, which compels them into their pacts and shapes their lives. This thirst drives warlocks into their pacts and shapes their later careers as well.

Stories of warlocks binding themselves to fiends are widely known. But many warlocks serve patrons that are not fiendish. Sometimes a traveler in the wilds comes to a strangely beautiful tower, meets its fey lord or lady, and stumbles into a pact without being fully aware of it. And sometimes, while poring over tomes of

The Warlock

Level	Proficiency Bonus	Features	Cantrips Known	Spells Known	Spell Slots	Slot Level	Invocations Known
1st	+2	Otherworldly Patron, Pact Magic	2	2	1	1st	—
2nd	+2	Eldritch Invocations	2	3	2	1st	2
3rd	+2	Pact Boon	2	4	2	2nd	2
4th	+2	Ability Score Improvement	3	5	2	2nd	2
5th	+3	—	3	6	2	3rd	3
6th	+3	Otherworldly Patron feature	3	7	2	3rd	3
7th	+3	—	3	8	2	4th	4
8th	+3	Ability Score Improvement	3	9	2	4th	4
9th	+4	—	3	10	2	5th	5
10th	+4	Otherworldly Patron feature	4	10	2	5th	5
11th	+4	Mystic Arcanum (6th level)	4	11	3	5th	5
12th	+4	Ability Score Improvement	4	11	3	5th	6
13th	+5	Mystic Arcanum (7th level)	4	12	3	5th	6
14th	+5	Otherworldly Patron feature	4	12	3	5th	6
15th	+5	Mystic Arcanum (8th level)	4	13	3	5th	7
16th	+5	Ability Score Improvement	4	13	3	5th	7
17th	+6	Mystic Arcanum (9th level)	4	14	4	5th	7
18th	+6	—	4	14	4	5th	8
19th	+6	Ability Score Improvement	4	15	4	5th	8
20th	+6	Eldritch Master	4	15	4	5th	8

forbidden lore, a brilliant but crazed student's mind is opened to realities beyond the material world and to the alien beings that dwell in the outer void.

Once a pact is made, a warlock's thirst for knowledge and power can't be slaked with mere study and research. No one makes a pact with such a mighty patron if he or she doesn't intend to use the power thus gained. Rather, the vast majority of warlocks spend their days in active pursuit of their goals, which typically means some kind of adventuring. Furthermore, the demands of their patrons drive warlocks toward adventure.

CREATING A WARLOCK

As you make your warlock character, spend some time thinking about your patron and the obligations that your pact imposes upon you. What led you to make the pact, and how did you make contact with your patron? Were you seduced into summoning a devil, or did you seek out the ritual that would allow you to make contact with an alien elder god? Did you search for your patron, or did your patron find and choose you? Do you chafe under the obligations of your pact or serve joyfully in anticipation of the rewards promised to you?

Work with your DM to determine how big a part your pact will play in your character's adventuring career.

Your patron's demands might drive you into adventures, or they might consist entirely of small favors you can do between adventures.

What kind of relationship do you have with your patron? Is it friendly, antagonistic, uneasy, or romantic? How important does your patron consider you to be? What part do you play in your patron's plans? Do you know other servants of your patron?

How does your patron communicate with you? If you have a familiar, it might occasionally speak with your patron's voice. Some warlocks find messages from their patrons etched on trees, mingled among tea leaves, or adrift in the clouds—messages that only the warlock can see. Other warlocks converse with their patrons in dreams or waking visions, or deal only with intermediaries.

QUICK BUILD

You can make a warlock quickly by following these suggestions. First, Charisma should be your highest ability score, followed by Constitution. Second, choose the charlatan background. Third, choose the *eldritch blast* and *chill touch* cantrips, along with the 1st-level spells *charm person* and *witch bolt*.

CLASS FEATURES

As a warlock, you gain the following class features.

HIT POINTS

Hit Dice: 1d8 per warlock level
Hit Points at 1st Level: 8 + your Constitution modifier
Hit Points at Higher Levels: 1d8 (or 5) + your Constitution modifier per warlock level after 1st

PROFICIENCIES

Armor: Light armor
Weapons: Simple weapons
Tools: None

Saving Throws: Wisdom, Charisma
Skills: Choose two skills from Arcana, Deception, History, Intimidation, Investigation, Nature, and Religion

EQUIPMENT

You start with the following equipment, in addition to the equipment granted by your background:

- (*a*) a light crossbow and 20 bolts or (*b*) any simple weapon
- (*a*) a component pouch or (*b*) an arcane focus
- (*a*) a scholar's pack or (*b*) a dungeoneer's pack
- Leather armor, any simple weapon, and two daggers

OTHERWORLDLY PATRON

At 1st level, you have struck a bargain with an otherworldly being of your choice: the Archfey, the Fiend, or the Great Old One, each of which is detailed at the end of the class description. Your choice grants you features at 1st level and again at 6th, 10th, and 14th level.

PACT MAGIC

Your arcane research and the magic bestowed on you by your patron have given you facility with spells. See chapter 10 for the general rules of spellcasting and chapter 11 for the warlock spell list.

CANTRIPS

You know two cantrips of your choice from the warlock spell list. You learn additional warlock cantrips of your choice at higher levels, as shown in the Cantrips Known column of the Warlock table.

SPELL SLOTS

The Warlock table shows how many spell slots you have. The table also shows what the level of those slots is; all of your spell slots are the same level. To cast one of your warlock spells of 1st level or higher, you must expend a spell slot. You regain all expended spell slots when you finish a short or long rest.

For example, when you are 5th level, you have two 3rd-level spell slots. To cast the 1st-level spell *thunderwave*, you must spend one of those slots, and you cast it as a 3rd-level spell.

SPELLS KNOWN OF 1ST LEVEL AND HIGHER

At 1st level, you know two 1st-level spells of your choice from the warlock spell list.

The Spells Known column of the Warlock table shows when you learn more warlock spells of your choice of 1st level and higher. A spell you choose must be of a level no higher than what's shown in the table's Slot Level column for your level. When you reach 6th level, for example, you learn a new warlock spell, which can be 1st, 2nd, or 3rd level.

Additionally, when you gain a level in this class, you can choose one of the warlock spells you know and replace it with another spell from the warlock spell list, which also must be of a level for which you have spell slots.

SPELLCASTING ABILITY

Charisma is your spellcasting ability for your warlock spells, so you use your Charisma whenever a spell refers to your spellcasting ability. In addition, you use your Charisma modifier when setting the saving throw DC for a warlock spell you cast and when making an attack roll with one.

> **Spell save DC** = 8 + your proficiency bonus + your Charisma modifier
>
> **Spell attack modifier** = your proficiency bonus + your Charisma modifier

SPELLCASTING FOCUS

You can use an arcane focus (see chapter 5, "Equipment") as a spellcasting focus for your warlock spells.

ELDRITCH INVOCATIONS

In your study of occult lore, you have unearthed eldritch invocations, fragments of forbidden knowledge that imbue you with an abiding magical ability.

At 2nd level, you gain two eldritch invocations of your choice. Your invocation options are detailed at the end of the class description. When you gain certain warlock levels, you gain additional invocations of your choice, as shown in the Invocations Known column of the Warlock table.

Additionally, when you gain a level in this class, you can choose one of the invocations you know and replace it with another invocation that you could learn at that level.

PACT BOON

At 3rd level, your otherworldly patron bestows a gift upon you for your loyal service. You gain one of the following features of your choice.

PACT OF THE CHAIN

You learn the *find familiar* spell and can cast it as a ritual. The spell doesn't count against your number of spells known.

When you cast the spell, you can choose one of the normal forms for your familiar or one of the following special forms: imp, pseudodragon, quasit, or sprite.

Additionally, when you take the Attack action, you can forgo one of your own attacks to allow your familiar to make one attack of its own with its reaction.

PACT OF THE BLADE

You can use your action to create a pact weapon in your empty hand. You can choose the form that this melee weapon takes each time you create it (see chapter 5 for weapon options). You are proficient with it while you wield it. This weapon counts as magical for the purpose of overcoming resistance and immunity to nonmagical attacks and damage.

Your pact weapon disappears if it is more than 5 feet away from you for 1 minute or more. It also disappears if you use this feature again, if you dismiss the weapon (no action required), or if you die.

You can transform one magic weapon into your pact weapon by performing a special ritual while you hold the weapon. You perform the ritual over the course of 1 hour, which can be done during a short rest. You can then dismiss the weapon, shunting it into an extradimensional space, and it appears whenever you create your pact weapon thereafter. You can't affect an artifact or a sentient weapon in this way. The weapon ceases being your pact weapon if you die, if you perform the 1-hour ritual on a different weapon, or if you use a 1-hour ritual to break your bond to it. The weapon appears at your feet if it is in the extradimensional space when the bond breaks.

Pact of the Tome

Your patron gives you a grimoire called a Book of Shadows. When you gain this feature, choose three cantrips from any class's spell list (the three needn't be from the same list). While the book is on your person, you can cast those cantrips at will. They don't count against your number of cantrips known. If they don't appear on the warlock spell list, they are nonetheless warlock spells for you.

If you lose your Book of Shadows, you can perform a 1-hour ceremony to receive a replacement from your patron. This ceremony can be performed during a short or long rest, and it destroys the previous book. The book turns to ash when you die.

Ability Score Improvement

When you reach 4th level, and again at 8th, 12th, 16th, and 19th level, you can increase one ability score of your choice by 2, or you can increase two ability scores of your choice by 1. As normal, you can't increase an ability score above 20 using this feature.

Mystic Arcanum

At 11th level, your patron bestows upon you a magical secret called an arcanum. Choose one 6th-level spell from the warlock spell list as this arcanum.

You can cast your arcanum spell once without expending a spell slot. You must finish a long rest before you can do so again.

At higher levels, you gain more warlock spells of your choice that can be cast in this way: one 7th-level spell at 13th level, one 8th-level spell at 15th level, and one 9th-level spell at 17th level. You regain all uses of your Mystic Arcanum when you finish a long rest.

Eldritch Master

At 20th level, you can draw on your inner reserve of mystical power while entreating your patron to regain expended spell slots. You can spend 1 minute entreating your patron for aid to regain all your expended spell slots from your Pact Magic feature. Once you regain spell slots with this feature, you must finish a long rest before you can do so again.

Your Pact Boon

Each Pact Boon option produces a special creature or an object that reflects your patron's nature.

Pact of the Chain. Your familiar is more cunning than a typical familiar. Its default form can be a reflection of your patron, with sprites and pseudodragons tied to the Archfey and imps and quasits tied to the Fiend. Because the Great Old One's nature is inscrutable, any familiar form is suitable for it.

Pact of the Blade. If your patron is the Archfey, your weapon might be a slender blade wrapped in leafy vines. If you serve the Fiend, your weapon could be an axe made of black metal and adorned with decorative flames. If your patron is the Great Old One, your weapon might be an ancient-looking spear, with a gemstone embedded in its head, carved to look like a terrible unblinking eye.

Pact of the Tome. Your Book of Shadows might be a fine, gilt-edged tome with spells of enchantment and illusion, gifted to you by the lordly Archfey. It could be a weighty tome bound in demon hide studded with iron, holding spells of conjuration and a wealth of forbidden lore about the sinister regions of the cosmos, a gift of the Fiend. Or it could be the tattered diary of a lunatic driven mad by contact with the Great Old One, holding scraps of spells that only your own burgeoning insanity allows you to understand and cast.

Otherworldly Patrons

The beings that serve as patrons for warlocks are mighty inhabitants of other planes of existence—not gods, but almost godlike in their power. Various patrons give their warlocks access to different powers and invocations, and expect significant favors in return.

Some patrons collect warlocks, doling out mystic knowledge relatively freely or boasting of their ability to bind mortals to their will. Other patrons bestow their power only grudgingly, and might make a pact with only one warlock. Warlocks who serve the same patron might view each other as allies, siblings, or rivals.

The Archfey

Your patron is a lord or lady of the fey, a creature of legend who holds secrets that were forgotten before the mortal races were born. This being's motivations are often inscrutable, and sometimes whimsical, and might involve a striving for greater magical power or the settling of age-old grudges. Beings of this sort include the Prince of Frost; the Queen of Air and Darkness, ruler of the Gloaming Court; Titania of the Summer Court; her consort Oberon, the Green Lord; Hyrsam, the Prince of Fools; and ancient hags.

Expanded Spell List

The Archfey lets you choose from an expanded list of spells when you learn a warlock spell. The following spells are added to the warlock spell list for you.

Archfey Expanded Spells

Spell Level	Spells
1st	*faerie fire, sleep*
2nd	*calm emotions, phantasmal force*
3rd	*blink, plant growth*
4th	*dominate beast, greater invisibility*
5th	*dominate person, seeming*

Fey Presence

Starting at 1st level, your patron bestows upon you the ability to project the beguiling and fearsome presence of the fey. As an action, you can cause each creature in a 10-foot cube originating from you to make a Wisdom saving throw against your warlock spell save DC. The creatures that fail their saving throws are all charmed or frightened by you (your choice) until the end of your next turn.

Once you use this feature, you can't use it again until you finish a short or long rest.

Misty Escape

Starting at 6th level, you can vanish in a puff of mist in response to harm. When you take damage, you can use your reaction to turn invisible and teleport up to 60 feet to an unoccupied space you can see. You remain invisible until the start of your next turn or until you attack or cast a spell.

Once you use this feature, you can't use it again until you finish a short or long rest.

Beguiling Defenses

Beginning at 10th level, your patron teaches you how to turn the mind-affecting magic of your enemies against them. You are immune to being charmed, and when another creature attempts to charm you, you can use your reaction to attempt to turn the charm back on that creature. The creature must succeed on a Wisdom saving throw against your warlock spell save DC or be charmed by you for 1 minute or until the creature takes any damage.

Dark Delirium

Starting at 14th level, you can plunge a creature into an illusory realm. As an action, choose a creature that you can see within 60 feet of you. It must make a Wisdom saving throw against your warlock spell save DC. On a failed save, it is charmed or frightened by you (your choice) for 1 minute or until your concentration is broken (as if you are concentrating on a spell). This effect ends early if the creature takes any damage.

Until this illusion ends, the creature thinks it is lost in a misty realm, the appearance of which you choose. The creature can see and hear only itself, you, and the illusion.

You must finish a short or long rest before you can use this feature again.

THE FIEND

You have made a pact with a fiend from the lower planes of existence, a being whose aims are evil, even if you strive against those aims. Such beings desire the corruption or destruction of all things, ultimately including you. Fiends powerful enough to forge a pact include demon lords such as Demogorgon, Orcus, Fraz'Urb-luu, and Baphomet; archdevils such as Asmodeus, Dispater, Mephistopheles, and Belial; pit fiends and balors that are especially mighty; and ultroloths and other lords of the yugoloths.

Expanded Spell List

The Fiend lets you choose from an expanded list of spells when you learn a warlock spell. The following spells are added to the warlock spell list for you.

Fiend Expanded Spells

Spell Level	Spells
1st	burning hands, command
2nd	blindness/deafness, scorching ray
3rd	fireball, stinking cloud
4th	fire shield, wall of fire
5th	flame strike, hallow

Dark One's Blessing

Starting at 1st level, when you reduce a hostile creature to 0 hit points, you gain temporary hit points equal to your Charisma modifier + your warlock level (minimum of 1).

Dark One's Own Luck

Starting at 6th level, you can call on your patron to alter fate in your favor. When you make an ability check or a saving throw, you can use this feature to add a d10 to your roll. You can do so after seeing the initial roll but before any of the roll's effects occur.

Once you use this feature, you can't use it again until you finish a short or long rest.

Fiendish Resilience

Starting at 10th level, you can choose one damage type when you finish a short or long rest. You gain resistance to that damage type until you choose a different one with this feature. Damage from magical weapons or silver weapons ignores this resistance.

Hurl Through Hell

Starting at 14th level, when you hit a creature with an attack, you can use this feature to instantly transport the target through the lower planes. The creature disappears and hurtles through a nightmare landscape.

At the end of your next turn, the target returns to the space it previously occupied, or the nearest unoccupied space. If the target is not a fiend, it takes 10d10 psychic damage as it reels from its horrific experience.

Once you use this feature, you can't use it again until you finish a long rest.

THE GREAT OLD ONE

Your patron is a mysterious entity whose nature is utterly foreign to the fabric of reality. It might come from the Far Realm, the space beyond reality, or it could be one of the elder gods known only in legends. Its motives are incomprehensible to mortals, and its knowledge so immense and ancient that even the greatest libraries pale in comparison to the vast secrets it holds. The Great Old One might be unaware of your existence or entirely indifferent to you, but the secrets you have learned allow you to draw your magic from it.

Entities of this type include Ghaunadar, called That Which Lurks; Tharizdun, the Chained God; Dendar, the Night Serpent; Zargon, the Returner; Great Cthulhu; and other unfathomable beings.

EXPANDED SPELL LIST

The Great Old One lets you choose from an expanded list of spells when you learn a warlock spell. The following spells are added to the warlock spell list for you.

GREAT OLD ONE EXPANDED SPELLS

Spell Level	Spells
1st	dissonant whispers, Tasha's hideous laughter
2nd	detect thoughts, phantasmal force
3rd	clairvoyance, sending
4th	dominate beast, Evard's black tentacles
5th	dominate person, telekinesis

AWAKENED MIND

Starting at 1st level, your alien knowledge gives you the ability to touch the minds of other creatures. You can telepathically speak to any creature you can see within 30 feet of you. You don't need to share a language with the creature for it to understand your telepathic utterances, but the creature must be able to understand at least one language.

ENTROPIC WARD

At 6th level, you learn to magically ward yourself against attack and to turn an enemy's failed strike into good luck for yourself. When a creature makes an attack roll against you, you can use your reaction to impose disadvantage on that roll. If the attack misses you, your next attack roll against the creature has advantage if you make it before the end of your next turn.

Once you use this feature, you can't use it again until you finish a short or long rest.

THOUGHT SHIELD

Starting at 10th level, your thoughts can't be read by telepathy or other means unless you allow it. You also have resistance to psychic damage, and whenever a creature deals psychic damage to you, that creature takes the same amount of damage that you do.

CREATE THRALL

At 14th level, you gain the ability to infect a humanoid's mind with the alien magic of your patron. You can use your action to touch an incapacitated humanoid. That creature is then charmed by you until a *remove curse* spell is cast on it, the charmed condition is removed from it, or you use this feature again.

You can communicate telepathically with the charmed creature as long as the two of you are on the same plane of existence.

ELDRITCH INVOCATIONS

If an eldritch invocation has prerequisites, you must meet them to learn it. You can learn the invocation at the same time that you meet its prerequisites. A level prerequisite refers to your level in this class.

AGONIZING BLAST

Prerequisite: eldritch blast cantrip

When you cast *eldritch blast*, add your Charisma modifier to the damage it deals on a hit.

ARMOR OF SHADOWS

You can cast *mage armor* on yourself at will, without expending a spell slot or material components.

ASCENDANT STEP

Prerequisite: 9th level

You can cast *levitate* on yourself at will, without expending a spell slot or material components.

BEAST SPEECH

You can cast *speak with animals* at will, without expending a spell slot.

BEGUILING INFLUENCE

You gain proficiency in the Deception and Persuasion skills.

BEWITCHING WHISPERS

Prerequisite: 7th level

You can cast *compulsion* once using a warlock spell slot. You can't do so again until you finish a long rest.

BOOK OF ANCIENT SECRETS

Prerequisite: Pact of the Tome feature

You can now inscribe magical rituals in your Book of Shadows. Choose two 1st-level spells that have the ritual tag from any class's spell list (the two needn't be from the same list). The spells appear in the book and don't count against the number of spells you know. With your Book of Shadows in hand, you can cast the chosen spells as rituals. You can't cast the spells except as rituals, unless you've learned them by some other means. You can also cast a warlock spell you know as a ritual if it has the ritual tag.

On your adventures, you can add other ritual spells to your Book of Shadows. When you find such a spell, you can add it to the book if the spell's level is equal to or less than half your warlock level (rounded up) and if you can spare the time to transcribe the spell. For each level of the spell, the transcription process takes 2 hours and costs 50 gp for the rare inks needed to inscribe it.

CHAINS OF CARCERI

Prerequisite: 15th level, Pact of the Chain feature

You can cast *hold monster* at will—targeting a celestial, fiend, or elemental—without expending a spell slot or material components. You must finish a long rest before you can use this invocation on the same creature again.

DEVIL'S SIGHT

You can see normally in darkness, both magical and nonmagical, to a distance of 120 feet.

DREADFUL WORD

Prerequisite: 7th level

You can cast *confusion* once using a warlock spell slot. You can't do so again until you finish a long rest.

ELDRITCH SIGHT

You can cast *detect magic* at will, without expending a spell slot.

Eldritch Spear

Prerequisite: eldritch blast cantrip

When you cast *eldritch blast*, its range is 300 feet.

Eyes of the Rune Keeper

You can read all writing.

Fiendish Vigor

You can cast *false life* on yourself at will as a 1st-level spell, without expending a spell slot or material components.

Gaze of Two Minds

You can use your action to touch a willing humanoid and perceive through its senses until the end of your next turn. As long as the creature is on the same plane of existence as you, you can use your action on subsequent turns to maintain this connection, extending the duration until the end of your next turn. While perceiving through the other creature's senses, you benefit from any special senses possessed by that creature, and you are blinded and deafened to your own surroundings.

Lifedrinker

Prerequisite: 12th level, Pact of the Blade feature

When you hit a creature with your pact weapon, the creature takes extra necrotic damage equal to your Charisma modifier (minimum 1).

Mask of Many Faces

You can cast *disguise self* at will, without expending a spell slot.

Master of Myriad Forms

Prerequisite: 15th level

You can cast *alter self* at will, without expending a spell slot.

Minions of Chaos

Prerequisite: 9th level

You can cast *conjure elemental* once using a warlock spell slot. You can't do so again until you finish a long rest.

Mire the Mind

Prerequisite: 5th level

You can cast *slow* once using a warlock spell slot. You can't do so again until you finish a long rest.

Misty Visions

You can cast *silent image* at will, without expending a spell slot or material components.

One with Shadows

Prerequisite: 5th level

When you are in an area of dim light or darkness, you can use your action to become invisible until you move or take an action or a reaction.

Otherworldly Leap

Prerequisite: 9th level

You can cast *jump* on yourself at will, without expending a spell slot or material components.

Repelling Blast

Prerequisite: eldritch blast cantrip

When you hit a creature with *eldritch blast*, you can push the creature up to 10 feet away from you in a straight line.

Sculptor of Flesh

Prerequisite: 7th level

You can cast *polymorph* once using a warlock spell slot. You can't do so again until you finish a long rest.

Sign of Ill Omen

Prerequisite: 5th level

You can cast *bestow curse* once using a warlock spell slot. You can't do so again until you finish a long rest.

Thief of Five Fates

You can cast *bane* once using a warlock spell slot. You can't do so again until you finish a long rest.

Thirsting Blade

Prerequisite: 5th level, Pact of the Blade feature

You can attack with your pact weapon twice, instead of once, whenever you take the Attack action on your turn.

Visions of Distant Realms

Prerequisite: 15th level

You can cast *arcane eye* at will, without expending a spell slot.

Voice of the Chain Master

Prerequisite: Pact of the Chain feature

You can communicate telepathically with your familiar and perceive through your familiar's senses as long as you are on the same plane of existence. Additionally, while perceiving through your familiar's senses, you can also speak through your familiar in your own voice, even if your familiar is normally incapable of speech.

Whispers of the Grave

Prerequisite: 9th level

You can cast *speak with dead* at will, without expending a spell slot.

Witch Sight

Prerequisite: 15th level

You can see the true form of any shapechanger or creature concealed by illusion or transmutation magic while the creature is within 30 feet of you and within line of sight.

WIZARD

Clad in the silver robes that denote her station, an elf closes her eyes to shut out the distractions of the battlefield and begins her quiet chant. Fingers weaving in front of her, she completes her spell and launches a tiny bead of fire toward the enemy ranks, where it erupts into a conflagration that engulfs the soldiers.

Checking and rechecking his work, a human scribes an intricate magic circle in chalk on the bare stone floor, then sprinkles powdered iron along every line and graceful curve. When the circle is complete, he drones a long incantation. A hole opens in space inside the circle, bringing a whiff of brimstone from the otherworldly plane beyond.

Crouching on the floor in a dungeon intersection, a gnome tosses a handful of small bones inscribed with mystic symbols, muttering a few words of power over them. Closing his eyes to see the visions more clearly, he nods slowly, then opens his eyes and points down the passage to his left.

Wizards are supreme magic-users, defined and united as a class by the spells they cast. Drawing on the subtle weave of magic that permeates the cosmos, wizards cast spells of explosive fire, arcing lightning, subtle deception, and brute-force mind control. Their magic conjures monsters from other planes of existence, glimpses the future, or turns slain foes into zombies. Their mightiest spells change one substance into another, call meteors down from the sky, or open portals to other worlds.

SCHOLARS OF THE ARCANE

Wild and enigmatic, varied in form and function, the power of magic draws students who seek to master its mysteries. Some aspire to become like the gods, shaping reality itself. Though the casting of a typical spell requires merely the utterance of a few strange words, fleeting gestures, and sometimes a pinch or clump of exotic materials, these surface components barely hint at the expertise attained after years of apprenticeship and countless hours of study.

Wizards live and die by their spells. Everything else is secondary. They learn new spells as they experiment and grow in experience. They can also learn them from other wizards, from ancient tomes or inscriptions, and from ancient creatures (such as the fey) that are steeped in magic.

The Wizard

Level	Proficiency Bonus	Features	Cantrips Known	Spell Slots per Spell Level								
				1st	2nd	3rd	4th	5th	6th	7th	8th	9th
1st	+2	Spellcasting, Arcane Recovery	3	2	—	—	—	—	—	—	—	—
2nd	+2	Arcane Tradition	3	3	—	—	—	—	—	—	—	—
3rd	+2	—	3	4	2	—	—	—	—	—	—	—
4th	+2	Ability Score Improvement	4	4	3	—	—	—	—	—	—	—
5th	+3	—	4	4	3	2	—	—	—	—	—	—
6th	+3	Arcane Tradition feature	4	4	3	3	—	—	—	—	—	—
7th	+3	—	4	4	3	3	1	—	—	—	—	—
8th	+3	Ability Score Improvement	4	4	3	3	2	—	—	—	—	—
9th	+4	—	4	4	3	3	3	1	—	—	—	—
10th	+4	Arcane Tradition feature	5	4	3	3	3	2	—	—	—	—
11th	+4	—	5	4	3	3	3	2	1	—	—	—
12th	+4	Ability Score Improvement	5	4	3	3	3	2	1	—	—	—
13th	+5	—	5	4	3	3	3	2	1	1	—	—
14th	+5	Arcane Tradition feature	5	4	3	3	3	2	1	1	—	—
15th	+5	—	5	4	3	3	3	2	1	1	1	—
16th	+5	Ability Score Improvement	5	4	3	3	3	2	1	1	1	—
17th	+6	—	5	4	3	3	3	2	1	1	1	1
18th	+6	Spell Mastery	5	4	3	3	3	3	1	1	1	1
19th	+6	Ability Score Improvement	5	4	3	3	3	3	2	1	1	1
20th	+6	Signature Spell	5	4	3	3	3	3	2	2	1	1

The Lure of Knowledge

Wizards' lives are seldom mundane. The closest a wizard is likely to come to an ordinary life is working as a sage or lecturer in a library or university, teaching others the secrets of the multiverse. Other wizards sell their services as diviners, serve in military forces, or pursue lives of crime or domination.

But the lure of knowledge and power calls even the most unadventurous wizards out of the safety of their libraries and laboratories and into crumbling ruins and lost cities. Most wizards believe that their counterparts in ancient civilizations knew secrets of magic that have been lost to the ages, and discovering those secrets could unlock the path to a power greater than any magic available in the present age.

Creating a Wizard

Creating a wizard character demands a backstory dominated by at least one extraordinary event. How did your character first come into contact with magic? How did you discover you had an aptitude for it? Do you have a natural talent, or did you simply study hard and practice incessantly? Did you encounter a magical creature or an ancient tome that taught you the basics of magic?

What drew you forth from your life of study? Did your first taste of magical knowledge leave you hungry for more? Have you received word of a secret repository of knowledge not yet plundered by any other wizard? Perhaps you're simply eager to put your newfound magical skills to the test in the face of danger.

Quick Build

You can make a wizard quickly by following these suggestions. First, Intelligence should be your highest ability score, followed by Constitution or Dexterity. If you plan to join the School of Enchantment, make Charisma your next-best score. Second, choose the sage background. Third, choose the *mage hand, light,* and *ray of frost* cantrips, along with the following 1st-level spells for your spellbook: *burning hands, charm person, feather fall, mage armor, magic missile,* and *sleep.*

Class Features

As a wizard, you gain the following class features.

Hit Points

Hit Dice: 1d6 per wizard level
Hit Points at 1st Level: 6 + your Constitution modifier
Hit Points at Higher Levels: 1d6 (or 4) + your Constitution modifier per wizard level after 1st

Proficiencies

Armor: None
Weapons: Daggers, darts, slings, quarterstaffs, light crossbows
Tools: None

Saving Throws: Intelligence, Wisdom
Skills: Choose two from Arcana, History, Insight, Investigation, Medicine, and Religion

Equipment

You start with the following equipment, in addition to the equipment granted by your background:

- (a) a quarterstaff or (b) a dagger
- (a) a component pouch or (b) an arcane focus
- (a) a scholar's pack or (b) an explorer's pack
- A spellbook

Spellcasting

As a student of arcane magic, you have a spellbook containing spells that show the first glimmerings of your true power. See chapter 10 for the general rules of spellcasting and chapter 11 for the wizard spell list.

Cantrips

At 1st level, you know three cantrips of your choice from the wizard spell list. You learn additional wizard cantrips of your choice at higher levels, as shown in the Cantrips Known column of the Wizard table.

> ### Your Spellbook
>
> The spells that you add to your spellbook as you gain levels reflect the arcane research you conduct on your own, as well as intellectual breakthroughs you have had about the nature of the multiverse. You might find other spells during your adventures. You could discover a spell recorded on a scroll in an evil wizard's chest, for example, or in a dusty tome in an ancient library.
>
> ***Copying a Spell into the Book.*** When you find a wizard spell of 1st level or higher, you can add it to your spellbook if it is of a spell level you can prepare and if you can spare the time to decipher and copy it.
>
> Copying that spell into your spellbook involves reproducing the basic form of the spell, then deciphering the unique system of notation used by the wizard who wrote it. You must practice the spell until you understand the sounds or gestures required, then transcribe it into your spellbook using your own notation.
>
> For each level of the spell, the process takes 2 hours and costs 50 gp. The cost represents material components you expend as you experiment with the spell to master it, as well as the fine inks you need to record it. Once you have spent this time and money, you can prepare the spell just like your other spells.
>
> ***Replacing the Book.*** You can copy a spell from your own spellbook into another book—for example, if you want to make a backup copy of your spellbook. This is just like copying a new spell into your spellbook, but faster and easier, since you understand your own notation and already know how to cast the spell. You need spend only 1 hour and 10 gp for each level of the copied spell.
>
> If you lose your spellbook, you can use the same procedure to transcribe the spells that you have prepared into a new spellbook. Filling out the remainder of your spellbook requires you to find new spells to do so, as normal. For this reason, many wizards keep backup spellbooks in a safe place.
>
> ***The Book's Appearance.*** Your spellbook is a unique compilation of spells, with its own decorative flourishes and margin notes. It might be a plain, functional leather volume that you received as a gift from your master, a finely bound gilt-edged tome you found in an ancient library, or even a loose collection of notes scrounged together after you lost your previous spellbook in a mishap.

Spellbook

At 1st level, you have a spellbook containing six 1st-level wizard spells of your choice. Your spellbook is the repository of the wizard spells you know, except your cantrips, which are fixed in your mind.

Preparing and Casting Spells

The Wizard table shows how many spell slots you have to cast your spells of 1st level and higher. To cast one of these spells, you must expend a slot of the spell's level or higher. You regain all expended spell slots when you finish a long rest.

You prepare the list of wizard spells that are available for you to cast. To do so, choose a number of wizard spells from your spellbook equal to your Intelligence modifier + your wizard level (minimum of one spell). The spells must be of a level for which you have spell slots.

For example, if you're a 3rd-level wizard, you have four 1st-level and two 2nd-level spell slots. With an Intelligence of 16, your list of prepared spells can include six spells of 1st or 2nd level, in any combination, chosen from your spellbook. If you prepare the 1st-level spell *magic missile*, you can cast it using a 1st-level or a 2nd-level slot. Casting the spell doesn't remove it from your list of prepared spells.

You can change your list of prepared spells when you finish a long rest. Preparing a new list of wizard spells requires time spent studying your spellbook and memorizing the incantations and gestures you must make to cast the spell: at least 1 minute per spell level for each spell on your list.

Spellcasting Ability

Intelligence is your spellcasting ability for your wizard spells, since you learn your spells through dedicated study and memorization. You use your Intelligence whenever a spell refers to your spellcasting ability. In addition, you use your Intelligence modifier when setting the saving throw DC for a wizard spell you cast and when making an attack roll with one.

Spell save DC = 8 + your proficiency bonus + your Intelligence modifier

Spell attack modifier = your proficiency bonus + your Intelligence modifier

Ritual Casting

You can cast a wizard spell as a ritual if that spell has the ritual tag and you have the spell in your spellbook. You don't need to have the spell prepared.

Spellcasting Focus

You can use an arcane focus (see chapter 5, "Equipment") as a spellcasting focus for your wizard spells.

Learning Spells of 1st Level and Higher

Each time you gain a wizard level, you can add two wizard spells of your choice to your spellbook for free. Each of these spells must be of a level for which you have spell slots, as shown on the Wizard table. On your adventures, you might find other spells that you can add to your spellbook (see the "Your Spellbook" sidebar).

Arcane Recovery

You have learned to regain some of your magical energy by studying your spellbook. Once per day when you finish a short rest, you can choose expended spell slots to recover. The spell slots can have a combined level that is equal to or less than half your wizard level (rounded up), and none of the slots can be 6th level or higher.

For example, if you're a 4th-level wizard, you can recover up to two levels worth of spell slots. You can recover either a 2nd-level spell slot or two 1st-level spell slots.

Arcane Tradition

When you reach 2nd level, you choose an arcane tradition, shaping your practice of magic through one of eight schools: Abjuration, Conjuration, Divination, Enchantment, Evocation, Illusion, Necromancy, or Transmutation, all detailed at the end of the class description.

Your choice grants you features at 2nd level and again at 6th, 10th, and 14th level.

Ability Score Improvement

When you reach 4th level, and again at 8th, 12th, 16th, and 19th level, you can increase one ability score of your choice by 2, or you can increase two ability scores of your choice by 1. As normal, you can't increase an ability score above 20 using this feature.

Spell Mastery

At 18th level, you have achieved such mastery over certain spells that you can cast them at will. Choose a 1st-level wizard spell and a 2nd-level wizard spell that are in your spellbook. You can cast those spells at their lowest level without expending a spell slot when you have them prepared. If you want to cast either spell at a higher level, you must expend a spell slot as normal.

By spending 8 hours in study, you can exchange one or both of the spells you chose for different spells of the same levels.

Signature Spells

When you reach 20th level, you gain mastery over two powerful spells and can cast them with little effort. Choose two 3rd-level wizard spells in your spellbook as your signature spells. You always have these spells prepared, they don't count against the number of spells you have prepared, and you can cast each of them once at 3rd level without expending a spell slot. When you do so, you can't do so again until you finish a short or long rest.

If you want to cast either spell at a higher level, you must expend a spell slot as normal.

Arcane Traditions

The study of wizardry is ancient, stretching back to the earliest mortal discoveries of magic. It is firmly established in the worlds of D&D, with various traditions dedicated to its complex study.

The most common arcane traditions in the multiverse revolve around the schools of magic. Wizards through the ages have cataloged thousands of spells, grouping them into eight categories called schools, as described in chapter 10. In some places, these traditions are literally schools; a wizard might study at the School of Illusion while another studies across town at the School of Enchantment. In other institutions, the schools are more like academic departments, with rival faculties competing for students and funding. Even wizards who train apprentices in the solitude of their own towers use the division of magic into schools as a learning device, since the spells of each school require mastery of different techniques.

School of Abjuration

The School of Abjuration emphasizes magic that blocks, banishes, or protects. Detractors of this school say that its tradition is about denial, negation rather than positive assertion. You understand, however, that ending harmful effects, protecting the weak, and banishing evil influences is anything but a philosophical void. It is a proud and respected vocation.

Called abjurers, members of this school are sought when baleful spirits require exorcism, when important locations must be guarded against magical spying, and when portals to other planes of existence must be closed.

Abjuration Savant

Beginning when you select this school at 2nd level, the gold and time you must spend to copy an abjuration spell into your spellbook is halved.

Arcane Ward

Starting at 2nd level, you can weave magic around yourself for protection. When you cast an abjuration spell of 1st level or higher, you can simultaneously use a strand of the spell's magic to create a magical ward on yourself that lasts until you finish a long rest. The ward has a hit point maximum equal to twice your wizard level + your Intelligence modifier. Whenever you take damage, the ward takes the damage instead. If this damage reduces the ward to 0 hit points, you take any remaining damage.

While the ward has 0 hit points, it can't absorb damage, but its magic remains. Whenever you cast an abjuration spell of 1st level or higher, the ward regains a number of hit points equal to twice the level of the spell.

Once you create the ward, you can't create it again until you finish a long rest.

Projected Ward

Starting at 6th level, when a creature that you can see within 30 feet of you takes damage, you can use your reaction to cause your Arcane Ward to absorb that damage. If this damage reduces the ward to 0 hit points, the warded creature takes any remaining damage.

Improved Abjuration

Beginning at 10th level, when you cast an abjuration spell that requires you to make an ability check as a part of casting that spell (as in *counterspell* and *dispel magic*), you add your proficiency bonus to that ability check.

object that you have seen. The object is visibly magical, radiating dim light out to 5 feet.

The object disappears after 1 hour, when you use this feature again, or if it takes any damage.

BENIGN TRANSPOSITION

Starting at 6th level, you can use your action to teleport up to 30 feet to an unoccupied space that you can see. Alternatively, you can choose a space within range that is occupied by a Small or Medium creature. If that creature is willing, you both teleport, swapping places.

Once you use this feature, you can't use it again until you finish a long rest or you cast a conjuration spell of 1st level or higher.

FOCUSED CONJURATION

Beginning at 10th level, while you are concentrating on a conjuration spell, your concentration can't be broken as a result of taking damage.

DURABLE SUMMONS

Starting at 14th level, any creature that you summon or create with a conjuration spell has 30 temporary hit points.

SCHOOL OF DIVINATION

The counsel of a diviner is sought by royalty and commoners alike, for all seek a clearer understanding of the past, present, and future. As a diviner, you strive to part the veils of space, time, and consciousness so that you can see clearly. You work to master spells of discernment, remote viewing, supernatural knowledge, and foresight.

DIVINATION SAVANT

Beginning when you select this school at 2nd level, the gold and time you must spend to copy a divination spell into your spellbook is halved.

PORTENT

Starting at 2nd level when you choose this school, glimpses of the future begin to press in on your awareness. When you finish a long rest, roll two d20s and record the numbers rolled. You can replace any attack roll, saving throw, or ability check made by you or a creature that you can see with one of these foretelling rolls. You must choose to do so before the roll, and you can replace a roll in this way only once per turn.

Each foretelling roll can be used only once. When you finish a long rest, you lose any unused foretelling rolls.

EXPERT DIVINATION

Beginning at 6th level, casting divination spells comes so easily to you that it expends only a fraction of your spellcasting efforts. When you cast a divination spell of 2nd level or higher using a spell slot, you regain one expended spell slot. The slot you regain must be of a level lower than the spell you cast and can't be higher than 5th level.

THE THIRD EYE

Starting at 10th level, you can use your action to increase your powers of perception. When you do so,

SPELL RESISTANCE

Starting at 14th level, you have advantage on saving throws against spells.

Furthermore, you have resistance against the damage of spells.

SCHOOL OF CONJURATION

As a conjurer, you favor spells that produce objects and creatures out of thin air. You can conjure billowing clouds of killing fog or summon creatures from elsewhere to fight on your behalf. As your mastery grows, you learn spells of transportation and can teleport yourself across vast distances, even to other planes of existence, in an instant.

CONJURATION SAVANT

Beginning when you select this school at 2nd level, the gold and time you must spend to copy a conjuration spell into your spellbook is halved.

MINOR CONJURATION

Starting at 2nd level when you select this school, you can use your action to conjure up an inanimate object in your hand or on the ground in an unoccupied space that you can see within 10 feet of you. This object can be no larger than 3 feet on a side and weigh no more than 10 pounds, and its form must be that of a nonmagical choose one of the following benefits, which lasts until you are incapacitated or you take a short or long rest. You can't use the feature again until you finish a rest.

Darkvision. You gain darkvision out to a range of 60 feet, as described in chapter 8, "Adventuring."

Ethereal Sight. You can see into the Ethereal Plane within 60 feet of you.

Greater Comprehension. You can read any language.

See Invisibility. You can see invisible creatures and objects within 10 feet of you that are within line of sight.

GREATER PORTENT

Starting at 14th level, the visions in your dreams intensify and paint a more accurate picture in your mind of what is to come. You roll three d20s for your Portent feature, rather than two.

SCHOOL OF ENCHANTMENT

As a member of the School of Enchantment, you have honed your ability to magically entrance and beguile other people and monsters. Some enchanters are peacemakers who bewitch the violent to lay down their arms and charm the cruel into showing mercy. Others are tyrants who magically bind the unwilling into their service. Most enchanters fall somewhere in between.

ENCHANTMENT SAVANT

Beginning when you select this school at 2nd level, the gold and time you must spend to copy an enchantment spell into your spellbook is halved.

HYPNOTIC GAZE

Starting at 2nd level when you choose this school, your soft words and enchanting gaze can magically enthrall another creature. As an action, choose one creature that you can see within 5 feet of you. If the target can see or hear you, it must succeed on a Wisdom saving throw against your wizard spell save DC or be charmed by you until the end of your next turn. The charmed creature's speed drops to 0, and the creature is incapacitated and visibly dazed.

On subsequent turns, you can use your action to maintain this effect, extending its duration until the end of your next turn. However, the effect ends if you move more than 5 feet away from the creature, if the creature can neither see nor hear you, or if the creature takes damage.

Once the effect ends, or if the creature succeeds on its initial saving throw against this effect, you can't use this feature on that creature again until you finish a long rest.

INSTINCTIVE CHARM

Beginning at 6th level, when a creature you can see within 30 feet of you makes an attack roll against you, you can use your reaction to divert the attack, provided that another creature is within the attack's range. The attacker must make a Wisdom saving throw against your wizard spell save DC. On a failed save, the attacker must target the creature that is closest to it, not including you or itself. If multiple creatures are closest, the attacker chooses which one to target.

On a successful save, you can't use this feature on the attacker again until you finish a long rest.

You must choose to use this feature before knowing whether the attack hits or misses. Creatures that can't be charmed are immune to this effect.

SPLIT ENCHANTMENT

Starting at 10th level, when you cast an enchantment spell of 1st level or higher that targets only one creature, you can have it target a second creature.

ALTER MEMORIES

At 14th level, you gain the ability to make a creature unaware of your magical influence on it. When you cast an enchantment spell to charm one or more creatures, you can alter one creature's understanding so that it remains unaware of being charmed.

Additionally, once before the spell expires, you can use your action to try to make the chosen creature forget some of the time it spent charmed. The creature must succeed on an Intelligence saving throw against your wizard spell save DC or lose a number of hours of its memories equal to 1 + your Charisma modifier (minimum 1). You can make the creature forget less time, and the amount of time can't exceed the duration of your enchantment spell.

SCHOOL OF EVOCATION

You focus your study on magic that creates powerful elemental effects such as bitter cold, searing flame, rolling thunder, crackling lightning, and burning acid. Some evokers find employment in military forces, serving as artillery to blast enemy armies from afar. Others use their spectacular power to protect the weak, while some seek their own gain as bandits, adventurers, or aspiring tyrants.

EVOCATION SAVANT

Beginning when you select this school at 2nd level, the gold and time you must spend to copy an evocation spell into your spellbook is halved.

SCULPT SPELLS

Beginning at 2nd level, you can create pockets of relative safety within the effects of your evocation spells. When you cast an evocation spell that affects other creatures that you can see, you can choose a number of them equal to 1 + the spell's level. The chosen creatures automatically succeed on their saving throws against the spell, and they take no damage if they would normally take half damage on a successful save.

POTENT CANTRIP

Starting at 6th level, your damaging cantrips affect even creatures that avoid the brunt of the effect. When a creature succeeds on a saving throw against your cantrip, the creature takes half the cantrip's damage (if any) but suffers no additional effect from the cantrip.

EMPOWERED EVOCATION

Beginning at 10th level, you can add your Intelligence modifier to one damage roll of any wizard evocation spell you cast.

Overchannel

Starting at 14th level, you can increase the power of your simpler spells. When you cast a wizard spell of 1st through 5th level that deals damage, you can deal maximum damage with that spell.

The first time you do so, you suffer no adverse effect. If you use this feature again before you finish a long rest, you take 2d12 necrotic damage for each level of the spell, immediately after you cast it. Each time you use this feature again before finishing a long rest, the necrotic damage per spell level increases by 1d12. This damage ignores resistance and immunity.

School of Illusion

You focus your studies on magic that dazzles the senses, befuddles the mind, and tricks even the wisest folk. Your magic is subtle, but the illusions crafted by your keen mind make the impossible seem real. Some illusionists—including many gnome wizards—are benign tricksters who use their spells to entertain. Others are more sinister masters of deception, using their illusions to frighten and fool others for their personal gain.

Illusion Savant

Beginning when you select this school at 2nd level, the gold and time you must spend to copy an illusion spell into your spellbook is halved.

Improved Minor Illusion

When you choose this school at 2nd level, you learn the *minor illusion* cantrip. If you already know this cantrip, you learn a different wizard cantrip of your choice. The cantrip doesn't count against your number of cantrips known.

When you cast *minor illusion,* you can create both a sound and an image with a single casting of the spell.

Malleable Illusions

Starting at 6th level, when you cast an illusion spell that has a duration of 1 minute or longer, you can use your action to change the nature of that illusion (using the spell's normal parameters for the illusion), provided that you can see the illusion.

Illusory Self

Beginning at 10th level, you can create an illusory duplicate of yourself as an instant, almost instinctual reaction to danger. When a creature makes an attack roll against you, you can use your reaction to interpose the illusory duplicate between the attacker and yourself. The attack automatically misses you, then the illusion dissipates.

Once you use this feature, you can't use it again until you finish a short or long rest.

Illusory Reality

By 14th level, you have learned the secret of weaving shadow magic into your illusions to give them a semi-reality. When you cast an illusion spell of 1st level or higher, you can choose one inanimate, nonmagical object that is part of the illusion and make that object real. You can do this on your turn as a bonus action while the spell is ongoing. The object remains real for 1 minute. For example, you can create an illusion of a bridge over a chasm and then make it real long enough for your allies to cross.

The object can't deal damage or otherwise directly harm anyone.

School of Necromancy

The School of Necromancy explores the cosmic forces of life, death, and undeath. As you focus your studies in this tradition, you learn to manipulate the energy that animates all living things. As you progress, you learn to sap the life force from a creature as your magic destroys its body, transforming that vital energy into magical power you can manipulate.

Most people see necromancers as menacing, or even villainous, due to the close association with death. Not all necromancers are evil, but the forces they manipulate are considered taboo by many societies.

Necromancy Savant

Beginning when you select this school at 2nd level, the gold and time you must spend to copy a necromancy spell into your spellbook is halved.

Grim Harvest

At 2nd level, you gain the ability to reap life energy from creatures you kill with your spells. Once per turn when you kill one or more creatures with a spell of 1st level or higher, you regain hit points equal to twice the spell's level, or three times its level if the spell belongs to the School of Necromancy. You don't gain this benefit for killing constructs or undead.

Undead Thralls

At 6th level, you add the *animate dead* spell to your spellbook if it is not there already. When you cast *animate dead,* you can target one additional corpse or pile of bones, creating another zombie or skeleton, as appropriate.

Whenever you create an undead using a necromancy spell, it has additional benefits:

- The creature's hit point maximum is increased by an amount equal to your wizard level.
- The creature adds your proficiency bonus to its weapon damage rolls.

Inured to Undeath

Beginning at 10th level, you have resistance to necrotic damage, and your hit point maximum can't be reduced. You have spent so much time dealing with undead and the forces that animate them that you have become inured to some of their worst effects.

Command Undead

Starting at 14th level, you can use magic to bring undead under your control, even those created by other wizards. As an action, you can choose one undead that you can see within 60 feet of you. That creature must make a Charisma saving throw against your wizard spell save DC. If it succeeds, you can't use this feature on it again. If it fails, it becomes friendly to you and obeys your commands until you use this feature again.

Intelligent undead are harder to control in this way. If the target has an Intelligence of 8 or higher, it has advantage on the saving throw. If it fails the saving throw and has an Intelligence of 12 or higher, it can repeat the saving throw at the end of every hour until it succeeds and breaks free.

School of Transmutation

You are a student of spells that modify energy and matter. To you, the world is not a fixed thing, but eminently mutable, and you delight in being an agent of change. You wield the raw stuff of creation and learn to alter both physical forms and mental qualities. Your magic gives you the tools to become a smith on reality's forge.

Some transmuters are tinkerers and pranksters, turning people into toads and transforming copper into silver for fun and occasional profit. Others pursue their magical studies with deadly seriousness, seeking the power of the gods to make and destroy worlds.

Transmutation Savant

Beginning when you select this school at 2nd level, the gold and time you must spend to copy a transmutation spell into your spellbook is halved.

Minor Alchemy

Starting at 2nd level when you select this school, you can temporarily alter the physical properties of one nonmagical object, changing it from one substance into another. You perform a special alchemical procedure on one object composed entirely of wood, stone (but not a gemstone), iron, copper, or silver, transforming it into a different one of those materials. For each 10 minutes you spend performing the procedure, you can transform up to 1 cubic foot of material. After 1 hour, or until you lose your concentration (as if you were concentrating on a spell), the material reverts to its original substance.

Transmuter's Stone

Starting at 6th level, you can spend 8 hours creating a transmuter's stone that stores transmutation magic. You can benefit from the stone yourself or give it to another creature. A creature gains a benefit of your choice as long as the stone is in the creature's possession. When you create the stone, choose the benefit from the following options:

- Darkvision out to a range of 60 feet, as described in chapter 8, "Adventuring"
- An increase to speed of 10 feet while the creature is unencumbered
- Proficiency in Constitution saving throws
- Resistance to acid, cold, fire, lightning, or thunder damage (your choice whenever you choose this benefit)

Each time you cast a transmutation spell of 1st level or higher, you can change the effect of your stone if the stone is on your person.

If you create a new transmuter's stone, the previous one ceases to function.

Shapechanger

At 10th level, you add the *polymorph* spell to your spellbook, if it is not there already. You can cast *polymorph* without expending a spell slot. When you do so, you can target only yourself and transform into a beast whose challenge rating is 1 or lower.

Once you cast *polymorph* in this way, you can't do so again until you finish a short or long rest, though you can still cast it normally using an available spell slot.

Master Transmuter

Starting at 14th level, you can use your action to consume the reserve of transmutation magic stored within your transmuter's stone in a single burst. When you do so, choose one of the following effects. Your transmuter's stone is destroyed and can't be remade until you finish a long rest.

Major Transformation. You can transmute one nonmagical object—no larger than a 5-foot cube—into another nonmagical object of similar size and mass and of equal or lesser value. You must spend 10 minutes handling the object to transform it.

Panacea. You remove all curses, diseases, and poisons affecting a creature that you touch with the transmuter's stone. The creature also regains all its hit points.

Restore Life. You cast the *raise dead* spell on a creature you touch with the transmuter's stone, without expending a spell slot or needing to have the spell in your spellbook.

Restore Youth. You touch the transmuter's stone to a willing creature, and that creature's apparent age is reduced by 3d10 years, to a minimum of 13 years. This effect doesn't extend the creature's lifespan.

CHAPTER 4: PERSONALITY AND BACKGROUND

HARACTERS ARE DEFINED BY MUCH MORE THAN their race and class. They're individuals with their own stories, interests, connections, and capabilities beyond those that class and race define. This chapter expounds on the details that distinguish characters from one another, including the basics of name and physical description, the rules of backgrounds and languages, and the finer points of personality and alignment.

CHARACTER DETAILS

Your character's name and physical description might be the first things that the other players at the table learn about you. It's worth thinking about how these characteristics reflect the character you have in mind.

NAME

Your character's race description includes sample names for members of that race. Put some thought into your name even if you're just picking one from a list.

SEX

You can play a male or female character without gaining any special benefits or hindrances. Think about how your character does or does not conform to the broader culture's expectations of sex, gender, and sexual behavior. For example, a male drow cleric defies the traditional gender divisions of drow society, which could be a reason for your character to leave that society and come to the surface.

TIKA AND ARTEMIS: CONTRASTING CHARACTERS

The details in this chapter make a big difference in setting your character apart from every other character. Consider the following two human fighters.

Hailing from the Dragonlance setting, Tika Waylan was a brash teenager who had a rough childhood. The daughter of a thief, she ran away from home and practiced her father's trade on the streets of Solace. When she tried to rob the proprietor of the Inn of the Last Home, he caught her and took her under his wing, giving her a job as a barmaid. But when the dragonarmies laid waste to the town of Solace and destroyed the inn, necessity forced Tika into adventure alongside the friends she'd known from her childhood. Her skill as a fighter (a frying pan remains one of her favorite weapons) combined with her history on the streets gave her skills invaluable in her adventuring career.

Artemis Entreri grew up on the streets of Calimport in the Forgotten Realms. He used his wits, strength, and agility to carve out his own territory in one of the city's hundreds of poor shanty towns. After several years, he attracted the notice of one of the most powerful thieves' guilds in the city, and he ascended the ranks of the guild quickly despite his youth. Artemis became the favored assassin of one of the city's pashas, who sent him to far-off Icewind Dale to recover some stolen gems. He's a professional killer, constantly challenging himself to improve his skills.

Tika and Artemis are both human and both fighters (with some experience as rogues), possessing similarly high Strength and Dexterity scores, but there the similarity ends.

You don't need to be confined to binary notions of sex and gender. The elf god Corellon Larethian is often seen as androgynous, for example, and some elves in the multiverse are made in Corellon's image. You could also play a female character who presents herself as a man, a man who feels trapped in a female body, or a bearded female dwarf who hates being mistaken for a male. Likewise, your character's sexual orientation is for you to decide.

HEIGHT AND WEIGHT

You can decide your character's height and weight, using the information provided in your race description or on the Random Height and Weight table. Think about what your character's ability scores might say about his or her height and weight. A weak but agile character might be thin. A strong and tough character might be tall or just heavy.

If you want to, you can roll randomly for your character's height and weight using the Random Height and Weight table. The dice roll given in the Height Modifier column determines the character's extra height (in inches) beyond the base height. That same number multiplied by the dice roll or quantity given in the Weight Modifier column determines the character's extra weight (in pounds) beyond the base weight.

RANDOM HEIGHT AND WEIGHT

Race	Base Height	Height Modifier	Base Weight	Weight Modifier
Human	4'8"	+2d10	110 lb.	× (2d4) lb.
Dwarf, hill	3'8"	+2d4	115 lb.	× (2d6) lb.
Dwarf, mountain	4'	+2d4	130 lb.	× (2d6) lb.
Elf, high	4'6"	+2d10	90 lb.	× (1d4) lb.
Elf, wood	4'6"	+2d10	100 lb.	× (1d4) lb.
Elf, drow	4'5"	+2d6	75 lb.	× (1d6) lb.
Halfling	2'7"	+2d4	35 lb.	× 1 lb.
Dragonborn	5'6"	+2d8	175 lb.	× (2d6) lb.
Gnome	2'11"	+2d4	35 lb.	× 1 lb.
Half-elf	4'9"	+2d8	110 lb.	× (2d4) lb.
Half-orc	4'10"	+2d10	140 lb.	× (2d6) lb.
Tiefling	4'9"	+2d8	110 lb.	× (2d4) lb.

For example, as a human, Tika has a height of 4 feet 8 inches plus 2d10 inches. Her player rolls 2d10 and gets a total of 12, so Tika stands 5 feet 8 inches tall. Then the player uses that same roll of 12 and multiplies it by 2d4 pounds. Her 2d4 roll is 3, so Tika weighs an extra 36 pounds (12 × 3) on top of her base 110 pounds, for a total of 146 pounds.

OTHER PHYSICAL CHARACTERISTICS

You choose your character's age and the color of his or her hair, eyes, and skin. To add a touch of distinctiveness, you might want to give your character an unusual or memorable physical characteristic, such as a scar, a limp, or a tattoo.

Tika and Artemis: Character Details

Consider how the names Tika Waylan and Artemis Entreri set these characters apart from each other and reflect their personalities. Tika is a young woman determined to prove that she's not just a kid any more, and her name makes her sound young and ordinary. Artemis Entreri comes from an exotic land and carries a more mysterious name.

Tika is nineteen years old at the start of her adventuring career and has auburn hair, green eyes, fair skin with freckles, and a mole on her right hip. Artemis is a small man, compact and all wiry muscle. He has angular features and high cheekbones, and he always seems in need of a shave. His raven-black hair is thick and full, but his eyes are gray and lifeless—betraying the emptiness of his life and soul.

Alignment

A typical creature in the worlds of Dungeons & Dragons has an alignment, which broadly describes its moral and personal attitudes. Alignment is a combination of two factors: one identifies morality (good, evil, or neutral), and the other describes attitudes toward society and order (lawful, chaotic, or neutral). Thus, nine distinct alignments define the possible combinations.

These brief summaries of the nine alignments describe the typical behavior of a creature with that alignment. Individuals might vary significantly from that typical behavior, and few people are perfectly and consistently faithful to the precepts of their alignment.

Lawful good (LG) creatures can be counted on to do the right thing as expected by society. Gold dragons, paladins, and most dwarves are lawful good.

Neutral good (NG) folk do the best they can to help others according to their needs. Many celestials, some cloud giants, and most gnomes are neutral good.

Chaotic good (CG) creatures act as their conscience directs, with little regard for what others expect. Copper dragons, many elves, and unicorns are chaotic good.

Lawful neutral (LN) individuals act in accordance with law, tradition, or personal codes. Many monks and some wizards are lawful neutral.

Neutral (N) is the alignment of those who prefer to steer clear of moral questions and don't take sides, doing what seems best at the time. Lizardfolk, most druids, and many humans are neutral.

Chaotic neutral (CN) creatures follow their whims, holding their personal freedom above all else. Many barbarians and rogues, and some bards, are chaotic neutral.

Lawful evil (LE) creatures methodically take what they want, within the limits of a code of tradition, loyalty, or order. Devils, blue dragons, and hobgoblins are lawful evil.

Neutral evil (NE) is the alignment of those who do whatever they can get away with, without compassion or qualms. Many drow, some cloud giants, and yugoloths are neutral evil.

Chaotic evil (CE) creatures act with arbitrary violence, spurred by their greed, hatred, or bloodlust. Demons, red dragons, and orcs are chaotic evil.

Alignment in the Multiverse

For many thinking creatures, alignment is a moral choice. Humans, dwarves, elves, and other humanoid races can choose whether to follow the paths of good or evil, law or chaos. According to myth, the good-aligned gods who created these races gave them free will to choose their moral paths, knowing that good without free will is slavery.

The evil deities who created other races, though, made those races to serve them. Those races have strong inborn tendencies that match the nature of their gods. Most orcs share the violent, savage nature of the orc god, Gruumsh, and are thus inclined toward evil. Even if an orc chooses a good alignment, it struggles against its innate tendencies for its entire life. (Even half-orcs feel the lingering pull of the orc god's influence.)

Alignment is an essential part of the nature of celestials and fiends. A devil does not choose to be lawful evil, and it doesn't tend toward lawful evil, but rather it is lawful evil in its essence. If it somehow ceased to be lawful evil, it would cease to be a devil.

Most creatures that lack the capacity for rational thought do not have alignments—they are **unaligned**. Such a creature is incapable of making a moral or ethical choice and acts according to its bestial nature. Sharks are savage predators, for example, but they are not evil; they have no alignment.

Dwarvish Script: Sample Alphabet

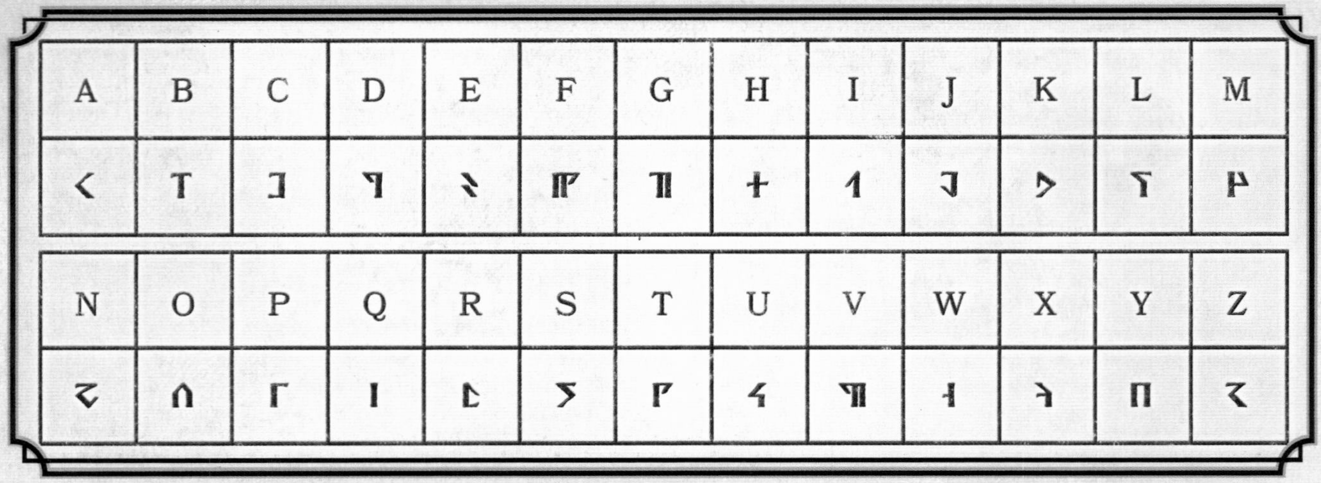
A B C D E F G H I J K L M
N O P Q R S T U V W X Y Z

LANGUAGES

Your race indicates the languages your character can speak by default, and your background might give you access to one or more additional languages of your choice. Note these languages on your character sheet.

Choose your languages from the Standard Languages table, or choose one that is common in your campaign. With your DM's permission, you can instead choose a language from the Exotic Languages table or a secret language, such as thieves' cant or the tongue of druids.

Some of these languages are actually families of languages with many dialects. For example, the Primordial language includes the Auran, Aquan, Ignan, and Terran dialects, one for each of the four elemental planes. Creatures that speak different dialects of the same language can communicate with one another.

STANDARD LANGUAGES

Language	Typical Speakers	Script
Common	Humans	Common
Dwarvish	Dwarves	Dwarvish
Elvish	Elves	Elvish
Giant	Ogres, giants	Dwarvish
Gnomish	Gnomes	Dwarvish
Goblin	Goblinoids	Dwarvish
Halfling	Halflings	Common
Orc	Orcs	Dwarvish

EXOTIC LANGUAGES

Language	Typical Speakers	Script
Abyssal	Demons	Infernal
Celestial	Celestials	Celestial
Draconic	Dragons, dragonborn	Draconic
Deep Speech	Mind flayers, beholders	—
Infernal	Devils	Infernal
Primordial	Elementals	Dwarvish
Sylvan	Fey creatures	Elvish
Undercommon	Underdark traders	Elvish

TIKA AND ARTEMIS: ALIGNMENT

Tika Waylan is neutral good, fundamentally good-hearted and striving to help others where she can. Artemis is lawful evil, unconcerned with the value of sentient life but at least professional in his approach to murder.

As an evil character, Artemis is not an ideal adventurer. He began his career as a villain, and only cooperates with heroes when he must—and when it's in his own best interests. In most games, evil adventurers cause problems in groups alongside others who don't share their interests and objectives. Generally, evil alignments are for villains and monsters.

PERSONAL CHARACTERISTICS

Fleshing out your character's personality—the array of traits, mannerisms, habits, beliefs, and flaws that give a person a unique identity—will help you bring him or her to life as you play the game. Four categories of characteristics are presented here: personality traits, ideals, bonds, and flaws. Beyond those categories, think about your character's favorite words or phrases, tics and habitual gestures, vices and pet peeves, and whatever else you can imagine.

Each background presented later in this chapter includes suggested characteristics that you can use to spark your imagination. You're not bound to those options, but they're a good starting point.

PERSONALITY TRAITS

Give your character two personality traits. Personality traits are small, simple ways to help you set your character apart from every other character. Your personality traits should tell you something interesting and fun about your character. They should be self-descriptions that are specific about what makes your character stand out. "I'm smart" is not a good trait, because it describes a lot of characters. "I've read every book in Candlekeep" tells you something specific about your character's interests and disposition.

Personality traits might describe the things your character likes, his or her past accomplishments, things your character dislikes or fears, your character's self-attitude or mannerisms, or the influence of his or her ability scores.

ELVISH SCRIPT: SAMPLE ALPHABET

Tika and Artemis: Personal Characteristics

Tika and Artemis have distinct personality traits. Tika Waylan dislikes boastfulness and has a fear of heights resulting from a bad fall during her career as a thief. Artemis Entreri is always prepared for the worst and moves with a quick, precise confidence.

Consider their ideals. Tika Waylan is innocent, almost childlike, believing in the value of life and the importance of appreciating everyone. Neutral good in alignment, she cleaves to ideals of life and respect. Artemis Entreri never allows his emotions to master him, and he constantly challenges himself to improve his skills. His lawful evil alignment gives him ideals of impartiality and a lust for power.

Tika Waylan's bond is to the Inn of the Last Home. The inn's proprietor gave her a new chance at life, and her friendship with her adventuring companions was forged during her time working there. Its destruction by the marauding dragonarmies gives Tika a very personal reason to hate them with a fiery passion. Her bond might be phrased as "I will do whatever it takes to punish the dragonarmies for the destruction of the Inn of the Last Home."

Artemis Entreri's bond is a strange, almost paradoxical relationship with Drizzt Do'Urden, his equal in swordplay and grim determination. In his first battle with Drizzt, Artemis recognized something of himself in his opponent, some indication that if his life had gone differently, he might have led a life more like the heroic drow's. From that moment, Artemis is more than a criminal assassin—he is an antihero, driven by his rivalry with Drizzt. His bond might be phrased as "I will not rest until I have proved myself better than Drizzt Do'Urden."

Each of these characters also has an important flaw. Tika Waylan is naive and emotionally vulnerable, younger than her companions and annoyed that they still think of her as the kid they knew years ago. She might even be tempted to act against her principles if she's convinced that a particular achievement would demonstrate her maturity. Artemis Entreri is completely walled off from any personal relationship and just wants to be left alone.

A useful place to start thinking about personality traits is to look at your highest and lowest ability scores and define one trait related to each. Either one could be positive or negative: you might work hard to overcome a low score, for example, or be cocky about your high score.

Ideals

Describe one ideal that drives your character. Your ideals are the things that you believe in most strongly, the fundamental moral and ethical principles that compel you to act as you do. Ideals encompass everything from your life goals to your core belief system.

Ideals might answer any of these questions: What are the principles that you will never betray? What would prompt you to make sacrifices? What drives you to act and guides your goals and ambitions? What is the single most important thing you strive for?

You can choose any ideals you like, but your character's alignment is a good place to start defining them. Each background in this chapter includes six suggested ideals. Five of them are linked to aspects of alignment: law, chaos, good, evil, and neutrality. The last one has more to do with the particular background than with moral or ethical perspectives.

Bonds

Create one bond for your character. Bonds represent a character's connections to people, places, and events in the world. They tie you to things from your background. They might inspire you to heights of heroism, or lead you to act against your own best interests if they are threatened. They can work very much like ideals, driving a character's motivations and goals.

Bonds might answer any of these questions: Whom do you care most about? To what place do you feel a special connection? What is your most treasured possession?

Your bonds might be tied to your class, your background, your race, or some other aspect of your character's history or personality. You might also gain new bonds over the course of your adventures.

Flaws

Finally, choose a flaw for your character. Your character's flaw represents some vice, compulsion, fear, or weakness—in particular, anything that someone else could exploit to bring you to ruin or cause you to act against your best interests. More significant than negative personality traits, a flaw might answer any of these questions: What enrages you? What's the one person, concept, or event that you are terrified of? What are your vices?

Draconic Script: Sample Alphabet

A	B	C	D	E	F	G	H	I	J	K	L	M

N	O	P	Q	R	S	T	U	V	W	X	Y	Z

Inspiration

Inspiration is a rule the Dungeon Master can use to reward you for playing your character in a way that's true to his or her personality traits, ideal, bond, and flaw. By using inspiration, you can draw on your personality trait of compassion for the downtrodden to give you an edge in negotiating with the Beggar Prince. Or inspiration can let you call on your bond to the defense of your home village to push past the effect of a spell that has been laid on you.

Gaining Inspiration

Your DM can choose to give you inspiration for a variety of reasons. Typically, DMs award it when you play out your personality traits, give in to the drawbacks presented by a flaw or bond, and otherwise portray your character in a compelling way. Your DM will tell you how you can earn inspiration in the game.

You either have inspiration or you don't—you can't stockpile multiple "inspirations" for later use.

Using Inspiration

If you have inspiration, you can expend it when you make an attack roll, saving throw, or ability check. Spending your inspiration gives you advantage on that roll.

Additionally, if you have inspiration, you can reward another player for good roleplaying, clever thinking, or simply doing something exciting in the game. When another player character does something that really contributes to the story in a fun and interesting way, you can give up your inspiration to give that character inspiration.

Backgrounds

Every story has a beginning. Your character's background reveals where you came from, how you became an adventurer, and your place in the world. Your fighter might have been a courageous knight or a grizzled soldier. Your wizard could have been a sage or an artisan. Your rogue might have gotten by as a guild thief or commanded audiences as a jester.

Choosing a background provides you with important story cues about your character's identity. The most important question to ask about your background is *what changed*? Why did you stop doing whatever your background describes and start adventuring? Where did you get the money to purchase your starting gear, or, if you come from a wealthy background, why don't you have *more* money? How did you learn the skills of your class? What sets you apart from ordinary people who share your background?

Tika and Artemis: Backgrounds

Tika Waylan and Artemis Entreri both lived their earliest years as street urchins. Tika's later career as a barmaid didn't really change her, so she might choose the urchin background, gaining proficiency in the Sleight of Hand and Stealth skills, and learning the tools of the thieving trade. Artemis is more defined by his criminal background, giving him skills in Deception and Stealth, as well as proficiency with the tools of thievery and poison.

The sample backgrounds in this chapter provide both concrete benefits (features, proficiencies, and languages) and roleplaying suggestions.

Proficiencies

Each background gives a character proficiency in two skills (described in chapter 7, "Using Ability Scores").

In addition, most backgrounds give a character proficiency with one or more tools (detailed in chapter 5, "Equipment").

If a character would gain the same proficiency from two different sources, he or she can choose a different proficiency of the same kind (skill or tool) instead.

Languages

Some backgrounds also allow characters to learn additional languages beyond those given by race. See "Languages" earlier in this chapter.

Equipment

Each background provides a package of starting equipment. If you use the optional rule from chapter 5 to spend coin on gear, you do not receive the starting equipment from your background.

Suggested Characteristics

A background contains suggested personal characteristics based on your background. You can pick characteristics, roll dice to determine them randomly, or use the suggestions as inspiration for characteristics of your own creation.

Customizing a Background

You might want to tweak some of the features of a background so it better fits your character or the campaign setting. To customize a background, you can replace one feature with any other one, choose any two skills, and choose a total of two tool proficiencies or languages from the sample backgrounds. You can either use the equipment package from your background or spend coin on gear as described in chapter 5. (If you spend coin, you can't also take the equipment package suggested for your class.) Finally, choose two personality

traits, one ideal, one bond, and one flaw. If you can't find a feature that matches your desired background, work with your DM to create one.

ACOLYTE

You have spent your life in the service of a temple to a specific god or pantheon of gods. You act as an intermediary between the realm of the holy and the mortal world, performing sacred rites and offering sacrifices in order to conduct worshipers into the presence of the divine. You are not necessarily a cleric—performing sacred rites is not the same thing as channeling divine power.

Choose a god, a pantheon of gods, or some other quasi-divine being from among those listed in appendix B or those specified by your DM, and work with your DM to detail the nature of your religious service. Were you a lesser functionary in a temple, raised from childhood to assist the priests in the sacred rites? Or were you a high priest who suddenly experienced a call to serve your god in a different way? Perhaps you were the leader of a small cult outside of any established temple structure, or even an occult group that served a fiendish master that you now deny.

Skill Proficiencies: Insight, Religion
Languages: Two of your choice
Equipment: A holy symbol (a gift to you when you entered the priesthood), a prayer book or prayer wheel, 5 sticks of incense, vestments, a set of common clothes, and a pouch containing 15 gp

FEATURE: SHELTER OF THE FAITHFUL

As an acolyte, you command the respect of those who share your faith, and you can perform the religious ceremonies of your deity. You and your adventuring companions can expect to receive free healing and care at a temple, shrine, or other established presence of your faith, though you must provide any material components needed for spells. Those who share your religion will support you (but only you) at a modest lifestyle.

You might also have ties to a specific temple dedicated to your chosen deity or pantheon, and you have a residence there. This could be the temple where you used to serve, if you remain on good terms with it, or a temple where you have found a new home. While near your temple, you can call upon the priests for assistance, provided the assistance you ask for is not hazardous and you remain in good standing with your temple.

SUGGESTED CHARACTERISTICS

Acolytes are shaped by their experience in temples or other religious communities. Their study of the history and tenets of their faith and their relationships to temples, shrines, or hierarchies affect their mannerisms and ideals. Their flaws might be some hidden hypocrisy or heretical idea, or an ideal or bond taken to an extreme.

d8	Personality Trait
1	I idolize a particular hero of my faith, and constantly refer to that person's deeds and example.
2	I can find common ground between the fiercest enemies, empathizing with them and always working toward peace.
3	I see omens in every event and action. The gods try to speak to us, we just need to listen
4	Nothing can shake my optimistic attitude.
5	I quote (or misquote) sacred texts and proverbs in almost every situation.
6	I am tolerant (or intolerant) of other faiths and respect (or condemn) the worship of other gods.
7	I've enjoyed fine food, drink, and high society among my temple's elite. Rough living grates on me.
8	I've spent so long in the temple that I have little practical experience dealing with people in the outside world.

d6	Ideal
1	**Tradition.** The ancient traditions of worship and sacrifice must be preserved and upheld. (Lawful)
2	**Charity.** I always try to help those in need, no matter what the personal cost. (Good)
3	**Change.** We must help bring about the changes the gods are constantly working in the world. (Chaotic)
4	**Power.** I hope to one day rise to the top of my faith's religious hierarchy. (Lawful)
5	**Faith.** I trust that my deity will guide my actions. I have faith that if I work hard, things will go well. (Lawful)
6	**Aspiration.** I seek to prove myself worthy of my god's favor by matching my actions against his or her teachings. (Any)

d6	Bond
1	I would die to recover an ancient relic of my faith that was lost long ago.
2	I will someday get revenge on the corrupt temple hierarchy who branded me a heretic.
3	I owe my life to the priest who took me in when my parents died.
4	Everything I do is for the common people.
5	I will do anything to protect the temple where I served.
6	I seek to preserve a sacred text that my enemies consider heretical and seek to destroy.

d6	Flaw
1	I judge others harshly, and myself even more severely.
2	I put too much trust in those who wield power within my temple's hierarchy.
3	My piety sometimes leads me to blindly trust those that profess faith in my god.
4	I am inflexible in my thinking.
5	I am suspicious of strangers and expect the worst of them.
6	Once I pick a goal, I become obsessed with it to the detriment of everything else in my life.

CHARLATAN

You have always had a way with people. You know what makes them tick, you can tease out their hearts' desires after a few minutes of conversation, and with a few leading questions you can read them like they were children's books. It's a useful talent, and one that you're perfectly willing to use for your advantage.

You know what people want and you deliver, or rather, you promise to deliver. Common sense should steer people away from things that sound too good to be true, but common sense seems to be in short supply when you're around. The bottle of pink-colored liquid will surely cure that unseemly rash, this ointment—nothing more than a bit of fat with a sprinkle of silver dust—can restore youth and vigor, and there's a bridge in the city that just happens to be for sale. These marvels sound implausible, but you make them sound like the real deal.

Skill Proficiencies: Deception, Sleight of Hand
Tool Proficiencies: Disguise kit, forgery kit
Equipment: A set of fine clothes, a disguise kit, tools of the con of your choice (ten stoppered bottles filled with colored liquid, a set of weighted dice, a deck of marked cards, or a signet ring of an imaginary duke), and a pouch containing 15 gp

FAVORITE SCHEMES

Every charlatan has an angle he or she uses in preference to other schemes. Choose a favorite scam or roll on the table below.

d6	Scam
1	I cheat at games of chance.
2	I shave coins or forge documents.
3	I insinuate myself into people's lives to prey on their weakness and secure their fortunes.
4	I put on new identities like clothes.
5	I run sleight-of-hand cons on street corners.
6	I convince people that worthless junk is worth their hard-earned money.

FEATURE: FALSE IDENTITY

You have created a second identity that includes documentation, established acquaintances, and disguises that allow you to assume that persona. Additionally, you can forge documents including official papers and personal letters, as long as you have seen an example of the kind of document or the handwriting you are trying to copy.

SUGGESTED CHARACTERISTICS

Charlatans are colorful characters who conceal their true selves behind the masks they construct. They reflect what people want to see, what they want to believe, and how they see the world. But their true selves are sometimes plagued by an uneasy conscience, an old enemy, or deep-seated trust issues.

d8	Personality Trait
1	I fall in and out of love easily, and am always pursuing someone.
2	I have a joke for every occasion, especially occasions where humor is inappropriate.
3	Flattery is my preferred trick for getting what I want.
4	I'm a born gambler who can't resist taking a risk for a potential payoff.
5	I lie about almost everything, even when there's no good reason to.
6	Sarcasm and insults are my weapons of choice.
7	I keep multiple holy symbols on me and invoke whatever deity might come in useful at any given moment.
8	I pocket anything I see that might have some value.

d6	Ideal
1	**Independence.** I am a free spirit—no one tells me what to do. (Chaotic)
2	**Fairness.** I never target people who can't afford to lose a few coins. (Lawful)
3	**Charity.** I distribute the money I acquire to the people who really need it. (Good)
4	**Creativity.** I never run the same con twice. (Chaotic)
5	**Friendship.** Material goods come and go. Bonds of friendship last forever. (Good)
6	**Aspiration.** I'm determined to make something of myself. (Any)

d6	Bond
1	I fleeced the wrong person and must work to ensure that this individual never crosses paths with me or those I care about.
2	I owe everything to my mentor—a horrible person who's probably rotting in jail somewhere.
3	Somewhere out there, I have a child who doesn't know me. I'm making the world better for him or her.
4	I come from a noble family, and one day I'll reclaim my lands and title from those who stole them from me.
5	A powerful person killed someone I love. Some day soon, I'll have my revenge.
6	I swindled and ruined a person who didn't deserve it. I seek to atone for my misdeeds but might never be able to forgive myself.

d6	Flaw
1	I can't resist a pretty face.
2	I'm always in debt. I spend my ill-gotten gains on decadent luxuries faster than I bring them in..
3	I'm convinced that no one could ever fool me the way I fool others.
4	I'm too greedy for my own good. I can't resist taking a risk if there's money involved.
5	I can't resist swindling people who are more powerful than me.
6	I hate to admit it and will hate myself for it, but I'll run and preserve my own hide if the going gets tough.

CRIMINAL

You are an experienced criminal with a history of breaking the law. You have spent a lot of time among other criminals and still have contacts within the criminal underworld. You're far closer than most people to the world of murder, theft, and violence that pervades the underbelly of civilization, and you have survived up to this point by flouting the rules and regulations of society.

Skill Proficiencies: Deception, Stealth
Tool Proficiencies: One type of gaming set, thieves' tools
Equipment: A crowbar, a set of dark common clothes including a hood, and a pouch containing 15 gp

CRIMINAL SPECIALTY

There are many kinds of criminals, and within a thieves' guild or similar criminal organization, individual members have particular specialties. Even criminals who operate outside of such organizations have strong preferences for certain kinds of crimes over others. Choose the role you played in your criminal life, or roll on the table below.

d8	Specialty	d8	Specialty
1	Blackmailer	5	Highway robber
2	Burglar	6	Hired killer
3	Enforcer	7	Pickpocket
4	Fence	8	Smuggler

FEATURE: CRIMINAL CONTACT

You have a reliable and trustworthy contact who acts as your liaison to a network of other criminals. You know how to get messages to and from your contact, even over great distances; specifically, you know the local messengers, corrupt caravan masters, and seedy sailors who can deliver messages for you.

SUGGESTED CHARACTERISTICS

Criminals might seem like villains on the surface, and many of them are villainous to the core. But some have an abundance of endearing, if not redeeming, characteristics. There might be honor among thieves, but criminals rarely show any respect for law or authority.

d8	Personality Trait
1	I always have a plan for what to do when things go wrong.
2	I am always calm, no matter what the situation. I never raise my voice or let my emotions control me.
3	The first thing I do in a new place is note the locations of everything valuable—or where such things could be hidden.
4	I would rather make a new friend than a new enemy.
5	I am incredibly slow to trust. Those who seem the fairest often have the most to hide.
6	I don't pay attention to the risks in a situation. Never tell me the odds.
7	The best way to get me to do something is to tell me I can't do it.
8	I blow up at the slightest insult.

d6	Ideal
1	**Honor.** I don't steal from others in the trade. (Lawful)
2	**Freedom.** Chains are meant to be broken, as are those who would forge them. (Chaotic)
3	**Charity.** I steal from the wealthy so that I can help people in need. (Good)
4	**Greed.** I will do whatever it takes to become wealthy. (Evil)
5	**People.** I'm loyal to my friends, not to any ideals, and everyone else can take a trip down the Styx for all I care. (Neutral)
6	**Redemption.** There's a spark of good in everyone. (Good)

d6	Bond
1	I'm trying to pay off an old debt I owe to a generous benefactor.
2	My ill-gotten gains go to support my family.
3	Something important was taken from me, and I aim to steal it back.
4	I will become the greatest thief that ever lived.
5	I'm guilty of a terrible crime. I hope I can redeem myself for it.
6	Someone I loved died because of I mistake I made. That will never happen again.

129

d6	Flaw
1	When I see something valuable, I can't think about anything but how to steal it.
2	When faced with a choice between money and my friends, I usually choose the money.
3	If there's a plan, I'll forget it. If I don't forget it, I'll ignore it.
4	I have a "tell" that reveals when I'm lying.
5	I turn tail and run when things look bad.
6	An innocent person is in prison for a crime that I committed. I'm okay with that.

VARIANT CRIMINAL: SPY

Although your capabilities are not much different from those of a burglar or smuggler, you learned and practiced them in a very different context: as an espionage agent. You might have been an officially sanctioned agent of the crown, or perhaps you sold the secrets you uncovered to the highest bidder.

ENTERTAINER

You thrive in front of an audience. You know how to entrance them, entertain them, and even inspire them. Your poetics can stir the hearts of those who hear you, awakening grief or joy, laughter or anger. Your music raises their spirits or captures their sorrow. Your dance steps captivate, your humor cuts to the quick. Whatever techniques you use, your art is your life.

Skill Proficiencies: Acrobatics, Performance
Tool Proficiencies: Disguise kit, one type of musical instrument
Equipment: A musical instrument (one of your choice), the favor of an admirer (love letter, lock of hair, or trinket), a costume, and a pouch containing 15 gp

ENTERTAINER ROUTINES

A good entertainer is versatile, spicing up every performance with a variety of different routines. Choose one to three routines or roll on the table below to define your expertise as an entertainer.

d10	Entertainer Routine	d10	Entertainer Routine
1	Actor	6	Instrumentalist
2	Dancer	7	Poet
3	Fire-eater	8	Singer
4	Jester	9	Storyteller
5	Juggler	10	Tumbler

FEATURE: BY POPULAR DEMAND

You can always find a place to perform, usually in an inn or tavern but possibly with a circus, at a theater, or even in a noble's court. At such a place, you receive free lodging and food of a modest or comfortable standard (depending on the quality of the establishment), as long as you perform each night. In addition, your performance makes you something of a local figure. When strangers recognize you in a town where you have performed, they typically take a liking to you.

SUGGESTED CHARACTERISTICS

Successful entertainers have to be able to capture and hold an audience's attention, so they tend to have flamboyant or forceful personalities. They're inclined toward the romantic and often cling to high-minded ideals about the practice of art and the appreciation of beauty.

d8	Personality Trait
1	I know a story relevant to almost every situation.
2	Whenever I come to a new place, I collect local rumors and spread gossip.
3	I'm a hopeless romantic, always searching for that "special someone."
4	Nobody stays angry at me or around me for long, since I can defuse any amount of tension.
5	I love a good insult, even one directed at me.
6	I get bitter if I'm not the center of attention.
7	I'll settle for nothing less than perfection.
8	I change my mood or my mind as quickly as I change key in a song.

d6 Ideal

1	**Beauty.** When I perform, I make the world better than it was. (Good)
2	**Tradition.** The stories, legends, and songs of the past must never be forgotten, for they teach us who we are. (Lawful)
3	**Creativity.** The world is in need of new ideas and bold action. (Chaotic)
4	**Greed.** I'm only in it for the money and fame. (Evil)
5	**People.** I like seeing the smiles on people's faces when I perform. That's all that matters. (Neutral)
6	**Honesty.** Art should reflect the soul; it should come from within and reveal who we really are. (Any)

d6 Bond

1	My instrument is my most treasured possession, and it reminds me of someone I love.
2	Someone stole my precious instrument, and someday I'll get it back.
3	I want to be famous, whatever it takes.
4	I idolize a hero of the old tales and measure my deeds against that person's.
5	I will do anything to prove myself superior to my hated rival.
6	I would do anything for the other members of my old troupe.

d6 Flaw

1	I'll do anything to win fame and renown.
2	I'm a sucker for a pretty face.
3	A scandal prevents me from ever going home again. That kind of trouble seems to follow me around.
4	I once satirized a noble who still wants my head. It was a mistake that I will likely repeat.
5	I have trouble keeping my true feelings hidden. My sharp tongue lands me in trouble.
6	Despite my best efforts, I am unreliable to my friends.

VARIANT ENTERTAINER: GLADIATOR

A gladiator is as much an entertainer as any minstrel or circus performer, trained to make the arts of combat into a spectacle the crowd can enjoy. This kind of flashy combat is your entertainer routine, though you might also have some skills as a tumbler or actor. Using your By Popular Demand feature, you can find a place to perform in any place that features combat for entertainment—perhaps a gladiatorial arena or secret pit fighting club. You can replace the musical instrument in your equipment package with an inexpensive but unusual weapon, such as a trident or net.

FOLK HERO

You come from a humble social rank, but you are destined for so much more. Already the people of your home village regard you as their champion, and your destiny calls you to stand against the tyrants and monsters that threaten the common folk everywhere.

Skill Proficiencies: Animal Handling, Survival
Tool Proficiencies: One type of artisan's tools, vehicles (land)
Equipment: A set of artisan's tools (one of your choice), a shovel, an iron pot, a set of common clothes, and a pouch containing 10 gp

DEFINING EVENT

You previously pursued a simple profession among the peasantry, perhaps as a farmer, miner, servant, shepherd, woodcutter, or gravedigger. But something happened that set you on a different path and marked you for greater things. Choose or randomly determine a defining event that marked you as a hero of the people.

d10 Defining Event

1	I stood up to a tyrant's agents.
2	I saved people during a natural disaster.
3	I stood alone against a terrible monster.
4	I stole from a corrupt merchant to help the poor.
5	I led a militia to fight off an invading army.
6	I broke into a tyrant's castle and stole weapons to arm the people.
7	I trained the peasantry to use farm implements as weapons against a tyrant's soldiers.
8	A lord rescinded an unpopular decree after I led a symbolic act of protest against it.
9	A celestial, fey, or similar creature gave me a blessing or revealed my secret origin.
10	Recruited into a lord's army, I rose to leadership and was commended for my heroism.

FEATURE: RUSTIC HOSPITALITY

Since you come from the ranks of the common folk, you fit in among them with ease. You can find a place to hide, rest, or recuperate among other commoners, unless you have shown yourself to be a danger to them. They will shield you from the law or anyone else searching for you, though they will not risk their lives for you.

SUGGESTED CHARACTERISTICS

A folk hero is one of the common people, for better or for worse. Most folk heroes look on their humble origins as a virtue, not a shortcoming, and their home communities remain very important to them.

d8 Personality Trait

1	I judge people by their actions, not their words.
2	If someone is in trouble, I'm always ready to lend help.
3	When I set my mind to something, I follow through no matter what gets in my way.
4	I have a strong sense of fair play and always try to find the most equitable solution to arguments.
5	I'm confident in my own abilities and do what I can to instill confidence in others.
6	Thinking is for other people. I prefer action.
7	I misuse long words in an attempt to sound smarter.
8	I get bored easily. When am I going to get on with my destiny?

d6	Ideal
1	**Respect.** People deserve to be treated with dignity and respect. (Good)
2	**Fairness.** No one should get preferential treatment before the law, and no one is above the law. (Lawful)
3	**Freedom.** Tyrants must not be allowed to oppress the people. (Chaotic)
4	**Might.** If I become strong, I can take what I want—what I deserve. (Evil)
5	**Sincerity.** There's no good in pretending to be something I'm not. (Neutral)
6	**Destiny.** Nothing and no one can steer me away from my higher calling. (Any)

d6	Bond
1	I have a family, but I have no idea where they are. One day, I hope to see them again.
2	I worked the land, I love the land, and I will protect the land.
3	A proud noble once gave me a horrible beating, and I will take my revenge on any bully I encounter.
4	My tools are symbols of my past life, and I carry them so that I will never forget my roots.
5	I protect those who cannot protect themselves.
6	I wish my childhood sweetheart had come with me to pursue my destiny.

d6	Flaw
1	The tyrant who rules my land will stop at nothing to see me killed.
2	I'm convinced of the significance of my destiny, and blind to my shortcomings and the risk of failure.
3	The people who knew me when I was young know my shameful secret, so I can never go home again.
4	I have a weakness for the vices of the city, especially hard drink.
5	Secretly, I believe that things would be better if I were a tyrant lording over the land.
6	I have trouble trusting in my allies.

GUILD ARTISAN

You are a member of an artisan's guild, skilled in a particular field and closely associated with other artisans. You are a well-established part of the mercantile world, freed by talent and wealth from the constraints of a feudal social order. You learned your skills as an apprentice to a master artisan, under the sponsorship of your guild, until you became a master in your own right.

Skill Proficiencies: Insight, Persuasion
Tool Proficiencies: One type of artisan's tools
Languages: One of your choice
Equipment: A set of artisan's tools (one of your choice), a letter of introduction from your guild, a set of traveler's clothes, and a pouch containing 15 gp

GUILD BUSINESS

Guilds are generally found in cities large enough to support several artisans practicing the same trade. However, your guild might instead be a loose network of artisans who each work in a different village within a larger realm. Work with your DM to determine the nature of your guild. You can select your guild business from the Guild Business table or roll randomly.

d20	Guild Business
1	Alchemists and apothecaries
2	Armorers, locksmiths, and finesmiths
3	Brewers, distillers, and vintners
4	Calligraphers, scribes, and scriveners
5	Carpenters, roofers, and plasterers
6	Cartographers, surveyors, and chart-makers
7	Cobblers and shoemakers
8	Cooks and bakers
9	Glassblowers and glaziers
10	Jewelers and gemcutters
11	Leatherworkers, skinners, and tanners
12	Masons and stonecutters
13	Painters, limners, and sign-makers
14	Potters and tile-makers
15	Shipwrights and sailmakers
16	Smiths and metal-forgers
17	Tinkers, pewterers, and casters
18	Wagon-makers and wheelwrights
19	Weavers and dyers
20	Woodcarvers, coopers, and bowyers

As a member of your guild, you know the skills needed to create finished items from raw materials (reflected in your proficiency with a certain kind of artisan's tools), as well as the principles of trade and good business practices. The question now is whether you abandon your trade for adventure, or take on the extra effort to weave adventuring and trade together.

FEATURE: GUILD MEMBERSHIP

As an established and respected member of a guild, you can rely on certain benefits that membership provides. Your fellow guild members will provide you with lodging and food if necessary, and pay for your funeral if needed. In some cities and towns, a guildhall offers a central place to meet other members of your profession, which can be a good place to meet potential patrons, allies, or hirelings.

Guilds often wield tremendous political power. If you are accused of a crime, your guild will support you if a good case can be made for your innocence or the crime is justifiable. You can also gain access to powerful political figures through the guild, if you are a member in good standing. Such connections might require the donation of money or magic items to the guild's coffers.

You must pay dues of 5 gp per month to the guild. If you miss payments, you must make up back dues to remain in the guild's good graces.

SUGGESTED CHARACTERISTICS

Guild artisans are among the most ordinary people in the world—until they set down their tools and take up an adventuring career. They understand the value of hard work and the importance of community, but they're vulnerable to sins of greed and covetousness.

d8	Personality Trait
1	I believe that anything worth doing is worth doing right. I can't help it—I'm a perfectionist.
2	I'm a snob who looks down on those who can't appreciate fine art.
3	I always want to know how things work and what makes people tick.
4	I'm full of witty aphorisms and have a proverb for every occasion.
5	I'm rude to people who lack my commitment to hard work and fair play.
6	I like to talk at length about my profession.
7	I don't part with my money easily and will haggle tirelessly to get the best deal possible.
8	I'm well known for my work, and I want to make sure everyone appreciates it. I'm always taken aback when people haven't heard of me.

d6	Ideal
1	**Community.** It is the duty of all civilized people to strengthen the bonds of community and the security of civilization. (Lawful)
2	**Generosity.** My talents were given to me so that I could use them to benefit the world. (Good)
3	**Freedom.** Everyone should be free to pursue his or her own livelihood. (Chaotic)
4	**Greed.** I'm only in it for the money. (Evil)
5	**People.** I'm committed to the people I care about, not to ideals. (Neutral)
6	**Aspiration.** I work hard to be the best there is at my craft. (Any)

d6	Bond
1	The workshop where I learned my trade is the most important place in the world to me.
2	I created a great work for someone, and then found them unworthy to receive it. I'm still looking for someone worthy.
3	I owe my guild a great debt for forging me into the person I am today.
4	I pursue wealth to secure someone's love.
5	One day I will return to my guild and prove that I am the greatest artisan of them all.
6	I will get revenge on the evil forces that destroyed my place of business and ruined my livelihood.

d6	Flaw
1	I'll do anything to get my hands on something rare or priceless.
2	I'm quick to assume that someone is trying to cheat me.
3	No one must ever learn that I once stole money from guild coffers.
4	I'm never satisfied with what I have—I always want more.
5	I would kill to acquire a noble title.
6	I'm horribly jealous of anyone who can outshine my handiwork. Everywhere I go, I'm surrounded by rivals.

VARIANT GUILD ARTISAN: GUILD MERCHANT

Instead of an artisans' guild, you might belong to a guild of traders, caravan masters, or shopkeepers. You don't craft items yourself but earn a living by buying and selling the works of others (or the raw materials artisans need to practice their craft). Your guild might be a large merchant consortium (or family) with interests across the region. Perhaps you transported goods from one place to another, by ship, wagon, or caravan, or bought them from traveling traders and sold them in your own little shop. In some ways, the traveling merchant's life lends itself to adventure far more than the life of an artisan.

Rather than proficiency with artisan's tools, you might be proficient with navigator's tools or an additional language. And instead of artisan's tools, you can start with a mule and a cart.

Hermit

You lived in seclusion—either in a sheltered community such as a monastery, or entirely alone—for a formative part of your life. In your time apart from the clamor of society, you found quiet, solitude, and perhaps some of the answers you were looking for.

Skill Proficiencies: Medicine, Religion
Tool Proficiencies: Herbalism kit
Languages: One of your choice
Equipment: A scroll case stuffed full of notes from your studies or prayers, a winter blanket, a set of common clothes, an herbalism kit, and 5 gp

Life of Seclusion

What was the reason for your isolation, and what changed to allow you to end your solitude? You can work with your DM to determine the exact nature of your seclusion, or you can choose or roll on the table below to determine the reason behind your seclusion.

d8	Life of Seclusion
1	I was searching for spiritual enlightenment.
2	I was partaking of communal living in accordance with the dictates of a religious order.
3	I was exiled for a crime I didn't commit.
4	I retreated from society after a life-altering event.
5	I needed a quiet place to work on my art, literature, music, or manifesto.
6	I needed to commune with nature, far from civilization.
7	I was the caretaker of an ancient ruin or relic.
8	I was a pilgrim in search of a person, place, or relic of spiritual significance.

Feature: Discovery

The quiet seclusion of your extended hermitage gave you access to a unique and powerful discovery. The exact nature of this revelation depends on the nature of your seclusion. It might be a great truth about the cosmos, the deities, the powerful beings of the outer planes, or the forces of nature. It could be a site that no one else has ever seen. You might have uncovered a fact that has long been forgotten, or unearthed some relic of the past that could rewrite history. It might be information that would be damaging to the people who or consigned you to exile, and hence the reason for your return to society.

Work with your DM to determine the details of your discovery and its impact on the campaign.

Suggested Characteristics

Some hermits are well suited to a life of seclusion, whereas others chafe against it and long for company. Whether they embrace solitude or long to escape it, the solitary life shapes their attitudes and ideals. A few are driven slightly mad by their years apart from society.

d8	Personality Trait
1	I've been isolated for so long that I rarely speak, preferring gestures and the occasional grunt.
2	I am utterly serene, even in the face of disaster.
3	The leader of my community had something wise to say on every topic, and I am eager to share that wisdom.
4	I feel tremendous empathy for all who suffer.
5	I'm oblivious to etiquette and social expectations.
6	I connect everything that happens to me to a grand, cosmic plan.
7	I often get lost in my own thoughts and contemplation, becoming oblivious to my surroundings.
8	I am working on a grand philosophical theory and love sharing my ideas.

d6	Ideal
1	**Greater Good.** My gifts are meant to be shared with all, not used for my own benefit. (Good)
2	**Logic.** Emotions must not cloud our sense of what is right and true, or our logical thinking. (Lawful)
3	**Free Thinking.** Inquiry and curiosity are the pillars of progress. (Chaotic)
4	**Power.** Solitude and contemplation are paths toward mystical or magical power. (Evil)
5	**Live and Let Live.** Meddling in the affairs of others only causes trouble. (Neutral)
6	**Self-Knowledge.** If you know yourself, there's nothing left to know. (Any)

d6	Bond
1	Nothing is more important than the other members of my hermitage, order, or association.
2	I entered seclusion to hide from the ones who might still be hunting me. I must someday confront them.
3	I'm still seeking the enlightenment I pursued in my seclusion, and it still eludes me.
4	I entered seclusion because I loved someone I could not have.
5	Should my discovery come to light, it could bring ruin to the world.
6	My isolation gave me great insight into a great evil that only I can destroy.

d6	Flaw
1	Now that I've returned to the world, I enjoy its delights a little too much.
2	I harbor dark, bloodthirsty thoughts that my isolation and meditation failed to quell.
3	I am dogmatic in my thoughts and philosophy.
4	I let my need to win arguments overshadow friendships and harmony.
5	I'd risk too much to uncover a lost bit of knowledge.
6	I like keeping secrets and won't share them with anyone.

OTHER HERMITS

This hermit background assumes a contemplative sort of seclusion that allows room for study and prayer. If you want to play a rugged wilderness recluse who lives off the land while shunning the company of other people, look at the outlander background. On the other hand, if you want to go in a more religious direction, the acolyte might be what you're looking for. Or you could even be a charlatan, posing as a wise and holy person and letting pious fools support you.

NOBLE

You understand wealth, power, and privilege. You carry a noble title, and your family owns land, collects taxes, and wields significant political influence. You might be a pampered aristocrat unfamiliar with work or discomfort, a former merchant just elevated to the nobility, or a disinherited scoundrel with a disproportionate sense of entitlement. Or you could be an honest, hard-working landowner who cares deeply about the people who live and work on your land, keenly aware of your responsibility to them.

Work with your DM to come up with an appropriate title and determine how much authority that title carries. A noble title doesn't stand on its own—it's connected to an entire family, and whatever title you hold, you will pass it down to your own children. Not only do you need to determine your noble title, but you should also work with the DM to describe your family and their influence on you.

Is your family old and established, or was your title only recently bestowed? How much influence do they wield, and over what area? What kind of reputation does your family have among the other aristocrats of the region? How do the common people regard them?

What's your position in the family? Are you the heir to the head of the family? Have you already inherited the title? How do you feel about that responsibility? Or are you so far down the line of inheritance that no one cares what you do, as long as you don't embarrass the family? How does the head of your family feel about your adventuring career? Are you in your family's good graces, or shunned by the rest of your family?

Does your family have a coat of arms? An insignia you might wear on a signet ring? Particular colors you wear all the time? An animal you regard as a symbol of your line or even a spiritual member of the family?

These details help establish your family and your title as features of the world of the campaign.

Skill Proficiencies: History, Persuasion
Tool Proficiencies: One type of gaming set
Languages: One of your choice
Equipment: A set of fine clothes, a signet ring, a scroll of pedigree, and a purse containing 25 gp

FEATURE: POSITION OF PRIVILEGE

Thanks to your noble birth, people are inclined to think the best of you. You are welcome in high society, and people assume you have the right to be wherever you are. The common folk make every effort to accommodate you and avoid your displeasure, and other people of high birth treat you as a member of the same social sphere. You can secure an audience with a local noble if you need to.

SUGGESTED CHARACTERISTICS

Nobles are born and raised to a very different lifestyle than most people ever experience, and their personalities reflect that upbringing. A noble title comes with a plethora of bonds—responsibilities to family, to other nobles (including the sovereign), to the people entrusted to the family's care, or even to the title itself. But this responsibility is often a good way to undermine a noble.

d8	Personality Trait
1	My eloquent flattery makes everyone I talk to feel like the most wonderful and important person in the world.
2	The common folk love me for my kindness and generosity.
3	No one could doubt by looking at my regal bearing that I am a cut above the unwashed masses.
4	I take great pains to always look my best and follow the latest fashions.
5	I don't like to get my hands dirty, and I won't be caught dead in unsuitable accommodations.
6	Despite my noble birth, I do not place myself above other folk. We all have the same blood.
7	My favor, once lost, is lost forever.
8	If you do me an injury, I will crush you, ruin your name, and salt your fields.

d6	Ideal
1	**Respect.** Respect is due to me because of my position, but all people regardless of station deserve to be treated with dignity. (Good)
2	**Responsibility.** It is my duty to respect the authority of those above me, just as those below me must respect mine. (Lawful)
3	**Independence.** I must prove that I can handle myself without the coddling of my family. (Chaotic)
4	**Power.** If I can attain more power, no one will tell me what to do. (Evil)
5	**Family.** Blood runs thicker than water. (Any)
6	**Noble Obligation.** It is my duty to protect and care for the people beneath me. (Good)

d6	Bond
1	I will face any challenge to win the approval of my family.
2	My house's alliance with another noble family must be sustained at all costs.
3	Nothing is more important than the other members of my family.
4	I am in love with the heir of a family that my family despises.
5	My loyalty to my sovereign is unwavering.
6	The common folk must see me as a hero of the people.

d6	Flaw
1	I secretly believe that everyone is beneath me.
2	I hide a truly scandalous secret that could ruin my family forever.
3	I too often hear veiled insults and threats in every word addressed to me, and I'm quick to anger.
4	I have an insatiable desire for carnal pleasures.
5	In fact, the world does revolve around me.
6	By my words and actions, I often bring shame to my family.

VARIANT NOBLE: KNIGHT

A knighthood is among the lowest noble titles in most societies, but it can be a path to higher status. If you wish to be a knight, choose the Retainers feature (see the sidebar) instead of the Position of Privilege feature. One of your commoner retainers is replaced by a noble who serves as your squire, aiding you in exchange for

---

VARIANT FEATURE: RETAINERS

If your character has a noble background, you may select this background feature instead of Position of Privilege.

You have the service of three retainers loyal to your family. These retainers can be attendants or messengers, and one might be a majordomo. Your retainers are commoners who can perform mundane tasks for you, but they do not fight for you, will not follow you into obviously dangerous areas (such as dungeons), and will leave if they are frequently endangered or abused.

---

training on his or her own path to knighthood. Your two remaining retainers might include a groom to care for your horse and a servant who polishes your armor (and even helps you put it on).

As an emblem of chivalry and the ideals of courtly love, you might include among your equipment a banner or other token from a noble lord or lady to whom you have given your heart—in a chaste sort of devotion. (This person could be your bond.)

OUTLANDER

You grew up in the wilds, far from civilization and the comforts of town and technology. You've witnessed the migration of herds larger than forests, survived weather more extreme than any city-dweller could comprehend, and enjoyed the solitude of being the only thinking creature for miles in any direction. The wilds are in your blood, whether you were a nomad, an explorer, a recluse, a hunter-gatherer, or even a marauder. Even in places where you don't know the specific features of the terrain, you know the ways of the wild.

Skill Proficiencies: Athletics, Survival
Tool Proficiencies: One type of musical instrument
Languages: One of your choice
Equipment: A staff, a hunting trap, a trophy from an animal you killed, a set of traveler's clothes, and a pouch containing 10 gp

ORIGIN

You've been to strange places and seen things that others cannot begin to fathom. Consider some of the distant lands you have visited, and how they impacted you. You can roll on the following table to determine your occupation during your time in the wild, or choose one that best fits your character.

d10	Origin	d10	Origin
1	Forester	6	Bounty hunter
2	Trapper	7	Pilgrim
3	Homesteader	8	Tribal nomad
4	Guide	9	Hunter-gatherer
5	Exile or outcast	10	Tribal marauder

FEATURE: WANDERER

You have an excellent memory for maps and geography, and you can always recall the general layout of terrain, settlements, and other features around you. In addition, you can find food and fresh water for yourself and up to five other people each day, provided that the land offers berries, small game, water, and so forth.

SUGGESTED CHARACTERISTICS

Often considered rude and uncouth among civilized folk, outlanders have little respect for the niceties of life in the cities. The ties of tribe, clan, family, and the natural world of which they are a part are the most important bonds to most outlanders.

d8	Personality Trait
1	I'm driven by a wanderlust that led me away from home.
2	I watch over my friends as if they were a litter of newborn pups.
3	I once ran twenty-five miles without stopping to warn to my clan of an approaching orc horde. I'd do it again if I had to.
4	I have a lesson for every situation, drawn from observing nature.
5	I place no stock in wealthy or well-mannered folk. Money and manners won't save you from a hungry owlbear.
6	I'm always picking things up, absently fiddling with them, and sometimes accidentally breaking them.
7	I feel far more comfortable around animals than people.
8	I was, in fact, raised by wolves.

d6	Ideal
1	**Change.** Life is like the seasons, in constant change, and we must change with it. (Chaotic)
2	**Greater Good.** It is each person's responsibility to make the most happiness for the whole tribe. (Good)
3	**Honor.** If I dishonor myself, I dishonor my whole clan. (Lawful)
4	**Might.** The strongest are meant to rule. (Evil)
5	**Nature.** The natural world is more important than all the constructs of civilization. (Neutral)
6	**Glory.** I must earn glory in battle, for myself and my clan. (Any)

d6	Bond
1	My family, clan, or tribe is the most important thing in my life, even when they are far from me.
2	An injury to the unspoiled wilderness of my home is an injury to me.
3	I will bring terrible wrath down on the evildoers who destroyed my homeland.
4	I am the last of my tribe, and it is up to me to ensure their names enter legend.
5	I suffer awful visions of a coming disaster and will do anything to prevent it.
6	It is my duty to provide children to sustain my tribe.

d6	Flaw
1	I am too enamored of ale, wine, and other intoxicants.
2	There's no room for caution in a life lived to the fullest.
3	I remember every insult I've received and nurse a silent resentment toward anyone who's ever wronged me.
4	I am slow to trust members of other races, tribes, and societies.
5	Violence is my answer to almost any challenge.
6	Don't expect me to save those who can't save themselves. It is nature's way that the strong thrive and the weak perish.

SAGE

You spent years learning the lore of the multiverse. You scoured manuscripts, studied scrolls, and listened to the greatest experts on the subjects that interest you. Your efforts have made you a master in your fields of study.

Skill Proficiencies: Arcana, History
Languages: Two of your choice
Equipment: A bottle of black ink, a quill, a small knife, a letter from a dead colleague posing a question you have not yet been able to answer, a set of common clothes, and a pouch containing 10 gp

SPECIALTY

To determine the nature of your scholarly training, roll a d8 or choose from the options in the table below.

d8	Specialty	d8	Specialty
1	Alchemist	5	Professor
2	Astronomer	6	Researcher
3	Discredited academic	7	Wizard's apprentice
4	Librarian	8	Scribe

FEATURE: RESEARCHER

When you attempt to learn or recall a piece of lore, if you do not know that information, you often know where and from whom you can obtain it. Usually, this information comes from a library, scriptorium, university, or a sage or other learned person or creature. Your DM might rule that the knowledge you seek is secreted away in an almost inaccessible place, or that it simply cannot be found. Unearthing the deepest secrets of the multiverse can require an adventure or even a whole campaign.

SUGGESTED CHARACTERISTICS

Sages are defined by their extensive studies, and their characteristics reflect this life of study. Devoted to scholarly pursuits, a sage values knowledge highly—sometimes in its own right, sometimes as a means toward other ideals.

d8	Personality Trait
1	I use polysyllabic words that convey the impression of great erudition.
2	I've read every book in the world's greatest libraries—or I like to boast that I have.
3	I'm used to helping out those who aren't as smart as I am, and I patiently explain anything and everything to others.
4	There's nothing I like more than a good mystery.
5	I'm willing to listen to every side of an argument before I make my own judgment.
6	I . . . speak . . . slowly . . . when talking . . . to idiots, . . . which . . . almost . . . everyone . . . is . . . compared . . . to me.
7	I am horribly, horribly awkward in social situations.
8	I'm convinced that people are always trying to steal my secrets.

d6	Ideal
1	**Knowledge.** The path to power and self-improvement is through knowledge. (Neutral)
2	**Beauty.** What is beautiful points us beyond itself toward what is true. (Good)
3	**Logic.** Emotions must not cloud our logical thinking. (Lawful)
4	**No Limits.** Nothing should fetter the infinite possibility inherent in all existence. (Chaotic)
5	**Power.** Knowledge is the path to power and domination. (Evil)
6	**Self-Improvement.** The goal of a life of study is the betterment of oneself. (Any)

d6	Bond
1	It is my duty to protect my students.
2	I have an ancient text that holds terrible secrets that must not fall into the wrong hands.
3	I work to preserve a library, university, scriptorium, or monastery.
4	My life's work is a series of tomes related to a specific field of lore.
5	I've been searching my whole life for the answer to a certain question.
6	I sold my soul for knowledge. I hope to do great deeds and win it back.

d6	Flaw
1	I am easily distracted by the promise of information.
2	Most people scream and run when they see a demon. I stop and take notes on its anatomy.
3	Unlocking an ancient mystery is worth the price of a civilization.
4	I overlook obvious solutions in favor of complicated ones.
5	I speak without really thinking through my words, invariably insulting others.
6	I can't keep a secret to save my life, or anyone else's.

Sailor

You sailed on a seagoing vessel for years. In that time, you faced down mighty storms, monsters of the deep, and those who wanted to sink your craft to the bottomless depths. Your first love is the distant line of the horizon, but the time has come to try your hand at something new.

Discuss the nature of the ship you previously sailed with your Dungeon Master. Was it a merchant ship, a naval vessel, a ship of discovery, or a pirate ship? How famous (or infamous) is it? Is it widely traveled? Is it still sailing, or is it missing and presumed lost with all hands?

What were your duties on board—boatswain, captain, navigator, cook, or some other position? Who were the captain and first mate? Did you leave your ship on good terms with your fellows, or on the run?

Skill Proficiencies: Athletics, Perception
Tool Proficiencies: Navigator's tools, vehicles (water)
Equipment: A belaying pin (club), 50 feet of silk rope, a lucky charm such as a rabbit foot or a small stone with a hole in the center (or you may roll for a random trinket on the Trinkets table in chapter 5), a set of common clothes, and a pouch containing 10 gp

Feature: Ship's Passage

When you need to, you can secure free passage on a sailing ship for yourself and your adventuring companions. You might sail on the ship you served on, or another ship you have good relations with (perhaps one captained by a former crewmate). Because you're calling in a favor, you can't be certain of a schedule or route that will meet your every need. Your Dungeon Master will determine how long it takes to get where you need to go. In return for your free passage, you and your companions are expected to assist the crew during the voyage.

Suggested Characteristics

Sailors can be a rough lot, but the responsibilities of life on a ship make them generally reliable as well. Life aboard a ship shapes their outlook and forms their most important attachments.

d8	Personality Trait
1	My friends know they can rely on me, no matter what.
2	I work hard so that I can play hard when the work is done.
3	I enjoy sailing into new ports and making new friends over a flagon of ale.
4	I stretch the truth for the sake of a good story.
5	To me, a tavern brawl is a nice way to get to know a new city.
6	I never pass up a friendly wager.
7	My language is as foul as an otyugh nest.
8	I like a job well done, especially if I can convince someone else to do it.

d6	Ideal
1	**Respect.** The thing that keeps a ship together is mutual respect between captain and crew. (Good)
2	**Fairness.** We all do the work, so we all share in the rewards. (Lawful)
3	**Freedom.** The sea is freedom—the freedom to go anywhere and do anything. (Chaotic)
4	**Mastery.** I'm a predator, and the other ships on the sea are my prey. (Evil)
5	**People.** I'm committed to my crewmates, not to ideals. (Neutral)
6	**Aspiration.** Someday I'll own my own ship and chart my own destiny. (Any)

d6	Bond
1	I'm loyal to my captain first, everything else second.
2	The ship is most important—crewmates and captains come and go.
3	I'll always remember my first ship.
4	In a harbor town, I have a paramour whose eyes nearly stole me from the sea.
5	I was cheated out of my fair share of the profits, and I want to get my due.
6	Ruthless pirates murdered my captain and crewmates, plundered our ship, and left me to die. Vengeance will be mine.

d6	Flaw
1	I follow orders, even if I think they're wrong.
2	I'll say anything to avoid having to do extra work.
3	Once someone questions my courage, I never back down no matter how dangerous the situation.
4	Once I start drinking, it's hard for me to stop.
5	I can't help but pocket loose coins and other trinkets I come across.
6	My pride will probably lead to my destruction.

Variant Sailor: Pirate

You spent your youth under the sway of a dread pirate, a ruthless cutthroat who taught you how to survive in a world of sharks and savages. You've indulged in larceny on the high seas and sent more than one deserving soul to a briny grave. Fear and bloodshed are no strangers to you, and you've garnered a somewhat unsavory reputation in many a port town.

If you decide that your sailing career involved piracy, you can choose the Bad Reputation feature (see sidebar) instead of the Ship's Passage feature.

Variant Feature: Bad Reputation

If your character has a sailor background, you may select this background feature instead of Ship's Passage.

No matter where you go, people are afraid of you due to your reputation. When you are in a civilized settlement, you can get away with minor criminal offenses, such as refusing to pay for food at a tavern or breaking down doors at a local shop, since most people will not report your activity to the authorities.

Soldier

War has been your life for as long as you care to remember. You trained as a youth, studied the use of weapons and armor, learned basic survival techniques, including how to stay alive on the battlefield. You might have been part of a standing national army or a mercenary company, or perhaps a member of a local militia who rose to prominence during a recent war.

When you choose this background, work with your DM to determine which military organization you were a part of, how far through its ranks you progressed, and what kind of experiences you had during your military career. Was it a standing army, a town guard, or a village militia? Or it might have been a noble's or merchant's private army, or a mercenary company.

Skill Proficiencies: Athletics, Intimidation
Tool Proficiencies: One type of gaming set, vehicles (land)
Equipment: An insignia of rank, a trophy taken from a fallen enemy (a dagger, broken blade, or piece of a banner), a set of bone dice or deck of cards, a set of common clothes, and a pouch containing 10 gp

Specialty

During your time as a soldier, you had a specific role to play in your unit or army. Roll a d8 or choose from the options in the table below to determine your role:

d8	Specialty	d8	Specialty
1	Officer	6	Quartermaster
2	Scout	7	Standard bearer
3	Infantry	8	Support staff (cook, blacksmith, or the like)
4	Cavalry		
5	Healer		

Feature: Military Rank

You have a military rank from your career as a soldier. Soldiers loyal to your former military organization still recognize your authority and influence, and they defer to you if they are of a lower rank. You can invoke your rank to exert influence over other soldiers and requisition simple equipment or horses for temporary use. You can also usually gain access to friendly military encampments and fortresses where your rank is recognized.

Suggested Characteristics

The horrors of war combined with the rigid discipline of military service leave their mark on all soldiers, shaping their ideals, creating strong bonds, and often leaving them scarred and vulnerable to fear, shame, and hatred.

d8	Personality Trait
1	I'm always polite and respectful.
2	I'm haunted by memories of war. I can't get the images of violence out of my mind.
3	I've lost too many friends, and I'm slow to make new ones.
4	I'm full of inspiring and cautionary tales from my military experience relevant to almost every combat situation.
5	I can stare down a hell hound without flinching.
6	I enjoy being strong and like breaking things.
7	I have a crude sense of humor.
8	I face problems head-on. A simple, direct solution is the best path to success.

d6	Ideal
1	**Greater Good.** Our lot is to lay down our lives in defense of others. (Good)
2	**Responsibility.** I do what I must and obey just authority. (Lawful)
3	**Independence.** When people follow orders blindly, they embrace a kind of tyranny. (Chaotic)
4	**Might.** In life as in war, the stronger force wins. (Evil)
5	**Live and Let Live.** Ideals aren't worth killing over or going to war for. (Neutral)
6	**Nation.** My city, nation, or people are all that matter. (Any)

d6	Bond
1	I would still lay down my life for the people I served with.
2	Someone saved my life on the battlefield. To this day, I will never leave a friend behind.
3	My honor is my life.
4	I'll never forget the crushing defeat my company suffered or the enemies who dealt it.
5	Those who fight beside me are those worth dying for.
6	I fight for those who cannot fight for themselves.

d6	Flaw
1	The monstrous enemy we faced in battle still leaves me quivering with fear.
2	I have little respect for anyone who is not a proven warrior.
3	I made a terrible mistake in battle that cost many lives, and I would do anything to keep that mistake secret.
4	My hatred of my enemies is blind and unreasoning.
5	I obey the law, even if the law causes misery.
6	I'd rather eat my armor than admit when I'm wrong.

URCHIN

You grew up on the streets alone, orphaned, and poor. You had no one to watch over you or to provide for you, so you learned to provide for yourself. You fought fiercely over food and kept a constant watch out for other desperate souls who might steal from you. You slept on rooftops and in alleyways, exposed to the elements, and endured sickness without the advantage of medicine or a place to recuperate. You've survived despite all odds, and did so through cunning, strength, speed, or some combination of each.

You begin your adventuring career with enough money to live modestly but securely for at least ten days. How did you come by that money? What allowed you to break free of your desperate circumstances and embark on a better life?

Skill Proficiencies: Sleight of Hand, Stealth
Tool Proficiencies: Disguise kit, thieves' tools
Equipment: A small knife, a map of the city you grew up in, a pet mouse, a token to remember your parents by, a set of common clothes, and a pouch containing 10 gp

FEATURE: CITY SECRETS
You know the secret patterns and flow to cities and can find passages through the urban sprawl that others would miss. When you are not in combat, you (and companions you lead) can travel between any two locations in the city twice as fast as your speed would normally allow.

SUGGESTED CHARACTERISTICS
Urchins are shaped by lives of desperate poverty, for good and for ill. They tend to be driven either by a commitment to the people with whom they shared life on the street or by a burning desire to find a better life—and maybe get some payback on all the rich people who treated them badly.

d8	Personality Trait
1	I hide scraps of food and trinkets away in my pockets.
2	I ask a lot of questions.
3	I like to squeeze into small places where no one else can get to me.
4	I sleep with my back to a wall or tree, with everything I own wrapped in a bundle in my arms.
5	I eat like a pig and have bad manners.
6	I think anyone who's nice to me is hiding evil intent.
7	I don't like to bathe.
8	I bluntly say what other people are hinting at or hiding.

d6	Ideal
1	**Respect.** All people, rich or poor, deserve respect. (Good)
2	**Community.** We have to take care of each other, because no one else is going to do it. (Lawful)
3	**Change.** The low are lifted up, and the high and mighty are brought down. Change is the nature of things. (Chaotic)
4	**Retribution.** The rich need to be shown what life and death are like in the gutters. (Evil)
5	**People.** I help the people who help me—that's what keeps us alive. (Neutral)
6	**Aspiration.** I'm going to prove that I'm worthy of a better life.

d6	Bond
1	My town or city is my home, and I'll fight to defend it.
2	I sponsor an orphanage to keep others from enduring what I was forced to endure.
3	I owe my survival to another urchin who taught me to live on the streets.
4	I owe a debt I can never repay to the person who took pity on me.
5	I escaped my life of poverty by robbing an important person, and I'm wanted for it.
6	No one else should have to endure the hardships I've been through.

d6	Flaw
1	If I'm outnumbered, I will run away from a fight.
2	Gold seems like a lot of money to me, and I'll do just about anything for more of it.
3	I will never fully trust anyone other than myself.
4	I'd rather kill someone in their sleep then fight fair.
5	It's not stealing if I need it more than someone else.
6	People who can't take care of themselves get what they deserve.

Chapter 5: Equipment

HE MARKETPLACE OF A LARGE CITY TEEMS with buyers and sellers of many sorts: dwarf smiths and elf woodcarvers, halfling farmers and gnome jewelers, not to mention humans of every shape, size, and color drawn from a spectrum of nations and cultures. In the largest cities, almost anything imaginable is offered for sale, from exotic spices and luxurious clothing to wicker baskets and practical swords.

For an adventurer, the availability of armor, weapons, backpacks, rope, and similar goods is of paramount importance, since proper equipment can mean the difference between life and death in a dungeon or the untamed wilds. This chapter details the mundane and exotic merchandise that adventurers commonly find useful in the face of the threats that the worlds of D&D present.

Starting Equipment

When you create your character, you receive equipment based on a combination of your class and background. Alternatively, you can start with a number of gold pieces based on your class and spend them on items from the lists in this chapter. See the Starting Wealth by Class table to determine how much gold you have to spend.

You decide how your character came by this starting equipment. It might have been an inheritance, or goods that the character purchased during his or her upbringing. You might have been equipped with a weapon, armor, and a backpack as part of military service. You might even have stolen your gear. A weapon could be a family heirloom, passed down from generation to generation until your character finally took up the mantle and followed in an ancestor's adventurous footsteps.

Starting Wealth by Class

Class	Funds
Barbarian	2d4 × 10 gp
Bard	5d4 × 10 gp
Cleric	5d4 × 10 gp
Druid	2d4 × 10 gp
Fighter	5d4 × 10 gp
Monk	5d4 gp
Paladin	5d4 × 10 gp
Ranger	5d4 × 10 gp
Rogue	4d4 × 10 gp
Sorcerer	3d4 × 10 gp
Warlock	4d4 × 10 gp
Wizard	4d4 × 10 gp

Wealth

Wealth appears in many forms in a D&D world. Coins, gemstones, trade goods, art objects, animals, and property can reflect your character's financial well-being. Members of the peasantry trade in goods, bartering for what they need and paying taxes in grain and cheese.

Members of the nobility trade either in legal rights, such as the rights to a mine, a port, or farmland, or in gold bars, measuring gold by the pound rather than by the coin. Only merchants, adventurers, and those offering professional services for hire commonly deal in coins.

Coinage

Common coins come in several different denominations based on the relative worth of the metal from which they are made. The three most common coins are the gold piece (gp), the silver piece (sp), and the copper piece (cp).

With one gold piece, a character can buy a bedroll, 50 feet of good rope, or a goat. A skilled (but not exceptional) artisan can earn one gold piece a day. The gold piece is the standard unit of measure for wealth, even if the coin itself is not commonly used. When merchants discuss deals that involve goods or services worth hundreds or thousands of gold pieces, the transactions don't usually involve the exchange of individual coins. Rather, the gold piece is a standard measure of value, and the actual exchange is in gold bars, letters of credit, or valuable goods.

One gold piece is worth ten silver pieces, the most prevalent coin among commoners. A silver piece buys a laborer's work for half a day, a flask of lamp oil, or a night's rest in a poor inn.

One silver piece is worth ten copper pieces, which are common among laborers and beggars. A single copper piece buys a candle, a torch, or a piece of chalk.

In addition, unusual coins made of other precious metals sometimes appear in treasure hoards. The electrum piece (ep) and the platinum piece (pp) originate from fallen empires and lost kingdoms, and they sometimes arouse suspicion and skepticism when used in transactions. An electrum piece is worth five silver pieces, and a platinum piece is worth ten gold pieces.

A standard coin weighs about a third of an ounce, so fifty coins weigh a pound.

Standard Exchange Rates

Coin	cp	sp	ep	gp	pp
Copper (cp)	1	1/10	1/50	1/100	1/1,000
Silver (sp)	10	1	1/5	1/10	1/100
Electrum (ep)	50	5	1	1/2	1/20
Gold (gp)	100	10	2	1	1/10
Platinum (pp)	1,000	100	20	10	1

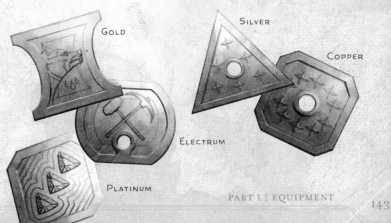

GOLD

SILVER

COPPER

ELECTRUM

PLATINUM

SELLING TREASURE

Opportunities abound to find treasure, equipment, weapons, armor, and more in the dungeons you explore. Normally, you can sell your treasures and trinkets when you return to a town or other settlement, provided that you can find buyers and merchants interested in your loot.

Arms, Armor, and Other Equipment. As a general rule, undamaged weapons, armor, and other equipment fetch half their cost when sold in a market. Weapons and armor used by monsters are rarely in good enough condition to sell.

Magic Items. Selling magic items is problematic. Finding someone to buy a potion or a scroll isn't too hard, but other items are out of the realm of most but the wealthiest nobles. Likewise, aside from a few common magic items, you won't normally come across magic items or spells to purchase. The value of magic is far beyond simple gold and should always be treated as such.

Gems, Jewelry, and Art Objects. These items retain their full value in the marketplace, and you can either trade them in for coin or use them as currency for other transactions. For exceptionally valuable treasures, the DM might require you to find a buyer in a large town or larger community first.

Trade Goods. On the borderlands, many people conduct transactions through barter. Like gems and art objects, trade goods—bars of iron, bags of salt, livestock, and so on—retain their full value in the market and can be used as currency.

ARMOR AND SHIELDS

D&D worlds are a vast tapestry made up of many different cultures, each with its own technology level. For this reason, adventurers have access to a variety of armor types, ranging from leather armor to chain mail to costly plate armor, with several other kinds of armor in between. The Armor table collects the most commonly available types of armor found in the game and separates them into three categories: light armor, medium armor, and heavy armor. Many warriors supplement their armor with a shield.

VARIANT: EQUIPMENT SIZES

In most campaigns, you can use or wear any equipment that you find on your adventures, within the bounds of common sense. For example, a burly half-orc won't fit in a halfling's leather armor, and a gnome would be swallowed up in a cloud giant's elegant robe.

The DM can impose more realism. For example, a suit of plate armor made for one human might not fit another one without significant alterations, and a guard's uniform might be visibly ill-fitting when an adventurer tries to wear it as a disguise.

Using this variant, when adventurers find armor, clothing, and similar items that are made to be worn, they might need to visit an armorsmith, tailor, leatherworker, or similar expert to make the item wearable. The cost for such work varies from 10 to 40 percent of the market price of the item. The DM can either roll 1d4 × 10 or determine the increase in cost based on the extent of the alterations required.

The Armor table shows the cost, weight, and other properties of the common types of armor worn in the worlds of D&D.

Armor Proficiency. Anyone can put on a suit of armor or strap a shield to an arm. Only those proficient in the armor's use know how to wear it effectively, however. Your class gives you proficiency with certain types of armor. If you wear armor that you lack proficiency with, you have disadvantage on any ability check, saving throw, or attack roll that involves Strength or Dexterity, and you can't cast spells.

Armor Class (AC). Armor protects its wearer from attacks. The armor (and shield) you wear determines your base Armor Class.

Heavy Armor. Heavier armor interferes with the wearer's ability to move quickly, stealthily, and freely. If the Armor table shows "Str 13" or "Str 15" in the Strength column for an armor type, the armor reduces the wearer's speed by 10 feet unless the wearer has a Strength score equal to or higher than the listed score.

Stealth. If the Armor table shows "Disadvantage" in the Stealth column, the wearer has disadvantage on Dexterity (Stealth) checks.

Shields. A shield is made from wood or metal and is carried in one hand. Wielding a shield increases your Armor Class by 2. You can benefit from only one shield at a time.

LIGHT ARMOR

Made from supple and thin materials, light armor favors agile adventurers since it offers some protection without sacrificing mobility. If you wear light armor, you add your Dexterity modifier to the base number from your armor type to determine your Armor Class.

Padded. Padded armor consists of quilted layers of cloth and batting.

Leather. The breastplate and shoulder protectors of this armor are made of leather that has been stiffened by being boiled in oil. The rest of the armor is made of softer and more flexible materials.

Studded Leather. Made from tough but flexible leather, studded leather is reinforced with close-set rivets or spikes.

MEDIUM ARMOR

Medium armor offers more protection than light armor, but it also impairs movement more. If you wear medium armor, you add your Dexterity modifier, to a maximum of +2, to the base number from your armor type to determine your Armor Class.

Hide. This crude armor consists of thick furs and pelts. It is commonly worn by barbarian tribes, evil humanoids, and other folk who lack access to the tools and materials needed to create better armor.

Chain Shirt. Made of interlocking metal rings, a chain shirt is worn between layers of clothing or leather. This armor offers modest protection to the wearer's upper body and allows the sound of the rings rubbing against one another to be muffled by outer layers.

Scale Mail. This armor consists of a coat and leggings (and perhaps a separate skirt) of leather covered with overlapping pieces of metal, much like the scales of a fish. The suit includes gauntlets.

Breastplate. This armor consists of a fitted metal chest piece worn with supple leather. Although it leaves the legs and arms relatively unprotected, this armor provides good protection for the wearer's vital organs while leaving the wearer relatively unencumbered.

Half Plate. Half plate consists of shaped metal plates that cover most of the wearer's body. It does not include leg protection beyond simple greaves that are attached with leather straps.

HEAVY ARMOR

Of all the armor categories, heavy armor offers the best protection. These suits of armor cover the entire body and are designed to stop a wide range of attacks. Only proficient warriors can manage their weight and bulk.

Heavy armor doesn't let you add your Dexterity modifier to your Armor Class, but it also doesn't penalize you if your Dexterity modifier is negative.

Ring Mail. This armor is leather armor with heavy rings sewn into it. The rings help reinforce the armor against blows from swords and axes. Ring mail is inferior to chain mail, and it's usually worn only by those who can't afford better armor.

Chain Mail. Made of interlocking metal rings, chain mail includes a layer of quilted fabric worn underneath the mail to prevent chafing and to cushion the impact of blows. The suit includes gauntlets.

Splint. This armor is made of narrow vertical strips of metal riveted to a backing of leather that is worn over cloth padding. Flexible chain mail protects the joints.

Plate. Plate consists of shaped, interlocking metal plates to cover the entire body. A suit of plate includes gauntlets, heavy leather boots, a visored helmet, and thick layers of padding underneath the armor. Buckles and straps distribute the weight over the body.

ARMOR

Armor	Cost	Armor Class (AC)	Strength	Stealth	Weight
Light Armor					
Padded	5 gp	11 + Dex modifier	—	Disadvantage	8 lb.
Leather	10 gp	11 + Dex modifier	—	—	10 lb.
Studded leather	45 gp	12 + Dex modifier	—	—	13 lb.
Medium Armor					
Hide	10 gp	12 + Dex modifier (max 2)	—	—	12 lb.
Chain shirt	50 gp	13 + Dex modifier (max 2)	—	—	20 lb.
Scale mail	50 gp	14 + Dex modifier (max 2)	—	Disadvantage	45 lb.
Breastplate	400 gp	14 + Dex modifier (max 2)	—	—	20 lb.
Half plate	750 gp	15 + Dex modifier (max 2)	—	Disadvantage	40 lb.
Heavy Armor					
Ring mail	30 gp	14	—	Disadvantage	40 lb.
Chain mail	75 gp	16	Str 13	Disadvantage	55 lb.
Splint	200 gp	17	Str 15	Disadvantage	60 lb.
Plate	1,500 gp	18	Str 15	Disadvantage	65 lb.
Shield					
Shield	10 gp	+2	—	—	6 lb.

Getting Into and Out of Armor

The time it takes to don or doff armor depends on the armor's category.

Don. This is the time it takes to put on armor. You benefit from the armor's AC only if you take the full time to don the suit of armor.

Doff. This is the time it takes to take off armor. If you have help, reduce this time by half.

Donning and Doffing Armor

Category	Don	Doff
Light Armor	1 minute	1 minute
Medium Armor	5 minutes	1 minute
Heavy Armor	10 minutes	5 minutes
Shield	1 action	1 action

Weapons

Your class grants proficiency in certain weapons, reflecting both the class's focus and the tools you are most likely to use. Whether you favor a longsword or a longbow, your weapon and your ability to wield it effectively can mean the difference between life and death while adventuring.

The Weapons table shows the most common weapons used in the worlds of D&D, their price and weight, the damage they deal when they hit, and any special properties they possess. Every weapon is classified as either melee or ranged. A **melee weapon** is used to attack a target within 5 feet of you, whereas a **ranged weapon** is used to attack a target at a distance.

Weapon Proficiency

Your race, class, and feats can grant you proficiency with certain weapons or categories of weapons. The two categories are **simple** and **martial**. Most people can use simple weapons with proficiency. These weapons include clubs, maces, and other weapons often found in the hands of commoners. Martial weapons, including swords, axes, and polearms, require more specialized training to use effectively. Most warriors use martial weapons because these weapons put their fighting style and training to best use.

Proficiency with a weapon allows you to add your proficiency bonus to the attack roll for any attack you make with that weapon. If you make an attack roll using a weapon with which you lack proficiency, you do not add your proficiency bonus to the attack roll.

Weapon Properties

Many weapons have special properties related to their use, as shown in the Weapons table.

Ammunition. You can use a weapon that has the ammunition property to make a ranged attack only if you have ammunition to fire from the weapon. Each time you attack with the weapon, you expend one piece of ammunition. Drawing the ammunition from a quiver, case, or other container is part of the attack (you need a free hand to load a one-handed weapon). At the end of the battle, you can recover half your expended ammunition by taking a minute to search the battlefield.

If you use a weapon that has the ammunition property to make a melee attack, you treat the weapon as an improvised weapon (see "Improvised Weapons" later in the section). A sling must be loaded to deal any damage when used in this way.

Finesse. When making an attack with a finesse weapon, you use your choice of your Strength or Dexterity modifier for the attack and damage rolls. You must use the same modifier for both rolls.

Heavy. Small creatures have disadvantage on attack rolls with heavy weapons. A heavy weapon's size and bulk make it too large for a Small creature to use effectively.

Light. A light weapon is small and easy to handle, making it ideal for use when fighting with two weapons. See the rules for two-weapon fighting in chapter 9.

Loading. Because of the time required to load this weapon, you can fire only one piece of ammunition from it when you use an action, bonus action, or reaction to fire it, regardless of the number of attacks you can normally make.

Range. A weapon that can be used to make a ranged attack has a range in parentheses after the ammunition or thrown property. The range lists two numbers. The first is the weapon's normal range in feet, and the second indicates the weapon's long range. When attacking a target beyond normal range, you have disadvantage on the attack roll. You can't attack a target beyond the weapon's long range.

Reach. This weapon adds 5 feet to your reach when you attack with it, as well as when determining your reach for opportunity attacks with it (see chapter 9).

Special. A weapon with the special property has unusual rules governing its use, explained in the weapon's description (see "Special Weapons" later in this section).

Thrown. If a weapon has the thrown property, you can throw the weapon to make a ranged attack. If the weapon is a melee weapon, you use the same ability modifier for that attack roll and damage roll that you would use for a melee attack with the weapon. For example, if you throw a handaxe, you use your Strength, but if you throw a dagger, you can use either your Strength or your Dexterity, since the dagger has the finesse property.

Two-Handed. This weapon requires two hands when you attack with it.

Versatile. This weapon can be used with one or two hands. A damage value in parentheses appears with the property—the damage when the weapon is used with two hands to make a melee attack.

Improvised Weapons

Sometimes characters don't have their weapons and have to attack with whatever is at hand. An improvised weapon includes any object you can wield in one or two hands, such as broken glass, a table leg, a frying pan, a wagon wheel, or a dead goblin.

Often, an improvised weapon is similar to an actual weapon and can be treated as such. For example, a table leg is akin to a club. At the DM's option, a character proficient with a weapon can use a similar object as if it were that weapon and use his or her proficiency bonus.

An object that bears no resemblance to a weapon deals 1d4 damage (the DM assigns a damage type appropriate to the object). If a character uses a ranged weapon to make a melee attack, or throws a melee weapon that does not have the thrown property, it also deals 1d4 damage. An improvised thrown weapon has a normal range of 20 feet and a long range of 60 feet.

SILVERED WEAPONS

Some monsters that have immunity or resistance to nonmagical weapons are susceptible to silver weapons, so cautious adventurers invest extra coin to plate their weapons with silver. You can silver a single weapon or ten pieces of ammunition for 100 gp. This cost represents not only the price of the silver, but the time and expertise needed to add silver to the weapon without making it less effective.

SPECIAL WEAPONS

Weapons with special rules are described here.

Lance. You have disadvantage when you use a lance to attack a target within 5 feet of you. Also, a lance requires two hands to wield when you aren't mounted.

Net. A Large or smaller creature hit by a net is restrained until it is freed. A net has no effect on creatures that are formless, or creatures that are Huge or larger. A creature can use its action to make a DC 10 Strength check, freeing itself or another creature within its reach on a success. Dealing 5 slashing damage to the net (AC 10) also frees the creature without harming it, ending the effect and destroying the net.

When you use an action, bonus action, or reaction to attack with a net, you can make only one attack regardless of the number of attacks you can normally make.

ADVENTURING GEAR

This section describes items that have special rules or require further explanation.

Acid. As an action, you can splash the contents of this vial onto a creature within 5 feet of you or throw the vial up to 20 feet, shattering it on impact. In either case, make a ranged attack against a creature or object, treating the acid as an improvised weapon. On a hit, the target takes 2d6 acid damage.

Alchemist's Fire. This sticky, adhesive fluid ignites when exposed to air. As an action, you can throw this flask up to 20 feet, shattering it on impact. Make a ranged attack against a creature or object, treating

Weapons

Name	Cost	Damage	Weight	Properties
Simple Melee Weapons				
Club	1 sp	1d4 bludgeoning	2 lb.	Light
Dagger	2 gp	1d4 piercing	1 lb.	Finesse, light, thrown (range 20/60)
Greatclub	2 sp	1d8 bludgeoning	10 lb.	Two-handed
Handaxe	5 gp	1d6 slashing	2 lb.	Light, thrown (range 20/60)
Javelin	5 sp	1d6 piercing	2 lb.	Thrown (range 30/120)
Light hammer	2 gp	1d4 bludgeoning	2 lb.	Light, thrown (range 20/60)
Mace	5 gp	1d6 bludgeoning	4 lb.	—
Quarterstaff	2 sp	1d6 bludgeoning	4 lb.	Versatile (1d8)
Sickle	1 gp	1d4 slashing	2 lb.	Light
Spear	1 gp	1d6 piercing	3 lb.	Thrown (range 20/60), versatile (1d8)
Simple Ranged Weapons				
Crossbow, light	25 gp	1d8 piercing	5 lb.	Ammunition (range 80/320), loading, two-handed
Dart	5 cp	1d4 piercing	1/4 lb.	Finesse, thrown (range 20/60)
Shortbow	25 gp	1d6 piercing	2 lb.	Ammunition (range 80/320), two-handed
Sling	1 sp	1d4 bludgeoning	—	Ammunition (range 30/120)
Martial Melee Weapons				
Battleaxe	10 gp	1d8 slashing	4 lb.	Versatile (1d10)
Flail	10 gp	1d8 bludgeoning	2 lb.	—
Glaive	20 gp	1d10 slashing	6 lb.	Heavy, reach, two-handed
Greataxe	30 gp	1d12 slashing	7 lb.	Heavy, two-handed
Greatsword	50 gp	2d6 slashing	6 lb.	Heavy, two-handed
Halberd	20 gp	1d10 slashing	6 lb.	Heavy, reach, two-handed
Lance	10 gp	1d12 piercing	6 lb.	Reach, special
Longsword	15 gp	1d8 slashing	3 lb.	Versatile (1d10)
Maul	10 gp	2d6 bludgeoning	10 lb.	Heavy, two-handed
Morningstar	15 gp	1d8 piercing	4 lb.	—
Pike	5 gp	1d10 piercing	18 lb.	Heavy, reach, two-handed
Rapier	25 gp	1d8 piercing	2 lb.	Finesse
Scimitar	25 gp	1d6 slashing	3 lb.	Finesse, light
Shortsword	10 gp	1d6 piercing	2 lb.	Finesse, light
Trident	5 gp	1d6 piercing	4 lb.	Thrown (range 20/60), versatile (1d8)
War pick	5 gp	1d8 piercing	2 lb.	—
Warhammer	15 gp	1d8 bludgeoning	2 lb.	Versatile (1d10)
Whip	2 gp	1d4 slashing	3 lb.	Finesse, reach
Martial Ranged Weapons				
Blowgun	10 gp	1 piercing	1 lb.	Ammunition (range 25/100), loading
Crossbow, hand	75 gp	1d6 piercing	3 lb.	Ammunition (range 30/120), light, loading
Crossbow, heavy	50 gp	1d10 piercing	18 lb.	Ammunition (range 100/400), heavy, loading, two-handed
Longbow	50 gp	1d8 piercing	2 lb.	Ammunition (range 150/600), heavy, two-handed
Net	1 gp	—	3 lb.	Special, thrown (range 5/15)

Adventuring Gear

Item	Cost	Weight
Abacus	2 gp	2 lb.
Acid (vial)	25 gp	1 lb.
Alchemist's fire (flask)	50 gp	1 lb.
Ammunition		
Arrows (20)	1 gp	1 lb.
Blowgun needles (50)	1 gp	1 lb.
Crossbow bolts (20)	1 gp	1½ lb.
Sling bullets (20)	4 cp	1½ lb.
Antitoxin (vial)	50 gp	—
Arcane focus		
Crystal	10 gp	1 lb.
Orb	20 gp	3 lb.
Rod	10 gp	2 lb.
Staff	5 gp	4 lb.
Wand	10 gp	1 lb.
Backpack	2 gp	5 lb.
Ball bearings (bag of 1,000)	1 gp	2 lb.
Barrel	2 gp	70 lb.
Basket	4 sp	2 lb.
Bedroll	1 gp	7 lb.
Bell	1 gp	—
Blanket	5 sp	3 lb.
Block and tackle	1 gp	5 lb.
Book	25 gp	5 lb.
Bottle, glass	2 gp	2 lb.
Bucket	5 cp	2 lb.
Caltrops (bag of 20)	1 gp	2 lb.
Candle	1 cp	—
Case, crossbow bolt	1 gp	1 lb.
Case, map or scroll	1 gp	1 lb.
Chain (10 feet)	5 gp	10 lb.
Chalk (1 piece)	1 cp	—
Chest	5 gp	25 lb.
Climber's kit	25 gp	12 lb.
Clothes, common	5 sp	3 lb.
Clothes, costume	5 gp	4 lb.
Clothes, fine	15 gp	6 lb.
Clothes, traveler's	2 gp	4 lb.
Component pouch	25 gp	2 lb.
Crowbar	2 gp	5 lb.
Druidic focus		
Sprig of mistletoe	1 gp	—
Totem	1 gp	—
Wooden staff	5 gp	4 lb.
Yew wand	10 gp	1 lb.
Fishing tackle	1 gp	4 lb.
Flask or tankard	2 cp	1 lb.
Grappling hook	2 gp	4 lb.
Hammer	1 gp	3 lb.
Hammer, sledge	2 gp	10 lb.
Healer's kit	5 gp	3 lb.

Item	Cost	Weight
Holy symbol		
Amulet	5 gp	1 lb.
Emblem	5 gp	—
Reliquary	5 gp	2 lb.
Holy water (flask)	25 gp	1 lb.
Hourglass	25 gp	1 lb.
Hunting trap	5 gp	25 lb.
Ink (1 ounce bottle)	10 gp	—
Ink pen	2 cp	—
Jug or pitcher	2 cp	4 lb.
Ladder (10-foot)	1 sp	25 lb.
Lamp	5 sp	1 lb.
Lantern, bullseye	10 gp	2 lb.
Lantern, hooded	5 gp	2 lb.
Lock	10 gp	1 lb.
Magnifying glass	100 gp	—
Manacles	2 gp	6 lb.
Mess kit	2 sp	1 lb.
Mirror, steel	5 gp	1/2 lb.
Oil (flask)	1 sp	1 lb.
Paper (one sheet)	2 sp	—
Parchment (one sheet)	1 sp	—
Perfume (vial)	5 gp	—
Pick, miner's	2 gp	10 lb.
Piton	5 cp	1/4 lb.
Poison, basic (vial)	100 gp	—
Pole (10-foot)	5 cp	7 lb.
Pot, iron	2 gp	10 lb.
Potion of healing	50 gp	1/2 lb.
Pouch	5 sp	1 lb.
Quiver	1 gp	1 lb.
Ram, portable	4 gp	35 lb.
Rations (1 day)	5 sp	2 lb.
Robes	1 gp	4 lb.
Rope, hempen (50 feet)	1 gp	10 lb.
Rope, silk (50 feet)	10 gp	5 lb.
Sack	1 cp	1/2 lb.
Scale, merchant's	5 gp	3 lb.
Sealing wax	5 sp	—
Shovel	2 gp	5 lb.
Signal whistle	5 cp	—
Signet ring	5 gp	—
Soap	2 cp	—
Spellbook	50 gp	3 lb.
Spikes, iron (10)	1 gp	5 lb.
Spyglass	1,000 gp	1 lb.
Tent, two-person	2 gp	20 lb.
Tinderbox	5 sp	1 lb.
Torch	1 cp	1 lb.
Vial	1 gp	—
Waterskin	2 sp	5 lb. (full)
Whetstone	1 cp	1 lb.

the alchemist's fire as an improvised weapon. On a hit, the target takes 1d4 fire damage at the start of each of its turns. A creature can end this damage by using its action to make a DC 10 Dexterity check to extinguish the flames.

Antitoxin. A creature that drinks this vial of liquid gains advantage on saving throws against poison for 1 hour. It confers no benefit to undead or constructs.

Arcane Focus. An arcane focus is a special item—an orb, a crystal, a rod, a specially constructed staff, a wand-like length of wood, or some similar item—designed to channel the power of arcane spells. A sorcerer, warlock, or wizard can use such an item as a spellcasting focus, as described in chapter 10.

Ball Bearings. As an action, you can spill these tiny metal balls from their pouch to cover a level, square area that is 10 feet on a side. A creature moving across the covered area must succeed on a DC 10 Dexterity saving throw or fall prone. A creature moving through the area at half speed doesn't need to make the save.

Block and Tackle. A set of pulleys with a cable threaded through them and a hook to attach to objects, a block and tackle allows you to hoist up to four times the weight you can normally lift.

Book. A book might contain poetry, historical accounts, information pertaining to a particular field of lore, diagrams and notes on gnomish contraptions, or just about anything else that can be represented using text or pictures. A book of spells is a spellbook (described later in this section).

Caltrops. As an action, you can spread a bag of caltrops to cover a square area that is 5 feet on a side. Any creature that enters the area must succeed on a DC 15 Dexterity saving throw or stop moving this turn and take 1 piercing damage. Taking this damage reduces the creature's walking speed by 10 feet until the creature regains at least 1 hit point. A creature moving through the area at half speed doesn't need to make the save.

Candle. For 1 hour, a candle sheds bright light in a 5-foot radius and dim light for an additional 5 feet.

Case, Crossbow Bolt. This wooden case can hold up to twenty crossbow bolts.

Case, Map or Scroll. This cylindrical leather case can hold up to ten rolled-up sheets of paper or five rolled-up sheets of parchment.

Chain. A chain has 10 hit points. It can be burst with a successful DC 20 Strength check.

Climber's Kit. A climber's kit includes special pitons, boot tips, gloves, and a harness. You can use the climber's kit as an action to anchor yourself; when you do, you can't fall more than 25 feet from the point where you anchored yourself, and you can't climb more than 25 feet away from that point without undoing the anchor.

Component Pouch. A component pouch is a small, watertight leather belt pouch that has compartments to hold all the material components and other special items you need to cast your spells, except for those components that have a specific cost (as indicated in a spell's description).

Crowbar. Using a crowbar grants advantage to Strength checks where the crowbar's leverage can be applied.

Druidic Focus. A druidic focus might be a sprig of mistletoe or holly, a wand or scepter made of yew or another special wood, a staff drawn whole out of a living tree, or a totem object incorporating feathers, fur, bones, and teeth from sacred animals. A druid can use such an object as a spellcasting focus, as described in chapter 10.

Fishing Tackle. This kit includes a wooden rod, silken line, corkwood bobbers, steel hooks, lead sinkers, velvet lures, and narrow netting.

Healer's Kit. This kit is a leather pouch containing bandages, salves, and splints. The kit has ten uses. As an action, you can expend one use of the kit to stabilize a creature that has 0 hit points, without needing to make a Wisdom (Medicine) check.

Holy Symbol. A holy symbol is a representation of a god or pantheon. It might be an amulet depicting a symbol representing a deity, the same symbol carefully engraved or inlaid as an emblem on a shield, or a tiny box holding a fragment of a sacred relic. Appendix B lists the symbols commonly associated with many gods in the multiverse. A cleric or paladin can use a holy symbol as a spellcasting focus, as described in chapter 10. To use the symbol in this way, the caster must hold it in hand, wear it visibly, or bear it on a shield.

Holy Water. As an action, you can splash the contents of this flask onto a creature within 5 feet of you or throw it up to 20 feet, shattering it on impact. In either case, make a ranged attack against a target creature, treating the holy water as an improvised weapon. If the target is a fiend or undead, it takes 2d6 radiant damage.

EQUIPMENT PACKS

The starting equipment you get from your class includes a collection of useful adventuring gear, put together in a pack. The contents of these packs are listed here. If you are buying your starting equipment, you can purchase a pack for the price shown, which might be cheaper than buying the items individually.

Burglar's Pack (16 gp). Includes a backpack, a bag of 1,000 ball bearings, 10 feet of string, a bell, 5 candles, a crowbar, a hammer, 10 pitons, a hooded lantern, 2 flasks of oil, 5 days rations, a tinderbox, and a waterskin. The pack also has 50 feet of hempen rope strapped to the side of it.

Diplomat's Pack (39 gp). Includes a chest, 2 cases for maps and scrolls, a set of fine clothes, a bottle of ink, an ink pen, a lamp, 2 flasks of oil, 5 sheets of paper, a vial of perfume, sealing wax, and soap.

Dungeoneer's Pack (12 gp). Includes a backpack, a crowbar, a hammer, 10 pitons, 10 torches, a tinderbox, 10 days of rations, and a waterskin. The pack also has 50 feet of hempen rope strapped to the side of it.

Entertainer's Pack (40 gp). Includes a backpack, a bedroll, 2 costumes, 5 candles, 5 days of rations, a waterskin, and a disguise kit.

Explorer's Pack (10 gp). Includes a backpack, a bedroll, a mess kit, a tinderbox, 10 torches, 10 days of rations, and a waterskin. The pack also has 50 feet of hempen rope strapped to the side of it.

Priest's Pack (19 gp). Includes a backpack, a blanket, 10 candles, a tinderbox, an alms box, 2 blocks of incense, a censer, vestments, 2 days of rations, and a waterskin.

Scholar's Pack (40 gp). Includes a backpack, a book of lore, a bottle of ink, an ink pen, 10 sheets of parchment, a little bag of sand, and a small knife.

A cleric or paladin may create holy water by performing a special ritual. The ritual takes 1 hour to perform, uses 25 gp worth of powdered silver, and requires the caster to expend a 1st-level spell slot.

Hunting Trap. When you use your action to set it, this trap forms a saw-toothed steel ring that snaps shut when a creature steps on a pressure plate in the center. The trap is affixed by a heavy chain to an immobile object, such as a tree or a spike driven into the ground. A creature that steps on the plate must succeed on a DC 13 Dexterity saving throw or take 1d4 piercing damage and stop moving. Thereafter, until the creature breaks free of the trap, its movement is limited by the length of the chain (typically 3 feet long). A creature can use its action to make a DC 13 Strength check, freeing itself or another creature within its reach on a success. Each failed check deals 1 piercing damage to the trapped creature.

Lamp. A lamp casts bright light in a 15-foot radius and dim light for an additional 30 feet. Once lit, it burns for 6 hours on a flask (1 pint) of oil.

Lantern, Bullseye. A bullseye lantern casts bright light in a 60-foot cone and dim light for an additional 60 feet. Once lit, it burns for 6 hours on a flask (1 pint) of oil.

Lantern, Hooded. A hooded lantern casts bright light in a 30-foot radius and dim light for an additional 30 feet. Once lit, it burns for 6 hours on a flask (1 pint) of oil. As an action, you can lower the hood, reducing the light to dim light in a 5-foot radius.

Lock. A key is provided with the lock. Without the key, a creature proficient with thieves' tools can pick this lock with a successful DC 15 Dexterity check. Your DM may decide that better locks are available for higher prices.

Magnifying Glass. This lens allows a closer look at small objects. It is also useful as a substitute for flint and steel when starting fires. Lighting a fire with a magnifying glass requires light as bright as sunlight to focus, tinder to ignite, and about 5 minutes for the fire to ignite. A magnifying glass grants advantage on any ability check made to appraise or inspect an item that is small or highly detailed.

Manacles. These metal restraints can bind a Small or Medium creature. Escaping the manacles requires a successful DC 20 Dexterity check. Breaking them requires a successful DC 20 Strength check. Each set of manacles comes with one key. Without the key, a creature proficient with thieves' tools can pick the manacles' lock with a successful DC 15 Dexterity check. Manacles have 15 hit points.

Mess Kit. This tin box contains a cup and simple cutlery. The box clamps together, and one side can be used as a cooking pan and the other as a plate or shallow bowl.

Oil. Oil usually comes in a clay flask that holds 1 pint. As an action, you can splash the oil in this flask onto a creature within 5 feet of you or throw it up to 20 feet, shattering it on impact. Make a ranged attack against a target creature or object, treating the oil as an improvised weapon. On a hit, the target is covered in oil. If the target takes any fire damage before the oil dries (after 1 minute), the target takes an additional 5 fire damage from the burning oil. You can also pour a flask of oil on the ground to cover a 5-foot-square area, provided that the surface is level. If lit, the oil burns for 2 rounds and deals 5 fire damage to any creature that enters the area or ends its turn in the area. A creature can take this damage only once per turn.

Poison, Basic. You can use the poison in this vial to coat one slashing or piercing weapon or up to three pieces of ammunition. Applying the poison takes an action. A creature hit by the poisoned weapon or ammunition must make a DC 10 Constitution saving throw or take 1d4 poison damage. Once applied, the poison retains potency for 1 minute before drying.

Potion of Healing. A character who drinks the magical red fluid in this vial regains 2d4 + 2 hit points. Drinking or administering a potion takes an action.

Pouch. A cloth or leather pouch can hold up to 20 sling bullets or 50 blowgun needles, among other things. A compartmentalized pouch for holding spell components is called a component pouch (described earlier in this section).

Quiver. A quiver can hold up to 20 arrows.

Ram, Portable. You can use a portable ram to break down doors. When doing so, you gain a +4 bonus on the Strength check. One other character can help you use the ram, giving you advantage on this check.

Rations. Rations consist of dry foods suitable for extended travel, including jerky, dried fruit, hardtack, and nuts.

Rope. Rope, whether made of hemp or silk, has 2 hit points and can be burst with a DC 17 Strength check.

Scale, Merchant's. A scale includes a small balance, pans, and a suitable assortment of weights up to 2 pounds. With it, you can measure the exact weight of small objects, such as raw precious metals or trade goods, to help determine their worth.

Spellbook. Essential for wizards, a spellbook is a leather-bound tome with 100 blank vellum pages suitable for recording spells.

Spyglass. Objects viewed through a spyglass are magnified to twice their size.

Tent. A simple and portable canvas shelter, a tent sleeps two.

Tinderbox. This small container holds flint, fire steel, and tinder (usually dry cloth soaked in light oil) used to kindle a fire. Using it to light a torch—or anything else with abundant, exposed fuel—takes an action. Lighting any other fire takes 1 minute.

Torch. A torch burns for 1 hour, providing bright light in a 20-foot radius and dim light for an additional 20 feet. If you make a melee attack with a burning torch and hit, it deals 1 fire damage.

CONTAINER CAPACITY

Container	Capacity
Backpack*	1 cubic foot/30 pounds of gear
Barrel	40 gallons liquid, 4 cubic feet solid
Basket	2 cubic feet/40 pounds of gear
Bottle	1½ pints liquid
Bucket	3 gallons liquid, 1/2 cubic foot solid
Chest	12 cubic feet/300 pounds of gear
Flask or tankard	1 pint liquid
Jug or pitcher	1 gallon liquid
Pot, iron	1 gallon liquid
Pouch	1/5 cubic foot/6 pounds of gear
Sack	1 cubic foot/30 pounds of gear
Vial	4 ounces liquid
Waterskin	4 pints liquid

* You can also strap items, such as a bedroll or a coil of rope, to the outside of a backpack.

Tools

A tool helps you to do something you couldn't otherwise do, such as craft or repair an item, forge a document, or pick a lock. Your race, class, background, or feats give you proficiency with certain tools. Proficiency with a tool allows you to add your proficiency bonus to any ability check you make using that tool. Tool use is not tied to a single ability, since proficiency with a tool represents broader knowledge of its use. For example, the DM might ask you to make a Dexterity check to carve a fine detail with your woodcarver's tools, or a Strength check to make something out of particularly hard wood.

Tools

Item	Cost	Weight
Artisan's tools		
Alchemist's supplies	50 gp	8 lb.
Brewer's supplies	20 gp	9 lb.
Calligrapher's supplies	10 gp	5 lb.
Carpenter's tools	8 gp	6 lb.
Cartographer's tools	15 gp.	6 lb.
Cobbler's tools	5 gp	5 lb.
Cook's utensils	1 gp	8 lb.
Glassblower's tools	30 gp	5 lb.
Jeweler's tools	25 gp	2 lb.
Leatherworker's tools	5 gp	5 lb.
Mason's tools	10 gp	8 lb.
Painter's supplies	10 gp	5 lb.
Potter's tools	10 gp	3 lb.
Smith's tools	20 gp	8 lb.
Tinker's tools	50 gp	10 lb.
Weaver's tools	1 gp	5 lb.
Woodcarver's tools	1 gp	5 lb.
Disguise kit	25 gp	3 lb.
Forgery kit	15 gp	5 lb.
Gaming set		
Dice set	1 sp	—
Dragonchess set	1 gp	1/2 lb.
Playing card set	5 sp	—
Three-Dragon Ante set	1 gp	—
Herbalism kit	5 gp	3 lb.
Musical instrument		
Bagpipes	30 gp	6 lb.
Drum	6 gp	3 lb.
Dulcimer	25 gp	10 lb.
Flute	2 gp	1 lb.
Lute	35 gp	2 lb.
Lyre	30 gp	2 lb.
Horn	3 gp	2 lb.
Pan flute	12 gp	2 lb.
Shawm	2 gp	1 lb.
Viol	30 gp	1 lb.
Navigator's tools	25 gp	2 lb.
Poisoner's kit	50 gp	2 lb.
Thieves' tools	25 gp	1 lb.
Vehicles (land or water)	*	*

* See the "Mounts and Vehicles" section.

Artisan's Tools. These special tools include the items needed to pursue a craft or trade. The table shows examples of the most common types of tools, each providing items related to a single craft. Proficiency with a set of artisan's tools lets you add your proficiency bonus to any ability checks you make using the tools in your craft. Each type of artisan's tools requires a separate proficiency.

Disguise Kit. This pouch of cosmetics, hair dye, and small props lets you create disguises that change your physical appearance. Proficiency with this kit lets you add your proficiency bonus to any ability checks you make to create a visual disguise.

Forgery Kit. This small box contains a variety of papers and parchments, pens and inks, seals and sealing wax, gold and silver leaf, and other supplies necessary to create convincing forgeries of physical documents. Proficiency with this kit lets you add your proficiency bonus to any ability checks you make to create a physical forgery of a document.

Gaming Set. This item encompasses a wide range of game pieces, including dice and decks of cards (for games such as Three-Dragon Ante). A few common examples appear on the Tools table, but other kinds of gaming sets exist. If you are proficient with a gaming set, you can add your proficiency bonus to ability checks you make to play a game with that set. Each type of gaming set requires a separate proficiency.

Herbalism Kit. This kit contains a variety of instruments such as clippers, mortar and pestle, and pouches and vials used by herbalists to create remedies and potions. Proficiency with this kit lets you add your proficiency bonus to any ability checks you make to identify or apply herbs. Also, proficiency with this kit is required to create antitoxin and *potions of healing*.

Musical Instrument. Several of the most common types of musical instruments are shown on the table as examples. If you have proficiency with a given musical instrument, you can add your proficiency bonus to any ability checks you make to play music with the instrument. A bard can use a musical instrument as a spellcasting focus, as described in chapter 10. Each type of musical instrument requires a separate proficiency.

Navigator's Tools. This set of instruments is used for navigation at sea. Proficiency with navigator's tools lets you chart a ship's course and follow navigation charts. In addition, these tools allow you to add your proficiency bonus to any ability check you make to avoid getting lost at sea.

Poisoner's Kit. A poisoner's kit includes the vials, chemicals, and other equipment necessary for the creation of poisons. Proficiency with this kit lets you add your proficiency bonus to any ability checks you make to craft or use poisons.

Thieves' Tools. This set of tools includes a small file, a set of lock picks, a small mirror mounted on a metal handle, a set of narrow-bladed scissors, and a pair of pliers. Proficiency with these tools lets you add your proficiency bonus to any ability checks you make to disarm traps or open locks.

MOUNTS AND VEHICLES

A good mount can help you move more quickly through the wilderness, but its primary purpose is to carry the gear that would otherwise slow you down. The Mounts and Other Animals table shows each animal's speed and base carrying capacity.

An animal pulling a carriage, cart, chariot, sled, or wagon can move weight up to five times its base carrying capacity, including the weight of the vehicle. If multiple animals pull the same vehicle, they can add their carrying capacity together.

Mounts other than those listed here are available in the worlds of D&D, but they are rare and not normally available for purchase. These include flying mounts (pegasi, griffons, hippogriffs, and similar animals) and even aquatic mounts (giant sea horses, for example). Acquiring such a mount often means securing an egg and raising the creature yourself, making a bargain with a powerful entity, or negotiating with the mount itself.

Barding. Barding is armor designed to protect an animal's head, neck, chest, and body. Any type of armor shown on the Armor table in this chapter can be purchased as barding. The cost is four times the equivalent armor made for humanoids, and it weighs twice as much.

Saddles. A military saddle braces the rider, helping you keep your seat on an active mount in battle. It gives you advantage on any check you make to remain mounted. An exotic saddle is required for riding any aquatic or flying mount.

Vehicle Proficiency. If you have proficiency with a certain kind of vehicle (land or water), you can add your proficiency bonus to any check you make to control that kind of vehicle in difficult circumstances.

Rowed Vessels. Keelboats and rowboats are used on lakes and rivers. If going downstream, add the speed of the current (typically 3 miles per hour) to the speed of

the vehicle. These vehicles can't be rowed against any significant current, but they can be pulled upstream by draft animals on the shores. A rowboat weighs 100 pounds, in case adventurers carry it over land.

MOUNTS AND OTHER ANIMALS

Item	Cost	Speed	Carrying Capacity
Camel	50 gp	50 ft.	480 lb.
Donkey or mule	8 gp	40 ft.	420 lb.
Elephant	200 gp	40 ft.	1,320 lb.
Horse, draft	50 gp	40 ft.	540 lb.
Horse, riding	75 gp	60 ft.	480 lb.
Mastiff	25 gp	40 ft.	195 lb.
Pony	30 gp	40 ft.	225 lb.
Warhorse	400 gp	60 ft.	540 lb.

TACK, HARNESS, AND DRAWN VEHICLES

Item	Cost	Weight
Barding	×4	×2
Bit and bridle	2 gp	1 lb.
Carriage	100 gp	600 lb.
Cart	15 gp	200 lb.
Chariot	250 gp	100 lb.
Feed (per day)	5 cp	10 lb.
Saddle		
Exotic	60 gp	40 lb.
Military	20 gp	30 lb.
Pack	5 gp	15 lb.
Riding	10 gp	25 lb.
Saddlebags	4 gp	8 lb.
Sled	20 gp	300 lb.
Stabling (per day)	5 sp	—
Wagon	35 gp	400 lb.

WATERBORNE VEHICLES

Item	Cost	Speed
Galley	30,000 gp	4 mph
Keelboat	3,000 gp	1 mph
Longship	10,000 gp	3 mph
Rowboat	50 gp	1½ mph
Sailing ship	10,000 gp	2 mph
Warship	25,000 gp	2½ mph

TRADE GOODS

Most wealth is not in coins. It is measured in livestock, grain, land, rights to collect taxes, or rights to resources (such as a mine or a forest).

Guilds, nobles, and royalty regulate trade. Chartered companies are granted rights to conduct trade along certain routes, to send merchant ships to various ports, or to buy or sell specific goods. Guilds set prices for the goods or services that they control, and determine who may or may not offer those goods and services. Merchants commonly exchange trade goods without using currency. The Trade Goods table shows the value of commonly exchanged goods.

TRADE GOODS

Cost	Goods
1 cp	1 lb. of wheat
2 cp	1 lb. of flour or one chicken
5 cp	1 lb. of salt
1 sp	1 lb. of iron or 1 sq. yd. of canvas
5 sp	1 lb. of copper or 1 sq. yd. of cotton cloth
1 gp	1 lb. of ginger or one goat
2 gp	1 lb. of cinnamon or pepper, or one sheep
3 gp	1 lb. of cloves or one pig
5 gp	1 lb. of silver or 1 sq. yd. of linen
10 gp	1 sq. yd. of silk or one cow
15 gp	1 lb. of saffron or one ox
50 gp	1 lb. of gold
500 gp	1 lb. of platinum

EXPENSES

When not descending into the depths of the earth, exploring ruins for lost treasures, or waging war against the encroaching darkness, adventurers face more mundane realities. Even in a fantastical world, people require basic necessities such as shelter, sustenance, and clothing. These things cost money, although some lifestyles cost more than others.

LIFESTYLE EXPENSES

Lifestyle expenses provide you with a simple way to account for the cost of living in a fantasy world. They cover your accommodations, food and drink, and all your other necessities. Furthermore, expenses cover the cost of maintaining your equipment so you can be ready when adventure next calls.

At the start of each week or month (your choice), choose a lifestyle from the Expenses table and pay the price to sustain that lifestyle. The prices listed are per day, so if you wish to calculate the cost of your chosen lifestyle over a thirty-day period, multiply the listed price by 30. Your lifestyle might change from one period to the next, based on the funds you have at your disposal, or you might maintain the same lifestyle throughout your character's career.

Your lifestyle choice can have consequences. Maintaining a wealthy lifestyle might help you make contacts with the rich and powerful, though you run the risk of attracting thieves. Likewise, living frugally might help you avoid criminals, but you are unlikely to make powerful connections.

LIFESTYLE EXPENSES

Lifestyle	Price/Day
Wretched	—
Squalid	1 sp
Poor	2 sp
Modest	1 gp
Comfortable	2 gp
Wealthy	4 gp
Aristocratic	10 gp minimum

Wretched. You live in inhumane conditions. With no place to call home, you shelter wherever you can, sneaking into barns, huddling in old crates, and relying on the good graces of people better off than you. A wretched lifestyle presents abundant dangers. Violence, disease, and hunger follow you wherever you go. Other wretched people covet your armor, weapons, and adventuring gear, which represent a fortune by their standards. You are beneath the notice of most people.

Squalid. You live in a leaky stable, a mud-floored hut just outside town, or a vermin-infested boarding house in the worst part of town. You have shelter from the elements, but you live in a desperate and often violent environment, in places rife with disease, hunger, and misfortune. You are beneath the notice of most people, and you have few legal protections. Most people at this lifestyle level have suffered some terrible setback. They might be disturbed, marked as exiles, or suffer from disease.

Poor. A poor lifestyle means going without the comforts available in a stable community. Simple food and lodgings, threadbare clothing, and unpredictable conditions result in a sufficient, though probably unpleasant, experience. Your accommodations might be a room in a flophouse or in the common room above a tavern. You benefit from some legal protections, but you still have to contend with violence, crime, and disease. People at this lifestyle level tend to be unskilled laborers, costermongers, peddlers, thieves, mercenaries, and other disreputable types.

Modest. A modest lifestyle keeps you out of the slums and ensures that you can maintain your equipment. You live in an older part of town, renting a room in a boarding house, inn, or temple. You don't go hungry or thirsty, and your living conditions are clean, if simple. Ordinary people living modest lifestyles include soldiers with families, laborers, students, priests, hedge wizards, and the like.

Comfortable. Choosing a comfortable lifestyle means that you can afford nicer clothing and can easily maintain your equipment. You live in a small cottage in a middle-class neighborhood or in a private room at a fine inn. You associate with merchants, skilled tradespeople, and military officers.

Wealthy. Choosing a wealthy lifestyle means living a life of luxury, though you might not have achieved the social status associated with the old money of nobility or royalty. You live a lifestyle comparable to that of a highly successful merchant, a favored servant of the royalty, or the owner of a few small businesses. You have respectable lodgings, usually a spacious home in a good part of town or a comfortable suite at a fine inn. You likely have a small staff of servants.

Aristocratic. You live a life of plenty and comfort. You move in circles populated by the most powerful people in the community. You have excellent lodgings, perhaps a townhouse in the nicest part of town or rooms in the finest inn. You dine at the best restaurants, retain the most skilled and fashionable tailor, and have servants attending to your every need. You receive invitations to the social gatherings of the rich and powerful, and spend evenings in the company of politicians, guild leaders, high priests, and nobility. You must also contend with the highest levels of deceit and treachery. The wealthier you are, the greater the chance you will be drawn into political intrigue as a pawn or participant.

FOOD, DRINK, AND LODGING

The Food, Drink, and Lodging table gives prices for individual food items and a single night's lodging. These prices are included in your total lifestyle expenses.

FOOD, DRINK, AND LODGING

Item	Cost
Ale	
Gallon	2 sp
Mug	4 cp
Banquet (per person)	10 gp
Bread, loaf	2 cp
Cheese, hunk	1 sp
Inn stay (per day)	
Squalid	7 cp
Poor	1 sp
Modest	5 sp
Comfortable	8 sp
Wealthy	2 gp
Aristocratic	4 gp
Meals (per day)	
Squalid	3 cp
Poor	6 cp
Modest	3 sp
Comfortable	5 sp
Wealthy	8 sp
Aristocratic	2 gp
Meat, chunk	3 sp
Wine	
Common (pitcher)	2 sp
Fine (bottle)	10 gp

SERVICES

Adventurers can pay nonplayer characters to assist them or act on their behalf in a variety of circumstances. Most such hirelings have fairly ordinary skills, while others are masters of a craft or art, and a few are experts with specialized adventuring skills.

Some of the most basic types of hirelings appear on the Services table. Other common hirelings include any of the wide variety of people who inhabit a typical town or city, when the adventurers pay them to perform a specific task. For example, a wizard might pay a carpenter to construct an elaborate chest (and its miniature replica) for use in the *Leomund's secret chest* spell. A fighter might commission a blacksmith to forge a special sword. A bard might pay a tailor to make exquisite clothing for an upcoming performance in front of the duke.

Other hirelings provide more expert or dangerous services. Mercenary soldiers paid to help the adventurers take on a hobgoblin army are hirelings, as are sages hired to research ancient or esoteric lore. If a high-level adventurer establishes a stronghold of some kind, he or she might hire a whole staff of servants and agents to run the place, from a castellan or steward to menial laborers to keep the stables clean. These hirelings often enjoy a long-term contract that includes a place to live within the stronghold as part of the offered compensation.

Skilled hirelings include anyone hired to perform a service that involves a proficiency (including weapon, tool, or skill): a mercenary, artisan, scribe, and so on. The pay shown is a minimum; some expert hirelings require more pay. Untrained hirelings are hired for menial work that requires no particular skill and can include laborers, porters, maids, and similar workers.

SPELLCASTING SERVICES

People who are able to cast spells don't fall into the category of ordinary hirelings. It might be possible to find someone willing to cast a spell in exchange for coin or favors, but it is rarely easy and no established pay rates exist. As a rule, the higher the level of the desired spell, the harder it is to find someone who can cast it and the more it costs.

Hiring someone to cast a relatively common spell of 1st or 2nd level, such as *cure wounds* or *identify*, is easy enough in a city or town, and might cost 10 to 50 gold pieces (plus the cost of any expensive material components). Finding someone able and willing to cast a higher-level spell might involve traveling to a large city, perhaps one with a university or prominent temple. Once found, the spellcaster might ask for a service instead of payment—the kind of service that only adventurers can provide, such as retrieving a rare item from a dangerous locale or traversing a monster-infested wilderness to deliver something important to a distant settlement.

TRINKETS

When you make your character, you can roll once on the Trinkets table to gain a trinket, a simple item lightly touched by mystery. The DM might also use this table. It can help stock a room in a dungeon or fill a creature's pockets.

SERVICES

Service	Pay
Coach cab	
Between towns	3 cp per mile
Within a city	1 cp
Hireling	
Skilled	2 gp per day
Untrained	2 sp per day
Messenger	2 cp per mile
Road or gate toll	1 cp
Ship's passage	1 sp per mile

TRINKETS

d100	Trinket
01	A mummified goblin hand
02	A piece of crystal that faintly glows in the moonlight
03	A gold coin minted in an unknown land
04	A diary written in a language you don't know
05	A brass ring that never tarnishes
06	An old chess piece made from glass
07	A pair of knucklebone dice, each with a skull symbol on the side that would normally show six pips
08	A small idol depicting a nightmarish creature that gives you unsettling dreams when you sleep near it
09	A rope necklace from which dangles four mummified elf fingers
10	The deed for a parcel of land in a realm unknown to you
11	A 1-ounce block made from an unknown material
12	A small cloth doll skewered with needles
13	A tooth from an unknown beast
14	An enormous scale, perhaps from a dragon
15	A bright green feather
16	An old divination card bearing your likeness
17	A glass orb filled with moving smoke
18	A 1-pound egg with a bright red shell
19	A pipe that blows bubbles
20	A glass jar containing a weird bit of flesh floating in pickling fluid
21	A tiny gnome-crafted music box that plays a song you dimly remember from your childhood
22	A small wooden statuette of a smug halfling
23	A brass orb etched with strange runes
24	A multicolored stone disk
25	A tiny silver icon of a raven
26	A bag containing forty-seven humanoid teeth, one of which is rotten

d100	Trinket
27	A shard of obsidian that always feels warm to the touch
28	A dragon's bony talon hanging from a plain leather necklace
29	A pair of old socks
30	A blank book whose pages refuse to hold ink, chalk, graphite, or any other substance or marking
31	A silver badge in the shape of a five-pointed star
32	A knife that belonged to a relative
33	A glass vial filled with nail clippings
34	A rectangular metal device with two tiny metal cups on one end that throws sparks when wet
35	A white, sequined glove sized for a human
36	A vest with one hundred tiny pockets
37	A small, weightless stone block
38	A tiny sketch portrait of a goblin
39	An empty glass vial that smells of perfume when opened
40	A gemstone that looks like a lump of coal when examined by anyone but you
41	A scrap of cloth from an old banner
42	A rank insignia from a lost legionnaire
43	A tiny silver bell without a clapper
44	A mechanical canary inside a gnomish lamp
45	A tiny chest carved to look like it has numerous feet on the bottom
46	A dead sprite inside a clear glass bottle
47	A metal can that has no opening but sounds as if it is filled with liquid, sand, spiders, or broken glass (your choice)
48	A glass orb filled with water, in which swims a clockwork goldfish
49	A silver spoon with an M engraved on the handle
50	A whistle made from gold-colored wood

d100	Trinket
51	A dead scarab beetle the size of your hand
52	Two toy soldiers, one with a missing head
53	A small box filled with different-sized buttons
54	A candle that can't be lit
55	A tiny cage with no door
56	An old key
57	An indecipherable treasure map
58	A hilt from a broken sword
59	A rabbit's foot
60	A glass eye
61	A cameo carved in the likeness of a hideous person
62	A silver skull the size of a coin
63	An alabaster mask
64	A pyramid of sticky black incense that smells very bad
65	A nightcap that, when worn, gives you pleasant dreams
66	A single caltrop made from bone
67	A gold monocle frame without the lens
68	A 1-inch cube, each side painted a different color
69	A crystal knob from a door
70	A small packet filled with pink dust
71	A fragment of a beautiful song, written as musical notes on two pieces of parchment
72	A silver teardrop earring made from a real teardrop
73	The shell of an egg painted with scenes of human misery in disturbing detail
74	A fan that, when unfolded, shows a sleeping cat
75	A set of bone pipes
76	A four-leaf clover pressed inside a book discussing manners and etiquette
77	A sheet of parchment upon which is drawn a complex mechanical contraption
78	An ornate scabbard that fits no blade you have found so far

d100	Trinket
79	An invitation to a party where a murder happened
80	A bronze pentacle with an etching of a rat's head in its center
81	A purple handkerchief embroidered with the name of a powerful archmage
82	Half of a floorplan for a temple, castle, or some other structure
83	A bit of folded cloth that, when unfolded, turns into a stylish cap
84	A receipt of deposit at a bank in a far-flung city
85	A diary with seven missing pages
86	An empty silver snuffbox bearing an inscription on the surface that says "dreams"
87	An iron holy symbol devoted to an unknown god
88	A book that tells the story of a legendary hero's rise and fall, with the last chapter missing
89	A vial of dragon blood
90	An ancient arrow of elven design
91	A needle that never bends
92	An ornate brooch of dwarven design
93	An empty wine bottle bearing a pretty label that says, "The Wizard of Wines Winery, Red Dragon Crush, 331422-W"
94	A mosaic tile with a multicolored, glazed surface
95	A petrified mouse
96	A black pirate flag adorned with a dragon's skull and crossbones
97	A tiny mechanical crab or spider that moves about when it's not being observed
98	A glass jar containing lard with a label that reads, "Griffon Grease"
99	A wooden box with a ceramic bottom that holds a living worm with a head on each end of its body
100	A metal urn containing the ashes of a hero

Chapter 6: Customization Options

HE COMBINATION OF ABILITY SCORES, RACE, class, and background defines your character's capabilities in the game, and the personal details you create set your character apart from every other character. Even within your class and race, you have options to fine-tune what your character can do. But this chapter is for players who—with the DM's permission—want to go a step further.

This chapter defines two optional sets of rules for customizing your character: multiclassing and feats. Multiclassing lets you combine classes together, and feats are special options you can choose instead of increasing your ability scores as you gain levels. Your DM decides whether these options are available in a campaign.

Multiclassing

Multiclassing allows you to gain levels in multiple classes. Doing so lets you mix the abilities of those classes to realize a character concept that might not be reflected in one of the standard class options.

With this rule, you have the option of gaining a level in a new class whenever you advance in level, instead of gaining a level in your current class. Your levels in all your classes are added together to determine your character level. For example, if you have three levels in wizard and two in fighter, you're a 5th-level character.

As you advance in levels, you might primarily remain a member of your original class with just a few levels in another class, or you might change course entirely, never looking back at the class you left behind. You might even start progressing in a third or fourth class. Compared to a single-class character of the same level, you'll sacrifice some focus in exchange for versatility.

Multiclassing Example

Gary is playing a 4th-level fighter. When his character earns enough experience points to reach 5th level, Gary decides that his character will multiclass instead of continuing to progress as a fighter. Gary's fighter has been spending a lot of time with Dave's rogue, and has even been doing some jobs on the side for the local thieves' guild as a bruiser. Gary decides that his character will multiclass into the rogue class, and thus his character becomes a 4th-level fighter and 1st-level rogue (written as fighter 4/rogue 1).

When Gary's character earns enough experience to reach 6th level, he can decide whether to add another fighter level (becoming a fighter 5/rogue 1), another rogue level (becoming a fighter 4/rogue 2), or a level in a third class, perhaps dabbling in wizardry thanks to the tome of mysterious lore he acquired (becoming a fighter 4/rogue 1/wizard 1).

Prerequisites

To qualify for a new class, you must meet the ability score prerequisites for both your current class and your new one, as shown in the Multiclassing Prerequisites table. For example, a barbarian who decides to multiclass into the druid class must have both Strength and Wisdom scores of 13 or higher. Without the full training that a beginning character receives, you must be a quick study in your new class, having a natural aptitude that is reflected by higher-than-average ability scores.

Multiclassing Prerequisites

Class	Ability Score Minimum
Barbarian	Strength 13
Bard	Charisma 13
Cleric	Wisdom 13
Druid	Wisdom 13
Fighter	Strength 13 or Dexterity 13
Monk	Dexterity 13 and Wisdom 13
Paladin	Strength 13 and Charisma 13
Ranger	Dexterity 13 and Wisdom 13
Rogue	Dexterity 13
Sorcerer	Charisma 13
Warlock	Charisma 13
Wizard	Intelligence 13

Experience Points

The experience point cost to gain a level is always based on your total character level, as shown in the Character Advancement table in chapter 1, not your level in a particular class. So, if you are a cleric 6/fighter 1, you must gain enough XP to reach 8th level before you can take your second level as a fighter or your seventh level as a cleric.

Hit Points and Hit Dice

You gain the hit points from your new class as described for levels after 1st. You gain the 1st-level hit points for a class only when you are a 1st-level character.

You add together the Hit Dice granted by all your classes to form your pool of Hit Dice. If the Hit Dice are the same die type, you can simply pool them together. For example, both the fighter and the paladin have a d10, so if you are a paladin 5/fighter 5, you have ten d10 Hit Dice. If your classes give you Hit Dice of different types, keep track of them separately. If you are a paladin 5/cleric 5, for example, you have five d10 Hit Dice and five d8 Hit Dice.

Proficiency Bonus

Your proficiency bonus is always based on your total character level, as shown in the Character Advancement table in chapter 1, not your level in a particular class. For example, if you are a fighter 3/rogue 2, you have the proficiency bonus of a 5th-level character, which is +3.

PROFICIENCIES

When you gain your first level in a class other than your initial class, you gain only some of new class's starting proficiencies, as shown in the Multiclassing Proficiencies table.

MULTICLASSING PROFICIENCIES

Class	Proficiencies Gained
Barbarian	Shields, simple weapons, martial weapons
Bard	Light armor, one skill of your choice, one musical instrument of your choice
Cleric	Light armor, medium armor, shields
Druid	Light armor, medium armor, shields (druids will not wear armor or use shields made of metal)
Fighter	Light armor, medium armor, shields, simple weapons, martial weapons
Monk	Simple weapons, shortswords
Paladin	Light armor, medium armor, shields, simple weapons, martial weapons
Ranger	Light armor, medium armor, shields, simple weapons, martial weapons, one skill from the class's skill list
Rogue	Light armor, one skill from the class's skill list, thieves' tools
Sorcerer	—
Warlock	Light armor, simple weapons
Wizard	—

CLASS FEATURES

When you gain a new level in a class, you get its features for that level. You don't, however, receive the class's starting equipment, and a few features have additional rules when you're multiclassing: Channel Divinity, Extra Attack, Unarmored Defense, and Spellcasting.

CHANNEL DIVINITY

If you already have the Channel Divinity feature and gain a level in a class that also grants the feature, you gain the Channel Divinity effects granted by that class, but getting the feature again doesn't give you an additional use of it. You gain additional uses only when you reach a class level that explicitly grants them to you. For example, if you are a cleric 6/paladin 4, you can use Channel Divinity twice between rests because you are high enough level in the cleric class to have more uses. Whenever you use the feature, you can choose any of the Channel Divinity effects available to you from your two classes.

EXTRA ATTACK

If you gain the Extra Attack class feature from more than one class, the features don't add together. You can't make more than two attacks with this feature unless it says you do (as the fighter's version of Extra Attack does). Similarly, the warlock's eldritch invocation Thirsting Blade doesn't give you additional attacks if you also have Extra Attack.

UNARMORED DEFENSE

If you already have the Unarmored Defense feature, you can't gain it again from another class.

SPELLCASTING

Your capacity for spellcasting depends partly on your combined levels in all your spellcasting classes and partly on your individual levels in those classes. Once you have the Spellcasting feature from more than one class, use the rules below. If you multiclass but have the Spellcasting feature from only one class, you follow the rules as described in that class.

Spells Known and Prepared. You determine what spells you know and can prepare for each class individually, as if you were a single-classed member of that class. If you are a ranger 4/wizard 3, for example, you know three 1st-level ranger spells based on your levels in the ranger class. As 3rd-level wizard, you know three wizard cantrips, and your spellbook contains ten wizard spells, two of which (the two you gained when you reached 3rd level as a wizard) can be 2nd-level spells. If your Intelligence is 16, you can prepare six wizard spells from your spellbook.

Each spell you know and prepare is associated with one of your classes, and you use the spellcasting ability of that class when you cast the spell. Similarly, a spellcasting focus, such as a holy symbol, can be used only for the spells from the class associated with that focus.

Spell Slots. You determine your available spell slots by adding together all your levels in the bard, cleric, druid, sorcerer, and wizard classes, half your levels (rounded down) in the paladin and ranger classes, and a third of your fighter or rogue levels (rounded down) if you have the Eldritch Knight or the Arcane Trickster feature. Use this total to determine your spell slots by consulting the Multiclass Spellcaster table.

If you have more than one spellcasting class, this table might give you spell slots of a level that is higher than the spells you know or can prepare. You can use those slots, but only to cast your lower-level spells. If a lower-level spell that you cast, like *burning hands*, has an enhanced effect when cast using a higher-level slot, you can use the enhanced effect, even though you don't have any spells of that higher level.

For example, if you are the aforementioned ranger 4/wizard 3, you count as a 5th-level character when determining your spell slots: you have four 1st-level slots, three 2nd-level slots, and two 3rd-level slots. However, you don't know any 3rd-level spells, nor do you know any 2nd-level ranger spells. You can use the spell slots of those levels to cast the spells you do know—and potentially enhance their effects.

Pact Magic. If you have both the Spellcasting class feature and the Pact Magic class feature from the warlock class, you can use the spell slots you gain from the Pact Magic feature to cast spells you know or have prepared from classes with the Spellcasting class feature, and you can use the spell slots you gain from the Spellcasting class feature to cast warlock spells you know.

Multiclass Spellcaster: Spell Slots per Spell Level

Lvl.	1st	2nd	3rd	4th	5th	6th	7th	8th	9th
1st	2	—	—	—	—	—	—	—	—
2nd	3	—	—	—	—	—	—	—	—
3rd	4	2	—	—	—	—	—	—	—
4th	4	3	—	—	—	—	—	—	—
5th	4	3	2	—	—	—	—	—	—
6th	4	3	3	—	—	—	—	—	—
7th	4	3	3	1	—	—	—	—	—
8th	4	3	3	2	—	—	—	—	—
9th	4	3	3	3	1	—	—	—	—
10th	4	3	3	3	2	—	—	—	—
11th	4	3	3	3	2	1	—	—	—
12th	4	3	3	3	2	1	—	—	—
13th	4	3	3	3	2	1	1	—	—
14th	4	3	3	3	2	1	1	—	—
15th	4	3	3	3	2	1	1	1	—
16th	4	3	3	3	2	1	1	1	—
17th	4	3	3	3	2	1	1	1	1
18th	4	3	3	3	3	1	1	1	1
19th	4	3	3	3	3	2	1	1	1
20th	4	3	3	3	3	2	2	1	1

FEATS

A feat represents a talent or an area of expertise that gives a character special capabilities. It embodies training, experience, and abilities beyond what a class provides.

At certain levels, your class gives you the Ability Score Improvement feature. Using the optional feats rule, you can forgo taking that feature to take a feat of your choice instead. You can take each feat only once, unless the feat's description says otherwise.

You must meet any prerequisite specified in a feat to take that feat. If you ever lose a feat's prerequisite, you can't use that feat until you regain the prerequisite. For example, the Grappler feat requires you to have a Strength of 13 or higher. If your Strength is reduced below 13 somehow—perhaps by a withering curse—you can't benefit from the Grappler feat until your Strength is restored.

ALERT

Always on the lookout for danger, you gain the following benefits:

- You gain a +5 bonus to initiative.
- You can't be surprised while you are conscious.
- Other creatures don't gain advantage on attack rolls against you as a result of being hidden from you.

ATHLETE

You have undergone extensive physical training to gain the following benefits:

- Increase your Strength or Dexterity score by 1, to a maximum of 20.
- When you are prone, standing up uses only 5 feet of your movement.
- Climbing doesn't cost you extra movement.
- You can make a running long jump or a running high jump after moving only 5 feet on foot, rather than 10 feet.

ACTOR

Skilled at mimicry and dramatics, you gain the following benefits:

- Increase your Charisma score by 1, to a maximum of 20.
- You have advantage on Charisma (Deception) and Charisma (Performance) checks when trying to pass yourself off as a different person.
- You can mimic the speech of another person or the sounds made by other creatures. You must have heard the person speaking, or heard the creature make the sound, for at least 1 minute. A successful Wisdom (Insight) check contested by your Charisma (Deception) check allows a listener to determine that the effect is faked.

CHARGER

When you use your action to Dash, you can use a bonus action to make one melee weapon attack or to shove a creature.

If you move at least 10 feet in a straight line immediately before taking this bonus action, you either gain a +5 bonus to the attack's damage roll (if you chose to make a melee attack and hit) or push the target up to 10 feet away from you (if you chose to shove and you succeed).

CROSSBOW EXPERT

Thanks to extensive practice with the crossbow, you gain the following benefits:

- You ignore the loading property of crossbows with which you are proficient.
- Being within 5 feet of a hostile creature doesn't impose disadvantage on your ranged attack rolls.
- When you use the Attack action and attack with a one-handed weapon, you can use a bonus action to attack with a hand crossbow you are holding.

DEFENSIVE DUELIST

Prerequisite: Dexterity 13 or higher

When you are wielding a finesse weapon with which you are proficient and another creature hits you with a melee attack, you can use your reaction to add your proficiency bonus to your AC for that attack, potentially causing the attack to miss you.

DUAL WIELDER

You master fighting with two weapons, gaining the following benefits:

- You gain a +1 bonus to AC while you are wielding a separate melee weapon in each hand.
- You can use two-weapon fighting even when the one-handed melee weapons you are wielding aren't light.
- You can draw or stow two one-handed weapons when you would normally be able to draw or stow only one.

DUNGEON DELVER

Alert to the hidden traps and secret doors found in many dungeons, you gain the following benefits:

- You have advantage on Wisdom (Perception) and Intelligence (Investigation) checks made to detect the presence of secret doors.
- You have advantage on saving throws made to avoid or resist traps.
- You have resistance to the damage dealt by traps.
- You can search for traps while traveling at a normal pace, instead of only at a slow pace.

DURABLE

Hardy and resilient, you gain the following benefits:

- Increase your Constitution score by 1, to a maximum of 20.

- When you roll a Hit Die to regain hit points, the minimum number of hit points you regain from the roll equals twice your Constitution modifier (minimum of 2).

ELEMENTAL ADEPT

Prerequisite: The ability to cast at least one spell

When you gain this feat, choose one of the following damage types: acid, cold, fire, lightning, or thunder.

Spells you cast ignore resistance to damage of the chosen type. In addition, when you roll damage for a spell you cast that deals damage of that type, you can treat any 1 on a damage die as a 2.

You can select this feat multiple times. Each time you do so, you must choose a different damage type.

GRAPPLER

Prerequisite: Strength 13 or higher

You've developed the skills necessary to hold your own in close-quarters grappling. You gain the following benefits:

- You have advantage on attack rolls against a creature you are grappling.
- You can use your action to try to pin a creature grappled by you. To do so, make another grapple check. If you succeed, you and the creature are both restrained until the grapple ends.

GREAT WEAPON MASTER

You've learned to put the weight of a weapon to your advantage, letting its momentum empower your strikes. You gain the following benefits:

- On your turn, when you score a critical hit with a melee weapon or reduce a creature to 0 hit points with one, you can make one melee weapon attack as a bonus action.
- Before you make a melee attack with a heavy weapon that you are proficient with, you can choose to take a −5 penalty to the attack roll. If the attack hits, you add +10 to the attack's damage.

HEALER

You are an able physician, allowing you to mend wounds quickly and get your allies back in the fight. You gain the following benefits:

- When you use a healer's kit to stabilize a dying creature, that creature also regains 1 hit point.
- As an action, you can spend one use of a healer's kit to tend to a creature and restore 1d6 + 4 hit points to it, plus additional hit points equal to the creature's maximum number of Hit Dice. The creature can't regain hit points from this feat again until it finishes a short or long rest.

HEAVILY ARMORED

Prerequisite: Proficiency with medium armor

You have trained to master the use of heavy armor, gaining the following benefits:

- Increase your Strength score by 1, to a maximum of 20.
- You gain proficiency with heavy armor.

HEAVY ARMOR MASTER

Prerequisite: Proficiency with heavy armor

You can use your armor to deflect strikes that would kill others. You gain the following benefits:

- Increase your Strength score by 1, to a maximum of 20.
- While you are wearing heavy armor, bludgeoning, piercing, and slashing damage that you take from nonmagical weapons is reduced by 3.

INSPIRING LEADER

Prerequisite: Charisma 13 or higher

You can spend 10 minutes inspiring your companions, shoring up their resolve to fight. When you do so, choose up to six friendly creatures (which can include yourself) within 30 feet of you who can see or hear you and who can understand you. Each creature can gain temporary hit points equal to your level + your Charisma modifier. A creature can't gain temporary hit points from this feat again until it has finished a short or long rest.

KEEN MIND

You have a mind that can track time, direction, and detail with uncanny precision. You gain the following benefits.

- Increase your Intelligence score by 1, to a maximum of 20.
- You always know which way is north.
- You always know the number of hours left before the next sunrise or sunset.
- You can accurately recall anything you have seen or heard within the past month.

LIGHTLY ARMORED

You have trained to master the use of light armor, gaining the following benefits:

- Increase your Strength or Dexterity score by 1, to a maximum of 20.
- You gain proficiency with light armor.

LINGUIST

You have studied languages and codes, gaining the following benefits:

- Increase your Intelligence score by 1, to a maximum of 20.
- You learn three languages of your choice.
- You can ably create written ciphers. Others can't decipher a code you create unless you teach them, they succeed on an Intelligence check (DC equal to your Intelligence score + your proficiency bonus), or they use magic to decipher it.

LUCKY

You have inexplicable luck that seems to kick in at just the right moment.

You have 3 luck points. Whenever you make an attack roll, an ability check, or a saving throw, you can spend one luck point to roll an additional d20. You can choose to spend one of your luck points after you roll the die, but before the outcome is determined. You choose which of the d20s is used for the attack roll, ability check, or saving throw.

You can also spend one luck point when an attack roll is made against you. Roll a d20, and then choose whether the attack uses the attacker's roll or yours.

If more than one creature spends a luck point to influence the outcome of a roll, the points cancel each other out; no additional dice are rolled.

You regain your expended luck points when you finish a long rest.

MAGE SLAYER

You have practiced techniques useful in melee combat against spellcasters, gaining the following benefits:

- When a creature within 5 feet of you casts a spell, you can use your reaction to make a melee weapon attack against that creature.
- When you damage a creature that is concentrating on a spell, that creature has disadvantage on the saving throw it makes to maintain its concentration.
- You have advantage on saving throws against spells cast by creatures within 5 feet of you.

MAGIC INITIATE

Choose a class: bard, cleric, druid, sorcerer, warlock, or wizard. You learn two cantrips of your choice from that class's spell list.

In addition, choose one 1st-level spell to learn from that same list. Using this feat, you can cast the spell once at its lowest level, and you must finish a long rest before you can cast it in this way again.

Your spellcasting ability for these spells depends on the class you chose: Charisma for bard, sorcerer, or warlock; Wisdom for cleric or druid; or Intelligence for wizard.

MARTIAL ADEPT

You have martial training that allows you to perform special combat maneuvers. You gain the following benefits:

- You learn two maneuvers of your choice from among those available to the Battle Master archetype in the fighter class. If a maneuver you use requires your target to make a saving throw to resist the maneuver's effects, the saving throw DC equals 8 + your proficiency bonus + your Strength or Dexterity modifier (your choice).
- You gain one superiority die, which is a d6 (this die is added to any superiority dice you have from another source). This die is used to fuel your maneuvers. A superiority die is expended when you use it. You regain your expended superiority dice when you finish a short or long rest.

MEDIUM ARMOR MASTER

Prerequisite: Proficiency with medium armor

You have practiced moving in medium armor to gain the following benefits:

- Wearing medium armor doesn't impose disadvantage on your Dexterity (Stealth) checks.
- When you wear medium armor, you can add 3, rather than 2, to your AC if you have a Dexterity of 16 or higher.

MOBILE

You are exceptionally speedy and agile. You gain the following benefits:

- Your speed increases by 10 feet.

- When you use the Dash action, difficult terrain doesn't cost you extra movement on that turn.
- When you make a melee attack against a creature, you don't provoke opportunity attacks from that creature for the rest of the turn, whether you hit or not.

MODERATELY ARMORED

Prerequisite: Proficiency with light armor

You have trained to master the use of medium armor and shields, gaining the following benefits:

- Increase your Strength or Dexterity score by 1, to a maximum of 20.
- You gain proficiency with medium armor and shields.

MOUNTED COMBATANT

You are a dangerous foe to face while mounted. While you are mounted and aren't incapacitated, you gain the following benefits:

- You have advantage on melee attack rolls against any unmounted creature that is smaller than your mount.
- You can force an attack targeted at your mount to target you instead.
- If your mount is subjected to an effect that allows it to make a Dexterity saving throw to take only half damage, it instead takes no damage if it succeeds on the saving throw, and only half damage if it fails.

OBSERVANT

Quick to notice details of your environment, you gain the following benefits:

- Increase your Intelligence or Wisdom score by 1, to a maximum of 20.
- If you can see a creature's mouth while it is speaking a language you understand, you can interpret what it's saying by reading its lips.
- You have a +5 bonus to your passive Wisdom (Perception) and passive Intelligence (Investigation) scores.

POLEARM MASTER

You gain the following benefits:

- When you take the Attack action and attack with only a glaive, halberd, or quarterstaff, you can use a bonus action to make a melee attack with the opposite end of the weapon. This attack uses the same ability modifier as the primary attack. The weapon's damage die for this attack is a d4, and it deals bludgeoning damage.
- While you are wielding a glaive, halberd, pike, or quarterstaff, other creatures provoke an opportunity attack from you when they enter the reach you have with that weapon.

RESILIENT

Choose one ability score. You gain the following benefits:

- Increase the chosen ability score by 1, to a maximum of 20.
- You gain proficiency in saving throws using the chosen ability.

Ritual Caster

Prerequisite: Intelligence or Wisdom 13 or higher

You have learned a number of spells that you can cast as rituals. These spells are written in a ritual book, which you must have in hand while casting one of them.

When you choose this feat, you acquire a ritual book holding two 1st-level spells of your choice. Choose one of the following classes: bard, cleric, druid, sorcerer, warlock, or wizard. You must choose your spells from that class's spell list, and the spells you choose must have the ritual tag. The class you choose also determines your spellcasting ability for these spells: Charisma for bard, sorcerer, or warlock; Wisdom for cleric or druid; or Intelligence for wizard.

If you come across a spell in written form, such as a magical *spell scroll* or a wizard's spellbook, you might be able to add it to your ritual book. The spell must be on the spell list for the class you chose, the spell's level can be no higher than half your level (rounded up), and

it must have the ritual tag. The process of copying the spell into your ritual book takes 2 hours per level of the spell, and costs 50 gp per level. The cost represents material components you expend as you experiment with the spell to master it, as well as the fine inks you need to record it.

Savage Attacker

Once per turn when you roll damage for a melee weapon attack, you can reroll the weapon's damage dice and use either total.

Sentinel

You have mastered techniques to take advantage of every drop in any enemy's guard, gaining the following benefits:

- When you hit a creature with an opportunity attack, the creature's speed becomes 0 for the rest of the turn.

- Creatures provoke opportunity attacks from you even if they take the Disengage action before leaving your reach.
- When a creature within 5 feet of you makes an attack against a target other than you (and that target doesn't have this feat), you can use your reaction to make a melee weapon attack against the attacking creature.

SHARPSHOOTER

You have mastered ranged weapons and can make shots that others find impossible. You gain the following benefits:

- Attacking at long range doesn't impose disadvantage on your ranged weapon attack rolls.
- Your ranged weapon attacks ignore half cover and three-quarters cover.
- Before you make an attack with a ranged weapon that you are proficient with, you can choose to take a –5 penalty to the attack roll. If the attack hits, you add +10 to the attack's damage.

SHIELD MASTER

You use shields not just for protection but also for offense. You gain the following benefits while you are wielding a shield:

- If you take the Attack action on your turn, you can use a bonus action to try to shove a creature within 5 feet of you with your shield.
- If you aren't incapacitated, you can add your shield's AC bonus to any Dexterity saving throw you make against a spell or other harmful effect that targets only you.
- If you are subjected to an effect that allows you to make a Dexterity saving throw to take only half damage, you can use your reaction to take no damage if you succeed on the saving throw, interposing your shield between yourself and the source of the effect.

SKILLED

You gain proficiency in any combination of three skills or tools of your choice.

SKULKER

Prerequisite: Dexterity 13 or higher

You are expert at slinking through shadows. You gain the following benefits:

- You can try to hide when you are lightly obscured from the creature from which you are hiding.
- When you are hidden from a creature and miss it with a ranged weapon attack, making the attack doesn't reveal your position.
- Dim light doesn't impose disadvantage on your Wisdom (Perception) checks relying on sight.

SPELL SNIPER

Prerequisite: The ability to cast at least one spell

You have learned techniques to enhance your attacks with certain kinds of spells, gaining the following benefits:

- When you cast a spell that requires you to make an attack roll, the spell's range is doubled.
- Your ranged spell attacks ignore half cover and three-quarters cover.
- You learn one cantrip that requires an attack roll. Choose the cantrip from the bard, cleric, druid, sorcerer, warlock, or wizard spell list. Your spellcasting ability for this cantrip depends on the spell list you chose from: Charisma for bard, sorcerer, or warlock; Wisdom for cleric or druid; or Intelligence for wizard.

TAVERN BRAWLER

Accustomed to rough-and-tumble fighting using whatever weapons happen to be at hand, you gain the following benefits:

- Increase your Strength or Constitution score by 1, to a maximum of 20.
- You are proficient with improvised weapons.
- Your unarmed strike uses a d4 for damage.
- When you hit a creature with an unarmed strike or an improvised weapon on your turn, you can use a bonus action to attempt to grapple the target.

TOUGH

Your hit point maximum increases by an amount equal to twice your level when you gain this feat. Whenever you gain a level thereafter, your hit point maximum increases by an additional 2 hit points.

WAR CASTER

Prerequisite: The ability to cast at least one spell

You have practiced casting spells in the midst of combat, learning techniques that grant you the following benefits:

- You have advantage on Constitution saving throws that you make to maintain your concentration on a spell when you take damage.
- You can perform the somatic components of spells even when you have weapons or a shield in one or both hands.
- When a hostile creature's movement provokes an opportunity attack from you, you can use your reaction to cast a spell at the creature, rather than making an opportunity attack. The spell must have a casting time of 1 action and must target only that creature.

WEAPON MASTER

You have practiced extensively with a variety of weapons, gaining the following benefits:

- Increase your Strength or Dexterity score by 1, to a maximum of 20.
- You gain proficiency with four weapons of your choice. Each one must be a simple or a martial weapon.

PART 2

Playing the Game

Chapter 7: Using Ability Scores

SIX ABILITIES PROVIDE A QUICK DESCRIPTION of every creature's physical and mental characteristics:

- **Strength**, measuring physical power
- **Dexterity**, measuring agility
- **Constitution**, measuring endurance
- **Intelligence**, measuring reasoning and memory
- **Wisdom**, measuring perception and insight
- **Charisma**, measuring force of personality

Is a character muscle-bound and insightful? Brilliant and charming? Nimble and hardy? Ability scores define these qualities—a creature's assets as well as weaknesses.

The three main rolls of the game—the ability check, the saving throw, and the attack roll—rely on the six ability scores. The book's introduction describes the basic rule behind these rolls: roll a d20, add an ability modifier derived from one of the six ability scores, and compare the total to a target number.

This chapter focuses on how to use ability checks and saving throws, covering the fundamental activities that creatures attempt in the game. Rules for attack rolls appear in chapter 9, "Combat."

Ability Scores and Modifiers

Each of a creature's abilities has a score, a number that defines the magnitude of that ability. An ability score is not just a measure of innate capabilities, but also encompasses a creature's training and competence in activities related to that ability.

A score of 10 or 11 is the normal human average, but adventurers and many monsters are a cut above average in most abilities. A score of 18 is the highest that a person usually reaches. Adventurers can have scores as high as 20, and monsters and divine beings can have scores as high as 30.

Each ability also has a modifier, derived from the score and ranging from –5 (for an ability score of 1) to +10 (for a score of 30). The Ability Scores and Modifiers table notes the ability modifiers for the range of possible ability scores, from 1 to 30.

Ability Scores and Modifiers

Score	Modifier	Score	Modifier
1	−5	16–17	+3
2–3	−4	18–19	+4
4–5	−3	20–21	+5
6–7	−2	22–23	+6
8–9	−1	24–25	+7
10–11	+0	26–27	+8
12–13	+1	28–29	+9
14–15	+2	30	+10

To determine an ability modifier without consulting the table, subtract 10 from the ability score and then divide the total by 2 (round down).

Because ability modifiers affect almost every attack roll, ability check, and saving throw, ability modifiers come up in play more often than their associated scores.

Advantage and Disadvantage

Sometimes a special ability or spell tells you that you have advantage or disadvantage on an ability check, a saving throw, or an attack roll. When that happens, you roll a second d20 when you make the roll. Use the higher of the two rolls if you have advantage, and use the lower roll if you have disadvantage. For example, if you have disadvantage and roll a 17 and a 5, you use the 5. If you instead have advantage and roll those numbers, you use the 17.

If multiple situations affect a roll and each one grants advantage or imposes disadvantage on it, you don't roll more than one additional d20. If two favorable situations grant advantage, for example, you still roll only one additional d20.

If circumstances cause a roll to have both advantage and disadvantage, you are considered to have neither of them, and you roll one d20. This is true even if multiple circumstances impose disadvantage and only one grants advantage or vice versa. In such a situation, you have neither advantage nor disadvantage.

When you have advantage or disadvantage and something in the game, such as the halfling's Lucky trait, lets you reroll the d20, you can reroll only one of the dice. You choose which one. For example, if a halfling has advantage or disadvantage on an ability check and rolls a 1 and a 13, the halfling could use the Lucky trait to reroll the 1.

You usually gain advantage or disadvantage through the use of special abilities, actions, or spells. Inspiration can also give a character advantage (as explained in chapter 4, "Personality and Background"). The DM can also decide that circumstances influence a roll in one direction or the other and grant advantage or impose disadvantage as a result.

Proficiency Bonus

Characters have a proficiency bonus determined by level, as detailed in chapter 1. Monsters also have this bonus, which is incorporated in their stat blocks. The bonus is used in the rules on ability checks, saving throws, and attack rolls.

Your proficiency bonus can't be added to a single die roll or other number more than once. For example, if two different rules say you can add your proficiency bonus to a Wisdom saving throw, you nevertheless add the bonus only once when you make the save.

Occasionally, your proficiency bonus might be multiplied or divided (doubled or halved, for example) before you apply it. For example, the rogue's Expertise feature doubles the proficiency bonus for certain ability checks. If a circumstance suggests that your proficiency bonus applies more than once to the same roll, you still add it only once and multiply or divide it only once.

By the same token, if a feature or effect allows you to multiply your proficiency bonus when making an ability check that wouldn't normally benefit from your proficiency bonus, you still don't add the bonus to the check. For that check your proficiency bonus is 0, given the fact that multiplying 0 by any number is still 0. For instance, if you lack proficiency in the History skill, you gain no benefit from a feature that lets you double your proficiency bonus when you make Intelligence (History) checks.

In general, you don't multiply your proficiency bonus for attack rolls or saving throws. If a feature or effect allows you to do so, these same rules apply.

ABILITY CHECKS

An ability check tests a character's or monster's innate talent and training in an effort to overcome a challenge. The DM calls for an ability check when a character or monster attempts an action (other than an attack) that has a chance of failure. When the outcome is uncertain, the dice determine the results.

For every ability check, the DM decides which of the six abilities is relevant to the task at hand and the difficulty of the task, represented by a Difficulty Class. The more difficult a task, the higher its DC. The Typical Difficulty Classes table shows the most common DCs.

TYPICAL DIFFICULTY CLASSES

Task Difficulty	DC
Very easy	5
Easy	10
Medium	15
Hard	20
Very hard	25
Nearly impossible	30

To make an ability check, roll a d20 and add the relevant ability modifier. As with other d20 rolls, apply bonuses and penalties, and compare the total to the DC. If the total equals or exceeds the DC, the ability check is a success—the creature overcomes the challenge at hand. Otherwise, it's a failure, which means the character or monster makes no progress toward the objective or makes progress combined with a setback determined by the DM.

CONTESTS

Sometimes one character's or monster's efforts are directly opposed to another's. This can occur when both of them are trying to do the same thing and only one can succeed, such as attempting to snatch up a magic ring that has fallen on the floor. This situation also applies when one of them is trying to prevent the other one from accomplishing a goal—for example, when a monster tries to force open a door that an adventurer

is holding closed. In situations like these, the outcome is determined by a special form of ability check, called a contest.

Both participants in a contest make ability checks appropriate to their efforts. They apply all appropriate bonuses and penalties, but instead of comparing the total to a DC, they compare the totals of their two checks. The participant with the higher check total wins the contest. That character or monster either succeeds at the action or prevents the other one from succeeding.

If the contest results in a tie, the situation remains the same as it was before the contest. Thus, one contestant might win the contest by default. If two characters tie in a contest to snatch a ring off the floor, neither character grabs it. In a contest between a monster trying to open a door and an adventurer trying to keep the door closed, a tie means that the door remains shut.

SKILLS

Each ability covers a broad range of capabilities, including skills that a character or a monster can be proficient in. A skill represents a specific aspect of an ability score, and an individual's proficiency in a skill demonstrates a focus on that aspect. (A character's starting skill proficiencies are determined at character creation, and a monster's skill proficiencies appear in the monster's stat block.)

For example, a Dexterity check might reflect a character's attempt to pull off an acrobatic stunt, to palm an object, or to stay hidden. Each of these aspects of Dexterity has an associated skill: Acrobatics, Sleight of Hand, and Stealth, respectively. So a character who has proficiency in the Stealth skill is particularly good at Dexterity checks related to sneaking and hiding.

The skills related to each ability score are shown in the following list. (No skills are related to Constitution.) See an ability's description in the later sections of this chapter for examples of how to use a skill associated with an ability.

Strength
Athletics

Dexterity
Acrobatics
Sleight of Hand
Stealth

Intelligence
Arcana
History
Investigation
Nature
Religion

Wisdom
Animal Handling
Insight
Medicine
Perception
Survival

Charisma
Deception
Intimidation
Performance
Persuasion

Sometimes, the DM might ask for an ability check using a specific skill—for example, "Make a Wisdom (Perception) check." At other times, a player might ask the DM if proficiency in a particular skill applies to a check. In either case, proficiency in a skill means an individual can add his or her proficiency bonus to ability checks that involve that skill. Without proficiency in the skill, the individual makes a normal ability check.

For example, if a character attempts to climb up a dangerous cliff, the Dungeon Master might ask for a Strength (Athletics) check. If the character is proficient in Athletics, the character's proficiency bonus is added to the Strength check. If the character lacks that proficiency, he or she just makes a Strength check.

VARIANT: SKILLS WITH DIFFERENT ABILITIES

Normally, your proficiency in a skill applies only to a specific kind of ability check. Proficiency in Athletics, for example, usually applies to Strength checks. In some situations, though, your proficiency might reasonably apply to a different kind of check. In such cases, the DM might ask for a check using an unusual combination of ability and skill, or you might ask your DM if you can apply a proficiency to a different check. For example, if you have to swim from an offshore island to the mainland, your DM might call for a Constitution check to see if you have the stamina to make it that far. In this case, your DM might allow you to apply your proficiency in Athletics and ask for a Constitution (Athletics) check. So if you're proficient in Athletics, you apply your proficiency bonus to the Constitution check just as you would normally do for a Strength (Athletics) check. Similarly, when your half-orc barbarian uses a display of raw strength to intimidate an enemy, your DM might ask for a Strength (Intimidation) check, even though Intimidation is normally associated with Charisma.

PASSIVE CHECKS

A passive check is a special kind of ability check that doesn't involve any die rolls. Such a check can represent the average result for a task done repeatedly, such as searching for secret doors over and over again, or can be used when the DM wants to secretly determine whether the characters succeed at something without rolling dice, such as noticing a hidden monster.

Here's how to determine a character's total for a passive check:

> 10 + all modifiers that normally apply to the check

If the character has advantage on the check, add 5. For disadvantage, subtract 5. The game refers to a passive check total as a **score**.

For example, if a 1st-level character has a Wisdom of 15 and proficiency in Perception, he or she has a passive Wisdom (Perception) score of 14.

The rules on hiding in the "Dexterity" section below rely on passive checks, as do the exploration rules in chapter 8, "Adventuring."

WORKING TOGETHER

Sometimes two or more characters team up to attempt a task. The character who's leading the effort—or the one with the highest ability modifier—can make an ability check with advantage, reflecting the help provided by the other characters. In combat, this requires the Help action (see chapter 9, "Combat").

A character can only provide help if the task is one that he or she could attempt alone. For example, trying to open a lock requires proficiency with thieves' tools, so a character who lacks that proficiency can't help another character in that task. Moreover, a character can help only when two or more individuals working together would actually be productive. Some tasks, such as threading a needle, are no easier with help.

GROUP CHECKS

When a number of individuals are trying to accomplish something as a group, the DM might ask for a group ability check. In such a situation, the characters who are skilled at a particular task help cover those who aren't.

To make a group ability check, everyone in the group makes the ability check. If at least half the group succeeds, the whole group succeeds. Otherwise, the group fails.

Group checks don't come up very often, and they're most useful when all the characters succeed or fail as a group. For example, when adventurers are navigating a swamp, the DM might call for a group Wisdom (Survival) check to see if the characters can avoid the quicksand, sinkholes, and other natural hazards of the environment. If at least half the group succeeds, the successful characters are able to guide their companions out of danger. Otherwise, the group stumbles into one of these hazards.

USING EACH ABILITY

Every task that a character or monster might attempt in the game is covered by one of the six abilities. This section explains in more detail what those abilities mean and the ways they are used in the game.

STRENGTH

Strength measures bodily power, athletic training, and the extent to which you can exert raw physical force.

STRENGTH CHECKS

A Strength check can model any attempt to lift, push, pull, or break something, to force your body through a space, or to otherwise apply brute force to a situation. The Athletics skill reflects aptitude in certain kinds of Strength checks.

Athletics. Your Strength (Athletics) check covers difficult situations you encounter while climbing, jumping, or swimming. Examples include the following activities:

- You attempt to climb a sheer or slippery cliff, avoid hazards while scaling a wall, or cling to a surface while something is trying to knock you off.
- You try to jump an unusually long distance or pull off a stunt midjump.
- You struggle to swim or stay afloat in treacherous currents, storm-tossed waves, or areas of thick seaweed. Or another creature tries to push or pull you underwater or otherwise interfere with your swimming.

Other Strength Checks. The DM might also call for a Strength check when you try to accomplish tasks like the following:

- Force open a stuck, locked, or barred door
- Break free of bonds
- Push through a tunnel that is too small
- Hang on to a wagon while being dragged behind it
- Tip over a statue
- Keep a boulder from rolling

ATTACK ROLLS AND DAMAGE

You add your Strength modifier to your attack roll and your damage roll when attacking with a melee weapon such as a mace, a battleaxe, or a javelin. You use melee weapons to make melee attacks in hand-to-hand combat, and some of them can be thrown to make a ranged attack.

LIFTING AND CARRYING

Your Strength score determines the amount of weight you can bear. The following terms define what you can lift or carry.

Carrying Capacity. Your carrying capacity is your Strength score multiplied by 15. This is the weight (in pounds) that you can carry, which is high enough that most characters don't usually have to worry about it.

Push, Drag, or Lift. You can push, drag, or lift a weight in pounds up to twice your carrying capacity (or 30 times your Strength score). While pushing or dragging weight in excess of your carrying capacity, your speed drops to 5 feet.

Size and Strength. Larger creatures can bear more weight, whereas Tiny creatures can carry less. For each size category above Medium, double the creature's carrying capacity and the amount it can push, drag, or lift. For a Tiny creature, halve these weights.

VARIANT: ENCUMBRANCE

The rules for lifting and carrying are intentionally simple. Here is a variant if you are looking for more detailed rules for determining how a character is hindered by the weight of equipment. When you use this variant, ignore the Strength column of the Armor table in chapter 5, "Equipment."

If you carry weight in excess of 5 times your Strength score, you are **encumbered**, which means your speed drops by 10 feet.

If you carry weight in excess of 10 times your Strength score, up to your maximum carrying capacity, you are instead **heavily encumbered**, which means your speed drops by 20 feet and you have disadvantage on ability checks, attack rolls, and saving throws that use Strength, Dexterity, or Constitution.

DEXTERITY

Dexterity measures agility, reflexes, and balance.

DEXTERITY CHECKS

A Dexterity check can model any attempt to move nimbly, quickly, or quietly, or to keep from falling on tricky footing. The Acrobatics, Sleight of Hand, and Stealth skills reflect aptitude in certain kinds of Dexterity checks.

Acrobatics. Your Dexterity (Acrobatics) check covers your attempt to stay on your feet in a tricky situation, such as when you're trying to run across a sheet of ice, balance on a tightrope, or stay upright on a rocking ship's deck. The DM might also call for a Dexterity (Acrobatics) check to see if you can perform acrobatic stunts, including dives, rolls, somersaults, and flips.

Sleight of Hand. Whenever you attempt an act of legerdemain or manual trickery, such as planting something on someone else or concealing an object on your person, make a Dexterity (Sleight of Hand) check. The DM might also call for a Dexterity (Sleight of Hand) check to determine whether you can lift a coin purse off another person or slip something out of another person's pocket.

Stealth. Make a Dexterity (Stealth) check when you attempt to conceal yourself from enemies, slink past guards, slip away without being noticed, or sneak up on someone without being seen or heard.

Other Dexterity Checks. The DM might call for a Dexterity check when you try to accomplish tasks like the following:

- Control a heavily laden cart on a steep descent
- Steer a chariot around a tight turn
- Pick a lock
- Disable a trap
- Securely tie up a prisoner
- Wriggle free of bonds
- Play a stringed instrument
- Craft a small or detailed object

ATTACK ROLLS AND DAMAGE

You add your Dexterity modifier to your attack roll and your damage roll when attacking with a ranged weapon, such as a sling or a longbow. You can also add your Dexterity modifier to your attack roll and your damage roll when attacking with a melee weapon that has the finesse property, such as a dagger or a rapier.

HIDING

The DM decides when circumstances are appropriate for hiding. When you try to hide, make a Dexterity (Stealth) check. Until you are discovered or you stop hiding, that check's total is contested by the Wisdom (Perception) check of any creature that actively searches for signs of your presence.

You can't hide from a creature that can see you clearly, and you give away your position if you make noise, such as shouting a warning or knocking over a vase.

An invisible creature can always try to hide. Signs of its passage might still be noticed, and it does have to stay quiet.

In combat, most creatures stay alert for signs of danger all around, so if you come out of hiding and approach a creature, it usually sees you. However, under certain circumstances, the DM might allow you to stay hidden as you approach a creature that is distracted, allowing you to gain advantage on an attack roll before you are seen.

Passive Perception. When you hide, there's a chance someone will notice you even if they aren't searching. To determine whether such a creature notices you, the DM compares your Dexterity (Stealth) check with that creature's passive Wisdom (Perception) score, which equals 10 + the creature's Wisdom modifier, as well as any other bonuses or penalties. If the creature has advantage, add 5. For disadvantage, subtract 5. For example, if a 1st-level character (with a proficiency bonus of +2) has a Wisdom of 15 (a +2 modifier) and proficiency in Perception, he or she has a passive Wisdom (Perception) of 14.

What Can You See? One of the main factors in determining whether you can find a hidden creature or object is how well you can see in an area, which might be **lightly** or **heavily obscured**, as explained in chapter 8, "Adventuring."

ARMOR CLASS

Depending on the armor you wear, you might add some or all of your Dexterity modifier to your Armor Class, as described in chapter 5, "Equipment."

INITIATIVE

At the beginning of every combat, you roll initiative by making a Dexterity check. Initiative determines the order of creatures' turns in combat, as described in chapter 9, "Combat."

CONSTITUTION

Constitution measures health, stamina, and vital force.

CONSTITUTION CHECKS

Constitution checks are uncommon, and no skills apply to Constitution checks, because the endurance this ability represents is largely passive rather than involving a specific effort on the part of a character or monster. A Constitution check can model your attempt to push beyond normal limits, however.

The DM might call for a Constitution check when you try to accomplish tasks like the following:

- Hold your breath
- March or labor for hours without rest
- Go without sleep
- Survive without food or water
- Quaff an entire stein of ale in one go

HIT POINTS

Your Constitution modifier contributes to your hit points. Typically, you add your Constitution modifier to each Hit Die you roll for your hit points.

If your Constitution modifier changes, your hit point maximum changes as well, as though you had the new modifier from 1st level. For example, if you raise your Constitution score when you reach 4th level and your Constitution modifier increases from +1 to +2, you adjust your hit point maximum as though the modifier had always been +2. So you add 3 hit points for your first three levels, and then roll your hit points for 4th level using your new modifier. Or if you're 7th level and some effect lowers your Constitution score so as to reduce your Constitution modifier by 1, your hit point maximum is reduced by 7.

INTELLIGENCE

Intelligence measures mental acuity, accuracy of recall, and the ability to reason.

INTELLIGENCE CHECKS

An Intelligence check comes into play when you need to draw on logic, education, memory, or deductive reasoning. The Arcana, History, Investigation, Nature, and Religion skills reflect aptitude in certain kinds of Intelligence checks.

Arcana. Your Intelligence (Arcana) check measures your ability to recall lore about spells, magic items, eldritch symbols, magical traditions, the planes of existence, and the inhabitants of those planes.

History. Your Intelligence (History) check measures your ability to recall lore about historical events, legendary people, ancient kingdoms, past disputes, recent wars, and lost civilizations.

Investigation. When you look around for clues and make deductions based on those clues, you make an Intelligence (Investigation) check. You might deduce the location of a hidden object, discern from the appearance of a wound what kind of weapon dealt it, or determine the weakest point in a tunnel that could cause it to collapse. Poring through ancient scrolls in search of a hidden fragment of knowledge might also call for an Intelligence (Investigation) check.

Nature. Your Intelligence (Nature) check measures your ability to recall lore about terrain, plants and animals, the weather, and natural cycles.

Religion. Your Intelligence (Religion) check measures your ability to recall lore about deities, rites and prayers, religious hierarchies, holy symbols, and the practices of secret cults.

Other Intelligence Checks. The DM might call for an Intelligence check when you try to accomplish tasks like the following:

- Communicate with a creature without using words
- Estimate the value of a precious item
- Pull together a disguise to pass as a city guard
- Forge a document
- Recall lore about a craft or trade
- Win a game of skill

Spellcasting Ability

Wizards use Intelligence as their spellcasting ability, which helps determine the saving throw DCs of spells they cast.

Wisdom

Wisdom reflects how attuned you are to the world around you and represents perceptiveness and intuition.

Wisdom Checks

A Wisdom check might reflect an effort to read body language, understand someone's feelings, notice things about the environment, or care for an injured person. The Animal Handling, Insight, Medicine, Perception, and Survival skills reflect aptitude in certain kinds of Wisdom checks.

Animal Handling. When there is any question whether you can calm down a domesticated animal, keep a mount from getting spooked, or intuit an animal's intentions, the DM might call for a Wisdom (Animal Handling) check. You also make a Wisdom (Animal Handling) check to control your mount when you attempt a risky maneuver.

Insight. Your Wisdom (Insight) check decides whether you can determine the true intentions of a creature, such as when searching out a lie or predicting someone's next move. Doing so involves gleaning clues from body language, speech habits, and changes in mannerisms.

Medicine. A Wisdom (Medicine) check lets you try to stabilize a dying companion or diagnose an illness.

Perception. Your Wisdom (Perception) check lets you spot, hear, or otherwise detect the presence of something. It measures your general awareness of your surroundings and the keenness of your senses.

Finding a Hidden Object

When your character searches for a hidden object such as a secret door or a trap, the DM typically asks you to make a Wisdom (Perception) check. Such a check can be used to find hidden details or other information and clues that you might otherwise overlook.

In most cases, you need to describe where you are looking in order for the DM to determine your chance of success. For example, a key is hidden beneath a set of folded clothes in the top drawer of a bureau. If you tell the DM that you pace around the room, looking at the walls and furniture for clues, you have no chance of finding the key, regardless of your Wisdom (Perception) check result. You would have to specify that you were opening the drawers or searching the bureau in order to have any chance of success.

For example, you might try to hear a conversation through a closed door, eavesdrop under an open window, or hear monsters moving stealthily in the forest. Or you might try to spot things that are obscured or easy to miss, whether they are orcs lying in ambush on a road, thugs hiding in the shadows of an alley, or candlelight under a closed secret door.

Survival. The DM might ask you to make a Wisdom (Survival) check to follow tracks, hunt wild game, guide your group through frozen wastelands, identify signs that owlbears live nearby, predict the weather, or avoid quicksand and other natural hazards.

Other Wisdom Checks. The DM might call for a Wisdom check when you try to accomplish tasks like the following:

- Get a gut feeling about what course of action to follow
- Discern whether a seemingly dead or living creature is undead

Spellcasting Ability

Clerics, druids, and rangers use Wisdom as their spellcasting ability, which helps determine the saving throw DCs of spells they cast.

Charisma

Charisma measures your ability to interact effectively with others. It includes such factors as confidence and eloquence, and it can represent a charming or commanding personality.

Charisma Checks

A Charisma check might arise when you try to influence or entertain others, when you try to make an impression or tell a convincing lie, or when you are navigating a tricky social situation. The Deception, Intimidation, Performance, and Persuasion skills reflect aptitude in certain kinds of Charisma checks.

Deception. Your Charisma (Deception) check determines whether you can convincingly hide the truth, either verbally or through your actions. This deception can encompass everything from misleading others through ambiguity to telling outright lies. Typical situations include trying to fast-talk a guard, con a merchant, earn money through gambling, pass yourself off in a disguise, dull someone's suspicions with false assurances, or maintain a straight face while telling a blatant lie.

Intimidation. When you attempt to influence someone through overt threats, hostile actions, and physical violence, the DM might ask you to make a Charisma (Intimidation) check. Examples include trying to pry information out of a prisoner, convincing street thugs to back down from a confrontation, or using the edge of a broken bottle to convince a sneering vizier to reconsider a decision.

Performance. Your Charisma (Performance) check determines how well you can delight an audience with music, dance, acting, storytelling, or some other form of entertainment.

Persuasion. When you attempt to influence someone or a group of people with tact, social graces, or good nature, the DM might ask you to make a Charisma (Persuasion) check. Typically, you use persuasion when acting in good faith, to foster friendships, make cordial requests, or exhibit proper etiquette. Examples of persuading others include convincing a chamberlain to let your party see the king, negotiating peace between warring tribes, or inspiring a crowd of townsfolk.

Other Charisma Checks. The DM might call for a Charisma check when you try to accomplish tasks like the following:

- Find the best person to talk to for news, rumors, and gossip
- Blend into a crowd to get the sense of key topics of conversation

Spellcasting Ability

Bards, paladins, sorcerers, and warlocks use Charisma as their spellcasting ability, which helps determine the saving throw DCs of spells they cast.

Saving Throws

A saving throw—also called a save—represents an attempt to resist a spell, a trap, a poison, a disease, or a similar threat. You don't normally decide to make a saving throw; you are forced to make one because your character or monster is at risk of harm.

To make a saving throw, roll a d20 and add the appropriate ability modifier. For example, you use your Dexterity modifier for a Dexterity saving throw.

A saving throw can be modified by a situational bonus or penalty and can be affected by advantage and disadvantage, as determined by the DM.

Each class gives proficiency in at least two saving throws. The wizard, for example, is proficient in Intelligence saves. As with skill proficiencies, proficiency in a saving throw lets a character add his or her proficiency bonus to saving throws made using a particular ability score. Some monsters have saving throw proficiencies as well.

The Difficulty Class for a saving throw is determined by the effect that causes it. For example, the DC for a saving throw allowed by a spell is determined by the caster's spellcasting ability and proficiency bonus.

The result of a successful or failed saving throw is also detailed in the effect that allows the save. Usually, a successful save means that a creature suffers no harm, or reduced harm, from an effect.

CHAPTER 8: ADVENTURING

ELVING INTO THE ANCIENT TOMB OF HORRORS, slipping through the back alleys of Waterdeep, hacking a fresh trail through the thick jungles on the Isle of Dread—these are the things that DUNGEONS & DRAGONS adventures are made of. Your character in the game might explore forgotten ruins and uncharted lands, uncover dark secrets and sinister plots, and slay foul monsters. And if all goes well, your character will survive to claim rich rewards before embarking on a new adventure.

This chapter covers the basics of the adventuring life, from the mechanics of movement to the complexities of social interaction. The rules for resting are also in this chapter, along with a discussion of the activities your character might pursue between adventures.

Whether adventurers are exploring a dusty dungeon or the complex relationships of a royal court, the game follows a natural rhythm, as outlined in the book's introduction:

1. The DM describes the environment.
2. The players describe what they want to do.
3. The DM narrates the results of their actions.

Typically, the DM uses a map as an outline of the adventure, tracking the characters' progress as they explore dungeon corridors or wilderness regions. The DM's notes, including a key to the map, describe what the adventurers find as they enter each new area. Sometimes, the passage of time and the adventurers' actions determine what happens, so the DM might use a timeline or a flowchart to track their progress instead of a map.

TIME

In situations where keeping track of the passage of time is important, the DM determines the time a task requires. The DM might use a different time scale depending on the context of the situation at hand. In a dungeon environment, the adventurers' movement happens on a scale of **minutes**. It takes them about a minute to creep down a long hallway, another minute to check for traps on the door at the end of the hall, and a good ten minutes to search the chamber beyond for anything interesting or valuable.

· In a city or wilderness, a scale of **hours** is often more appropriate. Adventurers eager to reach the lonely tower at the heart of the forest hurry across those fifteen miles in just under four hours' time.

For long journeys, a scale of **days** works best. Following the road from Baldur's Gate to Waterdeep, the adventurers spend four uneventful days before a goblin ambush interrupts their journey.

In combat and other fast-paced situations, the game relies on **rounds**, a 6-second span of time described in chapter 9, "Combat."

MOVEMENT

Swimming across a rushing river, sneaking down a dungeon corridor, scaling a treacherous mountain slope— all sorts of movement play a key role in D&D adventures.

The DM can summarize the adventurers' movement without calculating exact distances or travel times: "You travel through the forest and find the dungeon entrance late in the evening of the third day." Even in a dungeon, particularly a large dungeon or a cave network, the DM can summarize movement between encounters: "After killing the guardian at the entrance to the ancient dwarven stronghold, you consult your map, which leads you through miles of echoing corridors to a chasm bridged by a narrow stone arch."

Sometimes it's important, though, to know how long it takes to get from one spot to another, whether the answer is in days, hours, or minutes. The rules for determining travel time depend on two factors: the speed and travel pace of the creatures moving and the terrain they're moving over.

SPEED

Every character and monster has a speed, which is the distance in feet that the character or monster can walk in 1 round. This number assumes short bursts of energetic movement in the midst of a life-threatening situation.

The following rules determine how far a character or monster can move in a minute, an hour, or a day.

TRAVEL PACE

While traveling, a group of adventurers can move at a normal, fast, or slow pace, as shown on the Travel Pace table. The table states how far the party can move in a period of time and whether the pace has any effect. A fast pace makes characters less perceptive, while a slow pace makes it possible to sneak around and to search an area more carefully (see the "Activity While Traveling" section later in this chapter for more information).

Forced March. The Travel Pace table assumes that characters travel for 8 hours in day. They can push on beyond that limit, at the risk of exhaustion.

For each additional hour of travel beyond 8 hours, the characters cover the distance shown in the Hour column for their pace, and each character must make a Constitution saving throw at the end of the hour. The DC is 10 + 1 for each hour past 8 hours. On a failed saving throw, a character suffers one level of exhaustion (see appendix A).

Mounts and Vehicles. For short spans of time (up to an hour), many animals move much faster than humanoids. A mounted character can ride at a gallop for about an hour, covering twice the usual distance for a fast pace. If fresh mounts are available every 8 to 10 miles, characters can cover larger distances at this pace, but this is very rare except in densely populated areas.

Characters in wagons, carriages, or other land vehicles choose a pace as normal. Characters in a waterborne vessel are limited to the speed of the vessel (see chapter 5, "Equipment"), and they don't suffer penalties for a fast pace or gain benefits from a slow pace. Depending on the vessel and the size of the crew, ships might be able to travel for up to 24 hours per day.

Certain special mounts, such as a pegasus or griffon, or special vehicles, such as a *carpet of flying*, allow you to travel more swiftly. The *Dungeon Master's Guide* contains more information on special methods of travel.

TRAVEL PACE

	Distance Traveled per . . .			
Pace	Minute	Hour	Day	Effect
Fast	400 feet	4 miles	30 miles	−5 penalty to passive Wisdom (Perception) scores
Normal	300 feet	3 miles	24 miles	—
Slow	200 feet	2 miles	18 miles	Able to use stealth

DIFFICULT TERRAIN

The travel speeds given in the Travel Pace table assume relatively simple terrain: roads, open plains, or clear dungeon corridors. But adventurers often face dense forests, deep swamps, rubble-filled ruins, steep mountains, and ice-covered ground—all considered difficult terrain.

You move at half speed in difficult terrain—moving 1 foot in difficult terrain costs 2 feet of speed—so you can cover only half the normal distance in a minute, an hour, or a day.

SPECIAL TYPES OF MOVEMENT

Movement through dangerous dungeons or wilderness areas often involves more than simply walking. Adventurers might have to climb, crawl, swim, or jump to get where they need to go.

CLIMBING, SWIMMING, AND CRAWLING

While climbing or swimming, each foot of movement costs 1 extra foot (2 extra feet in difficult terrain), unless a creature has a climbing or swimming speed. At the DM's option, climbing a slippery vertical surface or one with few handholds requires a successful Strength (Athletics) check. Similarly, gaining any distance in rough water might require a successful Strength (Athletics) check.

JUMPING

Your Strength determines how far you can jump.

Long Jump. When you make a long jump, you cover a number of feet up to your Strength score if you move at least 10 feet on foot immediately before the jump. When you make a standing long jump, you can leap only half that distance. Either way, each foot you clear on the jump costs a foot of movement.

This rule assumes that the height of your jump doesn't matter, such as a jump across a stream or chasm. At your DM's option, you must succeed on a DC 10 Strength (Athletics) check to clear a low obstacle (no taller than a quarter of the jump's distance), such as a hedge or low wall. Otherwise, you hit it.

When you land in difficult terrain, you must succeed on a DC 10 Dexterity (Acrobatics) check to land on your feet. Otherwise, you land prone.

High Jump. When you make a high jump, you leap into the air a number of feet equal to 3 + your Strength modifier if you move at least 10 feet on foot immediately before the jump. When you make a standing high jump, you can jump only half that distance. Either way, each foot you clear on the jump costs a foot of movement. In some circumstances, your DM might allow you to make a Strength (Athletics) check to jump higher than you normally can.

You can extend your arms half your height above yourself during the jump. Thus, you can reach above you a distance equal to the height of the jump plus 1½ times your height.

ACTIVITY WHILE TRAVELING

As adventurers travel through a dungeon or the wilderness, they need to remain alert for danger, and some characters might perform other tasks to help the group's journey.

MARCHING ORDER

The adventurers should establish a marching order. A marching order makes it easier to determine which characters are affected by traps, which ones can spot hidden enemies, and which ones are the closest to those enemies when a fight breaks out.

A character might occupy the front rank, one or more middle ranks, or the back rank. Characters in the front and back ranks need enough room to travel side by side with others in their rank. When space is too tight, the marching order must change, usually by moving characters to a middle rank.

Fewer Than Three Ranks. If an adventuring party arranges its marching order with only two ranks, they are a front rank and a back rank. If there's only one rank, it's considered a front rank.

STEALTH

While traveling at a slow pace, the characters can move stealthily. As long as they're not in the open, they can try to surprise or sneak by other creatures they encounter. See the rules for hiding in chapter 7, "Using Ability Scores."

NOTICING THREATS

Use the passive Wisdom (Perception) scores of the characters to determine whether anyone in the group notices a hidden threat. The DM might decide that a threat can be noticed only by characters in a particular rank. For example, as the characters are exploring a maze of tunnels, the DM might decide that only those characters in the back rank have a chance to hear or spot a stealthy creature following the group, while characters in the front and middle ranks cannot.

While traveling at a fast pace, characters take a −5 penalty to their passive Wisdom (Perception) scores to notice hidden threats.

Encountering Creatures. If the DM determines that the adventurers encounter other creatures while they're traveling, it's up to both groups to decide what happens next. Either group might decide to attack, initiate a conversation, run away, or wait to see what the other group does.

Surprising Foes. If the adventurers encounter a hostile creature or group, the DM determines whether the adventurers or their foes might be surprised when combat erupts. See chapter 9 for more about surprise.

OTHER ACTIVITIES

Characters who turn their attention to other tasks as the group travels are not focused on watching for danger. These characters don't contribute their passive Wisdom (Perception) scores to the group's chance of noticing hidden threats. However, a character not watching for danger can do one of the following activities instead, or some other activity with the DM's permission.

Navigate. The character can try to prevent the group from becoming lost, making a Wisdom (Survival) check when the DM calls for it. (The *Dungeon Master's Guide* has rules to determine whether the group gets lost.)

Draw a Map. The character can draw a map that records the group's progress and helps the characters get back on course if they get lost. No ability check is required.

Track. A character can follow the tracks of another creature, making a Wisdom (Survival) check when the DM calls for it. (The *Dungeon Master's Guide* has rules for tracking.)

Forage. The character can keep an eye out for ready sources of food and water, making a Wisdom (Survival) check when the DM calls for it. (The *Dungeon Master's Guide* has rules for foraging.)

THE ENVIRONMENT

By its nature, adventuring involves delving into places that are dark, dangerous, and full of mysteries to be explored. The rules in this section cover some of the most important ways in which adventurers interact with the environment in such places. The *Dungeon Master's Guide* has rules covering more unusual situations.

FALLING

A fall from a great height is one of the most common hazards facing an adventurer. At the end of a fall, a creature takes 1d6 bludgeoning damage for every 10 feet it fell, to a maximum of 20d6. The creature lands prone, unless it avoids taking damage from the fall.

SUFFOCATING

A creature can hold its breath for a number of minutes equal to 1 + its Constitution modifier (minimum of 30 seconds).

When a creature runs out of breath or is choking, it can survive for a number of rounds equal to its Constitution modifier (minimum of 1 round). At the start of its next turn, it drops to 0 hit points and is dying, and it can't regain hit points or be stabilized until it can breathe again.

For example, a creature with a Constitution of 14 can hold its breath for 3 minutes. If it starts suffocating, it has 2 rounds to reach air before it drops to 0 hit points.

VISION AND LIGHT

The most fundamental tasks of adventuring—noticing danger, finding hidden objects, hitting an enemy in combat, and targeting a spell, to name just a few—rely heavily on a character's ability to see. Darkness and other effects that obscure vision can prove a significant hindrance.

A given area might be lightly or heavily obscured. In a **lightly obscured** area, such as dim light, patchy fog, or moderate foliage, creatures have disadvantage on Wisdom (Perception) checks that rely on sight.

A **heavily obscured** area—such as darkness, opaque fog, or dense foliage—blocks vision entirely. A creature effectively suffers from the blinded condition (see appendix A) when trying to see something in that area.

The presence or absence of light in an environment creates three categories of illumination: bright light, dim light, and darkness.

Bright light lets most creatures see normally. Even gloomy days provide bright light, as do torches, lanterns, fires, and other sources of illumination within a specific radius.

Dim light, also called shadows, creates a lightly obscured area. An area of dim light is usually a boundary between a source of bright light, such as a torch, and surrounding darkness. The soft light of twilight and dawn also counts as dim light. A particularly brilliant full moon might bathe the land in dim light.

Darkness creates a heavily obscured area. Characters face darkness outdoors at night (even most moonlit nights), within the confines of an unlit dungeon or a subterranean vault, or in an area of magical darkness.

BLINDSIGHT

A creature with blindsight can perceive its surroundings without relying on sight, within a specific radius. Creatures without eyes, such as oozes, and creatures with echolocation or heightened senses, such as bats and true dragons, have this sense.

DARKVISION

Many creatures in the worlds of D&D, especially those that dwell underground, have darkvision. Within a specified range, a creature with darkvision can see in

darkness as if the darkness were dim light, so areas of darkness are only lightly obscured as far as that creature is concerned. However, the creature can't discern color in darkness, only shades of gray.

TRUESIGHT

A creature with truesight can, out to a specific range, see in normal and magical darkness, see invisible creatures and objects, automatically detect visual illusions and succeed on saving throws against them, and perceives the original form of a shapechanger or a creature that is transformed by magic. Furthermore, the creature can see into the Ethereal Plane.

FOOD AND WATER

Characters who don't eat or drink suffer the effects of exhaustion (see appendix A). Exhaustion caused by lack of food or water can't be removed until the character eats and drinks the full required amount.

FOOD

A character needs one pound of food per day and can make food last longer by subsisting on half rations. Eating half a pound of food in a day counts as half a day without food.

A character can go without food for a number of days equal to 3 + his or her Constitution modifier (minimum 1). At the end of each day beyond that limit, a character automatically suffers one level of exhaustion.

A normal day of eating resets the count of days without food to zero.

WATER

A character needs one gallon of water per day, or two gallons per day if the weather is hot. A character who drinks only half that much water must succeed on a DC 15 Constitution saving throw or suffer one level of exhaustion at the end of the day. A character with access to even less water automatically suffers one level of exhaustion at the end of the day.

If the character already has one or more levels of exhaustion, the character takes two levels in either case.

INTERACTING WITH OBJECTS

A character's interaction with objects in an environment is often simple to resolve in the game. The player tells the DM that his or her character is doing something, such as moving a lever, and the DM describes what, if anything, happens.

For example, a character might decide to pull a lever, which might, in turn, raise a portcullis, cause a room to flood with water, or open a secret door in a nearby wall. If the lever is rusted in position, though, a character might need to force it. In such a situation, the DM might call for a Strength check to see whether the character can wrench the lever into place. The DM sets the DC for any such check based on the difficulty of the task.

Characters can also damage objects with their weapons and spells. Objects are immune to poison and psychic damage, but otherwise they can be affected by physical and magical attacks much like creatures

can. The DM determines an object's Armor Class and hit points, and might decide that certain objects have resistance or immunity to certain kinds of attacks. (It's hard to cut a rope with a club, for example.) Objects always fail Strength and Dexterity saving throws, and they are immune to effects that require other saves. When an object drops to 0 hit points, it breaks.

A character can also attempt a Strength check to break an object. The DM sets the DC for any such check.

SOCIAL INTERACTION

Exploring dungeons, overcoming obstacles, and slaying monsters are key parts of D&D adventures. No less important, though, are the social interactions that adventurers have with other inhabitants of the world.

Interaction takes on many forms. You might need to convince an unscrupulous thief to confess to some malfeasance, or you might try to flatter a dragon so that it will spare your life. The DM assumes the roles of any characters who are participating in the interaction that don't belong to another player at the table. Any such character is called a **nonplayer character** (NPC).

In general terms, an NPC's attitude toward you is described as friendly, indifferent, or hostile. Friendly NPCs are predisposed to help you, and hostile ones are inclined to get in your way. It's easier to get what you want from a friendly NPC, of course.

Social interactions have two primary aspects: roleplaying and ability checks.

ROLEPLAYING

Roleplaying is, literally, the act of playing out a role. In this case, it's *you* as a player determining how your character thinks, acts, and talks.

Roleplaying is a part of every aspect of the game, and it comes to the fore during social interactions. Your character's quirks, mannerisms, and personality influence how interactions resolve.

There are two styles you can use when roleplaying your character: the descriptive approach and the active approach. Most players use a combination of the two styles. Use whichever mix of the two works best for you.

DESCRIPTIVE APPROACH TO ROLEPLAYING

With this approach, you describe your character's words and actions to the DM and the other players. Drawing on your mental image of your character, you tell everyone what your character does and how he or she does it.

For instance, Chris plays Tordek the dwarf. Tordek has a quick temper and blames the elves of the Cloakwood for his family's misfortune. At a tavern, an obnoxious elf minstrel sits at Tordek's table and tries to strike up a conversation with the dwarf.

Chris says, "Tordek spits on the floor, growls an insult at the bard, and stomps over to the bar. He sits on a stool and glares at the minstrel before ordering another drink."

In this example, Chris has conveyed Tordek's mood and given the DM a clear idea of his character's attitude and actions.

When using descriptive roleplaying, keep the following things in mind:

- Describe your character's emotions and attitude.
- Focus on your character's intent and how others might perceive it.
- Provide as much embellishment as you feel comfortable with.

Don't worry about getting things exactly right. Just focus on thinking about what your character would do and describing what you see in your mind.

Active Approach to Roleplaying

If descriptive roleplaying tells your DM and your fellow players what your character thinks and does, active roleplaying *shows* them.

When you use active roleplaying, you speak with your character's voice, like an actor taking on a role. You might even echo your character's movements and body language. This approach is more immersive than descriptive roleplaying, though you still need to describe things that can't be reasonably acted out.

Going back to the example of Chris roleplaying Tordek above, here's how the scene might play out if Chris used active roleplaying:

Speaking as Tordek, Chris says in a gruff, deep voice, "I was wondering why it suddenly smelled awful in here. If I wanted to hear anything out of you, I'd snap your arm and enjoy your screams." In his normal voice, Chris then adds, "I get up, glare at the elf, and head to the bar."

Results of Roleplaying

The DM uses your character's actions and attitudes to determine how an NPC reacts. A cowardly NPC buckles under threats of violence. A stubborn dwarf refuses to let anyone badger her. A vain dragon laps up flattery.

When interacting with an NPC, pay close attention to the DM's portrayal of the NPC's mood, dialogue, and personality. You might be able to determine an NPC's personality traits, ideals, flaws, and bonds, then play on them to influence the NPC's attitude.

Interactions in D&D are much like interactions in real life. If you can offer NPCs something they want, threaten them with something they fear, or play on their sympathies and goals, you can use words to get almost anything you want. On the other hand, if you insult a proud warrior or speak ill of a noble's allies, your efforts to convince or deceive will fall short.

Ability Checks

In addition to roleplaying, ability checks are key in determining the outcome of an interaction.

Your roleplaying efforts can alter an NPC's attitude, but there might still be an element of chance in the situation. For example, your DM can call for a Charisma check at any point during an interaction if he or she wants the dice to play a role in determining an NPC's reactions. Other checks might be appropriate in certain situations, at your DM's discretion.

Pay attention to your skill proficiencies when thinking of how you want to interact with an NPC, and stack the deck in your favor by using an approach that relies on your best bonuses and skills. If the group needs to trick a guard into letting them into a castle, the rogue who is proficient in Deception is the best bet to lead the discussion. When negotiating for a hostage's release, the cleric with Persuasion should do most of the talking.

Resting

Heroic though they might be, adventurers can't spend every hour of the day in the thick of exploration, social interaction, and combat. They need rest—time to sleep and eat, tend their wounds, refresh their minds and spirits for spellcasting, and brace themselves for further adventure.

Adventurers can take short rests in the midst of an adventuring day and a long rest to end the day.

Short Rest

A short rest is a period of downtime, at least 1 hour long, during which a character does nothing more strenuous than eating, drinking, reading, and tending to wounds.

A character can spend one or more Hit Dice at the end of a short rest, up to the character's maximum number of Hit Dice, which is equal to the character's level. For each Hit Die spent in this way, the player rolls the die and adds the character's Constitution modifier to it. The character regains hit points equal to the total. The player can decide to spend an additional Hit Die after each roll. A character regains some spent Hit Dice upon finishing a long rest, as explained below.

Long Rest

A long rest is a period of extended downtime, at least 8 hours long, during which a character sleeps or performs light activity: reading, talking, eating, or standing watch for no more than 2 hours. If the rest is interrupted by a period of strenuous activity—at least 1 hour of walking, fighting, casting spells, or similar adventuring activity—the characters must begin the rest again to gain any benefit from it.

At the end of a long rest, a character regains all lost hit points. The character also regains spent Hit Dice, up to a number of dice equal to half of the character's total number of them (minimum of one die). For example, if a character has eight Hit Dice, he or she can regain four spent Hit Dice upon finishing a long rest.

A character can't benefit from more than one long rest in a 24-hour period, and a character must have at least 1 hit point at the start of the rest to gain its benefits.

Between Adventures

Between trips to dungeons and battles against ancient evils, adventurers need time to rest, recuperate, and prepare for their next adventure. Many adventurers also use this time to perform other tasks, such as crafting arms and armor, performing research, or spending their hard-earned gold.

In some cases, the passage of time is something that occurs with little fanfare or description. When starting a new adventure, the DM might simply declare that a certain amount of time has passed and allow you to describe in general terms what your character has been doing. At other times, the DM might want to keep track of just how much time is passing as events beyond your perception stay in motion.

LIFESTYLE EXPENSES

Between adventures, you choose a particular quality of life and pay the cost of maintaining that lifestyle, as described in chapter 5.

Living a particular lifestyle doesn't have a huge effect on your character, but your lifestyle can affect the way other individuals and groups react to you. For example, when you lead an aristocratic lifestyle, it might be easier for you to influence the nobles of the city than if you live in poverty.

DOWNTIME ACTIVITIES

Between adventures, the DM might ask you what your character is doing during his or her downtime. Periods of downtime can vary in duration, but each downtime activity requires a certain number of days to complete before you gain any benefit, and at least 8 hours of each day must be spent on the downtime activity for the day to count. The days do not need to be consecutive. If you have more than the minimum amount of days to spend, you can keep doing the same thing for a longer period of time, or switch to a new downtime activity.

Downtime activities other than the ones presented below are possible. If you want your character to spend his or her downtime performing an activity not covered here, discuss it with your DM.

CRAFTING

You can craft nonmagical objects, including adventuring equipment and works of art. You must be proficient with tools related to the object you are trying to create (typically artisan's tools). You might also need access to special materials or locations necessary to create it. For example, someone proficient with smith's tools needs a forge in order to craft a sword or suit of armor.

For every day of downtime you spend crafting, you can craft one or more items with a total market value not exceeding 5 gp, and you must expend raw materials worth half the total market value. If something you want to craft has a market value greater than 5 gp, you make progress every day in 5-gp increments until you reach the market value of the item. For example, a suit of plate armor (market value 1,500 gp) takes 300 days to craft by yourself.

Multiple characters can combine their efforts toward the crafting of a single item, provided that the characters all have proficiency with the requisite tools and are working together in the same place. Each character contributes 5 gp worth of effort for every day spent helping to craft the item. For example, three characters with the requisite tool proficiency and the proper facilities can craft a suit of plate armor in 100 days, at a total cost of 750 gp.

While crafting, you can maintain a modest lifestyle without having to pay 1 gp per day, or a comfortable lifestyle at half the normal cost (see chapter 5 for more information on lifestyle expenses).

PRACTICING A PROFESSION

You can work between adventures, allowing you to maintain a modest lifestyle without having to pay 1 gp per day (see chapter 5 for more information on lifestyle expenses). This benefit lasts as long you continue to practice your profession.

If you are a member of an organization that can provide gainful employment, such as a temple or a thieves' guild, you earn enough to support a comfortable lifestyle instead.

If you have proficiency in the Performance skill and put your performance skill to use during your downtime, you earn enough to support a wealthy lifestyle instead.

RECUPERATING

You can use downtime between adventures to recover from a debilitating injury, disease, or poison.

After three days of downtime spent recuperating, you can make a DC 15 Constitution saving throw. On a successful save, you can choose one of the following results:

- End one effect on you that prevents you from regaining hit points.
- For the next 24 hours, gain advantage on saving throws against one disease or poison currently affecting you.

RESEARCHING

The time between adventures is a great chance to perform research, gaining insight into mysteries that have unfurled over the course of the campaign. Research can include poring over dusty tomes and crumbling scrolls in a library or buying drinks for the locals to pry rumors and gossip from their lips.

When you begin your research, the DM determines whether the information is available, how many days of downtime it will take to find it, and whether there are any restrictions on your research (such as needing to seek out a specific individual, tome, or location). The DM might also require you to make one or more ability checks, such as an Intelligence (Investigation) check to find clues pointing toward the information you seek, or a Charisma (Persuasion) check to secure someone's aid. Once those conditions are met, you learn the information if it is available.

For each day of research, you must spend 1 gp to cover your expenses. This cost is in addition to your normal lifestyle expenses (as discussed in chapter 5).

TRAINING

You can spend time between adventures learning a new language or training with a set of tools. Your DM might allow additional training options.

First, you must find an instructor willing to teach you. The DM determines how long it takes, and whether one or more ability checks are required.

The training lasts for 250 days and costs 1 gp per day. After you spend the requisite amount of time and money, you learn the new language or gain proficiency with the new tool.

CHAPTER 9: COMBAT

HE CLATTER OF A SWORD STRIKING AGAINST a shield. The terrible rending sound as monstrous claws tear through armor. A brilliant flash of light as a ball of flame blossoms from a wizard's spell. The sharp tang of blood in the air, cutting through the stench of vile monsters. Roars of fury, shouts of triumph, cries of pain. Combat in D&D can be chaotic, deadly, and thrilling.

This chapter provides the rules you need for your characters and monsters to engage in combat, whether it is a brief skirmish or an extended conflict in a dungeon or on a field of battle. Throughout this chapter, the rules address you, the player or Dungeon Master. The Dungeon Master controls all the monsters and nonplayer characters involved in combat, and each other player controls an adventurer. "You" can also mean the character or monster that you control.

THE ORDER OF COMBAT

A typical combat encounter is a clash between two sides, a flurry of weapon swings, feints, parries, footwork, and spellcasting. The game organizes the chaos of combat into a cycle of rounds and turns. A **round** represents about 6 seconds in the game world. During a round, each participant in a battle takes a **turn**. The order of turns is determined at the beginning of a combat encounter, when everyone rolls initiative. Once everyone has taken a turn, the fight continues to the next round if neither side has defeated the other.

SURPRISE

A band of adventurers sneaks up on a bandit camp, springing from the trees to attack them. A gelatinous cube glides down a dungeon passage, unnoticed by the adventurers until the cube engulfs one of them. In these situations, one side of the battle gains surprise over the other.

The DM determines who might be surprised. If neither side tries to be stealthy, they automatically notice each other. Otherwise, the DM compares the Dexterity (Stealth) checks of anyone hiding with the passive Wisdom (Perception) score of each creature on the opposing side. Any character or monster that doesn't notice a threat is surprised at the start of the encounter.

If you're surprised, you can't move or take an action on your first turn of the combat, and you can't take a reaction until that turn ends. A member of a group can be surprised even if the other members aren't.

INITIATIVE

Initiative determines the order of turns during combat. When combat starts, every participant makes a Dexterity check to determine their place in the initiative order. The DM makes one roll for an entire group of identical creatures, so each member of the group acts at the same time.

The DM ranks the combatants in order from the one with the highest Dexterity check total to the one with the lowest. This is the order (called the initiative order) in which they act during each round. The initiative order remains the same from round to round.

If a tie occurs, the DM decides the order among tied DM-controlled creatures, and the players decide the order among their tied characters. The DM can decide the order if the tie is between a monster and a player character. Optionally, the DM can have the tied characters and monsters each roll a d20 to determine the order, highest roll going first.

YOUR TURN

On your turn, you can **move** a distance up to your speed and **take one action**. You decide whether to move first or take your action first. Your speed—sometimes called your walking speed—is noted on your character sheet.

The most common actions you can take are described in the "Actions in Combat" section later in this chapter. Many class features and other abilities provide additional options for your action.

The "Movement and Position" section later in this chapter gives the rules for your move.

You can forgo moving, taking an action, or doing anything at all on your turn. If you can't decide what to do on your turn, consider taking the Dodge or Ready action, as described in "Actions in Combat."

BONUS ACTIONS

Various class features, spells, and other abilities let you take an additional action on your turn called a bonus action. The Cunning Action feature, for example, allows a rogue to take a bonus action. You can take a bonus action only when a special ability, spell, or other feature of the game states that you can do something as a bonus action. You otherwise don't have a bonus action to take.

You can take only one bonus action on your turn, so you must choose which bonus action to use when you have more than one available.

You choose when to take a bonus action during your turn, unless the bonus action's timing is specified, and anything that deprives you of your ability to take actions also prevents you from taking a bonus action.

COMBAT STEP BY STEP

1. **Determine surprise.** The DM determines whether anyone involved in the combat encounter is surprised.
2. **Establish positions.** The DM decides where all the characters and monsters are located. Given the adventurers' marching order or their stated positions in the room or other location, the DM figures out where the adversaries are—how far away and in what direction.
3. **Roll initiative.** Everyone involved in the combat encounter rolls initiative, determining the order of combatants' turns.
4. **Take turns.** Each participant in the battle takes a turn in initiative order.
5. **Begin the next round.** When everyone involved in the combat has had a turn, the round ends. Repeat step 4 until the fighting stops.

Other Activity on Your Turn

Your turn can include a variety of flourishes that require neither your action nor your move.

You can communicate however you are able, through brief utterances and gestures, as you take your turn.

You can also interact with one object or feature of the environment for free, during either your move or your action. For example, you could open a door during your move as you stride toward a foe, or you could draw your weapon as part of the same action you use to attack.

If you want to interact with a second object, you need to use your action. Some magic items and other special objects always require an action to use, as stated in their descriptions.

The DM might require you to use an action for any of these activities when it needs special care or when it presents an unusual obstacle. For instance, the DM could reasonably expect you to use an action to open a stuck door or turn a crank to lower a drawbridge.

Reactions

Certain special abilities, spells, and situations allow you to take a special action called a reaction. A reaction is an instant response to a trigger of some kind, which can occur on your turn or on someone else's. The opportunity attack, described later in this chapter, is the most common type of reaction.

When you take a reaction, you can't take another one until the start of your next turn. If the reaction interrupts another creature's turn, that creature can continue its turn right after the reaction.

Movement and Position

In combat, characters and monsters are in constant motion, often using movement and position to gain the upper hand.

Interacting with Objects Around You

Here are a few examples of the sorts of thing you can do in tandem with your movement and action:

- draw or sheathe a sword
- open or close a door
- withdraw a potion from your backpack
- pick up a dropped axe
- take a bauble from a table
- remove a ring from your finger
- stuff some food into your mouth
- plant a banner in the ground
- fish a few coins from your belt pouch
- drink all the ale in a flagon
- throw a lever or a switch
- pull a torch from a sconce
- take a book from a shelf you can reach
- extinguish a small flame
- don a mask
- pull the hood of your cloak up and over your head
- put your ear to a door
- kick a small stone
- turn a key in a lock
- tap the floor with a 10-foot pole
- hand an item to another character

On your turn, you can move a distance up to your speed. You can use as much or as little of your speed as you like on your turn, following the rules here.

Your movement can include jumping, climbing, and swimming. These different modes of movement can be combined with walking, or they can constitute your entire move. However you're moving, you deduct the distance of each part of your move from your speed until it is used up or until you are done moving.

The "Special Types of Movement" section in chapter 8 gives the particulars for jumping, climbing, and swimming.

Breaking Up Your Move

You can break up your movement on your turn, using some of your speed before and after your action. For example, if you have a speed of 30 feet, you can move 10 feet, take your action, and then move 20 feet.

Moving between Attacks

If you take an action that includes more than one weapon attack, you can break up your movement even further by moving between those attacks. For example, a fighter who can make two attacks with the Extra Attack feature and who has a speed of 25 feet could move 10 feet, make an attack, move 15 feet, and then attack again.

Using Different Speeds

If you have more than one speed, such as your walking speed and a flying speed, you can switch back and forth between your speeds during your move. Whenever you switch, subtract the distance you've already moved from the new speed. The result determines how much farther you can move. If the result is 0 or less, you can't use the new speed during the current move.

For example, if you have a speed of 30 and a flying speed of 60 because a wizard cast the *fly* spell on you, you could fly 20 feet, then walk 10 feet, and then leap into the air to fly 30 feet more.

Difficult Terrain

Combat rarely takes place in bare rooms or on featureless plains. Boulder-strewn caverns, briar-choked forests, treacherous staircases—the setting of a typical fight contains difficult terrain.

Every foot of movement in difficult terrain costs 1 extra foot. This rule is true even if multiple things in a space count as difficult terrain.

Low furniture, rubble, undergrowth, steep stairs, snow, and shallow bogs are examples of difficult terrain. The space of another creature, whether hostile or not, also counts as difficult terrain.

Being Prone

Combatants often find themselves lying on the ground, either because they are knocked down or because they throw themselves down. In the game, they are prone, a condition described in appendix A.

You can **drop prone** without using any of your speed. **Standing up** takes more effort; doing so costs an amount of movement equal to half your speed. For example, if your speed is 30 feet, you must spend 15 feet of movement to stand up. You can't stand up if you don't have enough movement left or if your speed is 0.

To move while prone, you must **crawl** or use magic such as teleportation. Every foot of movement while crawling costs 1 extra foot. Crawling 1 foot in difficult terrain, therefore, costs 3 feet of movement.

Moving Around Other Creatures

You can move through a nonhostile creature's space. In contrast, you can move through a hostile creature's space only if the creature is at least two sizes larger or smaller than you. Remember that another creature's space is difficult terrain for you.

Whether a creature is a friend or an enemy, you can't willingly end your move in its space.

If you leave a hostile creature's reach during your move, you provoke an opportunity attack, as explained later in the chapter.

Flying Movement

Flying creatures enjoy many benefits of mobility, but they must also deal with the danger of falling. If a flying creature is knocked prone, has its speed reduced to 0, or is otherwise deprived of the ability to move, the creature falls, unless it has the ability to hover or it is being held aloft by magic, such as by the *fly* spell.

Creature Size

Each creature takes up a different amount of space. The Size Categories table shows how much space a creature of a particular size controls in combat. Objects sometimes use the same size categories.

Size Categories

Size	Space
Tiny	2½ by 2½ ft.
Small	5 by 5 ft.
Medium	5 by 5 ft.
Large	10 by 10 ft.
Huge	15 by 15 ft.
Gargantuan	20 by 20 ft. or larger

Space

A creature's space is the area in feet that it effectively controls in combat, not an expression of its physical dimensions. A typical Medium creature isn't 5 feet wide, for example, but it does control a space that wide. If a Medium hobgoblin stands in a 5-foot-wide doorway, other creatures can't get through unless the hobgoblin lets them.

A creature's space also reflects the area it needs to fight effectively. For that reason, there's a limit to the number of creatures that can surround another creature in combat. Assuming Medium combatants, eight creatures can fit in a 5-foot radius around another one.

Because larger creatures take up more space, fewer of them can surround a creature. If five Large creatures crowd around a Medium or smaller one, there's little room for anyone else. In contrast, as many as twenty Medium creatures can surround a Gargantuan one.

SQUEEZING INTO A SMALLER SPACE

A creature can squeeze through a space that is large enough for a creature one size smaller than it. Thus, a Large creature can squeeze through a passage that's only 5 feet wide. While squeezing through a space, a creature must spend 1 extra foot for every foot it moves there, and it has disadvantage on attack rolls and Dexterity saving throws. Attack rolls against the creature have advantage while it's in the smaller space.

ACTIONS IN COMBAT

When you take your action on your turn, you can take one of the actions presented here, an action you gained from your class or a special feature, or an action that you improvise. Many monsters have action options of their own in their stat blocks.

When you describe an action not detailed elsewhere in the rules, the DM tells you whether that action is possible and what kind of roll you need to make, if any, to determine success or failure.

ATTACK

The most common action to take in combat is the Attack action, whether you are swinging a sword, firing an arrow from a bow, or brawling with your fists.

With this action, you make one melee or ranged attack. See the "Making an Attack" section for the rules that govern attacks.

Certain features, such as the Extra Attack feature of the fighter, allow you to make more than one attack with this action.

CAST A SPELL

Spellcasters such as wizards and clerics, as well as many monsters, have access to spells and can use them to great effect in combat. Each spell has a casting time, which specifies whether the caster must use an action, a reaction, minutes, or even hours to cast the spell. Casting a spell is, therefore, not necessarily an action. Most spells do have a casting time of 1 action, so a spellcaster often uses his or her action in combat to cast such a spell. See chapter 10 for the rules on spellcasting.

DASH

When you take the Dash action, you gain extra movement for the current turn. The increase equals your speed, after applying any modifiers. With a speed of 30 feet, for example, you can move up to 60 feet on your turn if you dash.

Any increase or decrease to your speed changes this additional movement by the same amount. If your speed of 30 feet is reduced to 15 feet, for instance, you can move up to 30 feet this turn if you dash.

DISENGAGE

If you take the Disengage action, your movement doesn't provoke opportunity attacks for the rest of the turn.

DODGE

When you take the Dodge action, you focus entirely on avoiding attacks. Until the start of your next turn, any attack roll made against you has disadvantage if you can see the attacker, and you make Dexterity saving throws with advantage. You lose this benefit if you are incapacitated (as explained in appendix A) or if your speed drops to 0.

HELP

You can lend your aid to another creature in the completion of a task. When you take the Help action, the creature you aid gains advantage on the next ability check it makes to perform the task you are helping with, provided that it makes the check before the start of your next turn.

Alternatively, you can aid a friendly creature in attacking a creature within 5 feet of you. You feint, distract the target, or in some other way team up to make your ally's attack more effective. If your ally attacks the target before your next turn, the first attack roll is made with advantage.

HIDE

When you take the Hide action, you make a Dexterity (Stealth) check in an attempt to hide, following the rules in chapter 7 for hiding. If you succeed, you gain certain benefits, as described in the "Unseen Attackers and Targets" section later in this chapter.

READY

Sometimes you want to get the jump on a foe or wait for a particular circumstance before you act. To do so, you can take the Ready action on your turn, which lets you act using your reaction before the start of your next turn.

First, you decide what perceivable circumstance will trigger your reaction. Then, you choose the action you will take in response to that trigger, or you choose to move up to your speed in response to it. Examples include "If the cultist steps on the trapdoor, I'll pull the lever that opens it," and "If the goblin steps next to me, I move away."

When the trigger occurs, you can either take your reaction right after the trigger finishes or ignore the trigger. Remember that you can take only one reaction per round.

When you ready a spell, you cast it as normal but hold its energy, which you release with your reaction when the trigger occurs. To be readied, a spell must have a casting time of 1 action, and holding onto the spell's magic requires concentration (explained in chapter 10). If your concentration is broken, the spell dissipates without taking effect. For example, if you are concentrating on the *web* spell and ready *magic missile*, your *web* spell ends, and if you take damage before you release *magic missile* with your reaction, your concentration might be broken.

SEARCH

When you take the Search action, you devote your attention to finding something. Depending on the nature of your search, the DM might have you make a Wisdom (Perception) check or an Intelligence (Investigation) check.

USE AN OBJECT

You normally interact with an object while doing something else, such as when you draw a sword as part of an attack. When an object requires your action for its use, you take the Use an Object action. This action is also useful when you want to interact with more than one object on your turn.

MAKING AN ATTACK

Whether you're striking with a melee weapon, firing a weapon at range, or making an attack roll as part of a spell, an attack has a simple structure.

1. **Choose a target.** Pick a target within your attack's range: a creature, an object, or a location.
2. **Determine modifiers.** The DM determines whether the target has cover and whether you have advantage or disadvantage against the target. In addition, spells, special abilities, and other effects can apply penalties or bonuses to your attack roll.
3. **Resolve the attack.** You make the attack roll. On a hit, you roll damage, unless the particular attack has rules that specify otherwise. Some attacks cause special effects in addition to or instead of damage.

If there's ever any question whether something you're doing counts as an attack, the rule is simple: if you're making an attack roll, you're making an attack.

Attack Rolls

When you make an attack, your attack roll determines whether the attack hits or misses. To make an attack roll, roll a d20 and add the appropriate modifiers. If the total of the roll plus modifiers equals or exceeds the target's Armor Class (AC), the attack hits. The AC of a character is determined at character creation, whereas the AC of a monster is in its stat block.

Modifiers to the Roll

When a character makes an attack roll, the two most common modifiers to the roll are an ability modifier and the character's proficiency bonus. When a monster makes an attack roll, it uses whatever modifier is provided in its stat block.

Ability Modifier. The ability modifier used for a melee weapon attack is Strength, and the ability modifier used for a ranged weapon attack is Dexterity. Weapons that have the finesse or thrown property break this rule.

Some spells also require an attack roll. The ability modifier used for a spell attack depends on the spellcasting ability of the spellcaster, as explained in chapter 10.

Proficiency Bonus. You add your proficiency bonus to your attack roll when you attack using a weapon with which you have proficiency, as well as when you attack with a spell.

Rolling 1 or 20

Sometimes fate blesses or curses a combatant, causing the novice to hit and the veteran to miss.

If the d20 roll for an attack is a 20, the attack hits regardless of any modifiers or the target's AC. This is called a critical hit, which is explained later in this chapter.

If the d20 roll for an attack is a 1, the attack misses regardless of any modifiers or the target's AC.

Unseen Attackers and Targets

Combatants often try to escape their foes' notice by hiding, casting the invisibility spell, or lurking in darkness.

When you attack a target that you can't see, you have disadvantage on the attack roll. This is true whether you're guessing the target's location or you're targeting a creature you can hear but not see. If the target isn't in the location you targeted, you automatically miss, but the DM typically just says that the attack missed, not whether you guessed the target's location correctly.

When a creature can't see you, you have advantage on attack rolls against it. If you are hidden—both unseen and unheard—when you make an attack, you give away your location when the attack hits or misses.

RANGED ATTACKS

When you make a ranged attack, you fire a bow or a crossbow, hurl a handaxe, or otherwise send projectiles to strike a foe at a distance. A monster might shoot spines from its tail. Many spells also involve making a ranged attack.

RANGE

You can make ranged attacks only against targets within a specified range.

If a ranged attack, such as one made with a spell, has a single range, you can't attack a target beyond this range.

Some ranged attacks, such as those made with a longbow or a shortbow, have two ranges. The smaller number is the normal range, and the larger number is the long range. Your attack roll has disadvantage when your target is beyond normal range, and you can't attack a target beyond the long range.

RANGED ATTACKS IN CLOSE COMBAT

Aiming a ranged attack is more difficult when a foe is next to you. When you make a ranged attack with a weapon, a spell, or some other means, you have disadvantage on the attack roll if you are within 5 feet of a hostile creature who can see you and who isn't incapacitated.

MELEE ATTACKS

Used in hand-to-hand combat, a melee attack allows you to attack a foe within your reach. A melee attack typically uses a handheld weapon such as a sword, a warhammer, or an axe. A typical monster makes a melee attack when it strikes with its claws, horns, teeth, tentacles, or other body part. A few spells also involve making a melee attack.

Most creatures have a 5-foot **reach** and can thus attack targets within 5 feet of them when making a melee attack. Certain creatures (typically those larger than Medium) have melee attacks with a greater reach than 5 feet, as noted in their descriptions.

Instead of using a weapon to make a melee weapon attack, you can use an **unarmed strike**: a punch, kick, head-butt, or similar forceful blow (none of which count as weapons). On a hit, an unarmed strike deals bludgeoning damage equal to 1 + your Strength modifier. You are proficient with your unarmed strikes.

OPPORTUNITY ATTACKS

In a fight, everyone is constantly watching for a chance to strike an enemy who is fleeing or passing by. Such a strike is called an opportunity attack.

You can make an opportunity attack when a hostile creature that you can see moves out of your reach. To make the opportunity attack, you use your reaction to make one melee attack against the provoking

CONTESTS IN COMBAT

Battle often involves pitting your prowess against that of your foe. Such a challenge is represented by a contest. This section includes the most common contests that require an action in combat: grappling and shoving a creature. The DM can use these contests as models for improvising others.

creature. The attack occurs right before the creature leaves your reach.

You can avoid provoking an opportunity attack by taking the Disengage action. You also don't provoke an opportunity attack when you teleport or when someone or something moves you without using your movement, action, or reaction. For example, you don't provoke an opportunity attack if an explosion hurls you out of a foe's reach or if gravity causes you to fall past an enemy.

TWO-WEAPON FIGHTING

When you take the Attack action and attack with a light melee weapon that you're holding in one hand, you can use a bonus action to attack with a different light melee weapon that you're holding in the other hand. You don't add your ability modifier to the damage of the bonus attack, unless that modifier is negative.

If either weapon has the thrown property, you can throw the weapon, instead of making a melee attack with it.

GRAPPLING

When you want to grab a creature or wrestle with it, you can use the Attack action to make a special melee attack, a grapple. If you're able to make multiple attacks with the Attack action, this attack replaces one of them.

The target of your grapple must be no more than one size larger than you and must be within your reach. Using at least one free hand, you try to seize the target by making a grapple check instead of an attack roll: a Strength (Athletics) check contested by the target's Strength (Athletics) or Dexterity (Acrobatics) check (the target chooses the ability to use). If you succeed, you subject the target to the grappled condition (see appendix A). The condition specifies the things that end it, and you can release the target whenever you like (no action required).

Escaping a Grapple. A grappled creature can use its action to escape. To do so, it must succeed on a Strength (Athletics) or Dexterity (Acrobatics) check contested by your Strength (Athletics) check.

Moving a Grappled Creature. When you move, you can drag or carry the grappled creature with you, but your speed is halved, unless the creature is two or more sizes smaller than you.

SHOVING A CREATURE

Using the Attack action, you can make a special melee attack to shove a creature, either to knock it prone or push it away from you. If you're able to make multiple attacks with the Attack action, this attack replaces one of them.

The target must be no more than one size larger than you and must be within your reach. Instead of making an attack roll, you make a Strength (Athletics) check contested by the target's Strength (Athletics) or

Dexterity (Acrobatics) check (the target chooses the ability to use). If you win the contest, you either knock the target prone or push it 5 feet away from you.

COVER

Walls, trees, creatures, and other obstacles can provide cover during combat, making a target more difficult to harm. A target can benefit from cover only when an attack or other effect originates on the opposite side of the cover.

There are three degrees of cover. If a target is behind multiple sources of cover, only the most protective degree of cover applies; the degrees aren't added together. For example, if a target is behind a creature that gives half cover and a tree trunk that gives three-quarters cover, the target has three-quarters cover.

A target with **half cover** has a +2 bonus to AC and Dexterity saving throws. A target has half cover if an obstacle blocks at least half of its body. The obstacle might be a low wall, a large piece of furniture, a narrow tree trunk, or a creature, whether that creature is an enemy or a friend.

A target with **three-quarters cover** has a +5 bonus to AC and Dexterity saving throws. A target has three-quarters cover if about three-quarters of it is covered by an obstacle. The obstacle might be a portcullis, an arrow slit, or a thick tree trunk.

A target with **total cover** can't be targeted directly by an attack or a spell, although some spells can reach such a target by including it in an area of effect. A target has total cover if it is completely concealed by an obstacle.

DAMAGE AND HEALING

Injury and the risk of death are constant companions of those who explore the worlds of D&D. The thrust of a sword, a well-placed arrow, or a blast of flame from a *fireball* spell all have the potential to damage, or even kill, the hardiest of creatures.

HIT POINTS

Hit points represent a combination of physical and mental durability, the will to live, and luck. Creatures with more hit points are more difficult to kill. Those with fewer hit points are more fragile.

A creature's current hit points (usually just called hit points) can be any number from the creature's hit point maximum down to 0. This number changes frequently as a creature takes damage or receives healing.

Whenever a creature takes damage, that damage is subtracted from its hit points. The loss of hit points has no effect on a creature's capabilities until the creature drops to 0 hit points.

DAMAGE ROLLS

Each weapon, spell, and harmful monster ability specifies the damage it deals. You roll the damage die or dice, add any modifiers, and apply the damage to your target. Magic weapons, special abilities, and other factors can grant a bonus to damage. With a penalty, it is possible to deal 0 damage, but never negative damage.

When attacking with a **weapon**, you add your ability modifier—the same modifier used for the attack roll—to the damage. A **spell** tells you which dice to roll for damage and whether to add any modifiers.

If a spell or other effect deals damage to **more than one target** at the same time, roll the damage once for all of them. For example, when a wizard casts *fireball* or a cleric casts *flame strike*, the spell's damage is rolled once for all creatures caught in the blast.

CRITICAL HITS

When you score a critical hit, you get to roll extra dice for the attack's damage against the target. Roll all of the attack's damage dice twice and add them together. Then add any relevant modifiers as normal. To speed up play, you can roll all the damage dice at once.

For example, if you score a critical hit with a dagger, roll 2d4 for the damage, rather than 1d4, and then add your relevant ability modifier. If the attack involves other damage dice, such as from the rogue's Sneak Attack feature, you roll those dice twice as well.

DAMAGE TYPES

Different attacks, damaging spells, and other harmful effects deal different types of damage. Damage types have no rules of their own, but other rules, such as damage resistance, rely on the types.

The damage types follow, with examples to help a DM assign a damage type to a new effect.

Acid. The corrosive spray of a black dragon's breath and the dissolving enzymes secreted by a black pudding deal acid damage.

Bludgeoning. Blunt force attacks—hammers, falling, constriction, and the like—deal bludgeoning damage.

Cold. The infernal chill radiating from an ice devil's spear and the frigid blast of a white dragon's breath deal cold damage.

Fire. Red dragons breathe fire, and many spells conjure flames to deal fire damage.

Force. Force is pure magical energy focused into a damaging form. Most effects that deal force damage are spells, including *magic missile* and *spiritual weapon*.

Lightning. A *lightning bolt* spell and a blue dragon's breath deal lightning damage.

Necrotic. Necrotic damage, dealt by certain undead and a spell such as *chill touch*, withers matter and even the soul.

Piercing. Puncturing and impaling attacks, including spears and monsters' bites, deal piercing damage.

Poison. Venomous stings and the toxic gas of a green dragon's breath deal poison damage.

Psychic. Mental abilities such as a mind flayer's psionic blast deal psychic damage.

Radiant. Radiant damage, dealt by a cleric's *flame strike* spell or an angel's smiting weapon, sears the flesh like fire and overloads the spirit with power.

Slashing. Swords, axes, and monsters' claws deal slashing damage.

Thunder. A concussive burst of sound, such as the effect of the *thunderwave* spell, deals thunder damage.

Damage Resistance and Vulnerability

Some creatures and objects are exceedingly difficult or unusually easy to hurt with certain types of damage.

If a creature or an object has **resistance** to a damage type, damage of that type is halved against it. If a creature or an object has **vulnerability** to a damage type, damage of that type is doubled against it.

Resistance and then vulnerability are applied after all other modifiers to damage. For example, a creature has resistance to bludgeoning damage and is hit by an attack that deals 25 bludgeoning damage. The creature is also within a magical aura that reduces all damage by 5. The 25 damage is first reduced by 5 and then halved, so the creature takes 10 damage.

Multiple instances of resistance or vulnerability that affect the same damage type count as only one instance. For example, if a creature has resistance to fire damage as well as resistance to all nonmagical damage, the damage of a nonmagical fire is reduced by half against the creature, not reduced by three-quarters.

Healing

Unless it results in death, damage isn't permanent. Even death is reversible through powerful magic. Rest can restore a creature's hit points (as explained in chapter 8), and magical methods such as a *cure wounds* spell or a *potion of healing* can remove damage in an instant.

When a creature receives healing of any kind, hit points regained are added to its current hit points. A creature's hit points can't exceed its hit point maximum, so any hit points regained in excess of this number are lost. For example, a druid grants a ranger 8 hit points of healing. If the ranger has 14 current hit points and has a hit point maximum of 20, the ranger regains 6 hit points from the druid, not 8.

A creature that has died can't regain hit points until magic such as the *revivify* spell has restored it to life.

Dropping to 0 Hit Points

When you drop to 0 hit points, you either die outright or fall unconscious, as explained in the following sections.

Instant Death

Massive damage can kill you instantly. When damage reduces you to 0 hit points and there is damage remaining, you die if the remaining damage equals or exceeds your hit point maximum.

For example, a cleric with a maximum of 12 hit points currently has 6 hit points. If she takes 18 damage from an attack, she is reduced to 0 hit points, but 12 damage remains. Because the remaining damage equals her hit point maximum, the cleric dies.

Falling Unconscious

If damage reduces you to 0 hit points and fails to kill you, you fall unconscious (see appendix A). This unconsciousness ends if you regain any hit points.

> **Describing the Effects of Damage**
>
> Dungeon Masters describe hit point loss in different ways. When your current hit point total is half or more of your hit point maximum, you typically show no signs of injury. When you drop below half your hit point maximum, you show signs of wear, such as cuts and bruises. An attack that reduces you to 0 hit points strikes you directly, leaving a bleeding injury or other trauma, or it simply knocks you unconscious.

Death Saving Throws

Whenever you start your turn with 0 hit points, you must make a special saving throw, called a death saving throw, to determine whether you creep closer to death or hang onto life. Unlike other saving throws, this one isn't tied to any ability score. You are in the hands of fate now, aided only by spells and features that improve your chances of succeeding on a saving throw.

Roll a d20. If the roll is 10 or higher, you succeed. Otherwise, you fail. A success or failure has no effect by itself. On your third success, you become stable (see below). On your third failure, you die. The successes and failures don't need to be consecutive; keep track of both until you collect three of a kind. The number of both is reset to zero when you regain any hit points or become stable.

Rolling 1 or 20. When you make a death saving throw and roll a 1 on the d20, it counts as two failures. If you roll a 20 on the d20, you regain 1 hit point.

Damage at 0 Hit Points. If you take any damage while you have 0 hit points, you suffer a death saving throw failure. If the damage is from a critical hit, you suffer two failures instead. If the damage equals or exceeds your hit point maximum, you suffer instant death.

Stabilizing a Creature

The best way to save a creature with 0 hit points is to heal it. If healing is unavailable, the creature can at least be stabilized so that it isn't killed by a failed death saving throw.

You can use your action to administer first aid to an unconscious creature and attempt to stabilize it, which requires a successful DC 10 Wisdom (Medicine) check.

A **stable** creature doesn't make death saving throws, even though it has 0 hit points, but it does remain unconscious. The creature stops being stable, and must start making death saving throws again, if it takes any damage. A stable creature that isn't healed regains 1 hit point after 1d4 hours.

Monsters and Death

Most DMs have a monster die the instant it drops to 0 hit points, rather than having it fall unconscious and make death saving throws.

Mighty villains and special nonplayer characters are common exceptions; the DM might have them fall unconscious and follow the same rules as player characters.

Knocking a Creature Out

Sometimes an attacker wants to incapacitate a foe, rather than deal a killing blow. When an attacker reduces a creature to 0 hit points with a melee attack, the attacker can knock the creature out. The attacker can make this choice the instant the damage is dealt. The creature falls unconscious and is stable.

Temporary Hit Points

Some spells and special abilities confer temporary hit points to a creature. Temporary hit points aren't actual hit points; they are a buffer against damage, a pool of hit points that protect you from injury.

When you have temporary hit points and take damage, the temporary hit points are lost first, and any leftover damage carries over to your normal hit points. For example, if you have 5 temporary hit points and take 7 damage, you lose the temporary hit points and then take 2 damage.

Because temporary hit points are separate from your actual hit points, they can exceed your hit point maximum. A character can, therefore, be at full hit points and receive temporary hit points.

Healing can't restore temporary hit points, and they can't be added together. If you have temporary hit points and receive more of them, you decide whether to keep the ones you have or to gain the new ones. For example, if a spell grants you 12 temporary hit points when you already have 10, you can have 12 or 10, not 22.

If you have 0 hit points, receiving temporary hit points doesn't restore you to consciousness or stabilize you. They can still absorb damage directed at you while you're in that state, but only true healing can save you.

Unless a feature that grants you temporary hit points has a duration, they last until they're depleted or you finish a long rest.

Mounted Combat

A knight charging into battle on a warhorse, a wizard casting spells from the back of a griffon, or a cleric soaring through the sky on a pegasus all enjoy the benefits of speed and mobility that a mount can provide.

A willing creature that is at least one size larger than you and that has an appropriate anatomy can serve as a mount, using the following rules.

Mounting and Dismounting

Once during your move, you can mount a creature that is within 5 feet of you or dismount. Doing so costs an amount of movement equal to half your speed. For example, if your speed is 30 feet, you must spend 15 feet of movement to mount a horse. Therefore, you can't mount it if you don't have 15 feet of movement left or if your speed is 0.

If an effect moves your mount against its will while you're on it, you must succeed on a DC 10 Dexterity saving throw or fall off the mount, landing prone in a space within 5 feet of it. If you're knocked prone while mounted, you must make the same saving throw.

If your mount is knocked prone, you can use your reaction to dismount it as it falls and land on your feet. Otherwise, you are dismounted and fall prone in a space within 5 feet it.

Controlling a Mount

While you're mounted, you have two options. You can either control the mount or allow it to act independently. Intelligent creatures, such as dragons, act independently.

You can control a mount only if it has been trained to accept a rider. Domesticated horses, donkeys, and similar creatures are assumed to have such training. The initiative of a controlled mount changes to match yours when you mount it. It moves as you direct it, and it has only three action options: Dash, Disengage, and Dodge. A controlled mount can move and act even on the turn that you mount it.

An independent mount retains its place in the initiative order. Bearing a rider puts no restrictions on the actions the mount can take, and it moves and acts as it wishes. It might flee from combat, rush to attack and devour a badly injured foe, or otherwise act against your wishes.

In either case, if the mount provokes an opportunity attack while you're on it, the attacker can target you or the mount.

Underwater Combat

When adventurers pursue sahuagin back to their undersea homes, fight off sharks in an ancient shipwreck, or find themselves in a flooded dungeon room, they must fight in a challenging environment. Underwater the following rules apply.

When making a **melee weapon attack**, a creature that doesn't have a swimming speed (either natural or granted by magic) has disadvantage on the attack roll unless the weapon is a dagger, javelin, shortsword, spear, or trident.

A **ranged weapon attack** automatically misses a target beyond the weapon's normal range. Even against a target within normal range, the attack roll has disadvantage unless the weapon is a crossbow, a net, or a weapon that is thrown like a javelin (including a spear, trident, or dart).

Creatures and objects that are fully immersed in water have resistance to fire damage.

PART 3

The Rules of Magic

Chapter 10: Spellcasting

AGIC PERMEATES THE WORLDS OF D&D AND most often appears in the form of a spell. This chapter provides the rules for casting spells. Different character classes have distinctive ways of learning and preparing their spells, and monsters use spells in unique ways. Regardless of its source, a spell follows the rules here.

What Is a Spell?

A spell is a discrete magical effect, a single shaping of the magical energies that suffuse the multiverse into a specific, limited expression. In casting a spell, a character carefully plucks at the invisible strands of raw magic suffusing the world, pins them in place in a particular pattern, sets them vibrating in a specific way, and then releases them to unleash the desired effect—in most cases, all in the span of seconds.

Spells can be versatile tools, weapons, or protective wards. They can deal damage or undo it, impose or remove conditions (see appendix A), drain life energy away, and restore life to the dead.

Uncounted thousands of spells have been created over the course of the multiverse's history, and many of them are long forgotten. Some might yet lie recorded in crumbling spellbooks hidden in ancient ruins or trapped in the minds of dead gods. Or they might someday be reinvented by a character who has amassed enough power and wisdom to do so.

Spell Level

Every spell has a level from 0 to 9. A spell's level is a general indicator of how powerful it is, with the lowly (but still impressive) *magic missile* at 1st level and the earth-shaking *wish* at 9th. Cantrips—simple but powerful spells that characters can cast almost by rote— are level 0. The higher a spell's level, the higher level a spellcaster must be to use that spell.

Spell level and character level don't correspond directly. Typically, a character has to be at least 17th level, not 9th level, to cast a 9th-level spell.

Known and Prepared Spells

Before a spellcaster can use a spell, he or she must have the spell firmly fixed in mind, or must have access to the spell in a magic item. Members of a few classes, including bards and sorcerers, have a limited list of spells they know that are always fixed in mind. The same thing is true of many magic-using monsters. Other spellcasters, such as clerics and wizards, undergo a process of preparing spells. This process varies for different classes, as detailed in their descriptions.

Casting in Armor

Because of the mental focus and precise gestures required for spellcasting, you must be proficient with the armor you are wearing to cast a spell. You are otherwise too distracted and physically hampered by your armor for spellcasting.

In every case, the number of spells a caster can have fixed in mind at any given time depends on the character's level.

Spell Slots

Regardless of how many spells a caster knows or prepares, he or she can cast only a limited number of spells before resting. Manipulating the fabric of magic and channeling its energy into even a simple spell is physically and mentally taxing, and higher-level spells are even more so. Thus, each spellcasting class's description (except that of the warlock) includes a table showing how many spell slots of each spell level a character can use at each character level. For example, the 3rd-level wizard Umara has four 1st-level spell slots and two 2nd-level slots.

When a character casts a spell, he or she expends a slot of that spell's level or higher, effectively "filling" a slot with the spell. You can think of a spell slot as a groove of a certain size—small for a 1st-level slot, larger for a spell of higher level. A 1st-level spell fits into a slot of any size, but a 9th-level spell fits only in a 9th-level slot. So when Umara casts *magic missile,* a 1st-level spell, she spends one of her four 1st-level slots and has three remaining.

Finishing a long rest restores any expended spell slots (see chapter 8 for the rules on resting).

Some characters and monsters have special abilities that let them cast spells without using spell slots. For example, a monk who follows the Way of the Four Elements, a warlock who chooses certain eldritch invocations, and a pit fiend from the Nine Hells can all cast spells in such a way.

Casting a Spell at a Higher Level

When a spellcaster casts a spell using a slot that is of a higher level than the spell, the spell assumes the higher level for that casting. For instance, if Umara casts *magic missile* using one of her 2nd-level slots, that *magic missile* is 2nd level. Effectively, the spell expands to fill the slot it is put into.

Some spells, such as *magic missile* and *cure wounds,* have more powerful effects when cast at a higher level, as detailed in a spell's description.

Cantrips

A cantrip is a spell that can be cast at will, without using a spell slot and without being prepared in advance. Repeated practice has fixed the spell in the caster's mind and infused the caster with the magic needed to produce the effect over and over. A cantrip's spell level is 0.

Rituals

Certain spells have a special tag: ritual. Such a spell can be cast following the normal rules for spellcasting, or the spell can be cast as a ritual. The ritual version of a spell takes 10 minutes longer to cast than normal.

It also doesn't expend a spell slot, which means the ritual version of a spell can't be cast at a higher level.

To cast a spell as a ritual, a spellcaster must have a feature that grants the ability to do so. The cleric and the druid, for example, have such a feature. The caster must also have the spell prepared or on his or her list of spells known, unless the character's ritual feature specifies otherwise, as the wizard's does.

CASTING A SPELL

When a character casts any spell, the same basic rules are followed, regardless of the character's class or the spell's effects.

Each spell description in chapter 11 begins with a block of information, including the spell's name, level, school of magic, casting time, range, components, and duration. The rest of a spell entry describes the spell's effect.

CASTING TIME

Most spells require a single action to cast, but some spells require a bonus action, a reaction, or much more time to cast.

BONUS ACTION

A spell cast with a bonus action is especially swift. You must use a bonus action on your turn to cast the spell, provided that you haven't already taken a bonus action this turn. You can't cast another spell during the same turn, except for a cantrip with a casting time of 1 action.

REACTIONS

Some spells can be cast as reactions. These spells take a fraction of a second to bring about and are cast in response to some event. If a spell can be cast as a reaction, the spell description tells you exactly when you can do so.

LONGER CASTING TIMES

Certain spells (including spells cast as rituals) require more time to cast: minutes or even hours. When you cast a spell with a casting time longer than a single action or reaction, you must spend your action each turn casting the spell, and you must maintain your concentration while you do so (see "Concentration" below). If your concentration is broken, the spell fails, but you don't expend a spell slot. If you want to try casting the spell again, you must start over.

RANGE

The target of a spell must be within the spell's range. For a spell like *magic missile*, the target is a creature. For a spell like *fireball*, the target is the point in space where the ball of fire erupts.

Most spells have ranges expressed in feet. Some spells can target only a creature (including you) that you touch. Other spells, such as the *shield* spell, affect only you. These spells have a range of self.

Spells that create cones or lines of effect that originate from you also have a range of self, indicating that the origin point of the spell's effect must be you (see "Areas of Effect" later in the this chapter).

Once a spell is cast, its effects aren't limited by its range, unless the spell's description says otherwise.

COMPONENTS

A spell's components are the physical requirements you must meet in order to cast it. Each spell's description indicates whether it requires verbal (V), somatic (S), or material (M) components. If you can't provide one or more of a spell's components, you are unable to cast the spell.

VERBAL (V)

Most spells require the chanting of mystic words. The words themselves aren't the source of the spell's power; rather, the particular combination of sounds, with specific pitch and resonance, sets the threads of magic in motion. Thus, a character who is gagged or in an area of silence, such as one created by the *silence* spell, can't cast a spell with a verbal component.

SOMATIC (S)

Spellcasting gestures might include a forceful gesticulation or an intricate set of gestures. If a spell requires a somatic component, the caster must have free use of at least one hand to perform these gestures.

MATERIAL (M)

Casting some spells requires particular objects, specified in parentheses in the component entry. A character can use a **component pouch** or a **spellcasting focus** (found in chapter 5, "Equipment") in place of the components specified for a spell. But if a cost is indicated for a component, a character must have that specific component before he or she can cast the spell.

If a spell states that a material component is consumed by the spell, the caster must provide this component for each casting of the spell.

A spellcaster must have a hand free to access a spell's material components—or to hold a spellcasting focus—but it can be the same hand that he or she uses to perform somatic components.

DURATION

A spell's duration is the length of time the spell persists. A duration can be expressed in rounds, minutes, hours, or even years. Some spells specify that their effects last until the spells are dispelled or destroyed.

INSTANTANEOUS

Many spells are instantaneous. The spell harms, heals, creates, or alters a creature or an object in a way that can't be dispelled, because its magic exists only for an instant.

CONCENTRATION

Some spells require you to maintain concentration in order to keep their magic active. If you lose concentration, such a spell ends.

If a spell must be maintained with concentration, that fact appears in its Duration entry, and the spell specifies how long you can concentrate on it. You can end concentration at any time (no action required).

Normal activity, such as moving and attacking, doesn't interfere with concentration. The following factors can break concentration:

- **Casting another spell that requires concentration.** You lose concentration on a spell if you cast another spell that requires concentration. You can't concentrate on two spells at once.
- **Taking damage.** Whenever you take damage while you are concentrating on a spell, you must make a Constitution saving throw to maintain your concentration. The DC equals 10 or half the damage you take, whichever number is higher. If you take damage from multiple sources, such as an arrow and a dragon's breath, you make a separate saving throw for each source of damage.
- **Being incapacitated or killed.** You lose concentration on a spell if you are incapacitated or if you die.

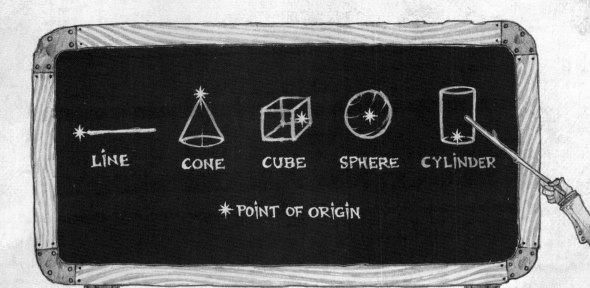

The DM might also decide that certain environmental phenomena, such as a wave crashing over you while you're on a storm-tossed ship, require you to succeed on a DC 10 Constitution saving throw to maintain concentration on a spell.

TARGETS

A typical spell requires you to pick one or more targets to be affected by the spell's magic. A spell's description tells you whether the spell targets creatures, objects, or a point of origin for an area of effect (described below).

Unless a spell has a perceptible effect, a creature might not know it was targeted by a spell at all. An effect like crackling lightning is obvious, but a more subtle effect, such as an attempt to read a creature's thoughts, typically goes unnoticed, unless a spell says otherwise.

A CLEAR PATH TO THE TARGET

To target something, you must have a clear path to it, so it can't be behind total cover.

If you place an area of effect at a point that you can't see and an obstruction, such as a wall, is between you and that point, the point of origin comes into being on the near side of that obstruction.

TARGETING YOURSELF

If a spell targets a creature of your choice, you can choose yourself, unless the creature must be hostile or specifically a creature other than you. If you are in the area of effect of a spell you cast, you can target yourself.

AREAS OF EFFECT

Spells such as *burning hands* and *cone of cold* cover an area, allowing them to affect multiple creatures at once.

A spell's description specifies its area of effect, which typically has one of five different shapes: cone, cube, cylinder, line, or sphere. Every area of effect has a **point of origin**, a location from which the spell's energy erupts. The rules for each shape specify how you position its point of origin. Typically, a point of origin is a point in space, but some spells have an area whose origin is a creature or an object.

A spell's effect expands in straight lines from the point of origin. If no unblocked straight line extends from the point of origin to a location within the area of effect, that location isn't included in the spell's area. To block one of these imaginary lines, an obstruction must provide total cover, as explained in chapter 9.

CONE

A cone extends in a direction you choose from its point of origin. A cone's width at a given point along its length is equal to that point's distance from the point of origin. A cone's area of effect specifies its maximum length.

A cone's point of origin is not included in the cone's area of effect, unless you decide otherwise.

CUBE

You select a cube's point of origin, which lies anywhere on a face of the cubic effect. The cube's size is expressed as the length of each side.

A cube's point of origin is not included in the cube's area of effect, unless you decide otherwise.

CYLINDER

A cylinder's point of origin is the center of a circle of a particular radius, as given in the spell description. The circle must either be on the ground or at the height of the spell effect. The energy in a cylinder expands in straight lines from the point of origin to the perimeter of the circle, forming the base of the cylinder. The spell's effect then shoots up from the base or down from the top, to a distance equal to the height of the cylinder.

A cylinder's point of origin is included in the cylinder's area of effect.

Line

A line extends from its point of origin in a straight path up to its length and covers an area defined by its width.

A line's point of origin is not included in the line's area of effect, unless you decide otherwise.

Sphere

You select a sphere's point of origin, and the sphere extends outward from that point. The sphere's size is expressed as a radius in feet that extends from the point.

A sphere's point of origin is included in the sphere's area of effect.

Saving Throws

Many spells specify that a target can make a saving throw to avoid some or all of a spell's effects. The spell specifies the ability that the target uses for the save and what happens on a success or failure.

The DC to resist one of your spells equals 8 + your spellcasting ability modifier + your proficiency bonus + any special modifiers.

Attack Rolls

Some spells require the caster to make an attack roll to determine whether the spell effect hits the intended target. Your attack bonus with a spell attack equals your spellcasting ability modifier + your proficiency bonus.

Most spells that require attack rolls involve ranged attacks. Remember that you have disadvantage on a ranged attack roll if you are within 5 feet of a hostile creature that can see you and that isn't incapacitated (see chapter 9).

Combining Magical Effects

The effects of different spells add together while the durations of those spells overlap. The effects of the same spell cast multiple times don't combine, however. Instead, the most potent effect—such as the highest bonus—from those castings applies while their durations overlap.

For example, if two clerics cast *bless* on the same target, that character gains the spell's benefit only once; he or she doesn't get to roll two bonus dice.

The Weave of Magic

The worlds within the D&D multiverse are magical places. All existence is suffused with magical power, and potential energy lies untapped in every rock, stream, and living creature, and even in the air itself. Raw magic is the stuff of creation, the mute and mindless will of existence, permeating every bit of matter and present in every manifestation of energy throughout the multiverse.

Mortals can't directly shape this raw magic. Instead, they make use of a fabric of magic, a kind of interface between the will of a spellcaster and the stuff of raw magic. The spellcasters of the Forgotten Realms call it the Weave and recognize its essence as the goddess Mystra, but casters have varied ways of naming and visualizing this interface. By any name, without the Weave, raw magic is locked away and inaccessible; the most powerful archmage can't light a candle with magic in an area where the Weave has been torn. But surrounded by the Weave, a spellcaster can shape lightning to blast foes, transport hundreds of miles in the blink of an eye, or even reverse death itself.

All magic depends on the Weave, though different kinds of magic access it in a variety of ways. The spells of wizards, warlocks, sorcerers, and bards are commonly called **arcane magic**. These spells rely on an understanding—learned or intuitive—of the workings of the Weave. The caster plucks directly at the strands of the Weave to create the desired effect. Eldritch knights and arcane tricksters also use arcane magic. The spells of clerics, druids, paladins, and rangers are called **divine magic**. These spellcasters' access to the Weave is mediated by divine power—gods, the divine forces of nature, or the sacred weight of a paladin's oath.

Whenever a magic effect is created, the threads of the Weave intertwine, twist, and fold to make the effect possible. When characters use divination spells such as *detect magic* or *identify*, they glimpse the Weave. A spell such as *dispel magic* smooths the Weave. Spells such as *antimagic field* rearrange the Weave so that magic flows around, rather than through, the area affected by the spell. And in places where the Weave is damaged or torn, magic works in unpredictable ways—or not at all.

Chapter 11: Spells

 HIS CHAPTER DESCRIBES THE MOST COMMON spells in the worlds of DUNGEONS & DRAGONS. The chapter begins with the spell lists of the spellcasting classes. The remainder contains spell descriptions, presented in alphabetical order by the name of the spell.

BARD SPELLS

CANTRIPS (0 LEVEL)
Blade Ward
Dancing Lights
Friends
Light
Mage Hand
Mending
Message
Minor Illusion
Prestidigitation
True Strike
Vicious Mockery

1ST LEVEL
Animal Friendship
Bane
Charm Person
Comprehend Languages
Cure Wounds
Detect Magic
Disguise Self
Dissonant Whispers
Faerie Fire
Feather Fall
Healing Word
Heroism
Identify
Illusory Script
Longstrider
Silent Image
Sleep
Speak with Animals
Tasha's Hideous Laughter
Thunderwave
Unseen Servant

2ND LEVEL
Animal Messenger
Blindness/Deafness
Calm Emotions
Cloud of Daggers
Crown of Madness
Detect Thoughts
Enhance Ability
Enthrall
Heat Metal

Hold Person
Invisibility
Knock
Lesser Restoration
Locate Animals or Plants
Locate Object
Magic Mouth
Phantasmal Force
See Invisibility
Shatter
Silence
Suggestion
Zone of Truth

3RD LEVEL
Bestow Curse
Clairvoyance
Dispel Magic
Fear
Feign Death
Glyph of Warding
Hypnotic Pattern
Leomund's Tiny Hut
Major Image
Nondetection
Plant Growth
Sending
Speak with Dead
Speak with Plants
Stinking Cloud
Tongues

4TH LEVEL
Compulsion
Confusion
Dimension Door
Freedom of Movement
Greater Invisibility
Hallucinatory Terrain
Locate Creature
Polymorph

5TH LEVEL
Animate Objects
Awaken
Dominate Person
Dream
Geas
Greater Restoration

Hold Monster
Legend Lore
Mass Cure Wounds
Mislead
Modify Memory
Planar Binding
Raise Dead
Scrying
Seeming
Teleportation Circle

6TH LEVEL
Eyebite
Find the Path
Guards and Wards
Mass Suggestion
Otto's Irresistible Dance
Programmed Illusion
True Seeing

7TH LEVEL
Etherealness
Forcecage
Mirage Arcane
Mordenkainen's
    Magnificent Mansion
Mordenkainen's Sword
Project Image
Regenerate
Resurrection
Symbol
Teleport

8TH LEVEL
Dominate Monster
Feeblemind
Glibness
Mind Blank
Power Word Stun

9TH LEVEL
Foresight
Power Word Heal
Power Word Kill
True Polymorph

CLERIC SPELLS

CANTRIPS (0 LEVEL)
Guidance
Light
Mending
Resistance
Sacred Flame
Spare the Dying
Thaumaturgy

1ST LEVEL
Bane
Bless
Command
Create or Destroy Water
Cure Wounds
Detect Evil and Good
Detect Magic
Detect Poison and Disease
Guiding Bolt
Healing Word
Inflict Wounds
Protection from
    Evil and Good
Purify Food and Drink
Sanctuary
Shield of Faith

2ND LEVEL
Aid
Augury
Blindness/Deafness
Calm Emotions
Continual Flame
Enhance Ability
Find Traps
Gentle Repose
Hold Person
Lesser Restoration
Locate Object
Prayer of Healing
Protection from Poison
Silence
Spiritual Weapon
Warding Bond
Zone of Truth

3RD LEVEL
Animate Dead
Beacon of Hope
Bestow Curse
Clairvoyance
Create Food and Water
Daylight
Dispel Magic
Feign Death
Glyph of Warding
Magic Circle
Mass Healing Word
Meld into Stone
Protection from Energy
Remove Curse
Revivify
Sending
Speak with Dead

Spirit Guardians
Tongues
Water Walk

4TH LEVEL
Banishment
Control Water
Death Ward
Divination
Freedom of Movement
Guardian of Faith
Locate Creature
Stone Shape

5TH LEVEL
Commune
Contagion
Dispel Evil and Good
Flame Strike
Geas
Greater Restoration
Hallow
Insect Plague
Legend Lore
Mass Cure Wounds
Planar Binding
Raise Dead
Scrying

6TH LEVEL
Blade Barrier
Create Undead
Find the Path
Forbiddance
Harm
Heal
Heroes' Feast
Planar Ally
True Seeing
Word of Recall

7TH LEVEL
Conjure Celestial
Divine Word
Etherealness
Fire Storm
Plane Shift
Regenerate
Resurrection
Symbol

8TH LEVEL
Antimagic Field
Control Weather
Earthquake
Holy Aura

9TH LEVEL
Astral Projection

Gate
Mass Heal
True Resurrection

DRUID SPELLS

CANTRIPS (0 LEVEL)
Druidcraft
Guidance
Mending
Poison Spray
Produce Flame
Resistance
Shillelagh
Thorn Whip

1ST LEVEL
Animal Friendship
Charm Person
Create or Destroy Water
Cure Wounds
Detect Magic
Detect Poison and Disease
Entangle
Faerie Fire
Fog Cloud
Goodberry
Healing Word
Jump
Longstrider
Purify Food and Drink
Speak with Animals
Thunderwave

2ND LEVEL
Animal Messenger
Barkskin
Beast Sense
Darkvision
Enhance Ability
Find Traps
Flame Blade
Flaming Sphere
Gust of Wind
Heat Metal
Hold Person
Lesser Restoration
Locate Animals or Plants
Locate Object
Moonbeam
Pass without Trace
Protection from Poison
Spike Growth

3RD LEVEL
Call Lightning
Conjure Animals
Daylight

Dispel Magic
Feign Death
Meld into Stone
Plant Growth
Protection from Energy
Sleet Storm
Speak with Plants
Water Breathing
Water Walk
Wind Wall

4TH LEVEL
Blight
Confusion
Conjure Minor Elementals
Conjure Woodland Beings
Control Water
Dominate Beast
Freedom of Movement
Giant Insect
Grasping Vine
Hallucinatory Terrain
Ice Storm
Locate Creature
Polymorph
Stone Shape
Stoneskin
Wall of Fire

5TH LEVEL
Antilife Shell
Awaken
Commune with Nature
Conjure Elemental
Contagion
Geas
Greater Restoration
Insect Plague
Mass Cure Wounds
Planar Binding
Reincarnate
Scrying
Tree Stride
Wall of Stone

6TH LEVEL
Conjure Fey
Find the Path
Heal
Heroes' Feast
Move Earth
Sunbeam
Transport via Plants
Wall of Thorns
Wind Walk

7TH LEVEL
Fire Storm

Mirage Arcane
Plane Shift
Regenerate
Reverse Gravity

8TH LEVEL
Animal Shapes
Antipathy/Sympathy
Control Weather
Earthquake
Feeblemind
Sunburst
Tsunami

9TH LEVEL
Foresight
Shapechange
Storm of Vengeance
True Resurrection

PALADIN SPELLS

1ST LEVEL
Bless
Command
Compelled Duel
Cure Wounds
Detect Evil and Good
Detect Magic
Detect Poison and Disease
Divine Favor
Heroism
Protection from
   Evil and Good
Purify Food and Drink
Searing Smite
Shield of Faith
Thunderous Smite
Wrathful Smite

2ND LEVEL
Aid
Branding Smite
Find Steed
Lesser Restoration
Locate Object
Magic Weapon
Protection from Poison
Zone of Truth

3RD LEVEL
Aura of Vitality
Blinding Smite
Create Food and Water
Crusader's Mantle
Daylight
Dispel Magic
Elemental Weapon

Magic Circle
Remove Curse
Revivify

4TH LEVEL
Aura of Life
Aura of Purity
Banishment
Death Ward
Locate Creature
Staggering Smite

5TH LEVEL
Banishing Smite
Circle of Power
Destructive Wave
Dispel Evil and Good
Geas
Raise Dead

RANGER SPELLS

1ST LEVEL
Alarm
Animal Friendship
Cure Wounds
Detect Magic
Detect Poison and Disease
Ensnaring Strike
Fog Cloud
Goodberry
Hail of Thorns
Hunter's Mark
Jump
Longstrider
Speak with Animals

2ND LEVEL
Animal Messenger
Barkskin
Beast Sense
Cordon of Arrows
Darkvision
Find Traps
Lesser Restoration
Locate Animals or Plants
Locate Object
Pass without Trace
Protection from Poison
Silence
Spike Growth

3RD LEVEL
Conjure Animals
Conjure Barrage
Daylight
Lightning Arrow
Nondetection

Plant Growth
Protection from Energy
Speak with Plants
Water Breathing
Water Walk
Wind Wall

4TH LEVEL
Conjure Woodland Beings
Freedom of Movement
Grasping Vine
Locate Creature
Stoneskin

5TH LEVEL
Commune with Nature
Conjure Volley
Swift Quiver
Tree Stride

SORCERER SPELLS

CANTRIPS (0 LEVEL)
Acid Splash
Blade Ward
Chill Touch
Dancing Lights
Fire Bolt
Friends
Light
Mage Hand
Mending
Message
Minor Illusion
Poison Spray
Prestidigitation
Ray of Frost
Shocking Grasp
True Strike

1ST LEVEL
Burning Hands
Charm Person
Chromatic Orb
Color Spray
Comprehend Languages
Detect Magic
Disguise Self
Expeditious Retreat
False Life
Feather Fall
Fog Cloud
Jump
Mage Armor
Magic Missile
Ray of Sickness
Shield
Silent Image

Sleep
Thunderwave
Witch Bolt

2ND LEVEL
Alter Self
Blindness/Deafness
Blur
Cloud of Daggers
Crown of Madness
Darkness
Darkvision
Detect Thoughts
Enhance Ability
Enlarge/Reduce
Gust of Wind
Hold Person
Invisibility
Knock
Levitate
Mirror Image
Misty Step
Phantasmal Force
Scorching Ray
See Invisibility
Shatter
Spider Climb
Suggestion
Web

3RD LEVEL
Blink
Clairvoyance
Counterspell
Daylight
Dispel Magic
Fear
Fireball
Fly
Gaseous Form
Haste
Hypnotic Pattern
Lightning Bolt
Major Image
Protection from Energy
Sleet Storm
Slow
Stinking Cloud
Tongues
Water Breathing
Water Walk

4TH LEVEL
Banishment
Blight
Confusion
Dimension Door
Dominate Beast

Greater Invisibility
Ice Storm
Polymorph
Stoneskin
Wall of Fire

5TH LEVEL
Animate Objects
Cloudkill
Cone of Cold
Creation
Dominate Person
Hold Monster
Insect Plague
Seeming
Telekinesis
Teleportation Circle
Wall of Stone

6TH LEVEL
Arcane Gate
Chain Lightning
Circle of Death
Disintegrate
Eyebite
Globe of Invulnerability
Mass Suggestion
Move Earth
Sunbeam
True Seeing

7TH LEVEL
Delayed Blast Fireball
Etherealness
Finger of Death
Fire Storm
Plane Shift
Prismatic Spray
Reverse Gravity
Teleport

8TH LEVEL
Dominate Monster
Earthquake
Incendiary Cloud
Power Word Stun
Sunburst

9TH LEVEL
Gate
Meteor Swarm
Power Word Kill
Time Stop
Wish

Warlock Spells

Cantrips (0 Level)
Blade Ward
Chill Touch
Eldritch Blast
Friends
Mage Hand
Minor Illusion
Poison Spray
Prestidigitation
True Strike

1st Level
Armor of Agathys
Arms of Hadar
Charm Person
Comprehend Languages
Expeditious Retreat
Hellish Rebuke
Hex
Illusory Script
Protection from
   Evil and Good
Unseen Servant
Witch Bolt

2nd Level
Cloud of Daggers
Crown of Madness
Darkness
Enthrall
Hold Person
Invisibility
Mirror Image
Misty Step
Ray of Enfeeblement
Shatter
Spider Climb
Suggestion

3rd Level
Counterspell
Dispel Magic
Fear
Fly
Gaseous Form
Hunger of Hadar
Hypnotic Pattern
Magic Circle
Major Image
Remove Curse
Tongues
Vampiric Touch

4th Level
Banishment
Blight

Dimension Door
Hallucinatory Terrain

5th Level
Contact Other Plane
Dream
Hold Monster
Scrying

6th Level
Arcane Gate
Circle of Death
Conjure Fey
Create Undead
Eyebite
Flesh to Stone
Mass Suggestion
True Seeing

7th Level
Etherealness
Finger of Death
Forcecage
Plane Shift

8th Level
Demiplane
Dominate Monster
Feeblemind
Glibness
Power Word Stun

9th Level
Astral Projection
Foresight
Imprisonment
Power Word Kill
True Polymorph

Wizard Spells

Cantrips (0 Level)
Acid Splash
Blade Ward
Chill Touch
Dancing Lights
Fire Bolt
Friends
Light
Mage Hand
Mending
Message
Minor Illusion
Poison Spray
Prestidigitation
Ray of Frost
Shocking Grasp
True Strike

1st Level
Alarm
Burning Hands
Charm Person
Chromatic Orb
Color Spray
Comprehend Languages
Detect Magic
Disguise Self
Expeditious Retreat
False Life
Feather Fall
Find Familiar
Fog Cloud
Grease
Identify
Illusory Script
Jump
Longstrider
Mage Armor
Magic Missile
Protection from
   Evil and Good
Ray of Sickness
Shield
Silent Image
Sleep
Tasha's Hideous Laughter
Tenser's Floating Disk
Thunderwave
Unseen Servant
Witch Bolt

2nd Level
Alter Self
Arcane Lock
Blindness/Deafness
Blur
Cloud of Daggers
Continual Flame
Crown of Madness
Darkness
Darkvision
Detect Thoughts
Enlarge/Reduce
Flaming Sphere
Gentle Repose
Gust of Wind
Hold Person
Invisibility
Knock
Levitate
Locate Object
Magic Mouth
Magic Weapon
Melf's Acid Arrow
Mirror Image

Misty Step
Nystul's Magic Aura
Phantasmal Force
Ray of Enfeeblement
Rope Trick
Scorching Ray
See Invisibility
Shatter
Spider Climb
Suggestion
Web

3rd Level
Animate Dead
Bestow Curse
Blink
Clairvoyance
Counterspell
Dispel Magic
Fear
Feign Death
Fireball
Fly
Gaseous Form
Glyph of Warding
Haste
Hypnotic Pattern
Leomund's Tiny Hut
Lightning Bolt
Magic Circle
Major Image
Nondetection
Phantom Steed
Protection from Energy
Remove Curse
Sending
Sleet Storm
Slow
Stinking Cloud
Tongues
Vampiric Touch
Water Breathing

4th Level
Arcane Eye
Banishment
Blight
Confusion
Conjure Minor Elementals
Control Water
Dimension Door
Evard's Black Tentacles
Fabricate
Fire Shield
Greater Invisibility
Hallucinatory Terrain
Ice Storm
Leomund's Secret Chest

Locate Creature
Mordenkainen's
    Faithful Hound
Mordenkainen's
    Private Sanctum
Otiluke's Resilient Sphere
Phantasmal Killer
Polymorph
Stone Shape
Stoneskin
Wall of Fire

5th Level

Animate Objects
Bigby's Hand
Cloudkill
Cone of Cold
Conjure Elemental
Contact Other Plane
Creation
Dominate Person
Dream
Geas
Hold Monster
Legend Lore
Mislead
Modify Memory
Passwall
Planar Binding
Rary's Telepathic Bond
Scrying
Seeming
Telekinesis
Teleportation Circle
Wall of Force
Wall of Stone

6th Level

Arcane Gate
Chain Lightning
Circle of Death
Contingency
Create Undead
Disintegrate
Drawmij's Instant
    Summons
Eyebite
Flesh to Stone
Globe of Invulnerability
Guards and Wards
Magic Jar
Mass Suggestion
Move Earth
Otiluke's Freezing Sphere
Otto's Irresistible Dance
Programmed Illusion

Sunbeam
True Seeing
Wall of Ice

7th Level

Delayed Blast Fireball
Etherealness
Finger of Death
Forcecage
Mirage Arcane
Mordenkainen's
    Magnificent Mansion
Mordenkainen's Sword
Plane Shift
Prismatic Spray
Project Image
Reverse Gravity
Sequester
Simulacrum
Symbol
Teleport

8th Level

Antimagic Field
Antipathy/Sympathy
Clone
Control Weather
Demiplane
Dominate Monster
Feeblemind
Incendiary Cloud
Maze
Mind Blank
Power Word Stun
Sunburst
Telepathy

9th Level

Astral Projection
Foresight
Gate
Imprisonment
Meteor Swarm
Power Word Kill
Prismatic Wall
Shapechange
Time Stop
True Polymorph
Weird
Wish

Spell Descriptions

The spells are presented in alphabetical order.

Acid Splash
Conjuration cantrip

Casting Time: 1 action
Range: 60 feet
Components: V, S
Duration: Instantaneous

You hurl a bubble of acid. Choose one creature within range, or choose two creatures within range that are within 5 feet of each other. A target must succeed on a Dexterity saving throw or take 1d6 acid damage.

This spell's damage increases by 1d6 when you reach 5th level (2d6), 11th level (3d6), and 17th level (4d6).

Aid
2nd-level abjuration

Casting Time: 1 action
Range: 30 feet
Components: V, S, M (a tiny strip of white cloth)
Duration: 8 hours

Your spell bolsters your allies with toughness and resolve. Choose up to three creatures within range. Each target's hit point maximum and current hit points increase by 5 for the duration.

At Higher Levels. When you cast this spell using a spell slot of 3rd level or higher, a target's hit points increase by an additional 5 for each slot level above 2nd.

Alarm
1st-level abjuration (ritual)

Casting Time: 1 minute
Range: 30 feet
Components: V, S, M (a tiny bell and a piece of fine silver wire)
Duration: 8 hours

You set an alarm against unwanted intrusion. Choose a door, a window, or an area within range that is no larger than a 20-foot cube. Until the spell ends, an alarm alerts you whenever a Tiny or larger creature touches or enters the warded area. When you cast the spell, you can designate creatures that won't set off the alarm. You also choose whether the alarm is mental or audible.

A mental alarm alerts you with a ping in your mind if you are within 1 mile of the warded area. This ping awakens you if you are sleeping.

An audible alarm produces the sound of a hand bell for 10 seconds within 60 feet.

Alter Self
2nd-level transmutation

Casting Time: 1 action
Range: Self
Components: V, S
Duration: Concentration, up to 1 hour

You assume a different form. When you cast the spell, choose one of the following options, the effects of which last for the duration of the spell. While the spell lasts, you can end one option as an action to gain the benefits of a different one.

Aquatic Adaptation. You adapt your body to an aquatic environment, sprouting gills and growing webbing between your fingers. You can breathe underwater and gain a swimming speed equal to your walking speed.

Change Appearance. You transform your appearance. You decide what you look like, including your height, weight, facial features, sound of your voice, hair length, coloration, and distinguishing characteristics, if any. You can make yourself appear as a member of another race, though none of your statistics change. You also can't appear as a creature of a different size than you, and your basic shape stays the same; if you're bipedal, you can't use this spell to become quadrupedal, for instance. At any time for the duration of the spell, you can use your action to change your appearance in this way again.

Natural Weapons. You grow claws, fangs, spines, horns, or a different natural weapon of your choice. Your unarmed strikes deal 1d6 bludgeoning, piercing, or slashing damage, as appropriate to the natural weapon you chose, and you are proficient with your unarmed strikes. Finally, the natural weapon is magic and you have a +1 bonus to the attack and damage rolls you make using it.

ANIMAL FRIENDSHIP
1st-level enchantment

Casting Time: 1 action
Range: 30 feet
Components: V, S, M (a morsel of food)
Duration: 24 hours

This spell lets you convince a beast that you mean it no harm. Choose a beast that you can see within range. It must see and hear you. If the beast's Intelligence is 4 or higher, the spell fails. Otherwise, the beast must succeed on a Wisdom saving throw or be charmed by you for the spell's duration. If you or one of your companions harms the target, the spells ends.

At Higher Levels. When you cast this spell using a spell slot of 2nd level or higher, you can affect one additional beast for each slot level above 1st.

ANIMAL MESSENGER
2nd-level enchantment (ritual)

Casting Time: 1 action
Range: 30 feet
Components: V, S, M (a morsel of food)
Duration: 24 hours

By means of this spell, you use an animal to deliver a message. Choose a Tiny beast you can see within range, such as a squirrel, a blue jay, or a bat. You specify a location, which you must have visited, and a recipient who matches a general description, such as "a man or woman dressed in the uniform of the town guard" or "a red-haired dwarf wearing a pointed hat." You also speak a message of up to twenty-five words. The target beast travels for the duration of the spell toward the specified

location, covering about 50 miles per 24 hours for a flying messenger, or 25 miles for other animals.

When the messenger arrives, it delivers your message to the creature that you described, replicating the sound of your voice. The messenger speaks only to a creature matching the description you gave. If the messenger doesn't reach its destination before the spell ends, the message is lost, and the beast makes its way back to where you cast this spell.

At Higher Levels. If you cast this spell using a spell slot of 3rd level or higher, the duration of the spell increases by 48 hours for each slot level above 2nd.

ANIMAL SHAPES
8th-level transmutation

Casting Time: 1 action
Range: 30 feet
Components: V, S
Duration: Concentration, up to 24 hours

Your magic turns others into beasts. Choose any number of willing creatures that you can see within range. You transform each target into the form of a Large or smaller beast with a challenge rating of 4 or lower. On subsequent turns, you can use your action to transform affected creatures into new forms.

The transformation lasts for the duration for each target, or until the target drops to 0 hit points or dies. You can choose a different form for each target. A target's game statistics are replaced by the statistics of the chosen beast, though the target retains its alignment and Intelligence, Wisdom, and Charisma scores. The target assumes the hit points of its new form, and when it reverts to its normal form, it returns to the number of hit points it had before it transformed. If it reverts as a result of dropping to 0 hit points, any excess damage carries over to its normal form. As long as the excess damage doesn't reduce the creature's normal form to 0 hit points, it isn't knocked unconscious. The creature is limited in the actions it can perform by the nature of its new form, and it can't speak or cast spells.

The target's gear melds into the new form. The target can't activate, wield, or otherwise benefit from any of its equipment.

ANIMATE DEAD
3rd-level necromancy

Casting Time: 1 minute
Range: 10 feet
Components: V, S, M (a drop of blood, a piece of flesh, and a pinch of bone dust)
Duration: Instantaneous

This spell creates an undead servant. Choose a pile of bones or a corpse of a Medium or Small humanoid within range. Your spell imbues the target with a foul mimicry of life, raising it as an undead creature. The target becomes a skeleton if you chose bones or a zombie if you chose a corpse (the DM has the creature's game statistics).

On each of your turns, you can use a bonus action to mentally command any creature you made with this spell if the creature is within 60 feet of you (if you control multiple creatures, you can command any or all of them at the same time, issuing the same command to each one). You decide what action the creature will take and where it will move during its next turn, or you can issue a general command, such as to guard a particular chamber or corridor. If you issue no commands, the creature only defends itself against hostile creatures. Once given an order, the creature continues to follow it until its task is complete.

The creature is under your control for 24 hours, after which it stops obeying any command you've given it. To maintain control of the creature for another 24 hours, you must cast this spell on the creature again before the current 24-hour period ends. This use of the spell reasserts your control over up to four creatures you have animated with this spell, rather than animating a new one.

At Higher Levels. When you cast this spell using a spell slot of 4th level or higher, you animate or reassert control over two additional undead creatures for each slot level above 3rd. Each of the creatures must come from a different corpse or pile of bones.

ANIMATE OBJECTS
5th-level transmutation

Casting Time: 1 action
Range: 120 feet
Components: V, S
Duration: Concentration, up to 1 minute

Objects come to life at your command. Choose up to ten nonmagical objects within range that are not being worn or carried. Medium targets count as two objects, Large targets count as four objects, Huge targets count as eight objects. You can't animate any object larger than Huge. Each target animates and becomes a creature under your control until the spell ends or until reduced to 0 hit points.

As a bonus action, you can mentally command any creature you made with this spell if the creature is within 500 feet of you (if you control multiple creatures, you can command any or all of them at the same time, issuing the same command to each one). You decide what action the creature will take and where it will move during its next turn, or you can issue a general command, such as to guard a particular chamber or corridor. If you issue no commands, the creature only defends itself against hostile creatures. Once given an order, the creature continues to follow it until its task is complete.

ANIMATED OBJECT STATISTICS

Size	HP	AC	Attack	Str	Dex
Tiny	20	18	+8 to hit, 1d4 + 4 damage	4	18
Small	25	16	+6 to hit, 1d8 + 2 damage	6	14
Medium	40	13	+5 to hit, 2d6 + 1 damage	10	12
Large	50	10	+6 to hit, 2d10 + 2 damage	14	10
Huge	80	10	+8 to hit, 2d12 + 4 damage	18	6

An animated object is a construct with AC, hit points, attacks, Strength, and Dexterity determined by its size. Its Constitution is 10 and its Intelligence and Wisdom are 3, and its Charisma is 1. Its speed is 30 feet; if the object lacks legs or other appendages it can use for locomotion, it instead has a flying speed of 30 feet and can hover. If the object is securely attached to a surface or a larger object, such as a chain bolted to a wall, its speed is 0. It has blindsight with a radius of 30 feet and is blind beyond that distance. When the animated object drops to 0 hit points, it reverts to its original object form, and any remaining damage carries over to its original object form.

If you command an object to attack, it can make a single melee attack against a creature within 5 feet of it. It makes a slam attack with an attack bonus and bludgeoning damage determined by its size. The DM might rule that a specific object inflicts slashing or piercing damage based on its form.

At Higher Levels. If you cast this spell using a spell slot of 6th level or higher, you can animate two additional objects for each slot level above 5th.

ANTILIFE SHELL
5th-level abjuration

Casting Time: 1 action
Range: Self (10-foot radius)
Components: V, S
Duration: Concentration, up to 1 hour

A shimmering barrier extends out from you in a 10-foot radius and moves with you, remaining centered on you and hedging out creatures other than undead and constructs. The barrier lasts for the duration.

The barrier prevents an affected creature from passing or reaching through. An affected creature can cast spells or make attacks with ranged or reach weapons through the barrier.

If you move so that an affected creature is forced to pass through the barrier, the spell ends.

ANTIMAGIC FIELD
8th-level abjuration

Casting Time: 1 action
Range: Self (10-foot-radius sphere)
Components: V, S, M (a pinch of powdered iron or iron filings)
Duration: Concentration, up to 1 hour

A 10-foot-radius invisible sphere of antimagic surrounds you. This area is divorced from the magical energy that suffuses the multiverse. Within the sphere, spells can't be cast, summoned creatures disappear, and even magic items become mundane. Until the spell ends, the sphere moves with you, centered on you.

Spells and other magical effects, except those created by an artifact or a deity, are suppressed in the sphere and can't protrude into it. A slot expended to cast a suppressed spell is consumed. While an effect is suppressed, it doesn't function, but the time it spends suppressed counts against its duration.

Targeted Effects. Spells and other magical effects, such as *magic missile* and *charm person*, that target a creature or an object in the sphere have no effect on that target.

Areas of Magic. The area of another spell or magical effect, such as *fireball*, can't extend into the sphere. If the sphere overlaps an area of magic, the part of the area that is covered by the sphere is suppressed. For example, the flames created by a *wall of fire* are suppressed within the sphere, creating a gap in the wall if the overlap is large enough.

Spells. Any active spell or other magical effect on a creature or an object in the sphere is suppressed while the creature or object is in it.

Magic Items. The properties and powers of magic items are suppressed in the sphere. For example, a *+1 longsword* in the sphere functions as a nonmagical longsword.

A magic weapon's properties and powers are suppressed if it is used against a target in the sphere or wielded by an attacker in the sphere. If a magic weapon or a piece of magic ammunition fully leaves the sphere (for example, if you fire a magic arrow or throw a magic spear at a target outside the sphere), the magic of the item ceases to be suppressed as soon as it exits.

Magical Travel. Teleportation and planar travel fail to work in the sphere, whether the sphere is the destination or the departure point for such magical travel. A portal to another location, world, or plane of existence, as well as an opening to an extradimensional space such as that created by the *rope trick* spell, temporarily closes while in the sphere.

Creatures and Objects. A creature or object summoned or created by magic temporarily winks out of existence in the sphere. Such a creature instantly reappears once the space the creature occupied is no longer within the sphere.

Dispel Magic. Spells and magical effects such as *dispel magic* have no effect on the sphere. Likewise, the spheres created by different *antimagic field* spells don't nullify each other.

ANTIPATHY/SYMPATHY
8th-level enchantment

Casting Time: 1 hour
Range: 60 feet
Components: V, S, M (either a lump of alum soaked in vinegar for the *antipathy* effect or a drop of honey for the *sympathy* effect)
Duration: 10 days

This spell attracts or repels creatures of your choice. You target something within range, either a Huge or smaller object or creature or an area that is no larger than a 200-foot cube. Then specify a kind of intelligent creature, such as red dragons, goblins, or vampires. You invest the target with an aura that either attracts or repels the specified creatures for the duration. Choose antipathy or sympathy as the aura's effect.

Antipathy. The enchantment causes creatures of the kind you designated to feel an intense urge to leave the area and avoid the target. When such a creature can see the target or comes within 60 feet of it, the creature must succeed on a Wisdom saving throw or become frightened. The creature remains frightened while it can see the target or is within 60 feet of it. While frightened by the target, the creature must use its movement to move to the nearest safe spot from which it can't see the target. If the creature moves more than 60 feet from the target and can't see it, the creature is no longer frightened, but the creature becomes frightened again if it regains sight of the target or moves within 60 feet of it.

Sympathy. The enchantment causes the specified creatures to feel an intense urge to approach the target while within 60 feet of it or able to see it. When such a creature can see the target or comes within 60 feet of it, the creature must succeed on a Wisdom saving throw or use its movement on each of its turns to enter the area or move within reach of the target. When the creature has done so, it can't willingly move away from the target.

If the target damages or otherwise harms an affected creature, the affected creature can make a Wisdom saving throw to end the effect, as described below.

Ending the Effect. If an affected creature ends its turn while not within 60 feet of the target or able to see it, the creature makes a Wisdom saving throw. On a successful save, the creature is no longer affected by the target and recognizes the feeling of repugnance or attraction as magical. In addition, a creature affected by the spell is allowed another Wisdom saving throw every 24 hours while the spell persists.

A creature that successfully saves against this effect is immune to it for 1 minute, after which time it can be affected again.

ARCANE EYE
4th-level divination

Casting Time: 1 action
Range: 30 feet
Components: V, S, M (a bit of bat fur)
Duration: Concentration, up to 1 hour

You create an invisible, magical eye within range that hovers in the air for the duration.

You mentally receive visual information from the eye, which has normal vision and darkvision out to 30 feet. The eye can look in every direction.

As an action, you can move the eye up to 30 feet in any direction. There is no limit to how far away from you the eye can move, but it can't enter another plane of existence. A solid barrier blocks the eye's movement, but the eye can pass through an opening as small as 1 inch in diameter.

ARCANE GATE
6th-level conjuration

Casting Time: 1 action
Range: 500 feet
Components: V, S
Duration: Concentration, up to 10 minutes

You create linked teleportation portals that remain open for the duration. Choose two points on the ground that you can see, one point within 10 feet of you and one point within 500 feet of you. A circular portal, 10 feet in diameter, opens over each point. If the portal would open in the space occupied by a creature, the spell fails, and the casting is lost.

The portals are two-dimensional glowing rings filled with mist, hovering inches from the ground and perpendicular to it at the points you choose. A ring is visible only from one side (your choice), which is the side that functions as a portal.

Any creature or object entering the portal exits from the other portal as if the two were adjacent to each other; passing through a portal from the nonportal side has no effect. The mist that fills each portal is opaque and blocks vision through it. On your turn, you can rotate the rings as a bonus action so that the active side faces in a different direction.

ARCANE LOCK
2nd-level abjuration

Casting Time: 1 action
Range: Touch
Components: V, S, M (gold dust worth at least 25 gp, which the spell consumes)
Duration: Until dispelled

You touch a closed door, window, gate, chest, or other entryway, and it becomes locked for the duration. You and the creatures you designate when you cast this spell can open the object normally. You can also set a password that, when spoken within 5 feet of the object, suppresses this spell for 1 minute. Otherwise, it is impassable until it is broken or the spell is dispelled or suppressed. Casting *knock* on the object suppresses *arcane lock* for 10 minutes.

While affected by this spell, the object is more difficult to break or force open; the DC to break it or pick any locks on it increases by 10.

ARMOR OF AGATHYS
1st-level abjuration

Casting Time: 1 action
Range: Self
Components: V, S, M (a cup of water)
Duration: 1 hour

A protective magical force surrounds you, manifesting as a spectral frost that covers you and your gear. You gain 5 temporary hit points for the duration. If a creature hits you with a melee attack while you have these hit points, the creature takes 5 cold damage.

At Higher Levels. When you cast this spell using a spell slot of 2nd level or higher, both the temporary hit points and the cold damage increase by 5 for each slot level above 1st.

ARMS OF HADAR
1st-level conjuration

Casting Time: 1 action
Range: Self (10-foot radius)
Components: V, S
Duration: Instantaneous

You invoke the power of Hadar, the Dark Hunger. Tendrils of dark energy erupt from you and batter all creatures within 10 feet of you. Each creature in that area must make a Strength saving throw. On a failed save, a target takes 2d6 necrotic damage and can't take reactions until its next turn. On a successful save, the creature takes half damage, but suffers no other effect.

At Higher Levels. When you cast this spell using a spell slot of 2nd level or higher, the damage increases by 1d6 for each slot level above 1st.

ASTRAL PROJECTION
9th-level necromancy

Casting Time: 1 hour
Range: 10 feet
Components: V, S, M (for each creature you affect with this spell, you must provide one jacinth worth at least 1,000 gp and one ornately carved bar of silver worth at least 100 gp, all of which the spell consumes)
Duration: Special

You and up to eight willing creatures within range project your astral bodies into the Astral Plane (the spell fails and the casting is wasted if you are already on that plane). The material body you leave behind is unconscious and in a state of suspended animation; it doesn't need food or air and doesn't age.

Your astral body resembles your mortal form in almost every way, replicating your game statistics and possessions. The principal difference is the addition of a silvery cord that extends from between your shoulder blades and trails behind you, fading to invisibility after 1 foot. This cord is your tether to your material body. As long as the tether remains intact, you can find your way home. If the cord is cut—something that can happen only when an effect specifically states that it does—your soul and body are separated, killing you instantly.

Your astral form can freely travel through the Astral Plane and can pass through portals there leading to any other plane. If you enter a new plane or return to the plane you were on when casting this spell, your body and possessions are transported along the silver cord, allowing you to re-enter your body as you enter the new plane. Your astral form is a separate incarnation. Any damage or other effects that apply to it have no effect on your physical body, nor do they persist when you return to it.

The spell ends for you and your companions when you use your action to dismiss it. When the spell ends, the affected creature returns to its physical body, and it awakens.

The spell might also end early for you or one of your companions. A successful *dispel magic* spell used against an astral or physical body ends the spell for that creature. If a creature's original body or its astral form drops to 0 hit points, the spell ends for that creature. If the spell ends and the silver cord is intact, the cord pulls the creature's astral form back to its body, ending its state of suspended animation.

If you are returned to your body prematurely, your companions remain in their astral forms and must find their own way back to their bodies, usually by dropping to 0 hit points.

AUGURY
2nd-level divination (ritual)

Casting Time: 1 minute
Range: Self
Components: V, S, M (specially marked sticks, bones, or similar tokens worth at least 25 gp)
Duration: Instantaneous

By casting gem-inlaid sticks, rolling dragon bones, laying out ornate cards, or employing some other divining tool, you receive an omen from an otherworldly entity about the results of a specific course of action that you plan to take within the next 30 minutes. The DM chooses from the following possible omens:

- *Weal*, for good results
- *Woe*, for bad results
- *Weal and woe*, for both good and bad results
- *Nothing*, for results that aren't especially good or bad

The spell doesn't take into account any possible circumstances that might change the outcome, such as the casting of additional spells or the loss or gain of a companion.

If you cast the spell two or more times before completing your next long rest, there is a cumulative 25 percent chance for each casting after the first that you get a random reading. The DM makes this roll in secret.

AURA OF LIFE
4th-level abjuration

Casting Time: 1 action
Range: Self (30-foot radius)
Components: V
Duration: Concentration, up to 10 minutes

Life-preserving energy radiates from you in an aura with a 30-foot radius. Until the spell ends, the aura moves with you, centered on you. Each nonhostile creature in the aura (including you) has resistance to necrotic damage, and its hit point maximum can't be reduced. In addition, a nonhostile, living creature regains 1 hit point when it starts its turn in the aura with 0 hit points.

AURA OF PURITY
4th-level abjuration

Casting Time: 1 action
Range: Self (30-foot radius)
Components: V
Duration: Concentration, up to 10 minutes

Purifying energy radiates from you in an aura with a 30-foot radius. Until the spell ends, the aura moves with you, centered on you. Each nonhostile creature in the aura (including you) can't become diseased, has resistance to poison damage, and has advantage on saving throws against effects that cause any of the following conditions: blinded, charmed, deafened, frightened, paralyzed, poisoned, and stunned.

AURA OF VITALITY
3rd-level evocation

Casting Time: 1 action
Range: Self (30-foot radius)
Components: V
Duration: Concentration, up to 1 minute

Healing energy radiates from you in an aura with a 30-foot radius. Until the spell ends, the aura moves with you, centered on you. You can use a bonus action to cause one creature in the aura (including you) to regain 2d6 hit points.

AWAKEN
5th-level transmutation

Casting Time: 8 hours
Range: Touch
Components: V, S, M (an agate worth at least 1,000 gp, which the spell consumes)
Duration: Instantaneous

After spending the casting time tracing magical pathways within a precious gemstone, you touch a Huge or smaller beast or plant. The target must have either no Intelligence score or an Intelligence of 3 or less. The target gains an Intelligence of 10. The target also gains the ability to speak one language you know. If the target is a plant, it gains the ability to move its limbs, roots, vines, creepers, and so forth, and it gains senses similar to a human's. Your DM chooses statistics appropriate for the awakened plant, such as the statistics for the awakened shrub or the awakened tree.

The awakened beast or plant is charmed by you for 30 days or until you or your companions do anything harmful to it. When the charmed condition ends, the awakened creature chooses whether to remain friendly to you, based on how you treated it while it was charmed.

BANE
1st-level enchantment

Casting Time: 1 action
Range: 30 feet
Components: V, S, M (a drop of blood)
Duration: Concentration, up to 1 minute

Up to three creatures of your choice that you can see within range must make Charisma saving throws. Whenever a target that fails this saving throw makes an attack roll or a saving throw before the spell ends, the target must roll a d4 and subtract the number rolled from the attack roll or saving throw.

At Higher Levels. When you cast this spell using a spell slot of 2nd level or higher, you can target one additional creature for each slot level above 1st.

BANISHING SMITE
5th-level abjuration

Casting Time: 1 bonus action
Range: Self
Components: V
Duration: Concentration, up to 1 minute

The next time you hit a creature with a weapon attack before this spell ends, your weapon crackles with force, and the attack deals an extra 5d10 force damage to the target. Additionally, if this attack reduces the target to 50 hit points or fewer, you banish it. If the target is native to a different plane of existence than the one you're on, the target disappears, returning to its home plane. If the target is native to the plane you're on, the creature vanishes into a harmless demiplane. While there, the target is incapacitated. It remains there until the spell ends, at which point the target reappears in the space it left or in the nearest unoccupied space if that space is occupied.

BANISHMENT
4th-level abjuration

Casting Time: 1 action
Range: 60 feet
Components: V, S, M (an item distasteful to the target)
Duration: Concentration, up to 1 minute

You attempt to send one creature that you can see within range to another plane of existence. The target must succeed on a Charisma saving throw or be banished.

If the target is native to the plane of existence you're on, you banish the target to a harmless demiplane. While there, the target is incapacitated. The target remains there until the spell ends, at which point the target reappears in the space it left or in the nearest unoccupied space if that space is occupied.

If the target is native to a different plane of existence than the one you're on, the target is banished with a faint popping noise, returning to its home plane. If the spell ends before 1 minute has passed, the target reappears in the space it left or in the nearest unoccupied space if that space is occupied. Otherwise, the target doesn't return.

At Higher Levels. When you cast this spell using a spell slot of 5th level or higher, you can target one additional creature for each slot level above 4th.

BARKSKIN
2nd-level transmutation

Casting Time: 1 action
Range: Touch
Components: V, S, M (a handful of oak bark)
Duration: Concentration, up to 1 hour

You touch a willing creature. Until the spell ends, the target's skin has a rough, bark-like appearance, and the target's AC can't be less than 16, regardless of what kind of armor it is wearing.

BEACON OF HOPE
3rd-level abjuration

Casting Time: 1 action
Range: 30 feet
Components: V, S
Duration: Concentration, up to 1 minute

This spell bestows hope and vitality. Choose any number of creatures within range. For the duration, each target has advantage on Wisdom saving throws and death saving throws, and regains the maximum number of hit points possible from any healing.

BEAST SENSE
2nd-level divination (ritual)

Casting Time: 1 action
Range: Touch
Components: S
Duration: Concentration, up to 1 hour

You touch a willing beast. For the duration of the spell, you can use your action to see through the beast's eyes and hear what it hears, and continue to do so until you use your action to return to your normal senses.

While perceiving through the beast's senses, you gain the benefits of any special senses possessed by that creature, though you are blinded and deafened to your own surroundings.

BESTOW CURSE
3rd-level necromancy

Casting Time: 1 action
Range: Touch
Components: V, S
Duration: Concentration, up to 1 minute

You touch a creature, and that creature must succeed on a Wisdom saving throw or become cursed for the duration of the spell. When you cast this spell, choose the nature of the curse from the following options:

- Choose one ability score. While cursed, the target has disadvantage on ability checks and saving throws made with that ability score.
- While cursed, the target has disadvantage on attack rolls against you.
- While cursed, the target must make a Wisdom saving throw at the start of each of its turns. If it fails, it wastes its action that turn doing nothing.
- While the target is cursed, your attacks and spells deal an extra 1d8 necrotic damage to the target.

A *remove curse* spell ends this effect. At the DM's option, you may choose an alternative curse effect, but it should be no more powerful than those described above. The DM has final say on such a curse's effect.

At Higher Levels. If you cast this spell using a spell slot of 4th level or higher, the duration is concentration, up to 10 minutes. If you use a spell slot of 5th level or higher, the duration is 8 hours. If you use a spell slot of 7th level or higher, the duration is 24 hours. If you use a 9th level spell slot, the spell lasts until it is dispelled. Using a spell slot of 5th level or higher grants a duration that doesn't require concentration.

BIGBY'S HAND
5th-level evocation

Casting Time: 1 action
Range: 120 feet
Components: V, S, M (an eggshell and a snakeskin glove)
Duration: Concentration, up to 1 minute

You create a Large hand of shimmering, translucent force in an unoccupied space that you can see within range. The hand lasts for the spell's duration, and it moves at your command, mimicking the movements of your own hand.

The hand is an object that has AC 20 and hit points equal to your hit point maximum. If it drops to 0 hit points, the spell ends. It has a Strength of 26 (+8) and a Dexterity of 10 (+0). The hand doesn't fill its space.

When you cast the spell and as a bonus action on your subsequent turns, you can move the hand up to 60 feet and then cause one of the following effects with it.

Clenched Fist. The hand strikes one creature or object within 5 feet of it. Make a melee spell attack for the hand using your game statistics. On a hit, the target takes 4d8 force damage.

Forceful Hand. The hand attempts to push a creature within 5 feet of it in a direction you choose. Make a check with the hand's Strength contested by the Strength (Athletics) check of the target. If the target is Medium or smaller, you have advantage on the check. If you succeed, the hand pushes the target up to 5 feet plus a number of feet equal to five times your spellcasting ability modifier. The hand moves with the target to remain within 5 feet of it.

Grasping Hand. The hand attempts to grapple a Huge or smaller creature within 5 feet of it. You use the hand's Strength score to resolve the grapple. If the target is Medium or smaller, you have advantage on the check. While the hand is grappling the target, you can use a bonus action to have the hand crush it. When you do so, the target takes bludgeoning damage equal to 2d6 + your spellcasting ability modifier.

Interposing Hand. The hand interposes itself between you and a creature you choose until you give the hand a different command. The hand moves to stay between you and the target, providing you with half cover against the target. The target can't move through the hand's space if its Strength score is less than or equal to the hand's Strength score. If its Strength score is higher than the hand's Strength score, the target can move toward you through the hand's space, but that space is difficult terrain for the target.

At Higher Levels. When you cast this spell using a spell slot of 6th level or higher, the damage from the clenched fist option increases by 2d8 and the damage from the grasping hand increases by 2d6 for each slot level above 5th.

BLADE BARRIER
6th-level evocation

Casting Time: 1 action
Range: 90 feet
Components: V, S
Duration: Concentration, up to 10 minutes

You create a vertical wall of whirling, razor-sharp blades made of magical energy. The wall appears within range and lasts for the duration. You can make a straight wall up to 100 feet long, 20 feet high, and 5 feet thick, or a ringed wall up to 60 feet in diameter, 20 feet high, and 5 feet thick. The wall provides three-quarters cover to creatures behind it, and its space is difficult terrain.

When a creature enters the wall's area for the first time on a turn or starts its turn there, the creature must make a Dexterity saving throw. On a failed save, the creature takes 6d10 slashing damage. On a successful save, the creature takes half as much damage.

BLADE WARD
Abjuration cantrip

Casting Time: 1 action
Range: Self
Components: V, S
Duration: 1 round

You extend your hand and trace a sigil of warding in the air. Until the end of your next turn, you have resistance against bludgeoning, piercing, and slashing damage dealt by weapon attacks.

BLESS
1st-level enchantment

Casting Time: 1 action
Range: 30 feet
Components: V, S, M (a sprinkling of holy water)
Duration: Concentration, up to 1 minute

You bless up to three creatures of your choice within range. Whenever a target makes an attack roll or a saving throw before the spell ends, the target can roll a d4 and add the number rolled to the attack roll or saving throw.

At Higher Levels. When you cast this spell using a spell slot of 2nd level or higher, you can target one additional creature for each slot level above 1st.

BLIGHT
4th-level necromancy

Casting Time: 1 action
Range: 30 feet
Components: V, S
Duration: Instantaneous

Necromantic energy washes over a creature of your choice that you can see within range, draining moisture and vitality from it. The target must make a Constitution saving throw. The target takes 8d8 necrotic damage on a failed save, or half as much damage on a successful one. This spell has no effect on undead or constructs.

If you target a plant creature or a magical plant, it makes the saving throw with disadvantage, and the spell deals maximum damage to it.

If you target a nonmagical plant that isn't a creature, such as a tree or shrub, it doesn't make a saving throw; it simply withers and dies.

At Higher Levels. When you cast this spell using a spell slot of 5th level or higher, the damage increases by 1d8 for each slot level above 4th.

BLINDING SMITE
3rd-level evocation

Casting Time: 1 bonus action
Range: Self
Components: V
Duration: Concentration, up to 1 minute

The next time you hit a creature with a melee weapon attack during this spell's duration, your weapon flares with bright light, and the attack deals an extra 3d8 radiant damage to the target. Additionally, the target must succeed on a Constitution saving throw or be blinded until the spell ends.

A creature blinded by this spell makes another Constitution saving throw at the end of each of its turns. On a successful save, it is no longer blinded.

BLINDNESS/DEAFNESS
2nd-level necromancy

Casting Time: 1 action
Range: 30 feet
Components: V
Duration: 1 minute

You can blind or deafen a foe. Choose one creature that you can see within range to make a Constitution saving throw. If it fails, the target is either blinded or deafened (your choice) for the duration. At the end of each of its turns, the target can make a Constitution saving throw. On a success, the spell ends.

At Higher Levels. When you cast this spell using a spell slot of 3rd level or higher, you can target one additional creature for each slot level above 2nd.

BLINK
3rd-level transmutation

Casting Time: 1 action
Range: Self
Components: V, S
Duration: 1 minute

Roll a d20 at the end of each of your turns for the duration of the spell. On a roll of 11 or higher, you vanish from your current plane of existence and appear in the Ethereal Plane (the spell fails and the casting is wasted if you were already on that plane). At the start of your next turn, and when the spell ends if you are on the Ethereal Plane, you return to an unoccupied space of your choice that you can see within 10 feet of the space you vanished from. If no unoccupied space is available within that range, you appear in the nearest unoccupied space (chosen at random if more than one space is equally near). You can dismiss this spell as an action.

While on the Ethereal Plane, you can see and hear the plane you originated from, which is cast in shades of gray, and you can't see anything there more than 60 feet away. You can only affect and be affected by other creatures on the Ethereal Plane. Creatures that aren't there can't perceive you or interact with you, unless they have the ability to do so.

BLUR
2nd-level illusion

Casting Time: 1 action
Range: Self
Components: V
Duration: Concentration, up to 1 minute

Your body becomes blurred, shifting and wavering to all who can see you. For the duration, any creature has disadvantage on attack rolls against you. An attacker is immune to this effect if it doesn't rely on sight, as with blindsight, or can see through illusions, as with truesight.

BRANDING SMITE
2nd-level evocation

Casting Time: 1 bonus action
Range: Self

Components: V
Duration: Concentration, up to 1 minute

The next time you hit a creature with a weapon attack before this spell ends, the weapon gleams with astral radiance as you strike. The attack deals an extra 2d6 radiant damage to the target, which becomes visible if it's invisible, and the target sheds dim light in a 5-foot radius and can't become invisible until the spell ends.

At Higher Levels. When you cast this spell using a spell slot of 3rd level or higher, the extra damage increases by 1d6 for each slot level above 2nd.

BURNING HANDS
1st-level evocation

Casting Time: 1 action
Range: Self (15-foot cone)
Components: V, S
Duration: Instantaneous

As you hold your hands with thumbs touching and fingers spread, a thin sheet of flames shoots forth from your outstretched fingertips. Each creature in a 15-foot cone must make a Dexterity saving throw. A creature takes 3d6 fire damage on a failed save, or half as much damage on a successful one.

The fire ignites any flammable objects in the area that aren't being worn or carried.

At Higher Levels. When you cast this spell using a spell slot of 2nd level or higher, the damage increases by 1d6 for each slot level above 1st.

CALL LIGHTNING
3rd-level conjuration

Casting Time: 1 action
Range: 120 feet
Components: V, S
Duration: Concentration, up to 10 minutes

A storm cloud appears in the shape of a cylinder that is 10 feet tall with a 60-foot radius, centered on a point you can see 100 feet directly above you. The spell fails if you can't see a point in the air where the storm cloud could appear (for example, if you are in a room that can't accommodate the cloud).

When you cast the spell, choose a point you can see within range. A bolt of lightning flashes down from the cloud to that point. Each creature within 5 feet of that point must make a Dexterity saving throw. A creature takes 3d10 lightning damage on a failed save, or half as much damage on a successful one. On each of your turns until the spell ends, you can use your action to call down lightning in this way again, targeting the same point or a different one.

If you are outdoors in stormy conditions when you cast this spell, the spell gives you control over the existing storm instead of creating a new one. Under such conditions, the spell's damage increases by 1d10.

At Higher Levels. When you cast this spell using a spell slot of 4th or higher level, the damage increases by 1d10 for each slot level above 3rd.

CALM EMOTIONS
2nd-level enchantment

Casting Time: 1 action
Range: 60 feet
Components: V, S
Duration: Concentration, up to 1 minute

You attempt to suppress strong emotions in a group of people. Each humanoid in a 20-foot-radius sphere centered on a point you choose within range must make a Charisma saving throw; a creature can choose to fail this saving throw if it wishes. If a creature fails its saving throw, choose one of the following two effects.

You can suppress any effect causing a target to be charmed or frightened. When this spell ends, any suppressed effect resumes, provided that its duration has not expired in the meantime.

Alternatively, you can make a target indifferent about creatures of your choice that it is hostile toward. This indifference ends if the target is attacked or harmed by a spell or if it witnesses any of its friends being harmed. When the spell ends, the creature becomes hostile again, unless the DM rules otherwise.

CHAIN LIGHTNING
6th-level evocation

Casting Time: 1 action
Range: 150 feet
Components: V, S, M (a bit of fur; a piece of amber, glass, or a crystal rod; and three silver pins)
Duration: Instantaneous

You create a bolt of lightning that arcs toward a target of your choice that you can see within range. Three bolts then leap from that target to as many as three other targets, each of which must be within 30 feet of the first target. A target can be a creature or an object and can be targeted by only one of the bolts.

A target must make a Dexterity saving throw. The target takes 10d8 lightning damage on a failed save, or half as much damage on a successful one.

At Higher Levels. When you cast this spell using a spell slot of 7th level or higher, one additional bolt leaps from the first target to another target for each slot level above 6th.

CHARM PERSON
1st-level enchantment

Casting Time: 1 action
Range: 30 feet
Components: V, S
Duration: 1 hour

You attempt to charm a humanoid you can see within range. It must make a Wisdom saving throw, and does so with advantage if you or your companions are fighting it. If it fails the saving throw, it is charmed by you until the spell ends or until you or your companions do anything harmful to it. The charmed creature regards you as a friendly acquaintance. When the spell ends, the creature knows it was charmed by you.

At Higher Levels. When you cast this spell using a spell slot of 2nd level or higher, you can target one

additional creature for each slot level above 1st. The creatures must be within 30 feet of each other when you target them.

CHILL TOUCH
Necromancy cantrip

Casting Time: 1 action
Range: 120 feet
Components: V, S
Duration: 1 round

You create a ghostly, skeletal hand in the space of a creature within range. Make a ranged spell attack against the creature to assail it with the chill of the grave. On a hit, the target takes 1d8 necrotic damage, and it can't regain hit points until the start of your next turn. Until then, the hand clings to the target.

If you hit an undead target, it also has disadvantage on attack rolls against you until the end of your next turn.

This spell's damage increases by 1d8 when you reach 5th level (2d8), 11th level (3d8), and 17th level (4d8).

CHROMATIC ORB
1st-level evocation

Casting Time: 1 action
Range: 90 feet
Components: V, S, M (a diamond worth at least 50 gp)
Duration: Instantaneous

You hurl a 4-inch-diameter sphere of energy at a creature that you can see within range. You choose acid, cold, fire, lightning, poison, or thunder for the type of orb you create, and then make a ranged spell attack against the target. If the attack hits, the creature takes 3d8 damage of the type you chose.

At Higher Levels. When you cast this spell using a spell slot of 2nd level or higher, the damage increases by 1d8 for each slot level above 1st.

CIRCLE OF DEATH
6th-level necromancy

Casting Time: 1 action
Range: 150 feet
Components: V, S, M (the powder of a crushed black pearl worth at least 500 gp)
Duration: Instantaneous

A sphere of negative energy ripples out in a 60-foot-radius sphere from a point within range. Each creature in that area must make a Constitution saving throw. A target takes 8d6 necrotic damage on a failed save, or half as much damage on a successful one.

At Higher Levels. When you cast this spell using a spell slot of 7th level or higher, the damage increases by 2d6 for each slot level above 6th.

CIRCLE OF POWER
5th-level abjuration

Casting Time: 1 action
Range: Self (30-foot radius)
Components: V
Duration: Concentration, up to 10 minutes

Divine energy radiates from you, distorting and diffusing magical energy within 30 feet of you. Until the spell ends, the sphere moves with you, centered on you. For the duration, each friendly creature in the area (including you) has advantage on saving throws against spells and other magical effects. Additionally, when an affected creature succeeds on a saving throw made against a spell or magical effect that allows it to make a saving throw to take only half damage, it instead takes no damage if it succeeds on the saving throw.

CLAIRVOYANCE
3rd-level divination

Casting Time: 10 minutes
Range: 1 mile
Components: V, S, M (a focus worth at least 100 gp, either a jeweled horn for hearing or a glass eye for seeing)
Duration: Concentration, up to 10 minutes

You create an invisible sensor within range in a location familiar to you (a place you have visited or seen before) or in an obvious location that is unfamiliar to you (such as behind a door, around a corner, or in a grove of trees). The sensor remains in place for the duration, and it can't be attacked or otherwise interacted with.

When you cast the spell, you choose seeing or hearing. You can use the chosen sense through the sensor as if you were in its space. As your action, you can switch between seeing and hearing.

A creature that can see the sensor (such as a creature benefiting from *see invisibility* or truesight) sees a luminous, intangible orb about the size of your fist.

CLONE
8th-level necromancy

Casting Time: 1 hour
Range: Touch
Components: V, S, M (a diamond worth at least 1,000 gp and at least 1 cubic inch of flesh of the creature that is to be cloned, which the spell consumes, and a vessel worth at least 2,000 gp that has a sealable lid and is large enough to hold a Medium creature, such as a huge urn, coffin, mud-filled cyst in the ground, or crystal container filled with salt water)
Duration: Instantaneous

This spell grows an inert duplicate of a living creature as a safeguard against death. This clone forms inside a sealed vessel and grows to full size and maturity after 120 days; you can also choose to have the clone be a younger version of the same creature. It remains inert and endures indefinitely, as long as its vessel remains undisturbed.

At any time after the clone matures, if the original creature dies, its soul transfers to the clone, provided that the soul is free and willing to return. The clone is physically identical to the original and has the same personality, memories, and abilities, but none of the original's equipment. The original creature's physical remains, if they still exist, become inert and can't thereafter be restored to life, since the creature's soul is elsewhere.

CLOUD OF DAGGERS
2nd-level conjuration

Casting Time: 1 action
Range: 60 feet
Components: V, S, M (a sliver of glass)
Duration: Concentration, up to 1 minute

You fill the air with spinning daggers in a cube 5 feet on each side, centered on a point you choose within range. A creature takes 4d4 slashing damage when it enters the spell's area for the first time on a turn or starts its turn there.

At Higher Levels. When you cast this spell using a spell slot of 3rd level or higher, the damage increases by 2d4 for each slot level above 2nd.

CLOUDKILL
5th-level conjuration

Casting Time: 1 action
Range: 120 feet
Components: V, S
Duration: Concentration, up to 10 minutes

You create a 20-foot-radius sphere of poisonous, yellow-green fog centered on a point you choose within range. The fog spreads around corners. It lasts for the duration or until strong wind disperses the fog, ending the spell. Its area is heavily obscured.

When a creature enters the spell's area for the first time on a turn or starts its turn there, that creature must make a Constitution saving throw. The creature takes 5d8 poison damage on a failed save, or half as much damage on a successful one. Creatures are affected even if they hold their breath or don't need to breathe.

The fog moves 10 feet away from you at the start of each of your turns, rolling along the surface of the ground. The vapors, being heavier than air, sink to the lowest level of the land, even pouring down openings.

At Higher Levels. When you cast this spell using a spell slot of 6th level or higher, the damage increases by 1d8 for each slot level above 5th.

COLOR SPRAY
1st-level illusion

Casting Time: 1 action
Range: Self (15-foot cone)
Components: V, S, M (a pinch of powder or sand that is colored red, yellow, and blue)
Duration: 1 round

A dazzling array of flashing, colored light springs from your hand. Roll 6d10; the total is how many hit points of creatures this spell can effect. Creatures in a 15-foot cone originating from you are affected in ascending order of their current hit points (ignoring unconscious creatures and creatures that can't see).

Starting with the creature that has the lowest current hit points, each creature affected by this spell is blinded until the spell ends. Subtract each creature's hit points from the total before moving on to the creature with the next lowest hit points. A creature's hit points must be equal to or less than the remaining total for that creature to be affected.

At Higher Levels. When you cast this spell using a spell slot of 2nd level or higher, roll an additional 2d10 for each slot level above 1st.

COMMAND
1st-level enchantment

Casting Time: 1 action
Range: 60 feet
Components: V
Duration: 1 round

You speak a one-word command to a creature you can see within range. The target must succeed on a Wisdom saving throw or follow the command on its next turn. The spell has no effect if the target is undead, if it doesn't understand your language, or if your command is directly harmful to it.

Some typical commands and their effects follow. You might issue a command other than one described here. If you do so, the DM determines how the target behaves. If the target can't follow your command, the spell ends.

Approach. The target moves toward you by the shortest and most direct route, ending its turn if it moves within 5 feet of you.

Drop. The target drops whatever it is holding and then ends its turn.

Flee. The target spends its turn moving away from you by the fastest available means.

Grovel. The target falls prone and then ends its turn.

Halt. The target doesn't move and takes no actions. A flying creature stays aloft, provided that it is able to do so. If it must move to stay aloft, it flies the minimum distance needed to remain in the air.

At Higher Levels. When you cast this spell using a spell slot of 2nd level or higher, you can affect one additional creature for each slot level above 1st. The creatures must be within 30 feet of each other when you target them.

COMMUNE
5th-level divination (ritual)

Casting Time: 1 minute
Range: Self
Components: V, S, M (incense and a vial of holy or unholy water)
Duration: 1 minute

You contact your deity or a divine proxy and ask up to three questions that can be answered with a yes or no. You must ask your questions before the spell ends. You receive a correct answer for each question.

Divine beings aren't necessarily omniscient, so you might receive "unclear" as an answer if a question pertains to information that lies beyond the deity's knowledge. In a case where a one-word answer could be misleading or contrary to the deity's interests, the DM might offer a short phrase as an answer instead.

If you cast the spell two or more times before finishing your next long rest, there is a cumulative 25 percent chance for each casting after the first that you get no answer. The DM makes this roll in secret.

Commune with Nature
5th-level divination (ritual)

Casting Time: 1 minute
Range: Self
Components: V, S
Duration: Instantaneous

You briefly become one with nature and gain knowledge of the surrounding territory. In the outdoors, the spell gives you knowledge of the land within 3 miles of you. In caves and other natural underground settings, the radius is limited to 300 feet. The spell doesn't function where nature has been replaced by construction, such as in dungeons and towns.

You instantly gain knowledge of up to three facts of your choice about any of the following subjects as they relate to the area:

- terrain and bodies of water
- prevalent plants, minerals, animals, or peoples
- powerful celestials, fey, fiends, elementals, or undead
- influence from other planes of existence
- buildings

For example, you could determine the location of powerful undead in the area, the location of major sources of safe drinking water, and the location of any nearby towns.

Compelled Duel
1st-level enchantment

Casting Time: 1 bonus action
Range: 30 feet
Components: V
Duration: Concentration, up to 1 minute

You attempt to compel a creature into a duel. One creature that you can see within range must make a Wisdom saving throw. On a failed save, the creature is drawn to you, compelled by your divine demand. For the duration, it has disadvantage on attack rolls against creatures other than you, and must make a Wisdom saving throw each time it attempts to move to a space that is more than 30 feet away from you; if it succeeds on this saving throw, this spell doesn't restrict the target's movement for that turn.

The spell ends if you attack any other creature, if you cast a spell that targets a hostile creature other than the target, if a creature friendly to you damages the target or casts a harmful spell on it, or if you end your turn more than 30 feet away from the target.

Comprehend Languages
1st-level divination (ritual)

Casting Time: 1 action
Range: Self
Components: V, S, M (a pinch of soot and salt)
Duration: 1 hour

For the duration, you understand the literal meaning of any spoken language that you hear. You also understand any written language that you see, but you must be touching the surface on which the words are written. It takes about 1 minute to read one page of text.

This spell doesn't decode secret messages in a text or a glyph, such as an arcane sigil, that isn't part of a written language.

Compulsion
4th-level enchantment

Casting Time: 1 action
Range: 30 feet
Components: V, S
Duration: Concentration, up to 1 minute

Creatures of your choice that you can see within range and that can hear you must make a Wisdom saving throw. A target automatically succeeds on this saving throw if it can't be charmed. On a failed save, a target is affected by this spell. Until the spell ends, you can use a bonus action on each of your turns to designate a direction that is horizontal to you. Each affected target must use as much of its movement as possible to move in that direction on its next turn. It can take its action before it moves. After moving in this way, it can make another Wisdom saving to try to end the effect.

A target isn't compelled to move into an obviously deadly hazard, such as a fire or pit, but it will provoke opportunity attacks to move in the designated direction.

Cone of Cold
5th-level evocation

Casting Time: 1 action
Range: Self (60-foot cone)
Components: V, S, M (a small crystal or glass cone)
Duration: Instantaneous

A blast of cold air erupts from your hands. Each creature in a 60-foot cone must make a Constitution saving throw. A creature takes 8d8 cold damage on a failed save, or half as much damage on a successful one.

A creature killed by this spell becomes a frozen statue until it thaws.

At Higher Levels. When you cast this spell using a spell slot of 6th level or higher, the damage increases by 1d8 for each slot level above 5th.

Confusion
4th-level enchantment

Casting Time: 1 action
Range: 90 feet
Components: V, S, M (three nut shells)
Duration: Concentration, up to 1 minute

This spell assaults and twists creatures' minds, spawning delusions and provoking uncontrolled action. Each creature in a 10-foot-radius sphere centered on a point you choose within range must succeed on a Wisdom saving throw when you cast this spell or be affected by it.

An affected target can't take reactions and must roll a d10 at the start of each of its turns to determine its behavior for that turn.

d10	Behavior
1	The creature uses all its movement to move in a random direction. To determine the direction, roll a d8 and assign a direction to each die face. The creature doesn't take an action this turn.
2–6	The creature doesn't move or take actions this turn.
7–8	The creature uses its action to make a melee attack against a randomly determined creature within its reach. If there is no creature within its reach, the creature does nothing this turn.
9–10	The creature can act and move normally.

At the end of each of its turns, an affected target can make a Wisdom saving throw. If it succeeds, this effect ends for that target.

At Higher Levels. When you cast this spell using a spell slot of 5th level or higher, the radius of the sphere increases by 5 feet for each slot level above 4th.

Conjure Animals
3rd-level conjuration

Casting Time: 1 action
Range: 60 feet
Components: V, S
Duration: Concentration, up to 1 hour

You summon fey spirits that take the form of beasts and appear in unoccupied spaces that you can see within range. Choose one of the following options for what appears:

- One beast of challenge rating 2 or lower
- Two beasts of challenge rating 1 or lower
- Four beasts of challenge rating 1/2 or lower
- Eight beasts of challenge rating 1/4 or lower

Each beast is also considered fey, and it disappears when it drops to 0 hit points or when the spell ends.

The summoned creatures are friendly to you and your companions. Roll initiative for the summoned creatures as a group, which has its own turns. They obey any verbal commands that you issue to them (no action required by you). If you don't issue any commands to them, they defend themselves from hostile creatures, but otherwise take no actions.

The DM has the creatures' statistics.

At Higher Levels. When you cast this spell using certain higher-level spell slots, you choose one of the summoning options above, and more creatures appear: twice as many with a 5th-level slot, three times as many with a 7th-level slot, and four times as many with a 9th-level slot.

Conjure Barrage
3rd-level conjuration

Casting Time: 1 action
Range: Self (60-foot cone)
Components: V, S, M (one piece of ammunition or a thrown weapon)
Duration: Instantaneous

You throw a nonmagical weapon or fire a piece of nonmagical ammunition into the air to create a cone of identical weapons that shoot forward and then disappear. Each creature in a 60-foot cone must succeed on a Dexterity saving throw. A creature takes 3d8 damage on a failed save, or half as much damage on a successful one. The damage type is the same as that of the weapon or ammunition used as a component.

Conjure Celestial
7th-level conjuration

Casting Time: 1 minute
Range: 90 feet
Components: V, S
Duration: Concentration, up to 1 hour

You summon a celestial of challenge rating 4 or lower, which appears in an unoccupied space that you can see within range. The celestial disappears when it drops to 0 hit points or when the spell ends.

The celestial is friendly to you and your companions for the duration. Roll initiative for the celestial, which has its own turns. It obeys any verbal commands that you issue to it (no action required by you), as long as they don't violate its alignment. If you don't issue any commands to the celestial, it defends itself from hostile creatures but otherwise takes no actions.

The DM has the celestial's statistics.

At Higher Levels. When you cast this spell using a 9th-level spell slot, you summon a celestial of challenge rating 5 or lower.

Conjure Elemental
5th-level conjuration

Casting Time: 1 minute
Range: 90 feet
Components: V, S, M (burning incense for air, soft clay for earth, sulfur and phosphorus for fire, or water and sand for water)
Duration: Concentration, up to 1 hour

You call forth an elemental servant. Choose an area of air, earth, fire, or water that fills a 10-foot cube within range. An elemental of challenge rating 5 or lower appropriate to the area you chose appears in an unoccupied space within 10 feet of it. For example, a fire elemental emerges from a bonfire, and an earth elemental rises up from the ground. The elemental disappears when it drops to 0 hit points or when the spell ends.

The elemental is friendly to you and your companions for the duration. Roll initiative for the elemental, which has its own turns. It obeys any verbal commands that you issue to it (no action required by you). If you don't issue any commands to the elemental, it defends itself from hostile creatures but otherwise takes no actions.

If your concentration is broken, the elemental doesn't disappear. Instead, you lose control of the elemental, it becomes hostile toward you and your companions, and it might attack. An uncontrolled elemental can't be dismissed by you, and it disappears 1 hour after you summoned it.

The DM has the elemental's statistics.

At Higher Levels. When you cast this spell using a spell slot of 6th level or higher, the challenge rating increases by 1 for each slot level above 5th.

Conjure Fey
6th-level conjuration

Casting Time: 1 minute
Range: 90 feet
Components: V, S
Duration: Concentration, up to 1 hour

You summon a fey creature of challenge rating 6 or lower, or a fey spirit that takes the form of a beast of challenge rating 6 or lower. It appears in an unoccupied space that you can see within range. The fey creature disappears when it drops to 0 hit points or when the spell ends.

The fey creature is friendly to you and your companions for the duration. Roll initiative for the creature, which has its own turns. It obeys any verbal commands that you issue to it (no action required by you), as long as they don't violate its alignment. If you don't issue any commands to the fey creature, it defends itself from hostile creatures but otherwise takes no actions.

If your concentration is broken, the fey creature doesn't disappear. Instead, you lose control of the fey creature, it becomes hostile toward you and your companions, and it might attack. An uncontrolled fey creature can't be dismissed by you, and it disappears 1 hour after you summoned it.

The DM has the fey creature's statistics.

At Higher Levels. When you cast this spell using a spell slot of 7th level or higher, the challenge rating increases by 1 for each slot level above 6th.

Conjure Minor Elementals
4th-level conjuration

Casting Time: 1 minute
Range: 90 feet
Components: V, S
Duration: Concentration, up to 1 hour

You summon elementals that appear in unoccupied spaces that you can see within range. You choose one the following options for what appears:

- One elemental of challenge rating 2 or lower
- Two elementals of challenge rating 1 or lower
- Four elementals of challenge rating 1/2 or lower
- Eight elementals of challenge rating 1/4 or lower.

An elemental summoned by this spell disappears when it drops to 0 hit points or when the spell ends.

The summoned creatures are friendly to you and your companions. Roll initiative for the summoned creatures as a group, which has its own turns. They obey any verbal commands that you issue to them (no action required by you). If you don't issue any commands to them, they defend themselves from hostile creatures, but otherwise take no actions.

The DM has the creatures' statistics.

At Higher Levels. When you cast this spell using certain higher-level spell slots, you choose one of the summoning options above, and more creatures appear: twice as many with a 6th-level slot and three times as many with an 8th-level slot.

Conjure Volley
5th-level conjuration

Casting Time: 1 action
Range: 150 feet
Components: V, S, M (one piece of ammunition or one thrown weapon)
Duration: Instantaneous

You fire a piece of nonmagical ammunition from a ranged weapon or throw a nonmagical weapon into the air and choose a point within range. Hundreds of duplicates of the ammunition or weapon fall in a volley from above and then disappear. Each creature in a 40-foot-radius, 20-foot-high cylinder centered on that point must make a Dexterity saving throw. A creature takes 8d8 damage on a failed save, or half as much damage on a successful one. The damage type is the same as that of the ammunition or weapon.

Conjure Woodland Beings
4th-level conjuration

Casting Time: 1 action
Range: 60 feet
Components: V, S, M (one holly berry per creature summoned)
Duration: Concentration, up to 1 hour

You summon fey creatures that appear in unoccupied spaces that you can see within range. Choose one of the following options for what appears:

- One fey creature of challenge rating 2 or lower
- Two fey creatures of challenge rating 1 or lower
- Four fey creatures of challenge rating 1/2 or lower
- Eight fey creatures of challenge rating 1/4 or lower

A summoned creature disappears when it drops to 0 hit points or when the spell ends.

The summoned creatures are friendly to you and your companions. Roll initiative for the summoned creatures as a group, which have their own turns. They obey any verbal commands that you issue to them (no action required by you). If you don't issue any commands to them, they defend themselves from hostile creatures, but otherwise take no actions.

The DM has the creatures' statistics.

At Higher Levels. When you cast this spell using certain higher-level spell slots, you choose one of the summoning options above, and more creatures appear: twice as many with a 6th-level slot and three times as many with an 8th-level slot.

Contact Other Plane
5th-level divination (ritual)

Casting Time: 1 minute
Range: Self
Components: V
Duration: 1 minute

You mentally contact a demigod, the spirit of a long-dead sage, or some other mysterious entity from another plane. Contacting this extraplanar intelligence can strain or even break your mind. When you cast this spell, make a DC 15 Intelligence saving throw. On a failure, you take 6d6 psychic damage and are insane until you finish a long rest. While insane, you can't take actions, can't understand what other creatures say, can't read, and speak only in gibberish. A *greater restoration* spell cast on you ends this effect.

On a successful save, you can ask the entity up to five questions. You must ask your questions before the spell ends. The DM answers each question with one word, such as "yes," "no," "maybe," "never," "irrelevant," or "unclear" (if the entity doesn't know the answer to the question). If a one-word answer would be misleading, the DM might instead offer a short phrase as an answer.

CONTAGION
5th-level necromancy

Casting Time: 1 action
Range: Touch
Component: V, S
Duration: 7 days

Your touch inflicts disease. Make a melee spell attack against a creature within your reach. On a hit, you afflict the creature with a disease of your choice from any of the ones described below.

At the end of each of the target's turns, it must make a Constitution saving throw. After failing three of these saving throws, the disease's effects last for the duration, and the creature stops making these saves. After succeeding on three of these saving throws, the creature recovers from the disease, and the spell ends.

Since this spell induces a natural disease in its target, any effect that removes a disease or otherwise ameliorates a disease's effects apply to it.

Blinding Sickness. Pain grips the creature's mind, and its eyes turn milky white. The creature has disadvantage on Wisdom checks and Wisdom saving throws and is blinded.

Filth Fever. A raging fever sweeps through the creature's body. The creature has disadvantage on Strength checks, Strength saving throws, and attack rolls that use Strength.

Flesh Rot. The creature's flesh decays. The creature has disadvantage on Charisma checks and vulnerability to all damage.

Mindfire. The creature's mind becomes feverish. The creature has disadvantage on Intelligence checks and Intelligence saving throws, and the creature behaves as if under the effects of the *confusion* spell during combat.

Seizure. The creature is overcome with shaking. The creature has disadvantage on Dexterity checks, Dexterity saving throws, and attack rolls that use Dexterity.

Slimy Doom. The creature begins to bleed uncontrollably. The creature has disadvantage on Constitution checks and Constitution saving throws. In addition, whenever the creature takes damage, it is stunned until the end of its next turn.

CONTINGENCY
6th-level evocation

Casting Time: 10 minutes
Range: Self

Components: V, S, M (a statuette of yourself carved from ivory and decorated with gems worth at least 1,500 gp)
Duration: 10 days

Choose a spell of 5th level or lower that you can cast, that has a casting time of 1 action, and that can target you. You cast that spell—called the contingent spell—as part of casting *contingency*, expending spell slots for both, but the contingent spell doesn't come into effect. Instead, it takes effect when a certain circumstance occurs. You describe that circumstance when you cast the two spells. For example, a *contingency* cast with *water breathing* might stipulate that *water breathing* comes into effect when you are engulfed in water or a similar liquid.

The contingent spell takes effect immediately after the circumstance is met for the first time, whether or not you want it to, and then *contingency* ends.

The contingent spell takes effect only on you, even if it can normally target others. You can use only one *contingency* spell at a time. If you cast this spell again, the effect of another *contingency* spell on you ends. Also, *contingency* ends on you if its material component is ever not on your person.

CONTINUAL FLAME
2nd-level evocation

Casting Time: 1 action
Range: Touch
Components: V, S, M (ruby dust worth 50 gp, which the spell consumes)
Duration: Until dispelled

A flame, equivalent in brightness to a torch, springs forth from an object that you touch. The effect looks like a regular flame, but it creates no heat and doesn't use oxygen. A *continual flame* can be covered or hidden but not smothered or quenched.

CONTROL WATER
4th-level transmutation

Casting Time: 1 action
Range: 300 feet
Components: V, S, M (a drop of water and a pinch of dust)
Duration: Concentration, up to 10 minutes

Until the spell ends, you control any freestanding water inside an area you choose that is a cube up to 100 feet on a side. You can choose from any of the following effects when you cast this spell. As an action on your turn, you can repeat the same effect or choose a different one.

Flood. You cause the water level of all standing water in the area to rise by as much as 20 feet. If the area includes a shore, the flooding water spills over onto dry land.

If you choose an area in a large body of water, you instead create a 20-foot tall wave that travels from one side of the area to the other and then crashes down. Any Huge or smaller vehicles in the wave's path are carried with it to the other side. Any Huge or smaller vehicles struck by the wave have a 25 percent chance of capsizing.

The water level remains elevated until the spell ends or you choose a different effect. If this effect produced a wave, the wave repeats on the start of your next turn while the flood effect lasts.

Part Water. You cause water in the area to move apart and create a trench. The trench extends across the spell's area, and the separated water forms a wall to either side. The trench remains until the spell ends or you choose a different effect. The water then slowly fills in the trench over the course of the next round until the normal water level is restored.

Redirect Flow. You cause flowing water in the area to move in a direction you choose, even if the water has to flow over obstacles, up walls, or in other unlikely directions. The water in the area moves as you direct it, but once it moves beyond the spell's area, it resumes its flow based on the terrain conditions. The water continues to move in the direction you chose until the spell ends or you choose a different effect.

Whirlpool. This effect requires a body of water at least 50 feet square and 25 feet deep. You cause a whirlpool to form in the center of the area. The whirlpool forms a vortex that is 5 feet wide at the base, up to 50 feet wide at the top, and 25 feet tall. Any creature or object in the water and within 25 feet of the vortex is pulled 10 feet toward it. A creature can swim away from the vortex by making a Strength (Athletics) check against your spell save DC.

When a creature enters the vortex for the first time on a turn or starts its turn there, it must make a Strength saving throw. On a failed save, the creature takes 2d8 bludgeoning damage and is caught in the vortex until the spell ends. On a successful save, the creature takes half damage, and isn't caught in the vortex. A creature caught in the vortex can use its action to try to swim away from the vortex as described above, but has disadvantage on the Strength (Athletics) check to do so.

The first time each turn that an object enters the vortex, the object takes 2d8 bludgeoning damage; this damage occurs each round it remains in the vortex.

CONTROL WEATHER
8th-level transmutation

Casting Time: 10 minutes
Range: Self (5-mile radius)
Components: V, S, M (burning incense and bits of earth and wood mixed in water)
Duration: Concentration, up to 8 hours

You take control of the weather within 5 miles of you for the duration. You must be outdoors to cast this spell. Moving to a place where you don't have a clear path to the sky ends the spell early.

When you cast the spell, you change the current weather conditions, which are determined by the DM based on the climate and season. You can change precipitation, temperature, and wind. It takes 1d4 × 10 minutes for the new conditions to take effect. Once they do so, you can change the conditions again. When the spell ends, the weather gradually returns to normal.

When you change the weather conditions, find a current condition on the following tables and change its stage by one, up or down. When changing the wind, you can change its direction.

PRECIPITATION

Stage	Condition
1	Clear
2	Light clouds
3	Overcast or ground fog
4	Rain, hail, or snow
5	Torrential rain, driving hail, or blizzard

TEMPERATURE

Stage	Condition
1	Unbearable heat
2	Hot
3	Warm
4	Cool
5	Cold
6	Arctic cold

WIND

Stage	Condition
1	Calm
2	Moderate wind
3	Strong wind
4	Gale
5	Storm

CORDON OF ARROWS
2nd-level transmutation

Casting Time: 1 action
Range: 5 feet
Components: V, S, M (four or more arrows or bolts)
Duration: 8 hours

You plant four pieces of nonmagical ammunition—arrows or crossbow bolts—in the ground within range and lay magic upon them to protect an area. Until the spell ends, whenever a creature other than you comes within 30 feet of the ammunition for the first time on a turn or ends its turn there, one piece of ammunition flies up to strike it. The creature must succeed on a Dexterity saving throw or take 1d6 piercing damage. The piece of ammunition is then destroyed. The spell ends when no ammunition remains.

When you cast this spell, you can designate any creatures you choose, and the spell ignores them.

At Higher Levels. When you cast this spell using a spell slot of 3rd level or higher, the amount of ammunition that can be affected increases by two for each slot level above 2nd.

COUNTERSPELL
3rd-level abjuration

Casting Time: 1 reaction, which you take when you see a creature within 60 feet of you casting a spell
Range: 60 feet
Components: S
Duration: Instantaneous

You attempt to interrupt a creature in the process of casting a spell. If the creature is casting a spell of 3rd level or lower, its spell fails and has no effect. If it is casting a spell of 4th level or higher, make an ability check using your spellcasting ability. The DC equals 10 + the spell's level. On a success, the creature's spell fails and has no effect.

At Higher Levels. When you cast this spell using a spell slot of 4th level or higher, the interrupted spell has no effect if its level is less than or equal to the level of the spell slot you used.

CREATE FOOD AND WATER
3rd-level conjuration

Casting Time: 1 action
Range: 30 feet
Components: V, S
Duration: Instantaneous

You create 45 pounds of food and 30 gallons of water on the ground or in containers within range, enough to sustain up to fifteen humanoids or five steeds for 24 hours. The food is bland but nourishing, and spoils if uneaten after 24 hours. The water is clean and doesn't go bad.

CREATE OR DESTROY WATER
1st-level transmutation

Casting Time: 1 action
Range: 30 feet
Components: V, S, M (a drop of water if creating water or a few grains of sand if destroying it)
Duration: Instantaneous

You either create or destroy water.

Create Water. You create up to 10 gallons of clean water within range in an open container. Alternatively, the water falls as rain in a 30-foot cube within range, extinguishing exposed flames in the area.

Destroy Water. You destroy up to 10 gallons of water in an open container within range. Alternatively, you destroy fog in a 30-foot cube within range.

At Higher Levels. When you cast this spell using a spell slot of 2nd level or higher, you create or destroy 10 additional gallons of water, or the size of the cube increases by 5 feet, for each slot level above 1st.

CREATE UNDEAD
6th-level necromancy

Casting Time: 1 minute
Range: 10 feet
Components: V, S, M (one clay pot filled with grave dirt, one clay pot filled with brackish water, and one 150 gp black onyx stone for each corpse)
Duration: Instantaneous

You can cast this spell only at night. Choose up to three corpses of Medium or Small humanoids within range. Each corpse becomes a ghoul under your control. (The DM has game statistics for these creatures.)

As a bonus action on each of your turns, you can mentally command any creature you animated with this spell if the creature is within 120 feet of you (if you control multiple creatures, you can command any or all of them at the same time, issuing the same command to each one). You decide what action the creature will take and where it will move during its next turn, or you can issue a general command, such as to guard a particular chamber or corridor. If you issue no commands, the creature only defends itself against hostile creatures. Once given an order, the creature continues to follow it until its task is complete.

The creature is under your control for 24 hours, after which it stops obeying any command you have given it. To maintain control of the creature for another 24 hours, you must cast this spell on the creature before the current 24-hour period ends. This use of the spell reasserts your control over up to three creatures you have animated with this spell, rather than animating new ones.

At Higher Levels. When you cast this spell using a 7th-level spell slot, you can animate or reassert control over four ghouls. When you cast this spell using an 8th-level spell slot, you can animate or reassert control over five ghouls or two ghasts or wights. When you cast this spell using a 9th-level spell slot, you can animate or reassert control over six ghouls, three ghasts or wights, or two mummies.

CREATION
5th-level illusion

Casting Time: 1 minute
Range: 30 feet
Components: V, S, M (a tiny piece of matter of the same type of the item you plan to create)
Duration: Special

You pull wisps of shadow material from the Shadowfell to create a nonliving object of vegetable matter within range: soft goods, rope, wood, or something similar. You can also use this spell to create mineral objects such as stone, crystal, or metal. The object created must be no larger than a 5-foot cube, and the object must be of a form and material that you have seen before.

The duration depends on the object's material. If the object is composed of multiple materials, use the shortest duration.

Material	Duration
Vegetable matter	1 day
Stone or crystal	12 hours
Precious metals	1 hour
Gems	10 minutes
Adamantine or mithral	1 minute

Using any material created by this spell as another spell's material component causes that spell to fail.

At Higher Levels. When you cast this spell using a spell slot of 6th level or higher, the cube increases by 5 feet for each slot level above 5th.

CROWN OF MADNESS
2nd-level enchantment

Casting Time: 1 action
Range: 120 feet
Components: V, S
Duration: Concentration, up to 1 minute

One humanoid of your choice that you can see within range must succeed on a Wisdom saving throw or become charmed by you for the duration. While the target is charmed in this way, a twisted crown of jagged iron appears on its head, and a madness glows in its eyes.

The charmed target must use its action before moving on each of its turns to make a melee attack against a creature other than itself that you mentally choose.

The target can act normally on its turn if you choose no creature or if none are within its reach.

On your subsequent turns, you must use your action to maintain control over the target, or the spell ends. Also, the target can make a Wisdom saving throw at the end of each of its turns. On a success, the spell ends.

CRUSADER'S MANTLE
3rd-level evocation

Casting Time: 1 action
Range: Self
Components: V
Duration: Concentration, up to 1 minute

Holy power radiates from you in an aura with a 30-foot radius, awakening boldness in friendly creatures. Until the spell ends, the aura moves with you, centered on you. While in the aura, each nonhostile creature in the aura (including you) deals an extra 1d4 radiant damage when it hits with a weapon attack.

CURE WOUNDS
1st-level evocation

Casting Time: 1 action
Range: Touch
Components: V, S
Duration: Instantaneous

A creature you touch regains a number of hit points equal to 1d8 + your spellcasting ability modifier. This spell has no effect on undead or constructs.

At Higher Levels. When you cast this spell using a spell slot of 2nd level or higher, the healing increases by 1d8 for each slot level above 1st.

DANCING LIGHTS
Evocation cantrip

Casting Time: 1 action
Range: 120 feet
Components: V, S, M (a bit of phosphorus or wychwood, or a glowworm)
Duration: Concentration, up to 1 minute

You create up to four torch-sized lights within range, making them appear as torches, lanterns, or glowing orbs that hover in the air for the duration. You can also combine the four lights into one glowing vaguely humanoid form of Medium size. Whichever form you choose, each light sheds dim light in a 10-foot radius.

As a bonus action on your turn, you can move the lights up to 60 feet to a new spot within range. A light must be within 20 feet of another light created by this spell, and a light winks out if it exceeds the spell's range.

DARKNESS
2nd-level evocation

Casting Time: 1 action
Range: 60 feet
Components: V, M (bat fur and a drop of pitch or piece of coal)
Duration: Concentration, up to 10 minutes

Magical darkness spreads from a point you choose within range to fill a 15-foot-radius sphere for the duration. The darkness spreads around corners. A creature with darkvision can't see through this darkness, and nonmagical light can't illuminate it.

If the point you choose is on an object you are holding or one that isn't being worn or carried, the darkness emanates from the object and moves with it. Completely covering the source of the darkness with an opaque object, such as a bowl or a helm, blocks the darkness.

If any of this spell's area overlaps with an area of light created by a spell of 2nd level or lower, the spell that created the light is dispelled.

DARKVISION
2nd-level transmutation

Casting Time: 1 action
Range: Touch
Components: V, S, M (either a pinch of dried carrot or an agate)
Duration: 8 hours

You touch a willing creature to grant it the ability to see in the dark. For the duration, that creature has darkvision out to a range of 60 feet.

DAYLIGHT
3rd-level evocation

Casting Time: 1 action
Range: 60 feet
Components: V, S
Duration: 1 hour

A 60-foot-radius sphere of light spreads out from a point you choose within range. The sphere is bright light and sheds dim light for an additional 60 feet.

If you chose a point on an object you are holding or one that isn't being worn or carried, the light shines from the object and moves with it. Completely covering the affected object with an opaque object, such as a bowl or a helm, blocks the light.

If any of this spell's area overlaps with an area of darkness created by a spell of 3rd level or lower, the spell that created the darkness is dispelled.

DEATH WARD
4th-level abjuration

Casting Time: 1 action
Range: Touch
Components: V, S
Duration: 8 hours

You touch a creature and grant it a measure of protection from death.

The first time the target would drop to 0 hit points as a result of taking damage, the target instead drops to 1 hit point, and the spell ends.

If the spell is still in effect when the target is subjected to an effect that would kill it instantaneously without dealing damage, that effect is instead negated against the target, and the spell ends.

DELAYED BLAST FIREBALL
7th-level evocation

Casting Time: 1 action

Range: 150 feet
Components: V, S, M (a tiny ball of bat guano and sulfur)
Duration: Concentration, up to 1 minute

A beam of yellow light flashes from your pointing finger, then condenses to linger at a chosen point within range as a glowing bead for the duration. When the spell ends, either because your concentration is broken or because you decide to end it, the bead blossoms with a low roar into an explosion of flame that spreads around corners. Each creature in a 20-foot-radius sphere centered on that point must make a Dexterity saving throw. A creature takes fire damage equal to the total accumulated damage on a failed save, or half as much damage on a successful one.

The spell's base damage is 12d6. If at the end of your turn the bead has not yet detonated, the damage increases by 1d6.

If the glowing bead is touched before the interval has expired, the creature touching it must make a Dexterity saving throw. On a failed save, the spell ends immediately, causing the bead to erupt in flame. On a successful save, the creature can throw the bead up to 40 feet. When it strikes a creature or a solid object, the spell ends, and the bead explodes.

The fire damages objects in the area and ignites flammable objects that aren't being worn or carried.

At Higher Levels. When you cast this spell using a spell slot of 8th level or higher, the base damage increases by 1d6 for each slot level above 7th.

DEMIPLANE
8th-level conjuration

Casting Time: 1 action
Range: 60 feet
Components: S
Duration: 1 hour

You create a shadowy door on a flat solid surface that you can see within range. The door is large enough to allow Medium creatures to pass through unhindered. When opened, the door leads to a demiplane that appears to be an empty room 30 feet in each dimension, made of wood or stone. When the spell ends, the door disappears, and any creatures or objects inside the demiplane remain trapped there, as the door also disappears from the other side.

Each time you cast this spell, you can create a new demiplane, or have the shadowy door connect to a demiplane you created with a previous casting of this spell. Additionally, if you know the nature and contents of a demiplane created by a casting of this spell by another creature, you can have the shadowy door connect to its demiplane instead.

DESTRUCTIVE WAVE
5th-level evocation

Casting Time: 1 action
Range: Self (30-foot radius)
Components: V
Duration: Instantaneous

You strike the ground, creating a burst of divine energy that ripples outward from you. Each creature you choose within 30 feet of you must succeed on a Constitution saving throw or take 5d6 thunder damage, as well as 5d6 radiant or necrotic damage (your choice), and be knocked prone. A creature that succeeds on its saving throw takes half as much damage and isn't knocked prone.

DETECT EVIL AND GOOD
1st-level divination

Casting Time: 1 action
Range: Self
Components: V, S
Duration: Concentration, up to 10 minutes

For the duration, you know if there is an aberration, celestial, elemental, fey, fiend, or undead within 30 feet of you, as well as where the creature is located. Similarly, you know if there is a place or object within 30 feet of you that has been magically consecrated or desecrated.

The spell can penetrate most barriers, but it is blocked by 1 foot of stone, 1 inch of common metal, a thin sheet of lead, or 3 feet of wood or dirt.

DETECT MAGIC
1st-level divination (ritual)

Casting Time: 1 action
Range: Self
Components: V, S
Duration: Concentration, up to 10 minutes

For the duration, you sense the presence of magic within 30 feet of you. If you sense magic in this way, you can use your action to see a faint aura around any visible creature or object in the area that bears magic, and you learn its school of magic, if any.

The spell can penetrate most barriers, but it is blocked by 1 foot of stone, 1 inch of common metal, a thin sheet of lead, or 3 feet of wood or dirt.

DETECT POISON AND DISEASE
1st-level divination (ritual)

Casting Time: 1 action
Range: Self
Components: V, S, M (a yew leaf)
Duration: Concentration, up to 10 minutes

For the duration, you can sense the presence and location of poisons, poisonous creatures, and diseases within 30 feet of you. You also identify the kind of poison, poisonous creature, or disease in each case.

The spell can penetrate most barriers, but it is blocked by 1 foot of stone, 1 inch of common metal, a thin sheet of lead, or 3 feet of wood or dirt.

DETECT THOUGHTS
2nd-level divination

Casting Time: 1 action
Range: Self
Components: V, S, M (a copper piece)
Duration: Concentration, up to 1 minute

For the duration, you can read the thoughts of certain creatures. When you cast the spell and as your action on each turn until the spell ends, you can focus your mind on any one creature that you can see within 30 feet of you. If the creature you choose has an Intelligence of 3 or lower or doesn't speak any language, the creature is unaffected.

You initially learn the surface thoughts of the creature—what is most on its mind in that moment. As an action, you can either shift your attention to another creature's thoughts or attempt to probe deeper into the same creature's mind. If you probe deeper, the target must make a Wisdom saving throw. If it fails, you gain insight into its reasoning (if any), its emotional state, and something that looms large in its mind (such as something it worries over, loves, or hates). If it succeeds, the spell ends. Either way, the target knows that you are probing into its mind, and unless you shift your attention to another creature's thoughts, the creature can use its action on its turn to make an Intelligence check contested by your Intelligence check; if it succeeds, the spell ends.

Questions verbally directed at the target creature naturally shape the course of its thoughts, so this spell is particularly effective as part of an interrogation.

You can also use this spell to detect the presence of thinking creatures you can't see. When you cast the spell or as your action during the duration, you can search for thoughts within 30 feet of you. The spell can penetrate barriers, but 2 feet of rock, 2 inches of any metal other than lead, or a thin sheet of lead blocks you. You can't detect a creature with an Intelligence of 3 or lower or one that doesn't speak any language.

Once you detect the presence of a creature in this way, you can read its thoughts for the rest of the duration as described above, even if you can't see it, but it must still be within range.

DIMENSION DOOR
4th-level conjuration

Casting Time: 1 action
Range: 500 feet
Components: V
Duration: Instantaneous

You teleport yourself from your current location to any other spot within range. You arrive at exactly the spot desired. It can be a place you can see, one you can visualize, or one you can describe by stating distance and direction, such as "200 feet straight downward" or "upward to the northwest at a 45-degree angle, 300 feet."

You can bring along objects as long as their weight doesn't exceed what you can carry. You can also bring one willing creature of your size or smaller who is carrying gear up to its carrying capacity. The creature must be within 5 feet of you when you cast this spell.

If you would arrive in a place already occupied by an object or a creature, you and any creature traveling with you each take 4d6 force damage, and the spell fails to teleport you.

DISGUISE SELF
1st-level illusion

Casting Time: 1 action
Range: Self
Components: V, S
Duration: 1 hour

You make yourself—including your clothing, armor, weapons, and other belongings on your person—look different until the spell ends or until you use your action to dismiss it. You can seem 1 foot shorter or taller and can appear thin, fat, or in between. You can't change your body type, so you must adopt a form that has the same basic arrangement of limbs. Otherwise, the extent of the illusion is up to you.

The changes wrought by this spell fail to hold up to physical inspection. For example, if you use this spell to add a hat to your outfit, objects pass through the hat, and anyone who touches it would feel nothing or would feel your head and hair. If you use this spell to appear thinner than you are, the hand of someone who reaches out to touch you would bump into you while it was seemingly still in midair.

To discern that you are disguised, a creature can use its action to inspect your appearance and must succeed on an Intelligence (Investigation) check against your spell save DC.

DISINTEGRATE
6th-level transmutation

Casting Time: 1 action
Range: 60 feet
Components: V, S, M (a lodestone and a pinch of dust)
Duration: Instantaneous

A thin green ray springs from your pointing finger to a target that you can see within range. The target can be a creature, an object, or a creation of magical force, such as the wall created by *wall of force*.

A creature targeted by this spell must make a Dexterity saving throw. On a failed save, the target takes 10d6 + 40 force damage. If this damage reduces the target to 0 hit points, it is disintegrated.

A disintegrated creature and everything it is wearing and carrying, except magic items, are reduced to a pile of fine gray dust. The creature can be restored to life only by means of a *true resurrection* or a *wish* spell.

This spell automatically disintegrates a Large or smaller nonmagical object or a creation of magical force. If the target is a Huge or larger object or creation of force, this spell disintegrates a 10-foot-cube portion of it. A magic item is unaffected by this spell.

At Higher Levels. When you cast this spell using a spell slot of 7th level or higher, the damage increases by 3d6 for each slot level above 6th.

DISPEL EVIL AND GOOD
5th-level abjuration

Casting Time: 1 action
Range: Self

Components: V, S, M (holy water or powdered silver and iron)
Duration: Concentration, up to 1 minute

Shimmering energy surrounds and protects you from fey, undead, and creatures originating from beyond the Material Plane. For the duration, celestials, elementals, fey, fiends, and undead have disadvantage on attack rolls against you.

You can end the spell early by using either of the following special functions.

Break Enchantment. As your action, you touch a creature you can reach that is charmed, frightened, or possessed by a celestial, an elemental, a fey, a fiend, or an undead. The creature you touch is no longer charmed, frightened, or possessed by such creatures.

Dismissal. As your action, make a melee spell attack against a celestial, an elemental, a fey, a fiend, or an undead you can reach. On a hit, you attempt to drive the creature back to its home plane. The creature must succeed on a Charisma saving throw or be sent back to its home plane (if it isn't there already). If they aren't on their home plane, undead are sent to the Shadowfell, and fey are sent to the Feywild.

DISPEL MAGIC
3rd-level abjuration

Casting Time: 1 action
Range: 120 feet
Components: V, S
Duration: Instantaneous

Choose one creature, object, or magical effect within range. Any spell of 3rd level or lower on the target ends. For each spell of 4th level or higher on the target, make an ability check using your spellcasting ability. The DC equals 10 + the spell's level. On a successful check, the spell ends.

At Higher Levels. When you cast this spell using a spell slot of 4th level or higher, you automatically end the effects of a spell on the target if the spell's level is equal to or less than the level of the spell slot you used.

DISSONANT WHISPERS
1st-level enchantment

Casting Time: 1 action
Range: 60 feet
Components: V
Duration: Instantaneous

You whisper a discordant melody that only one creature of your choice within range can hear, wracking it with terrible pain. The target must make a Wisdom saving throw. On a failed save, it takes 3d6 psychic damage and must immediately use its reaction, if available, to move as far as its speed allows away from you. The creature doesn't move into obviously dangerous ground, such as a fire or a pit. On a successful save, the target takes half as much damage and doesn't have to move away. A deafened creature automatically succeeds on the save.

At Higher Levels. When you cast this spell using a spell slot of 2nd level or higher, the damage increases by 1d6 for each slot level above 1st.

DIVINATION
4th-level divination (ritual)

Casting Time: 1 action
Range: Self
Components: V, S, M (incense and a sacrificial offering appropriate to your religion, together worth at least 25 gp, which the spell consumes)
Duration: Instantaneous

Your magic and an offering put you in contact with a god or a god's servants. You ask a single question concerning a specific goal, event, or activity to occur within 7 days. The DM offers a truthful reply. The reply might be a short phrase, a cryptic rhyme, or an omen.

The spell doesn't take into account any possible circumstances that might change the outcome, such as the casting of additional spells or the loss or gain of a companion.

If you cast the spell two or more times before finishing your next long rest, there is a cumulative 25 percent chance for each casting after the first that you get a random reading. The DM makes this roll in secret.

DIVINE FAVOR
1st-level evocation

Casting Time: 1 bonus action
Range: Self
Components: V, S
Duration: Concentration, up to 1 minute

Your prayer empowers you with divine radiance. Until the spell ends, your weapon attacks deal an extra 1d4 radiant damage on a hit.

DIVINE WORD
7th-level evocation

Casting Time: 1 bonus action
Range: 30 feet
Components: V
Duration: Instantaneous

You utter a divine word, imbued with the power that shaped the world at the dawn of creation. Choose any number of creatures you can see within range. Each creature that can hear you must make a Charisma saving throw. On a failed save, a creature suffers an effect based on its current hit points:

- 50 hit points or fewer: deafened for 1 minute
- 40 hit points or fewer: deafened and blinded for 10 minutes
- 30 hit points or fewer: blinded, deafened, and stunned for 1 hour
- 20 hit points or fewer: killed instantly

Regardless of its current hit points, a celestial, an elemental, a fey, or a fiend that fails its save is forced back to its plane of origin (if it isn't there already) and can't return to your current plane for 24 hours by any means short of a *wish* spell.

DOMINATE BEAST
4th-level enchantment

Casting Time: 1 action

Range: 60 feet
Components: V, S
Duration: Concentration, up to 1 minute

You attempt to beguile a beast that you can see within range. It must succeed on a Wisdom saving throw or be charmed by you for the duration. If you or creatures that are friendly to you are fighting it, it has advantage on the saving throw.

While the beast is charmed, you have a telepathic link with it as long as the two of you are on the same plane of existence. You can use this telepathic link to issue commands to the creature while you are conscious (no action required), which it does its best to obey. You can specify a simple and general course of action, such as "Attack that creature," "Run over there," or "Fetch that object." If the creature completes the order and doesn't receive further direction from you, it defends and preserves itself to the best of its ability.

You can use your action to take total and precise control of the target. Until the end of your next turn, the creature takes only the actions you choose, and doesn't do anything that you don't allow it to do. During this time, you can also cause the creature to use a reaction, but this requires you to use your own reaction as well.

Each time the target takes damage, it makes a new Wisdom saving throw against the spell. If the saving throw succeeds, the spell ends.

At Higher Levels. When you cast this spell with a 5th-level spell slot, the duration is concentration, up to 10 minutes. When you use a 6th-level spell slot, the duration is concentration, up to 1 hour. When you use a spell slot of 7th level or higher, the duration is concentration, up to 8 hours.

DOMINATE MONSTER
8th-level enchantment

Casting Time: 1 action
Range: 60 feet
Components: V, S
Duration: Concentration, up to 1 hour

You attempt to beguile a creature that you can see within range. It must succeed on a Wisdom saving throw or be charmed by you for the duration. If you or creatures that are friendly to you are fighting it, it has advantage on the saving throw.

While the creature is charmed, you have a telepathic link with it as long as the two of you are on the same plane of existence. You can use this telepathic link to issue commands to the creature while you are conscious (no action required), which it does its best to obey. You can specify a simple and general course of action, such as "Attack that creature," "Run over there," or "Fetch that object." If the creature completes the order and doesn't receive further direction from you, it defends and preserves itself to the best of its ability.

You can use your action to take total and precise control of the target. Until the end of your next turn, the creature takes only the actions you choose, and doesn't do anything that you don't allow it to do. During this time, you can also cause the creature to use a reaction, but this requires you to use your own reaction as well.

Each time the target takes damage, it makes a new Wisdom saving throw against the spell. If the saving throw succeeds, the spell ends.

At Higher Levels. When you cast this spell with a 9th-level spell slot, the duration is concentration, up to 8 hours.

DOMINATE PERSON
5th-level enchantment

Casting Time: 1 action
Range: 60 feet
Components: V, S
Duration: Concentration, up to 1 minute

You attempt to beguile a humanoid that you can see within range. It must succeed on a Wisdom saving throw or be charmed by you for the duration. If you or creatures that are friendly to you are fighting it, it has advantage on the saving throw.

While the target is charmed, you have a telepathic link with it as long as the two of you are on the same plane of existence. You can use this telepathic link to issue commands to the creature while you are conscious (no action required), which it does its best to obey. You can specify a simple and general course of action, such as "Attack that creature," "Run over there," or "Fetch that object." If the creature completes the order and doesn't receive further direction from you, it defends and preserves itself to the best of its ability.

You can use your action to take total and precise control of the target. Until the end of your next turn, the creature takes only the actions you choose, and doesn't do anything that you don't allow it to do. During this time you can also cause the creature to use a reaction, but this requires you to use your own reaction as well.

Each time the target takes damage, it makes a new Wisdom saving throw against the spell. If the saving throw succeeds, the spell ends.

At Higher Levels. When you cast this spell using a 6th-level spell slot, the duration is concentration, up to 10 minutes. When you use a 7th-level spell slot, the duration is concentration, up to 1 hour. When you use a spell slot of 8th level or higher, the duration is concentration, up to 8 hours.

DRAWMIJ'S INSTANT SUMMONS
6th-level conjuration (ritual)

Casting Time: 1 minute
Range: Touch
Components: V, S, M (a sapphire worth 1,000 gp)
Duration: Until dispelled

You touch an object weighing 10 pounds or less whose longest dimension is 6 feet or less. The spell leaves an invisible mark on its surface and invisibly inscribes the name of the item on the sapphire you use as the material component. Each time you cast this spell, you must use a different sapphire.

At any time thereafter, you can use your action to speak the item's name and crush the sapphire. The item instantly appears in your hand regardless of physical or planar distances, and the spell ends.

If another creature is holding or carrying the item, crushing the sapphire doesn't transport the item to you, but instead you learn who the creature possessing the object is and roughly where that creature is located at that moment.

Dispel magic or a similar effect successfully applied to the sapphire ends this spell's effect.

DREAM
5th-level illusion

Casting Time: 1 minute
Range: Special
Components: V, S, M (a handful of sand, a dab of ink, and a writing quill plucked from a sleeping bird)
Duration: 8 hours

This spell shapes a creature's dreams. Choose a creature known to you as the target of this spell. The target must be on the same plane of existence as you. Creatures that don't sleep, such as elves, can't be contacted by this spell. You, or a willing creature you touch, enters a trance state, acting as a messenger. While in the trance, the messenger is aware of his or her surroundings, but can't take actions or move.

If the target is asleep, the messenger appears in the target's dreams and can converse with the target as long as it remains asleep, through the duration of the spell. The messenger can also shape the environment of the dream, creating landscapes, objects, and other images. The messenger can emerge from the trance at any time, ending the effect of the spell early. The target recalls the dream perfectly upon waking. If the target is awake when you cast the spell, the messenger knows it, and can either end the trance (and the spell) or wait for the target to fall asleep, at which point the messenger appears in the target's dreams.

You can make the messenger appear monstrous and terrifying to the target. If you do, the messenger can deliver a message of no more than ten words and then the target must make a Wisdom saving throw. On a failed save, echoes of the phantasmal monstrosity spawn a nightmare that lasts the duration of the target's sleep and prevents the target from gaining any benefit from that rest. In addition, when the target wakes up, it takes 3d6 psychic damage.

If you have a body part, lock of hair, clipping from a nail, or similar portion of the target's body, the target makes its saving throw with disadvantage.

DRUIDCRAFT
Transmutation cantrip

Casting Time: 1 action
Range: 30 feet
Components: V, S
Duration: Instantaneous

Whispering to the spirits of nature, you create one of the following effects within range:

- You create a tiny, harmless sensory effect that predicts what the weather will be at your location for the next 24 hours. The effect might manifest as a golden orb for clear skies, a cloud for rain, falling snowflakes for snow, and so on. This effect persists for 1 round.
- You instantly make a flower blossom, a seed pod open, or a leaf bud bloom.
- You create an instantaneous, harmless sensory effect, such as falling leaves, a puff of wind, the sound of a small animal, or the faint odor of skunk. The effect must fit in a 5-foot cube.
- You instantly light or snuff out a candle, a torch, or a small campfire.

EARTHQUAKE
8th-level evocation

Casting Time: 1 action
Range: 500 feet
Components: V, S, M (a pinch of dirt, a piece of rock, and a lump of clay)
Duration: Concentration, up to 1 minute

You create a seismic disturbance at a point on the ground that you can see within range. For the duration, an intense tremor rips through the ground in a 100-foot-radius circle centered on that point and shakes creatures and structures in contact with the ground in that area.

The ground in the area becomes difficult terrain. Each creature on the ground that is concentrating must make a Constitution saving throw. On a failed save, the creature's concentration is broken.

When you cast this spell and at the end of each turn you spend concentrating on it, each creature on the ground in the area must make a Dexterity saving throw. On a failed save, the creature is knocked prone.

This spell can have additional effects depending on the terrain in the area, as determined by the DM.

Fissures. Fissures open throughout the spell's area at the start of your next turn after you cast the spell. A total of 1d6 such fissures open in locations chosen by the DM. Each is 1d10 × 10 feet deep, 10 feet wide, and extends from one edge of the spell's area to the opposite side. A creature standing on a spot where a fissure opens must succeed on a Dexterity saving throw or fall in. A creature that successfully saves moves with the fissure's edge as it opens.

A fissure that opens beneath a structure causes it to automatically collapse (see below).

Structures. The tremor deals 50 bludgeoning damage to any structure in contact with the ground in the area when you cast the spell and at the start of each of your turns until the spell ends. If a structure drops to 0 hit points, it collapses and potentially damages nearby creatures. A creature within half the distance of a structure's height must make a Dexterity saving throw. On a failed save, the creature takes 5d6 bludgeoning damage, is knocked prone, and is buried in the rubble, requiring a DC 20 Strength (Athletics) check as an action to escape. The DM can adjust the DC higher or lower, depending on the nature of the rubble. On a successful save, the creature takes half as much damage and doesn't fall prone or become buried.

ELDRITCH BLAST
Evocation cantrip

Casting Time: 1 action
Range: 120 feet
Components: V, S
Duration: Instantaneous

A beam of crackling energy streaks toward a creature within range. Make a ranged spell attack against the target. On a hit, the target takes 1d10 force damage.

The spell creates more than one beam when you reach higher levels: two beams at 5th level, three beams at 11th level, and four beams at 17th level. You can direct the beams at the same target or at different ones. Make a separate attack roll for each beam.

ELEMENTAL WEAPON
3rd-level transmutation

Casting Time: 1 action
Range: Touch
Components: V, S
Duration: Concentration, up to 1 hour

A nonmagical weapon you touch becomes a magic weapon. Choose one of the following damage types: acid, cold, fire, lightning, or thunder. For the duration, the weapon has a +1 bonus to attack rolls and deals an extra 1d4 damage of the chosen type when it hits.

At Higher Levels. When you cast this spell using a spell slot of 5th or 6th level, the bonus to attack rolls increases to +2 and the extra damage increases to 2d4. When you use a spell slot of 7th level or higher, the bonus increases to +3 and the extra damage increases to 3d4.

ENHANCE ABILITY
2nd-level transmutation

Casting Time: 1 action
Range: Touch
Components: V, S, M (fur or a feather from a beast)
Duration: Concentration, up to 1 hour.

You touch a creature and bestow upon it a magical enhancement. Choose one of the following effects; the target gains that effect until the spell ends.

Bear's Endurance. The target has advantage on Constitution checks. It also gains 2d6 temporary hit points, which are lost when the spell ends.

Bull's Strength. The target has advantage on Strength checks, and his or her carrying capacity doubles.

Cat's Grace. The target has advantage on Dexterity checks. It also doesn't take damage from falling 20 feet or less if it isn't incapacitated.

Eagle's Splendor. The target has advantage on Charisma checks.

Fox's Cunning. The target has advantage on Intelligence checks.

Owl's Wisdom. The target has advantage on Wisdom checks.

At Higher Levels. When you cast this spell using a spell slot of 3rd level or higher, you can target one additional creature for each slot level above 2nd.

ENLARGE/REDUCE
2nd-level transmutation

Casting Time: 1 action
Range: 30 feet
Components: V, S, M (a pinch of powdered iron)
Duration: Concentration, up to 1 minute

You cause a creature or an object you can see within range to grow larger or smaller for the duration. Choose either a creature or an object that is neither worn nor carried. If the target is unwilling, it can make a Constitution saving throw. On a success, the spell has no effect.

If the target is a creature, everything it is wearing and carrying changes size with it. Any item dropped by an affected creature returns to normal size at once.

Enlarge. The target's size doubles in all dimensions, and its weight is multiplied by eight. This growth increases its size by one category—from Medium to Large, for example. If there isn't enough room for the target to double its size, the creature or object attains the maximum possible size in the space available. Until the spell ends, the target also has advantage on Strength checks and Strength saving throws. The target's weapons also grow to match its new size. While these weapons are enlarged, the target's attacks with them deal 1d4 extra damage.

Reduce. The target's size is halved in all dimensions, and its weight is reduced to one-eighth of normal. This reduction decreases its size by one category—from Medium to Small, for example. Until the spell ends, the target also has disadvantage on Strength checks and Strength saving throws. The target's weapons also shrink to match its new size. While these weapons are reduced, the target's attacks with them deal 1d4 less damage (this can't reduce the damage below 1).

ENSNARING STRIKE
1st-level conjuration

Casting Time: 1 bonus action
Range: Self
Components: V
Duration: Concentration, up to 1 minute

The next time you hit a creature with a weapon attack before this spell ends, a writhing mass of thorny vines appears at the point of impact, and the target must succeed on a Strength saving throw or be restrained by the magical vines until the spell ends. A Large or larger creature has advantage on this saving throw. If the target succeeds on the save, the vines shrivel away.

While restrained by this spell, the target takes 1d6 piercing damage at the start of each of its turns. A creature restrained by the vines or one that can touch the creature can use its action to make a Strength check against your spell save DC. On a success, the target is freed.

At Higher Levels. If you cast this spell using a spell slot of 2nd level or higher, the damage increases by 1d6 for each slot level above 1st.

ENTANGLE
1st-level conjuration

Casting Time: 1 action
Range: 90 feet
Components: V, S
Duration: Concentration, up to 1 minute

Grasping weeds and vines sprout from the ground in a 20-foot square starting from a point within range. For the duration, these plants turn the ground in the area into difficult terrain.

A creature in the area when you cast the spell must succeed on a Strength saving throw or be restrained by the entangling plants until the spell ends. A creature restrained by the plants can use its action to make a Strength check against your spell save DC. On a success, it frees itself.

When the spell ends, the conjured plants wilt away.

ENTHRALL
2nd-level enchantment

Casting Time: 1 action
Range: 60 feet
Components: V, S
Duration: 1 minute

You weave a distracting string of words, causing creatures of your choice that you can see within range and that can hear you to make a Wisdom saving throw. Any creature that can't be charmed succeeds on this saving throw automatically, and if you or your companions are fighting a creature, it has advantage on the save. On a failed save, the target has disadvantage on Wisdom (Perception) checks made to perceive any creature other than you until the spell ends or until the target can no longer hear you. The spell ends if you are incapacitated or can no longer speak.

ETHEREALNESS
7th-level transmutation

Casting Time: 1 action
Range: Self
Components: V, S
Duration: Up to 8 hours

You step into the border regions of the Ethereal Plane, in the area where it overlaps with your current plane. You remain in the Border Ethereal for the duration or until you use your action to dismiss the spell. During this time, you can move in any direction. If you move up or down, every foot of movement costs an extra foot. You can see and hear the plane you originated from, but everything there looks gray, and you can't see anything more than 60 feet away.

While on the Ethereal Plane, you can only affect and be affected by other creatures on that plane. Creatures that aren't on the Ethereal Plane can't perceive you and can't interact with you, unless a special ability or magic has given them the ability to do so.

You ignore all objects and effects that aren't on the Ethereal Plane, allowing you to move through objects you perceive on the plane you originated from.

When the spell ends, you immediately return to the plane you originated from in the spot you currently occupy. If you occupy the same spot as a solid object or creature when this happens, you are immediately shunted to the nearest unoccupied space that you can occupy and take force damage equal to twice the number of feet you are moved.

This spell has no effect if you cast it while you are on the Ethereal Plane or a plane that doesn't border it, such as one of the Outer Planes.

At Higher Levels. When you cast this spell using a spell slot of 8th level or higher, you can target up to three willing creatures (including you) for each slot level above 7th. The creatures must be within 10 feet of you when you cast the spell.

EVARD'S BLACK TENTACLES
4th-level conjuration

Casting Time: 1 action
Range: 90 feet
Components: V, S, M (a piece of tentacle from a giant octopus or a giant squid)
Duration: Concentration, up to 1 minute

Squirming, ebony tentacles fill a 20-foot square on ground that you can see within range. For the duration, these tentacles turn the ground in the area into difficult terrain.

When a creature enters the affected area for the first time on a turn or starts its turn there, the creature must succeed on a Dexterity saving throw or take 3d6 bludgeoning damage and be restrained by the tentacles until the spell ends. A creature that starts its turn in the area and is already restrained by the tentacles takes 3d6 bludgeoning damage.

A creature restrained by the tentacles can use its action to make a Strength or Dexterity check (its choice) against your spell save DC. On a success, it frees itself.

EXPEDITIOUS RETREAT
1st-level transmutation

Casting Time: 1 bonus action
Range: Self
Components: V, S
Duration: Concentration, up to 10 minutes

This spell allows you to move at an incredible pace. When you cast this spell, and then as a bonus action on each of your turns until the spell ends, you can take the Dash action.

EYEBITE
6th-level necromancy

Casting Time: 1 action
Range: Self
Components: V, S
Duration: Concentration, up to 1 minute

For the spell's duration, your eyes become an inky void imbued with dread power. One creature of your choice within 60 feet of you that you can see must succeed on a Wisdom saving throw or be affected by one of the following effects of your choice for the duration. On each of your turns until the spell ends, you can use your action to target another creature but can't target a creature again if it has succeeded on a saving throw against this casting of *eyebite*.

Asleep. The target falls unconscious. It wakes up if it takes any damage or if another creature uses its action to shake the sleeper awake.

Panicked. The target is frightened of you. On each of its turns, the frightened creature must take the Dash action and move away from you by the safest and shortest available route, unless there is nowhere to move. If the target moves to a place at least 60 feet away from you where it can no longer see you, this effect ends.

Sickened. The target has disadvantage on attack rolls and ability checks. At the end of each of its turns, it can make another Wisdom saving throw. If it succeeds, the effect ends.

FABRICATE
4th-level transmutation

Casting Time: 10 minutes
Range: 120 feet
Components: V, S
Duration: Instantaneous

You convert raw materials into products of the same material. For example, you can fabricate a wooden bridge from a clump of trees, a rope from a patch of hemp, and clothes from flax or wool.

Choose raw materials that you can see within range. You can fabricate a Large or smaller object (contained within a 10-foot cube, or eight connected 5-foot cubes), given a sufficient quantity of raw material. If you are working with metal, stone, or another mineral substance, however, the fabricated object can be no larger than Medium (contained within a single 5-foot cube). The quality of objects made by the spell is commensurate with the quality of the raw materials.

Creatures or magic items can't be created or transmuted by this spell. You also can't use it to create items that ordinarily require a high degree of craftsmanship, such as jewelry, weapons, glass, or armor, unless you have proficiency with the type of artisan's tools used to craft such objects.

FAERIE FIRE
1st-level evocation

Casting Time: 1 action
Range: 60 feet
Components: V
Duration: Concentration, up to 1 minute

Each object in a 20-foot cube within range is outlined in blue, green, or violet light (your choice). Any creature in the area when the spell is cast is also outlined in light if it fails a Dexterity saving throw. For the duration, objects and affected creatures shed dim light in a 10-foot radius.

Any attack roll against an affected creature or object has advantage if the attacker can see it, and the affected creature or object can't benefit from being invisible.

FALSE LIFE
1st-level necromancy

Casting Time: 1 action
Range: Self
Components: V, S, M (a small amount of alcohol or distilled spirits)
Duration: 1 hour

Bolstering yourself with a necromantic facsimile of life, you gain 1d4 + 4 temporary hit points for the duration.

At Higher Levels. When you cast this spell using a spell slot of 2nd level or higher, you gain 5 additional temporary hit points for each slot level above 1st.

FEAR
3rd-level illusion

Casting Time: 1 action
Range: Self (30-foot cone)
Components: V, S, M (a white feather or the heart of a hen)
Duration: Concentration, up to 1 minute

You project a phantasmal image of a creature's worst fears. Each creature in a 30-foot cone must succeed on a Wisdom saving throw or drop whatever it is holding and become frightened for the duration.

While frightened by this spell, a creature must take the Dash action and move away from you by the safest available route on each of its turns, unless there is nowhere to move. If the creature ends its turn in a location where it doesn't have line of sight to you, the creature can make a Wisdom saving throw. On a successful save, the spell ends for that creature.

FEATHER FALL
1st-level transmutation

Casting Time: 1 reaction, which you take when you or a creature within 60 feet of you falls
Range: 60 feet
Components: V, M (a small feather or piece of down)
Duration: 1 minute

Choose up to five falling creatures within range. A falling creature's rate of descent slows to 60 feet per round until the spell ends. If the creature lands before the spell ends, it takes no falling damage and can land on its feet, and the spell ends for that creature.

FEEBLEMIND
8th-level enchantment

Casting Time: 1 action
Range: 150 feet
Components: V, S, M (a handful of clay, crystal, glass, or mineral spheres)
Duration: Instantaneous

You blast the mind of a creature that you can see within range, attempting to shatter its intellect and personality. The target takes 4d6 psychic damage and must make an Intelligence saving throw.

On a failed save, the creature's Intelligence and Charisma scores become 1. The creature can't cast spells, activate magic items, understand language, or communicate in any intelligible way. The creature can, however, identify its friends, follow them, and even protect them.

At the end of every 30 days, the creature can repeat its saving throw against this spell. If it succeeds on its saving throw, the spell ends.

The spell can also be ended by *greater restoration*, *heal*, or *wish*.

FEIGN DEATH
3rd-level necromancy (ritual)

Casting Time: 1 action
Range: Touch
Components: V, S, M (a pinch of graveyard dirt)
Duration: 1 hour

You touch a willing creature and put it into a cataleptic state that is indistinguishable from death.

For the spell's duration, or until you use an action to touch the target and dismiss the spell, the target appears dead to all outward inspection and to spells used to determine the target's status. The target is blinded and incapacitated, and its speed drops to 0. The target has resistance to all damage except psychic damage. If the target is diseased or poisoned when you cast the spell, or becomes diseased or poisoned while under the spell's effect, the disease and poison have no effect until the spell ends.

FIND FAMILIAR
1st-level conjuration (ritual)

Casting Time: 1 hour
Range: 10 feet
Components: V, S, M (10 gp worth of charcoal, incense, and herbs that must be consumed by fire in a brass brazier)
Duration: Instantaneous

You gain the service of a familiar, a spirit that takes an animal form you choose: bat, cat, crab, frog (toad), hawk, lizard, octopus, owl, poisonous snake, fish (quipper), rat, raven, sea horse, spider, or weasel. Appearing in an unoccupied space within range, the familiar has the statistics of the chosen form, though it is a celestial, fey, or fiend (your choice) instead of a beast.

Your familiar acts independently of you, but it always obeys your commands. In combat, it rolls its own initiative and acts on its own turn. A familiar can't attack, but it can take other actions as normal.

When the familiar drops to 0 hit points, it disappears, leaving behind no physical form. It reappears after you cast this spell again

While your familiar is within 100 feet of you, you can communicate with it telepathically. Additionally, as an action, you can see through your familiar's eyes and hear what it hears until the start of your next turn, gaining the benefits of any special senses that the familiar has. During this time, you are deaf and blind with regard to your own senses.

As an action, you can temporarily dismiss your familiar. It disappears into a pocket dimension where it awaits your summons. Alternatively, you can dismiss it forever. As an action while it is temporarily dismissed,

you can cause it to reappear in any unoccupied space within 30 feet of you.

You can't have more than one familiar at a time. If you cast this spell while you already have a familiar, you instead cause it to adopt a new form. Choose one of the forms from the above list. Your familiar transforms into the chosen creature.

Finally, when you cast a spell with a range of touch, your familiar can deliver the spell as if it had cast the spell. Your familiar must be within 100 feet of you, and it must use its reaction to deliver the spell when you cast it. If the spell requires an attack roll, you use your attack modifier for the roll.

FIND STEED
2nd-level conjuration

Casting Time: 10 minutes
Range: 30 feet
Components: V, S
Duration: Instantaneous

You summon a spirit that assumes the form of an unusually intelligent, strong, and loyal steed, creating a long-lasting bond with it. Appearing in an unoccupied space within range, the steed takes on a form that you choose: a warhorse, a pony, a camel, an elk, or a mastiff. (Your DM might allow other animals to be summoned as steeds.) The steed has the statistics of the chosen form, though it is a celestial, fey, or fiend (your choice) instead of its normal type. Additionally, if your steed has an Intelligence of 5 or less, its Intelligence becomes 6, and it gains the ability to understand one language of your choice that you speak.

Your steed serves you as a mount, both in combat and out, and you have an instinctive bond with it that allows you to fight as a seamless unit. While mounted on your steed, you can make any spell you cast that targets only you also target your steed.

When the steed drops to 0 hit points, it disappears, leaving behind no physical form. You can also dismiss your steed at any time as an action, causing it to disappear. In either case, casting this spell again summons the same steed, restored to its hit point maximum.

While your steed is within 1 mile of you, you can communicate with it telepathically.

You can't have more than one steed bonded by this spell at a time. As an action, you can release the steed from its bond at any time, causing it to disappear.

FIND THE PATH
6th-level divination

Casting Time: 1 minute
Range: Self
Components: V, S, M (a set of divinatory tools—such as bones, ivory sticks, cards, teeth, or carved runes—worth 100 gp and an object from the location you wish to find)
Duration: Concentration, up to 1 day

This spell allows you to find the shortest, most direct physical route to a specific fixed location that you are familiar with on the same plane of existence. If you

name a destination on another plane of existence, a
destination that moves (such as a mobile fortress), or a
destination that isn't specific (such as "a green dragon's
lair"), the spell fails.

For the duration, as long as you are on the same plane
of existence as the destination, you know how far it is
and in what direction it lies. While you are traveling
there, whenever you are presented with a choice of
paths along the way, you automatically determine which
path is the shortest and most direct route (but not
necessarily the safest route) to the destination.

FIND TRAPS
2nd-level divination

Casting Time: 1 action
Range: 120 feet
Components: V, S
Duration: Instantaneous

You sense the presence of any trap within range that
is within line of sight. A trap, for the purpose of this
spell, includes anything that would inflict a sudden or
unexpected effect you consider harmful or undesirable,
which was specifically intended as such by its creator.
Thus, the spell would sense an area affected by the
alarm spell, a *glyph of warding*, or a mechanical pit trap,
but it would not reveal a natural weakness in the floor,
an unstable ceiling, or a hidden sinkhole.

This spell merely reveals that a trap is present. You
don't learn the location of each trap, but you do learn the
general nature of the danger posed by a trap you sense.

FINGER OF DEATH
7th-level necromancy

Casting Time: 1 action
Range: 60 feet
Components: V, S
Duration: Instantaneous

You send negative energy coursing through a creature
that you can see within range, causing it searing pain.
The target must make a Constitution saving throw. It
takes 7d8 + 30 necrotic damage on a failed save, or half
as much damage on a successful one.

A humanoid killed by this spell rises at the start of
your next turn as a zombie that is permanently under
your command, following your verbal orders to the best
of its ability.

FIREBALL
3rd-level evocation

Casting Time: 1 action
Range: 150 feet
Components: V, S, M (a tiny ball of bat
  guano and sulfur)
Duration: Instantaneous

A bright streak flashes from your pointing finger to a
point you choose within range and then blossoms with
a low roar into an explosion of flame. Each creature
in a 20-foot-radius sphere centered on that point must
make a Dexterity saving throw. A target takes 8d6 fire

damage on a failed save, or half as much damage on a successful one.

The fire spreads around corners. It ignites flammable objects in the area that aren't being worn or carried.

At Higher Levels. When you cast this spell using a spell slot of 4th level or higher, the damage increases by 1d6 for each slot level above 3rd.

FIRE BOLT
Evocation cantrip

Casting Time: 1 action
Range: 120 feet
Components: V, S
Duration: Instantaneous

You hurl a mote of fire at a creature or object within range. Make a ranged spell attack against the target. On a hit, the target takes 1d10 fire damage. A flammable object hit by this spell ignites if it isn't being worn or carried.

This spell's damage increases by 1d10 when you reach 5th level (2d10), 11th level (3d10), and 17th level (4d10).

FIRE SHIELD
4th-level evocation

Casting Time: 1 action
Range: Self
Components: V, S, M (a bit of phosphorus or a firefly)
Duration: 10 minutes

Thin and wispy flames wreathe your body for the duration, shedding bright light in a 10-foot radius and dim light for an additional 10 feet. You can end the spell early by using an action to dismiss it.

The flames provide you with a warm shield or a chill shield, as you choose. The warm shield grants you resistance to cold damage, and the chill shield grants you resistance to fire damage.

In addition, whenever a creature within 5 feet of you hits you with a melee attack, the shield erupts with flame. The attacker takes 2d8 fire damage from a warm shield, or 2d8 cold damage from a cold shield.

FIRE STORM
7th-level evocation

Casting Time: 1 action
Range: 150 feet
Components: V, S
Duration: Instantaneous

A storm made up of sheets of roaring flame appears in a location you choose within range. The area of the storm consists of up to ten 10-foot cubes, which you can arrange as you wish. Each cube must have at least one face adjacent to the face of another cube. Each creature in the area must make a Dexterity saving throw. It takes 7d10 fire damage on a failed save, or half as much damage on a successful one.

The fire damages objects in the area and ignites flammable objects that aren't being worn or carried. If you choose, plant life in the area is unaffected by this spell.

FLAME BLADE
2nd-level evocation

Casting Time: 1 bonus action
Range: Self
Components: V, S, M (leaf of sumac)
Duration: Concentration, up to 10 minutes

You evoke a fiery blade in your free hand. The blade is similar in size and shape to a scimitar, and it lasts for the duration. If you let go of the blade, it disappears, but you can evoke the blade again as a bonus action.

You can use your action to make a melee spell attack with the fiery blade. On a hit, the target takes 3d6 fire damage.

The flaming blade sheds bright light in a 10-foot radius and dim light for an additional 10 feet.

At Higher Levels. When you cast this spell using a spell slot of 4th level or higher, the damage increases by 1d6 for every two slot levels above 2nd.

FLAME STRIKE
5th-level evocation

Casting Time: 1 action
Range: 60 feet
Components: V, S, M (pinch of sulfur)
Duration: Instantaneous

A vertical column of divine fire roars down from the heavens in a location you specify. Each creature in a 10-foot-radius, 40-foot-high cylinder centered on a point within range must make a Dexterity saving throw. A creature takes 4d6 fire damage and 4d6 radiant damage on a failed save, or half as much damage on a successful one.

At Higher Levels. When you cast this spell using a spell slot of 6th level or higher, the fire damage or the radiant damage (your choice) increases by 1d6 for each slot level above 5th.

FLAMING SPHERE
2nd-level conjuration

Casting Time: 1 action
Range: 60 feet
Components: V, S, M (a bit of tallow, a pinch of brimstone, and a dusting of powdered iron)
Duration: Concentration, up to 1 minute

A 5-foot-diameter sphere of fire appears in an unoccupied space of your choice within range and lasts for the duration. Any creature that ends its turn within 5 feet of the sphere must make a Dexterity saving throw. The creature takes 2d6 fire damage on a failed save, or half as much damage on a successful one.

As a bonus action, you can move the sphere up to 30 feet. If you ram the sphere into a creature, that creature must make the saving throw against the sphere's damage, and the sphere stops moving this turn.

When you move the sphere, you can direct it over barriers up to 5 feet tall and jump it across pits up to 10 feet wide. The sphere ignites flammable objects not being worn or carried, and it sheds bright light in a 20-foot radius and dim light for an additional 20 feet.

At Higher Levels. When you cast this spell using a spell slot of 3rd level or higher, the damage increases by 1d6 for each slot level above 2nd.

FLESH TO STONE

6th-level transmutation

Casting Time: 1 action
Range: 60 feet
Components: V, S, M (a pinch of lime, water, and earth)
Duration: Concentration, up to 1 minute

You attempt to turn one creature that you can see within range into stone. If the target's body is made of flesh, the creature must make a Constitution saving throw. On a failed save, it is restrained as its flesh begins to harden. On a successful save, the creature isn't affected.

A creature restrained by this spell must make another Constitution saving throw at the end of each of its turns. If it successfully saves against this spell three times, the spell ends. If it fails its saves three times, it is turned to stone and subjected to the petrified condition for the duration. The successes and failures don't need to be consecutive; keep track of both until the target collects three of a kind.

If the creature is physically broken while petrified, it suffers from similar deformities if it reverts to its original state.

If you maintain your concentration on this spell for the entire possible duration, the creature is turned to stone until the effect is removed.

FLY

3rd-level transmutation

Casting Time: 1 action
Range: Touch
Components: V, S, M (a wing feather from any bird)
Duration: Concentration, up to 10 minutes

You touch a willing creature. The target gains a flying speed of 60 feet for the duration. When the spell ends, the target falls if it is still aloft, unless it can stop the fall.

At Higher Levels. When you cast this spell using a spell slot of 4th level or higher, you can target one additional creature for each slot level above 3rd.

FOG CLOUD

1st-level conjuration

Casting Time: 1 action
Range: 120 feet
Components: V, S
Duration: Concentration, up to 1 hour

You create a 20-foot-radius sphere of fog centered on a point within range. The sphere spreads around corners, and its area is heavily obscured. It lasts for the duration or until a wind of moderate or greater speed (at least 10 miles per hour) disperses it.

At Higher Levels. When you cast this spell using a spell slot of 2nd level or higher, the radius of the fog increases by 20 feet for each slot level above 1st.

FORBIDDANCE

6th-level abjuration (ritual)

Casting Time: 10 minutes
Range: Touch
Components: V, S, M (a sprinkling of holy water, rare incense, and powdered ruby worth at least 1,000 gp)
Duration: 1 day

You create a ward against magical travel that protects up to 40,000 square feet of floor space to a height of 30 feet above the floor. For the duration, creatures can't teleport into the area or use portals, such as those created by the *gate* spell, to enter the area. The spell proofs the area against planar travel, and therefore prevents creatures from accessing the area by way of the Astral Plane, Ethereal Plane, Feywild, Shadowfell, or the *plane shift* spell.

In addition, the spell damages types of creatures that you choose when you cast it. Choose one or more of the following: celestials, elementals, fey, fiends, and undead. When a chosen creature enters the spell's area for the first time on a turn or starts its turn there, the creature takes 5d10 radiant or necrotic damage (your choice when you cast this spell).

When you cast this spell, you can designate a password. A creature that speaks the password as it enters the area takes no damage from the spell.

The spell's area can't overlap with the area of another *forbiddance* spell. If you cast *forbiddance* every day for 30 days in the same location, the spell lasts until it is dispelled, and the material components are consumed on the last casting.

FORCECAGE

7th-level evocation

Casting Time: 1 action
Range: 100 feet
Components: V, S, M (ruby dust worth 1,500 gp)
Duration: 1 hour

An immobile, invisible, cube-shaped prison composed of magical force springs into existence around an area you choose within range. The prison can be a cage or a solid box, as you choose.

A prison in the shape of a cage can be up to 20 feet on a side and is made from 1/2-inch diameter bars spaced 1/2 inch apart.

A prison in the shape of a box can be up to 10 feet on a side, creating a solid barrier that prevents any matter from passing through it and blocking any spells cast into or out from the area.

When you cast the spell, any creature that is completely inside the cage's area is trapped. Creatures only partially within the area, or those too large to fit inside the area, are pushed away from the center of the area until they are completely outside the area.

A creature inside the cage can't leave it by nonmagical means. If the creature tries to use teleportation or interplanar travel to leave the cage, it must first make a Charisma saving throw. On a success, the creature can use that magic to exit the cage. On a failure, the creature can't exit the cage and wastes the use of the spell or effect. The cage also extends into the Ethereal Plane, blocking ethereal travel.

This spell can't be dispelled by *dispel magic*.

FORESIGHT
9th-level divination

Casting Time: 1 minute
Range: Touch
Components: V, S, M (a hummingbird feather)
Duration: 8 hours

You touch a willing creature and bestow a limited ability to see into the immediate future. For the duration, the target can't be surprised and has advantage on attack rolls, ability checks, and saving throws. Additionally, other creatures have disadvantage on attack rolls against the target for the duration.

This spell immediately ends if you cast it again before its duration ends.

FREEDOM OF MOVEMENT
4th-level abjuration

Casting Time: 1 action
Range: Touch
Components: V, S, M (a leather strap, bound around the arm or a similar appendage)
Duration: 1 hour

You touch a willing creature. For the duration, the target's movement is unaffected by difficult terrain, and spells and other magical effects can neither reduce the target's speed nor cause the target to be paralyzed or restrained.

The target can also spend 5 feet of movement to automatically escape from nonmagical restraints, such as manacles or a creature that has it grappled. Finally, being underwater imposes no penalties on the target's movement or attacks.

FRIENDS
Enchantment cantrip

Casting Time: 1 action
Range: Self
Components: S, M (a small amount of makeup applied to the face as this spell is cast)
Duration: Concentration, up to 1 minute

For the duration, you have advantage on all Charisma checks directed at one creature of your choice that isn't hostile toward you. When the spell ends, the creature realizes that you used magic to influence its mood and becomes hostile toward you. A creature prone to violence might attack you. Another creature might seek retribution in other ways (at the DM's discretion), depending on the nature of your interaction with it.

GASEOUS FORM
3rd-level transmutation

Casting Time: 1 action
Range: Touch
Components: V, S, M (a bit of gauze and a wisp of smoke)
Duration: Concentration, up to 1 hour

You transform a willing creature you touch, along with everything it's wearing and carrying, into a misty cloud for the duration. The spell ends if the creature drops to 0 hit points. An incorporeal creature isn't affected.

While in this form, the target's only method of movement is a flying speed of 10 feet. The target can enter and occupy the space of another creature. The target has resistance to nonmagical damage, and it has advantage on Strength, Dexterity, and Constitution saving throws. The target can pass through small holes, narrow openings, and even mere cracks, though it treats liquids as though they were solid surfaces. The target can't fall and remains hovering in the air even when stunned or otherwise incapacitated.

While in the form of a misty cloud, the target can't talk or manipulate objects, and any objects it was carrying or holding can't be dropped, used, or otherwise interacted with. The target can't attack or cast spells.

GATE
9th-level conjuration

Casting Time: 1 action
Range: 60 feet
Components: V, S, M (a diamond worth at least 5,000 gp)
Duration: Concentration, up to 1 minute

You conjure a portal linking an unoccupied space you can see within range to a precise location on a different plane of existence. The portal is a circular opening, which you can make 5 to 20 feet in diameter. You can orient the portal in any direction you choose. The portal lasts for the duration.

The portal has a front and a back on each plane where it appears. Travel through the portal is possible only by moving through its front. Anything that does so is instantly transported to the other plane, appearing in the unoccupied space nearest to the portal.

Deities and other planar rulers can prevent portals created by this spell from opening in their presence or anywhere within their domains.

When you cast this spell, you can speak the name of a specific creature (a pseudonym, title, or nickname doesn't work). If that creature is on a plane other than the one you are on, the portal opens in the named creature's immediate vicinity and draws the creature through it to the nearest unoccupied space on your side of the portal. You gain no special power over the creature, and it is free to act as the DM deems appropriate. It might leave, attack you, or help you.

GEAS
5th-level enchantment

Casting Time: 1 minute
Range: 60 feet
Components: V
Duration: 30 days

You place a magical command on a creature that you can see within range, forcing it to carry out some service or refrain from some action or course of activity as you decide. If the creature can understand you, it must succeed on a Wisdom saving throw or become charmed by you for the duration. While the creature is charmed by you, it takes 5d10 psychic damage each time it acts in a manner directly counter to your instructions, but no more than once each day. A creature that can't understand you is unaffected by the spell.

You can issue any command you choose, short of an activity that would result in certain death. Should you issue a suicidal command, the spell ends.

You can end the spell early by using an action to dismiss it. A *remove curse*, *greater restoration*, or *wish* spell also ends it.

At Higher Levels. When you cast this spell using a spell slot of 7th or 8th level, the duration is 1 year. When you cast this spell using a spell slot of 9th level, the spell lasts until it is ended by one of the spells mentioned above.

GENTLE REPOSE
2nd-level necromancy (ritual)

Casting Time: 1 action
Range: Touch
Components: V, S, M (a pinch of salt and one copper piece placed on each of the corpse's eyes, which must remain there for the duration)
Duration: 10 days

You touch a corpse or other remains. For the duration, the target is protected from decay and can't become undead.

The spell also effectively extends the time limit on raising the target from the dead, since days spent under the influence of this spell don't count against the time limit of spells such as *raise dead*.

GIANT INSECT
4th-level transmutation

Casting Time: 1 action
Range: 30 feet
Components: V, S
Duration: Concentration, up to 10 minutes

You transform up to ten centipedes, three spiders, five wasps, or one scorpion within range into giant versions of their natural forms for the duration. A centipede becomes a giant centipede, a spider becomes a giant spider, a wasp becomes a giant wasp, and a scorpion becomes a giant scorpion.

Each creature obeys your verbal commands, and in combat, they act on your turn each round. The DM has the statistics for these creatures and resolves their actions and movement.

A creature remains in its giant size for the duration, until it drops to 0 hit points, or until you use an action to dismiss the effect on it.

The DM might allow you to choose different targets. For example, if you transform a bee, its giant version might have the same statistics as a giant wasp.

GLIBNESS
8th-level transmutation

Casting Time: 1 action
Range: Self
Components: V
Duration: 1 hour

Until the spell ends, when you make a Charisma check, you can replace the number you roll with a 15. Additionally, no matter what you say, magic that would determine if you are telling the truth indicates that you are being truthful.

GLOBE OF INVULNERABILITY
6th-level abjuration

Casting Time: 1 action
Range: Self (10-foot radius)
Components: V, S, M (a glass or crystal bead that shatters when the spell ends)
Duration: Concentration, up to 1 minute

An immobile, faintly shimmering barrier springs into existence in a 10-foot radius around you and remains for the duration.

Any spell of 5th level or lower cast from outside the barrier can't affect creatures or objects within it, even if the spell is cast using a higher level spell slot. Such a spell can target creatures and objects within the barrier, but the spell has no effect on them. Similarly, the area within the barrier is excluded from the areas affected by such spells.

At Higher Levels. When you cast this spell using a spell slot of 7th level or higher, the barrier blocks spells of one level higher for each slot level above 6th.

GLYPH OF WARDING
3rd-level abjuration

Casting Time: 1 hour
Range: Touch
Components: V, S, M (incense and powdered diamond worth at least 200 gp, which the spell consumes)
Duration: Until dispelled or triggered

When you cast this spell, you inscribe a glyph that harms other creatures, either upon a surface (such as a table or a section of floor or wall) or within an object that can be closed (such as a book, a scroll, or a treasure chest) to conceal the glyph. If you choose a surface, the glyph can cover an area of the surface no larger than 10 feet in diameter. If you choose an object, that object must remain in its place; if the object is moved more than 10 feet from where you cast this spell, the glyph is broken, and the spell ends without being triggered.

The glyph is nearly invisible and requires a successful Intelligence (Investigation) check against your spell save DC to be found.

You decide what triggers the glyph when you cast the spell. For glyphs inscribed on a surface, the most typical triggers include touching or standing on the glyph, removing another object covering the glyph, approaching within a certain distance of the glyph, or manipulating the object on which the glyph is inscribed. For glyphs inscribed within an object, the most common triggers include opening that object, approaching within a certain distance of the object, or seeing or reading the glyph. Once a glyph is triggered, this spell ends.

You can further refine the trigger so the spell activates only under certain circumstances or according to physical characteristics (such as height or weight), creature kind (for example, the ward could be set to affect aberrations or drow), or alignment. You can also set conditions for creatures that don't trigger the glyph, such as those who say a certain password.

When you inscribe the glyph, choose *explosive runes* or a *spell glyph.*

Explosive Runes. When triggered, the glyph erupts with magical energy in a 20-foot-radius sphere centered on the glyph. The sphere spreads around corners. Each creature in the area must make a Dexterity saving throw. A creature takes 5d8 acid, cold, fire, lightning, or thunder damage on a failed saving throw (your choice when you create the glyph), or half as much damage on a successful one.

Spell Glyph. You can store a prepared spell of 3rd level or lower in the glyph by casting it as part of creating the glyph. The spell must target a single creature or an area. The spell being stored has no immediate effect when cast in this way. When the glyph is triggered, the stored spell is cast. If the spell has a target, it targets the creature that triggered the glyph. If the spell affects an area, the area is centered on that creature. If the spell summons hostile creatures or creates harmful objects or traps, they appear as close as possible to the intruder and attack it. If the spell requires concentration, it lasts until the end of its full duration.

At Higher Levels. When you cast this spell using a spell slot of 4th level or higher, the damage of an *explosive runes* glyph increases by 1d8 for each slot level above 3rd. If you create a *spell glyph*, you can store any spell of up to the same level as the slot you use for the *glyph of warding.*

GOODBERRY
1st-level transmutation

Casting Time: 1 action
Range: Touch
Components: V, S, M (a sprig of mistletoe)
Duration: Instantaneous

Up to ten berries appear in your hand and are infused with magic for the duration. A creature can use its action to eat one berry. Eating a berry restores 1 hit point, and the berry provides enough nourishment to sustain a creature for one day.

The berries lose their potency if they have not been consumed within 24 hours of the casting of this spell.

GRASPING VINE
4th-level conjuration

Casting Time: 1 bonus action
Range: 30 feet
Components: V, S
Duration: Concentration, up to 1 minute

You conjure a vine that sprouts from the ground in an unoccupied space of your choice that you can see within range. When you cast this spell, you can direct the vine to lash out at a creature within 30 feet of it that you can see. That creature must succeed on a Dexterity saving throw or be pulled 20 feet directly toward the vine.

Until the spell ends, you can direct the vine to lash out at the same creature or another one as a bonus action on each of your turns.

GREASE
1st-level conjuration

Casting Time: 1 action
Range: 60 feet
Components: V, S, M (a bit of pork rind or butter)
Duration: 1 minute

Slick grease covers the ground in a 10-foot square centered on a point within range and turns it into difficult terrain for the duration.

When the grease appears, each creature standing in its area must succeed on a Dexterity saving throw or fall prone. A creature that enters the area or ends its turn there must also succeed on a Dexterity saving throw or fall prone.

GREATER INVISIBILITY
4th-level illusion

Casting Time: 1 action
Range: Touch
Components: V, S
Duration: Concentration, up to 1 minute

You or a creature you touch becomes invisible until the spell ends. Anything the target is wearing or carrying is invisible as long as it is on the target's person.

GREATER RESTORATION
5th-level abjuration

Casting Time: 1 action
Range: Touch
Components: V, S, M (diamond dust worth at least 100 gp, which the spell consumes)
Duration: Instantaneous

You imbue a creature you touch with positive energy to undo a debilitating effect. You can reduce the target's exhaustion level by one, or end one of the following effects on the target:

- One effect that charmed or petrified the target
- One curse, including the target's attunement to a cursed magic item
- Any reduction to one of the target's ability scores
- One effect reducing the target's hit point maximum

GUARDIAN OF FAITH
4th-level conjuration

Casting Time: 1 action
Range: 30 feet
Components: V
Duration: 8 hours

A Large spectral guardian appears and hovers for the duration in an unoccupied space of your choice that you

can see within range. The guardian occupies that space and is indistinct except for a gleaming sword and shield emblazoned with the symbol of your deity.

Any creature hostile to you that moves to a space within 10 feet of the guardian for the first time on a turn must succeed on a Dexterity saving throw. The creature takes 20 radiant damage on a failed save, or half as much damage on a successful one. The guardian vanishes when it has dealt a total of 60 damage.

GUARDS AND WARDS
6th-level abjuration

Casting Time: 10 minutes
Range: Touch
Components: V, S, M (burning incense, a small measure of brimstone and oil, a knotted string, a small amount of umber hulk blood, and a small silver rod worth at least 10 gp)
Duration: 24 hours

You create a ward that protects up to 2,500 square feet of floor space (an area 50 feet square, or one hundred 5-foot squares or twenty-five 10-foot squares). The warded area can be up to 20 feet tall, and shaped as you desire. You can ward several stories of a stronghold by dividing the area among them, as long as you can walk into each contiguous area while you are casting the spell.

When you cast this spell, you can specify individuals that are unaffected by any or all of the effects that you choose. You can also specify a password that, when spoken aloud, makes the speaker immune to these effects.

Guards and wards creates the following effects within the warded area.

Corridors. Fog fills all the warded corridors, making them heavily obscured. In addition, at each intersection or branching passage offering a choice of direction, there is a 50 percent chance that a creature other than you will believe it is going in the opposite direction from the one it chooses.

Doors. All doors in the warded area are magically locked, as if sealed by an *arcane lock* spell. In addition, you can cover up to ten doors with an illusion (equivalent to the illusory object function of the *minor illusion* spell) to make them appear as plain sections of wall.

Stairs. Webs fill all stairs in the warded area from top to bottom, as the *web* spell. These strands regrow in 10 minutes if they are burned or torn away while *guards and wards* lasts.

Other Spell Effect. You can place your choice of one of the following magical effects within the warded area of the stronghold.

- Place *dancing lights* in four corridors. You can designate a simple program that the lights repeat as long as *guards and wards* lasts.
- Place *magic mouth* in two locations.
- Place *stinking cloud* in two locations. The vapors appear in the places you designate; they return within 10 minutes if dispersed by wind while *guards and wards* lasts.
- Place a constant *gust of wind* in one corridor or room.

- Place a *suggestion* in one location. You select an area of up to 5 feet square, and any creature that enters or passes through the area receives the suggestion mentally.

The whole warded area radiates magic. A *dispel magic* cast on a specific effect, if successful, removes only that effect.

You can create a permanently guarded and warded structure by casting this spell there every day for one year.

GUIDANCE
Divination cantrip

Casting Time: 1 action
Range: Touch
Components: V, S
Duration: Concentration, up to 1 minute

You touch one willing creature. Once before the spell ends, the target can roll a d4 and add the number rolled to one ability check of its choice. It can roll the die before or after making the ability check. The spell then ends.

GUIDING BOLT
1st-level evocation

Casting Time: 1 action
Range: 120 feet
Components: V, S
Duration: 1 round

A flash of light streaks toward a creature of your choice within range. Make a ranged spell attack against the target. On a hit, the target takes 4d6 radiant damage, and the next attack roll made against this target before the end of your next turn has advantage, thanks to the mystical dim light glittering on the target until then.

At Higher Levels. When you cast this spell using a spell slot of 2nd level or higher, the damage increases by 1d6 for each slot level above 1st.

GUST OF WIND
2nd-level evocation

Casting Time: 1 action
Range: Self (60-foot line)
Components: V, S, M (a legume seed)
Duration: Concentration, up to 1 minute

A line of strong wind 60 feet long and 10 feet wide blasts from you in a direction you choose for the spell's duration. Each creature that starts its turn in the line must succeed on a Strength saving throw or be pushed 15 feet away from you in a direction following the line.

Any creature in the line must spend 2 feet of movement for every 1 foot it moves when moving closer to you.

The gust disperses gas or vapor, and it extinguishes candles, torches, and similar unprotected flames in the area. It causes protected flames, such as those of lanterns, to dance wildly and has a 50 percent chance to extinguish them.

As a bonus action on each of your turns before the spell ends, you can change the direction in which the line blasts from you.

HAIL OF THORNS
1st-level conjuration

Casting Time: 1 bonus action
Range: Self
Components: V
Duration: Concentration, up to 1 minute

The next time you hit a creature with a ranged weapon attack before the spell ends, this spell creates a rain of thorns that sprouts from your ranged weapon or ammunition. In addition to the normal effect of the attack, the target of the attack and each creature within 5 feet of it must make a Dexterity saving throw. A creature takes 1d10 piercing damage on a failed save, or half as much damage on a successful one.

At Higher Levels. If you cast this spell using a spell slot of 2nd level or higher, the damage increases by 1d10 for each slot level above 1st (to a maximum of 6d10).

HALLOW
5th-level evocation

Casting Time: 24 hours
Range: Touch
Components: V, S, M (herbs, oils, and incense worth at least 1,000 gp, which the spell consumes)
Duration: Until dispelled

You touch a point and infuse an area around it with holy (or unholy) power. The area can have a radius up to 60 feet, and the spell fails if the radius includes an area already under the effect a *hallow* spell. The affected area is subject to the following effects.

First, celestials, elementals, fey, fiends, and undead can't enter the area, nor can such creatures charm, frighten, or possess creatures within it. Any creature charmed, frightened, or possessed by such a creature is no longer charmed, frightened, or possessed upon entering the area. You can exclude one or more of those types of creatures from this effect.

Second, you can bind an extra effect to the area. Choose the effect from the following list, or choose an effect offered by the DM. Some of these effects apply to creatures in the area; you can designate whether the effect applies to all creatures, creatures that follow a specific deity or leader, or creatures of a specific sort, such as orcs or trolls. When a creature that would be affected enters the spell's area for the first time on a turn or starts its turn there, it can make a Charisma saving throw. On a success, the creature ignores the extra effect until it leaves the area.

Courage. Affected creatures can't be frightened while in the area.

Darkness. Darkness fills the area. Normal light, as well as magical light created by spells of a lower level than the slot you used to cast this spell, can't illuminate the area.

Daylight. Bright light fills the area. Magical darkness created by spells of a lower level than the slot you used to cast this spell can't extinguish the light.

Energy Protection. Affected creatures in the area have resistance to one damage type of your choice, except for bludgeoning, piercing, or slashing.

Energy Vulnerability. Affected creatures in the area have vulnerability to one damage type of your choice, except for bludgeoning, piercing, or slashing.

Everlasting Rest. Dead bodies interred in the area can't be turned into undead.

Extradimensional Interference. Affected creatures can't move or travel using teleportation or by extradimensional or interplanar means.

Fear. Affected creatures are frightened while in the area.

Silence. No sound can emanate from within the area, and no sound can reach into it.

Tongues. Affected creatures can communicate with any other creature in the area, even if they don't share a common language.

HALLUCINATORY TERRAIN
4th-level illusion

Casting Time: 10 minutes
Range: 300 feet
Components: V, S, M (a stone, a twig, and a bit of green plant)
Duration: 24 hours

You make natural terrain in a 150-foot cube in range look, sound, and smell like some other sort of natural terrain. Thus, open fields or a road can be made to resemble a swamp, hill, crevasse, or some other difficult or impassable terrain. A pond can be made to seem like a grassy meadow, a precipice like a gentle slope, or a rock-strewn gully like a wide and smooth road. Manufactured structures, equipment, and creatures within the area aren't changed in appearance.

The tactile characteristics of the terrain are unchanged, so creatures entering the area are likely to see through the illusion. If the difference isn't obvious by touch, a creature carefully examining the illusion can attempt an Intelligence (Investigation) check against your spell save DC to disbelieve it. A creature who discerns the illusion for what it is, sees it as a vague image superimposed on the terrain.

HARM
6th-level necromancy

Casting Time: 1 action
Range: 60 feet
Components: V, S
Duration: Instantaneous

You unleash a virulent disease on a creature that you can see within range. The target must make a Constitution saving throw. On a failed save, it takes 14d6 necrotic damage, or half as much damage on a successful save. The damage can't reduce the target's hit points below 1. If the target fails the saving throw, its hit point maximum is reduced for 1 hour by an amount equal to the necrotic damage it took. Any effect that removes a disease allows a creature's hit point maximum to return to normal before that time passes.

HASTE

3rd-level transmutation

Casting Time: 1 action
Range: 30 feet
Components: V, S, M (a shaving of licorice root)
Duration: Concentration, up to 1 minute

Choose a willing creature that you can see within range. Until the spell ends, the target's speed is doubled, it gains a +2 bonus to AC, it has advantage on Dexterity saving throws, and it gains an additional action on each of its turns. That action can be used only to take the Attack (one weapon attack only), Dash, Disengage, Hide, or Use an Object action.

When the spell ends, the target can't move or take actions until after its next turn, as a wave of lethargy sweeps over it.

HEAL

6th-level evocation

Casting Time: 1 action
Range: 60 feet
Components: V, S
Duration: Instantaneous

Choose a creature that you can see within range. A surge of positive energy washes through the creature, causing it to regain 70 hit points. This spell also ends blindness, deafness, and any diseases affecting the target. This spell has no effect on constructs or undead.

At Higher Levels. When you cast this spell using a spell slot of 7th level or higher, the amount of healing increases by 10 for each slot level above 6th.

HEALING WORD

1st-level evocation

Casting Time: 1 bonus action
Range: 60 feet
Components: V
Duration: Instantaneous

A creature of your choice that you can see within range regains hit points equal to 1d4 + your spellcasting ability modifier. This spell has no effect on undead or constructs.

At Higher Levels. When you cast this spell using a spell slot of 2nd level or higher, the healing increases by 1d4 for each slot level above 1st.

HEAT METAL

2nd-level transmutation

Casting Time: 1 action
Range: 60 feet
Components: V, S, M (a piece of iron and a flame)
Duration: Concentration, up to 1 minute

Choose a manufactured metal object, such as a metal weapon or a suit of heavy or medium metal armor, that you can see within range. You cause the object to glow red-hot. Any creature in physical contact with the object takes 2d8 fire damage when you cast the spell. Until the spell ends, you can use a bonus action on each of your subsequent turns to cause this damage again.

If a creature is holding or wearing the object and takes the damage from it, the creature must succeed on a Constitution saving throw or drop the object if it can. If it doesn't drop the object, it has disadvantage on attack rolls and ability checks until the start of your next turn.

At Higher Levels. When you cast this spell using a spell slot of 3rd level or higher, the damage increases by 1d8 for each slot level above 2nd.

HELLISH REBUKE

1st-level evocation

Casting Time: 1 reaction, which you take in response to being damaged by a creature within 60 feet of you that you can see
Range: 60 feet
Components: V, S
Duration: Instantaneous

You point your finger, and the creature that damaged you is momentarily surrounded by hellish flames. The creature must make a Dexterity saving throw. It takes 2d10 fire damage on a failed save, or half as much damage on a successful one.

At Higher Levels. When you cast this spell using a spell slot of 2nd level or higher, the damage increases by 1d10 for each slot level above 1st.

HEROES' FEAST

6th-level conjuration

Casting Time: 10 minutes
Range: 30 feet
Components: V, S , M (a gem-encrusted bowl worth at least 1,000 gp, which the spell consumes)
Duration: Instantaneous

You bring forth a great feast, including magnificent food and drink. The feast takes 1 hour to consume and disappears at the end of that time, and the beneficial effects don't set in until this hour is over. Up to twelve other creatures can partake of the feast.

A creature that partakes of the feast gains several benefits. The creature is cured of all diseases and poison, becomes immune to poison and being frightened, and makes all Wisdom saving throws with advantage. Its hit point maximum also increases by 2d10, and it gains the same number of hit points. These benefits last for 24 hours.

HEROISM

1st-level enchantment

Casting Time: 1 action
Range: Touch
Components: V, S
Duration: Concentration, up to 1 minute

A willing creature you touch is imbued with bravery. Until the spell ends, the creature is immune to being frightened and gains temporary hit points equal to your spellcasting ability modifier at the start of each of its turns. When the spell ends, the target loses any remaining temporary hit points from this spell.

At Higher Levels. When you cast this spell using a spell slot of 2nd level or higher, you can target one additional creature for each slot level above 1st.

HEX
1st-level enchantment

Casting Time: 1 bonus action
Range: 90 feet
Components: V, S, M (the petrified eye of a newt)
Duration: Concentration, up to 1 hour

You place a curse on a creature that you can see within range. Until the spell ends, you deal an extra 1d6 necrotic damage to the target whenever you hit it with an attack. Also, choose one ability when you cast the spell. The target has disadvantage on ability checks made with the chosen ability.

If the target drops to 0 hit points before this spell ends, you can use a bonus action on a subsequent turn of yours to curse a new creature.

A *remove curse* cast on the target ends this spell early.

At Higher Levels. When you cast this spell using a spell slot of 3rd or 4th level, you can maintain your concentration on the spell for up to 8 hours. When you use a spell slot of 5th level or higher, you can maintain your concentration on the spell for up to 24 hours.

HOLD MONSTER
5th-level enchantment

Casting Time: 1 action
Range: 90 feet
Components: V, S, M (a small, straight piece of iron)
Duration: Concentration, up to 1 minute

Choose a creature that you can see within range. The target must succeed on a Wisdom saving throw or be paralyzed for the duration. This spell has no effect on undead. At the end of each of its turns, the target can make another Wisdom saving throw. On a success, the spell ends on the target.

At Higher Levels. When you cast this spell using a spell slot of 6th level or higher, you can target one additional creature for each slot level above 5th. The creatures must be within 30 feet of each other when you target them.

HOLD PERSON
2nd-level enchantment

Casting Time: 1 action
Range: 60 feet
Components: V, S, M (a small, straight piece of iron)
Duration: Concentration, up to 1 minute

Choose a humanoid that you can see within range. The target must succeed on a Wisdom saving throw or be paralyzed for the duration. At the end of each of its turns, the target can make another Wisdom saving throw. On a success, the spell ends on the target.

At Higher Levels. When you cast this spell using a spell slot of 3rd level or higher, you can target one additional humanoid for each slot level above 2nd. The humanoids must be within 30 feet of each other when you target them.

HOLY AURA
8th-level abjuration

Casting Time: 1 action
Range: Self
Components: V, S, M (a tiny reliquary worth at least 1,000 gp containing a sacred relic, such as a scrap of cloth from a saint's robe or a piece of parchment from a religious text)
Duration: Concentration, up to 1 minute

Divine light washes out from you and coalesces in a soft radiance in a 30-foot radius around you. Creatures of your choice in that radius when you cast this spell shed dim light in a 5-foot radius and have advantage on all saving throws, and other creatures have disadvantage on attack rolls against them until the spell ends. In addition, when a fiend or an undead hits an affected creature with a melee attack, the aura flashes with brilliant light. The attacker must succeed on a Constitution saving throw or be blinded until the spell ends.

HUNGER OF HADAR
3rd-level conjuration

Casting Time: 1 action
Range: 150 feet
Components: V, S, M (a pickled octopus tentacle)
Duration: Concentration, up to 1 minute

You open a gateway to the dark between the stars, a region infested with unknown horrors. A 20-foot-radius sphere of blackness and bitter cold appears, centered on a point with range and lasting for the duration. This void is filled with a cacophony of soft whispers and slurping noises that can be heard up to 30 feet away. No light, magical or otherwise, can illuminate the area, and creatures fully within the area are blinded.

The void creates a warp in the fabric of space, and the area is difficult terrain. Any creature that starts its turn in the area takes 2d6 cold damage. Any creature that ends its turn in the area must succeed on a Dexterity saving throw or take 2d6 acid damage as milky, otherworldly tentacles rub against it.

HUNTER'S MARK
1st-level divination

Casting Time: 1 bonus action
Range: 90 feet
Components: V
Duration: Concentration, up to 1 hour

You choose a creature you can see within range and mystically mark it as your quarry. Until the spell ends, you deal an extra 1d6 damage to the target whenever you hit it with a weapon attack, and you have advantage on any Wisdom (Perception) or Wisdom (Survival) check you make to find it. If the target drops to 0 hit points before this spell ends, you can use a bonus action on a subsequent turn of yours to mark a new creature.

At Higher Levels. When you cast this spell using a spell slot of 3rd or 4th level, you can maintain your concentration on the spell for up to 8 hours. When you use a spell slot of 5th level or higher, you can maintain your concentration on the spell for up to 24 hours.

Hypnotic Pattern
3rd-level illusion

Casting Time: 1 action
Range: 120 feet
Components: S, M (a glowing stick of incense or a crystal vial filled with phosphorescent material)
Duration: Concentration, up to 1 minute

You create a twisting pattern of colors that weaves through the air inside a 30-foot cube within range. The pattern appears for a moment and vanishes. Each creature in the area who sees the pattern must make a Wisdom saving throw. On a failed save, the creature becomes charmed for the duration. While charmed by this spell, the creature is incapacitated and has a speed of 0.

The spell ends for an affected creature if it takes any damage or if someone else uses an action to shake the creature out of its stupor.

Ice Storm
4th-level evocation

Casting Time: 1 action
Range: 300 feet
Components: V, S, M (a pinch of dust and a few drops of water)
Duration: Instantaneous

A hail of rock-hard ice pounds to the ground in a 20-foot-radius, 40-foot-high cylinder centered on a point within range. Each creature in the cylinder must make a Dexterity saving throw. A creature takes 2d8 bludgeoning damage and 4d6 cold damage on a failed save, or half as much damage on a successful one.

Hailstones turn the storm's area of effect into difficult terrain until the end of your next turn.

At Higher Levels. When you cast this spell using a spell slot of 5th level or higher, the bludgeoning damage increases by 1d8 for each slot level above 4th.

Identify
1st-level divination (ritual)

Casting Time: 1 minute
Range: Touch
Components: V, S, M (a pearl worth at least 100 gp and an owl feather)
Duration: Instantaneous

You choose one object that you must touch throughout the casting of the spell. If it is a magic item or some other magic-imbued object, you learn its properties and how to use them, whether it requires attunement to use, and how many charges it has, if any. You learn whether any spells are affecting the item and what they are. If the item was created by a spell, you learn which spell created it.

If you instead touch a creature throughout the casting, you learn what spells, if any, are currently affecting it.

Illusory Script
1st-level illusion (ritual)

Casting Time: 1 minute
Range: Touch
Components: S, M (a lead-based ink worth at least 10 gp, which the spell consumes)
Duration: 10 days

You write on parchment, paper, or some other suitable writing material and imbue it with a potent illusion that lasts for the duration.

To you and any creatures you designate when you cast the spell, the writing appears normal, written in your hand, and conveys whatever meaning you intended when you wrote the text. To all others, the writing appears as if it were written in an unknown or magical script that is unintelligible. Alternatively, you can cause the writing to appear to be an entirely different message, written in a different hand and language, though the language must be one you know.

Should the spell be dispelled, the original script and the illusion both disappear.

A creature with truesight can read the hidden message.

Imprisonment
9th-level abjuration

Casting Time: 1 minute
Range: 30 feet
Components: V, S, M (a vellum depiction or a carved statuette in the likeness of the target, and a special component that varies according to the version of the spell you choose, worth at least 500 gp per Hit Die of the target)
Duration: Until dispelled

You create a magical restraint to hold a creature that you can see within range. The target must succeed on a Wisdom saving throw or be bound by the spell; if it succeeds, it is immune to this spell if you cast it again. While affected by this spell, the creature doesn't need to breathe, eat, or drink, and it doesn't age. Divination spells can't locate or perceive the target.

When you cast the spell, you choose one of the following forms of imprisonment.

Burial. The target is entombed far beneath the earth in a sphere of magical force that is just large enough to contain the target. Nothing can pass through the sphere, nor can any creature teleport or use planar travel to get into or out of it.

The special component for this version of the spell is a small mithral orb.

Chaining. Heavy chains, firmly rooted in the ground, hold the target in place. The target is restrained until the spell ends, and it can't move or be moved by any means until then.

The special component for this version of the spell is a fine chain of precious metal.

Hedged Prison. The spell transports the target into a tiny demiplane that is warded against teleportation and planar travel. The demiplane can be a labyrinth, a cage, a tower, or any similar confined structure or area of your choice.

The special component for this version of the spell is a miniature representation of the prison made from jade.

Minimus Containment. The target shrinks to a height of 1 inch and is imprisoned inside a gemstone or similar object. Light can pass through the gemstone normally (allowing the target to see out and other creatures to see in), but nothing else can pass through, even by means of teleportation or planar travel. The gemstone can't be cut or broken while the spell remains in effect.

The special component for this version of the spell is a large, transparent gemstone, such as a corundum, diamond, or ruby.

Slumber. The target falls asleep and can't be awoken. The special component for this version of the spell consists of rare soporific herbs.

Ending the Spell. During the casting of the spell, in any of its versions, you can specify a condition that will cause the spell to end and release the target. The condition can be as specific or as elaborate as you choose, but the DM must agree that the condition is reasonable and has a likelihood of coming to pass. The conditions can be based on a creature's name, identity, or deity but otherwise must be based on observable actions or qualities and not based on intangibles such as level, class, or hit points.

A *dispel magic* spell can end the spell only if it is cast as a 9th-level spell, targeting either the prison or the special component used to create it.

You can use a particular special component to create only one prison at a time. If you cast the spell again using the same component, the target of the first casting is immediately freed from its binding.

INCENDIARY CLOUD
8th-level conjuration

Casting Time: 1 action
Range: 150 feet
Components: V, S
Duration: Concentration, up to 1 minute

A swirling cloud of smoke shot through with white-hot embers appears in a 20-foot-radius sphere centered on a point within range. The cloud spreads around corners and is heavily obscured. It lasts for the duration or until a wind of moderate or greater speed (at least 10 miles per hour) disperses it.

When the cloud appears, each creature in it must make a Dexterity saving throw. A creature takes 10d8 fire damage on a failed save, or half as much damage on a successful one. A creature must also make this saving throw when it enters the spell's area for the first time on a turn or ends its turn there.

The cloud moves 10 feet directly away from you in a direction that you choose at the start of each of your turns.

INFLICT WOUNDS
1st-level necromancy

Casting Time: 1 action
Range: Touch
Components: V, S
Duration: Instantaneous

Make a melee spell attack against a creature you can reach. On a hit, the target takes 3d10 necrotic damage.

At Higher Levels. When you cast this spell using a spell slot of 2nd level or higher, the damage increases by 1d10 for each slot level above 1st.

INSECT PLAGUE

5th-level conjuration

Casting Time: 1 action
Range: 300 feet
Components: V, S, M (a few grains of sugar, some kernels of grain, and a smear of fat)
Duration: Concentration, up to 10 minutes

Swarming, biting locusts fill a 20-foot-radius sphere centered on a point you choose within range. The sphere spreads around corners. The sphere remains for the duration, and its area is lightly obscured. The sphere's area is difficult terrain.

When the area appears, each creature in it must make a Constitution saving throw. A creature takes 4d10 piercing damage on a failed save, or half as much damage on a successful one. A creature must also make this saving throw when it enters the spell's area for the first time on a turn or ends its turn there.

At Higher Levels. When you cast this spell using a spell slot of 6th level or higher, the damage increases by 1d10 for each slot level above 5th.

INVISIBILITY

2nd-level illusion

Casting Time: 1 action
Range: Touch
Components: V, S, M (an eyelash encased in gum arabic)
Duration: Concentration, up to 1 hour

A creature you touch becomes invisible until the spell ends. Anything the target is wearing or carrying is invisible as long as it is on the target's person. The spell ends for a target that attacks or casts a spell.

At Higher Levels. When you cast this spell using a spell slot of 3rd level or higher, you can target one additional creature for each slot level above 2nd.

JUMP

1st-level transmutation

Casting Time: 1 action
Range: Touch
Components: V, S, M (a grasshopper's hind leg)
Duration: 1 minute

You touch a creature. The creature's jump distance is tripled until the spell ends.

KNOCK

2nd-level transmutation

Casting Time: 1 action
Range: 60 feet
Components: V
Duration: Instantaneous

Choose an object that you can see within range. The object can be a door, a box, a chest, a set of manacles, a padlock, or another object that contains a mundane or magical means that prevents access.

A target that is held shut by a mundane lock or that is stuck or barred becomes unlocked, unstuck, or unbarred. If the object has multiple locks, only one of them is unlocked.

If you choose a target that is held shut with *arcane lock*, that spell is suppressed for 10 minutes, during which time the target can be opened and shut normally.

When you cast the spell, a loud knock, audible from as far away as 300 feet, emanates from the target object.

LEGEND LORE

5th-level divination

Casting Time: 10 minutes
Range: Self
Components: V, S, M (incense worth at least 250 gp, which the spell consumes, and four ivory strips worth at least 50 gp each)
Duration: Instantaneous

Name or describe a person, place, or object. The spell brings to your mind a brief summary of the significant lore about the thing you named. The lore might consist of current tales, forgotten stories, or even secret lore that has never been widely known. If the thing you named isn't of legendary importance, you gain no information. The more information you already have about the thing, the more precise and detailed the information you receive is.

The information you learn is accurate but might be couched in figurative language. For example, if you have a mysterious magic axe on hand, the spell might yield this information: "Woe to the evildoer whose hand touches the axe, for even the haft slices the hand of the evil ones. Only a true Child of Stone, lover and beloved of Moradin, may awaken the true powers of the axe, and only with the sacred word *Rudnogg* on the lips."

LEOMUND'S SECRET CHEST

4th-level conjuration

Casting Time: 1 action
Range: Touch
Components: V, S, M (an exquisite chest, 3 feet by 2 feet by 2 feet, constructed from rare materials worth at least 5,000 gp, and a Tiny replica made from the same materials worth at least 50 gp)
Duration: Instantaneous

You hide a chest, and all its contents, on the Ethereal Plane. You must touch the chest and the miniature replica that serves as a material component for the spell. The chest can contain up to 12 cubic feet of nonliving material (3 feet by 2 feet by 2 feet).

While the chest remains on the Ethereal Plane, you can use an action and touch the replica to recall the chest. It appears in an unoccupied space on the ground within 5 feet of you. You can send the chest back to the Ethereal Plane by using an action and touching both the chest and the replica.

After 60 days, there is a cumulative 5 percent chance per day that the spell's effect ends. This effect ends if you cast this spell again, if the smaller replica chest is destroyed, or if you choose to end the spell as an action. If the spell ends and the larger chest is on the Ethereal Plane, it is irretrievably lost.

LEOMUND'S TINY HUT
3rd-level evocation (ritual)

Casting Time: 1 minute
Range: Self (10-foot-radius hemisphere)
Components: V, S, M (a small crystal bead)
Duration: 8 hours

A 10-foot-radius immobile dome of force springs into existence around and above you and remains stationary for the duration. The spell ends if you leave its area.

Nine creatures of Medium size or smaller can fit inside the dome with you. The spell fails if its area includes a larger creature or more than nine creatures. Creatures and objects within the dome when you cast this spell can move through it freely. All other creatures and objects are barred from passing through it. Spells and other magical effects can't extend through the dome or be cast through it. The atmosphere inside the space is comfortable and dry, regardless of the weather outside.

Until the spell ends, you can command the interior to become dimly lit or dark. The dome is opaque from the outside, of any color you choose, but it is transparent from the inside.

LESSER RESTORATION
2nd-level abjuration

Casting Time: 1 action
Range: Touch
Components: V, S
Duration: Instantaneous

You touch a creature and can end either one disease or one condition afflicting it. The condition can be blinded, deafened, paralyzed, or poisoned.

LEVITATE
2nd-level transmutation

Casting Time: 1 action
Range: 60 feet
Components: V, S, M (either a small leather loop or a piece of golden wire bent into a cup shape with a long shank on one end)
Duration: Concentration, up to 10 minutes

One creature or object of your choice that you can see within range rises vertically, up to 20 feet, and remains suspended there for the duration. The spell can levitate a target that weighs up to 500 pounds. An unwilling creature that succeeds on a Constitution saving throw is unaffected.

The target can move only by pushing or pulling against a fixed object or surface within reach (such as a wall or a ceiling), which allows it to move as if it were climbing. You can change the target's altitude by up to 20 feet in either direction on your turn. If you are the target, you can move up or down as part of your move. Otherwise, you can use your action to move the target, which must remain within the spell's range.

When the spell ends, the target floats gently to the ground if it is still aloft.

LIGHT
Evocation cantrip

Casting Time: 1 action
Range: Touch
Components: V, M (a firefly or phosphorescent moss)
Duration: 1 hour

You touch one object that is no larger than 10 feet in any dimension. Until the spell ends, the object sheds bright light in a 20-foot radius and dim light for an additional 20 feet. The light can be colored as you like. Completely covering the object with something opaque blocks the light. The spell ends if you cast it again or dismiss it as an action.

If you target an object held or worn by a hostile creature, that creature must succeed on a Dexterity saving throw to avoid the spell.

LIGHTNING ARROW
3rd-level transmutation

Casting Time: 1 bonus action
Range: Self
Components: V, S
Duration: Concentration, up to 1 minute

The next time you make a ranged weapon attack during the spell's duration, the weapon's ammunition, or the weapon itself if it's a thrown weapon, transforms into a bolt of lightning. Make the attack roll as normal. The target takes 4d8 lightning damage on a hit, or half as much damage on a miss, instead of the weapon's normal damage.

Whether you hit or miss, each creature within 10 feet of the target must make a Dexterity saving throw. Each of these creatures takes 2d8 lightning damage on a failed save, or half as much damage on a successful one.

The piece of ammunition or weapon then returns to its normal form.

At Higher Levels. When you cast this spell using a spell slot of 4th level or higher, the damage for both effects of the spell increases by 1d8 for each slot level above 3rd.

LIGHTNING BOLT
3rd-level evocation

Casting Time: 1 action
Range: Self (100-foot line)
Components: V, S, M (a bit of fur and a rod of amber, crystal, or glass)
Duration: Instantaneous

A stroke of lightning forming a line 100 feet long and 5 feet wide blasts out from you in a direction you choose. Each creature in the line must make a Dexterity saving throw. A creature takes 8d6 lightning damage on a failed save, or half as much damage on a successful one.

The lightning ignites flammable objects in the area that aren't being worn or carried.

At Higher Levels. When you cast this spell using a spell slot of 4th level or higher, the damage increases by 1d6 for each slot level above 3rd.

LOCATE ANIMALS OR PLANTS
2nd-level divination (ritual)

Casting Time: 1 action
Range: Self
Components: V, S, M (a bit of fur from a bloodhound)
Duration: Instantaneous

Describe or name a specific kind of beast or plant. Concentrating on the voice of nature in your surroundings, you learn the direction and distance to the closest creature or plant of that kind within 5 miles, if any are present.

LOCATE CREATURE
4th-level divination

Casting Time: 1 action
Range: Self
Components: V, S, M (a bit of fur from a bloodhound)
Duration: Concentration, up to 1 hour

Describe or name a creature that is familiar to you. You sense the direction to the creature's location, as long as that creature is within 1,000 feet of you. If the creature is moving, you know the direction of its movement.

The spell can locate a specific creature known to you, or the nearest creature of a specific kind (such as a human or a unicorn), so long as you have seen such a creature up close—within 30 feet—at least once. If the creature you described or named is in a different form, such as being under the effects of a *polymorph* spell, this spell doesn't locate the creature.

This spell can't locate a creature if running water at least 10 feet wide blocks a direct path between you and the creature.

LOCATE OBJECT
2nd-level divination

Casting Time: 1 action
Range: Self
Components: V, S, M (a forked twig)
Duration: Concentration, up to 10 minutes

Describe or name an object that is familiar to you. You sense the direction to the object's location, as long as that object is within 1,000 feet of you. If the object is in motion, you know the direction of its movement.

The spell can locate a specific object known to you, as long as you have seen it up close—within 30 feet—at least once. Alternatively, the spell can locate the nearest object of a particular kind, such as a certain kind of apparel, jewelry, furniture, tool, or weapon.

This spell can't locate an object if any thickness of lead, even a thin sheet, blocks a direct path between you and the object.

LONGSTRIDER
1st-level transmutation

Casting Time: 1 action
Range: Touch
Components: V, S, M (a pinch of dirt)
Duration: 1 hour

You touch a creature. The target's speed increases by 10 feet until the spell ends.

At Higher Levels. When you cast this spell using a spell slot of 2nd level or higher, you can target one additional creature for each slot level above 1st.

MAGE ARMOR
1st-level abjuration

Casting Time: 1 action
Range: Touch
Components: V, S, M (a piece of cured leather)
Duration: 8 hours

You touch a willing creature who isn't wearing armor, and a protective magical force surrounds it until the spell ends. The target's base AC becomes 13 + its Dexterity modifier. The spell ends if the target dons armor or if you dismiss the spell as an action.

MAGE HAND
Conjuration cantrip

Casting Time: 1 action
Range: 30 feet
Components: V, S
Duration: 1 minute

A spectral, floating hand appears at a point you choose within range. The hand lasts for the duration or until you dismiss it as an action. The hand vanishes if it is ever more than 30 feet away from you or if you cast this spell again.

You can use your action to control the hand. You can use the hand to manipulate an object, open an unlocked door or container, stow or retrieve an item from an open container, or pour the contents out of a vial. You can move the hand up to 30 feet each time you use it.

The hand can't attack, activate magic items, or carry more than 10 pounds.

MAGIC CIRCLE
3rd-level abjuration

Casting Time: 1 minute
Range: 10 feet
Components: V, S, M (holy water or powdered silver and iron worth at least 100 gp, which the spell consumes)
Duration: 1 hour

You create a 10-foot-radius, 20-foot-tall cylinder of magical energy centered on a point on the ground that you can see within range. Glowing runes appear wherever the cylinder intersects with the floor or other surface.

Choose one or more of the following types of creatures: celestials, elementals, fey, fiends, or undead. The circle affects a creature of the chosen type in the following ways:

- The creature can't willingly enter the cylinder by nonmagical means. If the creature tries to use teleportation or interplanar travel to do so, it must first succeed on a Charisma saving throw.
- The creature has disadvantage on attack rolls against targets within the cylinder.
- Targets within the cylinder can't be charmed, frightened, or possessed by the creature.

When you cast this spell, you can elect to cause its magic to operate in the reverse direction, preventing a creature of the specified type from leaving the cylinder and protecting targets outside it.

At Higher Levels. When you cast this spell using a spell slot of 4th level or higher, the duration increases by 1 hour for each slot level above 3rd.

MAGIC JAR
6th-level necromancy

Casting Time: 1 minute
Range: Self
Components: V, S, M (a gem, crystal, reliquary, or some other ornamental container worth at least 500 gp)
Duration: Until dispelled

Your body falls into a catatonic state as your soul leaves it and enters the container you used for the spell's material component. While your soul inhabits the container, you are aware of your surroundings as if you were in the container's space. You can't move or use reactions. The only action you can take is to project your soul up to 100 feet out of the container, either returning to your living body (and ending the spell) or attempting to possess a humanoids body.

You can attempt to possess any humanoid within 100 feet of you that you can see (creatures warded by a *protection from evil and good* or *magic circle* spell can't be possessed). The target must make a Charisma saving throw. On a failure, your soul moves into the target's body, and the target's soul becomes trapped in the container. On a success, the target resists your efforts to possess it, and you can't attempt to possess it again for 24 hours.

Once you possess a creature's body, you control it. Your game statistics are replaced by the statistics of the creature, though you retain your alignment and your Intelligence, Wisdom, and Charisma scores. You retain the benefit of your own class features. If the target has any class levels, you can't use any of its class features.

Meanwhile, the possessed creature's soul can perceive from the container using its own senses, but it can't move or take actions at all.

While possessing a body, you can use your action to return from the host body to the container if it is within 100 feet of you, returning the host creature's soul to its body. If the host body dies while you're in it, the creature dies, and you must make a Charisma saving throw against your own spellcasting DC. On a success, you return to the container if it is within 100 feet of you. Otherwise, you die.

If the container is destroyed or the spell ends, your soul immediately returns to body. If your body is more than 100 feet away from you or if your body is dead when you attempt to return to it, you die. If another creature's soul is in the container when it is destroyed, the creature's soul returns to its body if the body is alive and within 100 feet. Otherwise, that creature dies.

When the spell ends, the container is destroyed.

MAGIC MISSILE
1st-level evocation

Casting Time: 1 action
Range: 120 feet
Components: V, S
Duration: Instantaneous

You create three glowing darts of magical force. Each dart hits a creature of your choice that you can see within range. A dart deals 1d4 + 1 force damage to its target. The darts all strike simultaneously, and you can direct them to hit one creature or several.

At Higher Levels. When you cast this spell using a spell slot of 2nd level or higher, the spell creates one more dart for each slot level above 1st.

MAGIC MOUTH
2nd-level illusion (ritual)

Casting Time: 1 minute
Range: 30 feet
Components: V, S, M (a small bit of honeycomb and jade dust worth at least 10 gp, which the spell consumes)
Duration: Until dispelled

You implant a message within an object in range, a message that is uttered when a trigger condition is met. Choose an object that you can see and that isn't being worn or carried by another creature. Then speak the message, which must be 25 words or less, though it can be delivered over as long as 10 minutes. Finally, determine the circumstance that will trigger the spell to deliver your message.

When that circumstance occurs, a magical mouth appears on the object and recites the message in your voice and at the same volume you spoke. If the object you chose has a mouth or something that looks like a mouth (for example, the mouth of a statue), the magical mouth appears there so that the words appear to come from the object's mouth. When you cast this spell, you can have the spell end after it delivers its message, or it can remain and repeat its message whenever the trigger occurs.

The triggering circumstance can be as general or as detailed as you like, though it must be based on visual or audible conditions that occur within 30 feet of the object. For example, you could instruct the mouth to speak when any creature moves within 30 feet of the object or when a silver bell rings within 30 feet of it.

MAGIC WEAPON
2nd-level transmutation

Casting Time: 1 bonus action
Range: Touch
Components: V, S
Duration: Concentration, up to 1 hour

You touch a nonmagical weapon. Until the spell ends, that weapon becomes a magic weapon with a +1 bonus to attack rolls and damage rolls.

At Higher Levels. When you cast this spell using a spell slot of 4th level or higher, the bonus increases to +2. When you use a spell slot of 6th level or higher, the bonus increases to +3.

MAJOR IMAGE
3rd-level illusion

Casting Time: 1 action
Range: 120 feet
Components: V, S, M (a bit of fleece)
Duration: Concentration, up to 10 minutes

You create the image of an object, a creature, or some other visible phenomenon that is no larger than a 20-foot cube. The image appears at a spot that you can see within range and lasts for the duration. It seems completely real, including sounds, smells, and temperature appropriate to the thing depicted. You can't create sufficient heat or cold to cause damage, a sound loud enough to deal thunder damage or deafen a creature, or a smell that might sicken a creature (like a troglodyte's stench).

As long as you are within range of the illusion, you can use your action to cause the image to move to any other spot within range. As the image changes location, you can alter its appearance so that its movements appear natural for the image. For example, if you create an image of a creature and move it, you can alter the image so that it appears to be walking. Similarly, you can cause the illusion to make different sounds at different times, even making it carry on a conversation, for example.

Physical interaction with the image reveals it to be an illusion, because things can pass through it. A creature that uses its action to examine the image can determine that it is an illusion with a successful Intelligence (Investigation) check against your spell save DC. If a creature discerns the illusion for what it is, the creature can see through the image, and its other sensory qualities become faint to the creature.

At Higher Levels. When you cast this spell using a spell slot of 6th level or higher, the spell lasts until dispelled, without requiring your concentration.

MASS CURE WOUNDS
5th-level evocation

Casting Time: 1 action
Range: 60 feet
Components: V, S
Duration: Instantaneous

A wave of healing energy washes out from a point of your choice within range. Choose up to six creatures in a 30-foot-radius sphere centered on that point. Each target regains hit points equal to 3d8 + your spellcasting ability modifier. This spell has no effect on undead or constructs.

At Higher Levels. When you cast this spell using a spell slot of 6th level or higher, the healing increases by 1d8 for each slot level above 5th.

MASS HEAL
9th-level evocation

Casting Time: 1 action
Range: 60 feet
Components: V, S
Duration: Instantaneous

A flood of healing energy flows from you into injured creatures around you. You restore up to 700 hit points, divided as you choose among any number of creatures that you can see within range. Creatures healed by this spell are also cured of all diseases and any effect making them blinded or deafened. This spell has no effect on undead or constructs.

MASS HEALING WORD
3rd-level evocation

Casting Time: 1 bonus action
Range: 60 feet
Components: V
Duration: Instantaneous

As you call out words of restoration, up to six creatures of your choice that you can see within range regain hit points equal to 1d4 + your spellcasting ability modifier. This spell has no effect on undead or constructs.

At Higher Levels. When you cast this spell using a spell slot of 4th level or higher, the healing increases by 1d4 for each slot level above 3rd.

MASS SUGGESTION
6th-level enchantment

Casting Time: 1 action
Range: 60 feet
Components: V, M (a snake's tongue and either a bit of honeycomb or a drop of sweet oil)
Duration: 24 hours

You suggest a course of activity (limited to a sentence or two) and magically influence up to twelve creatures of your choice that you can see within range and that can hear and understand you. Creatures that can't be charmed are immune to this effect. The suggestion must be worded in such a manner as to make the course of action sound reasonable. Asking the creature to stab itself, throw itself onto a spear, immolate itself, or do some other obviously harmful act automatically negates the effect of the spell.

Each target must make a Wisdom saving throw. On a failed save, it pursues the course of action you described to the best of its ability. The suggested course of action can continue for the entire duration. If the suggested activity can be completed in a shorter time, the spell ends when the subject finishes what it was asked to do.

You can also specify conditions that will trigger a special activity during the duration. For example, you might suggest that a group of soldiers give all their money to the first beggar they meet. If the condition isn't met before the spell ends, the activity isn't performed.

If you or any of your companions damage a creature affected by this spell, the spell ends for that creature.

At Higher Levels. When you cast this spell using a 7th-level spell slot, the duration is 10 days. When you use an 8th-level spell slot, the duration is 30 days. When you use a 9th-level spell slot, the duration is a year and a day.

MAZE
8th-level conjuration

Casting Time: 1 action
Range: 60 feet

Components: V, S
Duration: Concentration, up to 10 minutes

You banish a creature that you can see within range into a labyrinthine demiplane. The target remains there for the duration or until it escapes the maze.

The target can use its action to attempt to escape. When it does so, it makes a DC 20 Intelligence check. If it succeeds, it escapes, and the spell ends (a minotaur or goristro demon automatically succeeds).

When the spell ends, the target reappears in the space it left or, if that space is occupied, in the nearest unoccupied space.

MELD INTO STONE
3rd-level transmutation (ritual)

Casting Time: 1 action
Range: Touch
Components: V, S
Duration: 8 hours

You step into a stone object or surface large enough to fully contain your body, melding yourself and all the equipment you carry with the stone for the duration. Using your movement, you step into the stone at a point you can touch. Nothing of your presence remains visible or otherwise detectable by nonmagical senses.

While merged with the stone, you can't see what occurs outside it, and any Wisdom (Perception) checks you make to hear sounds outside it are made with disadvantage. You remain aware of the passage of time and can cast spells on yourself while merged in the stone. You can use your movement to leave the stone where you entered it, which ends the spell. You otherwise can't move.

Minor physical damage to the stone doesn't harm you, but its partial destruction or a change in its shape (to the extent that you no longer fit within it) expels you and deals 6d6 bludgeoning damage to you. The stone's complete destruction (or transmutation into a different substance) expels you and deals 50 bludgeoning damage to you. If expelled, you fall prone in an unoccupied space closest to where you first entered.

MELF'S ACID ARROW
2nd-level evocation

Casting Time: 1 action
Range: 90 feet
Components: V, S, M (powdered rhubarb leaf and an adder's stomach)
Duration: Instantaneous

A shimmering green arrow streaks toward a target within range and bursts in a spray of acid. Make a ranged spell attack against the target. On a hit, the target takes 4d4 acid damage immediately and 2d4 acid damage at the end of its next turn. On a miss, the arrow splashes the target with acid for half as much of the initial damage and no damage at the end of its next turn.

At Higher Levels. When you cast this spell using a spell slot of 3rd level or higher, the damage (both initial and later) increases by 1d4 for each slot level above 2nd.

MENDING
Transmutation cantrip

Casting Time: 1 minute
Range: Touch
Components: V, S, M (two lodestones)
Duration: Instantaneous

This spell repairs a single break or tear in an object you touch, such as a broken chain link, two halves of a broken key, a torn cloak, or a leaking wineskin. As long as the break or tear is no larger than 1 foot in any dimension, you mend it, leaving no trace of the former damage.

This spell can physically repair a magic item or construct, but the spell can't restore magic to such an object.

MESSAGE
Transmutation cantrip

Casting Time: 1 action
Range: 120 feet
Components: V, S, M (a short piece of copper wire)
Duration: 1 round

You point your finger toward a creature within range and whisper a message. The target (and only the target) hears the message and can reply in a whisper that only you can hear.

You can cast this spell through solid objects if you are familiar with the target and know it is beyond the barrier. Magical silence, 1 foot of stone, 1 inch of common metal, a thin sheet of lead, or 3 feet of wood blocks the spell. The spell doesn't have to follow a straight line and can travel freely around corners or through openings.

METEOR SWARM
9th-level evocation

Casting Time: 1 action
Range: 1 mile
Components: V, S
Duration: Instantaneous

Blazing orbs of fire plummet to the ground at four different points you can see within range. Each creature in a 40-foot-radius sphere centered on each point you choose must make a Dexterity saving throw. The sphere spreads around corners. A creature takes 20d6 fire damage and 20d6 bludgeoning damage on a failed save, or half as much damage on a successful one. A creature in the area of more than one fiery burst is affected only once.

The spell damages objects in the area and ignites flammable objects that aren't being worn or carried.

MIND BLANK
8th-level abjuration

Casting Time: 1 action
Range: Touch
Components: V, S
Duration: 24 hours

Until the spell ends, one willing creature you touch is immune to psychic damage, any effect that would sense its emotions or read its thoughts, divination spells, and the charmed condition. The spell even foils *wish* spells and spells or effects of similar power used to affect the target's mind or to gain information about the target.

MINOR ILLUSION
Illusion cantrip

Casting Time: 1 action
Range: 30 feet
Components: S, M (a bit of fleece)
Duration: 1 minute

You create a sound or an image of an object within range that lasts for the duration. The illusion also ends if you dismiss it as an action or cast this spell again.

If you create a sound, its volume can range from a whisper to a scream. It can be your voice, someone else's voice, a lion's roar, a beating of drums, or any other sound you choose. The sound continues unabated throughout the duration, or you can make discrete sounds at different times before the spell ends.

If you create an image of an object—such as a chair, muddy footprints, or a small chest—it must be no larger than a 5-foot cube. The image can't create sound, light, smell, or any other sensory effect. Physical interaction with the image reveals it to be an illusion, because things can pass through it.

If a creature uses its action to examine the sound or image, the creature can determine that it is an illusion with a successful Intelligence (Investigation) check against your spell save DC. If a creature discerns the illusion for what it is, the illusion becomes faint to the creature.

MIRAGE ARCANE
7th-level illusion

Casting Time: 10 minutes
Range: Sight
Components: V, S
Duration: 10 days

You make terrain in an area up to 1 mile square look, sound, smell, and even feel like some other sort of terrain. The terrain's general shape remains the same, however. Open fields or a road could be made to resemble a swamp, hill, crevasse, or some other difficult or impassable terrain. A pond can be made to seem like a grassy meadow, a precipice like a gentle slope, or a rock-strewn gully like a wide and smooth road.

Similarly, you can alter the appearance of structures, or add them where none are present. The spell doesn't disguise, conceal, or add creatures.

The illusion includes audible, visual, tactile, and olfactory elements, so it can turn clear ground into difficult terrain (or vice versa) or otherwise impede movement through the area. Any piece of the illusory terrain (such as a rock or stick) that is removed from the spell's area disappears immediately.

Creatures with truesight can see through the illusion to the terrain's true form; however, all other elements of the illusion remain, so while the creature is aware of the illusion's presence, the creature can still physically interact with the illusion.

MIRROR IMAGE
2nd-level illusion

Casting Time: 1 action
Range: Self
Components: V, S
Duration: 1 minute

Three illusory duplicates of yourself appear in your space. Until the spell ends, the duplicates move with you and mimic your actions, shifting position so it's impossible to track which image is real. You can use your action to dismiss the illusory duplicates.

Each time a creature targets you with an attack during the spell's duration, roll a d20 to determine whether the attack instead targets one of your duplicates.

If you have three duplicates, you must roll a 6 or higher to change the attack's target to a duplicate. With two duplicates, you must roll an 8 or higher. With one duplicate, you must roll an 11 or higher.

A duplicate's AC equals 10 + your Dexterity modifier. If an attack hits a duplicate, the duplicate is destroyed. A duplicate can be destroyed only by an attack that hits it. It ignores all other damage and effects. The spell ends when all three duplicates are destroyed.

A creature is unaffected by this spell if it can't see, if it relies on senses other than sight, such as blindsight, or if it can perceive illusions as false, as with truesight.

MISLEAD
5th-level illusion

Casting Time: 1 action
Range: Self
Components: S
Duration: Concentration, up to 1 hour

You become invisible at the same time that an illusory double of you appears where you are standing. The double lasts for the duration, but the invisibility ends if you attack or cast a spell.

You can use your action to move your illusory double up to twice your speed and make it gesture, speak, and behave in whatever way you choose.

You can see through its eyes and hear through its ears as if you were located where it is. On each of your turns as a bonus action, you can switch from using its senses to using your own, or back again. While you are using its senses, you are blinded and deafened in regard to your own surroundings.

MISTY STEP
2nd-level conjuration

Casting Time: 1 bonus action
Range: Self
Components: V
Duration: Instantaneous

Briefly surrounded by silvery mist, you teleport up to 30 feet to an unoccupied space that you can see.

MODIFY MEMORY
5th-level enchantment

Casting Time: 1 action
Range: 30 feet
Components: V, S
Duration: Concentration, up to 1 minute

You attempt to reshape another creature's memories. One creature that you can see must make a Wisdom saving throw. If you are fighting the creature, it has advantage on the saving throw. On a failed save, the target becomes charmed by you for the duration. The charmed target is incapacitated and unaware of its surroundings, though it can still hear you. If it takes any damage or is targeted by another spell, this spell ends, and none of the target's memories are modified.

While this charm lasts, you can affect the target's memory of an event that it experienced within the last 24 hours and that lasted no more than 10 minutes. You can permanently eliminate all memory of the event, allow the target to recall the event with perfect clarity and exacting detail, change its memory of the details of the event, or create a memory of some other event.

You must speak to the target to describe how its memories are affected, and it must be able to understand your language for the modified memories to take root. Its mind fills in any gaps in the details of your description. If the spell ends before you have finished describing the modified memories, the creature's memory isn't altered. Otherwise, the modified memories take hold when the spell ends.

A modified memory doesn't necessarily affect how a creature behaves, particularly if the memory contradicts the creature's natural inclinations, alignment, or beliefs. An illogical modified memory, such as implanting a memory of how much the creature enjoyed dousing itself in acid, is dismissed, perhaps as a bad dream. The DM might deem a modified memory too nonsensical to affect a creature in a significant manner.

A *remove curse* or *greater restoration* spell cast on the target restores the creature's true memory.

At Higher Levels. If you cast this spell using a spell slot of 6th level or higher, you can alter the target's memories of an event that took place up to 7 days ago (6th level), 30 days ago (7th level), 1 year ago (8th level), or any time in the creature's past (9th level).

MOONBEAM
2nd-level evocation

Casting Time: 1 action
Range: 120 feet
Components: V, S, M (several seeds of any moonseed plant and a piece of opalescent feldspar)
Duration: Concentration, up to 1 minute

A silvery beam of pale light shines down in a 5-foot-radius, 40-foot-high cylinder centered on a point within range. Until the spell ends, dim light fills the cylinder.

When a creature enters the spell's area for the first time on a turn or starts its turn there, it is engulfed in ghostly flames that cause searing pain, and it must make a Constitution saving throw. It takes 2d10 radiant damage on a failed save, or half as much damage on a successful one.

A shapechanger makes its saving throw with disadvantage. If it fails, it also instantly reverts to its original form and can't assume a different form until it leaves the spell's light.

On each of your turns after you cast this spell, you can use an action to move the beam 60 feet in any direction.

At Higher Levels. When you cast this spell using a spell slot of 3rd level or higher, the damage increases by 1d10 for each slot level above 2nd.

MORDENKAINEN'S FAITHFUL HOUND
4th-level conjuration

Casting Time: 1 action
Range: 30 feet
Components: V, S, M (a tiny silver whistle, a piece of bone, and a thread)
Duration: 8 hours

You conjure a phantom watchdog in an unoccupied space that you can see within range, where it remains for the duration, until you dismiss it as an action, or until you move more than 100 feet away from it.

The hound is invisible to all creatures except you and can't be harmed. When a Small or larger creature comes within 30 feet of it without first speaking the password that you specify when you cast this spell, the hound starts barking loudly. The hound sees invisible creatures and can see into the Ethereal Plane. It ignores illusions.

At the start of each of your turns, the hound attempts to bite one creature within 5 feet of it that is hostile to you. The hound's attack bonus is equal to your spellcasting ability modifier + your proficiency bonus. On a hit, it deals 4d8 piercing damage.

MORDENKAINEN'S MAGNIFICENT MANSION
7th-level conjuration

Casting Time: 1 minute
Range: 300 feet
Components: V, S, M (a miniature portal carved from ivory, a small piece of polished marble, and a tiny silver spoon, each item worth at least 5 gp)
Duration: 24 hours

You conjure an extradimensional dwelling in range that lasts for the duration. You choose where its one entrance is located. The entrance shimmers faintly and is 5 feet wide and 10 feet tall. You and any creature you designate when you cast the spell can enter the extradimensional dwelling as long as the portal remains open. You can open or close the portal if you are within 30 feet of it. While closed, the portal is invisible.

Beyond the portal is a magnificent foyer with numerous chambers beyond. The atmosphere is clean, fresh, and warm.

You can create any floor plan you like, but the space can't exceed 50 cubes, each cube being 10 feet on each side. The place is furnished and decorated as you choose. It contains sufficient food to serve a nine-course banquet for up to 100 people. A staff of 100 near-transparent servants attends all who enter. You

decide the visual appearance of these servants and their attire. They are completely obedient to your orders. Each servant can perform any task a normal human servant could perform, but they can't attack or take any action that would directly harm another creature. Thus the servants can fetch things, clean, mend, fold clothes, light fires, serve food, pour wine, and so on. The servants can go anywhere in the mansion but can't leave it. Furnishings and other objects created by this spell dissipate into smoke if removed from the mansion. When the spell ends, any creatures inside the extradimensional space are expelled into the open spaces nearest to the entrance.

MORDENKAINEN'S PRIVATE SANCTUM
4th-level abjuration

Casting Time: 10 minutes
Range: 120 feet
Components: V, S, M (a thin sheet of lead, a piece of opaque glass, a wad of cotton or cloth, and powdered chrysolite)
Duration: 24 hours

You make an area within range magically secure. The area is a cube that can be as small as 5 feet to as large as 100 feet on each side. The spell lasts for the duration or until you use an action to dismiss it.

When you cast the spell, you decide what sort of security the spell provides, choosing any or all of the following properties:

- Sound can't pass through the barrier at the edge of the warded area.
- The barrier of the warded area appears dark and foggy, preventing vision (including darkvision) through it.
- Sensors created by divination spells can't appear inside the protected area or pass through the barrier at its perimeter.
- Creatures in the area can't be targeted by divination spells.
- Nothing can teleport into or out of the warded area.
- Planar travel is blocked within the warded area.

Casting this spell on the same spot every day for a year makes this effect permanent.

At Higher Levels. When you cast this spell using a spell slot of 5th level or higher, you can increase the size of the cube by 100 feet for each slot level beyond 4th. Thus you could protect a cube that can be up to 200 feet on one side by using a spell slot of 5th level.

MORDENKAINEN'S SWORD
7th-level evocation

Casting Time: 1 action
Range: 60 feet
Components: V, S, M (a miniature platinum sword with a grip and pommel of copper and zinc, worth 250 gp)
Duration: Concentration, up to 1 minute

You create a sword-shaped plane of force that hovers within range. It lasts for the duration.

When the sword appears, you make a melee spell attack against a target of your choice within 5 feet of the sword. On a hit, the target takes 3d10 force damage.

Until the spell ends, you can use a bonus action on each of your turns to move the sword up to 20 feet to a spot you can see and repeat this attack against the same target or a different one.

MOVE EARTH
6th-level transmutation

Casting Time: 1 action
Range: 120 feet
Components: V, S, M (an iron blade and a small bag containing a mixture of soils—clay, loam, and sand)
Duration: Concentration, up to 2 hours

Choose an area of terrain no larger than 40 feet on a side within range. You can reshape dirt, sand, or clay in the area in any manner you choose for the duration. You can raise or lower the area's elevation, create or fill in a trench, erect or flatten a wall, or form a pillar. The extent of any such changes can't exceed half the area's largest dimension. So, if you affect a 40-foot square, you can create a pillar up to 20 feet high, raise or lower the square's elevation by up to 20 feet, dig a trench up to 20 feet deep, and so on. It takes 10 minutes for these changes to complete.

At the end of every 10 minutes you spend concentrating on the spell, you can choose a new area of terrain to affect.

Because the terrain's transformation occurs slowly, creatures in the area can't usually be trapped or injured by the ground's movement.

This spell can't manipulate natural stone or stone construction. Rocks and structures shift to accommodate the new terrain. If the way you shape the terrain would make a structure unstable, it might collapse.

Similarly, this spell doesn't directly affect plant growth. The moved earth carries any plants along with it.

NONDETECTION
3rd-level abjuration

Casting Time: 1 action
Range: Touch
Components: V, S, M (a pinch of diamond dust worth 25 gp sprinkled over the target, which the spell consumes)
Duration: 8 hours

For the duration, you hide a target that you touch from divination magic. The target can be a willing creature or a place or an object no larger than 10 feet in any dimension. The target can't be targeted by any divination magic or perceived through magical scrying sensors.

NYSTUL'S MAGIC AURA
2nd-level illusion

Casting Time: 1 action
Range: Touch
Components: V, S, M (a small square of silk)
Duration: 24 hours

You place an illusion on a creature or an object you touch so that divination spells reveal false information about it. The target can be a willing creature or an object that isn't being carried or worn by another creature.

When you cast the spell, choose one or both of the following effects. The effect lasts for the duration. If you cast this spell on the same creature or object every day for 30 days, placing the same effect on it each time, the illusion lasts until it is dispelled.

False Aura. You change the way the target appears to spells and magical effects, such as *detect magic*, that detect magical auras. You can make a nonmagical object appear magical, a magical object appear nonmagical, or change the object's magical aura so that it appears to belong to a specific school of magic that you choose. When you use this effect on an object, you can make the false magic apparent to any creature that handles the item.

Mask. You change the way the target appears to spells and magical effects that detect creature types, such as a paladin's Divine Sense or the trigger of a *symbol* spell. You choose a creature type and other spells and magical effects treat the target as if it were a creature of that type or of that alignment.

OTILUKE'S FREEZING SPHERE
6th-level evocation

Casting Time: 1 action
Range: 300 feet
Components: V, S, M (a small crystal sphere)
Duration: Instantaneous

A frigid globe of cold energy streaks from your fingertips to a point of your choice within range, where it explodes in a 60-foot-radius sphere. Each creature within the area must make a Constitution saving throw. On a failed save, a creature takes 10d6 cold damage. On a successful save, it takes half as much damage.

If the globe strikes a body of water or a liquid that is principally water (not including water-based creatures), it freezes the liquid to a depth of 6 inches over an area 30 feet square. This ice lasts for 1 minute. Creatures that were swimming on the surface of frozen water are trapped in the ice. A trapped creature can use an action to make a Strength check against your spell save DC to break free.

You can refrain from firing the globe after completing the spell, if you wish. A small globe about the size of a sling stone, cool to the touch, appears in your hand. At any time, you or a creature you give the globe to can throw the globe (to a range of 40 feet) or hurl it with a sling (to the sling's normal range). It shatters on impact, with the same effect as the normal casting of the spell. You can also set the globe down without shattering it. After 1 minute, if the globe hasn't already shattered, it explodes.

At Higher Levels. When you cast this spell using a spell slot of 7th level or higher, the damage increases by 1d6 for each slot level above 6th.

OTILUKE'S RESILIENT SPHERE
4th-level evocation

Casting Time: 1 action
Range: 30 feet
Components: V, S, M (a hemispherical piece of clear crystal and a matching hemispherical piece of gum arabic)
Duration: Concentration, up to 1 minute

A sphere of shimmering force encloses a creature or object of Large size or smaller within range. An unwilling creature must make a Dexterity saving throw. On a failed save, the creature is enclosed for the duration.

Nothing—not physical objects, energy, or other spell effects—can pass through the barrier, in or out, though a creature in the sphere can breathe there. The sphere is immune to all damage, and a creature or object inside can't be damaged by attacks or effects originating from outside, nor can a creature inside the sphere damage anything outside it.

The sphere is weightless and just large enough to contain the creature or object inside. An enclosed creature can use its action to push against the sphere's walls and thus roll the sphere at up to half the creature's speed. Similarly, the globe can be picked up and moved by other creatures.

A *disintegrate* spell targeting the globe destroys it without harming anything inside it.

OTTO'S IRRESISTIBLE DANCE
6th-level enchantment

Casting Time: 1 action
Range: 30 feet
Components: V
Duration: Concentration, up to 1 minute

Choose one creature that you can see within range. The target begins a comic dance in place: shuffling, tapping its feet, and capering for the duration. Creatures that can't be charmed are immune to this spell.

A dancing creature must use all its movement to dance without leaving its space and has disadvantage on Dexterity saving throws and attack rolls. While the target is affected by this spell, other creatures have advantage on attack rolls against it. As an action, a dancing creature makes a Wisdom saving throw to regain control of itself. On a successful save, the spell ends.

PASS WITHOUT TRACE
2nd-level abjuration

Casting Time: 1 action
Range: Self
Components: V, S, M (ashes from a burned leaf of mistletoe and a sprig of spruce)
Duration: Concentration, up to 1 hour

A veil of shadows and silence radiates from you, masking you and your companions from detection. For the duration, each creature you choose within 30 feet of you (including you) has a +10 bonus to Dexterity (Stealth) checks and can't be tracked except by magical means. A creature that receives this bonus leaves behind no tracks or other traces of its passage.

PASSWALL
5th-level transmutation

Casting Time: 1 action
Range: 30 feet
Components: V, S, M (a pinch of sesame seeds)
Duration: 1 hour

A passage appears at a point of your choice that you can see on a wooden, plaster, or stone surface (such as a wall, a ceiling, or a floor) within range, and lasts for the duration. You choose the opening's dimensions: up to 5 feet wide, 8 feet tall, and 20 feet deep. The passage creates no instability in a structure surrounding it.

When the opening disappears, any creatures or objects still in the passage created by the spell are safely ejected to an unoccupied space nearest to the surface on which you cast the spell.

PHANTASMAL FORCE
2nd-level illusion

Casting Time: 1 action
Range: 60 feet
Components: V, S, M (a bit of fleece)
Duration: Concentration, up to 1 minute

You craft an illusion that takes root in the mind of a creature that you can see within range. The target must make an Intelligence saving throw. On a failed save, you create a phantasmal object, creature, or other visible phenomenon of your choice that is no larger than a 10-foot cube and that is perceivable only to the target for the duration. This spell has no effect on undead or constructs.

The phantasm includes sound, temperature, and other stimuli, also evident only to the creature.

The target can use its action to examine the phantasm with an Intelligence (Investigation) check against your spell save DC. If the check succeeds, the target realizes that the phantasm is an illusion, and the spell ends.

While a target is affected by the spell, the target treats the phantasm as if it were real. The target rationalizes any illogical outcomes from interacting with the phantasm. For example, a target attempting to walk across a phantasmal bridge that spans a chasm falls once it steps onto the bridge. If the target survives the fall, it still believes that the bridge exists and comes up with some other explanation for its fall—it was pushed, it slipped, or a strong wind might have knocked it off.

An affected target is so convinced of the phantasm's reality that it can even take damage from the illusion. A phantasm created to appear as a creature can attack the target. Similarly, a phantasm created to appear as fire, a pool of acid, or lava can burn the target. Each round on your turn, the phantasm can deal 1d6 psychic damage to the target if it is in the phantasm's area or within 5 feet of the phantasm, provided that the illusion is of a creature or hazard that could logically deal damage, such as by attacking. The target perceives the damage as a type appropriate to the illusion.

PHANTASMAL KILLER
4th-level illusion

Casting Time: 1 action
Range: 120 feet
Components: V, S
Duration: Concentration, up to 1 minute

You tap into the nightmares of a creature you can see within range and create an illusory manifestation of its deepest fears, visible only to that creature. The target must make a Wisdom saving throw. On a failed save, the target becomes frightened for the duration. At the end of each of the target's turns before the spell ends, the target must succeed on a Wisdom saving throw or take 4d10 psychic damage. On a successful save, the spell ends.

At Higher Levels. When you cast this spell using a spell slot of 5th level or higher, the damage increases by 1d10 for each slot level above 4th.

PHANTOM STEED
3rd-level illusion (ritual)

Casting Time: 1 minute
Range: 30 feet
Components: V, S
Duration: 1 hour

A Large quasi-real, horselike creature appears on the ground in an unoccupied space of your choice within range. You decide the creature's appearance, but it is equipped with a saddle, bit, and bridle. Any of the equipment created by the spell vanishes in a puff of smoke if it is carried more than 10 feet away from the steed.

For the duration, you or a creature you choose can ride the steed. The creature uses the statistics for a riding horse, except it has a speed of 100 feet and can travel 10 miles in an hour, or 13 miles at a fast pace. When the spell ends, the steed gradually fades, giving the rider 1 minute to dismount. The spell ends if you use an action to dismiss it or if the steed takes any damage.

PLANAR ALLY
6th-level conjuration

Casting Time: 10 minutes
Range: 60 feet
Components: V, S
Duration: Instantaneous

You beseech an otherworldly entity for aid. The being must be known to you: a god, a primordial, a demon prince, or some other being of cosmic power. That entity sends a celestial, an elemental, or a fiend loyal to it to aid you, making the creature appear in an unoccupied space within range. If you know a specific creature's name, you can speak that name when you cast this spell to request that creature, though you might get a different creature anyway (DM's choice).

When the creature appears, it is under no compulsion to behave in any particular way. You can ask the creature to perform a service in exchange for payment, but it isn't obliged to do so. The requested task could range from simple (fly us across the chasm, or help us fight a battle) to complex (spy on our enemies, or protect us during our foray into the dungeon). You must be able to communicate with the creature to bargain for its services.

Payment can take a variety of forms. A celestial might require a sizable donation of gold or magic items to an allied temple, while a fiend might demand a living sacrifice or a gift of treasure. Some creatures might exchange their service for a quest undertaken by you.

As a rule of thumb, a task that can be measured in minutes requires a payment worth 100 gp per minute. A task measured in hours requires 1,000 gp per hour. And a task measured in days (up to 10 days) requires 10,000 gp per day. The DM can adjust these payments based on the circumstances under which you cast the spell. If the task is aligned with the creature's ethos, the payment might be halved or even waived. Nonhazardous tasks typically require only half the suggested payment, while especially dangerous tasks might require a greater gift. Creatures rarely accept tasks that seem suicidal.

After the creature completes the task, or when the agreed-upon duration of service expires, the creature returns to its home plane after reporting back to you, if appropriate to the task and if possible. If you are unable to agree on a price for the creature's service, the creature immediately returns to its home plane.

A creature enlisted to join your group counts as a member of it, receiving a full share of experience points awarded.

PLANAR BINDING
5th-level abjuration

Casting Time: 1 hour
Range: 60 feet
Components: V, S, M (a jewel worth at least 1,000 gp, which the spell consumes)
Duration: 24 hours

With this spell, you attempt to bind a celestial, an elemental, a fey, or a fiend to your service. The creature must be within range for the entire casting of the spell. (Typically, the creature is first summoned into the center of an inverted *magic circle* in order to keep it trapped while this spell is cast.) At the completion of the casting, the target must make a Charisma saving throw. On a failed save, it is bound to serve you for the duration. If the creature was summoned or created by another spell, that spell's duration is extended to match the duration of this spell.

A bound creature must follow your instructions to the best of its ability. You might command the creature to accompany you on an adventure, to guard a location, or to deliver a message. The creature obeys the letter of your instructions, but if the creature is hostile to you, it strives to twist your words to achieve its own objectives. If the creature carries out your instructions completely before the spell ends, it travels to you to report this fact if you are on the same plane of existence. If you are on a different plane of existence, it returns to the place where you bound it and remains there until the spell ends.

At Higher Levels. When you cast this spell using a spell slot of a higher level, the duration increases to 10 days with a 6th-level slot, to 30 days with a 7th-level slot, to 180 days with an 8th-level slot, and to a year and a day with a 9th-level spell slot.

Plane Shift

7th-level conjuration

Casting Time: 1 action
Range: Touch
Components: V, S, M (a forked, metal rod worth at least 250 gp, attuned to a particular plane of existence)
Duration: Instantaneous

You and up to eight willing creatures who link hands in a circle are transported to a different plane of existence. You can specify a target destination in general terms, such as the City of Brass on the Elemental Plane of Fire or the palace of Dispater on the second level of the Nine Hells, and you appear in or near that destination. If you are trying to reach the City of Brass, for example, you might arrive in its Street of Steel, before its Gate of Ashes, or looking at the city from across the Sea of Fire, at the DM's discretion.

Alternatively, if you know the sigil sequence of a teleportation circle on another plane of existence, this spell can take you to that circle. If the teleportation circle is too small to hold all the creatures you transported, they appear in the closest unoccupied spaces next to the circle.

You can use this spell to banish an unwilling creature to another plane. Choose a creature within your reach and make a melee spell attack against it. On a hit, the creature must make a Charisma saving throw. If the creature fails this save, it is transported to a random location on the plane of existence you specify. A creature so transported must find its own way back to your current plane of existence.

Plant Growth

3rd-level transmutation

Casting Time: 1 action or 8 hours
Range: 150 feet
Components: V, S
Duration: Instantaneous

This spell channels vitality into plants within a specific area. There are two possible uses for the spell, granting either immediate or long-term benefits.

If you cast this spell using 1 action, choose a point within range. All normal plants in a 100-foot radius centered on that point become thick and overgrown. A creature moving through the area must spend 4 feet of movement for every 1 foot it moves.

You can exclude one or more areas of any size within the spell's area from being affected.

If you cast this spell over 8 hours, you enrich the land. All plants in a half-mile radius centered on a point within range become enriched for 1 year. The plants yield twice the normal amount of food when harvested.

Poison Spray

Conjuration cantrip

Casting Time: 1 action
Range: 10 feet
Components: V, S
Duration: Instantaneous

You extend your hand toward a creature you can see within range and project a puff of noxious gas from your palm. The creature must succeed on a Constitution saving throw or take 1d12 poison damage.

This spell's damage increases by 1d12 when you reach 5th level (2d12), 11th level (3d12), and 17th level (4d12).

Polymorph

4th-level transmutation

Casting Time: 1 action
Range: 60 feet
Components: V, S, M (a caterpillar cocoon)
Duration: Concentration, up to 1 hour

This spell transforms a creature that you can see within range into a new form. An unwilling creature must make a Wisdom saving throw to avoid the effect. The spell has no effect on a shapechanger or a creature with 0 hit points.

The transformation lasts for the duration, or until the target drops to 0 hit points or dies. The new form can be any beast whose challenge rating is equal to or less than the target's (or the target's level, if it doesn't have a challenge rating). The target's game statistics, including mental ability scores, are replaced by the statistics of the chosen beast. It retains its alignment and personality.

The target assumes the hit points of its new form. When it reverts to its normal form, the creature returns to the number of hit points it had before it transformed. If it reverts as a result of dropping to 0 hit points, any excess damage carries over to its normal form. As long as the excess damage doesn't reduce the creature's normal form to 0 hit points, it isn't knocked unconscious.

The creature is limited in the actions it can perform by the nature of its new form, and it can't speak, cast spells, or take any other action that requires hands or speech.

The target's gear melds into the new form. The creature can't activate, use, wield, or otherwise benefit from any of its equipment.

Power Word Heal

9th-level evocation

Casting Time: 1 action
Range: Touch
Components: V, S
Duration: Instantaneous

A wave of healing energy washes over the creature you touch. The target regains all its hit points. If the creature is charmed, frightened, paralyzed, or stunned, the condition ends. If the creature is prone, it can use its reaction to stand up. This spell has no effect on undead or constructs.

Power Word Kill

9th-level enchantment

Casting Time: 1 action
Range: 60 feet
Components: V
Duration: Instantaneous

You utter a word of power that can compel one creature you can see within range to die instantly. If the creature you choose has 100 hit points or fewer, it dies. Otherwise, the spell has no effect.

POWER WORD STUN
8th-level enchantment

Casting Time: 1 action
Range: 60 feet
Components: V
Duration: Instantaneous

You speak a word of power that can overwhelm the mind of one creature you can see within range, leaving it dumbfounded. If the target has 150 hit points or fewer, it is stunned. Otherwise, the spell has no effect.

The stunned target must make a Constitution saving throw at the end of each of its turns. On a successful save, this stunning effect ends.

PRAYER OF HEALING
2nd-level evocation

Casting Time: 10 minutes
Range: 30 feet
Components: V
Duration: Instantaneous

Up to six creatures of your choice that you can see within range each regain hit points equal to 2d8 + your spellcasting ability modifier. This spell has no effect on undead or constructs.

At Higher Levels. When you cast this spell using a spell slot of 3rd level or higher, the healing increases by 1d8 for each slot level above 2nd.

PRESTIDIGITATION
Transmutation cantrip

Casting Time: 1 action
Range: 10 feet
Components: V, S
Duration: Up to 1 hour

This spell is a minor magical trick that novice spellcasters use for practice. You create one of the following magical effects within range:

- You create an instantaneous, harmless sensory effect, such as a shower of sparks, a puff of wind, faint musical notes, or an odd odor.
- You instantaneously light or snuff out a candle, a torch, or a small campfire.
- You instantaneously clean or soil an object no larger than 1 cubic foot.
- You chill, warm, or flavor up to 1 cubic foot of nonliving material for 1 hour.
- You make a color, a small mark, or a symbol appear on an object or a surface for 1 hour.
- You create a nonmagical trinket or an illusory image that can fit in your hand and that lasts until the end of your next turn.

If you cast this spell multiple times, you can have up to three of its non-instantaneous effects active at a time, and you can dismiss such an effect as an action.

PRISMATIC SPRAY
7th-level evocation

Casting Time: 1 action
Range: Self (60-foot cone)
Components: V, S
Duration: Instantaneous

Eight multicolored rays of light flash from your hand. Each ray is a different color and has a different power and purpose. Each creature in a 60-foot cone must make a Dexterity saving throw. For each target, roll a d8 to determine which color ray affects it.

1. Red. The target takes 10d6 fire damage on a failed save, or half as much damage on a successful one.

2. Orange. The target takes 10d6 acid damage on a failed save, or half as much damage on a successful one.

3. Yellow. The target takes 10d6 lightning damage on a failed save, or half as much damage on a successful one.

4. Green. The target takes 10d6 poison damage on a failed save, or half as much damage on a successful one.

5. Blue. The target takes 10d6 cold damage on a failed save, or half as much damage on a successful one.

6. Indigo. On a failed save, the target is restrained. It must then make a Constitution saving throw at the end of each of its turns. If it successfully saves three times, the spell ends. If it fails its save three times, it permanently turns to stone and is subjected to the petrified condition. The successes and failures don't need to be consecutive; keep track of both until the target collects three of a kind.

7. Violet. On a failed save, the target is blinded. It must then make a Wisdom saving throw at the start of your next turn. A successful save ends the blindness. If it fails that save, the creature is transported to another plane of existence of the DM's choosing and is no longer blinded. (Typically, a creature that is on a plane that isn't its home plane is banished home, while other creatures are usually cast into the Astral or Ethereal planes.)

8. Special. The target is struck by two rays. Roll twice more, rerolling any 8.

PRISMATIC WALL
9th-level abjuration

Casting Time: 1 action
Range: 60 feet
Components: V, S
Duration: 10 minutes

A shimmering, multicolored plane of light forms a vertical opaque wall—up to 90 feet long, 30 feet high, and 1 inch thick—centered on a point you can see within range. Alternatively, you can shape the wall into a sphere up to 30 feet in diameter centered on a point you choose within range. The wall remains in place for the duration. If you position the wall so that it passes through a space occupied by a creature, the spell fails, and your action and the spell slot are wasted.

The wall sheds bright light out to a range of 100 feet and dim light for an additional 100 feet. You and creatures you designate at the time you cast the spell can pass through and remain near the wall without harm. If another creature that can see the wall moves to within 20 feet of it or starts its turn there, the creature

must succeed on a Constitution saving throw or become blinded for 1 minute.

The wall consists of seven layers, each with a different color. When a creature attempts to reach into or pass through the wall, it does so one layer at a time through all the wall's layers. As it passes or reaches through each layer, the creature must make a Dexterity saving throw or be affected by that layer's properties as described below.

The wall can be destroyed, also one layer at a time, in order from red to violet, by means specific to each layer. Once a layer is destroyed, it remains so for the duration of the spell. A *rod of cancellation* destroys a *prismatic wall*, but an *antimagic field* has no effect on it.

1. Red. The creature takes 10d6 fire damage on a failed save, or half as much damage on a successful one. While this layer is in place, nonmagical ranged attacks can't pass through the wall. The layer can be destroyed by dealing at least 25 cold damage to it.

2. Orange. The creature takes 10d6 acid damage on a failed save, or half as much damage on a successful one. While this layer is in place, magical ranged attacks can't pass through the wall. The layer is destroyed by a strong wind.

3. Yellow. The creature takes 10d6 lightning damage on a failed save, or half as much damage on a successful one. This layer can be destroyed by dealing at least 60 force damage to it.

4. Green. The creature takes 10d6 poison damage on a failed save, or half as much damage on a successful one. A *passwall* spell, or another spell of equal or greater level that can open a portal on a solid surface, destroys this layer.

5. Blue. The creature takes 10d6 cold damage on a failed save, or half as much damage on a successful one. This layer can be destroyed by dealing at least 25 fire damage to it.

6. Indigo. On a failed save, the creature is restrained. It must then make a Constitution saving throw at the end of each of its turns. If it successfully saves three times, the spell ends. If it fails its save three times, it permanently turns to stone and is subjected to the petrified condition. The successes and failures don't need to be consecutive; keep track of both until the creature collects three of a kind.

While this layer is in place, spells can't be cast through the wall. The layer is destroyed by bright light shed by a *daylight* spell or a similar spell of equal or higher level.

7. Violet. On a failed save, the creature is blinded. It must then make a Wisdom saving throw at the start of your next turn. A successful save ends the blindness. If it fails that save, the creature is transported to another plane of the DM's choosing and is no longer blinded. (Typically, a creature that is on a plane that isn't its home plane is banished home, while other creatures are usually cast into the Astral or Ethereal planes.) This layer is destroyed by a *dispel magic* spell or a similar spell of equal or higher level that can end spells and magical effects.

PRODUCE FLAME
Conjuration cantrip

Casting Time: 1 action
Range: Self
Components: V, S
Duration: 10 minutes

A flickering flame appears in your hand. The flame remains there for the duration and harms neither you nor your equipment. The flame sheds bright light in a 10-foot radius and dim light for an additional 10 feet. The spell ends if you dismiss it as an action or if you cast it again.

You can also attack with the flame, although doing so ends the spell. When you cast this spell, or as an action on a later turn, you can hurl the flame at a creature within 30 feet of you. Make a ranged spell attack. On a hit, the target takes 1d8 fire damage.

This spell's damage increases by 1d8 when you reach 5th level (2d8), 11th level (3d8), and 17th level (4d8).

PROGRAMMED ILLUSION
6th-level illusion

Casting Time: 1 action
Range: 120 feet
Components: V, S, M (a bit of fleece and jade dust worth at least 25 gp)
Duration: Until dispelled

You create an illusion of an object, a creature, or some other visible phenomenon within range that activates when a specific condition occurs. The illusion is imperceptible until then. It must be no larger than a 30-foot cube, and you decide when you cast the spell how the illusion behaves and what sounds it makes. This scripted performance can last up to 5 minutes.

When the condition you specify occurs, the illusion springs into existence and performs in the manner you described. Once the illusion finishes performing, it disappears and remains dormant for 10 minutes. After this time, the illusion can be activated again.

The triggering condition can be as general or as detailed as you like, though it must be based on visual or audible conditions that occur within 30 feet of the area. For example, you could create an illusion of yourself to appear and warn off others who attempt to open a trapped door, or you could set the illusion to trigger only when a creature says the correct word or phrase.

Physical interaction with the image reveals it to be an illusion, because things can pass through it. A creature that uses its action to examine the image can determine that it is an illusion with a successful Intelligence (Investigation) check against your spell save DC. If a creature discerns the illusion for what it is, the creature can see through the image, and any noise it makes sounds hollow to the creature.

PROJECT IMAGE
7th-level illusion

Casting Time: 1 action
Range: 500 miles
Components: V, S, M (a small replica of you made from materials worth at least 5 gp)
Duration: Concentration, up to 1 day

You create an illusory copy of yourself that lasts for the duration. The copy can appear at any location within range that you have seen before, regardless of intervening obstacles. The illusion looks and sounds like you but is intangible. If the illusion takes any damage, it disappears, and the spell ends.

You can use your action to move this illusion up to twice your speed, and make it gesture, speak, and behave in whatever way you choose. It mimics your mannerisms perfectly.

You can see through its eyes and hear through its ears as if you were in its space. On your turn as a bonus action, you can switch from using its senses to using your own, or back again. While you are using its senses, you are blinded and deafened in regard to your own surroundings.

Physical interaction with the image reveals it to be an illusion, because things can pass through it. A creature that uses its action to examine the image can determine that it is an illusion with a successful Intelligence (Investigation) check against your spell save DC. If a creature discerns the illusion for what it is, the creature can see through the image, and any noise it makes sounds hollow to the creature.

PROTECTION FROM ENERGY
3rd-level abjuration

Casting Time: 1 action
Range: Touch
Components: V, S
Duration: Concentration, up to 1 hour

For the duration, the willing creature you touch has resistance to one damage type of your choice: acid, cold, fire, lightning, or thunder.

PROTECTION FROM EVIL AND GOOD
1st-level abjuration

Casting Time: 1 action
Range: Touch
Components: V, S, M (holy water or powdered silver and iron, which the spell consumes)
Duration: Concentration up to 10 minutes

Until the spell ends, one willing creature you touch is protected against certain types of creatures: aberrations, celestials, elementals, fey, fiends, and undead.

The protection grants several benefits. Creatures of those types have disadvantage on attack rolls against the target. The target also can't be charmed, frightened, or possessed by them. If the target is already charmed, frightened, or possessed by such a creature, the target has advantage on any new saving throw against the relevant effect.

PROTECTION FROM POISON
2nd-level abjuration

Casting Time: 1 action
Range: Touch
Components: V, S
Duration: 1 hour

You touch a creature. If it is poisoned, you neutralize the poison. If more than one poison afflicts the target, you neutralize one poison that you know is present, or you neutralize one at random.

For the duration, the target has advantage on saving throws against being poisoned, and it has resistance to poison damage.

PURIFY FOOD AND DRINK
1st-level transmutation (ritual)

Casting Time: 1 action
Range: 10 feet
Components: V, S
Duration: Instantaneous

All nonmagical food and drink within a 5-foot-radius sphere centered on a point of your choice within range is purified and rendered free of poison and disease.

RAISE DEAD
5th-level necromancy

Casting Time: 1 hour
Range: Touch
Components: V, S, M (a diamond worth at least 500 gp, which the spell consumes)
Duration: Instantaneous

You return a dead creature you touch to life, provided that it has been dead no longer than 10 days. If the creature's soul is both willing and at liberty to rejoin the body, the creature returns to life with 1 hit point.

This spell also neutralizes any poisons and cures nonmagical diseases that affected the creature at the time it died. This spell doesn't, however, remove magical diseases, curses, or similar effects; if these aren't first removed prior to casting the spell, they take effect when the creature returns to life. The spell can't return an undead creature to life.

This spell closes all mortal wounds, but it doesn't restore missing body parts. If the creature is lacking body parts or organs integral for its survival—its head, for instance—the spell automatically fails.

Coming back from the dead is an ordeal. The target takes a −4 penalty to all attack rolls, saving throws, and ability checks. Every time the target finishes a long rest, the penalty is reduced by 1 until it disappears.

RARY'S TELEPATHIC BOND
5th-level divination (ritual)

Casting Time: 1 action
Range: 30 feet
Components: V, S, M (pieces of eggshell from two different kinds of creatures)
Duration: 1 hour

You forge a telepathic link among up to eight willing creatures of your choice within range, psychically linking each creature to all the others for the duration. Creatures with Intelligence scores of 2 or less aren't affected by this spell.

Until the spell ends, the targets can communicate telepathically through the bond whether or not they have a common language. The communication is possible over any distance, though it can't extend to other planes of existence.

RAY OF ENFEEBLEMENT
2nd-level necromancy

Casting Time: 1 action
Range: 60 feet
Components: V, S
Duration: Concentration, up to 1 minute

A black beam of enervating energy springs from your finger toward a creature within range. Make a ranged spell attack against the target. On a hit, the target deals only half damage with weapon attacks that use Strength until the spell ends.

At the end of each of the target's turns, it can make a Constitution saving throw against the spell. On a success, the spell ends.

RAY OF FROST
Evocation cantrip

Casting Time: 1 action
Range: 60 feet
Components: V, S
Duration: Instantaneous

A frigid beam of blue-white light streaks toward a creature within range. Make a ranged spell attack against the target. On a hit, it takes 1d8 cold damage, and its speed is reduced by 10 feet until the start of your next turn.

The spell's damage increases by 1d8 when you reach 5th level (2d8), 11th level (3d8), and 17th level (4d8).

RAY OF SICKNESS
1st-level necromancy

Casting Time: 1 action
Range: 60 feet
Components: V, S
Duration: Instantaneous

A ray of sickening greenish energy lashes out toward a creature within range. Make a ranged spell attack against the target. On a hit, the target takes 2d8 poison damage and must make a Constitution saving throw. On a failed save, it is also poisoned until the end of your next turn.

At Higher Levels. When you cast this spell using a spell slot of 2nd level or higher, the damage increases by 1d8 for each slot level above 1st.

REGENERATE
7th-level transmutation

Casting Time: 1 minute
Range: Touch
Components: V, S, M (a prayer wheel and holy water)
Duration: 1 hour

You touch a creature and stimulate its natural healing ability. The target regains 4d8 + 15 hit points. For the duration of the spell, the target regains 1 hit point at the start of each of its turns (10 hit points each minute).

The target's severed body members (fingers, legs, tails, and so on), if any, are restored after 2 minutes. If you have the severed part and hold it to the stump, the spell instantaneously causes the limb to knit to the stump.

REINCARNATE
5th-level transmutation

Casting Time: 1 hour
Range: Touch
Components: V, S, M (rare oils and unguents worth at least 1,000 gp, which the spell consumes)
Duration: Instantaneous

You touch a dead humanoid or a piece of a dead humanoid. Provided that the creature has been dead no longer than 10 days, the spell forms a new adult body for it and then calls the soul to enter that body. If the target's soul isn't free or willing to do so, the spell fails.

The magic fashions a new body for the creature to inhabit, which likely causes the creature's race to change. The DM rolls a d100 and consults the following table to determine what form the creature takes when restored to life, or the DM chooses a form.

d100	Race
01–04	Dragonborn
05–13	Dwarf, hill
14–21	Dwarf, mountain
22–25	Elf, dark
26–34	Elf, high
35–42	Elf, wood
43–46	Gnome, forest
47–52	Gnome, rock
53–56	Half-elf
57–60	Half-orc
61–68	Halfling, lightfoot
69–76	Halfling, stout
77–96	Human
97–00	Tiefling

The reincarnated creature recalls its former life and experiences. It retains the capabilities it had in its original form, except it exchanges its original race for the new one and changes its racial traits accordingly.

REMOVE CURSE
3rd-level abjuration

Casting Time: 1 action
Range: Touch
Components: V, S
Duration: Instantaneous

At your touch, all curses affecting one creature or object end. If the object is a cursed magic item, its curse remains, but the spell breaks its owner's attunement to the object so it can be removed or discarded.

Resistance
Abjuration cantrip

Casting Time: 1 action
Range: Touch
Components: V, S, M (a miniature cloak)
Duration: Concentration, up to 1 minute

You touch one willing creature. Once before the spell ends, the target can roll a d4 and add the number rolled to one saving throw of its choice. It can roll the die before or after making the saving throw. The spell then ends.

Resurrection
7th-level necromancy

Casting Time: 1 hour
Range: Touch
Components: V, S, M (a diamond worth at least 1,000 gp, which the spell consumes)
Duration: Instantaneous

You touch a dead creature that has been dead for no more than a century, that didn't die of old age, and that isn't undead. If its soul is free and willing, the target returns to life with all its hit points.

This spell neutralizes any poisons and cures normal diseases afflicting the creature when it died. It doesn't, however, remove magical diseases, curses, and the like; if such effects aren't removed prior to casting the spell, they afflict the target on its return to life.

This spell closes all mortal wounds and restores any missing body parts.

Coming back from the dead is an ordeal. The target takes a −4 penalty to all attack rolls, saving throws, and ability checks. Every time the target finishes a long rest, the penalty is reduced by 1 until it disappears.

Casting this spell to restore life to a creature that has been dead for one year or longer taxes you greatly. Until you finish a long rest, you can't cast spells again, and you have disadvantage on all attack rolls, ability checks, and saving throws.

Reverse Gravity
7th-level transmutation

Casting Time: 1 action
Range: 100 feet
Components: V, S, M (a lodestone and iron filings)
Duration: Concentration, up to 1 minute

This spell reverses gravity in a 50-foot-radius, 100-foot high cylinder centered on a point within range. All creatures and objects that aren't somehow anchored to the ground in the area fall upward and reach the top of the area when you cast this spell. A creature can make a Dexterity saving throw to grab onto a fixed object it can reach, thus avoiding the fall.

If some solid object (such as a ceiling) is encountered in this fall, falling objects and creatures strike it just as they would during a normal downward fall. If an object or creature reaches the top of the area without striking anything, it remains there, oscillating slightly, for the duration.

At the end of the duration, affected objects and creatures fall back down.

Revivify
3rd-level necromancy

Casting Time: 1 action
Range: Touch
Components: V, S, M (diamonds worth 300 gp, which the spell consumes)
Duration: Instantaneous

You touch a creature that has died within the last minute. That creature returns to life with 1 hit point. This spell can't return to life a creature that has died of old age, nor can it restore any missing body parts.

Rope Trick
2nd-level transmutation

Casting Time: 1 action
Range: Touch
Components: V, S, M (powdered corn extract and a twisted loop of parchment)
Duration: 1 hour

You touch a length of rope that is up to 60 feet long. One end of the rope then rises into the air until the whole rope hangs perpendicular to the ground. At the upper end of the rope, an invisible entrance opens to an extradimensional space that lasts until the spell ends.

The extradimensional space can be reached by climbing to the top of the rope. The space can hold as many as eight Medium or smaller creatures. The rope can be pulled into the space, making the rope disappear from view outside the space.

Attacks and spells can't cross through the entrance into or out of the extradimensional space, but those inside can see out of it as if through a 3-foot-by-5-foot window centered on the rope.

Anything inside the extradimensional space drops out when the spell ends.

Sacred Flame
Evocation cantrip

Casting Time: 1 action
Range: 60 feet
Components: V, S
Duration: Instantaneous

Flame-like radiance descends on a creature that you can see within range. The target must succeed on a Dexterity saving throw or take 1d8 radiant damage. The target gains no benefit from cover for this saving throw.

The spell's damage increases by 1d8 when you reach 5th level (2d8), 11th level (3d8), and 17th level (4d8).

Sanctuary
1st-level abjuration

Casting Time: 1 bonus action
Range: 30 feet
Components: V, S, M (a small silver mirror)
Duration: 1 minute

You ward a creature within range against attack. Until the spell ends, any creature who targets the warded creature with an attack or a harmful spell must first make a Wisdom saving throw. On a failed save, the creature must choose a new target or lose the attack or spell. This spell doesn't protect the warded creature from area effects, such as the explosion of a fireball.

If the warded creature makes an attack or casts a spell that affects an enemy creature, this spell ends.

SCORCHING RAY
2nd-level evocation

Casting Time: 1 action
Range: 120 feet
Components: V, S
Duration: Instantaneous

You create three rays of fire and hurl them at targets within range. You can hurl them at one target or several.

Make a ranged spell attack for each ray. On a hit, the target takes 2d6 fire damage.

At Higher Levels. When you cast this spell using a spell slot of 3rd level or higher, you create one additional ray for each slot level above 2nd.

SCRYING
5th-level divination

Casting Time: 10 minutes
Range: Self
Components: V, S, M (a focus worth at least 1,000 gp, such as a crystal ball, a silver mirror, or a font filled with holy water)
Duration: Concentration, up to 10 minutes

You can see and hear a particular creature you choose that is on the same plane of existence as you. The target must make a Wisdom saving throw, which is modified by how well you know the target and the sort of physical connection you have to it. If a target knows you're casting this spell, it can fail the saving throw voluntarily if it wants to be observed.

Knowledge	Save Modifier
Secondhand (you have heard of the target)	+5
Firsthand (you have met the target)	+0
Familiar (you know the target well)	−5

Connection	Save Modifier
Likeness or picture	−2
Possession or garment	−4
Body part, lock of hair, bit of nail, or the like	−10

On a successful save, the target isn't affected, and you can't use this spell against it again for 24 hours.

On a failed save, the spell creates an invisible sensor within 10 feet of the target. You can see and hear through the sensor as if you were there. The sensor moves with the target, remaining within 10 feet of it for the duration. A creature that can see invisible objects sees the sensor as a luminous orb about the size of your fist.

Instead of targeting a creature, you can choose a location you have seen before as the target of this spell. When you do, the sensor appears at that location and doesn't move.

SEARING SMITE
1st-level evocation

Casting Time: 1 bonus action
Range: Self
Components: V
Duration: Concentration, up to 1 minute

The next time you hit a creature with a melee weapon attack during the spell's duration, your weapon flares with white-hot intensity, and the attack deals an extra 1d6 fire damage to the target and causes the target to ignite in flames. At the start of each of its turns until the spell ends, the target must make a Constitution saving throw. On a failed save, it takes 1d6 fire damage. On a successful save, the spell ends. If the target or a creature within 5 feet of it uses an action to put out the flames, or if some other effect douses the flames (such as the target being submerged in water), the spell ends.

At Higher Levels. When you cast this spell using a spell slot of 2nd level or higher, the initial extra damage dealt by the attack increases by 1d6 for each slot level above 1st.

SEE INVISIBILITY
2nd-level divination

Casting Time: 1 action
Range: Self
Components: V, S, M (a pinch of talc and a small sprinkling of powdered silver)
Duration: 1 hour

For the duration, you see invisible creatures and objects as if they were visible, and you can see into the Ethereal Plane. Ethereal creatures and objects appear ghostly and translucent.

SEEMING
5th-level illusion

Casting Time: 1 action
Range: 30 feet
Components: V, S
Duration: 8 hours

This spell allows you to change the appearance of any number of creatures that you can see within range. You give each target you choose a new, illusory appearance. An unwilling target can make a Charisma saving throw, and if it succeeds, it is unaffected by this spell.

The spell disguises physical appearance as well as clothing, armor, weapons, and equipment. You can make each creature seem 1 foot shorter or taller and appear thin, fat, or in between. You can't change a target's body type, so you must choose a form that has the same basic arrangement of limbs. Otherwise, the extent of the illusion is up to you. The spell lasts for the duration, unless you use your action to dismiss it sooner.

The changes wrought by this spell fail to hold up to physical inspection. For example, if you use this spell to add a hat to a creature's outfit, objects pass through the hat, and anyone who touches it would feel nothing or would feel the creature's head and hair. If you use this spell to appear thinner than you are, the hand of

someone who reaches out to touch you would bump into you while it was seemingly still in midair.

A creature can use its action to inspect a target and make an Intelligence (Investigation) check against your spell save DC. If it succeeds, it becomes aware that the target is disguised.

SENDING
3rd-level evocation

Casting Time: 1 action
Range: Unlimited
Components: V, S, M (a short piece of fine copper wire)
Duration: 1 round

You send a short message of twenty-five words or less to a creature with which you are familiar. The creature hears the message in its mind, recognizes you as the sender if it knows you, and can answer in a like manner immediately. The spell enables creatures with Intelligence scores of at least 1 to understand the meaning of your message.

You can send the message across any distance and even to other planes of existence, but if the target is on a different plane than you, there is a 5 percent chance that the message doesn't arrive.

SEQUESTER
7th-level transmutation

Casting Time: 1 action
Range: Touch
Components: V, S, M (a powder composed of diamond, emerald, ruby, and sapphire dust worth at least 5,000 gp, which the spell consumes)
Duration: Until dispelled

By means of this spell, a willing creature or an object can be hidden away, safe from detection for the duration. When you cast the spell and touch the target, it becomes invisible and can't be targeted by divination spells or perceived through scrying sensors created by divination spells.

If the target is a creature, it falls into a state of suspended animation. Time ceases to flow for it, and it doesn't grow older.

You can set a condition for the spell to end early. The condition can be anything you choose, but it must occur or be visible within 1 mile of the target. Examples include "after 1,000 years" or "when the tarrasque awakens." This spell also ends if the target takes any damage.

SHAPECHANGE
9th-level transmutation

Casting Time: 1 action
Range: Self
Components: V, S, M (a jade circlet worth at least 1,500 gp, which you must place on your head before you cast the spell)
Duration: Concentration, up to 1 hour

You assume the form of a different creature for the duration. The new form can be of any creature with a challenge rating equal to your level or lower. The creature can't be a construct or an undead, and you must have seen the sort of creature at least once. You transform into an average example of that creature, one without any class levels or the Spellcasting trait.

Your game statistics are replaced by the statistics of the chosen creature, though you retain your alignment and Intelligence, Wisdom, and Charisma scores. You also retain all of your skill and saving throw proficiencies, in addition to gaining those of the creature. If the creature has the same proficiency as you and the bonus listed in its statistics is higher than yours, use the creature's bonus in place of yours. You can't use any legendary actions or lair actions of the new form.

You assume the hit points and Hit Dice of the new form. When you revert to your normal form, you return to the number of hit points you had before you transformed. If you revert as a result of dropping to 0 hit points, any excess damage carries over to your normal form. As long as the excess damage doesn't reduce your normal form to 0 hit points, you aren't knocked unconscious.

You retain the benefit of any features from your class, race, or other source and can use them, provided that your new form is physically capable of doing so. You can't use any special senses you have (for example, darkvision) unless your new form also has that sense. You can only speak if the creature can normally speak.

When you transform, you choose whether your equipment falls to the ground, merges into the new form, or is worn by it. Worn equipment functions as normal. The DM determines whether it is practical for the new form to wear a piece of equipment, based on the creature's shape and size. Your equipment doesn't change shape or size to match the new form, and any equipment that the new form can't wear must either fall to the ground or merge into your new form. Equipment that merges has no effect in that state.

During this spell's duration, you can use your action to assume a different form following the same restrictions and rules for the original form, with one exception: if your new form has more hit points than your current one, your hit points remain at their current value.

SHATTER
2nd-level evocation

Casting Time: 1 action
Range: 60 feet
Components: V, S, M (a chip of mica)
Duration: Instantaneous

A sudden loud ringing noise, painfully intense, erupts from a point of your choice within range. Each creature in a 10-foot-radius sphere centered on that point must make a Constitution saving throw. A creature takes 3d8 thunder damage on a failed save, or half as much damage on a successful one. A creature made of inorganic material such as stone, crystal, or metal has disadvantage on this saving throw.

A nonmagical object that isn't being worn or carried also takes the damage if it's in the spell's area.

At Higher Levels. When you cast this spell using a spell slot of 3rd level or higher, the damage increases by 1d8 for each slot level above 2nd.

SHIELD
1st-level abjuration

Casting Time: 1 reaction, which you take when you are hit by an attack or targeted by the *magic missile* spell
Range: Self
Components: V, S
Duration: 1 round

An invisible barrier of magical force appears and protects you. Until the start of your next turn, you have a +5 bonus to AC, including against the triggering attack, and you take no damage from *magic missile*.

SHIELD OF FAITH
1st-level abjuration

Casting Time: 1 bonus action
Range: 60 feet
Components: V, S, M (a small parchment with a bit of holy text written on it)
Duration: Concentration, up to 10 minutes

A shimmering field appears and surrounds a creature of your choice within range, granting it a +2 bonus to AC for the duration.

SHILLELAGH
Transmutation cantrip

Casting Time: 1 bonus action
Range: Touch
Components: V, S, M (mistletoe, a shamrock leaf, and a club or quarterstaff)
Duration: 1 minute

The wood of a club or quarterstaff you are holding is imbued with nature's power. For the duration, you can use your spellcasting ability instead of Strength for the attack and damage rolls of melee attacks using that weapon, and the weapon's damage die becomes a d8. The weapon also becomes magical, if it isn't already. The spell ends if you cast it again or if you let go of the weapon.

SHOCKING GRASP
Evocation cantrip

Casting Time: 1 action
Range: Touch,
Components: V, S
Duration: Instantaneous

Lightning springs from your hand to deliver a shock to a creature you try to touch. Make a melee spell attack against the target. You have advantage on the attack roll if the target is wearing armor made of metal. On a hit, the target takes 1d8 lightning damage, and it can't take reactions until the start of its next turn.

The spell's damage increases by 1d8 when you reach 5th level (2d8), 11th level (3d8), and 17th level (4d8).

SILENCE
2nd-level illusion (ritual)

Casting Time: 1 action
Range: 120 feet
Components: V, S
Duration: Concentration, up to 10 minutes

For the duration, no sound can be created within or pass through a 20-foot-radius sphere centered on a point you choose within range. Any creature or object entirely inside the sphere is immune to thunder damage, and creatures are deafened while entirely inside it. Casting a spell that includes a verbal component is impossible there.

Silent Image
1st-level illusion

Casting Time: 1 action
Range: 60 feet
Components: V, S, M (a bit of fleece)
Duration: Concentration, up to 10 minutes

You create the image of an object, a creature, or some other visible phenomenon that is no larger than a 15-foot cube. The image appears at a spot within range and lasts for the duration. The image is purely visual; it isn't accompanied by sound, smell, or other sensory effects.

You can use your action to cause the image to move to any spot within range. As the image changes location, you can alter its appearance so that its movements appear natural for the image. For example, if you create an image of a creature and move it, you can alter the image so that it appears to be walking.

Physical interaction with the image reveals it to be an illusion, because things can pass through it. A creature that uses its action to examine the image can determine that it is an illusion with a successful Intelligence (Investigation) check against your spell save DC. If a creature discerns the illusion for what it is, the creature can see through the image.

Simulacrum
7th-level illusion

Casting Time: 12 hours
Range: Touch
Components: V, S, M (snow or ice in quantities sufficient to made a life-size copy of the duplicated creature; some hair, fingernail clippings, or other piece of that creature's body placed inside the snow or ice; and powdered ruby worth 1,500 gp, sprinkled over the duplicate and consumed by the spell)
Duration: Until dispelled

You shape an illusory duplicate of one beast or humanoid that is within range for the entire casting time of the spell. The duplicate is a creature, partially real and formed from ice or snow, and it can take actions and otherwise be affected as a normal creature. It appears to be the same as the original, but it has half the creature's hit point maximum and is formed without any equipment. Otherwise, the illusion uses all the statistics of the creature it duplicates.

The simulacrum is friendly to you and creatures you designate. It obeys your spoken commands, moving and acting in accordance with your wishes and acting on your turn in combat. The simulacrum lacks the ability to learn or become more powerful, so it never increases its level or other abilities, nor can it regain expended spell slots.

If the simulacrum is damaged, you can repair it in an alchemical laboratory, using rare herbs and minerals worth 100 gp per hit point it regains. The simulacrum lasts until it drops to 0 hit points, at which point it reverts to snow and melts instantly.

If you cast this spell again, any currently active duplicates you created with this spell are instantly destroyed.

Sleep
1st-level enchantment

Casting Time: 1 action
Range: 90 feet
Components: V, S, M (a pinch of fine sand, rose petals, or a cricket)
Duration: 1 minute

This spell sends creatures into a magical slumber. Roll 5d8; the total is how many hit points of creatures this spell can affect. Creatures within 20 feet of a point you choose within range are affected in ascending order of their current hit points (ignoring unconscious creatures).

Starting with the creature that has the lowest current hit points, each creature affected by this spell falls unconscious until the spell ends, the sleeper takes damage, or someone uses an action to shake or slap the sleeper awake. Subtract each creature's hit points from the total before moving on to the creature with the next lowest hit points. A creature's hit points must be equal to or less than the remaining total for that creature to be affected.

Undead and creatures immune to being charmed aren't affected by this spell.

At Higher Levels. When you cast this spell using a spell slot of 2nd level or higher, roll an additional 2d8 for each slot level above 1st.

Sleet Storm
3rd-level conjuration

Casting Time: 1 action
Range: 150 feet
Components: V, S, M (a pinch of dust and a few drops of water)
Duration: Concentration, up to 1 minute

Until the spell ends, freezing rain and sleet fall in a 20-foot-tall cylinder with a 40-foot radius centered on a point you choose within range. The area is heavily obscured, and exposed flames in the area are doused.

The ground in the area is covered with slick ice, making it difficult terrain. When a creature enters the spell's area for the first time on a turn or starts its turn there, it must make a Dexterity saving throw. On a failed save, it falls prone.

If a creature is concentrating in the spell's area, the creature must make a successful Constitution saving throw against your spell save DC or lose concentration.

Slow
3rd-level transmutation

Casting Time: 1 action
Range: 120 feet
Components: V, S, M (a drop of molasses)
Duration: Concentration, up to 1 minute

You alter time around up to six creatures of your choice in a 40-foot cube within range. Each target must succeed on a Wisdom saving throw or be affected by this spell for the duration.

An affected target's speed is halved, it takes a −2 penalty to AC and Dexterity saving throws, and it can't use reactions. On its turn, it can use either an action or a bonus action, not both. Regardless of the creature's abilities or magic items, it can't make more than one melee or ranged attack during its turn.

If the creature attempts to cast a spell with a casting time of 1 action, roll a d20. On an 11 or higher, the spell doesn't take effect until the creature's next turn, and the creature must use its action on that turn to complete the spell. If it can't, the spell is wasted.

A creature affected by this spell makes another Wisdom saving throw at the end of its turn. On a successful save, the effect ends for it.

Spare the Dying
Necromancy cantrip

Casting Time: 1 action
Range: Touch
Components: V, S
Duration: Instantaneous

You touch a living creature that has 0 hit points. The creature becomes stable. This spell has no effect on undead or constructs.

Speak with Animals
1st-level divination (ritual)

Casting Time: 1 action
Range: Self
Components: V, S
Duration: 10 minutes

You gain the ability to comprehend and verbally communicate with beasts for the duration. The knowledge and awareness of many beasts is limited by their intelligence, but at minimum, beasts can give you information about nearby locations and monsters, including whatever they can perceive or have perceived within the past day. You might be able to persuade a beast to perform a small favor for you, at the DM's discretion.

Speak with Dead
3rd-level necromancy

Casting Time: 1 action
Range: 10 feet
Components: V, S, M (burning incense)
Duration: 10 minutes

You grant the semblance of life and intelligence to a corpse of your choice within range, allowing it to answer the questions you pose. The corpse must still have a mouth and can't be undead. The spell fails if the corpse was the target of this spell within the last 10 days.

Until the spell ends, you can ask the corpse up to five questions. The corpse knows only what it knew in life, including the languages it knew. Answers are usually brief, cryptic, or repetitive, and the corpse is under no compulsion to offer a truthful answer if you are hostile to it or it recognizes you as an enemy. This spell doesn't return the creature's soul to its body, only its animating spirit. Thus, the corpse can't learn new information, doesn't comprehend anything that has happened since it died, and can't speculate about future events.

Speak with Plants
3rd-level transmutation

Casting Time: 1 action
Range: Self (30-foot radius)
Components: V, S
Duration: 10 minutes

You imbue plants within 30 feet of you with limited sentience and animation, giving them the ability to communicate with you and follow your simple commands. You can question plants about events in the spell's area within the past day, gaining information about creatures that have passed, weather, and other circumstances.

You can also turn difficult terrain caused by plant growth (such as thickets and undergrowth) into ordinary terrain that lasts for the duration. Or you can turn ordinary terrain where plants are present into difficult terrain that lasts for the duration, causing vines and branches to hinder pursuers, for example.

Plants might be able to perform other tasks on your behalf, at the DM's discretion. The spell doesn't enable plants to uproot themselves and move about, but they can freely move branches, tendrils, and stalks.

If a plant creature is in the area, you can communicate with it as if you shared a common language, but you gain no magical ability to influence it.

This spell can cause the plants created by the *entangle* spell to release a restrained creature.

Spider Climb
2nd-level transmutation

Casting Time: 1 action
Range: Touch
Components: V, S, M (a drop of bitumen and a spider)
Duration: Concentration, up to 1 hour

Until the spell ends, one willing creature you touch gains the ability to move up, down, and across vertical surfaces and upside down along ceilings, while leaving its hands free. The target also gains a climbing speed equal to its walking speed.

Spike Growth
2nd-level transmutation

Casting Time: 1 action
Range: 150 feet
Components: V, S, M (seven sharp thorns or seven small twigs, each sharpened to a point)
Duration: Concentration, up to 10 minutes

The ground in a 20-foot radius centered on a point within range twists and sprouts hard spikes and thorns. The area becomes difficult terrain for the duration. When a creature moves into or within the area, it takes 2d4 piercing damage for every 5 feet it travels.

The transformation of the ground is camouflaged to look natural. Any creature that can't see the area at the time the spell is cast must make a Wisdom (Perception) check against your spell save DC to recognize the terrain as hazardous before entering it.

SPIRIT GUARDIANS
3rd-level conjuration

Casting Time: 1 action
Range: Self (15-foot radius)
Components: V, S, M (a holy symbol)
Duration: Concentration, up to 10 minutes

You call forth spirits to protect you. They flit around you to a distance of 15 feet for the duration. If you are good or neutral, their spectral form appears angelic or fey (your choice). If you are evil, they appear fiendish.

When you cast this spell, you can designate any number of creatures you can see to be unaffected by it. An affected creature's speed is halved in the area, and when the creature enters the area for the first time on a turn or starts its turn there, it must make a Wisdom saving throw. On a failed save, the creature takes 3d8 radiant damage (if you are good or neutral) or 3d8 necrotic damage (if you are evil). On a successful save, the creature takes half as much damage.

At Higher Levels. When you cast this spell using a spell slot of 4th level or higher, the damage increases by 1d8 for each slot level above 3rd.

SPIRITUAL WEAPON
2nd-level evocation

Casting Time: 1 bonus action
Range: 60 feet
Components: V, S
Duration: 1 minute

You create a floating, spectral weapon within range that lasts for the duration or until you cast this spell again. When you cast the spell, you can make a melee spell attack against a creature within 5 feet of the weapon. On a hit, the target takes force damage equal to 1d8 + your spellcasting ability modifier.

As a bonus action on your turn, you can move the weapon up to 20 feet and repeat the attack against a creature within 5 feet of it.

The weapon can take whatever form you choose. Clerics of deities who are associated with a particular weapon (as St. Cuthbert is known for his mace and Thor for his hammer) make this spell's effect resemble that weapon.

At Higher Levels. When you cast this spell using a spell slot of 3rd level or higher, the damage increases by 1d8 for every two slot levels above 2nd.

STAGGERING SMITE
4th-level evocation

Casting Time: 1 bonus action
Range: Self
Components: V
Duration: Concentration, up to 1 minute

The next time you hit a creature with a melee weapon attack during this spell's duration, your weapon pierces both body and mind, and the attack deals an extra 4d6 psychic damage to the target. The target must make a Wisdom saving throw. On a failed save, it has disadvantage on attack rolls and ability checks, and can't take reactions, until the end of its next turn.

STINKING CLOUD
3rd-level conjuration

Casting Time: 1 action
Range: 90 feet
Components: V, S, M (a rotten egg or several skunk cabbage leaves)
Duration: Concentration, up to 1 minute

You create a 20-foot-radius sphere of yellow, nauseating gas centered on a point within range. The cloud spreads around corners, and its area is heavily obscured. The cloud lingers in the air for the duration.

Each creature that is completely within the cloud at the start of its turn must make a Constitution saving throw against poison. On a failed save, the creature spends its action that turn retching and reeling. Creatures that don't need to breathe or are immune to poison automatically succeed on this saving throw.

A moderate wind (at least 10 miles per hour) disperses the cloud after 4 rounds. A strong wind (at least 20 miles per hour) disperses it after 1 round.

STONE SHAPE
4th-level transmutation

Casting Time: 1 action
Range: Touch
Components: V, S, M (soft clay, which must be worked into roughly the desired shape of the stone object)
Duration: Instantaneous

You touch a stone object of Medium size or smaller or a section of stone no more than 5 feet in any dimension and form it into any shape that suits your purpose. So, for example, you could shape a large rock into a weapon, idol, or coffer, or make a small passage through a wall, as long as the wall is less than 5 feet thick. You could also shape a stone door or its frame to seal the door shut. The object you create can have up to two hinges and a latch, but finer mechanical detail isn't possible.

STONESKIN
4th-level abjuration

Casting Time: 1 action
Range: Touch
Components: V, S, M (diamond dust worth 100 gp, which the spell consumes)
Duration: Concentration, up to 1 hour

This spell turns the flesh of a willing creature you touch as hard as stone. Until the spell ends, the target has resistance to nonmagical bludgeoning, piercing, and slashing damage.

Storm of Vengeance
9th-level conjuration

Casting Time: 1 action
Range: Sight
Components: V, S
Duration: Concentration, up to 1 minute

A churning storm cloud forms, centered on a point you can see and spreading to a radius of 360 feet. Lightning flashes in the area, thunder booms, and strong winds roar. Each creature under the cloud (no more than 5,000 feet beneath the cloud) when it appears must make a Constitution saving throw. On a failed save, a creature takes 2d6 thunder damage and becomes deafened for 5 minutes.

Each round you maintain concentration on this spell, the storm produces additional effects on your turn.

Round 2. Acidic rain falls from the cloud. Each creature and object under the cloud takes 1d6 acid damage.

Round 3. You call six bolts of lightning from the cloud to strike six creatures or objects of your choice beneath the cloud. A given creature or object can't be struck by more than one bolt. A struck creature must make a Dexterity saving throw. The creature takes 10d6 lightning damage on a failed save, or half as much damage on a successful one.

Round 4. Hailstones rain down from the cloud. Each creature under the cloud takes 2d6 bludgeoning damage.

Round 5–10. Gusts and freezing rain assail the area under the cloud. The area becomes difficult terrain and is heavily obscured. Each creature there takes 1d6 cold damage. Ranged weapon attacks in the area are impossible. The wind and rain count as a severe distraction for the purposes of maintaining concentration on spells. Finally, gusts of strong wind (ranging from 20 to 50 miles per hour) automatically disperse fog, mists, and similar phenomena in the area, whether mundane or magical.

Suggestion
2nd-level enchantment

Casting Time: 1 action
Range: 30 feet
Components: V, M (a snake's tongue and either a bit of honeycomb or a drop of sweet oil)
Duration: Concentration, up to 8 hours

You suggest a course of activity (limited to a sentence or two) and magically influence a creature you can see within range that can hear and understand you. Creatures that can't be charmed are immune to this effect. The suggestion must be worded in such a manner as to make the course of action sound reasonable. Asking the creature to stab itself, throw itself onto a spear, immolate itself, or do some other obviously harmful act ends the spell.

The target must make a Wisdom saving throw. On a failed save, it pursues the course of action you described to the best of its ability. The suggested course of action can continue for the entire duration. If the suggested activity can be completed in a shorter time, the spell ends when the subject finishes what it was asked to do.

You can also specify conditions that will trigger a special activity during the duration. For example, you might suggest that a knight give her warhorse to the first beggar she meets. If the condition isn't met before the spell expires, the activity isn't performed.

If you or any of your companions damage the target, the spell ends.

Sunbeam
6th-level evocation

Casting Time: 1 action
Range: Self (60-foot line)
Components: V, S, M (a magnifying glass)
Duration: Concentration, up to 1 minute

A beam of brilliant light flashes out from your hand in a 5-foot-wide, 60-foot-long line. Each creature in the line must make a Constitution saving throw. On a failed save, a creature takes 6d8 radiant damage and is blinded until your next turn. On a successful save, it takes half as much damage and isn't blinded by this spell. Undead and oozes have disadvantage on this saving throw.

You can create a new line of radiance as your action on any turn until the spell ends.

For the duration, a mote of brilliant radiance shines in your hand. It sheds bright light in a 30-foot radius and dim light for an additional 30 feet. This light is sunlight.

Sunburst
8th-level evocation

Casting Time: 1 action
Range: 150 feet
Components: V, S, M (fire and a piece of sunstone)
Duration: Instantaneous

Brilliant sunlight flashes in a 60-foot radius centered on a point you choose within range. Each creature in that light must make a Constitution saving throw. On a failed save, a creature takes 12d6 radiant damage and is blinded for 1 minute. On a successful save, it takes half as much damage and isn't blinded by this spell. Undead and oozes have disadvantage on this saving throw.

A creature blinded by this spell makes another Constitution saving throw at the end of each of its turns. On a successful save, it is no longer blinded.

This spell dispels any darkness in its area that was created by a spell.

Swift Quiver
5th-level transmutation

Casting Time: 1 bonus action
Range: Touch
Components: V, S, M (a quiver containing at least one piece of ammunition)
Duration: Concentration, up to 1 minute

You transmute your quiver so it produces an endless supply of nonmagical ammunition, which seems to leap into your hand when you reach for it.

On each of your turns until the spell ends, you can use a bonus action to make two attacks with a weapon that uses ammunition from the quiver. Each time you make such a ranged attack, your quiver magically replaces the piece of ammunition you used with a similar piece of nonmagical ammunition. Any pieces of ammunition created by this spell disintegrate when the spell ends. If the quiver leaves your possession, the spell ends.

SYMBOL
7th-level abjuration

Casting Time: 1 minute
Range: Touch
Components: V, S, M (mercury, phosphorus, and powdered diamond and opal with a total value of at least 1,000 gp, which the spell consumes)
Duration: Until dispelled or triggered

When you cast this spell, you inscribe a harmful glyph either on a surface (such as a section of floor, a wall, or a table) or within an object that can be closed to conceal the glyph (such as a book, a scroll, or a treasure chest). If you choose a surface, the glyph can cover an area of the surface no larger than 10 feet in diameter. If you choose an object, that object must remain in its place; if the object is moved more than 10 feet from where you cast this spell, the glyph is broken, and the spell ends without being triggered.

The glyph is nearly invisible, requiring an Intelligence (Investigation) check against your spell save DC to find it.

You decide what triggers the glyph when you cast the spell. For glyphs inscribed on a surface, the most typical triggers include touching or stepping on the glyph, removing another object covering it, approaching within a certain distance of it, or manipulating the object that holds it. For glyphs inscribed within an object, the most common triggers are opening the object, approaching within a certain distance of it, or seeing or reading the glyph.

You can further refine the trigger so the spell is activated only under certain circumstances or according to a creature's physical characteristics (such as height or weight), or physical kind (for example, the ward could be set to affect hags or shapechangers). You can also specify creatures that don't trigger the glyph, such as those who say a certain password.

When you inscribe the glyph, choose one of the options below for its effect. Once triggered, the glyph glows, filling a 60-foot-radius sphere with dim light for 10 minutes, after which time the spell ends. Each creature in the sphere when the glyph activates is targeted by its effect, as is a creature that enters the sphere for the first time on a turn or ends its turn there.

Death. Each target must make a Constitution saving throw, taking 10d10 necrotic damage on a failed save, or half as much damage on a successful save.

Discord. Each target must make a Constitution saving throw. On a failed save, a target bickers and argues with other creatures for 1 minute. During this time, it is incapable of meaningful communication and has disadvantage on attack rolls and ability checks.

Fear. Each target must make a Wisdom saving throw and becomes frightened for 1 minute on a failed save. While frightened, the target drops whatever it is holding and must move at least 30 feet away from the glyph on each of its turns, if able.

Hopelessness. Each target must make a Charisma saving throw. On a failed save, the target is overwhelmed with despair for 1 minute. During this time, it can't attack or target any creature with harmful abilities, spells, or other magical effects.

Insanity. Each target must make an Intelligence saving throw. On a failed save, the target is driven insane for 1 minute. An insane creature can't take actions, can't understand what other creatures say, can't read, and speaks only in gibberish. The DM controls its movement, which is erratic.

Pain. Each target must make a Constitution saving throw and becomes incapacitated with excruciating pain for 1 minute on a failed save.

Sleep. Each target must make a Wisdom saving throw and falls unconscious for 10 minutes on a failed save. A creature awakens if it takes damage or if someone uses an action to shake or slap it awake.

Stunning. Each target must make a Wisdom saving throw and becomes stunned for 1 minute on a failed save.

TASHA'S HIDEOUS LAUGHTER
1st-level enchantment

Casting Time: 1 action
Range: 30 feet
Components: V, S, M (tiny tarts and a feather that is waved in the air)
Duration: Concentration, up to 1 minute

A creature of your choice that you can see within range perceives everything as hilariously funny and falls into fits of laughter if this spell affects it. The target must succeed on a Wisdom saving throw or fall prone, becoming incapacitated and unable to stand up for the duration. A creature with an Intelligence score of 4 or less isn't affected.

At the end of each of its turns, and each time it takes damage, the target can make another Wisdom saving throw. The target has advantage on the saving throw if it's triggered by damage. On a success, the spell ends.

TELEKINESIS
5th-level transmutation

Casting Time: 1 action
Range: 60 feet
Components: V, S
Duration: Concentration, up to 10 minutes

You gain the ability to move or manipulate creatures or objects by thought. When you cast the spell, and as your action each round for the duration, you can exert your will on one creature or object that you can see within range, causing the appropriate effect below. You can affect the same target round after round, or choose a new one at any time. If you switch targets, the prior target is no longer affected by the spell.

Creature. You can try to move a Huge or smaller creature. Make an ability check with your spellcasting ability contested by the creature's Strength check. If you win the contest, you move the creature up to 30 feet in any direction, including upward but not beyond the range of this spell. Until the end of your next turn, the creature is restrained in your telekinetic grip. A creature lifted upward is suspended in mid-air.

On subsequent rounds, you can use your action to attempt to maintain your telekinetic grip on the creature by repeating the contest.

Object. You can try to move an object that weighs up to 1,000 pounds. If the object isn't being worn or carried, you automatically move it up to 30 feet in any direction, but not beyond the range of this spell.

If the object is worn or carried by a creature, you must make an ability check with your spellcasting ability contested by that creature's Strength check. If you succeed, you pull the object away from that creature and can move it up to 30 feet in any direction but not beyond the range of this spell.

You can exert fine control on objects with your telekinetic grip, such as manipulating a simple tool, opening a door or a container, stowing or retrieving an item from an open container, or pouring the contents from a vial.

TELEPATHY
8th-level evocation

Casting Time: 1 action
Range: Unlimited
Components: V, S, M (a pair of linked silver rings)
Duration: 24 hours

You create a telepathic link between yourself and a willing creature with which you are familiar. The creature can be anywhere on the same plane of existence as you. The spell ends if you or the target are no longer on the same plane.

Until the spell ends, you and the target can instantaneously share words, images, sounds, and other sensory messages with one another through the link, and the target recognizes you as the creature it is communicating with. The spell enables a creature with an Intelligence score of at least 1 to understand the meaning of your words and take in the scope of any sensory messages you send to it.

TELEPORT
7th-level conjuration

Casting Time: 1 action
Range: 10 feet
Components: V
Duration: Instantaneous

This spell instantly transports you and up to eight willing creatures of your choice that you can see within range, or a single object that you can see within range, to a destination you select. If you target an object, it must be able to fit entirely inside a 10-foot cube, and it can't be held or carried by an unwilling creature.

The destination you choose must be known to you, and it must be on the same plane of existence as you. Your familiarity with the destination determines whether you arrive there successfully. The DM rolls d100 and consults the table.

Familiarity	Mishap	Similar Area	Off Target	On Target
Permanent circle	—	—	—	01–100
Associated object	—	—	—	01–100
Very familiar	01–05	06–13	14–24	25–100
Seen casually	01–33	34–43	44–53	54–100
Viewed once	01–43	44–53	54–73	74–100
Description	01–43	44–53	54–73	74–100
False destination	01–50	51–100	—	—

Familiarity. "Permanent circle" means a permanent teleportation circle whose sigil sequence you know. "Associated object" means that you possess an object taken from the desired destination within the last six months, such as a book from a wizard's library, bed linen from a royal suite, or a chunk of marble from a lich's secret tomb.

"Very familiar" is a place you have been very often, a place you have carefully studied, or a place you can see when you cast the spell. "Seen casually" is someplace you have seen more than once but with which you aren't very familiar. "Viewed once" is a place you have seen once, possibly using magic. "Description" is a place whose location and appearance you know through someone else's description, perhaps from a map.

"False destination" is a place that doesn't exist. Perhaps you tried to scry an enemy's sanctum but instead viewed an illusion, or you are attempting to teleport to a familiar location that no longer exists.

On Target. You and your group (or the target object) appear where you want to.

Off Target. You and your group (or the target object) appear a random distance away from the destination in a random direction. Distance off target is 1d10 × 1d10 percent of the distance that was to be traveled. For example, if you tried to travel 120 miles, landed off target, and rolled a 5 and 3 on the two d10s, then you would be off target by 15 percent, or 18 miles. The DM determines the direction off target randomly by rolling a d8 and designating 1 as north, 2 as northeast, 3 as east, and so on around the points of the compass. If you were teleporting to a coastal city and wound up 18 miles out at sea, you could be in trouble.

Similar Area. You and your group (or the target object) wind up in a different area that's visually or thematically similar to the target area. If you are heading for your home laboratory, for example, you might wind up in another wizard's laboratory or in an alchemical supply shop that has many of the same tools and implements as your laboratory. Generally, you appear in the closest similar place, but since the spell has no range limit, you could conceivably wind up anywhere on the plane.

Mishap. The spell's unpredictable magic results in a difficult journey. Each teleporting creature (or the target object) takes 3d10 force damage, and the DM rerolls on the table to see where you wind up (multiple mishaps can occur, dealing damage each time).

TELEPORTATION CIRCLE
5th-level conjuration

Casting Time: 1 minute
Range: 10 feet
Components: V, M (rare chalks and inks infused with precious gems with 50 gp, which the spell consumes)
Duration: 1 round

As you cast the spell, you draw a 10-foot-diameter circle on the ground inscribed with sigils that link your location to a permanent teleportation circle of your choice whose sigil sequence you know and that is on the same plane of existence as you. A shimmering portal opens within the circle you drew and remains open until the end of your next turn. Any creature that enters the portal instantly appears within 5 feet of the destination circle or in the nearest unoccupied space if that space is occupied.

Many major temples, guilds, and other important places have permanent teleportation circles inscribed somewhere within their confines. Each such circle includes a unique sigil sequence—a string of magical runes arranged in a particular pattern. When you first gain the ability to cast this spell, you learn the sigil sequences for two destinations on the Material Plane, determined by the DM. You can learn additional sigil sequences during your adventures. You can commit a new sigil sequence to memory after studying it for 1 minute.

You can create a permanent teleportation circle by casting this spell in the same location every day for one year. You need not use the circle to teleport when you cast the spell in this way.

TENSER'S FLOATING DISK
1st-level conjuration (ritual)

Casting Time: 1 action
Range: 30 feet
Components: V, S, M (a drop of mercury)
Duration: 1 hour

This spell creates a circular, horizontal plane of force, 3 feet in diameter and 1 inch thick, that floats 3 feet above the ground in an unoccupied space of your choice that you can see within range. The disk remains for the duration, and can hold up to 500 pounds. If more weight is placed on it, the spell ends, and everything on the disk falls to the ground.

The disk is immobile while you are within 20 feet of it. If you move more than 20 feet away from it, the disk follows you so that it remains within 20 feet of you. It can move across uneven terrain, up or down stairs, slopes and the like, but it can't cross an elevation change of 10 feet or more. For example, the disk can't move across a 10-foot-deep pit, nor could it leave such a pit if it was created at the bottom.

If you move more than 100 feet from the disk (typically because it can't move around an obstacle to follow you), the spell ends.

THAUMATURGY
Transmutation cantrip

Casting Time: 1 action
Range: 30 feet
Components: V
Duration: Up to 1 minute

You manifest a minor wonder, a sign of supernatural power, within range. You create one of the following magical effects within range:

- Your voice booms up to three times as loud as normal for 1 minute.
- You cause flames to flicker, brighten, dim, or change color for 1 minute.
- You cause harmless tremors in the ground for 1 minute.
- You create an instantaneous sound that originates from a point of your choice within range, such as a rumble of thunder, the cry of a raven, or ominous whispers.
- You instantaneously cause an unlocked door or window to fly open or slam shut.
- You alter the appearance of your eyes for 1 minute.

If you cast this spell multiple times, you can have up to three of its 1-minute effects active at a time, and you can dismiss such an effect as an action.

THORN WHIP
Transmutation cantrip

Casting Time: 1 action
Range: 30 feet
Components: V, S, M (the stem of a plant with thorns)
Duration: Instantaneous

You create a long, vine-like whip covered in thorns that lashes out at your command toward a creature in range. Make a melee spell attack against the target. If the attack hits, the creature takes 1d6 piercing damage, and if the creature is Large or smaller, you pull the creature up to 10 feet closer to you.

This spell's damage increases by 1d6 when you reach 5th level (2d6), 11th level (3d6), and 17th level (4d6).

THUNDEROUS SMITE
1st-level evocation

Casting Time: 1 bonus action
Range: Self
Components: V
Duration: Concentration, up to 1 minute

The first time you hit with a melee weapon attack during this spell's duration, your weapon rings with thunder that is audible within 300 feet of you, and the attack deals an extra 2d6 thunder damage to the target. Additionally, if the target is a creature, it must succeed on a Strength saving throw or be pushed 10 feet away from you and knocked prone.

THUNDERWAVE
1st-level evocation

Casting Time: 1 action
Range: Self (15-foot cube)

Components: V, S
Duration: Instantaneous

A wave of thunderous force sweeps out from you. Each creature in a 15-foot cube originating from you must make a Constitution saving throw. On a failed save, a creature takes 2d8 thunder damage and is pushed 10 feet away from you. On a successful save, the creature takes half as much damage and isn't pushed.

In addition, unsecured objects that are completely within the area of effect are automatically pushed 10 feet away from you by the spell's effect, and the spell emits a thunderous boom audible out to 300 feet.

At Higher Levels. When you cast this spell using a spell slot of 2nd level or higher, the damage increases by 1d8 for each slot level above 1st.

TIME STOP
9th-level transmutation

Casting Time: 1 action
Range: Self
Components: V
Duration: Instantaneous

You briefly stop the flow of time for everyone but yourself. No time passes for other creatures, while you take 1d4 + 1 turns in a row, during which you can use actions and move as normal.

This spell ends if one of the actions you use during this period, or any effects that you create during this period, affects a creature other than you or an object being worn or carried by someone other than you. In addition, the spell ends if you move to a place more than 1,000 feet from the location where you cast it.

TONGUES
3rd-level divination

Casting Time: 1 action
Range: Touch
Components: V, M (a small clay model of a ziggurat)
Duration: 1 hour

This spell grants the creature you touch the ability to understand any spoken language it hears. Moreover, when the target speaks, any creature that knows at least one language and can hear the target understands what it says.

TRANSPORT VIA PLANTS
6th-level conjuration

Casting Time: 1 action
Range: 10 feet
Components: V, S
Duration: 1 round

This spell creates a magical link between a Large or larger inanimate plant within range and another plant, at any distance, on the same plane of existence. You must have seen or touched the destination plant at least once before. For the duration, any creature can step into the target plant and exit from the destination plant by using 5 feet of movement.

TREE STRIDE
5th-level conjuration

Casting Time: 1 action
Range: Self
Components: V, S
Duration: Concentration, up to 1 minute

You gain the ability to enter a tree and move from inside it to inside another tree of the same kind within 500 feet. Both trees must be living and at least the same size as you. You must use 5 feet of movement to enter a tree. You instantly know the location of all other trees of the same kind within 500 feet and, as part of the move used to enter the tree, can either pass into one of those trees or step out of the tree you're in. You appear in a spot of your choice within 5 feet of the destination tree, using another 5 feet of movement. If you have no movement left, you appear within 5 feet of the tree you entered.

You can use this transportation ability once per round for the duration. You must end each turn outside a tree.

TRUE POLYMORPH
9th-level transmutation

Casting Time: 1 action
Range: 30 feet
Components: V, S, M (a drop of mercury, a dollop of gum arabic, and a wisp of smoke)
Duration: Concentration, up to 1 hour

Choose one creature or nonmagical object that you can see within range. You transform the creature into a different creature, the creature into an object, or the object into a creature (the object must be neither worn nor carried by another creature). The transformation lasts for the duration, or until the target drops to 0 hit points or dies. If you concentrate on this spell for the full duration, the transformation lasts until it is dispelled.

This spell has no effect on a shapechanger or a creature with 0 hit points. An unwilling creature can make a Wisdom saving throw, and if it succeeds, it isn't affected by this spell.

Creature into Creature. If you turn a creature into another kind of creature, the new form can be any kind you choose whose challenge rating is equal to or less than the target's (or its level, if the target doesn't have a challenge rating). The target's game statistics, including mental ability scores, are replaced by the statistics of the new form. It retains its alignment and personality.

The target assumes the hit points of its new form, and when it reverts to its normal form, the creature returns to the number of hit points it had before it transformed. If it reverts as a result of dropping to 0 hit points, any excess damage carries over to its normal form. As long as the excess damage doesn't reduce the creature's normal form to 0 hit points, it isn't knocked unconscious.

The creature is limited in the actions it can perform by the nature of its new form, and it can't speak, cast spells, or take any other action that requires hands or speech, unless its new form is capable of such actions.

The target's gear melds into the new form. The creature can't activate, use, wield, or otherwise benefit from any of its equipment.

Object into Creature. You can turn an object into any kind of creature, as long as the creature's size is no larger than the object's size and the creature's challenge rating is 9 or lower. The creature is friendly to you and your companions. It acts on each of your turns. You decide what action it takes and how it moves. The DM has the creature's statistics and resolves all of its actions and movement.

If the spell becomes permanent, you no longer control the creature. It might remain friendly to you, depending on how you have treated it.

Creature into Object. If you turn a creature into an object, it transforms along with whatever it is wearing and carrying into that form. The creature's statistics become those of the object, and the creature has no memory of time spent in this form, after the spell ends and it returns to its normal form.

TRUE RESURRECTION

9th-level necromancy

Casting Time: 1 hour
Range: Touch
Components: V, S, M (a sprinkle of holy water and diamonds worth at least 25,000 gp, which the spell consumes)
Duration: Instantaneous

You touch a creature that has been dead for no longer than 200 years and that died for any reason except old age. If the creature's soul is free and willing, the creature is restored to life with all its hit points.

This spell closes all wounds, neutralizes any poison, cures all diseases, and lifts any curses affecting the creature when it died. The spell replaces damaged or missing organs and limbs.

The spell can even provide a new body if the original no longer exists, in which case you must speak the creature's name. The creature then appears in an unoccupied space you choose within 10 feet of you.

TRUE SEEING

6th-level divination

Casting Time: 1 action
Range: Touch
Components: V, S, M (an ointment for the eyes that costs 25 gp; is made from mushroom powder, saffron, and fat; and is consumed by the spell)
Duration: 1 hour

This spell gives the willing creature you touch the ability to see things as they actually are. For the duration, the creature has truesight, notices secret doors hidden by magic, and can see into the Ethereal Plane, all out to a range of 120 feet.

TRUE STRIKE

Divination cantrip

Casting Time: 1 action
Range: 30 feet
Components: S
Duration: Concentration, up to 1 round

You extend your hand and point a finger at a target in range. Your magic grants you a brief insight into the target's defenses. On your next turn, you gain advantage on your first attack roll against the target, provided that this spell hasn't ended.

TSUNAMI

8th-level conjuration

Casting Time: 1 minute
Range: Sight
Components: V, S
Duration: Concentration, up to 6 rounds

A wall of water springs into existence at a point you choose within range. You can make the wall up to 300 feet long, 300 feet high, and 50 feet thick. The wall lasts for the duration.

When the wall appears, each creature within its area must make a Strength saving throw. On a failed save, a creature takes 6d10 bludgeoning damage, or half as much damage on a successful save.

At the start of each of your turns after the wall appears, the wall, along with any creatures in it, moves 50 feet away from you. Any Huge or smaller creature inside the wall or whose space the wall enters when it moves must succeed on a Strength saving throw or take 5d10 bludgeoning damage. A creature can take this damage only once per round. At the end of the turn, the wall's height is reduced by 50 feet, and the damage creatures take from the spell on subsequent rounds is reduced by 1d10. When the wall reaches 0 feet in height, the spell ends.

A creature caught in the wall can move by swimming. Because of the force of the wave, though, the creature must make a successful Strength (Athletics) check against your spell save DC in order to move at all. If it fails the check, it can't move. A creature that moves out of the area falls to the ground.

UNSEEN SERVANT

1st-level conjuration (ritual)

Casting Time: 1 action
Range: 60 feet
Components: V, S, M (a piece of string and a bit of wood)
Duration: 1 hour

This spell creates an invisible, mindless, shapeless force that performs simple tasks at your command until the spell ends. The servant springs into existence in an unoccupied space on the ground within range. It has AC 10, 1 hit point, and a Strength of 2, and it can't attack. If it drops to 0 hit points, the spell ends.

Once on each of your turns as a bonus action, you can mentally command the servant to move up to 15 feet and interact with an object. The servant can perform simple tasks that a human servant could do, such as fetching things, cleaning, mending, folding clothes, lighting fires, serving food, and pouring wine. Once you give the command, the servant performs the task to the best of its ability until it completes the task, then waits for your next command.

If you command the servant to perform a task that would move it more than 60 feet away from you, the spell ends.

Vampiric Touch
3rd-level necromancy

Casting Time: 1 action
Range: Self
Components: V, S
Duration: Concentration, up to 1 minute

The touch of your shadow-wreathed hand can siphon life force from others to heal your wounds. Make a melee spell attack against a creature within your reach. On a hit, the target takes 3d6 necrotic damage, and you regain hit points equal to half the amount of necrotic damage dealt. Until the spell ends, you can make the attack again on each of your turns as an action.

At Higher Levels. When you cast this spell using a spell slot of 4th level or higher, the damage increases by 1d6 for each slot level above 3rd.

Vicious Mockery
Enchantment cantrip

Casting Time: 1 action
Range: 60 feet
Components: V
Duration: Instantaneous

You unleash a string of insults laced with subtle enchantments at a creature you can see within range. If the target can hear you (though it need not understand you), it must succeed on a Wisdom saving throw or take 1d4 psychic damage and have disadvantage on the next attack roll it makes before the end of its next turn.

This spell's damage increases by 1d4 when you reach 5th level (2d4), 11th level (3d4), and 17th level (4d4).

Wall of Fire
4th-level evocation

Casting Time: 1 action
Range: 120 feet
Components: V, S, M (a small piece of phosphorus)
Duration: Concentration, up to 1 minute

You create a wall of fire on a solid surface within range. You can make the wall up to 60 feet long, 20 feet high, and 1 foot thick, or a ringed wall up to 20 feet in diameter, 20 feet high, and 1 foot thick. The wall is opaque and lasts for the duration.

When the wall appears, each creature within its area must make a Dexterity saving throw. On a failed save, a creature takes 5d8 fire damage, or half as much damage on a successful save.

One side of the wall, selected by you when you cast this spell, deals 5d8 fire damage to each creature that ends its turn within 10 feet of that side or inside the wall. A creature takes the same damage when it enters the wall for the first time on a turn or ends its turn there. The other side of the wall deals no damage.

At Higher Levels. When you cast this spell using a spell slot of 5th level or higher, the damage increases by 1d8 for each slot level above 4th.

Wall of Force
5th-level evocation

Casting Time: 1 action
Range: 120 feet
Components: V, S, M (a pinch of powder made by crushing a clear gemstone)
Duration: Concentration, up to 10 minutes

An invisible wall of force springs into existence at a point you choose within range. The wall appears in any orientation you choose, as a horizontal or vertical barrier or at an angle. It can be free floating or resting on a solid surface. You can form it into a hemispherical dome or a sphere with a radius of up to 10 feet, or you can shape a flat surface made up of ten 10-foot-by-10-foot panels. Each panel must be contiguous with another panel. In any form, the wall is 1/4 inch thick. It lasts for the duration. If the wall cuts through a creature's space when it appears, the creature is pushed to one side of the wall (your choice which side).

Nothing can physically pass through the wall. It is immune to all damage and can't be dispelled by *dispel magic*. A *disintegrate* spell destroys the wall instantly, however. The wall also extends into the Ethereal Plane, blocking ethereal travel through the wall.

Wall of Ice
6th-level evocation

Casting Time: 1 action
Range: 120 feet
Components: V, S, M (a small piece of quartz)
Duration: Concentration, up to 10 minutes

You create a wall of ice on a solid surface within range. You can form it into a hemispherical dome or a sphere with a radius of up to 10 feet, or you can shape a flat surface made up of ten 10-foot-square panels. Each panel must be contiguous with another panel. In any form, the wall is 1 foot thick and lasts for the duration.

If the wall cuts through a creature's space when it appears, the creature within its area is pushed to one side of the wall and must make a Dexterity saving throw. On a failed save, the creature takes 10d6 cold damage, or half as much damage on a successful save.

The wall is an object that can be damaged and thus breached. It has AC 12 and 30 hit points per 10-foot section, and it is vulnerable to fire damage. Reducing a 10-foot section of wall to 0 hit points destroys it and leaves behind a sheet of frigid air in the space the wall occupied. A creature moving through the sheet of frigid air for the first time on a turn must make a Constitution saving throw. That creature takes 5d6 cold damage on a failed save, or half as much damage on a successful one.

At Higher Levels. When you cast this spell using a spell slot of 7th level or higher, the damage the wall deals when it appears increases by 2d6, and the damage from passing through the sheet of frigid air increases by 1d6, for each slot level above 6th.

WALL OF STONE

5th-level evocation

Casting Time: 1 action
Range: 120 feet
Components: V, S, M (a small block of granite)
Duration: Concentration, up to 10 minutes

A nonmagical wall of solid stone springs into existence at a point you choose within range. The wall is 6 inches thick and is composed of ten 10-foot-by-10-foot panels. Each panel must be contiguous with at least one other panel. Alternatively, you can create 10-foot-by-20-foot panels that are only 3 inches thick.

If the wall cuts through a creature's space when it appears, the creature is pushed to one side of the wall (your choice). If a creature would be surrounded on all sides by the wall (or the wall and another solid surface), that creature can make a Dexterity saving throw. On a success, it can use its reaction to move up to its speed so that it is no longer enclosed by the wall.

The wall can have any shape you desire, though it can't occupy the same space as a creature or object. The wall doesn't need to be vertical or rest on any firm foundation. It must, however, merge with and be solidly supported by existing stone. Thus, you can use this spell to bridge a chasm or create a ramp.

If you create a span greater than 20 feet in length, you must halve the size of each panel to create supports. You can crudely shape the wall to create crenellations, battlements, and so on.

The wall is an object made of stone that can be damaged and thus breached. Each panel has AC 15 and 30 hit points per inch of thickness. Reducing a panel to 0 hit points destroys it and might cause connected panels to collapse at the DM's discretion.

If you maintain your concentration on this spell for its whole duration, the wall becomes permanent and can't be dispelled. Otherwise, the wall disappears when the spell ends.

WALL OF THORNS

6th-level conjuration

Casting Time: 1 action
Range: 120 feet
Components: V, S, M (a handful of thorns)
Duration: Concentration, up to 10 minutes

You create a wall of tough, pliable, tangled brush bristling with needle-sharp thorns. The wall appears within range on a solid surface and lasts for the duration. You choose to make the wall up to 60 feet long, 10 feet high, and 5 feet thick or a circle that has a 20-foot diameter and is up to 20 feet high and 5 feet thick. The wall blocks line of sight.

When the wall appears, each creature within its area must make a Dexterity saving throw. On a failed save, a creature takes 7d8 piercing damage, or half as much damage on a successful save.

A creature can move through the wall, albeit slowly and painfully. For every 1 foot a creature moves through the wall, it must spend 4 feet of movement. Furthermore, the first time a creature enters the wall on a turn or ends its turn there, the creature must make a Dexterity saving throw. It takes 7d8 slashing damage on a failed save, or half as much damage on a successful one.

At Higher Levels. When you cast this spell using a spell slot of 7th level or higher, both types of damage increase by 1d8 for each slot level above 6th.

WARDING BOND

2nd-level abjuration

Casting Time: 1 action
Range: Touch
Components: V, S, M (a pair of platinum rings worth at least 50 gp each, which you and the target must wear for the duration)
Duration: 1 hour

This spell wards a willing creature you touch and creates a mystic connection between you and the target until the spell ends. While the target is within 60 feet of you, it gains a +1 bonus to AC and saving throws, and it has resistance to all damage. Also, each time it takes damage, you take the same amount of damage.

The spell ends if you drop to 0 hit points or if you and the target become separated by more than 60 feet. It also ends if the spell is cast again on either of the connected creatures. You can also dismiss the spell as an action.

WATER BREATHING

3rd-level transmutation (ritual)

Casting Time: 1 action
Range: 30 feet
Components: V, S, M (a short reed or piece of straw)
Duration: 24 hours

This spell grants up to ten willing creatures you can see within range the ability to breathe underwater until the spell ends. Affected creatures also retain their normal mode of respiration.

WATER WALK

3rd-level transmutation (ritual)

Casting Time: 1 action
Range: 30 feet
Components: V, S, M (a piece of cork)
Duration: 1 hour

This spell grants the ability to move across any liquid surface—such as water, acid, mud, snow, quicksand, or lava—as if it were harmless solid ground (creatures crossing molten lava can still take damage from the heat). Up to ten willing creatures you can see within range gain this ability for the duration.

If you target a creature submerged in a liquid, the spell carries the target to the surface of the liquid at a rate of 60 feet per round.

WEB

2nd-level conjuration

Casting Time: 1 action
Range: 60 feet
Components: V, S, M (a bit of spiderweb)
Duration: Concentration, up to 1 hour

You conjure a mass of thick, sticky webbing at a point of your choice within range. The webs fill a 20-foot cube from that point for the duration. The webs are difficult terrain and lightly obscure their area.

If the webs aren't anchored between two solid masses (such as walls or trees) or layered across a floor, wall, or ceiling, the conjured web collapses on itself, and the spell ends at the start of your next turn. Webs layered over a flat surface have a depth of 5 feet.

Each creature that starts its turn in the webs or that enters them during its turn must make a Dexterity saving throw. On a failed save, the creature is restrained as long as it remains in the webs or until it breaks free.

A creature restrained by the webs can use its action to make a Strength check against your spell save DC. If it succeeds, it is no longer restrained.

The webs are flammable. Any 5-foot cube of webs exposed to fire burns away in 1 round, dealing 2d4 fire damage to any creature that starts its turn in the fire.

WEIRD
9th-level illusion

Casting Time: 1 action
Range: 120 feet
Components: V, S
Duration: Concentration, up to one minute

Drawing on the deepest fears of a group of creatures, you create illusory creatures in their minds, visible only to them. Each creature in a 30-foot-radius sphere centered on a point of your choice within range must make a Wisdom saving throw. On a failed save, a creature becomes frightened for the duration. The illusion calls on the creature's deepest fears, manifesting its worst nightmares as an implacable threat. At the end of each of the frightened creature's turns, it must succeed on a Wisdom saving throw or take 4d10 psychic damage. On a successful save, the spell ends for that creature.

WIND WALK
6th-level transmutation

Casting Time: 1 minute
Range: 30 feet
Components: V, S, M (fire and holy water)
Duration: 8 hours

You and up to ten willing creatures you can see within range assume a gaseous form for the duration, appearing as wisps of cloud. While in this cloud form, a creature has a flying speed of 300 feet and has resistance to damage from nonmagical weapons. The only actions a creature can take in this form are the Dash action or to revert to its normal form. Reverting takes 1 minute, during which time a creature is incapacitated and can't move. Until the spell ends, a creature can revert to cloud form, which also requires the 1-minute transformation.

If a creature is in cloud form and flying when the effect ends, the creature descends 60 feet per round for 1 minute until it lands, which it does safely. If it can't land after 1 minute, the creature falls the remaining distance.

WIND WALL
3rd-level evocation

Casting Time: 1 action
Range: 120 feet
Components: V, S, M (a tiny fan and a feather of exotic origin)
Duration: Concentration, up to 1 minute

A wall of strong wind rises from the ground at a point you choose within range. You can make the wall up to 50 feet long, 15 feet high, and 1 foot thick. You can shape the wall in any way you choose so long as it makes one continuous path along the ground. The wall lasts for the duration.

When the wall appears, each creature within its area must make a Strength saving throw. A creature takes 3d8 bludgeoning damage on a failed save, or half as much damage on a successful one.

The strong wind keeps fog, smoke, and other gases at bay. Small or smaller flying creatures or objects can't pass through the wall. Loose, lightweight materials brought into the wall fly upward. Arrows, bolts, and other ordinary projectiles launched at targets behind the wall are deflected upward and automatically miss. (Boulders hurled by giants or siege engines, and similar projectiles, are unaffected.) Creatures in gaseous form can't pass through it.

WISH
9th-level conjuration

Casting Time: 1 action
Range: Self
Components: V
Duration: Instantaneous

Wish is the mightiest spell a mortal creature can cast. By simply speaking aloud, you can alter the very foundations of reality in accord with your desires.

The basic use of this spell is to duplicate any other spell of 8th level or lower. You don't need to meet any requirements in that spell, including costly components. The spell simply takes effect.

Alternatively, you can create one of the following effects of your choice:

- You create one object of up to 25,000 gp in value that isn't a magic item. The object can be no more than

300 feet in any dimension, and it appears in an unoccupied space you can see on the ground.

- You allow up to twenty creatures that you can see to regain all hit points, and you end all effects on them described in the *greater restoration* spell.
- You grant up to ten creatures that you can see resistance to a damage type you choose.
- You grant up to ten creatures you can see immunity to a single spell or other magical effect for 8 hours. For instance, you could make yourself and all your companions immune to a lich's life drain attack.
- You undo a single recent event by forcing a reroll of any roll made within the last round (including your last turn). Reality reshapes itself to accommodate the new result. For example, a *wish* spell could undo an opponent's successful save, a foe's critical hit, or a friend's failed save. You can force the reroll to be made with advantage or disadvantage, and you can choose whether to use the reroll or the original roll.

You might be able to achieve something beyond the scope of the above examples. State your wish to the DM as precisely as possible. The DM has great latitude in ruling what occurs in such an instance; the greater the wish, the greater the likelihood that something goes wrong. This spell might simply fail, the effect you desire might only be partly achieved, or you might suffer some unforeseen consequence as a result of how you worded the wish. For example, wishing that a villain were dead might propel you forward in time to a period when that villain is no longer alive, effectively removing you from the game. Similarly, wishing for a legendary magic item or artifact might instantly transport you to the presence of the item's current owner.

The stress of casting this spell to produce any effect other than duplicating another spell weakens you. After enduring that stress, each time you cast a spell until you finish a long rest, you take 1d10 necrotic damage per level of that spell. This damage can't be reduced or prevented in any way. In addition, your Strength drops to 3, if it isn't 3 or lower already, for 2d4 days. For each of those days that you spend resting and doing nothing more than light activity, your remaining recovery time decreases by 2 days. Finally, there is a 33 percent chance that you are unable to cast *wish* ever again if you suffer this stress.

WITCH BOLT
1st-level evocation

Casting Time: 1 action
Range: 30 feet
Components: V, S, M (a twig from a tree that has been struck by lightning)
Duration: Concentration, up to 1 minute

A beam of crackling, blue energy lances out toward a creature within range, forming a sustained arc of lightning between you and the target. Make a ranged spell attack against that creature. On a hit, the target takes 1d12 lightning damage, and on each of your turns for the duration, you can use your action to deal 1d12 lightning damage to the target automatically. The spell ends if you use your action to do anything else. The spell

also ends if the target is ever outside the spell's range or if it has total cover from you.

At Higher Levels. When you cast this spell using a spell slot of 2nd level or higher, the initial damage increases by 1d12 for each slot level above 1st.

WORD OF RECALL
6th-level conjuration

Casting Time: 1 action
Range: 5 feet
Components: V
Duration: Instantaneous

You and up to five willing creatures within 5 feet of you instantly teleport to a previously designated sanctuary. You and any creatures that teleport with you appear in the nearest unoccupied space to the spot you designated when you prepared your sanctuary (see below). If you cast this spell without first preparing a sanctuary, the spell has no effect.

You must designate a sanctuary by casting this spell within a location, such as a temple, dedicated to or strongly linked to your deity. If you attempt to cast the spell in this manner in an area that isn't dedicated to your deity, the spell has no effect.

WRATHFUL SMITE
1st-level evocation

Casting Time: 1 bonus action
Range: Self
Components: V
Duration: Concentration, up to 1 minute

The next time you hit with a melee weapon attack during this spell's duration, your attack deals an extra 1d6 psychic damage. Additionally, if the target is a creature, it must make a Wisdom saving throw or be frightened of you until the spell ends. As an action, the creature can make a Wisdom check against your spell save DC to steel its resolve and end this spell.

ZONE OF TRUTH
2nd-level enchantment

Casting Time: 1 action
Range: 60 feet
Components: V, S
Duration: 10 minutes

You create a magical zone that guards against deception in a 15-foot-radius sphere centered on a point of your choice within range. Until the spell ends, a creature that enters the spell's area for the first time on a turn or starts its turn there must make a Charisma saving throw. On a failed save, a creature can't speak a deliberate lie while in the radius. You know whether each creature succeeds or fails on its saving throw.

An affected creature is aware of the spell and can thus avoid answering questions to which it would normally respond with a lie. Such a creature can be evasive in its answers as long as it remains within the boundaries of the truth.

APPENDIX A: CONDITIONS

CONDITIONS ALTER A CREATURE'S CAPABILITIES IN a variety of ways and can arise as a result of a spell, a class feature, a monster's attack, or other effect. Most conditions, such as blinded, are impairments, but a few, such as invisible, can be advantageous.

A condition lasts either until it is countered (the prone condition is countered by standing up, for example) or for a duration specified by the effect that imposed the condition.

If multiple effects impose the same condition on a creature, each instance of the condition has its own duration, but the condition's effects don't get worse. A creature either has a condition or doesn't.

The following definitions specify what happens to a creature while it is subjected to a condition.

BLINDED

- A blinded creature can't see and automatically fails any ability check that requires sight.
- Attack rolls against the creature have advantage, and the creature's attack rolls have disadvantage.

CHARMED

- A charmed creature can't attack the charmer or target the charmer with harmful abilities or magical effects.
- The charmer has advantage on any ability check to interact socially with the creature.

DEAFENED

- A deafened creature can't hear and automatically fails any ability check that requires hearing.

FRIGHTENED

- A frightened creature has disadvantage on ability checks and attack rolls while the source of its fear is within line of sight.
- The creature can't willingly move closer to the source of its fear.

GRAPPLED

- A grappled creature's speed becomes 0, and it can't benefit from any bonus to its speed.
- The condition ends if the grappler is incapacitated (see the condition).
- The condition also ends if an effect removes the grappled creature from the reach of the grappler or grappling effect, such as when a creature is hurled away by the *thunderwave* spell.

INCAPACITATED

- An incapacitated creature can't take actions or reactions.

BLINDED

FRIGHTENED

CHARMED

PETRIFIED

INVISIBLE

- An invisible creature is impossible to see without the aid of magic or a special sense. For the purpose of hiding, the creature is heavily obscured. The creature's location can be detected by any noise it makes or any tracks it leaves.
- Attack rolls against the creature have disadvantage, and the creature's attack rolls have advantage.

PARALYZED

- A paralyzed creature is incapacitated (see the condition) and can't move or speak.
- The creature automatically fails Strength and Dexterity saving throws.
- Attack rolls against the creature have advantage.
- Any attack that hits the creature is a critical hit if the attacker is within 5 feet of the creature.

PETRIFIED

- A petrified creature is transformed, along with any nonmagical object it is wearing or carrying, into a solid inanimate substance (usually stone). Its weight increases by a factor of ten, and it ceases aging.
- The creature is incapacitated (see the condition), can't move or speak, and is unaware of its surroundings.
- Attack rolls against the creature have advantage.
- The creature automatically fails Strength and Dexterity saving throws.
- The creature has resistance to all damage.
- The creature is immune to poison and disease, although a poison or disease already in its system is suspended, not neutralized.

EXHAUSTION

Some special abilities and environmental hazards, such as starvation and the long-term effects of freezing or scorching temperatures, can lead to a special condition called exhaustion. Exhaustion is measured in six levels. An effect can give a creature one or more levels of exhaustion, as specified in the effect's description.

Level	Effect
1	Disadvantage on ability checks
2	Speed halved
3	Disadvantage on attack rolls and saving throws
4	Hit point maximum halved
5	Speed reduced to 0
6	Death

If an already exhausted creature suffers another effect that causes exhaustion, its current level of exhaustion increases by the amount specified in the effect's description.

A creature suffers the effect of its current level of exhaustion as well as all lower levels. For example, a creature suffering level 2 exhaustion has its speed halved and has disadvantage on ability checks.

An effect that removes exhaustion reduces its level as specified in the effect's description, with all exhaustion effects ending if a creature's exhaustion level is reduced below 1.

Finishing a long rest reduces a creature's exhaustion level by 1, provided that the creature has also ingested some food and drink.

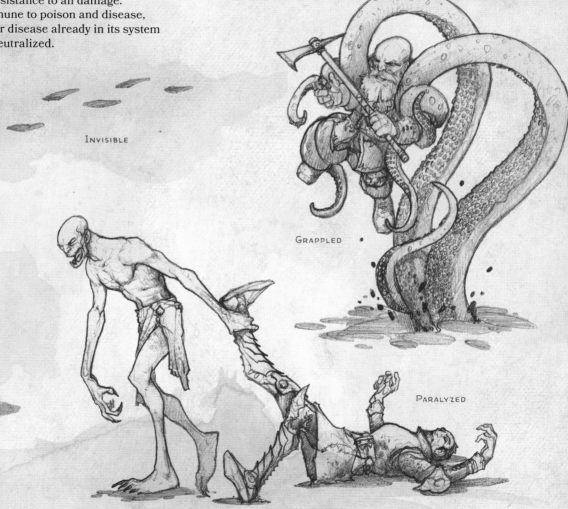

INVISIBLE

GRAPPLED

PARALYZED

DEAFENED

POISONED

- A poisoned creature has disadvantage on attack rolls and ability checks.

PRONE

- A prone creature's only movement option is to crawl, unless it stands up and thereby ends the condition.
- The creature has disadvantage on attack rolls.
- An attack roll against the creature has advantage if the attacker is within 5 feet of the creature. Otherwise, the attack roll has disadvantage.

RESTRAINED

- A restrained creature's speed becomes 0, and it can't benefit from any bonus to its speed.
- Attack rolls against the creature have advantage, and the creature's attack rolls have disadvantage.
- The creature has disadvantage on Dexterity saving throws.

STUNNED

- A stunned creature is incapacitated (see the condition), can't move, and can speak only falteringly.
- The creature automatically fails Strength and Dexterity saving throws.
- Attack rolls against the creature have advantage.

UNCONSCIOUS

- An unconscious creature is incapacitated (see the condition), can't move or speak, and is unaware of its surroundings
- The creature drops whatever it's holding and falls prone.
- The creature automatically fails Strength and Dexterity saving throws.
- Attack rolls against the creature have advantage.
- Any attack that hits the creature is a critical hit if the attacker is within 5 feet of the creature.

PRONE

RESTRAINED

POISONED

UNCONSCIOUS

STUNNED

APPENDIX B: GODS OF THE MULTIVERSE

RELIGION IS AN IMPORTANT PART OF LIFE IN THE worlds of the D&D multiverse. When gods walk the world, clerics channel divine power, evil cults perform dark sacrifices in subterranean lairs, and shining paladins stand like beacons against the darkness, it's hard to be ambivalent about the deities and deny their existence.

Many people in the worlds of D&D worship different gods at different times and circumstances. People in the Forgotten Realms, for example, might pray to Sune for luck in love, make an offering to Waukeen before heading to the market, and pray to appease Talos when a severe storm blows in—all in the same day. Many people have a favorite among the gods, one whose ideals and teachings they make their own. And a few people dedicate themselves entirely to a single god, usually serving as a priest or champion of that god's ideals.

Your DM determines which gods, if any, are worshiped in his or her campaign. From among the gods available, you can choose a single deity for your character to serve, worship, or pay lip service to. Or you can pick a few that your character prays to most often. Or just make a mental note of the gods who are revered in your DM's campaign so you can invoke their names when appropriate. If you're playing a cleric or a character with the Acolyte background, decide which god your deity serves or served, and consider the deity's suggested domains when selecting your character's domain.

D&D PANTHEONS

Each world in the D&D multiverse has its own pantheons of deities, ranging in size from the teeming pantheons of the Forgotten Realms and Greyhawk to the more focused religions of Eberron and Dragonlance. Many of the nonhuman races worship the same gods on different worlds—Moradin, for example, is revered by dwarves of the Forgotten Realms, Greyhawk, and many other worlds.

THE FORGOTTEN REALMS

Dozens of deities are revered, worshiped, and feared throughout the world of the Forgotten Realms. At least thirty deities are widely known across the Realms, and many more are worshiped locally, by individual tribes, small cults, or certain sects of larger religious temples.

THE LIFE AND DEATH DOMAINS

Many deities in this section suggest the Life domain, particularly if they are closely associated with healing, protection, childbirth, nurturing, or fertility. As described in the chapter 3, though, the Life domain is incredibly broad, and a cleric of any non-evil deity can choose it.

A number of other deities, mostly evil ones, suggest the Death domain, which is detailed in the *Dungeon Master's Guide*. Most clerics who choose this domain are evil NPCs, but if you want to worship a god of death, consult your Dungeon Master.

GREYHAWK

The gods of Greyhawk come from at least four different pantheons, representing the faiths of the various ethnic groups that populated the continent of Oerik over the ages. As a result, there's a great deal of overlap in their portfolios: Pelor is the Flan god of the sun and Pholtus is the Oeridian sun god, for example.

DRAGONLANCE

The gods of the world of Krynn are three families: seven gods of good headed by Paladine and Mishakal, seven of neutrality headed by Gilean, and seven of evil headed by Takhisis and Sargonnas. These deities have been called by many different names and held in varying levels of esteem by different peoples and cultures through the world's history, but they are the only gods of this world—their place fixed in the stars as constellations.

EBERRON

The world of Eberron has many different religions, but the most important revolves around a pantheon called the Sovereign Host and their malign shadow, the Dark Six. The gods of the Sovereign Host are thought to have dominion over every aspect of existence, and to speak with a unified voice. But the Dark Six are the primitive, bloody, and cruel gods who offer a dissenting voice.

Eberron's other religions are very different from the traditional D&D pantheons. The monotheistic Church of the Silver Flame is devoted to fighting against evil in the world, but plagued by corruption in its own ranks. The philosophy of the Blood of Vol teaches that divinity lies within all mortal beings and reveres the undead who have secured that immortality. Various mad cults are devoted to the demons and horrors imprisoned in Eberron's Underdark (called Khyber, the Dragon Below). The followers of the Path of Light believe that the world is heading toward a glorious future where the shadows that cloud this world will be transformed into light. And two related nations of elves revere their ancestral spirits: the Undying Court, preserved as spirits or even undead forms, and the glorified Spirits of the Past, the great heroes of ancient wars.

NONHUMAN DEITIES

Certain gods closely associated with nonhuman races are revered on many different worlds, though not always in the same way. The nonhuman races of the Forgotten Realms and Greyhawk share these deities.

Nonhuman races often have whole pantheons of their own. Besides Moradin, for example, the dwarf gods include Moradin's wife, Berronar Truesilver, and a number of other gods thought to be their children and grandchildren: Abbathor, Clangeddin Silverbeard, Dugmaren Brightmantle, Dumathoin, Gorm Gulthyn, Haela Brightaxe, Marthammor Duin, Sharindlar, Thard Harr, and Vergadain. Individual clans and kingdoms of dwarves might revere some, all, or none of these deities, and some have other gods unknown (or known by other names) to outsiders.

DEITIES OF THE FORGOTTEN REALMS

Deity	Alignment	Suggested Domains	Symbol
Auril, goddess of winter	NE	Nature, Tempest	Six-pointed snowflake
Azuth, god of wizards	LN	Knowledge	Left hand pointing upward, outlined in fire
Bane, god of tyranny	LE	War	Upright black right hand, thumb and fingers together
Beshaba, goddess of misfortune	CE	Trickery	Black antlers
Bhaal, god of murder	NE	Death	Skull surrounded by a ring of blood droplets
Chauntea, goddess of agriculture	NG	Life	Sheaf of grain or a blooming rose over grain
Cyric, god of lies	CE	Trickery	White jawless skull on black or purple sunburst
Deneir, god of writing	NG	Knowledge	Lit candle above an open eye
Eldath, goddess of peace	NG	Life, Nature	Waterfall plunging into still pool
Gond, god of craft	N	Knowledge	Toothed cog with four spokes
Helm, god of protection	LN	Life, Light	Staring eye on upright left gauntlet
Ilmater, god of endurance	LG	Life	Hands bound at the wrist with red cord
Kelemvor, god of the dead	LN	Death	Upright skeletal arm holding balanced scales
Lathander, god of birth and renewal	NG	Life, Light	Road traveling into a sunrise
Leira, goddess of illusion	CN	Trickery	Point-down triangle containing a swirl of mist
Lliira, goddess of joy	CG	Life	Triangle of three six-pointed stars
Loviatar, goddess of pain	LE	Death	Nine-tailed barbed scourge
Malar, god of the hunt	CE	Nature	Clawed paw
Mask, god of thieves	CN	Trickery	Black mask
Mielikki, goddess of forests	NG	Nature	Unicorn's head
Milil, god of poetry and song	NG	Light	Five-stringed harp made of leaves
Myrkul, god of death	NE	Death	White human skull
Mystra, goddess of magic	NG	Knowledge	Circle of seven stars, or nine stars encircling a flowing red mist, or a single star
Oghma, god of knowledge	N	Knowledge	Blank scroll
Savras, god of divination and fate	LN	Knowledge	Crystal ball containing many kinds of eyes
Selûne, goddess of the moon	CG	Knowledge, Life	Pair of eyes surrounded by seven stars
Shar, goddess of darkness and loss	NE	Death, Trickery	Black disk encircled with a border
Silvanus, god of wild nature	N	Nature	Oak leaf
Sune, goddess of love and beauty	CG	Life, Light	Face of a beautiful red-haired woman
Talona, goddess of disease and poison	CE	Death	Three teardrops on a triangle
Talos, god of storms	CE	Tempest	Three lightning bolts radiating from a central point
Tempus, god of war	N	War	Upright flaming sword
Torm, god of courage and self-sacrifice	LG	War	White right gauntlet
Tymora, goddess of good fortune	CG	Trickery	Face-up coin
Tyr, god of justice	LG	War	Balanced scales resting on a warhammer
Umberlee, goddess of the sea	CE	Tempest	Wave curling left and right
Waukeen, goddess of trade	N	Knowledge, Trickery	Upright coin with Waukeen's profile facing left

DEITIES OF GREYHAWK

Deity	Alignment	Suggested Domains	Symbol
Beory, goddess of nature	N	Nature	Green disk
Boccob, god of magic	N	Knowledge	Eye within a pentagram
Celestian, god of stars and wanderers	N	Knowledge	Arc of seven stars inside a circle
Ehlonna, goddess of woodlands	NG	Life, Nature	Unicorn horn
Erythnul, god of envy and slaughter	CE	War	Blood drop
Fharlanghn, god of horizons and travel	NG	Knowledge, Trickery	Circle crossed by a curved horizon line
Heironeous, god of chivalry and valor	LG	War	Lightning bolt
Hextor, god of war and discord	LE	War	Six arrows facing downward in a fan
Kord, god of athletics and sport	CG	Tempest, War	Four spears and four maces radiating out from a central point
Incabulos, god of plague and famine	NE	Death	Reptilian eye with a horizontal diamond
Istus, goddess of fate and destiny	N	Knowledge	Weaver's spindle with three strands
Iuz, god of pain and oppression	CE	Death	Grinning human skull
Nerull, god of death	NE	Death	Skull with either a sickle or a scythe
Obad-Hai, god of nature	N	Nature	Oak leaf and acorn
Olidammara, god of revelry	CN	Trickery	Laughing mask
Pelor, god of the sun and healing	NG	Life, Light	Sun
Pholtus, god of light and law	LG	Light	Silver sun or full moon partially eclipsed by a smaller crescent moon
Ralishaz, god of ill luck and insanity	CN	Trickery	Three bone fate-casting sticks
Rao, god of peace and reason	LG	Knowledge	White heart
St. Cuthbert, god of common sense and zeal	LN	Knowledge	Circle at the center of a starburst of lines
Tharizdun, god of eternal darkness	CE	Trickery	Dark spiral or inverted ziggurat
Trithereon, god of liberty and retribution	CG	War	Triskelion
Ulaa, goddess of hills and mountains	LG	Life, War	Mountain with a circle at its heart
Vecna, god of evil secrets	NE	Knowledge	Hand with eye in the palm
Wee Jas, goddess of magic and death	LN	Death, Knowledge	Red skull in front of fireball

DEITIES OF DRAGONLANCE

The Gods of Good	Alignment	Suggested Domains	Symbol
Paladine, god of rulers and guardians	LG	War	Silver triangle
Branchala, god of music	NG	Light	Bard's harp
Habbakuk, god of animal life and the sea	NG	Nature, Tempest	Blue bird
Kiri-Jolith, god of honor and war	LG	War	Bison's horns
Majere, god of meditation and order	LG	Knowledge	Copper spider
Mishakal, goddess of healing	LG	Knowledge, Life	Blue infinity sign
Solinari, god of good magic	LG	no clerics	White circle or sphere

The Gods of Neutrality	Alignment	Suggested Domains	Symbol
Gilean, god of knowledge	N	Knowledge	Open book
Chislev, goddess of nature	N	Nature	Feather
Reorx, god of craft	N	Knowledge	Forging hammer
Shinare, goddess of wealth and trade	N	Knowledge, Trickery	Griffon's wing
Sirrion, god of fire and change	N	Nature	Multi-colored fire
Zivilyn, god of wisdom	N	Knowledge	Great green or gold tree
Lunitari, goddess of neutral magic	N	no clerics	Red circle or sphere

The Gods of Evil	Alignment	Suggested Domains	Symbol
Takhisis, goddess of night and hatred	LE	Death	Black crescent
Chemosh, god of the undead	LE	Death	Yellow skull
Hiddukel, god of lies and greed	CE	Trickery	Broken merchant's scales
Morgion, god of disease and secrecy	NE	Death	Hood with two red eyes
Sargonnas, god of vengeance and fire	LE	War	Stylized red condor
Zeboim, goddess of the sea and storms	CE	Tempest	Turtle shell
Nuitari, god of evil magic	LE	no clerics	Black circle or sphere

DEITIES OF EBERRON

The Sovereign Host	Alignment	Suggested Domains	Symbol
Arawai, goddess of fertility	NG	Life, Nature	Sheaf of wheat tied with green ribbon
Aureon, god of law and knowledge	LN	Knowledge	Open tome
Balinor, god of beasts and the hunt	N	Life, Nature	Pair of antlers
Boldrei, goddess of community and home	LG	Life	Fire in a stone hearth
Dol Arrah, goddess of sunlight and honor	LG	Light, War	Rising sun
Dol Dorn, god of strength at arms	CG	War	Longsword crossed over a shield
Kol Korran, god of trade and wealth	N	Trickery	Nine-sided gold coin
Olladra, goddess of good fortune	NG	Life, Trickery	Domino
Onatar, god of craft	NG	Knowledge	Crossed hammer and tongs

The Dark Six	Alignment	Suggested Domains	Symbol
The Devourer, god of nature's wrath	NE	Tempest	Bundle of five sharpened bones
The Fury, goddess of wrath and madness	NE	War	Winged wyrm with woman's head and upper body
The Keeper, god of greed and death	NE	Death	Dragonshard stone in the shape of a fang
The Mockery, god of violence and treachery	NE	War	Five blood-spattered tools
The Shadow, god of dark magic	CE	Knowledge	Obsidian tower
The Traveler, deity of chaos and change	CN	Knowledge, Trickery	Four crossed, rune-inscribed bones

Other Faiths of Eberron	Alignment	Suggested Domains	Symbol
The Silver Flame, deity of protection and good	LG	Life, Light, War	Flame drawn on silver or molded from silver
The Blood of Vol, philosophy of immortality and undeath	LN	Death, Life	Stylized dragon skull on red teardrop gem
Cults of the Dragon Below, deities of madness	NE	Trickery	Varies
The Path of Light, philosophy of light and self-improvement	LN	Life, Light	Brilliant crystal
The Undying Court, elven ancestors	NG	Knowledge, Life	Varies
The Spirits of the Past, elven ancestors	CG	War	Varies

NONHUMAN DEITIES

Deity	Alignment	Suggested Domains	Symbol
Bahamut, dragon god of good	LG	Life, War	Dragon's head in profile
Blibdoolpoolp, kuo-toa goddess	NE	Death	Lobster head or black pearl
Corellon Larethian, elf deity of art and magic	CG	Light	Quarter moon or starburst
Deep Sashelas, elf god of the sea	CG	Nature, Tempest	Dolphin
Eadro, merfolk deity of the sea	N	Nature, Tempest	Spiral design
Garl Glittergold, gnome god of trickery and wiles	LG	Trickery	Gold nugget
Grolantor, hill giant god of war	CE	War	Wooden club
Gruumsh, orc god of storms and war	CE	Tempest, War	Unblinking eye
Hruggek, bugbear god of violence	CE	War	Morningstar
Kurtulmak, kobold god of war and mining	LE	War	Gnome skull
Laogzed, troglodyte god of hunger	CE	Death	Image of the lizard/toad god
Lolth, drow goddess of spiders	CE	Trickery	Spider
Maglubiyet, goblinoid god of war	LE	War	Bloody axe
Moradin, dwarf god of creation	LG	Knowledge	Hammer and anvil
Rillifane Rallathil, wood elf god of nature	CG	Nature	Oak
Sehanine Moonbow, elf goddess of the moon	CG	Knowledge	Crescent moon
Sekolah, sahuagin god of the hunt	LE	Nature, Tempest	Shark
Semuanya, lizardfolk deity of survival	N	Life	Egg
Skerrit, centaur and satyr god of nature	N	Nature	Oak growing from acorn
Skoraeus Stonebones, god of stone giants and art	N	Knowledge	Stalactite
Surtur, god of fire giants and craft	LE	Knowledge, War	Flaming sword
Thrym, god of frost giants and strength	CE	War	White double-bladed axe
Tiamat, dragon goddess of evil	LE	Trickery	Dragon head with five claw marks
Yondalla, halfling goddess of fertility and protection	LG	Life	Shield

Fantasy-Historical Pantheons

The Celtic, Egyptian, Greek, and Norse pantheons are fantasy interpretations of historical religions from our world's ancient times. They include deities that are most appropriate for use in a D&D game, divorced from their historical context in the real world and united into pantheons that serve the needs of the game.

The Celtic Pantheon

It's said that something wild lurks in the heart of every soul, a space that thrills to the sound of geese calling at night, to the whispering wind through the pines, to the unexpected red of mistletoe on an oak—and it is in this space that the Celtic gods dwell. They sprang from the brook and stream, their might heightened by the strength of the oak and the beauty of the woodlands and open moor. When the first forester dared put a name to the face seen in the bole of a tree or the voice babbling in a brook, these gods forced themselves into being.

The Celtic gods are as often served by druids as by clerics, for they are closely aligned with the forces of nature that druids revere.

The Greek Pantheon

The gods of Olympus make themselves known with the gentle lap of waves against the shores and the crash of the thunder among the cloud-enshrouded peaks. The thick boar-infested woods and the sere, olive-covered hillsides hold evidence of their passing. Every aspect of nature echoes with their presence, and they've made a place for themselves inside the human heart, too.

The Egyptian Pantheon

These gods are a young dynasty of an ancient divine family, heirs to the rulership of the cosmos and the maintenance of the divine principle of Ma'at—the fundamental order of truth, justice, law, and order that puts gods, mortal pharaohs, and ordinary men and women in their logical and rightful place in the universe.

The Egyptian pantheon is unusual in having three gods with the Death domain of different alignments. Anubis is the lawful neutral god of the afterlife, who judges the souls of the dead. Set is a chaotic evil god of murder, perhaps best known for killing his brother Osiris. And Nephthys is a chaotic good goddess of mourning. Thus, although most clerics of the Death domain (found in the *Dungeon Master's Guide*) are villainous characters, clerics who serve Anubis or Nephthys need not be.

THE NORSE PANTHEON

Where the land plummets from the snowy hills into the icy fjords below, where the longboats draw up on to the beach, where the glaciers flow forward and retreat with every fall and spring—this is the land of the Vikings, the home of the Norse pantheon. It's a brutal clime, and one that calls for brutal living. The warriors of the land have had to adapt to the harsh conditions in order to survive, but they haven't been too twisted by the needs of their environment. Given the necessity of raiding for food and wealth, it's surprising the mortals turned out as well as they did. Their powers reflect the need these warriors had for strong leadership and decisive action. Thus, they see their deities in every bend of a river, hear them in the crash of the thunder and the booming of the glaciers, and smell them in the smoke of a burning longhouse.

The Norse pantheon includes two main families, the Aesir (deities of war and destiny) and the Vanir (gods of fertility and prosperity). Once enemies, these two families are now closely allied against their common enemies, the giants (including the gods Surtur and Thrym). Like the gods of Greyhawk, gods in different families sometimes have overlap in their spheres of influence: Frey (of the Vanir) and Odur (of the Aesir) are both associated with the sun, for example.

CELTIC DEITIES

Deity	Alignment	Suggested Domains	Symbol
The Daghdha, god of weather and crops	CG	Nature, Trickery	Bubbling cauldron or shield
Arawn, god of life and death	NE	Life, Death	Black star on gray background
Belenus, god of sun, light, and warmth	NG	Light	Solar disk and standing stones
Brigantia, goddess of rivers and livestock	NG	Life	Footbridge
Diancecht, god of medicine and healing	LG	Life	Crossed oak and mistletoe branches
Dunatis, god of mountains and peaks	N	Nature	Red sun-capped mountain peak
Goibhniu, god of smiths and healing	NG	Knowledge, Life	Giant mallet over sword
Lugh, god of arts, travel, and commerce	CN	Knowledge, Life	Pair of long hands
Manannan mac Lir, god of oceans and sea creatures	LN	Nature, Tempest	Wave of white water on green
Math Mathonwy, god of magic	NE	Knowledge	Staff
Morrigan, goddess of battle	CE	War	Two crossed spears
Nuada, god of war and warriors	N	War	Silver hand on black background
Oghma, god of speech and writing	NG	Knowledge	Unfurled scroll
Silvanus, god of nature and forests	N	Nature	Summer oak tree

GREEK DEITIES

Deity	Alignment	Suggested Domains	Symbol
Zeus, god of the sky, ruler of the gods	N	Tempest	Fist full of lightning bolts
Aphrodite, goddess of love and beauty	CG	Light	Sea shell
Apollo, god of light, music, and healing	CG	Knowledge, Life, Light	Lyre
Ares, god of war and strife	CE	War	Spear
Artemis, goddess of hunting and childbirth	NG	Life, Nature	Bow and arrow on lunar disk
Athena, goddess of wisdom and civilization	LG	Knowledge, War	Owl
Demeter, goddess of agriculture	NG	Life	Mare's head
Dionysus, god of mirth and wine	CN	Life	Thyrsus (staff tipped with pine cone)
Hades, god of the underworld	LE	Death	Black ram
Hecate, goddess of magic and the moon	CE	Knowledge, Trickery	Setting moon
Hephaestus, god of smithing and craft	NG	Knowledge	Hammer and anvil
Hera, goddess of marriage and intrigue	CN	Trickery	Fan of peacock feathers
Hercules, god of strength and adventure	CG	Tempest, War	Lion's head
Hermes, god of travel and commerce	CG	Trickery	Caduceus (winged staff and serpents)
Hestia, goddess of home and family	NG	Life	Hearth
Nike, goddess of victory	LN	War	Winged woman
Pan, god of nature	CN	Nature	Syrinx (pan pipes)
Poseidon, god of the sea and earthquakes	CN	Tempest	Trident
Tyche, goddess of good fortune	N	Trickery	Red pentagram

Egyptian Deities

Deity	Alignment	Suggested Domains	Symbol
Re-Horakhty, god of the sun, ruler of the gods	LG	Life, Light	Solar disk encircled by serpent
Anubis, god of judgment and death	LN	Death	Black jackal
Apep, god of evil, fire, and serpents	NE	Trickery	Flaming snake
Bast, goddess of cats and vengeance	CG	War	Cat
Bes, god of luck and music	CN	Trickery	Image of the misshapen deity
Hathor, goddess of love, music, and motherhood	NG	Life, Light	Horned cow's head with lunar disk
Imhotep, god of crafts and medicine	NG	Knowledge	Step pyramid
Isis, goddess of fertility and magic	NG	Knowledge, Life	Ankh and star
Nephthys, goddess of death and grief	CG	Death	Horns around a lunar disk
Osiris, god of nature and the underworld	LG	Life, Nature	Crook and flail
Ptah, god of crafts, knowledge, and secrets	LN	Knowledge	Bull
Set, god of darkness and desert storms	CE	Death, Tempest, Trickery	Coiled cobra
Sobek, god of water and crocodiles	LE	Nature, Tempest	Crocodile head with horns and plumes
Thoth, god of knowledge and wisdom	N	Knowledge	Ibis

Norse Deities

Deity	Alignment	Suggested Domains	Symbol
Odin, god of knowledge and war	NG	Knowledge, War	Watching blue eye
Aegir, god of the sea and storms	NE	Tempest	Rough ocean waves
Balder, god of beauty and poetry	NG	Life, Light	Gem-encrusted silver chalice
Forseti, god of justice and law	N	Light	Head of a bearded man
Frey, god of fertility and the sun	NG	Life, Light	Ice-blue greatsword
Freya, goddess of fertility and love	NG	Life	Falcon
Frigga, goddess of birth and fertility	N	Life, Light	Cat
Heimdall, god of watchfulness and loyalty	LG	Light, War	Curling musical horn
Hel, goddess of the underworld	NE	Death	Woman's face, rotting on one side
Hermod, god of luck	CN	Trickery	Winged scroll
Loki, god of thieves and trickery	CE	Trickery	Flame
Njord, god of sea and wind	NG	Nature, Tempest	Gold coin
Odur, god of light and the sun	CG	Light	Solar disk
Sif, goddess of war	CG	War	Upraised sword
Skadi, god of earth and mountains	N	Nature	Mountain peak
Surtur, god of fire giants and war	LE	War	Flaming sword
Thor, god of storms and thunder	CG	Tempest, War	Hammer
Thrym, god of frost giants and cold	CE	War	White double-bladed axe
Tyr, god of courage and strategy	LN	Knowledge, War	Sword
Uller, god of hunting and winter	CN	Nature	Longbow

APPENDIX C: THE PLANES OF EXISTENCE

NCREDIBLY VAST IS THE COSMOS OF THE DUNGEONS & DRAGONS game, which teems with a multitude of worlds as well as myriad alternate dimensions of reality, called the **planes of existence**. It encompasses every world where Dungeon Masters run their adventures, all within the relatively mundane realm of the Material Plane. Beyond that plane are domains of raw elemental matter and energy, realms of pure thought and ethos, the homes of demons and angels, and the dominions of the gods.

Many spells and magic items can draw energy from these planes, summon the creatures that dwell there, communicate with their denizens, and allow adventurers to travel there. As your character achieves greater power and higher levels, you might undertake a quest to rescue a friend from the horrific depths of the Abyss, or find yourself hoisting a tankard with the friendly giants of Ysgard. You might walk on streets made of solid fire or test your mettle on a battlefield where the fallen are resurrected with each dawn.

THE MATERIAL PLANE

The Material Plane is the nexus where the philosophical and elemental forces that define the other planes collide in the jumbled existence of mortal life and mundane matter. All the worlds of D&D exist within the Material Plane, making it the starting point for most campaigns and adventures. The rest of the multiverse is defined in relation to the Material Plane.

The worlds of the Material Plane are infinitely diverse, for they reflect the creative imagination of the DMs who set their games there, as well as the players whose heroes adventure there. They include magic-wasted desert planets and island-dotted water worlds, worlds where magic combines with advanced technology and others trapped in an endless Stone Age, worlds where the gods walk and places they have abandoned.

The best-known worlds in the multiverse are the ones that have been published as official campaign settings for the D&D game over the years—Greyhawk, Blackmoor, Dragonlance, the Forgotten Realms, Mystara, Birthright, Dark Sun, and Eberron, among others. Each of these worlds boasts its own cast of heroic adventurers and scheming villains, its own ancient ruins and forgotten artifacts, its own dungeons and its own dragons. But if your campaign takes place on one of these worlds, it belongs to your DM—you might imagine it as one of thousands of parallel versions of the world, which might diverge wildly from the published version.

MATERIAL ECHOES

The Material Plane is a richly magical place, and its magical nature is reflected in the two planes that share its central place in the multiverse. The Feywild and the Shadowfell are parallel dimensions occupying the same cosmological space, so they are often called echo planes or mirror planes to the Material Plane. The worlds and landscapes of these planes mirror the natural world of the Material Plane but reflect those features into different forms—more marvelous and magical in the Feywild, distorted and colorless in the Shadowfell. Where a volcano stands in the Material Plane, a mountain topped with skyscraper-sized crystals that glow with internal fire towers in the Feywild, and a jagged rock outcropping resembling a skull marks the spot on the Shadowfell.

The **Feywild**, also called the Plane of Faerie, is a land of soft lights and wonder, a country of little people with great desires, a place of music and death. It is a realm of eternal twilight, with slow lanterns bobbing in the gentle breeze and huge fireflies buzzing through groves and fields. The sky is alight with the faded colors of the setting, or perhaps rising, sun. But, in fact, the sun never truly sets or rises; it remains stationary, dusky and low in the sky. Away from the settled areas ruled by the Seelie Court, the land is a tangle of sharp-toothed brambles and syrupy fens—perfect territory for the Unseelie to hunt their prey. Fey creatures, such as those brought to the world by *conjure woodland beings* and similar spells, dwell in the Feywild.

The **Shadowfell**, also called the Plane of Shadow, is a darkly lighted dimension, a world of black and white where color has been leached from everything. It is a place of toxic darkness that hates the light, where the sky is a black vault with neither sun nor stars.

POSITIVE PLANE

OUTER PLANES

NEGATIVE PLANE

POSITIVE AND NEGATIVE PLANES

Like a dome above the other planes, the **Positive Plane** is the source of radiant energy and the raw life force that suffuses all living beings, from the puny to the sublime. Its dark reflection is the **Negative Plane**, the source of necrotic energy that destroys the living and animates the undead.

BEYOND THE MATERIAL

Beyond the Material Plane, the various planes of existence are realms of myth and mystery. They're not simply other worlds, but different qualities of being, formed and governed by spiritual and elemental principles abstracted from the ordinary world.

PLANAR TRAVEL

When adventurers travel into other planes of existence, they are undertaking a legendary journey across the thresholds of existence to a mythic destination where they strive to complete their quest. Such a journey is the stuff of legend. Braving the realms of the dead, seeking out the celestial servants of a deity, or bargaining with an efreeti in its home city will be the subject of song and story for years to come.

Travel to the planes beyond the Material Plane can be accomplished in two ways: by casting a spell or by using a planar portal.

Spells. A number of spells allow direct or indirect access to other planes of existence. *Plane shift* and *gate* can transport adventurers directly to any other plane of existence, with different degrees of precision. *Etherealness* allows adventurers to enter the Ethereal Plane and travel from there to any of the planes it touches—the Shadowfell, the Feywild, or the Elemental Planes. And the *astral projection* spell lets adventurers project themselves into the Astral Plane and travel to the Outer Planes.

Portals. A portal is a general term for a stationary interplanar connection that links a specific location on one plane to a specific location on another. Some portals are like doorways, a clear window, or a fog-shrouded passage, and simply stepping through it effects the interplanar travel. Others are locations—circles of standing stones, soaring towers, sailing ships, or even whole towns—that exist in multiple planes at once or flicker from one plane to another in turn. Some are vortices, typically joining an Elemental Plane with a very similar location on the Material Plane, such as the heart of a volcano (leading to the Plane of Fire) or the depths of the ocean (to the Plane of Water).

TRANSITIVE PLANES

The Ethereal Plane and the Astral Plane are called the Transitive Planes. They are mostly featureless realms that serve primarily as ways to travel from one plane to another. Spells such as *etherealness* and *astral projection* allow characters to enter these planes and traverse them to reach the planes beyond.

The **Ethereal Plane** is a misty, fog-bound dimension that is sometimes described as a great ocean. Its shores, called the Border Ethereal, overlap the Material Plane and the Inner Planes, so that every location on those planes has a corresponding location on the Ethereal Plane. Certain creatures can see into the Border Ethereal, and the *see invisibility* and *true seeing* spell grant that ability. Some magical effects also extend from the Material Plane into the Border Ethereal, particularly effects that use force energy such as *forcecage* and *wall*

of force. The depths of the plane, the Deep Ethereal, are a region of swirling mists and colorful fogs.

The **Astral Plane** is the realm of thought and dream, where visitors travel as disembodied souls to reach the planes of the divine and demonic. It is a great, silvery sea, the same above and below, with swirling wisps of white and gray streaking among motes of light resembling distant stars. Erratic whirlpools of color flicker in midair like spinning coins. Occasional bits of solid matter can be found here, but most of the Astral Plane is an endless, open domain.

INNER PLANES

The Inner Planes surround and enfold the Material Plane and its echoes, providing the raw elemental substance from which all the worlds were made. The four **Elemental Planes**—Air, Earth, Fire, and Water—form a ring around the Material Plane, suspended within the churning **Elemental Chaos**.

At their innermost edges, where they are closest to the Material Plane (in a conceptual if not a literal geographical sense), the four Elemental Planes resemble a world in the Material Plane. The four elements mingle together as they do in the Material Plane, forming land, sea, and sky. Farther from the Material Plane, though, the Elemental Planes are both alien and hostile. Here, the elements exist in their purest form—great expanses of solid earth, blazing fire, crystal-clear water, and unsullied air. These regions are little-known, so when discussing the Plane of Fire, for example, a speaker usually means just the border region. At the farthest extents of the Inner Planes, the pure elements dissolve and bleed together into an unending tumult of clashing energies and colliding substance, the Elemental Chaos.

OUTER PLANES

If the Inner Planes are the raw matter and energy that makes up the multiverse, the Outer Planes are the direction, thought and purpose for such construction. Accordingly, many sages refer to the Outer Planes as divine planes, spiritual planes, or godly planes, for the Outer Planes are best known as the homes of deities.

When discussing anything to do with deities, the language used must be highly metaphorical. Their actual homes are not literally "places" at all, but exemplify the idea that the Outer Planes are realms of thought and spirit. As with the Elemental Planes, one can imagine the perceptible part of the Outer Planes as a sort of border region, while extensive spiritual regions lie beyond ordinary sensory experience.

Even in those perceptible regions, appearances can be deceptive. Initially, many of the Outer Planes appear hospitable and familiar to natives of the Material Plane. But the landscape can change at the whims of the powerful forces that live on the Outer Planes. The desires of the mighty forces that dwell on these planes can remake them completely, effectively erasing and rebuilding existence itself to better fulfill their own needs.

Distance is a virtually meaningless concept on the Outer Planes. The perceptible regions of the planes often seem quite small, but they can also stretch on to what seems like infinity. It might be possible to take a guided tour of the Nine Hells, from the first layer to the ninth, in a single day—if the powers of the Hells desire it. Or it could take weeks for travelers to make a grueling trek across a single layer.

The most well-known Outer Planes are a group of sixteen planes that correspond to the eight alignments (excluding neutrality) and the shades of distinction between them.

OUTER PLANES

Outer Plane	Alignment
Mount Celestia, the Seven Heavens of	LG
Bytopia, the Twin Paradises of	NG, LG
Elysium, the Blessed Fields of	NG
The Beastlands, the Wilderness of	NG, CG
Arborea, the Olympian Glades of	CG
Ysgard, the Heroic Domains of	CN, CG
Limbo, the Ever-Changing Chaos of	CN
Pandemonium, the Windswept Depths of	CN, CE
The Abyss, the Infinite Layers of	CE
Carceri, the Tarterian Depths of	NE, CE
Hades, the Gray Waste of	NE
Gehenna, the Bleak Eternity of	NE, LE
The Nine Hells (of Baator)	LE
Acheron, the Infinite Battlefield of	LN, LE
Mechanus, the Clockwork Nirvana of	LN
Arcadia, the Peaceable Kingdoms of	LN, LG

The planes with some element of good in their nature are called the **Upper Planes**. Celestial creatures such as angels and pegasi dwell in the Upper Planes. Planes with some element of evil are the **Lower Planes**. Fiends such as demons, devils, and yugoloths dwell in the Lower Planes. A plane's alignment is its essence, and a character whose alignment doesn't match the plane's experiences a profound sense of dissonance there. When a good creature visits Elysium, for example, it feels in tune with the plane, but an evil creature feels out of tune and more than a little uncomfortable.

OTHER PLANES

Existing somehow between or beyond the known planes of existence are a variety of other realms.

SIGIL AND THE OUTLANDS

The Outlands is the plane between the Outer Planes, a plane of neutrality, but not the neutrality of nothingness. Instead it incorporates a little of everything, keeping it all in a paradoxical balance—simultaneously concordant and in opposition. It is a broad region of varied terrain, with open prairies, towering mountains, and twisting, shallow rivers, strongly resembling an ordinary world of the Material Plane.

The Outlands is circular, like a great wheel—in fact, those who envision the Outer Planes as a wheel point to the Outlands as proof, calling it a microcosm of the planes. That argument might be circular, however, for it is possible that the arrangement of the Outlands inspired the idea of the Great Wheel in the first place.

Around the outside edge of the circle, evenly spaced, are the **gate-towns**: sixteen settlements, each built around a portal leading to one of the Outer Planes. Each town shares many of the characteristics of the plane where its gate leads.

At the center of the Outlands, like the axle of the planar wheel, the Spire shoots impossibly high into the sky. Above this thin peak floats the ring-shaped city of Sigil, the City of Doors. This bustling planar metropolis holds countless portals to other planes and worlds.

Sigil is a trader's city. Goods, merchandise, and information come to it from across the planes. There is a brisk trade in information about the planes, in particular in the command words or items required for the operation of particular portals. These portal keys are highly sought after, and many travelers within the city are looking for a particular portal or a portal key to allow them to continue on their way.

DEMIPLANES

Demiplanes are small extradimensional spaces with their own unique rules. They are pieces of reality that don't seem to fit anywhere else. Demiplanes come into being by a variety of means. Some are created by spells, such as *demiplane,* or generated at the desire of a powerful deity or other force. They may exist naturally, as a fold of existing reality that has been pinched off from the rest of the multiverse, or as a baby universe growing in power. A given demiplane can be entered through a single point where it touches another plane. Theoretically, a *plane shift* spell can also carry travelers to a demiplane, but the proper frequency required for the tuning fork is extremely hard to acquire. The *gate* spell is more reliable, assuming the caster knows of the demiplane.

THE FAR REALM

The Far Realm is beyond the known multiverse. In fact, it might be an entirely separate multiverse with its own physical and magical laws. Where stray energies from the Far Realm leak onto another plane, life and matter are warped and twisted into alien shapes that defy ordinary geometry and biology.

The entities that abide in the Far Realm are too alien for a normal mind to accept without damage. Titanic creatures swim through nothingness, preoccupied with madness. Unspeakable things whisper awful truths to those who dare listen. For mortals, knowledge of the Far Realm is a triumph of mind over the rude boundaries of matter, space, and eventually sanity.

There are no known portals to the Far Realm, or at least none that are still viable. Ancient elves once pierced the boundary of eons with a vast portal to the Far Realm within a mountain called Firestorm Peak, but their civilization imploded in bloody terror and the portal's location—even its home world—is long-forgotten. Other portals might still exist, marked by the alien forces leaking through to corrupt the Material Plane around them.

APPENDIX D: CREATURE STATISTICS

 PELLS AND CLASS FEATURES ALLOW CHARACTERS to transform into animals, summon creatures to serve as familiars, and create undead. Statistics for such creatures are grouped in this appendix for your convenience. For information on how to read a stat block, see the *Monster Manual*.

BAT

Tiny beast, unaligned

Armor Class 12
Hit Points 1 (1d4 − 1)
Speed 5 ft., fly 30 ft.

STR	DEX	CON	INT	WIS	CHA
2 (−4)	15 (+2)	8 (−1)	2 (−4)	12 (+1)	4 (−3)

Senses blindsight 60 ft., passive Perception 11
Languages —
Challenge 0 (10 XP)

Echolocation. While it can't hear, the bat has no blindsight.

Keen Hearing. The bat has advantage on Wisdom (Perception) checks that rely on hearing.

ACTIONS

Bite. *Melee Weapon Attack:* +0 to hit, reach 5 ft., one creature. *Hit:* 1 piercing damage.

BLACK BEAR

Medium beast, unaligned

Armor Class 11 (natural armor)
Hit Points 19 (3d8 + 6)
Speed 40 ft., climb 30 ft.

STR	DEX	CON	INT	WIS	CHA
15 (+2)	10 (+0)	14 (+2)	2 (−4)	12 (+1)	7 (−2)

Skills Perception +3
Senses passive Perception 13
Languages —
Challenge 1/2 (100 XP)

Keen Smell. The bear has advantage on Wisdom (Perception) checks that rely on smell.

ACTIONS

Multiattack. The bear makes two attacks: one with its bite and one with its claws.

Bite. *Melee Weapon Attack:* +3 to hit, reach 5 ft., one target. *Hit:* 5 (1d6 + 2) piercing damage.

Claws. *Melee Weapon Attack:* +3 to hit, reach 5 ft., one target. *Hit:* 7 (2d4 + 2) slashing damage.

BOAR

Medium beast, unaligned

Armor Class 11 (natural armor)
Hit Points 11 (2d8 + 2)
Speed 40 ft.

STR	DEX	CON	INT	WIS	CHA
13 (+1)	11 (+0)	12 (+1)	2 (−4)	9 (−1)	5 (−3)

Senses passive Perception 9
Languages —
Challenge 1/4 (50 XP)

Charge. If the boar moves at least 20 feet straight toward a creature right before hitting it with a tusk attack, the target takes an extra 3 (1d6) slashing damage and must succeed on a DC 11 Strength saving throw or be knocked prone.

Relentless (Recharges after the Boar Finishes a Short or Long Rest). If the boar takes 7 damage or less that would reduce it to 0 hit points, it is reduced to 1 hit point instead.

ACTIONS

Tusk. *Melee Weapon Attack:* +3 to hit, reach 5 ft., one target. *Hit:* 4 (1d6 + 1) slashing damage.

BROWN BEAR

Large beast, unaligned

Armor Class 11 (natural armor)
Hit Points 34 (4d10 + 12)
Speed 40 ft., climb 30 ft.

STR	DEX	CON	INT	WIS	CHA
19 (+4)	10 (+0)	16 (+3)	2 (−4)	13 (+1)	7 (−2)

Skills Perception +3
Senses passive Perception 13
Languages —
Challenge 1 (200 XP)

Keen Smell. The bear has advantage on Wisdom (Perception) checks that rely on smell.

ACTIONS

Multiattack. The bear makes two attacks: one with its bite and one with its claws.

Bite. *Melee Weapon Attack:* +5 to hit, reach 5 ft., one target. *Hit:* 8 (1d8 + 4) piercing damage.

Claws. *Melee Weapon Attack:* +5 to hit, reach 5 ft., one target. *Hit:* 11 (2d6 + 4) slashing damage.

CAT

Tiny beast, unaligned

Armor Class 12
Hit Points 2 (1d4)
Speed 40 ft., climb 30 ft.

STR	DEX	CON	INT	WIS	CHA
3 (−4)	15 (+2)	10 (+0)	3 (−4)	12 (+1)	7 (−2)

Skills Perception +3, Stealth +4
Senses passive Perception 13
Languages —
Challenge 0 (10 XP)

Keen Smell. The cat has advantage on Wisdom (Perception) checks that rely on smell.

ACTIONS

Claws. *Melee Weapon Attack:* +0 to hit, reach 5 ft., one target. *Hit:* 1 slashing damage.

CONSTRICTOR SNAKE

Large beast, unaligned

Armor Class 12
Hit Points 13 (2d10 + 2)
Speed 30 ft., swim 30 ft.

STR	DEX	CON	INT	WIS	CHA
15 (+2)	14 (+2)	12 (+1)	1 (−5)	10 (+0)	3 (−4)

Senses blindsight 10 ft., passive Perception 10
Languages —
Challenge 1/4 (50 XP)

ACTIONS

Bite. *Melee Weapon Attack:* +4 to hit, reach 5 ft., one creature. *Hit:* 5 (1d6 + 2) piercing damage.

Constrict. *Melee Weapon Attack:* +4 to hit, reach 5 ft., one creature. *Hit:* 6 (1d8 + 2) bludgeoning damage, and the target is grappled (escape DC 14). Until this grapple ends, the creature is restrained, and the snake can't constrict another target.

CROCODILE

Large beast, unaligned

Armor Class 12 (natural armor)
Hit Points 19 (3d10 + 3)
Speed 20 ft., swim 30 ft.

STR	DEX	CON	INT	WIS	CHA
15 (+2)	10 (+0)	13 (+1)	2 (−4)	10 (+0)	5 (−3)

Skills Stealth +2
Senses passive Perception 10
Languages —
Challenge 1/2 (100 XP)

Hold Breath. The crocodile can hold its breath for 15 minutes.

ACTIONS

Bite. *Melee Weapon Attack:* +4 to hit, reach 5 ft., one target. *Hit:* 7 (1d10 + 2) piercing damage, and the target is grappled (escape DC 12). Until this grapple ends, the target is restrained, and the crocodile can't bite another target.

DIRE WOLF

Large beast, unaligned

Armor Class 14 (natural armor)
Hit Points 37 (5d10 + 10)
Speed 50 ft.

STR	DEX	CON	INT	WIS	CHA
17 (+3)	15 (+2)	15 (+2)	3 (−4)	12 (+1)	7 (−2)

Skills Perception +3, Stealth +4
Senses passive Perception 13
Languages —
Challenge 1 (200 XP)

Keen Hearing and Smell. The wolf has advantage on Wisdom (Perception) checks that rely on hearing or smell.

Pack Tactics. The wolf has advantage on attack rolls against a creature if at least one of the wolf's allies is within 5 feet of the creature and isn't incapacitated.

ACTIONS

Bite. *Melee Weapon Attack:* +5 to hit, reach 5 ft., one target. *Hit:* 10 (2d6 + 3) piercing damage. If the target is a creature, it must succeed on a DC 13 Strength saving throw or be knocked prone.

FROG

Tiny beast, unaligned

Armor Class 11
Hit Points 1 (1d4 − 1)
Speed 20 ft., swim 20 ft.

STR	DEX	CON	INT	WIS	CHA
1 (−5)	13 (+1)	8 (−1)	1 (−5)	8 (−1)	3 (−4)

Skills Perception +1, Stealth +3
Senses darkvision 30 ft., passive Perception 11
Languages —
Challenge 0 (0 XP)

Amphibious. The frog can breathe air and water.

Standing Leap. As part of its movement and without a running start, the frog can long jump up to 10 feet and high jump up to 5 feet.

GIANT EAGLE
Large beast, neutral good

Armor Class 13
Hit Points 26 (4d10 + 4)
Speed 10 ft., fly 80 ft.

STR	DEX	CON	INT	WIS	CHA
16 (+3)	17 (+3)	13 (+1)	8 (−1)	14 (+2)	10 (+0)

Skills Perception +4
Senses passive Perception 14
Languages Giant Eagle, understands Common and Auran but doesn't speak them
Challenge 1 (200 XP)

Keen Sight. The eagle has advantage on Wisdom (Perception) checks that rely on sight.

ACTIONS

Multiattack. The eagle makes two attacks: one with its beak and one with its talons.

Beak. *Melee Weapon Attack:* +5 to hit, reach 5 ft., one target. *Hit:* 6 (1d6 + 3) piercing damage.

Talons. *Melee Weapon Attack:* +5 to hit, reach 5 ft., one target. *Hit:* 10 (2d6 + 3) slashing damage.

GIANT SPIDER
Large beast, unaligned

Armor Class 14 (natural armor)
Hit Points 26 (4d10 + 4)
Speed 30 ft., climb 30 ft.

STR	DEX	CON	INT	WIS	CHA
14 (+2)	16 (+3)	12 (+1)	2 (−4)	11 (+0)	4 (−3)

Skills Stealth +7
Senses blindsight 10 ft., darkvision 60 ft., passive Perception 10
Languages —
Challenge 1 (200 XP)

Spider Climb. The spider can climb difficult surfaces, including upside down on ceilings, without needing to make an ability check.

Web Sense. While in contact with a web, the spider knows the exact location of any other creature in contact with the same web.

Web Walker. The spider ignores movement restrictions caused by webbing.

ACTIONS

Bite. *Melee Weapon Attack:* +5 to hit, reach 5 ft., one creature. *Hit:* 7 (1d8 + 3) piercing damage, and the target must make a DC 11 Constitution saving throw, taking 9 (2d8) poison damage on a failed save, or half as much damage on a successful one. If the poison damage reduces the target to 0 hit points, the target is stable but poisoned for 1 hour, even after regaining hit points, and is paralyzed while poisoned in this way.

Web (Recharge 5–6). *Ranged Weapon Attack:* +5 to hit, range 30/60 ft., one creature. *Hit:* The target is restrained by webbing. As an action, the restrained target can make a DC 12 Strength check, bursting the webbing on a success. The webbing can also be attacked and destroyed (AC 10; hp 5; vulnerability to fire damage; immunity to bludgeoning, poison, and psychic damage).

HAWK (FALCON)
Tiny beast, unaligned

Armor Class 13
Hit Points 1 (1d4 − 1)
Speed 10 ft., fly 60 ft.

STR	DEX	CON	INT	WIS	CHA
5 (−3)	16 (+3)	8 (−1)	2 (−4)	14 (+2)	6 (−2)

Skills Perception +4
Senses passive Perception 14
Languages —
Challenge 0 (10 XP)

Keen Sight. The hawk has advantage on Wisdom (Perception) checks that rely on sight.

ACTIONS

Talons. *Melee Weapon Attack:* +5 to hit, reach 5 ft., one target. *Hit:* 1 slashing damage.

IMP
Tiny fiend (devil, shapechanger), lawful evil

Armor Class 13
Hit Points 10 (3d4 + 3)
Speed 20 ft., fly 40 ft. (20 ft. in rat form; 20 ft., fly 60 ft. in raven form; 20 ft., climb 20 ft. in spider form)

STR	DEX	CON	INT	WIS	CHA
6 (−2)	17 (+3)	13 (+1)	11 (+0)	12 (+1)	14 (+2)

Skills Deception +4, Insight +3, Persuasion +4, Stealth +5
Damage Resistances cold; bludgeoning, piercing, and slashing from nonmagical weapons that aren't silvered
Damage Immunities fire, poison
Condition Immunities poisoned
Senses darkvision 120 ft., passive Perception 11
Languages Infernal, Common
Challenge 1 (200 XP)

Shapechanger. The imp can use its action to polymorph into the beast form of a rat, a raven, or a spider, or into its devil form. Its statistics are the same in each form, except for the speed changes noted. Any equipment it is wearing or carrying is not transformed. It reverts to its devil form if it dies.

Devil's Sight. Magical darkness doesn't impede the imp's darkvision.

Magic Resistance. The imp has advantage on saving throws against spells and other magical effects.

ACTIONS

Sting (Bite in Beast Form). *Melee Weapon Attack:* +5 to hit, reach 5 ft., one creature. *Hit:* 5 (1d4 + 3) piercing damage, and the target must make on a DC 11 Constitution saving throw, taking 10 (3d6) poison damage on a failed save, or half as much damage on a successful one.

Invisibility. The imp magically turns invisible until it attacks or until its concentration ends (as if concentrating on a spell). Any equipment the imp wears or carries is invisible with it.

LION
Large beast, unaligned

Armor Class 12
Hit Points 26 (4d10 + 4)
Speed 50 ft.

STR	DEX	CON	INT	WIS	CHA
17 (+3)	15 (+2)	13 (+1)	3 (−4)	12 (+1)	8 (−1)

Skills Perception +3, Stealth +6
Senses passive Perception 13
Languages —
Challenge 1 (200 XP)

Keen Smell. The lion has advantage on Wisdom (Perception) checks that rely on smell.

Pack Tactics. The lion has advantage on attack rolls against a creature if at least one of the lion's allies is within 5 feet of the creature and isn't incapacitated.

Pounce. If the lion moves at least 20 feet straight toward a target right before hitting it with a claw attack, the target must succeed on a DC 13 Strength saving throw or be knocked prone. If the target is prone, the lion can take a bonus action to make one bite attack against it.

Running Leap. As part of its movement and after a 10-foot running start, the lion can long jump up to 25 feet.

ACTIONS

Bite. *Melee Weapon Attack:* +5 to hit, reach 5 ft., one target. *Hit:* 7 (1d8 + 3) piercing damage.

Claw. *Melee Weapon Attack:* +5 to hit, reach 5 ft., one target. *Hit:* 6 (1d6 + 3) slashing damage.

MASTIFF
Medium beast, unaligned

Armor Class 12
Hit Points 5 (1d8 + 1)
Speed 40 ft.

STR	DEX	CON	INT	WIS	CHA
13 (+1)	14 (+2)	12 (+1)	3 (−4)	12 (+1)	7 (−2)

Skills Perception +3
Senses passive Perception 13
Languages —
Challenge 1/8 (25 XP)

Keen Hearing and Smell. The mastiff has advantage on Wisdom (Perception) checks that rely on hearing or smell.

ACTIONS

Bite. *Melee Weapon Attack:* +3 to hit, reach 5 ft., one target. *Hit:* 4 (1d6 + 1) piercing damage. If the target is a creature, it must succeed on a DC 11 Strength saving throw or be knocked prone.

MULE
Medium beast, unaligned

Armor Class 10
Hit Points 11 (2d8 + 2)
Speed 40 ft.

STR	DEX	CON	INT	WIS	CHA
14 (+2)	10 (+0)	13 (+1)	2 (−4)	10 (+0)	5 (−3)

Senses passive Perception 10
Languages —
Challenge 1/8 (25 XP)

Beast of Burden. The mule is considered to be a Large animal for the purpose of determining its carrying capacity.

Sure-Footed. The mule has advantage on Strength and Dexterity saving throws made against effects that would knock it prone.

ACTIONS

Hooves. *Melee Weapon Attack:* +2 to hit, reach 5 ft., one target. *Hit:* 4 (1d4 + 2) bludgeoning damage.

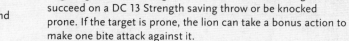

IMP

Owl

Tiny beast, unaligned

Armor Class 11
Hit Points 1 (1d4 − 1)
Speed 5 ft., fly 60 ft.

STR	DEX	CON	INT	WIS	CHA
3 (−4)	13 (+1)	8 (−1)	2 (−4)	12 (+1)	7 (−2)

Skills Perception +3, Stealth +3
Senses darkvision 120 ft., passive Perception 13
Languages —
Challenge 0 (10 XP)

Flyby. The owl provokes no opportunity attacks when it flies out of an enemy's reach.

Keen Hearing and Sight. The owl has advantage on Wisdom (Perception) checks that rely on hearing or sight.

Actions

Talons. *Melee Weapon Attack:* +3 to hit, reach 5 ft., one target. *Hit:* 1 slashing damage.

Panther

Medium beast, unaligned

Armor Class 12
Hit Points 13 (3d8)
Speed 50 ft., climb 40 ft.

STR	DEX	CON	INT	WIS	CHA
14 (+2)	15 (+2)	10 (+0)	3 (−4)	14 (+2)	7 (−2)

Skills Perception +4, Stealth +6
Senses passive Perception 14
Languages —
Challenge 1/4 (50 XP)

Keen Smell. The panther has advantage on Wisdom (Perception) checks that rely on smell.

Pounce. If the panther moves at least 20 feet straight toward a creature right before hitting it with a claw attack, the target must succeed on a DC 12 Strength saving throw or be knocked prone. If the target is prone, the panther can take a bonus action to make one bite attack against it.

Actions

Bite. *Melee Weapon Attack:* +4 to hit, reach 5 ft., one target. *Hit:* 5 (1d6 + 2) piercing damage.

Claw. *Melee Weapon Attack:* +4 to hit, reach 5 ft., one target. *Hit:* 4 (1d4 + 2) slashing damage.

Poisonous Snake

Tiny beast, unaligned

Armor Class 13
Hit Points 2 (1d4)
Speed 30 ft., swim 30 ft.

STR	DEX	CON	INT	WIS	CHA
2 (−4)	16 (+3)	11 (+0)	1 (−5)	10 (+0)	3 (−4)

Senses blindsight 10 ft., passive Perception 10
Languages —
Challenge 1/8 (25 XP)

Actions

Bite. *Melee Weapon Attack:* +5 to hit, reach 5 ft., one target. *Hit:* 1 piercing damage, and the target must make a DC 10 Constitution saving throw, taking 5 (2d4) poison damage on a failed save, or half as much damage on a successful one.

Pseudodragon

Tiny dragon, neutral good

Armor Class 13 (natural armor)
Hit Points 7 (2d4 + 2)
Speed 15 ft., fly 60 ft.

STR	DEX	CON	INT	WIS	CHA
6 (−2)	15 (+2)	13 (+1)	10 (+0)	12 (+1)	10 (+0)

Skills Perception +3, Stealth +4
Senses blindsight 10 ft., darkvision 60 ft., passive Perception 13
Languages understands Common and Draconic but doesn't speak
Challenge 1/4 (50 XP)

Keen Senses. The pseudodragon has advantage on Wisdom (Perception) checks that rely on sight, hearing, or smell.

Magic Resistance. The pseudodragon has advantage on saving throws against spells and other magical effects.

Limited Telepathy. The pseudodragon can magically communicate simple ideas, emotions, and images telepathically with any creature within 100 feet of it that can understand a language.

Actions

Bite. *Melee Weapon Attack:* +4 to hit, reach 5 ft., one target. *Hit:* 4 (1d4 + 2) piercing damage.

Sting. *Melee Weapon Attack:* +4 to hit, reach 5 ft., one creature. *Hit:* 4 (1d4 + 2) piercing damage, and the target must succeed on a DC 11 Constitution saving throw or become poisoned for 1 hour. If the saving throw fails by 5 or more, the target falls unconscious for the same duration, or until it takes damage or another creature uses an action to wake it.

QUASIT

Tiny fiend (demon, shapechanger), chaotic evil

Armor Class 13
Hit Points 7 (3d4)
Speed 40 ft. (10 ft., fly 40 ft. in bat form; 40 ft., climb 40 ft. in centipede form; 40 ft., swim 40 ft. in toad form)

STR	DEX	CON	INT	WIS	CHA
5 (−3)	17 (+3)	10 (+0)	7 (−2)	10 (+0)	10 (+0)

Skills Stealth +5
Damage Resistances cold, fire, lightning; bludgeoning, piercing, and slashing from nonmagical weapons
Damage Immunities poison
Condition Immunities poisoned
Senses darkvision 120 ft., passive Perception 10
Languages Abyssal, Common
Challenge 1 (200 XP)

Shapechanger. The quasit can use its action to polymorph into the beast form of a bat, centipede, or toad, or into its demon form. Its statistics are the same in each form, except for the speed changes noted. Any equipment it is wearing or carrying is not transformed. It reverts to its demon form if it dies.

Magic Resistance. The quasit has advantage on saving throws against spells and other magical effects.

ACTIONS

Claws (Bite in Beast Form). *Melee Weapon Attack:* +4 to hit, reach 5 ft., one target. *Hit:* 5 (1d4 + 3) piercing damage. If the target is a creature, it must succeed on a DC 10 Constitution saving throw or take 5 (2d4) poison damage and become poisoned for 1 minute. The creature can repeat the saving throw at the end of each of its turns, ending the effect early on a success.

Scare (1/Day). One creature of the quasit's choice within 20 feet of it must succeed on a DC 10 Wisdom saving throw or be frightened for 1 minute. The target can repeat the saving throw at the end of each of its turns, with disadvantage if the quasit is within line of sight, ending the effect early on a success.

Invisibility. The quasit magically turns invisible until it attacks or uses Scare, or until its concentration ends (as if concentrating on a spell). Any equipment the quasit wears or carries is invisible with it.

RAT

Tiny beast, unaligned

Armor Class 10
Hit Points 1 (1d4 − 1)
Speed 20 ft.

STR	DEX	CON	INT	WIS	CHA
2 (−4)	11 (+0)	9 (−1)	2 (−4)	10 (+0)	4 (−3)

Senses darkvision 30 ft., passive Perception 10
Languages —
Challenge 0 (10 XP)

Keen Smell. The rat has advantage on Wisdom (Perception) checks that rely on smell.

ACTIONS

Bite. *Melee Weapon Attack:* +0 to hit, reach 5 ft., one target. *Hit:* 1 piercing damage.

RAVEN

Tiny beast, unaligned

Armor Class 12
Hit Points 1 (1d4 − 1)
Speed 10 ft., fly 50 ft.

STR	DEX	CON	INT	WIS	CHA
2 (−4)	14 (+2)	8 (−1)	2 (−4)	12 (+1)	6 (−2)

Skills Perception +3
Senses passive Perception 13
Languages —
Challenge 0 (10 XP)

Mimicry. The raven can mimic simple sounds it has heard, such as a person whispering, a baby crying, or an animal chittering. A creature that hears the sounds can tell they are imitations with a successful DC 10 Wisdom (Insight) check.

ACTIONS

Beak. *Melee Weapon Attack:* +4 to hit, reach 5 ft., one target. *Hit:* 1 piercing damage.

REEF SHARK

Medium beast, unaligned

Armor Class 12 (natural armor)
Hit Points 22 (4d8 + 4)
Speed 0 ft., swim 40 ft.

STR	DEX	CON	INT	WIS	CHA
14 (+2)	13 (+1)	13 (+1)	1 (−5)	10 (+0)	4 (−3)

Skills Perception +2
Senses blindsight 30 ft., passive Perception 12
Languages —
Challenge 1/2 (100 XP)

Pack Tactics. The shark has advantage on attack rolls against a creature if at least one of the shark's allies is within 5 feet of the creature and isn't incapacitated.

Water Breathing. The shark can breathe only underwater.

ACTIONS

Bite. *Melee Weapon Attack:* +4 to hit, reach 5 ft., one target. *Hit:* 6 (1d8 + 2) piercing damage.

RIDING HORSE
Large beast, unaligned

Armor Class 10
Hit Points 13 (2d10 + 2)
Speed 60 ft.

STR	DEX	CON	INT	WIS	CHA
16 (+3)	10 (+0)	12 (+1)	2 (−4)	11 (+0)	7 (−2)

Senses passive Perception 10
Languages —
Challenge 1/4 (50 XP)

ACTIONS

Hooves. *Melee Weapon Attack:* +2 to hit, reach 5 ft., one target. *Hit:* 8 (2d4 + 3) bludgeoning damage.

SKELETON
Medium undead, lawful evil

Armor Class 13 (armor scraps)
Hit Points 13 (2d8 + 4)
Speed 30 ft.

STR	DEX	CON	INT	WIS	CHA
10 (+0)	14 (+2)	15 (+2)	6 (−2)	8 (−1)	5 (−3)

Damage Vulnerabilities bludgeoning
Damage Immunities poison
Condition Immunities exhaustion, poisoned
Senses darkvision 60 ft., passive Perception 9
Languages understands all languages it knew in life but can't speak
Challenge 1/4 (50 XP)

ACTIONS

Shortsword. *Melee Weapon Attack:* +4 to hit, reach 5 ft., one target. *Hit:* 5 (1d6 + 2) piercing damage.

Shortbow. *Ranged Weapon Attack:* +4 to hit, range 80/320 ft., one target. *Hit:* 5 (1d6 + 2) piercing damage.

SPRITE
Tiny fey, neutral good

Armor Class 15 (leather armor)
Hit Points 2 (1d4)
Speed 10 ft., fly 40 ft.

STR	DEX	CON	INT	WIS	CHA
3 (−4)	18 (+4)	10 (+0)	14 (+2)	13 (+1)	11 (+0)

Skills Perception +3, Stealth +8
Senses passive Perception 13
Languages Common, Elvish, Sylvan
Challenge 1/4 (50 XP)

ACTIONS

Longsword. *Melee Weapon Attack:* +2 to hit, reach 5 ft., one target. *Hit:* 1 slashing damage.

SKELETON

Shortbow. *Ranged Weapon Attack:* +6 to hit, range 40/160 ft., one target. *Hit:* 1 piercing damage, and the target must succeed on a DC 10 Constitution saving throw or become poisoned for 1 minute. If its saving throw result is 5 or lower, the poisoned target falls unconscious for the same duration, or until it takes damage or another creature takes an action to shake it awake.

Heart Sight. The sprite touches a creature and magically knows the creature's current emotional state. If the target fails a DC 10 Charisma saving throw, the sprite also knows the creature's alignment. Celestials, fiends, and undead automatically fail the saving throw.

Invisibility. The sprite magically turns invisible until it attacks or casts a spell, or until its concentration ends (as if casting a spell). Any equipment the sprite wears or carries is invisible with it.

VARIANT: WARHORSE ARMOR

An armored warhorse has an Armor Class based on the type of barding worn (see chapter 5 for more information on barding). Its Armor Class includes the horse's Dexterity modifier, where applicable.

AC	Barding	AC	Barding
12	Leather	16	Chain mail
13	Studded leather	17	Splint
14	Ring mail	18	Plate
15	Scale mail		

TIGER

Large beast, unaligned

Armor Class 12
Hit Points 37 (5d10 + 10)
Speed 40 ft.

STR	DEX	CON	INT	WIS	CHA
17 (+3)	15 (+2)	14 (+2)	3 (−4)	12 (+1)	8 (−1)

Skills Perception +3, Stealth +6
Senses darkvision 60 ft., passive Perception 13
Languages —
Challenge 1 (200 XP)

Keen Smell. The tiger has advantage on Wisdom (Perception) checks that rely on smell.

Pounce. If the tiger moves at least 20 feet straight toward a creature right before hitting it with a claw attack, the target must succeed on a DC 13 Strength saving throw or be knocked prone. If the target is prone, the tiger can take a bonus action to make one bite attack against it.

ACTIONS

Bite. *Melee Weapon Attack:* +5 to hit, reach 5 ft., one target. *Hit:* 8 (1d10 + 3) piercing damage.

Claw. *Melee Weapon Attack:* +5 to hit, reach 5 ft., one target. *Hit:* 7 (1d8 + 3) slashing damage.

WARHORSE

Large beast, unaligned

Armor Class 11
Hit Points 19 (3d10 + 3)
Speed 60 ft.

STR	DEX	CON	INT	WIS	CHA
18 (+4)	12 (+1)	13 (+1)	2 (−4)	12 (+1)	7 (−2)

Senses passive Perception 11
Languages —
Challenge 1/2 (100 XP)

Trampling Charge. If the horse moves at least 20 feet straight toward a creature right before hitting it with a hooves attack, the target must succeed on a DC 14 Strength saving throw or be knocked prone. If the target is prone, the horse can take a bonus action to make another attack with its hooves against the target.

ACTIONS

Hooves. *Melee Weapon Attack:* +4 to hit, reach 5 ft., one target. *Hit:* 11 (2d6 + 4) bludgeoning damage.

WOLF

Medium beast, unaligned

Armor Class 13 (natural armor)
Hit Points 11 (2d8 + 2)
Speed 40 ft.

STR	DEX	CON	INT	WIS	CHA
12 (+1)	15 (+2)	12 (+1)	3 (−4)	12 (+1)	6 (−2)

Skills Perception +3, Stealth +4
Senses passive Perception 13
Languages —
Challenge 1/4 (50 XP)

Keen Hearing and Smell. The wolf has advantage on Wisdom (Perception) checks that rely on hearing or smell.

Pack Tactics. The wolf has advantage on attack rolls against a creature if at least one of the wolf's allies is within 5 feet of the creature and isn't incapacitated.

ACTIONS

Bite. *Melee Weapon Attack:* +4 to hit, reach 5 ft., one target. *Hit:* 7 (2d4 + 2) piercing damage. If the target is a creature, it must succeed on a DC 11 Strength saving throw or be knocked prone.

ZOMBIE

Medium undead, neutral evil

Armor Class 8
Hit Points 22 (3d8 + 9)
Speed 20 ft.

STR	DEX	CON	INT	WIS	CHA
13 (+1)	6 (−2)	16 (+3)	3 (−4)	6 (−2)	5 (−3)

Saving Throws Wis +0
Damage Immunities poison
Condition Immunities poisoned
Senses darkvision 60 ft., passive Perception 8
Languages understands the languages it knew in life but can't speak
Challenge 1/4 (50 XP)

Undead Fortitude. If damage reduces the zombie to 0 hit points, it must make a Constitution saving throw with a DC of 5 + the damage taken, unless the damage is radiant or from a critical hit. On a success, the zombie drops to 1 hit point instead.

ACTIONS

Slam. *Melee Weapon Attack:* +3 to hit, reach 5 ft., one target. *Hit:* 4 (1d6 + 1) bludgeoning damage.

APPENDIX E: INSPIRATIONAL READING

 INSPIRATION FOR ALL OF THE FANTASY WORK I HAVE *done stems directly from the love my father showed when I was a lad, for he spent many hours telling me stories he made up as he went along, tales of cloaked old men who could grant wishes, of magic rings and enchanted swords, or wicked sorcerers and dauntless swordsmen. . . . All of us tend to get ample helpings of fantasy when we are very young, from fairy tales such as those written by the Brothers Grimm and Andrew Lang. This often leads to reading books of mythology, paging through bestiaries, and consultation of compilations of the myths of various lands and peoples. Upon such a base I built my interest in fantasy, being an avid reader of all science fiction and fantasy literature since 1950. The following authors were of particular inspiration to me.*

—E. Gary Gygax, Dungeon Master's Guide *(1979)*

A great deal of fantasy literature has been published since the co-creator of DUNGEONS & DRAGONS wrote those words, including breakthrough works set in the shared worlds of D&D. The following list includes Gary's original list and some additional works that have inspired the game's designers in the years since.

Ahmed, Saladin. *Throne of the Crescent Moon*.

Alexander, Lloyd. *The Book of Three* and the rest of the Chronicles of Prydain series.

Anderson, Poul. *The Broken Sword*, *The High Crusade*, and *Three Hearts and Three Lions*.

Anthony, Piers. *Split Infinity* and the rest of the Apprentice Adept series.

Augusta, Lady Gregory. *Gods and Fighting Men*.

Bear, Elizabeth. *Range of Ghosts* and the rest of the Eternal Sky trilogy.

Bellairs, John. *The Face in the Frost*.

Brackett, Leigh. *The Best of Leigh Brackett*, *The Long Tomorrow*, and *The Sword of Rhiannon*.

Brooks, Terry. *The Sword of Shannara* and the rest of the Shannara novels.

Brown, Fredric. *Hall of Mirrors* and *What Mad Universe*.

Bulfinch, Thomas. *Bulfinch's Mythology*.

Burroughs, Edgar Rice. *At the Earth's Core* and the rest of the Pellucidar series, *Pirates of Venus* and the rest of the Venus series, and *A Princess of Mars* and the rest of the Mars series.

Carter, Lin. *Warrior of World's End* and the rest of the World's End series.

Cook, Glen. *The Black Company* and the rest of the Black Company series.

de Camp, L. Sprague. *The Fallible Fiend* and *Lest Darkness Fall*.

de Camp, L. Sprague & Fletcher Pratt. *The Compleat Enchanter* and the rest of the Harold Shea series, and *Carnelian Cube*.

Derleth, August and H.P. Lovecraft. *Watchers out of Time*.

Dunsany, Lord. *The Book of Wonder*, *The Essential Lord Dunsany Collection*, *The Gods of Pegana*, *The King of Elfland's Daughter*, *Lord Dunsany Compendium*, and *The Sword of Welleran and Other Tales*.

Farmer, Philip Jose. *Maker of Universes* and the rest of the World of Tiers series.

Fox, Gardner. *Kothar and the Conjurer's Curse* and the rest of the Kothar series, and *Kyrik and the Lost Queen* and the rest of the Kyrik series.

Froud, Brian & Alan Lee. *Faeries*.

Hickman, Tracy & Margaret Weis. *Dragons of Autumn Twilight* and the rest of the Chronicles Trilogy.

Hodgson, William Hope. *The Night Land*.

Howard, Robert E. *The Coming of Conan the Cimmerian* and the rest of the Conan series.

Jemisin, N.K. *The Hundred Thousand Kingdoms* and the rest of the Inheritance series, *The Killing Moon*, and *The Shadowed Sun*.

Jordan, Robert. *The Eye of the World* and the rest of the Wheel of Time series.

Kay, Guy Gavriel. *Tigana*.

King, Stephen. *The Eyes of the Dragon*.

Lanier, Sterling. *Hiero's Journey* and *The Unforsaken Hiero*.

LeGuin, Ursula. *A Wizard of Earthsea* and the rest of the Earthsea series.

Leiber, Fritz. *Swords and Deviltry* and the rest of the Fafhrd & Gray Mouser series.

Lovecraft, H.P. *The Complete Works*.

Lynch, Scott. *The Lies of Locke Lamora* and the rest of the Gentlemen Bastard series.

Martin, George R.R. *A Game of Thrones* and the rest of the Song of Ice and Fire series.

McKillip, Patricia. *The Forgotten Beasts of Eld*.

Merritt, A. *Creep, Shadow, Creep*; *Dwellers in the Mirage*; and *The Moon Pool*.

Miéville, China. *Perdido Street Station* and the other Bas-Lag novels.

Moorcock, Michael. *Elric of Melniboné* and the rest of the Elric series, and *The Jewel in the Skull* and the rest of the Hawkmoon series.

Norton, Andre. *Quag Keep* and *Witch World*.

Offutt, Andrew J., ed. *Swords against Darkness III*.

Peake, Mervyn. *Titus Groan* and the rest of the Gormenghast series.

Pratchett, Terry. *The Colour of Magic* and the rest of the Discworld series.

Pratt, Fletcher. *Blue Star*.

Rothfuss, Patrick. *The Name of the Wind* and the rest of the Kingkiller series.

Saberhagen, Fred. *The Broken Lands* and *Changeling Earth*.

Salvatore, R.A. *The Crystal Shard* and the rest of The Legend of Drizzt.

Sanderson, Brandon. *Mistborn* and the rest of the Mistborn trilogy.

Smith, Clark Ashton. *The Return of the Sorcerer*.

St. Clair, Margaret. *Change the Sky and Other Stories*, *The Shadow People*, and *Sign of the Labrys*.

Tolkien, J.R.R. *The Hobbit*, *The Lord of the Rings*, and *The Silmarillion*.

Tolstoy, Nikolai. *The Coming of the King*.

Vance, Jack. *The Dying Earth* and *The Eyes of the Overworld*.

Weinbaum, Stanley. *Valley of Dreams* and *The Worlds of If*.

Wellman, Manly Wade. *The Golgotha Dancers*.

Williamson, Jack. *The Cosmic Express* and *The Pygmy Planet*.

Wolfe, Gene. *The Shadow of the Torturer* and the rest of The Book of the New Sun.

Zelazny, Roger. *Jack of Shadows* and *Nine Princes in Amber* and the rest of the Amber series.

DUNGEONS & DRAGONS®

CHARACTER NAME

| CLASS & LEVEL | BACKGROUND | PLAYER NAME |
| RACE | ALIGNMENT | EXPERIENCE POINTS |

STRENGTH

DEXTERITY

CONSTITUTION

INTELLIGENCE

WISDOM

CHARISMA

INSPIRATION

PROFICIENCY BONUS

○ ____ Strength
○ ____ Dexterity
○ ____ Constitution
○ ____ Intelligence
○ ____ Wisdom
○ ____ Charisma

SAVING THROWS

○ ____ Acrobatics (Dex)
○ ____ Animal Handling (Wis)
○ ____ Arcana (Int)
○ ____ Athletics (Str)
○ ____ Deception (Cha)
○ ____ History (Int)
○ ____ Insight (Wis)
○ ____ Intimidation (Cha)
○ ____ Investigation (Int)
○ ____ Medicine (Wis)
○ ____ Nature (Int)
○ ____ Perception (Wis)
○ ____ Performance (Cha)
○ ____ Persuasion (Cha)
○ ____ Religion (Int)
○ ____ Sleight of Hand (Dex)
○ ____ Stealth (Dex)
○ ____ Survival (Wis)

SKILLS

PASSIVE WISDOM (PERCEPTION)

OTHER PROFICIENCIES & LANGUAGES

ARMOR CLASS

INITIATIVE

SPEED

Hit Point Maximum ____

CURRENT HIT POINTS

TEMPORARY HIT POINTS

Total ____

HIT DICE

SUCCESSES ○─○─○
FAILURES ○─○─○

DEATH SAVES

| NAME | ATK BONUS | DAMAGE/TYPE |

ATTACKS & SPELLCASTING

CP
SP
EP
GP
PP

EQUIPMENT

PERSONALITY TRAITS

IDEALS

BONDS

FLAWS

FEATURES & TRAITS

CHARACTER NAME

AGE   HEIGHT   WEIGHT

EYES   SKIN   HAIR

CHARACTER APPEARANCE

NAME

SYMBOL

ALLIES & ORGANIZATIONS

ADDITIONAL FEATURES & TRAITS

CHARACTER BACKSTORY

TREASURE